D1225886

MONASTIC WISDOM SERIES: NUMBER SIXTY-ONE

The Collected Works

Saint Rafael Arnaiz

Translated by Catherine Addington

*Edited and introduced by
Sr. María Gonzalo-García, OCSO*

α

Cistercian Publications
www.cistercianpublications.org

LITURGICAL PRESS
Collegeville, Minnesota
www.litpress.org

A Cistercian Publications title published by Liturgical Press

Cistercian Publications
Editorial Offices
161 Grosvenor Street
Athens, Ohio 45701
www.cistercianpublications.org

The works in this volume are translated from Arnaiz Barón, Saint Rafael, *Hermano San Rafael: Obras completas,* ed. Alberico Feliz Carbajal, OCSO, 6th ed. Burgos: Monte Carmelo, 2011.

1   2   3   4   5   6   7   8   9

Library of Congress Cataloging-in-Publication Data

Names: Arnáiz Barón, Rafael, Saint, 1911–1938, author. | Addington, Catherine, translator.
Title: The collected works / Saint Rafael Arnaiz ; translated by Catherine Addington ; edited and introduced by Sr. María Gonzalo-García, OCSO.
Other titles: Works. English
Description: Collegeville, Minnesota : Cistercian Publications, LITURGICAL PRESS, 2022. | Series: Monastic wisdom series ; number 61 | Includes bibliographical references. | Summary: "When he was twenty-one years old, Saint Rafael Arnaiz left behind the comforts of his wealthy family and an unfinished degree in architecture to join the Trappist-Cistercian abbey of San Isidro de Dueñas. A sudden onset of diabetes and the beginning of the Spanish Civil War (1936–1939) turned his monastic journey into an unusual one. Rafael developed a solid spirituality, which in its simplicity is a straight path to holiness. He has been compared to mystics like Teresa of Avila and John of the Cross, whose writings inspired him, and his theology of the cross, born from his prayer, places him in continuity with the best of the monastic tradition. In his letters and journals, compiled in this volume, he speaks of the joys and struggles of striving to live for God alone"— Provided by publisher.
Identifiers: LCCN 2021047389 (print) | LCCN 2021047390 (ebook) | ISBN 9780879070618 (paperback) | ISBN 9780879071615 (epub) | ISBN 9780879071615 (pdf)
Subjects: LCSH: Arnaiz Barón, Rafael, Saint, 1911-1938—Correspondence. | Spirituality—Catholic Church. | Trappists—Spain.
Classification: LCC BX4705.A727 A2 2022 (print) | LCC BX4705.A727 (ebook) | DDC 271/.1202—dc23/eng/20211228
LC record available at https://lccn.loc.gov/2021047389
LC ebook record available at https://lccn.loc.gov/2021047390

Contents

II. *A Heart Filled with Joy and Love*: Joining the Monastery

III. *I Thought That God Was Abandoning Me*: Struck by Illness

V. *The Circus Clown:* The Last One in the Community

Drawings and Paintings

Numbers below preceded by a hashmark identify the numbered item in the work below, so, e.g., #207 is Rafael's letter to his brother Leopoldo on page 694.

Cover: *Incola ego in terra*, a holy card painted by Rafael (see #207). Source: LPM 225.

Title page: A deer and the cross (see #137). Source: LPM 234.

Illustrations

#30 (p. 86):   A drawing of a monk sitting at a desk and writing. Source: LPM 231.

#83 (p. 305):   A holy card featuring a quotation from Saint John of the Cross: "I will not gather flowers, / nor fear wild beasts; / I will go beyond strong men and frontiers." Source: LPM 213.

#87 (p. 328: above text):   Two Christmas sketches. Source: LPM 183.

#87 (p. 332):   "Knowing how to wait" ("*Saber esperar*"), a holy card for Leopoldo Barón. Source: LPM 215.

#94 (p. 366):   Saint Francis of Assisi. Source: LPM 203.

#103 (p. 389):   Landscape of the monastery. Source: LPM 199.

#103 (p. 395):   Saint Bernard of Clairvaux. Source: LPM 197.

#108 (p. 413):   Cover drawing for Meditations of a Trappist. Source: LPM 239.

#117 (p. 435):   "Why would God create flies?" Source: LPM 231.

#119 (p. 439):   A meadow outside the monastery. Source: LPM 229.

#120 (p. 441):   A ship in fair weather. Source: LPM 229.

Color Images

Samples of Rafael's art before he entered the monastery

An exaggerated portrait of a man in watercolor. Source: LPM 41.

A playful line drawing of children playing music. Source: LPM 63.

One of a series of sketches in pen and watercolor commissioned by his mother, portraying costume designs for a theater performance she directed. Source: LPM 44.

Covers Rafael painted for his uncle's books

A cover for *Él* (Madrid: Editorial Voluntad, 1930). Source: LPM 224.

A cover for *Del campo de batalla a la Trapa: El hermano Gabriel* (Madrid: Librería Religiosa Hernández, 1931). Source: LPM 224.

Holy cards painted by Rafael

Incola ego sum in terra, "I am a stranger and pilgrim on earth" (see #207). Source: LPM 225.

Omnis terra adoret te, "All the earth worships you" (see #207). Source: LPM 225.

"I have chosen the way of truth" (see #207). Source: LPM 219.

"I will not gather flowers, / nor fear wild beasts; / I will go beyond strong men and frontiers" (see #83). Source: LPM 213.

"The tranquil night / at the time of the rising dawn, / silent music, / sounding solitude, / the supper that refreshes, and deepens love" (SJC 474). Source: LPM 211.

The Holy Face of Jesus, painted as a mural above the staircase at his parents' residence in Villasandino. Source: LPM 175.

Abbreviations

LPM   *La pintura mensaje del Hermano Rafael*
Antonio Cobos Soto. *La pintura mensaje del hermano Rafael: estudio crítico de la obra pictórica del venerable Rafael Arnáiz Barón, monje trapense.* Burgos: Monte Carmelo y Monasterio Cisterciense de San Isidro de Dueñas, 1989.

OC   *Obras completas*
Saint Rafael Arnáiz Barón. *Hermano San Rafael: Obras completas.* Edited by Alberico Feliz Carbajal, OCSO. 6th ed. Burgos: Monte Carmelo, 2011.

RB   *Rule of Saint Benedict*
Saint Benedict. *RB 1980: The Rule of Saint Benedict in English.* Ed. Timothy Fry. Collegeville, MN: Liturgical Press, 2019.

SJC   *The Collected Works of Saint John of the Cross*
Saint John of the Cross. *The Collected Works of Saint John of the Cross.* Translated by Kieran Kavanaugh and Otilio Rodriguez. Washington, DC: ICS Publications, 1991.

STA   *The Collected Works of Saint Teresa of Ávila*
Saint Teresa of Ávila. *The Collected Works of Saint Teresa of Ávila.* Translated by Kieran Kavanaugh and Otilio Rodriguez. Washington, DC: ICS Publications, 1976.

Summ   *Summarium*
Giulio Dante. *Summarium.* In *Palentina Canonizationis servi Dei Raphaélis Arnáiz Barón, Ordinis Cisterciensium Reformatorum Oblati, Positio super virtutibus* by Congregatio pro Causis Sanctorum, Rome: Tip. Guerra, 1987. 1–265.

VE   *Vida y escritos*
Saint Rafael Arnáiz Barón. *Vida y escritos de Fray María Rafael Arnáiz Barón: monje trapense.* Edited by Mercedes Barón y Torres. Madrid: P. S. Editorial, 1974.

Oviedo

Villasandino Burgos

Venta de Baños
(La Trapa)

Toro

Ávila

Madrid

"Upheld by Him"

A Saint in the Making

God alone . . . How difficult it is to understand and live these
words, but once you do, even if just for a moment . . . once your
soul has realized that it belongs to God, that it is His possession . . .
that Jesus dwells within it, despite its wretchedness and weakness
. . . once your eyes are opened to the light of faith and hope . . .
Once you understand the purpose of life, which is to live for God
and for Him alone, there is nothing in the world that can trouble
your soul. . . . God alone! How sweet it is to live like this![1]

These words capture the inner current within Saint Rafael Arnaiz's
life. "God alone," *sólo Dios*, was his battle cry. It is also a door he left open
behind him, an access to that which we often can't name but for which
our hearts ache. Even though Rafael's main intention in writing was to
expand his soul in prayer and praise to God, he also desired that those
who happened to read any of his words would come closer to God. He had
himself received abundant guidance from the writings of great spiritual
masters such as Saint John of the Cross and Saint Teresa of Ávila, Saint
Benedict, Saint Bernard of Clairvaux, and some of the main proponents
of the *Devotio Moderna* movement.

---

1. Rafael Arnaiz, *The Collected Works* (CW), trans. Catherine Addington, MW 61
(Collegeville, MN: Cistercian Publications, 2022); Rafael Arnáiz Barón, *Obras Completas*
(OC), 6th ed. (Burgos: Monte Carmelo, 2011), 795. Rafael's works cited in the introduction
and in the translation below are identified by item number in the English, here CW 201.

As a rich young man of the twentieth century, Rafael weighed all the possibilities that life offered him against a single offer: "Follow me" (Matt 4:19). He sold everything and followed the Master who was calling him. Most of us would like to have what he found as he advanced on the path of discipleship: love, peace, and joy. However, we carefully try to avoid the struggle involved in the process. That is why, even though Rafael is not a complicated writer, there is something counterintuitive in his writings. If we are aware and honest, as we read through his letters and meditations we may realize we are experiencing a similar interior resistance to what we feel when we hear the Beatitudes, something like, "are you sure there is not an easier way to happiness?" From the many valuable lessons that can be learned from the writings of this saint, I believe the main one is the secret of the cross:[2] only by our walking the way of the cross is love set in order in us,[3] and our desire for lasting happiness fulfilled.

Rafael didn't write like a theologian. His brief life didn't allow him to elaborate a synthesis of his own experience. He himself was aware of the effect that rapid changes and the constant need to adapt to new situations had on him as he wrote, "The Lord has given me so many ups and downs in so few years that at times I am utterly perplexed. But when I serenely contemplate all the wonders He has done in me, despite my resistance . . . then my perplexity is transformed into a marvelous light that speaks to me of God's greatness and infinite mercy."[4]

On the other hand, Rafael's mission, what he describes as the occupation of the Trappist, to "love God and let ourselves be loved by Him,"[5] remained the same. Love is the key to his life and writings, as he wrote to his aunt María in one of his letters: "Love God and *nothing* else . . . That's what I'm saying in my letters, in all of them . . . Don't read anything else into them . . ."[6]

In his pages, we find the unfolding of his spiritual path he himself walked through the stages of his interior pilgrimage. And his spiritual

2. CW 140.
3. Saint Rafael's life embodies to perfection the Cistercian ideal that authors like Saint Bernard of Clairvaux proposed, as it is expressed in the Vulgate translation of these words of the Song of Songs, "He set love in order in me" (Song 2:4).
4. CW 168.
5. CW 51.
6. CW 85.

landscapes changed fast—his initial sunny descriptions of the life in the monastery during his "monastic honeymoon" contrast vividly with the darkness of confusion and pain when he was struck by illness. Each of his statements needs to be judged not so much in itself but as a part, a stepping stone, preparing for the next grace to be received and embraced. Out of context, some of Rafael's expressions are shocking and could be misleading. As parts of the whole, however, as colors or lines on a great and luminous canvas, they are simply perfect. Therefore we need to follow his journey to the end if we want to be able to understand what our brother meant and, ultimately, what we can learn from him. In some way, the life of each true Christian can only be understood if we read it like Christ's, in the light of the resurrection.

Rafael took the straight path to holiness, that is, the cross, without making excuses. His message, being so contrary to that of the prevalent culture, is desperately needed.[7] For this reason we are glad that Rafael's voice may now reach the people of the English-speaking world with the good news of hope.

All the World Can Give:
Early Years and Vocational Discernment[8]

Saint Rafael Arnaiz in His Historical Context

The interaction between God's grace and the personal traits and historical context of the life of each saint—a mixture of failures and victories—is always surprising. Seeing Saint Rafael framed in his concrete circumstances gives a better understanding of the power that led him and his free response to it.

Rafael Arnaiz Barón[9] was born in the city of Burgos, Spain, on April 9, 1911, and died at the Trappist-Cistercian monastery of San Isidro de Dueñas on April 26, 1938. The twenty-seven years of his life comprise

7. CW 53: "I sincerely believe, abuela, that the world has lost its mind . . . and is on its way to losing its heart, which would be even worse."

8. CW 1–24.

9. Traditionally Spaniards have two last names: the first one is the father's and the second the mother's—women don't change their maiden name when they marry. Rafael's full name is Rafael Arnaiz Barón.

some of the most difficult years of Spanish contemporary history and its bloodiest war: the Spanish Civil War (1936–1939).

The socio-cultural context into which Rafael was born was complex and rich. The loss in 1898 of the last Spanish colonies—the Philippines, Cuba, and Puerto Rico—had initiated the search for a new national identity that nurtured a cultural revival. At the same time, a new social balance was needed that would incorporate the growing working class, which was concentrated in the main cities, and the new business bourgeoisie. The lack of dialogue and understanding among different groups and factions—those in favor of the monarchy and the defenders of the Republic as a form of government, traditionalists and socialists, proletariat and the bourgeois—led to constant and unresolved tensions among the different social forces. The situation of the Roman Catholic Church was not separate from these conflicts, which erupted in the religious persecution that began during the years of the Republic (1931–1936) and continued during the Civil War. During this period, over 4,000 members of the Catholic clergy, about 2,500 men and women religious, and more than 3,000 lay people were killed because they refused to deny their Christian faith.

Saint Rafael Arnaiz's Family Environment

Rafael was blessed with a loving family who helped him grow humanly and spiritually. Cherished by his parents and three younger siblings, he remained deeply attached to them during his whole life. Because of his affectionate nature, separation from them was always a struggle. But while this attachment was an important source of emotional pain for Rafael, his parents' courageous example in accepting the religious vocation of their firstborn son gave him strength to persevere not only for his own sanctification but also for theirs.

Rafael's parents, Rafael Arnaiz and Mercedes Barón, belonged to the Spanish upper class, connected with the nobility and the wealthy families who owned large estates. The code of impeccable dressing and refinement at table, as well as other expressions of their social status, was however not at odds with the sincere practice of the Christian faith that permeated the ordinary life of the family.

Rafael's father had degrees in law and forestry engineering. A lover of both nature and literature, he maintained a personal library of some six thousand books. Because of his work as a forestry engineer, the family moved from Burgos to Oviedo in 1922. Mercedes Barón was highly esteemed in aristocratic society because of her elegance and sensitivity, and her talents for literature and music. While the father was clearly the head of the family, she was in charge of the spiritual education of the children. The religious vocations of three of their four children speak of the spirit prevalent in their home. After Rafael's death, Luis Fernando (1913–1999) would join the Carthusians, and the younger Mercedes (1917–1946) the Ursulines, but only for a short period, as tuberculosis forced her to leave and took her life when she was twenty-eight years old. Only Leopoldo (1915–1999) married; he had a family of twelve children.

Among the members of Rafael's extended family, Leopoldo Barón (Rafael's mother's youngest brother, affectionately called "Polín") and his wife, María del Socorro Osorio de Moscoso, the duke and duchess of Maqueda, deserve special mention because of their great influence in the development of Rafael's vocation. As Rafael writes in a letter to his aunt, "The Lord used you and Uncle Polín to plant a seed in me, and it has taken a long time to grow . . . and I don't know whether it'll produce flowers or thorns, but either way, it comes from God."[10] The largest amount of Rafael's correspondence was addressed to them. These letters are a privileged witness not only of Rafael's spiritual evolution but also of his desire to share the graces he was receiving, to foster in others the love he himself had for God and the Virgin Mary.

Rafael visited his aunt and uncle many times. His stay with them during the summer of 1929 at their country estate in Pedrosillo, close to the city of Ávila, influenced him deeply as he assumed the numerous religious practices of their pseudo-monastic life. After an adult conversion, Leopoldo Barón had seriously considered becoming a Trappist, and after his death in 1952, his wife entered the Discalced Carmelite Monastery of the Incarnation in Ávila.

During Rafael's first visits, his uncle and aunt introduced him to the writings of Saint John of the Cross and Saint Teresa of Ávila, writers who would have great influence in the development of Rafael's spirituality. Leopoldo's attraction to the monastic way of life was the source of Rafael's early glimmers of the Trappist vocation. His uncle also organized the first

10. CW 72.

quick visit that Rafael would make to the Trappist monastery of San Isidro de Dueñas, popularly known as "La Trapa."

Because of his frequent stays with his aunt and uncle, Rafael was for them one more of their five children. However, as the nephew advanced so quickly on the way of the Spirit, they started addressing each other as *brother* and *sister*. Ultimately, much to Rafael's distress and amusement, the aunt and uncle became his spiritual disciples.

Rafael's family household also included a number of servants. It is noteworthy that their family didn't pay attention to the differences in social classes, unlike the general custom in Spanish society of the time. A simple example of this fact is Rafael's great affection for Rosa Calvo, a poor lottery administrator. In two of his letters, we find Rafael entrusting himself to her prayers while remembering their conversations about God at her workplace, where there were "very few *pesetas* inside . . . but a whole lot of love for God."[11]

This particular aspect of Rafael's education was a good preparation for him to accept community life at the monastery, where a common law of work and mutual respect applies to all. According to the Rule of Saint Benedict, no differences are to be made in the reception of brothers or their rank in community, no matter their previous social status, and "Great care and concern are to be shown in receiving poor people and pilgrims, because in them more particularly Christ is received."[12]

Saint Rafael Arnaiz's Personality and Education

Rafael's early writings, along with the numerous testimonies of those who knew him well, provide valuable material for understanding his luminous personality, a personality that is partly shown in his later writings, where his suffering comes to the fore. Balancing the two realities is necessary for understanding the multifaceted aspects of this rich young soul.

Rafael was unusually talented. Testimonies from his years as a student in Jesuit schools, initially in Burgos and later in Oviedo, speak about his good academic results and religious piety—he belonged to the Sodality

11. CW 8 and 49.

12. *RB 1980: The Rule of Saint Benedict 1980,* ed. Timothy Fry (Collegeville, MN: Liturgical Press, 1981), 259, 271–73, on the offering of sons by nobles and the poor, and 279–81 on community rank (RB 53.15; 59:1-7; 63:1-9).

of Mary Immaculate of his school and, later, to the Nocturnal Adoration society and other religious organizations. The fact that he easily passed the difficult entrance exams for the prestigious School of Architecture in Madrid is also proof of his quick intelligence and self-confidence.[13] He also excelled in other areas, like playing various musical instruments without formal training, and being an excellent dancer. His artistic interest and capacity for drawing and painting were much more than a lifelong hobby for him. At the age of fifteen, he had already begun private lessons with the well-known artist Eugenio Tamayo.

Rafael's personality was magnetic. He intentionally brought joy wherever he went. He easily became the center of conversations and games thanks to his natural elegance and irresistible sense of humor. Along these lines, he tended to exaggerate his own imperfections as a way of laughing at himself. Awareness of this tendency is necessary to arrive at an accurate picture of some of the situations he describes.

Rafael's capacity for taking himself lightly was the counterpart of what he himself called his "excessive sensitivity."[14] His affectionate nature would bring him both great joys and great sorrows. When he pondered God's love for him, he described his soul as "a burning volcano about to erupt."[15] Often, his gratitude and the desire to love in return overwhelmed him: "My soul is full and running over. You've put so much love into such a miserable little soul, Lord!"[16]

Given the particular circumstances of his monastic journey, Rafael had to say goodbye to his family on four occasions. Each separation was an agonizing struggle. Joining a Trappist monastery at the time required a radical rupture from family and friends. Given the remarkably affectionate relationships in his family circle, and the pampered life he had lived so far, his impending separation from his family felt even starker. He so feared breaking the news to his family before his first departure to the monastery that he had initially decided to enter directly and only tell his parents when he had already been admitted as a novice. Fortunately, his uncle Polín, with the help of the papal nuncio to Spain, Monsignor

---

13. Rafael's own words on June 23, 1930, after he took one of his exams are eloquent in this respect. See CW 2.

14. CW 51.

15. CW 75.

16. CW 211.

Federico Tedeschini, was able to dissuade him from that approach. While they supported him in his resolution, they encouraged him to receive his parents' blessing before departing.

As a young man, Rafael was full of lofty ideals. When he entered the monastery, the monks looked like angels to him, living only for God. Coming to terms with the reality of human weakness still present in those who had dedicated their lives to God cost him many tears. His natural sensitivity and affectionate personality needed to be purified through the process of learning to love in and with God's love; only then would he discover a new peace, which he called "serenity."[17]

A Heart Filled with Joy and Love: Joining the Monastery[18]

Rafael visited the Trappist-Cistercian monastery of San Isidro de Due-ñas, in the Spanish region of Palencia, for the first time on September 23, 1930. He was nineteen years old. This first quick visit, when he stayed only overnight, left what was already an indelible mark on his soul, captivating his spiritual and aesthetic sensitivity.

After that short visit he did not go back to the monastery until September 1931, for an eight-day stay. His first written impressions of the life at La Trapa come from that time. But it was not till the summer of 1932, during an eight-day retreat at the monastery, preached by one of the monks, Father Armando Regolf, that Rafael seems to have come to a decision about his vocation. It was then a well-pondered decision when in November 1933 he finally wrote to the abbot of San Isidro, Dom Félix Alonso García, requesting to be admitted as a novice. He clearly stated his reasons for this request in this short but eloquent letter: "I am not motivated to change my life in this way because of sadness or suffering or disappointment or disillusionment with the world . . . I have all that it can give me. God, in His infinite goodness, has given me such gifts in this life, many more than I deserve . . . As such, my reverend Father, if you receive me into your community alongside your sons, be assured that you will be receiving only a heart filled with joy and much love for God."[19]

17. CW 159.
18. CW 25–34.
19. CW 12.

On January 15, 1934, at the age of twenty-two, Rafael left behind a promising career as an architect and his comfortable and warm family environment to join the Cistercian Order of the Strict Observance at the Abbey of San Isidro de Dueñas. He knew that a very different life from the one he had lived so far awaited him, and he embraced it with heroic enthusiasm and his characteristic sense of humor. His letters to his family from this time are full of his youthful and fresh spirit, ready to overcome any obstacles for love of God and with the help of Our Blessed Mother. His vivid descriptions of his personal struggle to overcome drowsiness, cold, and hunger as he adjusted to the austerities of Trappist life—even stricter during the Lenten season—prove Rafael's readiness to do whatever it took to become a saint. This determination and his surrender to the Lord's will would be the constant response to grace by the new novice.

Rafael took upon himself the yoke of Saint Benedict's Rule, faithfully obeying those in authority in the community (the abbot, his novice master, and his confessor), learning to use a hoe to join in the manual labor on the fields around the abbey, and many other practices foreign to him and even contrary to his personality. The strict silence of the cloister, which he loved, forced him at first to find new venues for his joy, as he had to repress his desire to whistle or spontaneously break into song when feelings of gratitude bubbled up in his heart. But after four months of full observation of monastery practices, when the victory over his natural tendencies felt so much closer, an unexpected challenge presented itself. His unwavering search for God had to take another shape, a more internal form of obedience: adjusting to often unplanned and unwanted events with renewed trust and love. Through this new attitude of constant listening and surrendering to God, Rafael rediscovered his call and his own way of observing the Rule.

I Thought That God Was Abandoning Me: Struck by Illness[20]

Except for a dangerous bacterial infection that Rafael suffered when he was nine years old, he had been healthy as a boy and young adult. In May 1934, however, symptoms of diabetes appeared. This illness, which ultimately took his life, arrived without previous warnings. Did the strict

20. CW 35–63.

fasting during Lent soon after his entrance trigger this bodily reaction? It is hard to know. At the time, knowledge about and measures of dealing with diabetes were rather limited. The effects of the illness, including his loss of about fifty pounds in a week, were so alarming that Rafael was forced to leave the monastery on May 26, 1934. Brokenhearted and almost blind, he was driven by his father back to the family home. Rafael would have preferred to stay at La Trapa, even if it meant his death, but he obeyed and returned to the world he had thought he had left once and for all. His abbot hoped that the more favorable conditions of his family environment and the best medical treatment would save his life, but, as an unusual concession, he gave Rafael his novice habit to be used as a shroud if necessary.

Almost a year and a half would pass until Rafael was able to return to his beloved Trapa. Once he had survived the imminent danger, he quickly recovered, thanks to insulin injections and a rigorous diet. Everyone hoped for a complete cure, and soon his doctor supported a prompt return to the monastery. The initially bewildered Rafael clung to those hopes, constantly dreaming of rejoining his brothers in the monastic choir and the quiet row of monks walking toward the fields for work.

The tension in Spanish society had been on the rise, until in October 1934 it exploded in the so-called "Revolución de Asturias," a strike undertaken by regional miners against the central government, lasting from the fourth to the nineteenth of the month. The Arnaiz house was occupied, first by the local police and then by rebel forces, and bullet-ridden for nine days, while churches and other buildings in the city were burned down and many priests and religious were killed. Rafael remained the moral support of his family during the horror of those days, but his health again suffered from the great stress and lack of food.

Shaped in His Hands: A Path of Oblation[21]

On November 21, 1934, Rafael made a quick visit to La Trapa. In *Mi Rafael*, Juan Antonio Martínez Camino, SJ, gives abundant details about

---

21. CW 64–101.

this important visit.[22] When Rafael spoke with his abbot and novice master, he had to acknowledge that he was still not cured from his diabetes. They both recommended that he wait to return to the monastery until he could follow the full observance of the Rule. As a diabetic, he could not follow the monastic diet, which was considered an essential ascetical practice.

Brokenhearted by this new delay and, even worse, by the fact that he had no guarantee of being able to resume his novitiate, Rafael asked for the advice of Fr. Teófilo Sandoval, his first confessor at the abbey and the one who later initiated his canonization process.[23] From the conversation came a glimmer of light. At first, Fr. Teófilo set before him other possibilities: why didn't he join the Benedictines, where the food regimen was less strict? It was neither the first nor the last time that Rafael had to patiently listen to someone trying to dissuade him from rejoining the Trappists. But when Fr. Teófilo saw that Rafael had made up his mind, he mentioned the oblate state as a way for him to return to the community.

The word *oblate* has different meanings even within the Benedictine tradition. In contemporary Trappist monasteries, it is a way of following the monastic life with some restrictions or mitigations, and without religious vows. This was something of an accommodation of a state recognized by canon law to fit Rafael's particular case—the oblate status was not designed for accepting young sick members, but rather for older candidates or those incapable of completing formal studies for the priesthood, which at that time was the norm for the choir monks. For someone of Rafael's social status, following this path was a humiliation, as in practice, oblates were seen as second-class monks. When the abbot, Fr. Félix, was presented with this new possibility, he didn't dismiss it, but he reiterated his earlier advice to wait and see whether full recovery was possible.

Rafael returned to his parents' house with this new option in mind, but before he was able to recognize in it the path to holiness that the Lord was

---

22. Juan Antonio Martínez Camino, *Mi Rafael* (Bilbao: Desclée De Brouwer, 2003), 97–101.

23. Fr. Teófilo was instrumental in the preservation of Rafael's writings, which he carefully compiled soon after the death of his spiritual son. Early on, he had become aware of Rafael's greatness of soul. Later, when he was no longer Rafael's confessor, he encouraged him to write, hoping that Rafael would be able to share with him his journal entries once he had finished his novitiate and was free to choose a confessor.

opening for him, he had to deal with his own feelings of disappointment in realizing that his cherished dreams of becoming a Cistercian monk and, one day, a priest, had come to an end. He would never be able to make religious vows in the Order. Rafael entered a dark period of sadness, discouragement, and confusion. He wrote, "Sometimes I think that, truly, I don't deserve to be a son of the Cistercian Order, that I've been dreaming too loftily for such a lowly person."[24]

During this season of uncertainty and sorrow he began to learn what it meant to surrender his will to God's at a deeper level. He remained mostly silent, because some lessons require stillness to be faithfuly learned. Only then were his peace and joy finally restored. Now he was able to see with new clarity the work God had been doing in his soul, and how this work had been made possible by his diabetes. Before his return to La Trapa, his understanding of the Cistercian vocation had acquired new vistas.

At last, on October 9, 1935, Rafael wrote to the abbot requesting his entrance as an oblate. His petition was accepted. But one final battle still remained to be fought, a struggle that repeated itself each time he had to leave his family home. The very intense correspondence that he maintained with the duke and duchess of Maqueda, and more particularly with his aunt María Osorio, provided a formidable support for him in the strife of the last three months before his entry. The mutual deep affection between aunt and nephew was no doubt a source of consolation, but even more crucial was the fact these letters became his only outlet for the overpowering feelings of love, joy, and awe for the Lord acting in his soul, which overwhelmed him at times. Although Rafael told his aunt to destroy his letters after she read them, she, aware of the treasure embodied in those missives, didn't do as he had asked.

The Circus Clown: The Last One in the Community[25]

Rafael returned to the monastery on January 11, 1936, for what would be the longest of his stays: eight and a half months. As he arrived, he was given back his novice's habit, and soon afterward he started his studies

24. CW 61.
25. CW 102–33.

for the priesthood—unheard of for oblates. It is possible that the abbot still hoped that Rafael would recover and then return to the ranks of the choir monks; in any case, his support for Rafael's working toward the priesthood showed his love and appreciation for his spiritual son. However, the abbot's support was not shared by the whole community. Many brothers did not understand the purpose of Rafael's return. One of those who did not agree was Fr. Pío Martínez,[26] a mentally unbalanced monk with whom Rafael had to eat in the infirmary. Fr. Pío, who was a torment for the whole community, constantly challenged Rafael to return to his parents' home, and he openly despised him for the diet his diabetes obliged him to follow. What agony these experiences must have been for Rafael's sensitive soul! But Rafael never complained.

Many other trials served Rafael as oportunities to grow in love and humility. Fr. Marcelo León, the novice master who had always been so affectionate with him, had died before his return, and the new novice master, Fr. José Olmedo, didn't get to know Rafael and the unusual path through which he was called to fulfill his monastic vocation. Rafael had to undergo the same lack of understanding from the monk assigned to the novices as confessor after his return. Because of this change, he was not able to continue with Fr. Teófilo, who had guided him so wisely, as his confessor.

Alone, and having to face his new situation in the community, Rafael suffered a short period of confusion—had he deceived himself about his vocation?—but he soon overcame this trial. Important interior changes were rapidly taking place. As he explained to his aunt María in a letter written less than a month and a half after his return, "I 'rejoice in my uselessness,' which has helped me to gain knowledge of myself, to uproot so much of my self-love, and to praise God."[27] He considered himself the "circus clown" of La Trapa.[28] The truth is that he was being instructed in the foolishness of the cross.

Despite these challenges, Rafael's adaptation was good. Except for his meals, he was able to move from the infirmary to the common dormitory, and he joined the community for the liturgical prayer in the choir and the

26. OC 840–42.
27. CW 105.
28. CW 113.

work in the fields. His words describing Vespers, the evening prayer, depict perfectly not only his love for the monastic liturgy, but the state of his soul:

> Those moments of great solemnity during the psalmody, with great peace in one's heart, bring such consolation! . . . The hour of Vespers contains so much joy! What a happy thought, that the day is now spent . . . and it was spent before the Tabernacle of the Lord . . . The soul is so moved upon having completed another day in the Lord's service. Our hearts are so grateful for the sublime privilege of having been able to spend the day singing before the Lord . . .[29]

During these months Rafael greatly benefited from the care of Br. Tescelino, the infirmarian, who also became his friend, and later his confidant and the recipient of some of his letters. In one letter to his father Rafael witnesses to the care Br. Tescelino gave him: "I can tell you that I honestly don't concern *myself* with my illness at all. In his charity, Brother Tescelino, the infirmarian, makes up for that . . . He gives me insulin, takes care of me, checks my levels every eight days, weighs me, etc."[30]

But the beginning of the Spanish Civil War put an abrupt end to Rafael's second stay at La Trapa. His first reflections on the war portray the uncertainty and lack of clear information at the monastery. Soon after the uprising on July 18, 1936, Spain was divided into two major zones, usually called the "National" and the "Republican" zones. Palencia, where the monastery of San Isidro is located, remained in the National zone and far from the first lines of battle. This fact allowed those who were not forced to leave the monastery to continue the monastic routine relatively undisturbed.

Fighting under Christ's Standard: Saint Rafael Arnaiz and the Spanish Civil War

On September 29, 1936, Rafael and about thirty of the other young monks had to leave the monastery when they were called up to render military service to the rightist faction, the National side, of the Spanish Civil War. Twice Rafael experienced the humiliation of being declared

---

29. CW 116.
30. CW 103.

unfit because of his diabetes. The results of the analysis performed on him showed very high levels of blood sugar, the sign that his illness was progressing.[31] While he waited for the paperwork to release him from military service, he lived with his family, who had sought refuge in the village of Villasandino, in the province of Burgos. During these months he was able to see firsthand some of the devastation caused by the war.

The Spanish Civil War and the religious persecution that started during the Republic and escalated during the years of the war were complex realities because of both their causes and their growth. Economic and political tensions were at play, but Rafael's vision of the events of the war was not reduced to or determined by either an economic or a political interpretation of the events. To understand his stance on the war and perhaps to learn from it, we will do well to distance ourselves from a simplistic labeling of either faction. Rafael was himself cautious about trying to interpret what was happening or even about praying for a specific outcome: "I tell the Lord that since I don't understand His plans . . . He ought to do whatever He wants, and I just offer my prayers and supplications so that He might make use of them, for He knows better than I do what their intention ought to be. Thus I avoid asking for the wrong thing."[32]

Rafael's approach to the war was not ideological; he remained consistent with the principle that guided his whole life: "God alone." He was undoubtedly familiar with Saint Ignatius's meditation in the *Spiritual Exercises,* where he places the retreatant on a battle field with two leaders, Christ and Satan, each trying to gather as many as possible to fight under their standard, but using opposite strategies.[33] The decision that mattered to Rafael was under which standard to fight. For him the answer was clear: choosing God alone rather than temporal enterprises, political parties, or other institutions, which, as he constantly repeated, always disappoint.

---

31. The second exam was performed while he was with staying with his family. Even though he was receiving all the care his mother could lavish on him, the results were the same as when he was at the monastery, showing the little understanding of diabetes at that time and the fact that Rafael was never able to know how to respond properly to the symptoms of diabetes.

32. CW 149.

33. David L. Fleming, *The Spiritual Exercises of Saint Ignatius: A Literal Translation & A Contemporary Reading* (St. Louis, MO: The Institute of Jesuit Sources, 1978), 84–91.

xxxvi   *The Collected Works*

In his reflections, Rafael speaks against any form of false religious fervor or political vision more intent on human pursuits than on God. Given his upbringing as a pampered child, Rafael's social conscience was remarkable. Even before the beginning of the war, he openly commented on the reality of social injustice, and he was quick to blame the rich rather than the poor for the increasing unrest that he observed in Oviedo's poor neighborhoods:

> If the idea of God is taken from the poor, they have nothing else left; their desperation is justifiable, their hatred for the rich is natural, their desire for revolution and anarchy is logical. And if the idea of God is a nuisance to the rich, and they do not heed the precepts of the Gospel and the teachings of Jesus . . . then they shouldn't complain. If their selfishness hinders them from drawing near to the poor, they should not be surprised when the latter plan to take what they have by force.[34]

When Rafael wrote that his brother Fernando, fighting with the National soldiers, was "firing cannons against God's enemies,"[35] he was not making a political statement; he was pointing out the supernatural forces that are at play in human affairs and, more concretely in this case, of the anticlerical violence that he had experienced firsthand. He knew of the war between good and evil in his own heart, and of his own need for purification. Similarly, he could recognize the same reality occurring among his contemporaries: "Spain needed to be shaken up . . . It needed to be made clean . . . It needed to react . . . It even needs martyrs to die for it. And God's mercy is permitting a war to break out."[36] Far from being rigid or out of touch with reality, Rafael's vision shows a deeper perception of the circumstances in which he was immersed; there he could recognize God's Providence, acting as the Lord of history while respecting human freedom. Rafael's words show faith in practice, not in theory: "Nothing happens in this world that He has not foreseen in His infinite goodness, and creatures will not go any further than God allows them to."[37] At the

34. CW 51.
35. CW 149.
36. CW 123.
37. CW 111.

same time, he does not recoil from telling God, "Lord, be careful what You're doing, because I have a brother on the front lines!"[38]

Above all, Rafael clearly understood that he also had a war to fight, as he did until the end. He soon became aware of the martyrdom God was asking of him: "The Trappist's martyrdom is not at the stake or down the barrel of a gun . . . God asks something else of us. God asks us to live this life while we are still separated from Him, and for a little while, we suffer the hardships of the body, the miseries of the spirit, and the weaknesses of the flesh . . . Behold, the true martyrdom of one who loves God and yearns for the peace of eternal life."[39] To carry on his spiritual battle without further delay, Rafael returned to the monastery on December 6, 1936.

A Deer that Thirsts: The Interior Trappist[40]

This was Rafael's shortest stay, two months. Without the care of a proper infirmarian, his health rapidly began to deteriorate. Initially, he reassumed the monastic rhythm in its entirety except for the meals, which he continued to have in the infirmary. But in January his state worsened, and he was confined to the infirmary. Finally, to prevent a diabetic coma, he left once again on February 7, 1937.

Despite the shortness of this stay at the monastery, Rafael's experience during these two months was crucial for the full development of what Antonio María Martín Fernández-Gallardo, OCSO, describes as the "interior Trappist."[41] Rafael's center is not in the exterior La Trapa but the hidden God who waits for him at La Trapa.

The unfavorable circumstances because of the Civil War that Rafael experienced when he returned to the monastery additionally enhanced the spiritual path that he was already following. The exterior elements of the Trappist life, which he had once identified as the perfection of the Trappist vocation, were now of relative unimportance. He focused totally on the interior search for God in love and desire: the soul of the Rule of Saint Benedict and Cistercian mysticism. Despite the fact that Rafael was

38. CW 149.
39. CW 112.
40. CW 134–58.
41. Antonio María Martín Fernández-Gallardo, *San Rafael Arnáiz Barón: Vida y mensaje del Hermano Rafael*, 2nd ed. (Madrid: Edibesa, 2009), 163.

not able to make full use of the ordinary means provided by the monastic life to support a monk in this search—such as work with the community or full participation in the Divine Office—the monastery remained the place where he was able to respond most fully to the call he had received to live for God alone. His cell had become for him "my heaven on earth."[42]

When Rafael was forced once again to return to his family environment, even though it was hard for him to leave, he didn't protest; he was convinced that, "He [God] is taking me away from here . . . He must bring me back to live within these walls once more . . . I'm so sure that I am to die a Trappist!"[43] As he left, he took with him the essence of the monastic silence and solitude, his love for Scripture, and humble service to all around him. His fidelity to these monastic values and practices, deeply internalized and cherished, allowed the interior Trappist to continue growing and developing outside the monastery walls.

Rafael joined his parents, his brother Leopoldo, and his sister Mercedes in the village of Villasandino, in Burgos province, as they had to abandon their family home in Oviedo and seek refuge in the country, far from the battle lines. Rafael's brother, Fernando, interrupted his studies in Belgium to enroll voluntarily in the National army.

Rafael remained in the family circle from February 7, 1937, to December 15, 1937. During some of these months, he also enjoyed the company of his beloved Aunt María and Uncle Leopoldo (Polín) and their children. It is easy to imagine Rafael surrounded by the kind of affection to which his heart so naturally inclined. Despite the horrors of the war, life in the village unfolded in relative peace. They were far from the front lines and sheltered by the National forces, which had their center in the town of Burgos. In this context, Rafael was once more able to adapt the monastic balance of work and prayer to his new circumstances. He combined the work of maintenance and improvement of the family property with long hours of silent prayer and meditation on the Word of God, in the solitude of the parish church and walking alone across the fields. He also devoted himself to painting, pouring into his art both the peace and the suffering in his heart. Gradually, as his body recovered its strength, his soul mustered all the graces received on his journey so far to face the last stage of his pilgrimage. Now that he was com-

42. CW 157.
43. CW 158.

pletely aware of what was awaiting him at the monastery, he shuddered. He needed to be strengthened by God's grace to undergo the hardships of bodily hunger caused by his illness, and his heart's loneliness caused by his isolation.

Once again, some people advised him to be prudent, to follow another path, to wait, but he also heard another voice. He described it in this way to Br. Tescelino: "If you saw the tenderness in Jesus' eyes, you wouldn't say any of that. Rather, you'd get up from your bed without a care in the world, without thinking about yourself at all, and you'd join Jesus' retinue, even if you were the last one . . . you hear, the *last one* . . . and you'd tell Him, 'I'm coming, Lord. I don't care about my illness, or death, or eating, or sleeping . . . If You'll have me, I will go.'"[44]

It is Love . . . : The Ultimate Sacrifice of Praise[45]

Just before his last departure from the monastery, Rafael wrote with conviction, trusting in God's plan for him, "If God grants me the grace and health to do so, I will leave it all behind again, not three or four times . . . but a thousand times over, if necessary."[46] Now, on December 15, 1937, he fulfills these words, clinging to the cross. He had dried his tears as he crossed the monastery threshold, when he met Fr. Teófilo in the monastery cloister. He told him with assurance, "I am coming for good, I come to die here."[47] What did he mean?

Rafael's decision was not a search for death. As his letters show, his upbringing, the love of his family and friends, had provided him with a solid and wholesome human foundation. Yes, as he himself had written, he was sensitive, and accordingly he suffered greatly at times, but he was equally equipped with a great capacity for experiencing joy, love, wonder, and all that is beautiful, true, and good. He returned to the monastery not as a victim of external circumstances or a destructive vision of God's will, but as one who yearns for more, as one who has discovered that the human horizon is too small because sooner or later it is bound to end. He knew, now through his own experience, that the only door through which

---

44. CW 166.
45. CW 170–208.
46. CW 158.
47. Arnáiz Barón, OC #858, n. 1033.

to enter and receive life in abundance is the cross. This door for him was at San Isidro, as he wrote: "I see La Trapa, I see a cross, and there I go."[48]

The day after Rafael returned, in the first entry of the journal that he entitled "God and My Soul"—the most personal of his writings because it was destined to be read only by Fr. Teófilo when he became his confessor once again—he specified the reasons that had brought him back:

> I have come for the following reasons:
>
> 1. Because I believe that here in the monastery I can better follow my vocation of loving God on the cross and in sacrifice.
>
> 2. In order to help my brothers in the fight, because Spain is at war.
>
> 3. In order to make use of the rest of the time that God has given me in this life, and make haste in learning to love His cross.[49]

These were Rafael's principal motives for returning. It would not take him too long to became aware of the Lord's own reasons for calling him back to his side at the tabernacle. Remaining attentive to the voice of his Master and waiting for his final call, Rafael was to be consumed by the living flame of love, on which he had often meditated when reading the poems of Saint John of the Cross. He recorded the longing that filled him: "The only thing that disturbs the silence of my cell is a desire for God . . . A prayer bursts forth from my sick lips . . . Saint John of the Cross composed it . . . It's just a line from one of his poems: 'Tear through the veil of this sweet encounter.'"[50]

And God finally tore the veil. Three important milestones led to this event, when he who had found his delight in the chanted choral office was able to complete his ultimate sacrifice of praise. Rafael's self-oblation included the offering of his will, a vow always to love Jesus, and, finally, the gift of his life to God.

In the midst of his loneliness, intensified during these festive days, and putting his trust in God, he gave himself to him in his weakness: "On Christmas Eve I gave the Lord, the Child Jesus, the last of what was left of my will. I gave Him even my littlest desires . . . So what is left? . . .

Nothing. Not even my desire to die. Now, I am nothing but God's possession. But Lord, what a poor little thing You possess!"[51]

Rafael was never able to make religious vows. However, on New Year's Day 1938, his vow always to love Jesus became his path of consecration. He described it in this way:

> I made a vow at prayer this morning. I made a *vow to love Jesus always*. I have realized what my vocation is. I am not a religious . . . I am not a layman . . . I am nothing . . . Blessed be God, I am nothing but a soul in love with Christ. He wants nothing but my love, and He wants it detached from everything and everyone else . . . A life of love, that is my Rule . . . my vow . . . That is my only reason for living.[52]

Before his final entrance, Rafael had promised Br. Tescelino, his former infirmarian, that he would do all that was in his power to take care of his illness. However, because of both his situation at the monastery and his deficient understanding of how best to treat his diabetes, his health kept deteriorating. He was aware of that fact, and it became a source of interior conflict for him. The offering of his life to God, which he made on February 27, put an end to this: "Today, I offered the Lord the only thing I had left . . . my life. I laid it down at His feet, so that He might accept it, use it however He wants, and take it away whenever He wants, for whatever He wants . . ."[53]

Rafael turned to Mary as his intercessor to present the gift of himself to God: "I asked the Virgin Mary to intercede for me with Jesus, so that He will accept my offering. What a great joy it would be if God were to accept it! What a joy it would be to die for Jesus . . . and for Jesus to offer my life to the Eternal Father in reparation for the sins of the world."[54]

The Father accepted this offering and united Rafael's oblation to the sacrifice of his own Son for the salvation of the world. There was no better sign of that acceptance than on Easter Sunday, when Rafael received the cowl and the black scapular, the monastic garment that monks and nuns

51. CW 172.
52. CW 175.
53. CW 187.
54. CW 187.

regularly receive in a public celebration after professing their solemn vows. In this case, it was an exceptional favor granted by Dom Félix Alonso, abbot of San Isidro, in a private ceremony in his office. As Rafael told his brother Leopoldo in his last letter, "Father Abbot gave me the black scapular and cowl, so other than the crown, I look just like a real monk now."[55] He looked like what he had become, one who, according to the Rule of Saint Benedict, had been willing to share in the sufferings of Christ so that he might also deserve to share in his kingdom.[56]

Now everything was accomplished. God had finished his masterpiece, apparently at the same time having covered the eyes of all so that they might not see that he was ready to call Rafael to himself. On April 21, Easter Thursday, Rafael's father came to visit him, and found him better than ever, radiant, peaceful, and happy. Only a day afterward, Rafael took to bed; even the doctor who was called to attend to him didn't notice the gravity of his state. Five days later, on April 26, Rafael died from a diabetic coma.

Having been born on a Palm Sunday, April 9, 1911, Rafael soon learned to cling to the cross of Christ. Its weight did not crush him, but lifted him up until he reached "the measure of the full stature of Christ" (Eph 4:13) and heard Christ's voice saying, "Come, share your master's joy" (Matt 25:23).

The Secret of the Cross: Saint Rafael Arnaiz's Spiritual Path

Whether he intended it or not, Rafael benefited from one of the positive outcomes of journaling: gaining clarity. He was not afraid of experiencing his feelings in all their intensity, without censoring them. As he wrote, he was presenting the whole of his experience to God, even though he could not fully understand it. Witnessing the way divine grace gradually led him and recreated him from within invites readers to have a similar attitude not only toward God but toward themselves. So often saints are presented as if one day they had crossed the threshold of holiness and

---

55. CW 207.
56. RB Prol. 50.

left behind all forms of confusion, temptation, or discouragement. But Rafael's recorded reflections and struggles reveal a saint in the making, striving to discern and embrace ever more fully the motions of the Holy Spirit in him. He didn't have a long battle against mortal sin—according to reliable witnesses, he never lived a life of vice, despite the fact that sometimes he uses expressions that may sound as if this were so. But in writing his thoughts, he left a record of the way God was winning Rafael for himself. His journal entry on the Wednesday of Holy Week in 1938, only thirteen days before his death, clearly shows this process still taking place. He begins with harsh words towards himself in his inability to do anything for Jesus, but as the words fill up the page, he becomes aware of his mistake, and he comes to this conclusion: "My God, my God, help me to humbly do Your will. Help me to serve You, loving my own weakness and uselessness. . . Lord, Lord, look at my intentions, and *purify them.*"[57]

Being able to contemplate a saint in progress is at the same time comforting and demanding. He himself wonders, "My Lord, I spend my life wallowing in my own misery, and at the same time I don't dream of anything but You, I don't live for anything but You. How does that make sense?"[58]

The most challenging aspect of these words consists in his understanding of holiness as an attainable goal, but only if one truly wants it: "The interior life . . . the spiritual life, a life of prayer. My God! Surely all that ought to be difficult! But it's not at all. Remove from your heart what's in the way and you'll find God. That's it."[59]

Removing what's in the way: that's the key, but what is it? Rafael repeatedly affirms that our own failures and misery are not the key, and they should not deter us from pressing forward on the path of love and holiness. Shortly before his death, he wrote, "My Jesus, how much I love you, despite what I am . . . , and the worse and more miserable I am, the more I love you, and I will love you always and *I will cling to you and I won't let you go.*"[60] As Cistercian contemplative authors insist, the true spiritual journey begins with self-knowledge and the recognition of our

57. CW 203.
58. CW 202.
59. CW 156.
60. CW 202.

xliv The Collected Works

own misery.[61] However, this sobering acknowledgement is balanced by the astonishing fact that human desire for God is but a poor reflection of the divine desire for us. God is the one who initiated and supports our search for him. Moreover, in Rafael's words, "The world doesn't see, it's blind, and God needs love, so much love."[62] This, of course, is not a theological statement, but a condensed expression of Rafael's basic experience of God. God needs our love because he truly longs for us; his love is real, more real than any human love. This is nothing but the experience of the people of Israel, whose God was jealous for his people. And it is the experience of the New Testament writers, who portrayed Jesus as deeply moved with compassion, and dying with a thirst beyond that of the body. If we thirst for God, and God thirsts for us, what prevents these two thirsts from encountering and satisfying each other in the full communion of love? Rafael came to this realization: "I was searching for God, but I was also searching for His creatures, and I was searching for myself; and God wants me all to Himself."[63] Human love needs to be purified—our desires need to be set in order—so that we who search can be found and transformed by the God who searches for us in love.

As Rafael discerned that he was being called to become a Trappist, he thought his vocation implied the sacrifice of his attachment to his family as well as other loves or desires such as those that had led him to become a student of architecture. Still, despite the different context and circumstances, he managed to transfer much of his natural affection to his new brothers. Similarly, he exchanged his older dreams for his new ideal of becoming a monk and a priest. His early descriptions of fraternal charity at La Trapa are eloquent: "There, we love one another deeply and truly; our love for God unites us in spirit, while our bodies are united by the Rule, by penance, and sometimes by suffering . . . As for the heart, ours is also very united . . . in silence we tell it . . . 'If you knew how beautiful it is to be a Trappist!!!' "[64]

61. See Bernard of Clairvaux, *The Steps of Humility and Pride*, trans. M. Ambrose Conway, Cistercian Fathers series 13 (Kalamazoo, MI: Cistercian Publications, 1989), 47.
62. CW 72.
63. CW 64.
64. CW 53.

Clinging to grace and to his own strong resolution, he had fought and overcome drowsiness, cold, and the hunger caused by the severe Lenten fasts. He had fought and overcome when his body had finally yielded to the discipline of the Trappist life. But the sudden disruption caused by the onset of his diabetes helped him to realize that God wanted more: he wanted his whole heart. Now, misunderstood, humiliated, and partly isolated from the community, Rafael began to learn that the process that leads to the complete surrender of the heart requires a different pedagogy from that of mastery over the physical body. Paradoxically, this same body, which seemed to have put an end to his dreams, was going to open up for him the possibility of discovering how to give his heart totally to God through his weakness. Thus began the process that would lead him to discover the secret that many saints had unveiled before him. He was ready to receive the "secret of the cross," ready to discover that the cross we so often reject is the only access to the love we yearn for. In Rafael's words, "What great intimacy Jesus has with those who mourn! Blessed are our tears, sorrows, and illnesses, which are our treasures, all that we possess. They make us draw near to Jesus, since the love we have for Him is so little, so feeble, so weak that it is not enough on its own . . . !"[65]

Our love is never enough; it is too weak and fickle to respond to the voice whispering, "Love me, suffer with me, I am Jesus."[66] This was Rafael's calling. Love had always been his goal. When he was only twenty-three years old, he had clearly expressed it in a letter to a layman, Marino del Hierro: "We must love Him above all things. And how hard that is! Only the saints achieved that . . . This must be our one and only, unchanging aspiration. Once we have achieved it, we shall have neither sorrows nor joys, nor shall we be here nor there . . . it will all be the same to us, for *everything* will be God, and we shall love Him more than we do anyone else, and our very being and feeling shall all disappear before Him."[67]

With a heart as sensitive as his, Rafael could intuit that his love had to be more than those ever-changing feelings. To love God above all also means to love him always, no matter what, particularly in times of trial.

65. CW 162.
66. CW 185.
67. CW 46.

Little by little, the cross appeared clearer and clearer in his horizon as the only way to his goal, a goal that he himself would not achieve but that the cross would achieve for him. He wrote, "My Jesus, how good you are. You do everything so marvelously well. You show me the way; You show me the goal. The way is the sweet cross . . . , it is sacrifice, renunciation . . . And the goal? The goal it's you, and only you . . ."[68]

The Master himself had clearly established the cross as the door to discipleship when he said, "If anyone wants to come after me, he must deny himself, take up his cross, and follow me" (Matt 16:24). However, the human resistance to the cross, particularly one's own, remains. Rafael's writings are a formidable witness of the way a heart can be changed from resistance to the love of the cross. Loving the cross: this was the key to Rafael's holiness, his joy, and his peace, a secret he opens up as he explains:

> May those who encounter these pages understand that death to the world is birth in God, that within the austerities of a life of silence and solitude is found the sweet joy of a heart whose happiness lies in simplicity and openness, and that while anyone who follows Christ undoubtedly follows Him down the only path, which is the cross . . . I believe it is in loving the cross that all things have been achieved.[69]

But why? Why did the love of the cross change everything for Rafael? Because only the cross can disarm and starve the ego that wants to control all that is—including God—as people's constant planning shows. Self-will cannot overcome self-will. This is the fundamental problem, precisely because, as Rafael clearly understood, the ego is the major hindrance on the path to God and holiness. In this letter to his Aunt María, Rafael describes with absolute lucidity what comprises the process of spiritual transformation as he experienced it:

> I don't know how to explain it, something that truly hinders us . . . perhaps you'll understand: when you place yourself at the foot of the tabernacle, and look at Jesus, and contemplate His wounds, and cry at His feet, and you realize that in the face of Christ's immense love,

68. CW 202.
69. CW 153.

you disappear, *your* tears disappear, your entire soul is overwhelmed
and becomes like a tiny speck of sand in the vastness of the sea . . .
Then you'll neither suffer nor rejoice, for everything is God. God
fills it all. You won't even have *desires*. Then when someone asks you,
"What's going on with you? . . . Are you suffering? Why are you
crying? What do you want?" maybe you'll smile and say, "Who, me?
Sweet Jesus! I'm nothing, I want nothing, don't ask about me . . .
I don't know . . . Talk to me about God instead. Then you'll see
how God fills it all . . . you'll come to realize that you aren't all that
concerned with *yourself* anymore. You'll realize that all you want is to
invite others into the tenderness that Jesus has placed in your heart.[70]

In his prayer before the tabernacle, Rafael stood face to face with the
crucified Lord. In his wounds, he discovered not only "Christ's immense
love," but the immense value of his own cross. Only our own cross, the
one given, not chosen, like his illness, can hollow us, open up within us
the access to the core of our being. There, and there only, can we experience that "God fills it all," because the ego has been moved out of the way.
Enveloped in his love, "you disappear," and so do tears or laughter, or any
desire but the desire for "God alone" and to share with others this love,
the tenderness that one receives.

The constant external and internal changes in Rafael's life taught him
the truth that we often refuse to accept: we are not in control. Alterna-
tion is part of the spiritual journey; however, true faith and love occur at
a much deeper level and cannot be identified with the peaks and valleys of
religious fervor. Remaining still under the provident hand of God, Rafael
was made whole; the barriers built by his ego were demolished under the
sign of the cross. While everything passed and even collapsed, including
his own country, the cross remained: the still point on an ever-changing
horizon. He clung to it in the Benedictine fashion: through obedience
and humility. Immediately after his final entrance, he wrote of his desire
"To be the last in everything, except obedience."[71] To belong to God, and
God alone, meant humbly accepting God's will as manifested through the
monastic superiors and all the circumstances of his life. This was his Rule.

70. CW 160.
71. CW 170.

Similarly, the strict Trappist silence was for him the privileged expression of his fundamental attitude of surrender. Rafael was often so moved inwardly that he longed to cry out his love for Christ in the streets, like a madman. But he found in silence a better way of preaching, and a constant form of praise. As he advanced carrying his cross on the path of total detachment from the self, his soul changed in a way that amazed him. He discovered what he called "serenity," the fruit of what the Jesuit tradition calls "holy indifference." He explains it in this way: "It's not that I forget my desires, but that they have become so unimportant and irrelevant that they are not simply forgotten but in fact *disappear*. My spirit is left only with a great contentment, realizing that all it earnestly desires is to do what God wants from me, and a great joy, realizing I have been relieved of a very great burden and that I am free from my will, which I have laid down next to that of Jesus."[72]

To become one will with the beloved in reality, not at the level of thought or feeling, that's the ripe fruit of love, a fruit that the tree of the cross bore for Rafael. His cross was real too. His physical pain was substantial, with constant hunger and thirst, and increasing bodily frailty. In spite of this suffering, his greatest sacrifice was isolation. Often, loneliness and the cross became the same reality to him as he describes it: "My God . . . My God, teach me to love your cross. Teach me to love absolute solitude, away from everything and everyone. I understand, Lord, that *this* is how You want me, that *this* is the only way that You can win over this heart of mine."[73] However, as Rafael responded to the call that led him to the desert to speak to his heart, and detached himself from any other source of comfort, he found in his solitude the consolation that came from the Lord, the only thing that could fully satisfy him. He describes it in these terms:

> I desired only to profoundly love the Lord who, in His great good-
> ness, was consoling my heart, which was thirsty for something *I*
> *couldn't name* and searched for among creatures in vain. Without
> the noise of words, the Lord helped me to understand that He is
> what my soul desires . . . That He is Truth, Life, and Love . . . And

72. CW 201.
73. CW 179.

that so long as I have Him . . . What am I looking for? What am I asking for? . . . What do I want?[74]

Rafael did stop searching, asking, or wanting anything but Christ, and him crucified. Joined to his Master through the pain of his own cross, his only desire was to respond in love to the one who was nothing but love for him, even in his weakness. He had written, "Jesus needs souls who listen to him in silence."[75] Now that the cross had opened the passage to the space within him where the multiplicity of desires, emotions, and memories were either silenced or forgotten, he could truly listen to the voice of Christ, who explained to him the secret of the cross. Nineteen days before his death, with great difficulty, he tried to confide in his journal something of what the Master was teaching him:

> Christ Jesus, teach me to suffer . . . But I know . . . a gentle inner voice explains to me everything . . . something I feel within me that is coming from you, and that I don't know how to explain, deciphers so great a mystery that man cannot understand . . . I, Lord, in my own way, do understand it. It is love . . . in that is everything . . . I see it, Lord . . . I need no more, I need no more . . . it is love, who would be able to explain the love of Christ?[76]

As a faithful follower of the Cistercian tradition, Rafael's devotion to Our Lady was great, to her who had become his sweetness and support. Her presence is pervasive throughout his writings. Unbeknownst to him, his desire to remain continually at the foot of the cross mirrors the attitude of Mary, the mother of Jesus. His eagerness to do more—everything and anything for love of Christ—was channeled into this quiet sacrifice of praise, standing in total surrender near his crucified Lord. As did Mary, he united his oblation to Christ's, and he experienced his soul's expanding and overflowing in love for his brothers, Spain, and the whole world. It could not be otherwise: the total surrender to God, and God alone, allows us to become total gift for our brothers and sisters. Once again,

74. CW 202.
75. CW 200.
76. CW 200.

he marveled at the change the Lord had accomplished in his heart. Now he could love others as they were and not as he wanted them to be. He could even laugh at situations that had formerly been the source of disappointment or humiliation. He had finally fully embodied his vocation to be an oblate, and on his last Holy Thursday, he couldn't help but exclaim, "Lord, take me and give yourself to the world."[77]

Rafael's final journal entry can be easily misunderstood and interpreted as the bitter taste of disappointment after a difficult life. His last written words were, "I am coming to see, with complete clarity, that those who focus on earth and its creatures are wasting their time . . . Only Jesus can fill the heart and soul."[78] My interpretation is different. I recognize in them the distilled wisdom of one who, having had it all, has found "the better part" (Luke 10:42) and knows well the difference between what is worth it and what is not. Nevertheless, there is no denying that his life was marked by suffering. His holiness doesn't reside in it, though. He wrote, "It's so hard to explain why suffering can be loved! But I think it can be explained, because it's not a question of loving suffering *itself*, but rather what suffering is in Christ. Those who love Christ love His cross."[79] As in Saint Paul's writings, Rafael's interior world hinges around this little word: *in*. His illness and emotional pain, the concrete shape of his cross, became precious to him because they were the locus always accessible to him, allowing him to live in Christ. The same reality is offered to all disciples willing to take up their cross.

The monastery became Rafael's school of the cross, a school where Christ is the teacher who atop Calvary proclaims the true science:[80] how to suffer well, knowing how "to love and wait in hope."[81] This is a practical science that is ultimately learned through the experience of suffering,[82] but also through a particular discipline that includes solitude, recollection, and silence.[83] Through this discipline, the monastic *conversatio*, Rafael acquired

77. CW 204.
78. CW 206.
79. CW 196.
80. See CW 200.
81. CW106.
82. CW 180.
83. CW 140.

the knowledge that allowed him to penetrate the mystery of life and death, of suffering and love, hidden in Christ crucified and in his own cross.

Rafael advanced through his personal desert, as had the many monks and nuns who had preceded him. Silence, solitude, and joyful penance purified his desire and set his love in order, and the water that flowed from the rock quenched his thirst. Christ crucified, struck like the rock at Horeb,[84] became his all. Following in his footsteps, Rafael remained in faith and trust even when he himself was struck by life, because he knew well that the hand that guides our history heals even when it wounds. With gratitude, he carried in his body and soul the marks of the cross that was saving him, signs of the most unexpected beatitude. In his own words: "I don't know . . . if I keep writing, I'll get lost in thought. All I can say is that I have found true happiness in loving the cross of Christ. I am happy, completely happy, more than anyone could ever imagine . . . But I am of no importance . . . God alone."[85]

Sr. María Gonzalo-García, OCSO
Our Lady of the Angels Monastery
Crozet, Virginia
April 9, 2021

---

84. *Strike the rock, and the water will flow from it for the people to drink* (Exod 17:6).
85. CW 186.

A Note on the Translation

I have grounded my approach to this translation in the values that Rafael himself embraced as the governing principles of his life in the monastery: the vows of obedience, stability, and fidelity to the monastic way of life[1] outlined in the Rule of Saint Benedict. While Rafael was an oblate who never formally made these vows, he nevertheless lived them, and as his translator, I felt compelled to follow his example.

For translators, the value of obedience is obvious in that we voluntarily bind ourselves to the style and message of our authors. In this project, that has meant obeying Rafael not just as an author, but as an editor and designer of his own work. For this reason, the selection of writings presented here is comprehensive, omitting only a few letters from his youth, from which a representative sample has instead been taken: a series of logistical letters to his parents and drawing tutor, three postcards, a stray page from his student agenda, and three undated scraps, including two comical poems that do not lend themselves to translation.[2] Otherwise, we have sought to present as complete a picture of Rafael's spiritual journey as possible by representing his writings across a variety of genres and audiences.

While the majority of Rafael's writings are epistolary, including letters, postcards, and dedications written in books or on the backs of holy cards, he also kept journals. In some of these journals, he privately prayed, reflected on his own spiritual journey, and joked that his prolific writing was a way of channeling some of his chattiness within the loneliness of

---

1. The Latin expression for this last vow is *conversatio morum*, literally translated as "conversion of life" or "conversion of manners."

2. In OC, the omitted entries are numbered #2, 3, 5, 10–12, and 14 (letters from Rafael's youth); #17, 21, 22, 26, 29–31, 33, 36, and 60 (logistical letters); #24, 25, and 71 (postcards); #19 (agenda page); #233 and 234 (poems); and #244 (undated scrap).

the infirmary. On other occasions, as with his journal *Meditations of a Trappist*, Rafael created coherent literary works that he revised, re-copied, and illustrated for a possible future audience. Similarly, he compiled a series of notebooks, designated *Notes I, II,* and *III,* in which he copied passages from his favorite spiritual writers, added his own meditations, and illustrated their pages using collage and drawing techniques. When Rafael shifts from intimate confidant to audience-conscious writer, this translation shifts with him.

In order to make those shifts, I have drawn on the bibliographical work of Juan Antonio Martínez Camino, SJ, and Alberico Feliz Carbajal, OCSO, whose studies of Rafael's manuscripts enabled me to present his works in chronological order, restore his illustrations to their intended placement within the text, and illuminate the historical context for these writings in footnotes. For the sake of consistency with the existing body of scholarship, this edition uses the titles added by Rafael's first editors, his mother Mercedes Barón Torres and his confessor Teófilo Sandoval, but it always identifies their authors. Meanwhile, I replicated Rafael's own patterns of emphasis. I used italics where he used a single underline, but otherwise I repeated his idiosyncratic punctuation habits exactly: his unusual spacing, unconventional use of ellipses, double underlining, multiple exclamation marks, and devout capitalization of pronouns when referring to God and Mary. I did, however, correct other inconsistencies in capitalization and unintentional errors in spelling and grammar.

In addition to reflecting Rafael's genre and style, I have made an effort to preserve his humanity and growth rather than allow stale hagiographic practice to tempt me to cover over his faults. When he refers to a female boarder as "*histérica*," I let him call her "hysterical"; when he belittled his classmates' performance on an exam ("*había algunos que merecían tres o cuatro en vez de uno*"), I make sure he's just as sassy about it in English ("there were some people who should have gotten a Y or a Z instead of an F").[3] After all, the spiritual significance of saints is that they were sinners in whom divine love worked wonders. For my part, I have done my best not to introduce any new biases into the text. When faced with the challenge of linguistic gender, for instance, I refrained from defaulting to the pseudogeneric masculine

---

3. See #2 in Rafael's writings below, which appear in chronological order and are numbered accordingly. They therefore differ from the numbering in the Spanish edition.

common in both English and Spanish (where "men" and "*los hombres*" have been used to mean "humanity"). Instead, I used gender-neutral language in English that reflects the deeper meaning of Rafael's words in Spanish: when he writes that Jesus was crucified "*para todos los hombres*," he does truly mean "for all humanity."[4] At other moments, however, Rafael's use of gendered language was a reflection of the circumstances of his vocation. Rafael was a man in a community comprised wholly of men; when he defaulted to masculine pronouns to describe his life at the monastery, he was not excluding anyone. Taking this reality into account, I have retained male pronouns when Rafael's use of them is specific to his experience.

That specificity is ultimately what makes reading Rafael such a joy, a joy I hope to have communicated to the English-language reader by following the principle of stability. For a Trappist, stability entails remaining in a specific monastery for the rest of one's life. This vow is rooted in the "threefold love" of one's religious vocation in general, the Trappist-Cistercian Order in which that calling is lived, and one's monastery in particular.[5] This threefold love is unmistakable in Rafael, who always wrote of his vocation in terms of the abbey at San Isidro de Dueñas. He saw himself as called not just to generically devout Catholicism or to religious life in general, but to a life lived for God in a specific monastery in a sparse Castilian river valley—circumstances that were not at all immaterial to him, but gifts of Divine Providence, the very stuff of his salvation.

This principle of stability led me to translate Rafael in a way that retains the markings of his circumstances. I hope to have preserved his voice in his time and place, a Spanish man of the early twentieth century who spoke with the elegance of his education and the humor of his youth. The most distinctive aspect of Rafael's style is his humorous tone and familiar register, which I attempted to capture in its lively modernity without introducing anachronisms.[6] Rafael was ever lighthearted, whether he was writing an apology ("whatever needs forgiving, there's always something"),[7] recounting

---

4. #12.

5. *La vida cisterciense en el monasterio de San Isidro de Dueñas* (Burgos: Tipografía de «El Monte Carmelo», 1923), 63.

6. In this regard, I have found the following resource invaluable: C. O. Sylvester Mawson, *Roget's International Thesaurus of English Words and Phrases* (New York: Thomas Y. Crowell Company, 1925).

7. #103.

his onion-peeling duties ("they aren't all exactly tears of compunction, as you can imagine"),[8] giving thanks for the end of a fast ("the two fried eggs tasted like heaven to me"),[9] or making self-deprecating jokes ("I'll always be your nephew . . . You know, the slightly wacky one who used to twirl around by the radio, and then go visit nuns").[10]

I also followed the spirit of stability in conserving markers not just of his personality, but of his Spanish identity. In addition to allowing him to keep his familiar units of measurement[11] and currency,[12] I also left names in Spanish, as "Mamá" and "Papá" are hardly ambiguous, and "La Trapa" is no more foreign than "La Trappe." Elsewhere, footnotes have been provided to explain the cultural context of irreplaceable Spanish terms (as with, for example, Rafael's delightful fixation with turrón.)[13]

Even more than obedience and stability, fidelity to the monastic way of life is the Trappist value that shines forth most brilliantly in Rafael, as he continually strove to lay aside all manner of personal preferences and habits in the interest of pursuing God alone. By pushing back against the ego and pointing toward God, monastic fidelity urges ever greater simplicity, which in my case has meant restraint not just in the translation itself but in my use of footnotes. I have restricted my editorial interventions to those most essential to facilitate the reader's encounter with Rafael's spirituality, which naturally entailed many notes on his life and historical context. However, this edition does not seek to be a comprehensive critical edition of Rafael's work,[14] but rather a definitive source text for English-language readers.

8. #105.

9. #33.

10. #106.

11. E.g., "A few *meters* short of the convent door, I stopped at a stream by the side of the road and cooled myself off" (#10, emphasis added).

12. E.g., "I need to pay the practicum fees, which will be some 50 pesetas, and get a drawing board from the school, which is 25 pesetas. I'm sure I'll have to pay the 'teacher' his 10 duros in advance, and I have to pay the boarding house through the end of the month" (#7).

13. A type of nougat, traditionally eaten in Spain at Christmastime (see e.g. #87).

14. For the critical edition of Rafael's work, see *Hermano San Rafael: Obras completas,* ed. Alberico Feliz Carbajal, OCSO (Burgos: Monte Carmelo, 2011).

Moreover, monastic fidelity is a challenge to both Trappists and their translators to understand the project of conforming one's individuality to a collective lifestyle as enriching, not repressive. Translators already reject romantic notions of individual creativity, instead placing value on collaboration not only with an author, but with the communities that author belonged to, as well as readers of both source and target languages. In that spirit, I draw a connection between the communal nature of Rafael's own language and the communal approach I have taken to this translation. When Rafael used terminology particular to his Trappist community, I was grateful to be able to consult the Trappist community at Our Lady of the Angels Monastery in Crozet, Virginia, for appropriate English equivalents. Thanks to them, for example, Rafael's need for exceptions ("*alivios*") to the community diet were translated using the term in English-language monastic usage, *indulgences*, rather than the more literal *reprieves*. Similarly, when Rafael used vocabulary drawn from his Jesuit schooling or his devotion to the Carmelite saints, I was able to draw on English-language writings about these spiritualities to ensure that I used the terms these communities would use among themselves. To that end, Rafael speaks of *consolation, desolation,* and spiritual *dryness* when pulling from Saint Ignatius of Loyola, and *recollection* when invoking the methods of Saint Teresa of Ávila.

As I celebrate this translation as a collective enterprise, I must thank Sr. María Gonzalo-García, OCSO, for entrusting me with Rafael's writings and for rigorously assuring this translation's accuracy; our editor at Cistercian Publications, Dr. Marsha Dutton, for her excellent guidance throughout this process; my academic advisor, Dr. Allison Bigelow, for her support in the dissertation phase of this project; Dr. Jane Mooney, for laying the foundation for this translation; and the Department of Spanish, Italian & Portuguese at the University of Virginia as well as Dr. Louis Carnendran, whose funding made this translation possible. To all the friends of Saint Rafael who contributed their ideas, prayers, and enthusiasm along the way, my sincerest thanks.

Catherine Addington, PhD
Charlottesville, Virginia
April 23, 2021

The
Collected
Works

I. *All the World Can Give*

Early Years and
Vocational Discernment

1. To Rafael Arnaiz Sánchez de la Campa[1]

Madrid, April 2, 1921[2]

My dearest Papá,

I got here in good shape and without getting queasy at all. I didn't have time to write you yesterday. I'm sending you this postcard I painted. I'm very happy. Yesterday I went to my cousins' house.[3]

Give the little ones lots of kisses for me.[4] A big hug from your son,

Rafael

1. Rafael Arnaiz Sánchez de la Campa (1882–1949) was Saint Rafael's father and namesake.

2. Rafael was ten years old when he wrote this postcard from Madrid, where he accompanied his mother, Mercedes Barón Torres, on a trip to visit his sick grandmother, Fernanda Torres Erro.

3. My cousins: The four children of Fernanda Barón Torres (the twin sister of Mercedes, Rafael's mother) and her husband Francisco Fontanals. Their names were Paco, Álvaro, Enrique, and Fernanda. The Fontanals-Barón family lived on Calle Atocha in Madrid (Saint Rafael Arnáiz Barón, Hermano San Rafael: *Obras completas*, ed. Alberico Feliz Carbajal, 6th ed. [Burgos: Monte Carmelo, 2011], 30; hereafter OC).

4. The little ones: Rafael's three siblings, Luis Fernando (b. 1913), Leopoldo (b. 1914), and Mercedes, better known as "Merceditas" (b. 1917).

2. *To Rafael Arnaiz Sánchez de la Campa*

Pedrosillo (Ávila), June 23, 1930[1]

My dearest father,

I haven't written you for a few days now, and although of course I have no excuse, I must tell you I've been very busy in every way.

Happily, I just finished my exam in statue drawing. They gave us Michelangelo's Moses, which you'll be familiar with, and I got a very good spot, to the side. I started out very calmly and coolly, despite the hour they'd scheduled for us, which was 9pm–1am. The exam lasts three days, and people fail the exam because they get tired. It's less an exam and more an endurance test. Not for me, though. I took a liking to the figure, so I enjoyed starting it and had no setbacks. It didn't seem as though it took that long to me. If I may say so, it turned out rather well, and I'm just being honest, I wouldn't have traded my drawing for that of any of the other seventy students who were in the class. Then again, I wasn't surprised at how many people failed. There were some people who should have gotten a Y or a Z instead of an F.

I'm exceedingly hopeful, and I'd be very surprised if I fail. It will be as God wishes it. Since I've worked hard during the course, I hope it will go well.

They'll send my grades to Pedrosillo, and I'll tell you how it went. As you can imagine, my heart has been pounding for a few days now.

On the feast of Corpus Christi,[2] I went to see Uncle Juan Antonio in Ciempozuelos.[3] As soon as I arrived, I ran into the doctor who is attending

1. Pedrosillo was the Ávila estate of Rafael's maternal uncle, Leopoldo Barón, and his wife, María Osorio, whom he was visiting. In 1930, when he wrote the letters and postcards that follow, Rafael was nineteen years old.

2. Corpus Christi: In 1930, the feast of the Body and Blood of Christ, which is celebrated on the Thursday after Trinity Sunday, fell on June 19.

3. Juan Antonio: Juan Antonio Arnaiz Sánchez de la Campa, Rafael's only paternal uncle. At the time, he was a patient at St. Joseph Psychiatric Hospital (Sanatorio Psiquiátrico

him. He's a very friendly man. He asked me who I was going to see, and when I gave him Uncle's information, he told me that my arrival was providential, because the patient in question wanted to leave the very next day at all costs, and he was very determined to do so, but the doctor was convinced that he would be cured if he stayed. We went to go see him, and between the doctor and me, we convinced him to stay. The doctor told him that he'd been tricking him over the past four days, and instead of giving him the four centigrams of pantopon[4] he'd been receiving daily, he'd gone the whole day with just half a centigram without even noticing it, because he'd been given the same injections at the same times every day. That proves that it's all just his imagination, and the doctor is certain that he can take it away completely within just a few days, and then his leg can heal, and he might even leave the hospital on foot if possible. In light of this, and other reasons, Uncle decided to stay; I don't know how long.

He told me not to tell you all these details and just to say that he's doing very well, and indeed he is. Afterward Luis Quílez came to see him, and he gave me a ride back in his car. I'd gone by train, because it's 38 kilometers on foot, which would have tired me out quite a bit.[5] I met his wife and children, and they told me to give their regards to Aunt Petra and to all of you.[6]

The doctor's address is: Don José González Pinto
St. Joseph Psychiatric Hospital
Brothers Hospitallers of St. John of God
Ciempozuelos (Madrid)

I couldn't see the director because he was busy with the procession they were having,[7] but if you write somebody, the doctor's your best bet.

---

de San Jose) in Ciempozuelos, Spain, outside Madrid. The hospital is run by the Brothers Hospitallers of Saint John of God, a Spanish religious order founded in 1572.

4. Pantopon: An opiate sometimes used as an alternative to morphine.

5. 38 kilometers is equivalent to 23.6 miles.

6. Petra Sánchez de la Campa y Tasquer, Rafael's paternal great-aunt, who was living with the Arnaiz-Barón family in Oviedo at the time.

7. The feast of Corpus Christi is traditionally celebrated with a eucharistic procession.

Afterward, I had dinner at my grandmother's place.[8] She's doing well now, and one of these days she'll go outside and head home to Toro. The next day, at 10:05, I went to Ávila, having sent notice via telegram the previous day. I've already arrived, and I'm sure the telegram will get here one of these days. I mention it because if you want to congratulate me or tell me something via telegram, make sure to give it time, because nothing gets here.

I'd ask you, if you haven't already packed the trunk, to please put a set of strings in there, and some picks, and a patch, and a banjo tuning key, and don't forget to put some candy or something for my cousins.[9] And just so you know, tomorrow, June 24, is Aunt María's name day, just for your own awareness. And don't forget to put a little pack of Capstans in there for me.[10] I'm sure you thinking "all right, that's a bit much," and if that's the case send me a letter or give me a call, whatever's easiest for you. But for goodness' sake, do send me something.

Forgive me for being such a bossy, boring bum, but since I don't see you anymore, please at least remind me that you exist and that I have parents and brothers and a sister and an aunt, all of whom are very loving and write me long letters all the time . . . Ahem . . . Ahem . . .

As you can imagine, I'm loving Pedrosillo. Today I went into Ávila with Uncle Polín to go to the cattle market, and we bought two pairs of oxen. We managed to bargain one down to 7.525 reales[11] by haggling for an hour and a half . . . It's so much fun. The cattle prices are higher than they were last year.

I'm doing some sketches for the stained-glass windows for the chapel.[12] We spend all day with water pumps and shovels and hoes. The house is a mess because they're getting some work done, so there's nowhere to sit down, and cigarette butts all over the floor. Aunt María's molars are killing her; the poor thing is out of sorts. Mademoiselle can't speak Spanish, and

8. My grandmother: Fernanda Torres Erro.

9. My cousins: The five children of Leopoldo Barón and María Osorio: Dolores, Leopoldo, Pilar, Fernando, and Blanca.

10. Capstans: Capstan is a British brand of cigarettes.

11. Reales: Before the introduction of the euro, the peseta was the currency of Spain. A real was equivalent to 25 céntimos, or one-quarter of a peseta.

12. Rafael designed the stained-glass windows for the chapel at Pedrosillo.

my cousins are always in the way . . . but we're all doing well, everybody is healthy and happy. What more could you want? I suppose you're all doing well too, and all very healthy.

Well, I'll leave it there, it's 11 o'clock now, and tomorrow we have Mass at 7:30, so we need to get up at the crack of dawn.

Give lots of hugs to my aunt[13] for me, and to your children. All my affection to you and my mother. Your son, who is thinking of you,

Rafael

Don't forget about the trunk with everything I asked for (if you haven't already sent it).

13. His great-aunt Petra.

3. *Postcards from Salamanca*[1]

Salamanca, July 12, 1930

To his brother Luis Fernando

A million hugs from your brother, who is thinking of you very much in this blessed place,

Rafael

To his brother Leopoldo

Another million hugs, so you don't fight with your brother Fernando, from your other brother,

Rafael

To his siblings

A very tiny, microscopic kiss from your brother, who is your senior in age, dignity, and self-control,

Rafael

To his drawing instructor Eugenio Tamayo

Thinking of you fondly in this city of such beauty, with so many interesting monuments,

Rafael

1. After visiting his maternal grandmother and aunt in Toro in the summer of 1930, Rafael headed home to Oviedo. On the way, he stopped in Salamanca, sending these four postcards from there.

4. To Mercedes Barón Torres

Pedrosillo (Ávila), July 18, 1930

My dearest mother,

You can't imagine how much I miss the violin and updates from you. What's going on? Please, all of you, try not to forget about your son, who loves you so much and is sending a thousand hugs your way.

5. To Leopoldo Barón[1]

Oviedo, October 11, 1930

Dearest Uncle Polín,

I could have written you earlier, but I've been on the move constantly these past few days. Now that I am at home and at ease, with my student life starting to return to normal and my spirit starting to calm down, I am taking this opportunity to trouble you with these lines.

What do you want me to tell you? What I saw and experienced in La Trapa,[2] the impression that this holy monastery made on me, cannot be explained. Or at least, I don't know how to explain it, only God does.

In any case, I will give you an account of what I did and saw.

You left me on the train with Aunt María's relative, to whom I paid no attention, for when I told him that I was going to La Trapa he was very startled and left me in peace.[3]

I arrived at the station in a suffocating heat. I left my things with the baggage master; with my coat, my hand luggage, and much excitement, I took to the road, without speaking to anyone. It is three kilometers away, and I thought I would never arrive. How the sun beat down! A few meters short of the convent door, I stopped at a stream by the side of the road and cooled myself off.[4] Once I was rested I called the gatehouse, and

---

1. Leopoldo Barón Torres, Rafael's maternal uncle, became Duke of Maqueda through marriage. Known to Rafael by his nickname, Polín, he had a strong influence on his nephew's vocation.

2. La Trapa: Refers throughout to the Cistercian Abbey of San Isidro (Abadía Cisterciense de San Isidro) in Dueñas, Palencia, Spain. Its popular nickname of "La Trapa" originates from the Monastery of La Trappe in France; from that monastery emerged the Order of Cistercians of the Strict Observance, known as the Trappists, to which the monks at San Isidro belong.

3. Aunt María: María del Socorro Osorio de Moscoso y Reynoso, Duchess of Maqueda.

4. Convent: While today this term is commonly used for communities of women religious, historically it referred to either men or women. Rafael uses the terms *monastery* (*monasterio*) and *convent* (*convento*) interchangeably in reference to La Trapa.

out came a most obliging brother to whom I gave your letter for Father Armando.[5] He brought me to a small room that was in the gatehouse, where it appeared that Brother Bartolomé—that's the name of the porter—had been sewing at the window, since there were needles, bobbins, and everything else one might need. Then he had me go up to a little room in the guesthouse where I waited for Father Armando, who treated me far better than I deserve. I told him what you already know; one can see that he loves you very much. I expressed to him my desire to remain a few hours in the monastery.

From this moment I began to see clearly and became intimately ashamed of myself: when upon entering the church to greet the Lord, I saw the monks chanting in the choir, and that altar with that Virgin; I saw the respect that the monks have in church and, most of all, I heard a *Salve* that . . . dear Uncle Polín, only God knows what I felt . . . I did not know how to pray before.[6]

At eleven o'clock at night I got up, got dressed, and went down to the church, thinking that it was two in the morning. Then at four Father Armando said Mass for me, and I assisted him.

I saw, of course, the whole convent. And Father Abbot, and Brother Carmelo, who was not in the tailor shop because he was sick.[7] I gave him a hug, and he told me through signs to give you one in return.[8] I saw it all. You already know it better than I do, and so I cannot tell you anything new. At eight, a car passed by on the road headed to the station. God, who is so good, wanted me to miss it, and I had to stay all morning until two in the afternoon.

5. A most obliging brother: Brother Bartolomé Aparicio Pérez was the porter in September 1930 when Rafael visited for the first time. Father Armando: Father Armando Regolf Santcher.

6. *Salve:* The *Salve Regina*, or "Hail Holy Queen," is a hymn to Mary, regularly sung after Compline in Cistercian houses.

7. Father Abbot: Dom Félix Alonso García was the abbot of San Isidro de Dueñas at this time. In the Western church, the title of abbot is used for male monastic superiors, whom Cistercians address using the appellation "Dom." Brother Carmelo: Brother Carmelo Mansuelo de Santiago.

8. Through signs: The practice of communication through simple hand signing has a long history in the Cistercian order, and in the monastic tradition more broadly.

Then I went into the field. I saw the monks with their big hats, working in the sun. If you saw how small they seem on those plains, so vast, with so much sky, and yet, in the eyes of God, it must seem quite different. And don't think that upon seeing and admiring them I felt envy, no, for you have taught me something very important that I have heard you say many times: that one may go toward God on many paths and in very different ways. Some fly, others walk, and others, most people, stumble. And since God wants it that way, then so do I.

Finally I had to leave the monastery, and I took to the road again on foot. I was not sad when I left, but I do intend to return, and to return for a few days.

You cannot fully comprehend my joy at La Trapa, but if you know the monks and you know me, you can begin to imagine it. I will remember that day my whole life, and at moments when I lose heart, I remember my brothers, their monastery, and their customs, and I am very much encouraged.

When I arrived at the station, dealing with men after having been among angels—it produced a certain disgust in me, to be frank with you. When I saw the train arriving in all its imposing grandiosity, I wanted to throw away my luggage and return to La Trapa.

Father Armando told me that not now, but when I finish my degree, they will need me. In short, may it be as God wills. And may He forgive us all when, as you say, we try to "put Him right" and think that we know better than He does what is best for us . . . when what we should do is leave ourselves in His hands and, of course, do all that we can on our part while He takes care of the rest.

Fr. Armando told me that he would not be at the convent in November, since he has to go direct a retreat elsewhere, so if you want to see him you need to go now, in October, or in December. And when you go, if possible, remember me while you are there, greet Father Armando and Brother Bartolomé for me. And again, only if possible—because that day I did not remember anything or anyone.

You were right when you said that I would thank you for this visit; how right you were. I will never be able to thank you enough, or Aunt María either, for what you have done for me. For while it is true that we must put up with one another's frailties and weaknesses, you had no obligation to put up with me for four months. And I realize that at times I must have been tiresome or impertinent, for which I hope you will be able to forgive me.

Afterward, in Burgos with Uncle Álvaro, I was very happy, and he would not let me leave, so much so that I have been in Oviedo with my parents, brothers, and sister only four days.[9]

I received the trunk. I forgot about your books; if it is no trouble please send them whenever you like, since my father wants to give them to the Catholic Action library, and if we had them here I would not ask you for them.[10] Now I will dedicate myself to *ruminating*[11] over them a little at a time.

I am sending you some holy cards from Father Aramburu, who is very elderly, but remembered me well and recognized me, though he can hardly see and cannot write.[12]

I am also sending you greetings and hugs from everyone. I have already started my university classes, and on Monday I start drawing classes.

We are going to found a chapter of Los Luises at the Jesuit rectory.[13]

And I have nothing else to tell you, other than that it has been raining all morning and I hope it will stay that way all day.

My parents, brothers, and sister are eagerly awaiting me. If you write me sometime, tell me all the news; you know I will thank you for it.

When are you going to Madrid? What are my cousins up to? Has Aunt María gone on the Exercises? . . . Did the tractor arrive? . . . And whatever else you think of. If you tell me, you will give me great joy, which God will return to you.

---

9. Uncle Álvaro: Don Álvaro Barón Torres, Rafael's maternal uncle.

10. Catholic Action (Acción Católica): an association of lay Catholics that began in response to anticlerical regimes across Europe in the nineteenth century and developed into groups with a variety of missions, from local parish evangelization to nationwide Social Democratic movements.

11. Emphasis in the original throughout, unless otherwise stated.

12. Father Aramburu: Father Ignacio María Aramburu, S.J. (1852–1935), one of Rafael's former schoolteachers at Colegio de la Merced in Burgos.

13. Los Luises: A confraternity of university students, formally named the Congregation of Our Lady of Good Counsel and Saint Louis Gonzaga (La Congregación de Nuestra Señora del Buen Consejo y San Luis Gonzaga). Better known by their nickname, Los Luises were an apostolate of the Jesuit fathers in Spain.

Tomorrow, the 12th, is the feast of Our Lady of the Pillar.[14] I do not know if that is Pilar's name day, but just in case, give her a hug from me, and the same to her brothers and sisters.[15]

And tell Polín[16] to remember that he has my address written down, so he should not forget to send me a few lines.

Do not laugh at my letter, for though it be poorly written and may say many silly things, good will and a little affection can make up for all its faults. Since I want to tell you all many things, and I have few words for them, everything comes out all tangled, and sometimes it does not make any sense. Especially my thoughts about La Trapa, of which I have enough to go on about for many days.

Fr. Armando told me that I ought not to come during the winter since I would have a difficult time with the cold, so I will go next year around this time, when no one else is around, to spend at least eight days there. This time only two priests and I were there.

Fr. Armando gave me a little book[17] about Cistercian life, and a life of Father Marie Éphrem,[18] a Trappist; if you don't have them, don't hesitate to ask Father Armando for them, you'll like them.

What moved me most was the *Salve* at dusk before bed. If we don't sing it like that at Pedrosillo next year, I'm not coming. It was sublime. Singing as they sing, with that fervor, it is impossible that the Virgin could not be pleased with them or would fail to give them all sorts of blessings . . . They are all so content and joyful, not a sad face to be seen, quite the opposite, and time flies for them. Brother Bartolomé told me he had been in the convent for twenty years and felt as if he had entered yesterday.

---

14. Our Lady of the Pillar: La Virgen del Pilar refers to the apparition of Mary to Saint James while he was preaching in Zaragoza, now part of Spain and home to her major shrine.

15. Pilar: Rafael's cousin, the daughter of Leopoldo Barón and María Osorio.

16. Polín: Rafael's cousin, the son of Leopoldo Barón and María Osorio, his father's namesake.

17. A little book: [Author unknown], *La vida cisterciense en el monasterio de San Isidro de Dueñas* (Burgos: Tipografía de «El Monte Carmelo», 1923). This book, printed for the monastery's use, is an extract of a work by Dom Vital Lehodey, abbot of Abbaye Notre-Dame de Grâce, Bricquebec, France, from 1895–1929. That longer work was later translated into English as *A Spiritual Directory for Religious* (Trappist, KY: Abbey of Our Lady of Gethsemani, 1946).

18. *The Life of Father Maria Ephraim* (Philadelphia: H. & C. McGrath, 1856).

Have you noticed the Virgin? The austerity of the main altar? Without rugs or flowers, only six candles and a cross: it is truly a Cistercian altar, where the tabernacle reigns above all.

While an older priest celebrated the conventual Mass, I heard the bells, up above the church there, deep and deliberate, the stillness of the monks, the soft, gentle light of the church, so that when it was time for the elevation, one would have needed to have such little faith to . . . I cannot explain it. When one feels a somewhat tender emotion, or when the soul feels something supernatural, trying to express it in words becomes somewhat grotesque. I think that in order to speak of God in certain ways, human language is very poor and spoils everything, or at least it cannot render the true meaning.

I assure you, I do not know what I am saying. If I say something ridiculous, I promise it is with the best of intentions.

If you have been patient enough to read up to this point, give Father Justo[19] my best if you see him sometime.

Hugs and kisses to my cousins, to Aunt María, and to you—I do not think I need to say it so many times; I am sending you all my affection and gratitude.

Rafael

19. Father Justo: Don Justo Sánchez Muñoz (1879–1951), a priest who was good friends with Rafael's aunt and uncle for many years and was their official chaplain in their positions as Duchess and Duke of Maqueda.

6. *To María Osorio*

Oviedo, March 15, 1931

Dearest Aunt María,

I do not ask your forgiveness for not having written you sooner, but rather I ask it of Him to whom I am answerable for my great laziness. I hope, with His help and what little willpower I have, to correct this odious fault of mine. I do not ask your forgiveness, because among those who are truly human, forgiveness is granted without being asked.

I have nothing to say that could be of interest to you, as my life goes on in the utmost peace of both spirit and body, always trying to be better and to *improve* what I can in those around me. Perhaps I am mistaken and they are better than I am, for at times I am very vain and proud, and in God's eyes I may not be a publican, but rather a Pharisee . . . How weak we are . . . But no, with his help I cast aside those moments of weakness and discouragement completely, and every day I am more content with this life that offers me a thousand reasons and occasions to praise God.

Most of all, I greatly enjoy knowing and seeing more clearly every day, and in my eagerness to teach everyone around me and guide them toward that light, sometimes . . . I go too far. That is sad, but what would you say if, one time, while going for a walk, you happened upon an enormous valley with splendid views, fertile soil, sun, flowers, all sorts of plants—that is, a landscape that the human mind can barely imagine, of which you had only seen one little nook or corner? If you realized what a marvelous treasure you had found, what would you do? Well, the most logical thing to do would be to tell the whole world, all your friends, your family—in a word, anyone who will listen—and to try to guide them toward that paradise, explain to them what you have seen, and aim to convince them to go there. I think that is what anyone would do, anyone who is not the least bit selfish. But well, if after you had explained all that to them, they were to say to you, "Everything you're saying is great, but in order to get there I would have to climb and clamber and make an effort, and honestly, I don't think it's all that you're making it out to be . . . besides, not everyone can go there . . ."

That is quite sad if you are making an effort to show others the way, the simplest and easiest way as I see it, for all you have to do is keep going, never stopping no matter what surprises you encounter, remembering that what you seek is waiting for you at the end with open arms.

I hope, with my little experience, to follow in this way and to bring many people along with me. For if our Lord made use of twelve fishermen to convert the whole world, so too will he help me with this good desire; sometimes God makes use of the most insignificant things to touch a man's heart.

Do not think me disheartened—on the contrary, I have made much progress in this task, which is of course an unending one.

The worst part, you know, is that I am the one who is most in need. Preaching is very simple; the hard thing is to practice what one preaches, and by divine will, I am by no means a saint, but a mere creature with a few sparks of fervor.

If you think of your nephew sometime, pray for him, since your prayers reach Him better than mine do, and pray for my intentions.

Since it was you who began this work, do not abandon it. . . . How good you are. I will never be able to repay you for what you have made of me . . . Luckily, I am not the one destined to give you the recompense you deserve. God will reward you.

What I really miss is someone to talk to about all this, but God has a different plan for me. He does not want to give me any friends, so I have to walk with Him alone, which is much better, for *true* loneliness is sad, whereas the solitude of one who is with God is not sad at all.

Forgive me for all this foolishness. Maybe I did sit down to write and say a bunch of silly things in such a short amount of time, but that's what happens when you speak without thinking.

Papá, who has a heart of gold, bought me a wonderful missal with Vespers the other day.

I am reading and rereading Uncle Polín's books, and I like them more every day. I rather feel like asking him to send me the last one he wrote.[1]

---

1. The last one he wrote: His uncle translated the biography of French soldier turned Trappist monk Gabriel Mossier: Dom Antoine de Bourg, *Del campo de batalla a la trapa:*

Tell him not to forget that he promised to send me the biography of
Father Doyle.[2]

Truth be told I do nothing but ask for things. I am exceedingly eager
for summer to arrive so that I can see you all again and embrace you, for
as much as I may regret it my heart is still very much bound to this earth.
You know that your nephew truly loves you.

Give my cousins many hugs, and as for you, receive all the affection
you wish from your nephew

Rafael

Send me news of the matter regarding Uncle Álvaro. Mamá will write
you all when she has resolved the question of the Chaplaincy.

Send me whatever news you have of my grandmother, too.

El hermano Gabriel (Madrid: Librería Religiosa Hernández, 1931). Rafael painted the cover,
which inspired him to make his first visit to La Trapa; see Antonio María Martín Fernández-
Gallardo, *San Rafael Arnáiz Barón: Vida y mensaje* (Madrid: Edibesa, 2009), 38.

2. Alfred O'Rahilly, *Father William Doyle, S.J.* (London: Longmans, Green & Co.,
1922). The Spanish edition was translated by Aurelio Ubierna (Ávila: Imp. Casa Social
Católica, 1929).

7. Impressions of La Trapa

September 1931[1]

In La Trapa, the Rule is arranged so wisely that while the monks must struggle against cold, hunger, and fatigue . . . it doesn't kill them.[2]

Everything goes so well when everything is done for the love of God.

I met with a wise and happy man, the porter of La Trapa.[3] He told me, "True happiness is found in God, and only in Him; and true wisdom lies in recognizing Him as Master and Lord of all creation."

I am convinced . . . whoever seeks God finds Him.[4]

You hear many bells at the monastery. Some are high pitched and crystal clear, like the one at the guesthouse; others musical, like those of the clocks that sing in the cloisters; others are strong and vibrant, like those that call the monks to the refectory and the chapterhouse . . . And finally, the deep resounding tower bells that sound only for church services, or to call the monks to the choir to pray . . . Bells ring in the convent all day and night . . . A monk said to me, "Bells in the cloister do not bother us, on the contrary: whether they sound in the silence of the night or when we are working, the bells console us and seem to speak to us." . . . A bell in a silent monastery is the voice of God.

---

1. Rafael was twenty years old when he wrote Impressions of La Trapa, which he copied into the end of a notebook that he filled with quotations from saints and Scripture, pasted-in holy cards, and illustrations (Juan Antonio Martínez Camino, *Mi Rafael: el Beato Rafael Arnáiz, según el Padre Teófilo Sandoval, su confesor, intérprete y editor* [Bilbao: Desclée de Brouwer, 2003], 156–57). For more on this notebook, titled Notes I, see #209, n. 1.

2. The Rule: The Trappists follow the Rule of Saint Benedict, a model for living in monastic community written by Saint Benedict of Nursia in the sixth century. All further references will use the abbreviation RB and cite the following edition: *RB 1980: The Rule of Saint Benedict in English*, ed. Timothy Fry (Collegeville, MN: Liturgical Press, 2019).

3. The porter of La Trapa: Rafael may have been referring either to Brother Justo García Hidalgo or to Father Buenaventura Ramos Caballero here.

4. Matt 7:8.

I have been feeling deeply ashamed of myself. Trappist monks wear coarse black wool, rough and stiff. They put it on when they profess and they are shrouded in it when they die[5] . . . In my room, I see my silk neckties hanging up . . . a serious cause for reflection, and at the same time a trifle, one that makes me blush, realizing that one can hide such foolish vanity in a ridiculous piece of cloth.

People say that the silence of the monastery is sad, and hard to maintain under the Rule[6] . . . Nothing could be more wrong than such an opinion . . . The silence of La Trapa is the most cheerful celebration imaginable . . . Oh! If God let us see into the heart of another, then we would see within the soul of a Trappist—who looks miserable on the outside and lives in silence—a glorious song of jubilation bursting forth constantly and abundantly, full of love and joy, for his Creator, his God, his loving Father who cares for him and consoles him . . . The silence of the monastery is not sad, quite the opposite; one could say that there is nothing more joyful than the silence of a Trappist.

It is six in the morning . . . It is very cold and rainy . . . From the window in my room I can see a line of monks leaving through the convent gate in silence, carrying shovels, picks, and hoes as they go to work . . . They head out with their hoods up and wearing durable work boots, like the ones used by farmers around here . . . Raindrops fall upon the monks like bullets . . . They are going to work far away from the convent . . . On the road, they come across a luxurious automobile, which slows down upon seeing the strange retinue . . . But the monks take no notice. They cross and keep walking.

The occupants of the car, startled, contemplate them with curiosity. Once their surprise has dissipated, the noise of the engine makes itself heard once again in a violent start, launching the vehicle back onto the paved road at full speed . . . The incident has no great importance of itself, each goes his own way, that's all . . . But looking closely, what different

5. When they profess: Trappists are first clothed with the white religious habit when they enter the novitiate and receive a black scapular when they first profess religious vows. While the rough, brownish garment Rafael refers to may have been a house robe, all of the monks' garments were made out of simple, rough fabrics.

6. "Monks should diligently cultivate silence at all times, but especially at night" (RB 42.1).

paths men take through this life!. . . On the one hand, the man running at high speed does not pause for even a moment to think or reflect, because all the baggage he carries around this world hinders and overwhelms him . . . Always, always running at high speed down a paved road. . . And on the other, a few men are going in the opposite direction, in silence and on foot, letting the raindrops soak their clothes, not looking at what happens around them; for they have mapped out a straight path and want to reach its end without stumbling, and so they cannot stop . . .

Lord! You descended to the Virgin's womb and let Yourself be crucified for all humanity. . . For everyone, without distinction. And yet how differently they repay You.

And from the window in my room this morning, I could see that contrast clearly, and with it a rather strange reality. In the world, since everyone speaks at once, no one can understand one another, and they can only hear the noise of an engine, whereas here, no one speaks, and they understand one another so well! But the explanation is rather obvious: the former speak to the world in shouts, and the latter speak to God in silence.

How well they understand one another. How quickly, upon contemplating the Trappists, the Savior's divine words in the Sermon on the Mount come to one's soul: *Blessed are the meek, for they will inherit the earth.*[7]

Nobody prays to the Virgin Mary as Trappists do. Such tenderness and affection our Mother must have for them, for her sons who venerate her with such love. I think that in heaven, the souls of Trappists form a crown for the Virgin Mary, and with infinite exaltation, they never cease to repeat the words of our father Saint Bernard, who, in a moment of ardent love for his Mother, once exclaimed, "*O clemens, o pia, o dulcis Virgo Maria!*"[8]

When Trappists are at prayer, for a moment they cease to be men of earth and become true angels who, much like those in heaven, do noth-

---

7. Matt 5:5.

8. *O clemens, o pia, o dulcis Virgo Maria*: Translating to "O clement, o loving, o sweet Virgin Mary," this is the final line of the Latin hymn *Salve Regina* ("Hail Holy Queen"); see #5, n. 6. While the hymn's composition is generally credited to the 11th-century monk Bl. Hermann of Reichenau, this final invocation is traditionally attributed to Saint Bernard of Clairvaux.

ing more than praise God: He who is thrice Mighty, thrice Immortal, and thrice Holy.[9]

At certain moments in a Trappist's prayer, God our Lord, in his infinite goodness, cannot help but descend to the choir where his sons are singing and take pity on them—when, hearts repentant of their sins and faces cast toward the earth, their low, measured voices let forth that exclamation that I have heard so many times, but never before as at La Trapa: *"Kyrie eleison, Christe eleison, Kyrie eleison."*[10]

The Trappists who have been ordained *in sacris*[11] sing the Divine Office[12] day and night, that liturgical song of the church, its ultimate prayer. The prayers of their brothers, the lay brothers,[13] consist of Our Fathers and Hail Marys in Latin, which in the course of the day rise up to heaven by the thousands . . . Humble offerings that must please God much more than many works that in the world are called charitable and that nevertheless conceal such vanity and self-love. How much more worthy in the eyes of God is one Hail Mary offered from the heart than the greatest deed done without pure love for God.

The Trappist lives in God and for God, who is his only reason to exist in the world . . . How different they are from certain souls who call themselves Christian, yet treat God as if he were of no consequence, merely

9. Thrice Mighty, Thrice Immortal, Thrice Holy: a reference to the Trisagion ("Holy God, Holy Mighty, Holy Immortal, have mercy on us"), an ancient prayer of the universal church generally recited in sets of three. In the Roman Rite, this prayer is primarily used in the liturgy for Good Friday, but it also forms part of the hour of Prime in certain monastic communities.

10. *Kyrie eleison, Christe eleison, Kyrie eleison*: a Greek prayer forming part of the Roman Rite of the Mass, "Lord have mercy, Christ have mercy, Lord have mercy."

11. *In sacris*: Under holy orders, and therefore under the obligation to pray the Divine Office.

12. Divine Office: Also known as the Liturgy of the Hours, the Divine Office is the prayer of the whole church, structured around the psalms and offered at set times, or Hours, throughout the day. The canonical Hours include Vigils, Lauds, Prime, Terce, Sext, None, Vespers, and Compline (see RB 16 and 17); for the schedule at San Isidro, see #29.

13. From the foundation of the Cistercian Order, the lay brothers were professed members of the Order who prayed a simplified Divine Office and devoted additional time to manual labor. This distinction between lay brothers and choir monks, who were also priests, ended with the Decree of Unification of December 1965.

someone to deal with at eight in the morning and leave behind at nine—
until the next day at the same time, only to forget him again.

In speaking of Trappists, one compares them to other souls without
wishing to . . . And it should not be like that; everyone offers what is
given to them to offer and what has been entrusted to them by God.
Comparisons—I was going to say that they are abhorrent. I will say, rather,
that they are not charitable . . . But, nevertheless, the difference is such
that one cannot help but fall into them. For setting aside the few little
shining lights in this world, one could say that it is ruled by darkness,
whereas here in La Trapa, it is never night and it is always day.

Every day hundreds of poor people come to the gate to ask for food,
which is never denied them.[14] That does not stop them from breaking the
brothers' windows from time to time.

The conventual Mass at the monastery is at ten in the morning, and
it is celebrated with such devotion and heard by the monks with such
profound respect that a man of little faith can only lower his head and
exclaim, "Lord, Lord!" How many times have I attended the divine Sacrifice with my soul absent . . . Forgive me, Lord, I knew not what I was
doing; in my littleness and wretchedness, I will never come to understand
the immense love of a God who humbles himself to come down among
his creatures only to be mistreated or to go unnoticed . . . But one cannot
say this of a Cistercian monastery. The monks attend the divine Sacrifice
not just with their bodies but with their souls . . . Everything is respect,
everything shows veneration and love for their God.

The smallest details in the liturgy can escape the most stringent academics, but not a Trappist, precisely because he lives it . . . No little bells
ring during the Mass, nor can anything be heard other than the monks'
slow and deliberate chanting and the priest's prayers . . . And when coming to the canon,[15] a Trappist gets up and rings the tower bells so that the

14. Hundreds of poor citizens who lived on the outskirts of Palencia depended on San
Isidro for their daily meals—and particularly for bread. Food shortages were exacerbated
during the Spanish Civil War, which officially began in 1936, as bread and other staples
were rationed. After the war, the ruler of Spain, Francisco Franco, banned the monastery
from distributing food, for fear that photographs of long lines stretching down the road
would be used as evidence against his government (OC 83).

15. Canon: in the Roman Rite, the "canon of the Mass" refers to the Eucharistic Prayer.

lay brothers, who are going about their work in the fields, may leave their tools behind for a moment. Lifting their eyes to heaven, they give thanks to God, for in those moments the great mystery that astonishes the soul is being prepared . . . The God of all creation is coming down into the world to be sacrificed, and to take refuge in the soul of a Trappist.

Nevertheless, let us not be fooled by our senses, which tend to be deceptive . . . Far beyond all the little details that impress a visitor, there is a certain something, a certain mystery that cannot be expressed in words and cannot be understood without faith . . . As such, in La Trapa the common saying comes to pass: "Many look, but only a few see" . . . La Trapa and the life of its monks may be moving to an artist, or to anyone who possesses a high degree of sensitivity, as they may be moved by a painting or a sonata . . .

But a Christian who has faith sees something more than that in La Trapa . . . He sees God clearly . . . He comes away edified in the faith, and if the Lord gives him the grace, he comes away knowing himself a little better . . . And there, alone with God and his conscience, he begins to change his way of thinking, his way of feeling, and most important, his way of acting in the world.

8. To Rosa Calvo[1]

Oviedo, January 10, 1932[2]

Dearest Aunt Ropi,

See, I am calling you my aunt, even though we once agreed—I don't know if you'll remember this—that you and I had a much closer relationship than that, so it would seem much more appropriate to me to begin this letter by saying, "My dear sister Rosa."

I am sure it will be a surprise to receive a letter from me. Perhaps you will not even remember who I am, but I'll remind you. The writer of this letter is that boy who, on a certain day that the Lord saw fit to choose, accompanied a holy man to the city of Toro. That holy man was Uncle Polín, and his companion was your humble servant, who had the fortune of stumbling through life with the affection and example of good people.

And so, dearest Rosa, now you must know who I am.

So now, you must be asking yourself, "why is Rafael writing me?" Well, for a very simple reason: your brother Rafael thinks of Rosa often, and is making use of a free moment to let her know that, and to tell her that in such times as these, when God has permitted that men should fight among themselves as if they were not brothers, that hatred and vengeance should be unleashed upon the world, and that God's creatures should rebel against their Creator . . . In such times, souls who suffer when God suffers and try with their small, meager love to return that immense, infinite love of the Master for his children ought to be united, consoling and aiding and comforting one another, so that, with hearts and prayers united, we might ask God to take pity on the world. Let us pray with Saint Teresa: "Lord,

---

1. Rosa Calvo was a friend who worked as a lottery administrator in Toro, where Rafael's maternal grandmother lived. Rafael wrote this letter from his family's home.
2. Rafael was twenty-one years old when he wrote #8 and #9.

either bring the world to an end or provide a remedy for these very serious evils." And afterwards she added, "Do it, Lord; if You will You can."[3]

That is, this saint asked Him to provide a remedy if He wanted, for He could if He wanted to. And so, dear Rosa, let's not worry; for if He wants to, He will fix everything. May his divine will be done, for just as we men and women do not understand the Lord's designs, neither do we understand what is good for us nor that He orders things toward our good and His greater glory.

We used to talk so much, didn't we? Do you remember those times we spent at the Lottery, when we'd talk about God and humanity and La Trapa? Do you remember how my grandmother or Aunt María would ask "where's Rafael?" and they would already know, "either with Uncle Polín, or with Rosa at the lottery."

Perhaps someday we can resume our visits once more, even though . . . it doesn't really matter, right? . . . We must take them up again if God wills it, but somewhere else where nobody will interrupt us. . . . Let's wait, though, let's wait, for the day is not far off. Let's not force it, or worry about having a good time down here or trying to do what is most pleasing to us, completely failing to remember that neither our will, nor our whims, nor even our heart should guide us—as if all those things were ours!—but rather it is His will alone that we should obey. And so, dear Rosa, do not worry about anything, or shed tears in anyone's absence, or grow sad over what we see as misfortune. Let's just wait, and wait with our hearts lifted up in peace and our souls at rest in God, for once you have and possess God, what more could you want? You have everything.

Well, dear Rosa, forgive me. I sound like a church lady's prayerbook. Sometimes my pen gets ahead of me and I don't know what I'm saying anymore, or who I'm saying it to. How absurd, to recommend peace and joy to you, when what I should do is ask you for some of the peace and joy you already have! I'm being silly.

---

3. "Well, what is this, my Lord and my God! Either bring the world to an end or provide a remedy for these very serious evils. . . . I beseech You, Eternal Father, that You suffer them no longer. Stop this fire, Lord, for if You will You can" (Saint Teresa of Ávila, *The Way of Perfection* [Washington, DC: ICS Publications, 2013], 393, chap. 35.4).

Well, leaving all that aside, tell me how you are, how the lottery[4] is going, how your uncle is, if you are cold, etc. . . . You know I care about everything going on with you, although I know perfectly well that you are not going to write me, nor do I ask you to. In fact I forbid you to, because I know it hurts your eyes. So don't think I will be offended or anything, quite the contrary. I'll keep writing you all the same, even if I don't have anything in particular to tell you, other than that I start classes tomorrow, Monday, at the university, that my brothers and sisters are doing well and my parents too, etc. . . .

What you can do is, when Uncle Polín next comes to Toro, send me word through him. And one thing I will ask of you: when you are with the Master in the mornings, tell Him not to let me fall from His hands. You'll say I'm a bit selfish, but there's nothing to be done about that; I rely on and trust in your prayers more than mine, which always reach Him cold and scattered. In any case, I will remember you in prayer too. Or rather, I remember you very often, so you should not forget that we came to an agreement last year, and I very much need the prayers of those whom He indulges with such affection as He does you.

I'll stop here, my dear sister Rosa; I have faith in you. With all my affection, your brother in Christ,

Rafael

4. The Spanish state lottery is an incredibly popular institution, running several games a week building up to the famous annual Christmas lottery. Official lottery outlets like the one Rosa Calvo worked at in Toro are often busy, centrally located community hotspots.

9. *To Luis Fernando Arnaiz Barón*

Madrid, November 4, 1932[1]

My dear brother Fernando,

I was very grateful to receive your letter, because you are the only one in the family who tells stories with any detail. You just have one tiny flaw as a writer, which is that your letters would strain anyone's lungs, let me tell you . . . You know that I like to read with emphasis and pausing after each period, and breathing after each comma . . . So, I started to read, and when I finished, they had to hook me up to an oxygen tank to get artificial respiration going . . . My darling boy . . . you do realize that you wrote ten pages without a comma or one measly period . . . I mean that's fifteen minutes talking without stopping to breathe, which I assure you is extremely unpleasant and poorly tolerated. When you write, please do me the favor of putting a comma every five words, a few question marks, ellipses, exclamation points, quotation marks, etc. All the marks you can think of, and if you don't know where to put them, just do it randomly, or you can make yourself an easy writing rule like this one: put a comma after words that end in o, a period and a comma after stressed words that end in s, an exclamation point after irregular verbs, and so on and so forth . . . You just have to put something, whatever it may be, because you have no business making your fellow man go fifteen minutes without breath.

Anyway, you're getting better at spelling . . . And I won't say anything else about your letter, because it's not as if you wrote me so that I could evaluate you, of course not . . . When a letter arrives from your brother, it's all the same whether it has errors or not . . . and to tell you the truth, I prefer letters with spelling errors to those without. Writing errors reveal

1. Rafael studied architecture at the Higher Technical School of Architecture of Madrid (Escuela Técnica Superior de Arquitectura de Madrid, ETSAM). During his studies, he stayed at a boarding house in the Palacio de la Prensa ("Press Palace"), just off the Plaza de Callao, which is the main square in the university neighborhood (OC 31).

the personality of the one who is writing, his temperament and way of being, and if we were all to write the same way, with our silent letters all in place, minding our p's and q's, then the epistolary genre would lose all its charm . . . Leave writing without spelling errors to the academics, those useless gentlemen with their glasses and their petulance and their strange words, fabricated by the Royal Spanish Academy every time you forget an accent mark[2] . . . Ugh! Pay them no mind; you write however you want (but use some commas, for God's sake) and don't worry about anything else.

For example, how much more expressive it is to say: "The clifs wer steip, the see wuz chopy, and off inn the distants the son hidded behind red clowds."

Such a paragraph is far more expressive than one like this: "The colorless, turbulent liquid with which the deep oleaginous expanse and its gleaming edges crashed—no, splashed—over the marbled granite rock of the shore's unfeeling crags resembled a shining sea of classical beauty."

All right, I think by now I will have convinced you . . . and if not, suit yourself.

I bought myself a bird, which cost me two pesetas.[3] I keep him in a cage with some lettuce, and I give him bird seed . . . If he doesn't die on me by December, I'll bring him back home with me . . . It's stupendously corny, this business of having a bird by the window to monkey around with from time to time.

The alumna[4] gave us three carnations, which we've put in a vase with some water, next to the bird . . . As you can see, the corniness continues . . . the bird, the flowers, and—brace yourself—a gramophone playing tangos . . . The alumna also left us the gramophone, because it turns out it doesn't fit in her room. Trust me, her room is so small that three people

2. Royal Spanish Academy: A government institution dedicated to conserving the Spanish language, best known for its rigorous dictionary.

3. Pesetas: The peseta was the currency of Spain before the adoption of the euro in 2002.

4. Alumna: Rafael refers to this fellow guest at the boarding house only as "la licenciada," a woman with a university degree, uncommon in 1932. Her name is unknown, but Rafael's friend Juan Vallaure mentioned her in his testimony for Rafael's cause: "There was a woman staying at the [Plaza de] Callao boarding house who was older than we were . . . [Rafael] had a friendly relationship with her, perfectly normal and sincere" (Summ 169).

couldn't stand in it, and of course, a portable gramophone takes up quite a bit of space . . . I'm telling you that girl is a gem . . . She got rid of all the stains on my coat for me, and is going to mend Juan's[5] raincoat for him, and today she invited us for *buñuelos de viento*.[6] All this in exchange for just a bit of conversation, and she talks enough for fourteen people—not to mention the hysterical laugh she lets out in the dining room. One time they had to give her an injection to calm her down.

After praying the rosary we went out into the hall and danced a *jota*.[7] Afterwards we performed the *Tenorio*,[8] and there I was, donning a red quilt with a paintbrush tucked into my hat, saying to Doña Inés, "Oh, my angel of love, do you see . . . ?"[9] when we heard some applause coming from the patio. It was the landlady of the boarding house, along with all the maids . . . I didn't know what to do with the quilt, so we had to keep going . . . Anyway, the last thing you'd expect your brother to be doing . . . the *Tenorio* . . . but there was nothing else we could do . . . I had to do something to justify what I was doing with a quilt and a paintbrush in the band of my hat.

I'm sending you an article that I read in a French newspaper that I bought. Since it's about aviation, you'll enjoy it, and you can use it to practice translating . . . It's very interesting. I'm also sending your preparation materials, and . . . I still haven't gone to Cuatro Vientos[10] . . . Look, it's a trek.

5. Juan: Juan Vallaure Fernández-Peña (1910–1975), Rafael's close friend, classmate, and roommate at the boarding house. He went on to become an architect in Oviedo and was an important witness in the beatification process. He named one of his sons after Rafael.

6. *Buñuelos de viento*: A pastry popular in Madrid.

7. *Jota*: A Spanish dance with many regional variations, often accompanied by castanets.

8. *Tenorio*: The longest-running play in Spain, Don Juan Tenorio was written by José Zorrilla in 1844. In it, the infamous womanizer Don Juan ultimately begs for mercy and is accompanied to heaven by the saintly Doña Inés, whom he had abandoned and caused to die of heartbreak.

9. "Oh, my angel of love": Don Juan's romantic overture to Doña Inés after kidnapping her from a convent (José Zorrilla, *Don Juan Tenorio* [Project Gutenberg, 2001], I.IV.III).

10. Cuatro Vientos: An airfield at the edge of Madrid.

Tell your mother that the stamps she sent me are much more useful than the calcium supplements, which I took two boxes of . . . These are at least good for something.

I am in good health, and you? Good, glad to hear it.

The price of canaries has fallen 5 cents, from 70 to 65. A stroke of luck.

This hooded pajama concept sounds excellent. I suppose it looks like this [*a drawing follows*]. Am I right? . . . From the description you gave me, I'm sure you look very imposing in it, although it's much more like Leopoldo[11] to wear such a thing. Moreover I figure [*another drawing follows*] that he's still playing with that yo-yo, so obviously I imagine him wearing a bathrobe[12] . . . and of course, lounging around in a bathrobe, he must be very bored, and the yo-yo thus represents a diversion.

I'm also sending you a triptych of mine. As you'll see I look very irritated, as when something's been confiscated from you.

I'll send you the photographs of Toledo when they are developed, probably in Oviedo, because Juan has the negatives and they turn out much better in Oviedo.[13] Their work is much better there, and they use better paper, and whatnot . . . photographs from Oviedo have a certain quality the ones from Madrid just don't have . . . Of course, it's not all that important, what do I know . . . but they are cheaper, I think . . . but even that doesn't really matter because I think we have about 30 negatives, and at a rate of 15 or 20 cents, it'll only cost about a duro[14] . . . Are you following all this? . . . Well, I figure you are, and if not, well . . . suit yourself.

Your cigar idea—that is, your cigar *bands* idea—seems very good to me, a very wise move . . . go on, keep collecting things and you'll see if your grandchildren make fun of you . . . Well, I'd prefer a collection of cigar bands to having a bird and some birdseed . . . don't you think? Well, nothing to be done about that.

Mamá asked me if this house had heating . . . Tell her that we have to shut the radiators, because if we don't, we'll roast . . . The whole house has central heating, and the cold season "officially" began on the first of

---

11. Leopoldo: Their younger brother, Leopoldo Arnaiz Barón.
12. Bathrobe: What Rafael drew next to the original text.
13. Toledo: Rafael was in Toledo with Juan Vallaure on October 12 and 13, 1932.
14. Duro: A five-peseta coin.

November, so I don't even want to tell you what the house is like right now . . . like an oven . . . and I got another cold, so I've spent all day expelling mucous substances . . . what a mess . . . and what I feel worst about is that now I have to wash more handkerchiefs . . . I am a disaster with this blessed secretion.

My class schedule begins with calculus, from eight to nine in the morning, with a gentleman who explains mathematics from memory, doesn't call on anyone, and instead of passing around an attendance sheet, asks everyone in class one by one what our names are. It takes forever, of course, because he has to make a new list every day . . . He says he doesn't write down absences, but rather attendances . . . So of course, somebody comes up to him one day and says, "Señor Cámara, would you please do me the favor of excusing my absence yesterday, because I couldn't come for such and such a reason . . . ?" And Señor Cámara responds, "No, because I haven't marked you down as absent. You can be absent all you want because I don't mark absences, I mark attendances." But then later, after the exam, he'll say, "You're doing well, but you have a forty-seven-and-a-half percent attendance rate, and for me you need at least a seventy percent . . ." Anyway, his bookkeeping is absurd . . . Such strange things happen at this school.

From nine to ten I have descriptive geometry, with Señor Mosteiro. He is a very pompous gentleman who looks like Muñoz Seca[15] [*a drawing follows*] and lectures about geometry without getting up from his seat, making a student stand at the blackboard and do whatever he says, and whoever understands it understands it, and whoever doesn't better deal with it . . .

There are about seventy students in that class, fifteen enrolled and the rest auditing. Of the fifteen who are enrolled, ten of them are repeating the course because that man is a monster; I'm telling you, you get out of one bad situation only to end up someplace worse.

We're like little schoolboys or worse. Plus, in some of the less decent classrooms, we have to take notes on our laps, and whoever gets there first takes the seats up front to be able to hear, because anyone in the back might

15. Muñoz Seca: Pablo Muñoz Seca (1879–1936), a comedic playwright and actor known for his handlebar mustache.

as well not be in class. The real work has to get done at home, because the school itself is just for introducing yourself and getting instructions, because the matter of learning . . . what Mosteiro does can be done by anybody looking at a book.

Next month we'll start practicums, and those take a lot of time. Anyway . . . at ten I go home to study and at noon I go to Mass or I keep studying, or rather, deciphering my class notes. I eat at two. Afterwards I do nothing. At four I take the metro and get off at Goya to go to my friend Evia's house. He and I study for calculus together until six-thirty or so, and after *merienda*,[16] I go back home and study for descriptive geometry. If I have time, I write letters to family or I go for a walk. Then, at nine-thirty, I have dinner. Afterwards, you can guess. And so, little by little, we get by.

I have just received 50 pesetas from my father, whom I thank profusely. Now all that remains is for me to receive the trunk. I went by the post office again today and it's still not here, but I await the Pamplona sausage with great excitement.

Anyway, I'm writing this letter in fits and starts, so as you can tell it's all over the place, but that's the only way I can write. I don't have time to sit and write nonsense for two hours straight, so perhaps this letter is dated one way now and will arrive with a different date entirely, but I suppose you won't mind.

Today Atilano, Vallaure, and I went up to Cerro de los Ángeles,[17] not on any pilgrimage, mind you, but just because it's the first Friday of the month so Father Colón had to go preach a sermon and we shared a taxi. There were very few people there, and it was delightful; Juan, who'd never been there before, liked it very much.

I have nothing to tell you about Madrid and its residents. People keep going, some fast and others slow, depending on what they have to do, and foot traffic is far too busy . . . Lots of begging, lottery-ticket sellers, and taxis . . . honking, stomping, lights going on and off, shop windows showing off expensive things; and meanwhile, the sky, which is the most beautiful part of Madrid, is cut to pieces, injured by the endless cables of its

16. *Merienda*: A light meal, often involving a hot beverage and a sandwich or sweets. It generally falls in the late afternoon, between lunch and dinner.

17. Cerro de los Ángeles: A hill in Getafe, just south of Madrid. The Monument to the Sacred Heart of Jesus was built there in 1916, along with a 14th-century monastery dedicated to Our Lady of the Angels—the hill's namesake.

trams and the eaves of its buildings . . . and you can't look up, because if
you do, your foot will get stomped on or your handkerchief will get stolen
(note that I don't say your wallet, because I don't carry one).

The porter here is all shoulders, with hair like a brush and a scar over
his eye, always staring at the ground [*a drawing follows*] when anybody
contradicts him. The elevator operator collects postage stamps and film-
star trading cards. The boarding-house cook is very skinny and ignorant,
and Juan is always laying it on thick with her: the rice was *so tasty*, the soup
was *delicious*, even the most overdone meat *she cooks just right* . . . And
of course, she does take care when she pleases, like with baked apples or
purée . . . In any case, every day he goes by the kitchen and gives her a
"menu," but she says, "Nah, yer jus' bein' selfish!"

They've put a new carpet in the hall, and it's made me absolutely hopeless, because the moment I see a long strip of fabric with fringe at each side
stretched out on the floor . . . I am filled with an unbearable urge to do
somersaults, starting at one end and going all the way to the other. But
since I suffer the misfortune of not knowing how, upon simply opening
the door and seeing that carpet—so new, grey with red stripes—I run
straight back to my room. And when I leave again, I don't look down at
the floor, because if I do, something takes over my body, something like
vertigo . . . and a desperate desire to put my hands on the soft, springy
floor, squat down, throw my feet in the air, trace half a circumference with
them, and place them once more on the floor, in front of my neck . . .
and thus, spinning at great velocity, pulling off a double somersault just
short of the door . . . Oh! It's horrible what comes over me, having to
run away without setting foot on the carpet, my eyes glued to the ceiling
. . . because if I look down, I'm telling you, I'm either losing my eyesight
or my head . . . That blessed carpet is making me sick. I'd rather have to
cross a ravine on a plank than have to slowly traverse that long grey-and-
red strip laid over the floor of my hall.

Well, I've got nothing else to tell you.

Now I'm listening to Godard's *Jocelyn*[18] on the gramophone . . . It's
making my blood boil!! Mamá might understand why. But nothing to be
done about that. Anyway, I'll leave you here for now. I have to go cut the

18. *Jocelyn*: An opera by the French composer Benjamin Godard that premiered in 1888,
Jocelyn centers on the temptation of a young seminarian by a passionate love.

carnations' stems and change out the water. The bird has made himself a ball of feathers [*a drawing follows*] and will only show his tail . . . I don't know where his head is. It seems to me, at least, that he is in a deep sleep, but I'm sure when Juan comes he'll wake up . . . I know him. Anyway, it's the next day.

I just got home from class and sat down to continue this letter . . . I don't remember anymore when I started it, but I do know when I'll end it . . . right now. Besides, today is Saturday, so it won't do to leave unfinished business.

Sundays are for resting and nothing else . . . Tomorrow morning I am going to the Monumental Cinema[19] at eleven-thirty to listen to Arbós[20] conduct his orchestra. I'll send Mamá my review, to show her that I can handle anything, and perhaps I'll agree with Turina.[21]

Well, that's all for now. I have things to do, and later I'll go post this "kolossal" letter.

An affectionate goodbye to you and the whole family, with all the hugs and kisses you'd like.

y.b.b.w.h.h. (1)

Rafael

(1) = your big brother, with a handshake and a hug.[22]

19. Monumental Cinema: A movie theatre and concert hall, now known as the Teatro Monumental.

20. Arbós: Enrique Fernández Arbós (1863–1939), a Spanish conductor and composer.

21. Turina: Joaquín Turina Pérez (1882–1936), a composer and music critic for the Madrid daily *El Debate*.

22. His mother responded to this letter on November 13, 1932, saying, "My dear son: We all read your letter to Fernando a couple of times, but especially your father, who enjoyed reading it out loud, and of course we spent a good while talking about you and your life. Thank God, the letter made it clear you're in good spirits, you must have been to play Don Juan in front of the landlady and the other guests . . ." (OC 107–8).

10. To Rafael Arnaiz Sánchez de la Campa and Mercedes Barón Torres

Madrid, October 21, 1933[1]

My dearest parents,

At last I have a free moment, so I've decided to send you some details about my life in Madrid. You already know that I haven't been able to enroll yet . . . the chaos[2] goes on but I am doing well, thanks be to God.

If they let me enroll in everything I've requested, I won't even have time to breathe, but I am dead set on making up for the year I lost last year[3] . . . and if it's up to me . . . so be it.

We have started classes, of course I have my first class at nine in the morning and don't finish until six in the afternoon. We started Infinitesimal Calculus with a teacher who is a force to be reckoned with. On the first day he recommended texts in German and Russian on mechanics, because he also teaches a course on that.

He started by taking differential calculus for granted, so integral calculus is now in full swing . . . I had no idea what he was talking about so I got distracted. See I have the misfortune of having previously studied with Señor Frontera, God forgive him for having passed me. As a result, four other students in the same boat have started to meet for two hours of tutoring on integral calculus every day with a sixth-year, who also has another degree already. He charges us ten duros each every month, and we are studying ferociously, because besides Calculus, there will be two other

1. Rafael was twenty-two years old when he wrote ##10–34. The individual letters, dedications to holy cards, etc. of Rafael as translated here are numbered sequentially throughout the volume and cited according to those numbers.

2. Chaos: As the capital of Spain, Madrid experienced the country's ongoing political turmoil acutely. Rafael wrote this letter just before the infamously violent, polarizing elections of November 1933, one of the key events leading up to the Spanish Civil War (1936–1939).

3. The year I lost: From January 25 to July 26, 1933, Rafael completed his compulsory military service in the Spanish Army Corps of Engineers (Cuerpo de Ingenieros).

sets of exams—one at the end of January, another in June. I need to pass in January and get it out of the way, so I spend nearly all my time on it. I will also probably be taking Construction I and Detail Drawing. I don't really know, I just go to class as if I were taking them . . . It's up to the registrar.

I get up at seven-thirty every day, believe it or not. But it's true, because when I was here before, I had the good habit of going to Communion every day, and I have found that starting the day by placing yourself in God's hands makes everything go better and makes study much more profitable. If it were not for the Master who helps me so much, I would be completely useless, and besides, I have to be accountable to somebody for my actions, both the good and the bad, right?

Afterwards I go to the classes that I need, depending on the day of the week (I'll send you my schedule when it's set in stone), etc. . . . From six-thirty to eight-thirty I have Calculus, after dinner I study Descriptive Geometry, and I end up going to bed exhausted, but satisfied that the day has ended . . . If it weren't for that—for my studies, my responsibilities, my classes, being so busy I don't even have time for *merienda*, etc.—a quiet life in Madrid would be dreadful to me. So I am not complaining about work, quite the contrary, it's a matter of keeping busy all day.

Well, on to another topic.

I don't remember what day Espinosa told me that he needed 520 pesetas to pay the inheritance tax. The next day I went to see Alvear, he told me he was just about to call me that morning, because he was going to Italy that very night . . . anyway, he gave me 500 pesetas. I gave them to Espinosa, and he told me that near the beginning of next month, on the 4th or 5th, he would return to the bank with all the documentation and would give me whatever was left of the pesetas if anything was left. That's all.

On Sunday[4] I was in Ávila with Uncle Polín, who is always affectionate toward me, and wants me to come as often as I can, so we can enjoy the country air and take walks together on Sundays. I found him looking well, not at all serious, and he is taking care of himself now, not moving around at all, and eating enough. I hope, God willing, that he is on the mend, because he only had one major episode of fatigue last season; for now, Uncle Álvaro is taking care of all his affairs.

---

4. Sunday: October 15, that is, the feast of Saint Teresa of Ávila.

I suppose my grandmother will come to Madrid soon, to spend the season with my aunt and uncle.[5]

The rest of the family, as usual. Today is Saturday, though not really, because I still had Calculus, and tomorrow I have to clean up my Descriptive Geometry notes, or else maybe I would have gone to Ávila, because going there means a lot to me . . . Nothing to be done about that, first things first. Besides, it costs 7.80 pesetas each way, and those ten duros for the calculus tutor add up, and what you spend in one place has to come from somewhere else.

Anyway, on that note, you know it's always hard for me to say so . . . I need money, as I am sure you can guess, and as I will demonstrate throughout the following.

The "Electrolux"[6] money is gone, and it's been gone for a while.

I have to register for a greater number of courses, and I need to pay the practicum fees, which will be some 50 pesetas, and get a drawing board from the school, which is 25 pesetas. I'm sure I'll have to pay the "teacher"[7] his 10 duros in advance, and I have to pay the boarding house through the end of the month. I have to buy some books and other little things that I need. I still have 150 pesetas, because Juan paid me already. So if you send me 250 pesetas, I'll have enough, because my budget (which I am very much simplifying) is as follows:

Registration fees	200, perhaps less	
Practicum fees	50	
Drawing board from the school	25	
Boarding house	150	
Tutor	50	
Books and other little things	25	
	500	
I have	150	
I need	350	goodness gracious!!

5. Aunt and uncle: Rafael's great-aunt and great-uncle, María de los Dolores Sánchez Lafuente and Leopoldo Torres Erro, the Marchioness and Marquess of San Miguel de Grox. (Because of their noble title, Rafael sometimes called them "Aunt and Uncle San Miguel.") Leopoldo's sister, Fernanda Torres, was Rafael's maternal grandmother.

6. Electrolux: A vacuum cleaner. Rafael had sold one earlier, but that money ran out.

7. "Teacher": In referring to his calculus tutor here, Rafael uses the English word *teacher*.

Well, that's fine, but that's not actually the math I expect. Registration fees should be lower, depending on how many classes they let me enroll in, so taking into consideration what's left over, that should be 300 pesetas rather than 350 in the end . . . that's right, some 300 rather than 350, that's it.

Good Lord! What a mess, it's always like this, I never have a clue how much money I have or spend or need. Look, please just send me 250, and if I need anything else, I'll ask you for it.

Oh, that reminds me—Espinosa's fees, when should I pay them? When he charges me for the banking matter, or before? Probably before, because he'll be giving me the papers all in order any day now, I suppose, and he won't be waiting around for me to pay him. Look, send me 300 pesetas so I can pay him, because I owe him 20 pesetas (it was 520, and I only gave him 500).

Or, look, don't send me anything, and then we can be done already. Let's do a test and see if I can sort this out on my own.

I have accounted for everything I spent: I paid some late bills to some magazines, two laundresses, and then the trip to Ávila, which cost me 16 pesetas. I went to Nocturnal Adoration for four months over the summer, somebody gave me a counterfeit duro, I don't know what to do with it, two dozen eggs, three taxis, five basic textbooks, tobacco . . . Anyway, a real mess; my suitcase is full of loose change.

Good Lord, it's not that I disregard money entirely, for it is my father's noble occupation, and I don't know how to earn it. But at times I feel like throwing it away, when I see how poorly I use it and the messes it gets me into.

All right, new paragraph, it's nine-fifty, and tomorrow, which is Sunday, I need to get up at dawn, but since I don't have class, instead of going to Mass early, I'll go at nine. Then maybe I'll go to Aunt and Uncle San Miguel's house, and tomorrow night I'll go to Uncle Paco's[8] house for dinner.

Has Antonio[9] gotten over his cold?

---

8. Paco: Rafael's uncle, Don Francisco Fontanals. He was married to Rafael's aunt, Fernanda Barón Torres, the twin sister of Rafael's mother Mercedes.

9. Antonio: Probably a servant in the Arnaiz-Barón household (OC n. 386).

I think you can send me 250 pesetas. I'll have enough, and if I need anything I'll telephone you, and I'll spend that fake duro—let's see if they'll take it at the telephone exchange, since they're foreign-owned, and the operators aren't very bright . . . yep, I don't think I'd feel bad about it. I don't know how I ended up with it, it's practically shouting that it's made of lead, plus it's all bent out of shape.

Well, that's all. Hope you're well, hugs to everybody.

This will go unsigned, since it's anonymous.

11. *Rafael's Daily Schedule in Madrid*[1]

October 1933

6:30 to 7	Mass
7 to 9	Study Descriptive Geometry and Perspective
9 to 1	Classes
1 to 2	Rest or walk
2 to 3	Lunch
3 to 3:30	Rest
3:30 to 5	Class at the Architecture School
5 to 6	Study Calculus and Mechanics
6 to 6:30	Merienda
6:30 to 7:30	Calculus tutoring
7:30 to 8:30	Study Calculus and Mechanics
8:30 to 9	Visit with the Master
9 to 10	Dinner
10 to 10:30	Study Art History and Construction
11:30	Rosary
12	Go to sleep.

1. The following words are written in big red letters next to the hours listed on this schedule: ALL FOR JESUS.

12. To Dom Félix Alonso García[1]

Ávila, November 19, 1933

Reverend Father,

I don't know if you will remember me, for it has been some time, about three years,[2] since I was last able to spend a few days at La Trapa. Even so, since that time, the Lord our God has been working within me in such a way that He has formed in me the firm intention to give myself to Him with all my heart and body and soul, and in order to fulfill my intention and resolution, and, moreover, trusting in God's help, it is my desire to enter the Cistercian Order. This is, in short, my Reverend Father, the reason that I am requesting an interview with you as soon as possible, so that your reverence might lend me your help and counsel.

I believe that I can rely on God, and in Him alone I trust, but as I take my first steps, I also trust in the charity of your reverence, whom I already regard as a father, and whom I beg to admit me as his son.

I am in Ávila with my aunt and uncle, awaiting your reply with the natural anxiety of one who wishes to give everything to God.

On the other hand, I have only to add that I am not motivated to change my life in this way because of sadness or suffering or disappointment or disillusionment with the world . . . I have all that it can give me. God, in His infinite goodness, has given me such gifts in this life, many more than I deserve . . . As such, my reverend Father, if you receive me into your community alongside your sons, be assured that you will be receiving only a heart filled with joy and much love for God.

---

1. Dom Félix Alonso García was the abbot of the monastery of San Isidro de Dueñas.

2. Rafael refers to the three years that had passed since his first visit to La Trapa, in September 1930, but he had in fact been to the monastery since then. He had done a retreat there from June 17–26, 1932 (OC 88).

Awaiting your reply, and humbly asking your blessing, your son in Jesus and Mary,

Rafael Arnaiz

c/o San Juan de la Cruz 4, Ávila[3]

3. The novice master, Father Marcelo León Fernández, responded to this letter on November 21, inviting Rafael to an interview. Rafael went to the monastery on the 24th, stayed the night, and returned to Ávila on the 25th having been admitted to the novitiate.

13. Dedication of a Holy Card to Leopoldo Barón

Ávila, November 22, 1933

A great many tabernacles exist across the face of the earth, but there is only one God, who is our eucharistic Lord: a consoling truth that unites the monk in his choir to the missionary among unbelievers to the priest in his parish. There is neither distance in space nor in time . . . at the foot of the tabernacle we are all near; God unites us. Let us ask Him, through Mary's intercession, that one day in heaven we might contemplate this God who, for love of humanity, hides Himself under the species of bread and wine. May it be so.

Rafael

14. To Rafael Arnaiz Sánchez de la Campa and Mercedes Barón Torres

Madrid, November 28, 1933

My dearest parents,

Forgive me for always failing to meet my obligations toward you, as usual . . . A leopard can't change its spots. I knew you would be satisfied with me being in Ávila on Sunday, and next Sunday I'm not sure what I'll do, although Uncle Polín is pleading with me to come back again, and his insistence is so great and my resistance is so little . . . that . . . I don't know. I don't make plans from one day to the next; God guides me and He knows how to do it.

There is one thing I have done without consulting you, because in truth there wasn't time. And besides, knowing that if I hadn't done it, you would have, it was a matter of conscience for me. It has to do with Uncle Polín. As you know, he has put the famous crown[1] up for sale, and it hasn't sold. He put Pedrosillo up for sale at any price, and it hasn't sold. He has Tímulos[2] up for rent and it hasn't been rented. And the bank has come calling, and so have his landlord and the butcher, etc. . . . And at home, *eight pesetas* without any more in sight, because everything depended on the sale of the jewel, and it's not selling . . .

Do you understand now why he's been sick? . . . I have been living in close proximity to his true *misery*, and although he did not wish it, because the money is not mine, he has had no choice but to allow me to lend him a thousand pesetas. The providence of God is watching over him and has made use of me in this matter. But, as I am sure you will understand, I was moved by my great affection for Uncle Polín, and I know you will not think poorly of

1. The famous crown: Rafael's aunt and uncle, María Osorio and Leopoldo Barón, were selling off some of their family assets because of financial troubles. The crown mentioned here may be a ducal coronet that María inherited along with her title as Duchess of Maqueda.

2. Tímulos: A small hamlet outside Toro, home to a hermitage to which Rafael may be referring.

this. And on the other hand, it is very painful for me to be there at his house, eating bread that I know very well has not been paid for in quite some time.

He will never complain, nor will he ask for anything himself, even if his children go hungry. But that is what we are for, those of us who are more or less secure.

He put up a real fight, but when you have no choice but to accept, because if not you will risk the same thing that everyone who sees hunger on the horizon is risking, you have no choice but to humble yourself and get through it . . .

I have always been something more than a nephew to Uncle Polín, and he has been something more than an uncle to me . . . The bond of Christian charity unites us, and that is something much greater than kinship.

Of course he will pay me back when the crown sells, or when Pedrosillo does, and though they can be very detached from earthly things, I understand perfectly well what that means. But don't you worry, nothing can get him down. He is always in good spirits, and last week he gained a pound and a half . . . It's clear that God loves him very much, for God's love is a cross . . . and he carries it joyfully. He turned to Aunt María's family, but that's no family at all . . .

Well, I paid 97 pesetas to Espinosa, and 500 to Alvear, plus a bit of his advance and fees. Essentially, with the 100 you sent me, I paid the boarding house, and now I've had to start paying back what I hadn't paid before. Between this that and the other thing, as of today, November 27,[3] I have 600 pesetas left, plus the thousand that Uncle Polín owes me.

Every day I find money more bothersome . . . everybody is dependent on those rotten pesetas, which provide only irritation and envy, and really rather little in the way of satisfaction. I do not ask God for anything more than what is necessary to cover the essentials, and if I can use what is left over to relieve my brother, then I shall, though what is truly beautiful is not giving away what is left over, but rather forfeiting what I spend on impulses, stupid luxuries, and nonsense, of which we will someday give a strict account to God . . . At times, my dear parents, I am deeply ashamed of myself. Of course it is so easy to give away what is not your own . . . but I hope that you will understand, and take care of this.

---

3. November 27: Probably an error, as the letter was dated and posted on November 28.

Uncle Polín thought about writing you the other day, but I told him to wait until I had written you myself, so I could fill you in; if I have acted wrongly . . . I don't know. I did so with the best of intentions and nothing more.

Long live the social revolution!!![4] Long live Larramendi!![5] Don't vote for the radicals!!![6] Long live the Christmas holidays, which will start any day now! Long live descriptive geometry! As you can see, long live everything. I never say die, it's not in my nature.

Tell Leopoldo that I was very grateful to receive his letter.

Great-uncle Leopoldo[7] is getting better now from his cold, which had him in bed for a few days and gave us quite a scare, because the doctor told us he had fluid building up at the base of his lung. Poor old man, he has so little left to overcome in this life, and it'll be the best day when he brings us joy by going up to heaven. I know that no human being says that sort of thing, but since I am a Christian I do say it . . . for the greatest mercy of God is a good death. That's how everything ends: crowns for sale, pesetas, descriptive geometry, right down the list of everything surrounding us . . . and then only one thing remains . . . God.

Well, my dear parents, pardon me this digression; the only great consolation available to every creature is to rise up above all these human trivialities for a moment to contemplate the one and only Truth.

Give my regards to everyone, including Ladreda,[8] who was just elected, and the Ursuline sisters, and everyone in Laspra,[9] etc. . . . , etc. . . . As for you, receive all my love as your son,

Rafael

4. Long live the social revolution!!!: "¡Viva la revolución social!" was a rallying cry for the Spanish Socialist Workers' Party, which lost power in the November 1933 elections.

5. Larramendi: Luis Hernando Larramendi (1882–1957), a politician who advocated monarchism and institutional support for the Catholic Church.

6. Radicals: The Radical Republican Party was founded as a socialist party but had become a center-right group by November 1933. It had a history of anticlericalism.

7. Great-uncle Leopoldo: Don Leopoldo Torres Erro.

8. Ladreda: José María Fernández Ladreda, the former mayor of Oviedo, who had just been elected to represent the city in the Spanish legislature. He was a right-wing monarchist who would later collaborate with the Franco regime during and after the Spanish Civil War.

9. Laspra: San Martín de Laspra, a small beach town north of Oviedo, with a parish church of the same name.

15. To Fr. Marcelo León[1]

Ávila, December 3, 1933

My dear Master,

Since I left the abbey, my spirit has not ceased to be among my monastic brothers for even a moment, although I have had to attend to all the business that I left unfinished in Madrid—all of which is now, thanks be to God, resolved. I will tell you what I have been up to since you saw me off.

I left Venta de Baños that Saturday, and spent Sunday and Monday in Ávila with my beloved aunt and uncle. On Tuesday I went to Madrid. If living in that city took a lot of effort and self-mortification before, the days I spent there now were relatively *easy*, seeing as—God willing—they shall be the last. Just remembering that the novices were surely praying for me has given me, and will continue to give me, the strength to follow in the way of the Lord, which of course is a cross, but a blessed cross when embraced for love of Christ.

Everything has been arranged. I said goodbye to my professors, my friends, and my family.[2] Of course, nobody knows that the trip I have planned will last my whole life, and I have left everyone under the impression that I will return in January after the holidays. So, nobody knows anything, except a friend of mine,[3] a classmate who is taking care of all my books and other things that seem so important to us as we go about the world, though in reality, understood rightly, they are nothing more than whims, luxuries, and little vanities.

I am already halfway there; what remains, as you know . . . is my parents. It is true that I have left behind the big dream of my degree, as well as the sincere affection of many people. To tell you the truth, it hasn't been

1. Fr. Marcelo León was the master of novices at San Isidro.
2. My family: Rafael is referring to family members in Madrid: the Fontanals-Barón family, and the Marquess and Marchioness of San Miguel y Grox. See #10, nn. 5, 8.
3. A friend of mine: His close friend and fellow boarder, Juan Vallaure.

that difficult, for two very simple reasons. First, the consideration that my sacrifice is pleasing in the eyes of God, who shall repay me in a way that people generally cannot understand, but that I can perceive from within my wretchedness. And second, because for a long time now my spirit has been growing more detached from things and closer to God. As I see this moment approaching, I am flooded with joy, and I am confident that God will continue giving me that joy, thus untying those knots of care and affection with which all creatures are tethered to the earth.

As I mentioned, Father, I spent the week in Madrid, and yesterday, December 2, I came to Ávila, in order to leave from here for Oviedo to wage the final battle: my parents. I will probably leave around December 8, and I will be there for . . . well, Father, I don't know how long. Following your advice, I will prepare the way little by little, and when it seems prudent, I will ask God for strength—for me and for my parents—and I will ask their permission, and without further delay, the master of novices will have me digging up roots in Venta de Baños . . .[4]

For now everything is in the hands of God and of the Blessed Virgin, to whom I must especially devote my affection and love, for She is to be my *only Mother* for what remains of my life.

How happy I am, Father, to know I am so loved by Our Lady, and how good God is with me, who treats me thus without my deserving it; at times I fear not knowing how to return His love, for my conduct has always been rather middling, and I have neither devotion nor mortification nor anything that really distinguishes me from others, and nevertheless, you see, my good God bestows upon me favors that I do not deserve . . . Mysteries of His will that make us think and reflect on many things . . . for truly, humanity deserved nothing, but still our Lord came down to be nailed to a cross . . . He gives us everything, and when we give Him a little bit, we call it a sacrifice; it seems to me the word is ill used in such a case . . .

When I do my *examen*[5] and look inside myself a little, I can see clearly that I do nothing more than follow the dictates of my heart toward God,

---

4. Venta de Baños: The town where the monastery of San Isidro de Dueñas was located.
5. *Examen*: A daily examination of conscience as recommended by Saint Ignatius of Loyola.

eager to fill myself with Him and nothing more. The real sacrifice would be to remain tethered to the world, and not to be able to sing to Him day and night in choir . . .

Forgive me, Father, for having digressed so much in this letter. What I do ask of you is that you might do me the kindness of answering me before I go to Oviedo, telling me what you think of what I plan to do, and your opinion about what I have done; your counsel will be followed as if it were a commandment, for I already consider myself a novice. If you give me some encouragement, I will be grateful to you for it, and if you merely oblige me with a line or two saying that my letter arrived, I will be grateful for that too, for I do not wish to bother you more than necessary.

Give my kind regards to Father Abbot, and I ask your blessing and your prayers as your novice

Rafael

Write me here, at my aunt and uncle's house in Ávila, San Juan de la Cruz 4.

16. To Fernanda Torres

Ávila del Rey, December 7, 1933

My dearest grandmother,

Uncle Polín tells me that today is the anniversary of your wedding day; this is the first time that I've written you on this day, but better late than never. My grandfather[1] in heaven will be pleased that it is your oldest grandson who, after so many years, is wishing you joy on this day.

From the letters you write to Uncle Polín, I can see clearly that some of your days are full of sadness and gray thoughts, as you say. It is very true that you have been through a lot, and you still have something left to go through . . . but, *abuelita*, if you look up to heaven for a moment, you'll see that all you can do is give infinite thanks, for you may be satisfied that you have given the world a large Christian family that gives much glory to God.

I do not want to minimize your sorrows. What I do want is to see a heart that is joyful in the midst of all the dejection that people and illness can cause . . . It all amounts to child's play compared to the great Truth . . . the only Truth, who is God, and the knowledge that we are sustained by Him gives us the strength for many things, even things that are considered heroic in the eyes of others, but as I am telling you, even those same heroic deeds are fun and games in the eyes of God . . . and very simple ones at that, you need only do one thing . . . which is to surrender yourself to Him in such a way that we have to contribute nothing more than our own good will . . .

I read somewhere, I don't know where, that *if you seek God, you will find Him*[2] . . . All that matters is seeking Him, and once you have found him, I promise you, *abuelita*, there will be no more pain, or joy, or anything else . . . there will be nothing but Him who fills and floods everything . . . And that is not a birthright for privileged souls, no. Every creature

---

1. My grandfather: His maternal grandfather, Álvaro Barón Cea-Bermúdez.

2. *If you seek God, you will find Him:* Among other biblical references, Matt 7:8: *everyone who searches finds.*

can find Him, but you must not search for Him among people and their affection, nor among material things and the world . . . neither will you find Him while looking for comfort and calm . . . To find Him, you must seek Him in the cross, in self-renunciation and sacrifice . . . That is when God reveals himself to us, and precludes us from seeing anything else, for He is so *absorbing* that there is no longer anything beyond Him.

Seize this moment, *abuela*, for God loves you so much in giving you a cross, so you are already well on your way, and need not look for one yourself.

Anyway, I'm writing you all these things that you already know, and they're inappropriate coming from your lowly grandson Rafael who has so much to learn from others, but the goodness of my desire ought to offset this little mystical-ascetic pedantry. I sound like a newly hatched Dominican, taking his first steps toward a sermon . . . Perhaps these are just quirks of youth.

These days, I'm finishing up my pleasant electoral holiday with my beloved aunt and uncle, and I'll be starting my Christmas holiday with my parents and brothers and sister . . . The truth is that with so much love on all sides and so many holidays . . . the cross I can offer to God is a little one, for I can assure you, *abuelita*, that I am completely happy . . . and the day that I make up my mind to seek God as I ought, it will cost me dearly, and I assure you that I am already quite impatient for it.

Well, nothing else for today. A great big hug from your grandson, who is very much counting on your prayers,

Rafael

Don't say anything to Aunt María,[3] because honestly I can't think of anything to tell her . . . An affectionate, courteous greeting . . . for the sake of "what people might say" . . . but nothing else, from her nephew who doesn't care for her at all.

---

3. Aunt María: María Josefa Barón Torres, Rafael's maternal aunt, who lived with Fernanda.

17. To Fr. Marcelo León

Ávila, December 8, 1933
Feast of the Immaculate Conception

My dearest Father Master,[1]

I received great consolation from your charitable, caring letter, may God reward you. This letter is to tell you that on Sunday[2] I will leave Ávila for Venta de Baños, and I will arrive on the express train, just like the other day.

The holidays have begun, and my trip home approaches. The moment when I will tell my parents is frightening, because of circumstances that I want to explain to you myself, as I promised; for because of my own weakness, I see myself in grave danger, and in such moments, the only things I care about are God and my vocation. Therefore, I am coming to the monastery now so that you can counsel me, and to surrender myself entirely to the will of my superiors, which to me, in this case, represents the will of God.

Regarding my books, drawing tools, and work implements, yes, I left him[3] everything conditionally, thinking that if the community would find them useful, then tomorrow . . . although of course I am coming to the monastery *completely* alone . . . I suppose you will understand perfectly what I am trying to say. I will be useful to the community in all that is asked of me, but my interests will be left at the door . . . My only interest is God.

---

1. Father Master: A title used for the master of novices, a professed monk who is tasked with the spiritual formation of novices as they begin religious life. See Thomas Merton, *Monastic Observances: Initiation into the Monastic Tradition 5*, ed. Patrick F. O'Connell, MW 25 (Collegeville, MN: Cistercian Publications, 2010), 260.

2. Rafael ended up leaving on Monday, December 11, rather than Sunday, December 10.

3. I left him everything: Rafael's friend Juan Vallaure.

I will travel with a close friend[4] who will help me around my parents. Right now they are the only anxiety I have, since they are unaware of all this.

Today, on this feast of the Immaculate Conception, I am uniting myself spiritually with my brother novices, so that She might enlighten us all, and that through her intercession, our Lord God might gladly accept what I am going to offer him with all my heart.

Give my kind regards to Father Abbot, and as for you, my dear Father, I ask your prayers and your blessing as your novice.[5]

Rafael

4. A close friend: Again, Juan Vallaure.
5. Rafael was not yet technically a novice, not yet having been clothed with the habit. However, he signed off as "your novice" here as a mark of respect for his novice master, whom he already considered an authority over him.

18. To Fernanda Torres

Ávila, December 10, 1933

My dearest *abuelita*,

Today Uncle Polín gave me your letter to read, and from it I can tell that, of course, you translated correctly. I did not intend for you to find out, for one rather simple reason: my parents don't know anything . . . And I *have been admitted* into La Trapa for fifteen days now. As you can imagine, I think only of the great favor that God has granted me, and I never cease to give Him thanks . . . I came to tell Uncle Polín about it the first time I came to Ávila; I went to Venta de Baños[1] . . . I am in correspondence with the master of novices, and tomorrow, Monday, I am going to La Trapa to get some advice, and then off to Oviedo to tell my parents, who should be *the first* to know about it, and should hear it from me . . . It is a duty for me and a kindness that they deserve; so the only people in the family who know about it are you and Aunt María, and my beloved Uncle Polín and Aunt María . . . I must ask you, therefore, for absolute discretion, but probably not for long, since my parents may find out as early as next week, as I will surely be in Oviedo by Wednesday.[2]

I know that the news did not catch you by surprise, and I hope it will not catch my parents by surprise either. For years now I have been thinking about it, and for years now God has been calling me, sweetly and gently. And so for me there is only one thing to do: go . . . Of course, in order to do that, I have to get up and destroy a lot of things . . . but such destruction is momentary . . . later, when the wounds have been healed and God has taken possession of us, the love that we seemed at first to leave behind will grow stronger and above all purer . . . that love is purified in God. Thus, with some in the world and others in the monastery choir, people

---

1. I went to Venta de Baños: Rafael is referring to his recent visit of November 24, 1933.
2. Wednesday: December 13, 1933.

come to identify with one another more and to love one another more, because true love is rooted in Christ and nourished by charity.

Don't think that I am going far away . . . on the contrary, I am going closer to God, and if through my prayers and sacrifices I can help others to grow closer to Him . . . what more could I ask, what more could I desire? . . . And so, I am not leaving behind the affection of my loved ones, which is very beautiful and very human . . . but rather I want to transform it into sublime, divine love.

My dear grandmother, what I do beg of you is that you ask God to give strength to my parents, and even more than strength, understanding. As for me, may God enlighten me and light my way in this endeavor, which seems heroic in the eyes of men, but in reality is nothing more than a way of returning the many benefits that the Lord has given me.

And please, *never* tell anyone that I told you before my parents . . . Things turned out that way, blessed be God, but that was not my intention.

Praise God, *abuelita*, praise Him at all times,[3] even when sorrows imprison us, even when our hearts are torn open, even when desolation overpowers us. Praise God at all times; there is no other prayer that God appreciates more, nor is there any other prayer that brings us closer to Him. That prayer will soon become my life . . . A life that will be spent in the choir, at work, and in silence, and that can be reduced to just one thing: praising God at all times.

Many things are coming to mind, and I would tell you those many things, but when love is true and deep, words express it poorly. Be content, then, with my silence, which perhaps you will understand better; after all, it is merely a foretaste of monastic silence.

My letter is not a farewell, either. Christians never bid one another farewell. God is our end, and there we will meet one another for all eternity . . . What do a few years matter, next to all that? Nothing, absolutely nothing . . . Impatience for our arrival makes them long, but God's help makes them short, so that they pass without our noticing. All we have to do is make good use of them, for there is only a little time to do good, and a long time to do evil.

---

3. See Ps 34:1: *I will bless the Lord at all times: his praise shall continually be in my mouth.*

Give Aunt María a big long hug for me. She already knows that the affection I have for her is real. As for you, *abuelita*, what do you want me to say? You already know what I am sending for you. I await only your blessing as your oldest grandchild

Rafael

19. To Fr. Marcelo León

Oviedo, December 17, 1933

My dear Father Master,

I should have written you days ago. Forgive my delay, but it is difficult to express the state of my soul in a letter; only God knows it, and I offer Him what I am going through these days. I am living in my parents' home, and right now they are completely happy to have me at their side . . . I still haven't said anything, because everything renders me defenseless: a show of affection here, a kindness from my mother there . . . but this situation is becoming unsustainable. On the other hand, I can't give the news a little bit at a time, because they haven't noticed anything different about me, since I have been thinking and acting this same way for a long time. That is, if I bring up La Trapa in conversation, it doesn't take them by surprise . . . because they're used to it by now. If I hint at any conversation about this topic, the same thing happens. They just think: that's Rafael for you . . . And so I have no choice but to give the news all of a sudden, just telling them that you are expecting me, and that I am leaving . . . and believe me, Father, I lack the strength to inflict the wound—though not on myself, for I am already bleeding from it . . .

Pray for me, dear Father, that God might sustain me in these difficult moments in which circumstances ordained by God have placed me. I am giving up everything, but I am doing it little by little, and every day, every hour that passes, every detail of my home life reminds me of that. It's as if I were about to undergo an operation, and with complete calm, even taking pleasure in it, I were to prepare the instruments and all the details myself . . . And my very nature and my selfishness are shouting at me: "Enough already! . . . Enough!" Soon, then; I don't know how long I can resist. When you have to operate, operate fast; if you have to cut open and wound, the sooner the better . . .

And it's not that my vocation is in danger. On the contrary, I am more content every day with the path on which I have set out, and more resolved in everything. For me, God comes first, and with His help I will be able to overcome His creatures. If the only thing I can offer Him is a bloodied heart, it is because that is what He wanted, and He will take care of healing it, for it shall be all His.

I have such a desire, Father, to be among my brother novices and leave all this behind at once . . . I am writing you from a warm room, with rugs, good lighting, and my soft, clean bed; in a word, all the comfort and convenience that modern life can provide . . . But when I think of the dormitory[1] at La Trapa, I would trade it all for that, and a hundred times over.

Today I went to hear a sermon and receive Benediction at the Dominican convent,[2] and my mother, because it was a bit cold, insisted that I take the car, and if you knew how much I have reflected on and considered that detail . . . Anyway, Father, what's the point of bothering you with all the details of my life? In short, what seemed of no importance to me before is now affecting me very much, and if I could move to the monastery through thought alone, I would do it . . .

But God is asking me for my parents' sacrifice, as well as my own . . . then may it be done. I am counting not on my own strength, but on the help of God and the Blessed Virgin. It will all be done; to do otherwise would be cowardice.

Tell the novices not to be anxious for my arrival, but rather to pray that the Lord's will be done in me.

I await your letter eagerly, but I ask that you send it by way of *San Juan de la Cruz 4, Ávila*, at my aunt and uncle's house,[3] and they will take care of sending it to me without my parents finding out. Until now I have never kept any secrets from them, and so I haven't minded that they read the letters I receive, but now, as long as I haven't told them yet, I don't want . . . good Father, you understand.

---

1. Dormitory: Here Rafael uses the Spanish word *camarilla*, meaning a shared dormitory divided with partitions, as distinct from *celda*, meaning the standard individual monastic cell.

2. Dominican convent: Convento de Santo Domingo in Oviedo, where the Dominican friars also have a chapel and a school.

3. My aunt and uncle's house: the Ávila residence of María Osorio and Leopoldo Barón.

I haven't done anything yet about the required documentation, not even finding out which Burgos parish I am confirmed and baptized in.[4]

Nothing more to tell you now; give my kind regards to Father Abbot, and I await your prayers and blessing as your novice

Rafael

Argüelles 39, Oviedo.[5]

4. Rafael was baptized on April 21, 1911, in the parish of Santa Águeda, Burgos, and confirmed on December 1, 1913, at the Colegio del Niño Jesús (School of the Child Jesus), Burgos. Sacramental records are a typical requirement for an application to enter religious life.

5. Argüelles 39: The address of Rafael's parents' home in Oviedo, from which he sent this letter.

20. *To Leopoldo Barón*

Oviedo, December 17, 1933

Dearest Uncle Polín,

Just a quick note to ask you for a favor. You will undoubtedly receive a letter for me from my home in Venta de Baños;[1] I beg you to send it to me with a quick note from you so that my parents don't find out, because they still know absolutely nothing, and right now are completely happy to have me at their side.

These days I've been telling one lie after another; or rather, I've been hiding the truth. I don't know how long God will give me the strength to do it, but I'm telling you, in my current state, anything can render me defenseless: a show of affection, my mother's kindness, my father's excitement. I am making a mighty effort, since my body is at home with my family, while my spirit is ever further away.

How much God asks of me!!! For He not only asks me to leave everything behind, but also, before leaving it for good, He asks me to savor it. It is hard to undergo an operation, but still harder to have to prepare all the instruments oneself and even take pleasure in the preparations.

I don't think I have to explain any of this to you. You understand perfectly well, and you know that God will forgive me for all this rather human weakness.

My mother is playing the piano. . . I have to leave. . . If I keep quiet, I suffer greatly; if my joy brings joy to my parents, I suffer even more . . . How good God is, Uncle Polín, who makes me suffer for His sake. For if it were not for Him, I would not have to tear my own heart out piece by piece, slowly, as I am now.

But look . . . let's leave the doing to Him. May His will be done in me. Are you better now?

1. My home in Venta de Baños: That is, the monastery.

When I arrived at La Trapa the other day,[2] and I laid at the foot of the altar what I had just done in Ávila,[3] I was utterly content, believe me. When I left, I asked the Virgin to be with me, to accompany me and guide my steps . . . the last steps I would take among men . . . so when I falter, I remember Her, and as I know that She is waiting for me at the monastery, just thinking of Her gives me strength to carry on . . . and I carry on.

Listen, the novices were very happy the other day because they thought I was there to stay, and as we heard the high Mass, the one who rings the bell[4] brought me a bench. When he was returning from work, I crossed paths with them on the way, because I was heading out, and he smiled at me as if to say, "Let's see if you come back soon . . . and take courage, the Virgin is at your side . . ." And I'm telling you, just for the friendly smile of that bell-ringing novice at a stranger—when all he knew about me was that I am in the world, fighting to detach myself from it—just for that kindness alone, my trip to the monastery was worth it . . . I'm just telling you this, because only you understand me.

But anyway, I don't want to go on rambling. If I were to start talking, I'd be up tonight until three in the morning, but since I don't have anyone to talk to, I'll share my thoughts in silence with God. He has taken that away from me, the consolation of others, so that I might seek Him alone and communicate with Him alone.

I am not asking for your prayers, or for Aunt María's, because I know that you are both already offering them generously.

My dearest aunt and uncle . . . I have done you wrong by giving you so much only then to have to take it away from you.

There are so many things coming to mind now that I didn't say to you, that my stupid tears kept me from saying, but there is so much I want to say to you, too much to say now. In heaven you will hear it all; for now, leave me alone. Then, upon finding myself alone, I will live more for God, and God will be more pleased with me.

2. The other day: December 11, 1933, when Rafael met with the master of novices to ask for his advice about breaking the news to his parents.

3. What I had just done in Ávila: Rafael requested permission to enter La Trapa by letter while he was staying with his aunt and uncle in Ávila.

4. The one who rings the bell: Brother María Damián Yáñez Neira, who would become Rafael's co-novice and eventually one of his biographers.

Forgive me, I don't know what I'm saying. I'd gladly take a glass of Cointreau; that would get rid of this lump in my throat that won't let me swallow. Anyway, I'll stop now because it's now one in the morning and I've already got two letters here, one for you and the other for Father Master.[5] This is the only time I can use, when everyone is quiet and in bed, and tonight it seems that I've "let go of my inhibitions" while writing.

How's it going with the crown? See, I'm paying attention to everything.

Don't worry about the money I left with you. One of these days my parents will write you.

Goodbye, my dearest aunt and uncle, and let us prepare ourselves, for beyond all these small matters that occupy us creatures, in six days the Savior of the world will come down to be born in a manger, in complete poverty, with the greatest vulnerability.

I wish you a Christmas season full of happiness with your children . . . As it is the feast of the Christian home, I will try not to spoil it for my parents and brothers and sister. If I don't spend the season as I have in the past, that is, *humanly* happy, spiritually I am even more so, for this is the first time in my twenty-two years that I have something worthy to offer the Child Jesus.

Sending you both a great big hug, your son,

Rafael

The day that I leave for good, I will write you, just as I promised. Take the novice master's letter out of its envelope, so you both can read it as you have every right to, but also so that it takes up less space.

---

5. Father Master: a title used for the master of novices, Fr. Marcelo León (see #17).

21. To Fr. Marcelo León

Oviedo, January 1, 1934

My dear Master,

I received your kind letter on December 26, and I was most grateful for it. It gave me great consolation; for I am used to not receiving encouragement from anyone, and to considering myself to be so alone that, although I have God as my sole confidant, my weakness often seeks out human consolation. Of course, to me you are my true brothers, and I consider the voice of my superiors to be the voice of God Himself. And it's becoming clear to me that when God calls a soul, He wants that soul so detached from everything that He takes away even the material consolation of other creatures, and when the soul realizes it is alone, helpless, and seemingly deprived of everything . . . that is when, as I understand it, God is closest to the soul, and when the voice of His divine will can be heard most clearly.

Dear Father, things are much the same, but the moment approaches, and I would be lying if I said that I don't fear it. At the same time, I have great confidence in God's protection, which leads me to keep going and face it all.

Truly, God's enemy is attacking me on all fronts. He has overcome me a few times, but in spite of everything, I haven't lost even a "millimeter" of ground, as you say. His victories are over my senses, and it's not that I want to make excuses for myself, quite the opposite. But since you have been in the world, you know this word, *comfort*, which is like a god these days, adored by idolaters, and since that is what surrounds me, comfort and convenience, the enemy is using that to try and mislead me . . . But my spirit is with God, and not only have I not lost even a "millimeter" in my resolution, but in fact I have advanced some "meters." The more temptations I have, the steadier I will be on my path—not because of my own merits, of which I have none, and not because I think I am invincible, but rather because Our Lady is behind me. When I last left the monastery, I entrusted myself to Her care, and I believe I am thoroughly protected by Her.

I have let these days go by, since it didn't seem like the right time to say anything, but one of these days I will start by telling my mother, for whom I ask your prayers.

Tomorrow I am going to visit the parish priest to ask him for the document I need.[1] And so, *little by little*, I will get where my fervent straining toward God has been wanting to go all at once . . . There are so many lessons we can draw from everything, even from our own weaknesses.

If you only knew, Father, how much dead weight I have to leave behind before presenting myself to God. Oh, people don't understand us at all!! Even leading a pious life, you end up with so much dirt on your hands! . . . But in general, people are satisfied with very little. If you receive communion often, and say the rosary from time to time, that's enough for them to start calling you holy. They'll even put you on the altar if you're not careful . . . But that's not how God, who sees all and knows all, judges things . . . fortunately.

The monastery will be two things for me: first, a corner of the world where I can praise God night and day without obstacles, and second, a purgatory on earth where I can become purified, become perfect, and become holy . . . Saying it like that, so casually . . . "become holy" . . . it seems like an aspiration that's a bit . . . I don't know how to put it, but that's the truth. I want to be holy in the eyes of God, not in those of men; a holiness that develops in the choir, in the fields, and above all, a holiness that develops in silence and that only God knows about, that not even I should discover, for then it would not be true holiness . . .

I recently read some verses that said, "Virtue that goes forth with great display is hardly virtue."[2] Well, forgive me for going on so long with my

---

1. The document I need: A statement of good moral and religious conduct; an aspirant to religious life often needs a recommendation from a parish priest. Rafael's family belonged to the parish of San Juan el Real, Oviedo, whose pastor was Fr. Bernardino González.

2. José María Pemán, *A Saint in a Hurry: El divino impaciente* (London: Sands and Co., 1935), 41. Pemán's play, which premiered in 1933, recounts the life of the Jesuit co-founder and missionary Saint Francis Xavier and was written in response to the legal dissolution of the Jesuits under the Second Spanish Republic the previous year. See Niceto Alcalá-Zamora y Torres and Álvaro Albornoz y Liminiana, "Ministerio de Justicia: Decreto," *Gaceta de Madrid* 24 (Jan. 1932): 610–11.

stupid fantasies. I will be content with whatever God wishes, and what He permits me to be. I surrender my will and my good desires to Him. May He do the rest.

If you write to me, please do me the kindness of doing just what you did the other day, using my beloved uncle in Ávila as our intermediary.

The days are getting longer on me the more time I take to join my dear brother Trappists.

Happy New Year to Father Abbot and the community. With love from your novice, who commends himself to your prayers,

Rafael Arnaiz

22. *To Dom Félix Alonso García*

Oviedo, January 9, 1934

Rev. Father,

First of all, may God be praised, and let us give Him infinite thanks for the many blessings that we receive from Him and do not deserve.

Today you will receive a letter from my father, to whose generous Christian words I have nothing further to add.

My intention was to leave the house after just getting permission from my parents, but my father said that he has to do his duty, and he will take me to the monastery himself, and so, I think I should do my duty too, by obeying. Moreover, I think that once the sacrifice has been made, God will be satisfied that he made it so completely, all the way to the end, and although I trust in neither my own strength nor that of my parents, I have absolute confidence in God, who has not failed me until now, and I hope never will.

I cannot find the words to express the state of my soul, but Your Reverence will understand me perfectly. Things have been very painful for me, especially as I have been watching my parents suffer, but at the same time I have experienced consolation in understanding that their suffering is Christian and their sacrifice is pleasing in the eyes of God.

I don't deserve such parents as I have. I don't want to drag these days out too much, so I beg Your Reverence with all my might to write my father as soon as possible, telling him that we can come to the monastery.

I desire it with all my heart, and along with my tears and my broken heart, I also have a joy and a contentment and a calmness of spirit that are hard to understand. Truly, on a human level, what I am going through is very strange.

Please pray a lot for my parents, that God may help them in these difficult moments.

Greet Father Master and the community for me. I ask your blessing as your son in Christ,

Rafael Arnaiz

23. *To María Osorio and Leopoldo Barón*

Oviedo, January 12, 1934

My dearest aunt and uncle,

Just a quick note so that this letter goes out today.

I have nothing to say to you, because I have too few words to communicate it all, and the only thing I can say is that I haven't done anything. The Lord has done everything, absolutely everything. If you only knew how much He loves me, and how He has sustained me, and is sustaining me now! You would never ask Him for anything again, nor offer Him anything. It would all be reduced to praising Him without ceasing, blessing Him, and extolling Him, and continually singing a glorious song of thanksgiving and gratitude.

Lord, Lord, I ask *nothing* of you, because I already have You who are everything! Merely permit me to join the choir of angels, archangels, and cherubim, and all the heavenly host, and for my heart here on earth to fly up to heaven and sing, *Glory to God in the highest heaven, and on earth peace among those whom He favors!*[1]

If only you could see how happy I am to know that God has accepted what I have offered Him. Not what I have offered Him, which is worth little, but rather what my parents have so generously offered Him . . . What great souls!

What a great responsibility I have undertaken! But the Blessed Virgin is helping me in such a way that I can almost physically feel it. I want to pour my heart out, but what I have inside me is so great that I cannot, for if my joy is great, then great too—so great—is my sorrow . . . but much greater is my love for God . . . if not, this wouldn't be possible.

I can't yet tell you when I am leaving, because I am waiting for a letter from my good Father Abbot.

1. Luke 2:14.

Things have gone much as the Nuncio[2] told me they would. My father did not only give me his permission, but in fact he is going to *offer me* himself; I am not running away from home, but rather I will bid my mother farewell . . . I am counting on neither my own strength nor that of my parents . . . I am counting on the help of the Virgin and the strength given by a God like ours.

The Nuncio's words come to mind: "Vocations must be pursued in such a way that it is not just pleasing in the eyes of God, but gentle and sweet in the eyes of others. That is, without violence or convulsions, but the other way around: pleasantly." When this is possible, as it is in my case, it must be done this way. Perhaps you suffer more this way, I'm not saying you don't, but in the eyes of God it is more meritorious, don't you think?

Anyway, I'll write you when I am in my monastery.

I'm sending you this money for my grandmother, but I'm sending it to you because I don't know if she is in Madrid or not. Careful now, don't you think that I've gone and stolen anything! My aunt gave me a few pesetas, in case I needed anything, but the first thing I thought of was you, and my grandmother, among others . . . I hope that this will not offend you, good sir.

If she is still staying with you, give her a big hug from me. As for you, my dearest aunt and uncle, nothing, because as you can tell, your nephew doesn't care much for you at all

Rafael

2. The Nuncio: Monsignor Federico Tedeschini served as the apostolic nuncio, or papal diplomat, in Spain from 1921 to 1935. Leopoldo Barón introduced him to his nephew in 1933 while Rafael was deciding how to break the news about his vocation to his parents (OC 133).

24. Dedication of a Little Office
to Mercedes Barón Torres[1]

January 14, 1934

Mother . . . I am giving everything to Him . . . everything I am and everything I am worth, I am giving to Him with all my good will and sincerity, and now I only ask Him to accept it . . . Ask Him for this too, Mother, and tell Him, "Lord, my son is offering You his life and his works, and is surrendering himself entirely to You; do not reject his offering, for although it may always be imperfect, he is doing it for pure love of You . . . Accept my son, Lord; a mother is begging you."

And so you, in the world, and I, in the monastery, both have something to offer to God. I offer Him all that I am, and you offer your son,

Rafael

---

1. Little Office: The Little Office of the Blessed Virgin Mary is a devotion to Mary that shares the structure of the monastic hours. Before the Second Vatican Council, it was often said as an addition to the Divine Office among religious, or as a replacement for it among laity.

25. Dedication of a Holy Card
to Mercedes Barón Torres

January 14, 1934

The only consolation that we creatures can have is to delight in God, and that is why I am going to La Trapa. There, seven times a day, I will sing canticles in His honor, just as King David did.[1] Remember, then, whenever you raise your eyes to God, that your son Rafael is in a choir of men on earth singing with joy in imitation of the angels in heaven, "Hosanna in the highest." Remember that he will never retire any evening without having first offered a devout *Salve*[2] to the Blessed Virgin for his father, his mother, his brothers, and his sister, so that soon, up above, we might all keep singing with joy to a God as good as Jesus.

1. Ps 119:164: *Seven times a day I praise you for your righteous ordinances.*
2. See note on the *Salve Regina* in #5, n. 6.

II. *A Heart Filled with Joy and Love*

Joining the Monastery

26. *To Mercedes Barón Torres*

the guesthouse at La Trapa,
January 16, 1934

My dearest mother,

Just a quick note to let you know that soon, at two in the afternoon, I will be entering the community and will go to the choir at Vespers; of course if I am happy, I hope that you are too.

Yesterday my father left me here. He spent a long time with Rev. Fr. Abbot. Afterwards I went to the *Salve*, then I had dinner and went to bed. Today I got up late and spent a good while with Father Master. He told me that he'd come look for me at two.

I suppose you will all be together in Oviedo now, giving thanks to God at all times for the great blessing He has given us; I, at least, do not cease giving Him thanks for everything.

I wanted to tell you so many things but I don't have the words for any of them. All of you are in my heart, especially you, my dear mother. Did you like the dedications I wrote for you?[1]

Keep praising God for everything, and asking the Blessed Virgin to pray for my perseverance, for if we receive anything from God it is always through Her intercession.

Now they are distributing food to the poor; Father told me that yesterday there were more than a hundred of them.[2]

It is splendidly sunny out today, not like yesterday, which was rather gloomy.

Right now I am impatiently awaiting the Novice Master and wanting it to be time for me to take my place in choir already. How happy I will be, dear Mother. Look, my first prayers will be a hymn of thanksgiving for God

---

1. The dedications I wrote for you: See #24 and #25.
2. See #7, n. 14.

that will burst forth from my heart, but afterwards, for whom will I pray if not for my parents? That is the one thing that I think can console you.

I will write you more slowly when the Novice Master gives me permission to do so. For today, be content with knowing that your son is content, that he is praying a lot for you all, and that he is in the hands of the Virgin, who is the protectress of the Order.

Without further ado, know of all your son's love as he asks for your blessing,

Rafael

I really want a smoke, but I don't know what's going on with me. Somehow I end up forgetting that I want to.

27. To Rafael Arnaiz Sánchez de la Campa and Mercedes Barón Torres

La Trapa, January 23, 1934[1]

It is six-thirty in the morning, and I am overcome with drowsiness. Brother Damián[2] noticed, and he signed to me that I won't fall asleep if I write, and I'll be able to keep my eyes open more easily that way . . . So without further ado beyond a Hail Mary, I have taken up pen and paper and begun to write.

I have been in the monastery for exactly eight days, in which I have tried to submit everything in my power to the Rule,[3] and for now all I can say is that I am very sleepy . . . I go to bed at seven in the evening, and with the grace of God, I fall asleep immediately. At one, the pain in my lower back wakes me up, since it's not exactly a feather mattress that I'm sleeping on. I change position at one, as I was saying, and just when I think I've fallen asleep again . . . Bong! The bell tells me that it's two and that I have to go down to Matins . . . I don't doubt it for a minute, not even a second. I just put on my slippers and coat, since I sleep in my clothes, and then wash my face a little. And then, thinking of God, with a joyful heart, I go down the novitiate stairs at full speed and enter the church, where my God is in the tabernacle waiting for His monks to start singing His praises . . . And once there, in the choir of a Cistercian abbey, fifty men begin to live the monastic day, gazing down and singing the words the angel spoke to Mary: "Hail Mary, full of grace, the Lord is with you."[4]

---

1. Although this was originally intended as an exercise to keep him awake, Rafael did end up attaching this sheet of paper (#27) and the following one (#28) to a letter to his parents dated January 29, 1934 (#29). See OC 185.
2. Brother María Damián Yáñez Neira (see #20, n. 4).
3. The Rule: The Rule of Saint Benedict (see #7, n. 2).
4. Luke 1:28.

I think that at that moment, the Queen of Heaven must look upon her sons with tenderness, and God Himself must delight in Mary . . . And so it is well worth the effort to get up at two and be a little sleepy.

Well, Brother Damián was right, I'm not sleepy anymore. Blasted nature, what a pain you are!! But I hope that with God's help I will conquer and master you, and for that, I need only one thing, persistence and prayer . . . and surely, without even realizing it, after a certain amount of time I won't be as sleepy as I am now, but nothing to be done about that . . . even the apostles fell asleep in the garden,[5] and left Jesus all alone . . . and they're apostles, so what am I, a poor sinner, to do?

5. Matt 26:40-46; Mark 14:37-42; Luke 22:45-46.

28. To Rafael Arnaiz Sánchez de la Campa and Mercedes Barón Torres[1]

La Trapa, January 24, 1934

How beautiful silence is! Especially here in La Trapa, where we all understand one another with a simple look; but above all, God understands us, and I think that is enough . . . The Rule of Saint Benedict is admirable, but silence is what gives it the quality of holiness.[2] That joyful silence of the cloister and the gardens, where everything falls silent, except the birds who sing to God.

I live together with three novices[3] who, since I have been here, have not spoken to me except through signing.[4] I already know how to make a few signs, but . . . how I'd like to say a paragraph or two to my beloved brothers! I'm convinced that silence helps one hold onto God's presence . . . but it is also a great penance, especially at certain moments and certain times. For example, when it's a splendid day out, and you're going to work in the fields, and working in the fields is cheerful; well, the cheerfulness that you'd like to express by jumping around and singing, you have to quiet it down instead, and offer it to God in silence . . . And that is rather beautiful, but you have to get used to it. I told Father Master that sometimes I feel like crying out, and he told me to channel that energy into singing in choir, and so that's what I do.

1. A loose sheet of paper included with a letter to his parents. See #27, n. 1.
2. On the Rule and on monastic silence, see #7, nn. 2, 6.
3. The three other novices were Brother María Isidro David (Felipe) Ortega, who left the monastery upon being drafted during the Spanish Civil War (1936–1939) and eventually became a doctor; Brother María Bernardo Michelena Castañeda, who spent most of his monastic life as a chaplain to Trappist nuns in Japan; and Brother María Damián Yáñez Neira, who moved to the Trappist monastery of Oseira in Galicia, Spain. Brothers Bernardo and Damián both attended Rafael's beatification in Rome on September 27, 1992.
4. On monastic sign language see #5, n. 8.

As you can see, life at La Trapa boils down to singing in choir and singing out of choir; sometimes shouting out, other times in silence, but the song is the same. And although my own is rather poor, and sometimes I sing it quite sleepily, I think God will accept it, and I pray to the Blessed Virgin that it may be so.

This morning, January 24, it was snowy, so after high Mass, we'll go to the chocolate factory to wrap chocolates.[5] I'm really slow, but lucky for me, I don't get paid by the piece. We have two hours of work, that is, two hours of absolute silence, and I promise I don't get tired or bored, because what I do is think. When I say it like that, it sounds absurd, because everybody thinks, but it's not like that—thinking is a difficult thing. Of course I mean thinking well, thinking in an orderly fashion, so as to benefit from it; thinking calmly, getting hold of your imagination and taking it where you will . . . I devote myself to all that while I wrap up chocolates, and if I pray a Hail Mary from time to time, I get even more out of the work, and the chocolate is wrapped better. Here in La Trapa you may be asked to do anything except waste time.

5. Until 1960, the monks at San Isidro de Dueñas made part of their income by making chocolate. As Rafael implies, novices generally worked in the fields unless the ground was too frozen, and then they might be assigned to the chocolate factory or the kitchen for the day.

29. To Mercedes Barón Torres

La Trapa, January 29, 1934

My dearest mother,

I hope you aren't cranky that your son didn't write you earlier, but you must know that here in La Trapa nothing is up to us, but rather to our superiors, and in this case, it is Father Master who has the final say. I got permission to write you yesterday, that is, Sunday, but I was with my father so I couldn't.[1] He'll tell you how I seemed and how I'm doing. . . In short, very well.

I appreciated your letter very much, and so did Father Master. He told me that it was written in a very literary style with great Christian sentiment, and that he was going to ask your permission to copy it . . . Of course I am proud of my parents, and praising God in them.

Today it has been fifteen days since I came to the monastery, but it feels as if I just arrived yesterday. I have adjusted very well to the Rule. Upon first glance, seen from the outside, it seems very hard, but the only hard thing here is my bed . . . Everything else is austere, but not inhumane, far from it.

If only you knew what great peace we breathe here, what silent joy fills the abbey; it cannot be explained, for that joy and that peace are God who reigns in the house, and He is the only focal point of monastic life.

All of a Cistercian monk's activity revolves around the tabernacle. The hours of the Divine Office in choir are never tiresome; the hours spent in church seem mere minutes . . . Faith tells us that we are praising God, and God is there, so nearby, just a few steps away in the tabernacle . . . What does the world know about a Trappist monastery?! I am ever more grateful to God for my vocation, and I ask Him to carry me from Venta de Baños to heaven, so that face to face with Him, as Saint Thérèse says,[2] I can keep on singing.

---

1. Rafael's father, Rafael Arnaiz Sánchez de la Campa, visited him on January 28, 1934.
2. "Notwithstanding my exceeding littleness, I dare to gaze upon the Divine Sun of Love, and I burn to dart upwards unto Him! . . . With daring self-abandonment there will I

There are so many things I could tell you, but my pen is rather uninspired, and would not be able to put into words what I am feeling . . . I am content, utterly content, for God loves me so much, and the Blessed Virgin helps me in such a way . . . as only She knows how.

Now I'm going to tell you what I enjoy most and what I find hardest . . . you can guess at both. What I like best is being in Choir, and what I find hardest is getting up at two, because here there's none of that "first one eye and then the other" business, no thinking about it and then going back to sleep again . . . No, at the sound of the bell, before it has even stopped ringing, we should already be on our feet, dressed, and with our shoes on, because the bell rings at two and Matins begins ten minutes later.

Your intention to pray the Little Office of the Blessed Virgin Mary at the same time seems a little over the top to me, because look:

Matins and Lauds   at 2:10 in the morning

Prime   at 5:30 in the morning

Terce and Sext   at 7:45 in the morning

None   at 11:07 in the morning

Vespers   at 4:30 in the afternoon

Compline   at 6:30 in the evening[3]

That's when we pray the Hours in the winter, the schedule varies in the summer.

Now we are going to the conventual Mass, that is, at 7:45. First we pray Terce, then we have Mass, and afterwards Sext. Then we go to work, whether that's pulling up vines or wrapping chocolate bars at the factory. It depends on the weather, because when there's frost, the ground is very hard and it's cold out.

Well . . . that's all for today.

I'm sending you two other pieces of paper that I scribbled on other day.

---

remain until death, my gaze fixed upon that Divine Sun" (Saint Thérèse of Lisieux Martin, *The Story of a Soul*, in *Soeur Thérèse of Lisieux: The Little Flower of Jesus*, trans. Thomas Taylor [London: Burns, Oates, & Washbourne, 1922], 187).

3. For the Divine Office, see #7, n. 12; for the Little Office, see #24, n. 1.

Don't be alarmed by the different paper, here we make use of everything and everything is useful.

If you see any friends of mine, give them my regards. I won't name them, but since there are so few of them, there's no need. But do give them to Mr. Fernando Vallaure[4] in particular.

As for you, and my brothers and sister, what can I say? . . . Only that I think of you all when I should, and where I should.

Now we are going to None and then to the refectory, to eat our "daily bread," since we just came from the chocolate factory.

I don't know when I will write you next . . . whenever they order me to. Right now I am coming from the refectory. We had black beans, milk, bread, wine, and nuts. What do you think of the menu? . . . In a little bit we'll have class on the Constitutions of the Order,[5] and then we'll go to work . . . I'm telling you, not a minute is to be wasted.

I think of you all often, and at the happiest moments, for I should so like for you to be able to participate in the joys of a Trappist novitiate.

Give my aunt[6] many hugs from me, and the same to my brothers and sister. Nothing for my father, as I just saw him yesterday. As for you, all my love as your novice Rafael, who as promised remembers you *every* day at 6:45 after praying the *Salve* to the Blessed Virgin (don't get the idea that I think of my family at set times . . .). Oh, I'll never learn how to write seriously.

Without further ado, a big hug from your son

Rafael

---

4. Mr. Fernando Vallaure: The father of Rafael's close friend Juan Vallaure; see #9, n. 5.

5. The Constitutions of the Order: "The meaning of the word 'constitutions': a rule is the norm of living by which the monk attains to his end, union with God. Constitutions are particular statutes, added to the Rule, approved by the Holy See. . . . The Constitutions interpret and apply the Rule to our way of life" (Thomas Merton, *Charter, Customs, and Constitutions of the Cistercians: Initiation into the Monastic Tradition 7*, ed. Patrick F. O'Connell, MW 41 [Collegeville, MN: Cistercian Publications, 2015], 57). San Isidro de Dueñas was governed by the 1924 Constitutions, translated into English as *Constitutions of the Order of Cistercians of the Strict Observance* (Dublin: M. H. Gill & Sons, 1925).

6. My aunt: Petra Sánchez de la Campa y Tasquer, Rafael's paternal great-aunt, who was living with the Arnaiz-Barón family in Oviedo at the time.

30. To Mercedes Barón Torres

La Trapa, January 30, 1934

My dearest mother,

My letter can't go out today, so I have time to fill up another sheet of paper for you.

I am longing for the day when I receive the habit, which I suspect will be in the next fifteen days or so, since I have to have been a postulant for at least a month. I don't know what name I will be given, but Father Master told me it's possible that I'll keep my own, since there isn't another Rafael in the monastery.[1]

For yesterday's work, we moved sacks of potatoes from the warehouse to the monastery. I'm telling you, I'm very good at loading and unloading sacks. After work, I go and make sure what I've done is all accounted for. That is, I go to the chapel and tell the Master[2] all about it, and whenever I go to see Him, I have something for Him to take note of, so that later He can pay my wages all at once. One day it's a few vines pulled or holes filled, another day it's chocolates wrapped, another it's rooms swept, etc. . . . At the end of the day, I'm just doing business, and I'm telling you, with a Master as generous as mine, it's a profitable business indeed.

The other day I was in the chapel alone. I'd just come back from the factory, where I had been wrapping chocolates. And there in the chapel it was just God and me, ready to report back to Him. On my knees before the Tabernacle, my soul offered my most recent work to God, those two

---

1. In Rafael's monastery, postulants received a religious name along with the habit upon entering the novitiate. The religious name could be the same as the postulant's baptismal name, provided no one else in the community already had it. Generally, a postulant would not receive a double name (e.g. "Jude Thaddeus," "Francis Xavier") except to add a form of Mary (e.g. "María Damián," "María Marcelo").

2. Master: Rafael uses the title "Master" on its own to refer to Jesus in the Eucharist, as distinct from "Father Master," a title used for the master of novices (see #17, n. 1).

hours wrapping chocolates in silence, and one of those things that happen sometimes, in fact happened to me . . . You'll see . . .

In an outburst of enthusiasm, I addressed the following prayer to my God: "Lord, you are so high up, and I am here below, where, in a more or less generous way, a poor Trappist wants to send You a humble gift, and all he has to give You right now is the work of wrapping up a few dozen pieces of chocolate . . . and believe me, if I could rise up to heaven to give You my offering myself, and then come back down to the chocolate factory at La Trapa, I would . . . believe me."

And since foolish things occur to me even in prayer, as I was getting up I thought, "I could really use an airplane." And just as I'd said that, the silence of the Castilian skies was broken by the powerful motor of an airplane that just so happened to be flying over the monastery.

Believe me, I was going to get up, but I stayed there on my knees, and now I didn't say anything to God . . . I just thought about the airplane that I had imagined passing by La Trapa, picking up chocolates from a novice who couldn't fly, and then, rudders and controls all aiming for the heavens, went to deliver them to God . . . And the Master stayed in the tabernacle, and His servant stayed on his knees and in silence, listening to the noise of the powerful motor fading as it flew away at full speed through the Castilian skies.

Anyway, I didn't come to La Trapa to write literature . . . I just do that without even trying.

Today a magnificent frost fell, and at five o'clock this morning the moonlight was so bright you could read by it . . . Just a few moments ago, in choir, my lips spoke the words of the *Benedicite*,[3] "Ice and cold, bless the Lord; sun, sky, and stars, bless the Lord," so when I left the church it didn't bother me that it was below freezing, for it was exactly the cold that I was feeling that was blessing the Lord. But nevertheless, we are very weak, and so while my soul was close to God, my body was close to the novitiate radiator.

3. *Benedicite*: A canticle, also called the Song of Creation, taken from Dan 3:56-88 and included in the Divine Office (see #7, n. 12). Rafael combines verses 69 (*Bless the Lord, ice and cold*), 62 (*Bless the Lord, sun and moon*), and 63 (*Bless the Lord, stars of heaven*).

I don't know when this letter will go out. Today is the 31st, and right now, it's five in the morning (just to give you more detail).

Today we sang the Office for the Dead[4] with solemnity, because today is one of the Order's anniversaries. It is truly marvelous, and has filled me with great fervor. If one wanted to write the psalms of the Office for the Dead anew, it would be impossible . . . My head and heart are so full . . . I can't explain what I felt in choir this morning, but despite my not understanding Latin, David's[5] words filled my soul in such a way that I drew close to God, in order to beg His mercy and to ask Him to stay His wrath on the great and sublime day of the resurrection.

This morning, when I was singing in choir, I didn't know what I was praying for, but I did know that I was praying for something very great, something that human understanding cannot comprehend.

The cold days persist, and so do the bitter frosts, and yesterday the wind was so strong that it whistled as it grazed the tower steeple and swayed the cypress trees in the cemetery. At Vespers, only two things could be heard in the monastery: the wind as it ran across the plains, and the song of the psalmody; nature and men joined in offering our praises to God. The wind caressed the monastery, grazing the bells, and the monks in choir caressed Jesus in the tabernacle with the psalms.

I could write so many things. To me, this life that seems monotonous has so many charms, and I do not tire of it for even a moment. Each hour is different. Though they are all exteriorly the same, interiorly they are not, just as all Masses are not the same, and each time you go to choir the Office seems different, or at least it does to me. Of course, that doesn't mean that one day the lentils taste like partridge and another day they taste like *tortilla de patatas*,[6] no . . . lentils will always be lentils as long as I am in the monastery, but despite everything, I eat them with great pleasure, because I season them with two things: hunger and love of God. Just like that, there's no food I can resist.

---

4. Office for the Dead: The Office for the Dead is a cycle in the Liturgy of the Hours (see #7, n. 12) prayed in intercession for souls in purgatory. Cistercian monasteries have historically recited it with great frequency, particularly for the deceased members of the Order, as Rafael implies here.

5. David: i.e. King David, traditionally identified as the author of the Psalms.

6. *Tortilla de patatas*: potato omelette, a common dish in Spanish cuisine.

The sun has already risen. In just a moment we will go to conventual Mass and then to work. And so, little by little, little by little, one day after the other, we wait patiently for God to call us to keep blessing Him for all eternity, but without having to package chocolates or eat lentils.

Truly, whenever I remember that work lasts but a day while rest lasts an eternity, I can do anything with pleasure and joy . . . it all comes and goes.

Well, that seems like enough paper to me, don't you think?

I ask you, my dear mother, to remember me in your prayers; I think it unnecessary to remind you.

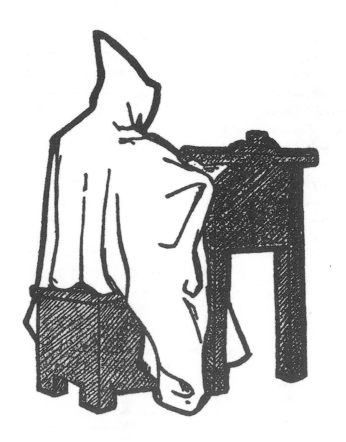

31. To Mercedes Barón Torres

La Trapa, February 18, 1934
First Sunday of Lent

My dearest mother,

As of just an hour ago, your son is no longer simply Rafael, but now his name is Brother María Rafael[1] . . . aren't you pleased? I know you are, because I still have the same name as I did before, but adding the name of the Blessed Virgin Mary, and rather than "*Don*"[2] . . . "Brother" . . . My dearest mother, I am so happy. Today I was given the habit; I am greatly moved, and can do nothing more than bless God who loves me so much.

I'm writing you today as a special favor, and just to give you the news.[3] Father Master gave me your letter, which I enjoyed very much, this morning after the ceremony, for it had arrived on exactly the day that I was beginning my retreat[4] . . . so he did not give it to me until today . . . Of course I will write you a long, lengthy letter when I can; right now, during Holy Lent, we devote ourselves to much greater silence, recollection, and prayer, and we neither write nor receive letters . . . So you will have to wait a few days then.

Father Master told me to tell you not to visit so soon, because it is way too cold to stay in the guesthouse now. But rather come in June, or sometime around then, when it will be much more lovely and pleasant, flowers in bloom . . . the fields will be splendid. At any rate, you won't be in the guesthouse with your teeth chattering.

1. In accordance with the Trappist convention at the time, Rafael retained his baptismal name. The addition of *María* would only be used in writing, not to address him in public or private (see #30, n. 1).

2. Don: In Spanish, the honorific *Don* was historically used to address nobility but by the twentieth century had a general connotation of respect.

3. During Lent, the monks were usually not permitted to write or receive letters.

4. Before receiving the habit and entering the novitiate, postulants would prepare by undertaking an eight-day retreat.

I'm all white now, at least on the outside;[5] now I'm going to make every effort to be so on the inside too, which is the most important thing . . . Today I renewed all my good intentions and resolutions . . . I offered my sacrifice to Jesus in Holy Communion—along with that of my parents, don't think that I've forgotten about you. After being clothed as a novice, and seeing myself so loved by my brothers, my soul is so content that it can only praise God in all things . . . The heart of a novice, full of love for God, cannot be comprehended . . . My dearest mother, it is a very great thing . . . very great. I cannot put it into words.

I should so like for my letter to be longer, but I've already told you the reasons for its brevity. Don't measure my love by sheets of paper . . . May it be enough for you to know that your son is content, happy, just as you say Saint Teresa would want, for she indeed said that "a sad saint would be a sorry saint"[6] . . . but don't worry, here in La Trapa is where I have seen the most joy gathered together . . . And besides, God treats us so well that we cannot be sad . . . that would be a sin against Him.

I'm as bald as a billiard ball now . . . well, not as much as a billiard ball, no . . . I have a little more hair than that.[7]

I'll have many things to tell you when you come visit . . . I think when you see me, I won't be as clean as I am today, looking like a novice fresh out of the package.

As you know, I haven't been feeling well, but I'm telling you that myself so you know I'm not hiding anything from you . . . But I was just doing the same thing as all my brothers who had the flu. We all spent two or three days in the infirmary. Fortunately, the epidemic is over . . . I can't tell you how charitably they treat the sick here. During those days, I didn't observe the community schedule, and afterwards, when you get out of the infirmary, for eight days they give you what they call "indulgences" at mealtimes, that is, eggs or something else that's special.

It's true, the life here is hard, but everything is so well arranged that it becomes not just tolerable, but pleasant . . . The hood does make life a bit

5. Cistercian novices receive an all-white habit. Upon profession of vows, the novice's white scapular is replaced with a black one.

6. This adage, which Rafael attributes to Saint Teresa of Ávila, is more often attributed to Saint Francis de Sales, though it does not appear in the writings of either saint.

7. Rafael is referring to the practice of tonsure, which involves shaving the top of one's head upon entrance into the novitiate as a sign of transition into religious life.

hotter though . . . I'm telling you, when summer arrives . . . I'm going to melt away little by little, and one day they'll go looking for Brother M. Rafael and find nothing more than a habit.

The cloak, scapular, tunic, shirt, stockings, and slippers are all made from the same fabric: white wool; the only exception is the undergarments, which are rougher and a brownish-gray color. I promise, I'm very comfortable.

I am ever more convinced that God made La Trapa for me, and me for La Trapa. It is clear that the only actionable science in this world is to place ourselves where God intended us to be . . . and, once we have come to know His will, to surrender ourselves to Him wholeheartedly.

The last prayers I said as a layman were a few Hail Marys to the Blessed Virgin, and as for the first ones I said as a novice, I'm not sure . . . because when I was kneeling in the middle of the chapterhouse, and all my brother monks were singing the *Benedictus* solemnly[8] . . . my soul was before God, and I offered my sacrifice to Him with a heart overflowing with joy, but also some very obvious tears . . . I believe that at that moment the angels, upon seeing me cry, sang the *Benedictus* too . . . But now I can die happy . . . now I am a Trappist. Pray to God that I might persevere, and I am praying for you too . . . Much is demanded of me, for much has been given to me.[9]

If only you could see how much we love one another here at La Trapa; today, naturally, anyone I come across in the hallway gives me a hug . . . And in silence we gladden one another.

Well, I'll tell you much more in my next letter, but for now I am going to focus on observing Lent devoutly, for the sake of all those in the world today who do not remember to think of God.

Sending you all a hug and even more, your son the Cistercian novice,

Brother María Rafael

I will send you the *Salve*[10] soon, but first you have to come hear it.

---

8. Novices are clothed in chapter, or the community gathering space, rather than in the chapel, as a sign of entering into the community more fully. After the novice receives the habit and his or her religious name, the community sings the *Benedictus*, or Canticle of Zechariah (Luke 1:68-79), as a song of thanksgiving.

9. Luke 12:48.

10. See #5, n. 8. Rafael is referring to the musical notation used at the monastery.

32. To Rafael Arnaiz Sánchez de la Campa

La Trapa, February 19, 1934

My dearest father,

Yesterday, when I gave Father Master the letter I'd written, he gave me yours and told me to answer it, and to ask you the following question on behalf of Father Abbot.[1] He asked me to tell you that eight or ten years ago they planted some live oaks here . . . about twenty or thirty of them, and they turned out all twisted and going every which way. So it's a matter of fixing them . . . Some say that we ought to cut them down and let them grow back, others say to prune them and guide them with stakes . . . What do you think?[2] . . . Make sure to say specifically what needs to be done . . . and I'm sure if you figure it out, Rev. Fr. will name you the Certified Technical Advisor of the Trappist Monastery of San Isidro.

It seems very good to me that you should go about your life as always . . . that's the natural thing, and it's what God asks of you . . . Each of us should play the part that God has given us to perform in this great comedy, as Calderón says in *The Great Theater of the World*.[3] Some in the world, others in the cloister, with the difference being that those who are in the cloister should not think of the world; as for those who are in the world, what they should do is think of God . . . The thing is simple enough; I will not attain more glory for being in the convent, nor will you attain less for not being in one . . . For at the hour when God calls us forth to Judgment, of me He shall demand having been a good Trappist, and of you, having been a good forest engineer and Christian father . . . which is what, with God's help, you are.

---

1. Father Abbot: Dom Félix Alonso García (see #5, n. 7).

2. Rafael's father, Rafael Arnaiz Sánchez de la Campa, was a forest engineer.

3. "Ages ago I cast mankind to be / My company, and they're the ones who'll act / In this great theater of the world. / I'll give a part to each one that appears" (Pedro Calderón de la Barca, "The Great Theater of the World," trans. Rick Davis, *Theater* 34, no. 1 [January 2004]: 130).

You've told me to pray for your needs . . . and who doesn't have needs?
. . . But don't worry, your son thinks of you more than you realize . . .
I will pray for your spiritual needs and also for your material ones . . .
You know, that's what I do. Let's see if God wants Fernando to continue
with the Bank of Spain[4] . . . You ask men to put in a good word, which
is necessary, and I'll ask God to do the same . . . maybe God will listen to
me . . . not because of my merits, but because I'm a tremendous flatterer.
May He forgive me, if what I say to Him causes offense.

In yesterday's letter I told you that I'd burst into tears in chapter, but the
great flood actually came at collation in the refectory, because they gave
us white beans with carrots and then salad, which we prepared ourselves,
made of beets and some green leaves, I don't know what they were, and
. . . oh! something terrible, one of those long onions that's thick as a cigar
and about eight inches long. It reminded me a lot of my mother, who likes
them so much, and I don't know if it was the memory of my mother or the
provocation of the onion, but the thing is, my eyes got all red and tears
streamed abundantly down my cheeks . . . Now, just between us . . . I
think that it was the onion that made me cry.

I'm a rather dissolute monk . . . unfortunately . . . I'm in a good
mood, just as I always am, but since I can't talk or shout or run, I have to
swallow it . . . So maybe I get a terrible urge to whistle when I see my
brothers, and myself among them, with our hoods up and eating onions
. . . A thousand ideas for mischief come to mind, because while I always
see the sublime side of La Trapa, I see the amusing side of it too . . . Well,
that seems like a contradiction, to say La Trapa is an amusing place . . . but
the thing is, I never get bored, I don't even know what that word means.

All right, I'm going to see if I can finish this letter, because I'm telling
you, I don't have time for anything . . . The days fly by . . . I've hardly
gotten up when it's already time to go to bed . . . Here we live by the
minute, and we make the most of them all. Everything is so regimented
that the things you do, one after the other, switching off with the Divine
Office—that is, during what we call "intervals,"[5] which are set aside for

4. Rafael's brother, Luis Fernando, was studying aeronautical engineering in Belgium at
the time. He signed up for the competitive examinations required to work at the Bank of
Spain, but in the end he did not go through with them (OC 211).

5. Intervals: In the monastic schedule, any time not officially assigned to work or prayer
is referred to as an "interval." Monks and nuns may use this "free time" as they see fit.

study or reading or prayer—they go by quite quickly. And then the same happens with the hours you spend in church . . . when you're in choir with the psalter[6] in front of you, hour after hour can pass by without you even noticing. Plus, there's something different each day of the year, whether in the Office at church or in our schedule, our work, our food . . . , etc.

In short, I'm very happy, and I want you to be too. If there's one thing in the world that concerns me, it's my parents . . . and since coming here, I love you even more . . . God doesn't ask me to stop loving you, quite the opposite . . . He just tells me, "You shall love the Lord your God above all things."[7] As such, what He asks of me is to love Him first, and then my parents . . . I imagine you won't be jealous of such a great Lord.

The weather is splendid these days, and it hasn't rained since I got here . . . Every day I see the sunrise . . . Here, I won't have the whole of nature to enjoy . . . but I do have a sky that's so blue . . . that it gives glory to God. Above all, what reigns in this holy house is a splendid peace, the greatest that men can give . . . Such a great peace in God.

Well, my dearest father, don't forget about the problem of the live oaks; give us the specifics I've asked for right away.

I'm so glad that Jaime[8] comes by the house. He's one of the few real friends I've had; give him a hug for me, I'll write him one of these days.

With nothing else to tell you now, give my aunt[9] many kisses for me, and all the love imaginable to you. With the Blessed Virgin's help, share it with the whole family. A big hug from your son, the newest novice of La Trapa,

Br. María Rafael

---

6. Psalter: an arrangement of the Psalms for use in the Liturgy of the Hours.

7. See Lev 19:18; Deut 6:5; Luke 10:27.

8. Jaime Suárez Ordóñez (d. 1969), one of Rafael's good friends. A pharmacist, he visited La Trapa frequently, especially during Holy Week, and hoped to become a Trappist himself (OC 213).

9. Petra Sánchez de la Campa y Tasquer (see #2, n. 6).

33. To Rafael Arnaiz Sánchez de la Campa and Mercedes Barón Torres

La Trapa, April 1, 1934

My dearest parents,

I imagine you've been waiting eagerly for the letter that I promised at the beginning of Lent. Everything comes and goes.

Today, Easter Sunday, Father Master summoned me, gave me some paper, and ordered me to write to you; of course, in this case I submit to holy obedience with great joy. Without further ado than a Hail Mary, so that God might enlighten my words, I will begin to tell you what I have been doing these forty days.

It's pretty quick to tell, since, trying to imitate Jesus in the desert, what I've been doing these forty days is fasting, prayer, and penance . . . and nothing else, because all that is quite enough. Don't think that long, sad faces abound during this time of the liturgical year, on account of the fast . . . none of that . . . We experience hunger, but joyfully, because it is for God's sake . . . and you can rest assured that I've never been so content getting up from the table as I was on certain Fridays, after having eaten nothing more than bread and water.

Of course, Lent in La Trapa is very hard, but it's manageable—just look at the proof: here I am, still alive to praise God more and more each day.

But the clouds parted, mourning has changed into delight and joy, the King of Heaven is praised by all the angels, and a thunderous "alleluia" echoes in every corner of the world, resounding from the Catholic Church . . . I am proud to be a son of the Church[1] and to be able to sing my praises to God too, here in the choir of a Trappist monastery.

---

1. With her dying words, Saint Teresa of Ávila is famously said to have thanked God for making her a "daughter of the Church." See Silverio de Santa Teresa, ed., *Procesos de beatificación y canonización de Santa Teresa de Jesús* (Burgos: Tipografía de «El Monte Carmelo», 1934), 105.

Everything has its reward, in heaven and sometimes on earth too . . .
Today Reverend Father Abbot awarded the community an "indulgence"[2]
for how well we've been singing these days: two fried eggs and a cup of
coffee. As you can see, there are special things here in La Trapa too sometimes . . . The two fried eggs tasted like heaven to me.

Now the summer schedule starts; we take an hour's *siesta*, because
instead of sleeping for seven hours, we sleep for six. We go out to work
in the fields at six in the morning; it's still pretty chilly out at that hour,
because we're in April, but by the time June and July come around, it'll
be pleasant. I am more content every day with being a Trappist monk;
that is a priceless thing. How many things I would tell you if I had more
time, but I'm short on it. I'll say it again, here I cannot do what I please,
but rather what I am ordered to do.

Recently I've had to sing some readings from the pulpit at Matins[3]
and I'm telling you I've never been in such a fix. My voice was trembling,
singing either way too high or too low, tripping on my cape as I climbed
up the stairs, in short, a real disaster. But it can't be helped; when I found
myself up at the pulpit at three in the morning, looking out over all the
shaved bald heads of the monks, the letters danced around the lectionary
and I suddenly forgot how to pronounce Latin. I was striking out.

I've also been an altar server, or rather, a "candle snuffer," which is a job
I like very much. Also, don't get me wrong, it has its importance. Here
at La Trapa, any ceremony acquires a great importance; to light or snuff
out a candle, one must follow all the rubrics laid out by the Laws of the
Order . . . Everything is accounted for: the steps, the minutes, the bowing.

In church we are always ceremonial.[4] We do not speak for any reason
or make any signs; we walk slowly, making no noise; we bow deeply to the
Lord who is in the tabernacle . . . In short, what divine worship ought to

---

2. Indulgence: A reprieve from the usual monastic fare at mealtimes (see #31). While
the same term is used in English, monastic *indulgences* (in Spanish, *alivios*) are not related
to the practice of performing acts of prayer and penance to remit punishment for sin (*in-
dulgencias*).

3. Matins: The first hour of the Liturgy of the Hours, also known as Vigils or the Office
of Readings.

4. Ceremonial: "When moving about the church, one must do so ceremonially, that is,
with the sleeves of the cowl hanging down; novices should keep their arms tilted down
underneath their capes . . ." (*Book of Usages*, cited in OC 219; emphasis in the original).

be and demands. This delights me. You know that I've never liked informalities anywhere, least of all at church. You could say that Trappists are formed exclusively for God. First they form the soul, but then the body and its manners . . . and it's not that I wish to praise my Order above any other, but you could say that when it comes to celebrating worship, the Trappist way is the most elegant . . . How I would have liked for you all to see all the ceremonies of Holy Week.

The most insignificant details are arranged mathematically, as is the only way not to make a mess of things.

In any case, this life is so different from the one I led up until now that you can't imagine it, no matter how much I tell you . . . All the details of my life are in the book of *Usages*, which you have at home. That is, in regards to the external aspects . . . in regards to my soul, what can I say? . . . God loves me so much! . . . I have so much peace in my soul, more than I could explain . . . With every day that goes by, I bless God even more, for having chosen me from among so many without my deserving it.

People have such a different idea of what a Trappist monastery is . . . How many of them would feel sorry for me, or even be frightened of my way of life, without even suspecting that here in the very renunciation of self and total surrender to God, one finds the only thing that makes life worth living . . . which is peace in God.

My sole pursuit is loving God. That fills up everything, and every moment of the day.

During my free time I study singing and music theory, I practice the Divine Office, I read Saint Teresa, and in this way, in silence, whole days and months go by without even noticing . . . I am truly amazed that, despite waking up at two and going to bed at eight, I don't have time for anything.

Besides, you can't imagine how pleasant it is not to know anything about the world . . . In the two and a half months I've been here, I've learned just two pieces of news. The first one Father Abbot told us in chapter, when he told us one Friday in Lent that we'd be offering our procession around the cloister that day, singing the penitential psalms, so that the good side might win out in the government crisis[5] . . . but he told us nothing else, so I still don't know if it's been resolved.

---

5. The government crisis: The abbot most likely alluded to an ongoing legislative battle over the allocation of state funds to the church (see María Concepción Marcos del Olmo,

The other one was from Father Sub-Master,[6] who for some reason told me that the king of Belgium[7] had died. That's all that has reached me this whole time . . . and I have no desire to know anything else.

What gives me the most joy is thinking about how this peace will be eternal. The day I die, all I will be doing is multiplying it on a scale that I can't even imagine.

Love for created beings ends at death . . . Desire for human glory fades away into nothing; only love for God grows with death . . . And so what I have, I have forever, the faith tells me so, whereas what I have left behind in the world is just on loan for a few years . . . and then . . . nothing.

That's why, my dearest parents, when I am so happy here in my monastery, merely a tunic and a white cape for my riches, seeing that one needs nothing more than that to be happy on this earth, I think of you. And I have the most ardent desire to be able to convey to you what I feel in those moments, to say to you and my brothers and sister, "Don't worry about the world and its affairs, don't let the future disturb you, leave it in God's hands; don't take an interest in earthly things, because they are a *waste of time*.[8] Turn to God and in Him you will find peace, first here on earth and then in heaven . . ."

In certain moments, I want to impart my soul to you, my love for God, so that you might see that your son has found the true way . . . and, as the Gospel says,[9] a treasure, one that he has set about digging up without a moment's hesitation . . . But at the same time, since I am not selfish, I want to call my brothers and sister[10] and tell them, "Come with me, and

---

"La movilización eclesiástica en defensa de sus haberes: una reacción ante la política religiosa republicana (1931–1934)," *Diacronie* 41 [January 2020]: 1–21). While the issue was resolved in the short term with the promulgation of the pro-clerical Law of Clerical Pensions (Ley de Haberes Pasivos del Clero) on April 6, 1934, the question of state support for the Catholic Church would remain a key issue in the forthcoming Spanish Civil War and beyond.

6. Father Sub-Master: Father Francisco Díez Martínez (1907–1954). The sub-master assists the master of novices with the formation of the postulants and novices at the beginning of their religious life.

7. The king of Belgium: Albert I, who died in a mountaineering accident on February 17, 1934.

8. See 1 John 2:15-17; Col 3:2.

9. See Matt 13:44.

10. Two of Rafael's three siblings did enter religious life. His brother Luis Fernando entered the Carthusians, an order of monks founded by Saint Bruno of Cologne in 1084

you'll see what I'm telling you is true . . . Seek God and you will find Him, and once you've found Him, know that nothing and no one will take Him from you."

Well, there you have my sermon. Truth be told I don't know how I come up with them. The day you come to see me I'll give you a little lecture, the whole bit.

Now we're going to Vespers, since it's about four.

I think I'm getting used to the hood . . . or rather, I'm getting used to everything. The body is a creature of habit, and one must simply learn to master it.

Do what Father Master told you, and don't come yet, because it's still cold in the guesthouse, but in the spring it'll be very pleasant.

Just now Father Master gave me a letter from my mother and told me to answer it; so I shall.

First of all, I'm not a friar, for the record . . . I'm a monk, which is not the same thing. Second, my head isn't behind a hood, but rather my hood is behind my head . . . which is not the same thing.

What you shouldn't do is worry about whether my hands are using a paintbrush or a hoe . . . in the eyes of God it's all the same, so long as they are being used for His greater glory . . . and He can be praised through anything . . . With the hoe in the fields, with the pen at home . . . with the thurible[11] in church, so long as you don't put them down . . . so that one day you can present yourself before God and, showing Him your hands covered in calluses and chilblains,[12] say to Him, "Lord, the works I have carried out are poor and insignificant, my hands have labored poorly . . . but, Lord, I did it all in Your name, and every time my body bent down over the ground to earn my daily bread, my heart was lifted up to You so that I might someday gain heaven." It is a great consolation to have calluses for love of God.

I am infinitely grateful that you see God's will in that of my superiors, for it is so . . . Take good care of my aunt, for the sick and the elderly are a wellspring for charity . . . Do it all with patience, with affection,

---

(Burgos). His sister Mercedes joined the Ursulines, an order of cloistered nuns dedicated to education and founded by Saint Angela Merici in 1535.

11. Thurible: A censer used to burn incense, often carried by an altar server.

12. Chilblains: Blisters caused by the cold. Unlike most buildings in the 1930s, the monastery did not have heating, and the winters in Palencia are wet, cold, and long.

tolerating rudeness and dirty looks at times . . . and if our sacrifices are not recognized or understood by others, all the better, for thus they are more pleasing to God, whose sacrifice on the cross was not recognized either . . . and He told us Himself that if we gave a cup of water in His name, we would rejoice in Him in heaven.[13]

Charity, what a beautiful virtue! In it is contained patience, self-denial, meekness, gentleness . . . well, in a word, holiness. As such, seize the opportunities that God places within your reach, and don't squander them, for soon enough we will have to account for our actions before God.

Now I'm going to deal with Fernando. All he has to do is to not make a fool of himself and to follow his diet down to the letter, and if he wants to get well, he should come to La Trapa. I promise him that here there's not even the slightest chance of liver attacks . . . Oh, it's difficult? Yes, I know, but if he won't do it for his health, he should do it for love of God, and I'm sure he'd be cured.

I can personally testify that one can live on beans, potatoes, boiled beets, wine, and bread alone . . . And if he's good, and behaves himself, they might give him a couple of eggs and a bit of coffee every two or three months.

Of course at first it takes a while to get used to it . . . and sometimes it makes you cry.

I remember the third day I was in the monastery. They hadn't given me anything other than white beans one day, black beans the next, and pinto beans the next, and since I am a soft, stupid glutton, I was going upstairs from the refectory to the novitiate thinking about how that was going to be my food *for the rest of my life*, and I started crying cats and dogs. And now, when I remember that, I start laughing, and the days they don't give me beans I miss them . . . And it's true that our brother the cook works miracles with a handful of the aforementioned legumes and a bit of salt and water, or at least they seem like miracles to me. I wouldn't trade my bowl, my silent meal, and my joyful heart for the best menu on offer at Lhardy[14] . . . So, Fernandillo, cheer up and play nice with the vegetables.

---

13. Matt 10:42; Mark 9:41.
14. Lhardy: An elegant French restaurant in Madrid.

I haven't heard a word from Juan.[15] I'm glad he comes by the house, he's a good kid and I love him very much.

I'm also glad that my letters make you happy, even if my words fall too short to fully express what I'm feeling. I hope that, in spite of it all, you understand me perfectly.

You've asked me for details of my life, but you already know them all. In any case, here they are.

I've learned how to shave with a razor without cutting myself. My sleeves are way too short for me. Today we ate white beans, milk, and walnuts . . . All through Lent they took away the milk and dessert, leaving only the beans . . . At night they gave us a plate of potatoes or lentils and six ounces of bread . . . and at six in the morning, half an ounce of chocolate and one ounce of bread. That was the hardest thing about Lent for me, since on the days we got up at one, when the Divine Office went on a bit longer, we'd be fasting for six or seven hours at a time, and then afterwards they'd give you a tiny piece of bread the size of two duros . . . well, you go hungry, that's all . . . Now we take all the bread we want. In spite of it all, I'm in stupendous health, and giving infinite thanks to God who gives me the strength for everything.

More details: I know how to peel potatoes now, with all my typical elegance. When you read in the lives of the saints about how they devoted themselves to humble duties, as if it were a remarkable thing, you think nothing of it . . . but in reality, it's no big deal knowing how to handle a broom, it's all relative. Back home, if I were to put an apron on and help the housekeeper wash the stairs, it would have attracted attention . . . just as it would here if someone were to sit in the refectory and give a little clap to call over a waiter . . . Here we all sweep and help each other with everything . . . Last week my esteemed Father Master was serving food . . . This morning a respectable priest with white hair[16] helped me wrap chocolates, and later I helped him at the conventual Mass.

So, life at La Trapa is not well understood, because it is compared with the world, but in truth, life in the world is completely different.

15. Juan: Rafael's close friend Juan Vallaure (see #9, n. 5).
16. Father Eugenio (Juan) Díez Ubierna (1873–1940).

At work, at mealtimes, and at rest, and in the cemetery, we are all equal . . . even though there is a pyramid from Reverend Father Abbot down to the newest novice, on which each of us has his place, his role, and his dignity. That is, in a Cistercian monastery, hierarchy and equality are blended together: it is a perfect society, as much as can be expected among men.

When you sing Gounod's[17] *Ave Maria*, don't think of me at all. It's better for you to think of the Virgin; you'll get more out of it that way, and it'll sound better.

No memory of me should make you sad, on the contrary . . . let's not waste tears.

Anytime you remember me and are sad, think of the Virgin Mary, for She too had to sacrifice a lot. I am glad that my father didn't stop by, because if they didn't let him see me, it would have been hard on him and on me too. It's good not to force things. You can imagine that, naturally, the novitiate is the most secluded part of religious life.

I would have a lot of things to say to you too, and I wanted to pour my heart out on paper, but you'll have to be content with my good wishes. I want to finish this letter now, as it's going on longer than it should, so I'll leave it until next time.

Give out all the good wishes you'd like on my behalf. All my love, your son,

Br. M. Rafael ✠

17. Charles Gounod (1813–1893), French composer.

34. *To Rafael Arnaiz Sánchez de la Campa*

La Trapa, April 8, 1934

My dearest father,

You are never a bother, no matter what you wish to discuss. To answer your question, I took the proof of payment for the 750 pesetas to the major's office at Cuartel de la Montaña,[1] Regiment of Sappers and Miners;[2] I believe they gave me a receipt, which, if I kept it, you will find in one of the white envelopes where I put all my Madrid documents . . . I don't know where the envelopes are . . . but in any case, if you don't find the receipt among my papers, I don't think it will be difficult to get them to give you a duplicate . . . since they have the proof of payment there . . . If you need to get in touch with one of the soldiers, take the matter up with Mr. Luis Díaz Iglesias, who is a non-commissioned officer,[3] and a very good person who liked me a lot. I can tell you nothing more about the matter at hand.

I suppose you already have in your possession a long letter that I wrote you the other day, giving you details of my life. I have nothing to add to it. I continue to pray for you, which is the only way I can pay back some of what I owe you all.

Before coming to the monastery, I dreamed of finishing my degree so that I could use my first earnings to help my father out . . . and I used to think about what I'd do with the thousand pesetas I'd earn from my first

---

1. Cuartel de la Montaña: These barracks, constructed in the nineteenth century, were located on a hill in western Madrid known as La Montaña de Príncipe Pío.

2. Regiment of Sappers and Miners: The formal name (Regimiento de Zapadores-Minadores) of the Spanish army's regiment of combat engineers, formed in 1802.

3. Non-commissioned officer: Rafael refers to Díaz Iglesias as a sub-official, indicating that he earned his position through enlisted service. His rank at the time was brigada (the eighth enlisted grade), which is roughly equivalent to a master sergeant in the U.S. Army (Prieto, Diario Oficial del Ministerio de Defensa Nacional, 446).

project . . . Of course, they wouldn't be for me . . . my parents came first . . . But things have changed . . . The future architect has become a monk; projects for human glory have become a desire for the glory of God . . . And so I have changed from a student into a novice. My ambitions to earn money will become a vow of poverty . . . but don't worry, what hasn't changed, and never will, is that I am your son. So while I can't help you with money I don't earn, you can be assured that the first prayers that rose up from me, after taking on my new state in life, were for my father and mother . . . My earnings aren't meant for this earth, so you don't have the pleasure of saying, "We have a son whose worth astonishes the world. His reputation precedes him among men, by whom he is highly regarded; he stores up treasures,[4] from which he supports his parents . . ."

Instead of that whole magnificent song and dance, which I'll never be able to provide, since my merits are few and far between, you can exclaim, "We have a son whom nobody knows. He is poorer than a church mouse . . . he is a Trappist who lives in the peace and grace of God in his monastery. He does not help us materially, because he cannot, for he earns nothing more than his keep, but in exchange, he is storing up for his parents treasures that human beings cannot appreciate, because they know nothing about them. One day, before God, he will be able to offer up his parents and brothers and sister. He will say to them, 'My sacrifices have been accepted by God, and I have offered them to Him in your name. So while you thought that your son would be good for nothing, he was at the feet of Jesus, interceding for his parents.'" So, as you can see, in one way or another, I am keeping the commandment to honor my father and mother.

I'm so sorry about Aunt Petra,[5] I can imagine the scene from here . . . I don't want to annoy you as I did the other day by telling you to have patience . . . I'm sure you already have the necessary amount . . . Try to attend to her spiritual matters as much as possible, so that she doesn't give you a scare one of these days. Though it seems irresponsible to me at her age, it's not our business, but rather God's. All we can do is provide the necessary means.

4. Stores up treasures: see Matt 6:19-21.
5. Rafael's great-aunt, who was living with his parents at the time; see #2, n. 6.

II. A Heart Filled with Joy and Love 103

Father Eufrasio,[6] the superior of the Carmelite Fathers, told me that he'd come by the house sometime. Has he? You can trust him, he's very good.

How did Fernando's retreat go? I've asked God to use it to make him very good.

I have nothing new to tell you . . . Today, which is Sunday, it's raining and the sky is gloomy; it reminds me of those gray Asturian[7] days.

Well, that's all for today; I don't want to go on too long as I did the other day. With a pen in my hand, I never rest, and the sad thing is that I say nothing of substance. The one detail of the day that I'll share is that the organ stopped working. The newest novice is the one who has to operate it by hand,[8] so I've spent the day raising my prayers to God with my own strength, and now my arms are sore.

I'll also say, in case you're interested, that it's still raining . . . And . . . nothing else in particular. I'll just repeat that you aren't bothering me, as you say in your letter, when you write me about these matters . . . You have to keep in mind that I'm not dead yet.

Of course, I'm happy not talking about pesetas, and it's hard to believe that my letters aren't to ask you for money as they used to be. All those incomprehensible combinations of subtraction and addition, totals and deductions, just so that later, in sum, I could panhandle my father . . . all that's history now.

Well, I'll leave you now, I still have a lot to do, like the Stations of the Cross and praying the Rosary to our Holy Mother . . . Listen, don't stop praying it, even though I'm not there. I often remember my mother's velocity. Now I pray it alone, but always as if I were praying it with you, and I believe that the Virgin receives your prayers and mine at the same time, even if they are offered at different times . . .

6. Padre Eufrasio: Father Eufrasio del Niño Jesús Barredo Fernández, prior of the Discalced Carmelites at Oviedo, and Rafael's former confessor (OC 209). He later became a martyr of the religious persecution during the Spanish Civil War and was beatified in 2007.

7. Rafael was raised in Oviedo, the capital of the province of Asturias in northwestern Spain.

8. It was a custom at San Isidro that the newest novice was in charge of this routine maintenance. Normally the pipe organ relied on an electrical current to fill its bellows with air, but when the power was out, it had to be pumped up manually.

Truly, it is a great consolation for Christians to know that we are so united . . . Where there is faith, there is no distance in time or space, no parents, no children; only one thing exists, and that is God, and there we shall all end up sooner or later.

A million hugs from your son,

Br. M. Rafael

III. I Thought That God Was Abandoning Me

Struck by Illness

35. *To Leopoldo Barón*

Oviedo, June 3, 1934[1]

My dearest Uncle Polín,

I was waiting for your letter, I knew you'd be the first one to write me . . . May God return to you the consolation I received from it. Now, in turn, I will give you the news you've asked for. I didn't do it before only because it was physically impossible, my eyesight is very poor at the moment, and I get worn out quickly. I have to use my father's glasses for everything, and they're for farsightedness . . . The doctor says it'll pass when I am stronger.[2]

What's happening to me is very simple; in short, God loves me very much . . . I was happy in La Trapa. I considered myself the most fortunate of mortals, having managed to detach myself from earthly creatures, aspiring to nothing more than God . . . But I still had one thing left: love for La Trapa. So Jesus, who is very selfish when it comes to His children's love, wanted me to detach myself from my beloved monastery too, even if just temporarily.

This trial that I am enduring is difficult, very difficult, but I am not shaken, nor afraid, nor have I ceased to trust in God. More and more, I see His hand in everything that happens to me, and truly, it is so sweet to abandon yourself to such a good Father. There are so many things I would tell you if I were with you. You talk of my troubles, but I say to you, blessed is the one who suffers for Christ, and woe to the one who sees his desires fulfilled on earth.[3]

The congratulations you sent were given to me by my confessor[4] in La Trapa with tears in his eyes. If only you knew what that was like, Uncle Polín . . . I have left behind such profound affection . . . If you could see how we Trappists love one another in silence . . . Nobody knows what

---

1. In ##35–60, Rafael is twenty-three years old.

2. Poor eyesight is a symptom of diabetes; in Rafael's case, it was temporary.

3. See Luke 6:20–26.

4. My confessor: Father Teófilo Sandoval Fernández (1902–2000), who would later become the vice-postulator of Rafael's cause for canonization.

it is to cry for a brother as he leaves, a brother to whom you have not said a word in four months.

Well, when we see each other we'll talk at length, I wouldn't know how to express my feelings to you in a letter. What I will do is explain my illness to you in detail.

In four months of novitiate, not even one bad headache; stupendous health, loving life . . . Then weeding season starts. First few days in the fields are good, praising God among the wheat; one day I feel very tired, the next day even more so; the next I can't take it anymore, and, while my brothers work, I sit down . . . I am exhausted. Two or three days before I eliminated a tremendous amount of urine, there were nights when I got up six times . . . Father Master doesn't let me go out into the field; I stay in the house, washing lettuce; the next day, after the Virgin's Matins,[5] at three in the morning, I can't be in choir any longer and I go up to bed. The next day, Rev. Fr.[6] comes up to the novitiate and sends me to the infirmary for a few days.

The infirmarian[7] analyzes my urine and gets worried. The doctor[8] arrives and says that I have to get into treatment immediately and it's impossible at the monastery. The next day my father arrives with the car. I arrived in Oviedo at four in the afternoon, and by six they had given me my first injection of "insulin," which they say is the only thing that cures it.[9]

I have high levels of sugar, and I had acetone.[10] I'm on a diet where I have to weigh everything I eat, gram by gram; I'm terribly hungry, and so weak that reading makes me dizzy and walking makes me tired, I can hardly see . . . It has all been a matter of six or seven days, but there have been days when I've lost two kilos.[11]

5. The Virgin's Matins: matins from the Little Office (see #24, n. 1).

6. Rev. Fr.: The abbot, Dom Félix Alonso García (see #5, n. 7).

7. The infirmarian: Father Vicente Pardo Feliú (1883–1955) oversaw the community infirmary.

8. The doctor: Clemente Cilleruelo y Arizón was the local doctor who served the monastery.

9. Insulin was first used in the treatment of diabetes just twelve years earlier, in 1922. It was still being studied and would not have been as well known to the average person in Rafael's time as it is today. Rafael encloses the word in quotation marks.

10. Acetone: High levels of acetone in the blood and urine are a common first symptom in previously undiagnosed diabetics.

11. Two kilos: Equivalent to four and a half pounds.

They do an analysis twice a day, and they give me three injections a day too . . . Some real medical revelry. I'm not in any pain or discomfort; I spend all day sitting down not doing anything.

I brought my habit with me, but I haven't put it on.

This illness is a very long one, and I don't know when I'll be able to go back to my monastery. And I don't know when it will be, but God tells me that I will die a Trappist; now all I can do is put my life in His hands, and I promise you that I have. I can do nothing more, and besides, I know that the Blessed Virgin has not abandoned me.

You can't imagine how sorry I am about Pilar,[12] but there's no need to worry. God gives health and God takes it away . . . and He knows what He is doing. I've been at heaven's door (forgive my presumption), just a matter of hours away, and nevertheless, God said to me: Wait . . . and I'll wait as long as God wants me to.

I hope to see you when you come to Covadonga,[13] so that there, at the feet of the Virgin, we might speak of God . . . Neither your troubles nor mine are worth talking about. What difference does health make over sickness, or wealth over poverty, when you have God?

Oh, Uncle Polín, how great the Lord is! And how little are we. I've changed a lot these past four months. God has spoiled me so much, and made me see things that I didn't see before.

Well, that's all for today. Another day I'll write you with more details, but don't worry about my health, there's no need. Give Aunt María and the cousins a big hug for me, and all my love to you as your nephew and brother in Jesus and Mary,

Rafael

If you have some time, send me a quick note.

12. Pilar: Rafael's cousin, a daughter of Leopoldo Barón and María Osorio. She was sick at the time.

13. Covadonga: A Marian pilgrimage site in Asturias, a short journey from where Rafael was staying at his parents' home in Oviedo.

36. To Fr. Marcelo León

Oviedo, June 11, 1934

My dear and respected Father Master,

I beg your forgiveness for my tardiness in writing you with news of my health, but a sick man can be forgiven for this small transgression.

I continue to improve, though very slowly, and now I am recovering the strength I'd lost . . . These last few days, I've been able to go receive the Lord. Of course, I can't go on foot, despite the short distance between my house and the church. This afternoon I'll go out for the first time, to go for a drive.

I'm still on a very strict diet, scrupulously weighing the amounts, in order to find out the number of "carbohydrates" that my body can tolerate and correlate that with the amount of "insulin" they have to give me . . . They do two urine analyses per day, and they give me three injections of "insulin" per day too. I'm telling you, Father, I'm hungrier than I was during Lent.

The doctor says I'll have to keep doing this all summer, but that I'll recover . . . That's what I want, so that I can return to my monastery, even if some time has to pass before I can follow the normal diet at La Trapa . . . Meanwhile, everything is in God's hands. He is the one who can resolve it all, and I am in His hands.

My mood varies . . . All this was so sudden, and so fast, that I've been stupefied for days, without realizing what was going on inside me, just bewildered. This lifestyle change is so radical, it wouldn't be like this if it weren't . . . I thought that God was taking me up to heaven, but it seems that the hour of my liberation has not yet come, and that He wants me here on earth for a little longer still . . . May His will be done and not my own.[1]

1. See Matt 6:10; 26:39-42.

When I went to La Trapa, I surrendered to Him all I had and all I possessed: my soul and my body . . . My surrender was absolute and total. It is utterly just, then, that God should now do with me as He wishes and as He pleases, without a single complaint or rebellious move on my part.

God is my absolute master, and I am His servant, who keeps quiet and obeys . . . Sometimes I wonder, "What does God want from me?" . . . But as David says, "Who is man to know God's designs?"[2] Therefore, the best thing to do is close your eyes and let Him carry you, for He knows what is good for us.

I was too happy at La Trapa; the trial He has required of me is a hard one, but with His help I will come out on the other side of it, and here, there, or wherever I am, I will keep going forward without losing ground. "I have put my hand to the plow and cannot look back."[3]

God not only accepted my sacrifice, when I left the world, but He has also asked me for a still greater sacrifice, which was returning to it . . . For how long? . . . That's up to God. He gives health, and He takes it away . . . We human beings can do nothing more than trust in His divine providence, knowing that what He does is well done, even if *at first glance* it might go against our desires. But I believe that true perfection is to have no desire other than "may His will be done in us."[4]

God, in His infinite wisdom, does not ask us what we desire in order to give it to us immediately, because generally we don't know what we need for our salvation. Rather, working far above our reason and the designs of His creatures, He carries us, brings us along, and tests us in a thousand ways . . . and we say, "Lord, why are you doing this?" . . . and it seems that God responds, "Trust Me. You are like children, and in order to reach the kingdom of My Father, you cannot go it alone, nor do you know the way; I will take you there . . . Follow me, even if it goes against your desires . . ." The kingdom of God is subjected to violence,[5] . . . and to reach the end, we must not go by the way we choose, for, children that we are in the eyes of God, we hardly even know how to walk . . . "Trust Me," Jesus says, "And I will lead you."

2. Ps 8:4: "What are human beings that you are mindful of them, mortals that you care for them?" Compare Isa 40:13; Rom 11:34; 1 Cor 2:16.

3. See Luke 9:62.

4. See Matt 6:10; 26:39, 42.

5. See Matt 11:12; Luke 16:16.

My dear Father Master . . . I am letting Jesus lead me . . . When I was happier . . . When I saw my future as a Cistercian monk clearly before me, when I desired nothing more from the world and my *only desire* was to be among my brothers in the religious life until death . . . Jesus says, "Now, an illness, and get out" . . . Well all right, *fiat*[6] . . . What else can I do?

And so, Father, you can see that I am at peace. The circumstances in which I find myself do not depend on me. Therefore, as it is God who has taken me out of the novitiate, if He wants to, He will be the one to lead me back there.

I have so many things to say to the priests and the novices and the oblates . . . But I think my silence will be more eloquent than anything I could say in a letter . . . I've left so much sincere affection behind in La Trapa, and it will never be forgotten. I won't ask you to give my regards to anyone in particular, because I'd have to start listing off the whole community; although I am here bodily, spiritually I am very often in choir.

I get up late, I go to bed late, I spend all day at home doing nothing because reading strains my eyes quite a bit and I can't do it, and I don't have the energy for anything else . . . I go through all the armchairs in the house so as not to sit in the same one all the time, and so as not to keep secrets from you, I'll confess that I've started smoking again.

I don't put on my habit, in order not to call attention to myself. I put it away carefully; for me, it was a consolation to bring it with me.

I don't receive anyone. The first few days, that was because I was too out of it. Now, it's because what they have to say doesn't interest me a whit, as you will easily understand. And while there are people who truly care for me, there's also a lot of curiosity. You don't see a Trappist every day.

The other day Father Felipe[7] came by the house, I hadn't met him before. He had come to see his family, and on the way he stopped by to meet me. He's very kind and must be very good.

6. Fiat: From the Latin version of Mary's words in Luke 1:38, *Let it be with me according to your word.*

7. Father Felipe (Joaquín) Álvarez Vázquez (1876–1955). He had been a priest of the diocese of Oviedo before entering San Isidro in 1910. He then served as the chaplain of the Trappist nuns at Alloz, in Navarre, and later spent several years in the monastery at Oseira, in Galicia.

I have nothing more to tell you . . . Forgive me for how rushed these lines have been, but you know how I write—a lot, fast, and badly, but that's me. I'll save the formal letters for somebody who isn't my Father Master.

I trust in the prayers that the novices and oblates will be offering to the Blessed Virgin on my behalf; naturally, I have more faith in them than I do in the doctors, may God forgive them for making me endure so much hunger . . . I'm telling you, Father, it's dreadful. It is, after all, a characteristic of the illness.

With nothing more to add, give my regards to Rev. Fr. Abbot and convey my sincere affection to the novices. Awaiting your blessing and your prayers, your novice,

Brother María Rafael

37. To Leopoldo Barón

Oviedo, June 17, 1934
Fourth Sunday after Pentecost

Dearest Uncle Polín,

To answer your letter, I'm doing much better, thanks be to God, and according to the doctor this goes very quickly. True, the medicines I'm using aren't the most common, but the prayers of my brother novices are worth more than all the doctors and medicines put together . . . In any case, it's going to take me at least the summer, and afterwards I'll start a diet much like the one at La Trapa, to see how my body responds to it, and then hopefully I'll be able to continue my life as a "poor Trappist," as you say.

I trust deeply in God. Surely He will carry me back to the monastery; I think of nothing else all day . . . The choir . . . the fields . . . the silence, the joyful peace of the cemetery . . . my brothers, my habit, my cell . . . my tabernacle of La Trapa . . . everything I won with sacrifices and tears collapsed over something so insignificant as a bit of sugar in the blood . . . How great God is, Uncle Polín, who uses the smallest, most insignificant things to show us our own smallness and wretchedness, and to make us understand that we are nothing without Him.

I was too happy at La Trapa. I can promise you that while the life there is hard, very hard, God is so close by that you don't even notice the austerity of the Rule. I breathed in joy through every pore . . . God was my one and only desire, and I felt Him so close to me that I forgot about everything else.

It's also true that, at first, it made me cry sometimes. After all, I am a human creature with a heart and feelings, and some things cannot be helped.

I remember my first days as a postulant, when we went out to the fields in a single file line . . . Every novice carrying his hoe, and I was last . . . We set out for the vineyard in silence . . . it was terribly cold . . . the ground was hard from the frost, and on top of all that, I was so tired I could hardly stay awake . . . The work boss[1] divided up the tasks, we crossed ourselves and prayed a Hail Mary, and we got to work.

Well, more than once in those days I watered the clods of dirt that I pulled up with my hoe with teardrops the size of oranges. I recovered quickly, remembering the question that our holy father Saint Bernard would ask himself: "Bernard, what have you come for?" [2] I would then redouble my efforts, and if anyone had been very close to me, they'd have heard me sing something that goes like this: "*Virgen del santo Recuerdo, que nunca te podré olvidar.*"[3] For me that was the cure . . . singing to the Virgin . . . If only you knew how Our Lady has treated me . . . ! We will never fully grasp, Uncle Polín, how much Mary loves us.

The other day I broke down crying again, you know why? Every time I remember, I laugh . . . Well it's simple. One morning at five o'clock, hunger (it was Lent), exhaustion, and cold all got together, and between the three of them they gave my miserable body, so accustomed to comfort, such a thrashing that it began to produce tears . . . I can assure you that it is difficult to master one's flesh, but with God's great assistance, which He lends to the Trappists, you can make of it whatever you wish . . . I am convinced that without a very special grace, a Trappist could not go on living.

Well, just so you know everything, when I was most moved to tears was . . . at my mother's letters.

I tell you all this so that you might grasp the misery of your nephew, who, despite his great love for God, surrendered himself to Him without as much generosity as he ought to have . . . But he got through postu-

---

1. Work boss: A term in use among Trappists to refer to the monk or nun who organizes the community's work and assigns tasks for the day.

2. "He constantly said in his heart and even often on his lips, 'Bernard, Bernard, what have you come for?'" (William of Saint-Thierry, Arnold of Bonneval, and Geoffrey of Auxerre, *The First Life of Bernard of Clairvaux*, trans. Hilary Costello, CF 36 [Collegeville, MN: Cistercian Publications, 2015], 22).

3. The first line of a hymn to the Virgin Mary (OC 257), lit. "Our Lady of Remembrance, I'll never be able to forget you." The Spanish Jesuits had a particular devotion to Our Lady of Remembrance, for whom their most famous school (Colegio Nuestra Señora del Recuerdo, Madrid) was named. Rafael may have learned the hymn as a schoolchild, as he attended Jesuit schools throughout his youth.

lancy and then came the novitiate, and though his body kept causing him trouble, he didn't listen to it anymore . . . I was after one thing and one thing only; I wanted to draw close to God. And in truth, I didn't do anything, it was God who drew close to me. I offered myself to Him, He accepted me . . . and as the proof of it, He has sent me back to the world with an illness . . . Blessed be God! Now what I ask of Him is to let me recover, so that I can return to the monastery with my brothers. I ask Him for health so that I can give it right back to Him again . . . I have no other use for it. Among human beings, things aren't so great, as you say . . . Of course Trappists are human beings too, but . . . ? . . . you know what I mean.

I have one thing to say that you'll be happy to hear. You and I, before my *escape* from the world, didn't know what a Trappist monastery was. We suspected, correctly, that it was the closest thing to heaven that the world had . . . Well, now I'm telling you that we underestimated it, and you have *no idea* what is enclosed within a Cistercian monastery . . . Believe me, and you will understand, that after one comes to know and experience monastic life, no other way will do. There I found something so very rare and strange in this world . . . it's called *love* of neighbor, and charity.

Well . . . if I knew how to put them into words, there are so many things I would tell you about, things that I know would make you shed tears of happiness . . . But I'll leave all that for when we see one another face to face, which I hope will be soon. The more beautiful thing would be to say that I'll tell you everything when we see each other in heaven, but surely up there we won't have time to waste on such trifles, don't you think? . . . But while we are here on earth, no matter how high up you might be, I know you must have some interest in the trifles of your more-than-a-nephew, Brother María Rafael . . . on the other hand, I'd hate to be a nuisance.

You asked me if I knew Mr. Pedro Sánchez del Río, I think I mentioned him to you one time . . . He is an *intimate* friend of mine, and there are many things I have only told him . . . He is a man of God, if not a saint, for as we've already agreed, the word *saint* is applied too liberally; he is a man given over to God, a man who is *truly* virtuous . . . Yes, I can assure you I know him well . . . You're sure to like him. If you want to tell him something, you can do so in full confidence.

I was very grateful to Aunt María[4] for her letter, knowing how little she likes to write. I know that you both remember me before the Tabernacle, and at the feet of Mary above all. I, on the other hand . . . I'm such an idiot! What can I say?

I'm so sorry about Pili[5] . . . she's so good and kind to her cousin Rafael. Tell her for me that I'll be sending a surprise for her soon, and if she's sick, I am too, so she ought to ask God to make us both better soon. That's what I'm doing.

Aunt María tells me that you aren't taking care of yourself and that I should encourage you to let yourself be taken care of. Good Lord, Uncle Polín, you're too old for this. But I'll just share with you a reflection that I am doing myself. "God has sent me this illness, why? To humble me . . . So, humble yourself." I know it's hard to be at the mercy of broth and injections and schedules and doctors . . . Man provides the means and God provides everything else . . . There's nothing else we can do.

When I left the monastery, Father Abbot said to me, "You must return, therefore, I charge you to obey the doctor as if he were Father Master . . ." And so, obedience takes part in my recovery. Do the same thing . . . obey, and don't misbehave.

I have nothing else in particular to tell you. Everyone is doing well here, thank God, there's no news.

One of these days I'll write my grandmother and Aunt María Barón,[6] but not until they've left Madrid, because Mamá and Merceditas[7] are going there for some tests. They'll give her news of her grandson.

I'm so glad that Anita[8] thought of me. When you write to her, you can tell her that this Trappist, whenever he prayed for the missions, never

---

4. Aunt María: María Osorio, who was married to Leopoldo Barón.

5. Pili: Rafael's cousin Pilar.

6. My grandmother and Aunt María Barón: Fernanda Torres Erro, Rafael's maternal grandmother, and María Josefa Barón Torres, his maternal aunt, who lived together.

7. Mamá and Merceditas: Rafael's mother, Mercedes, and his sister, also named Mercedes (nicknamed Merceditas), visited Madrid and made a trip to the monastery of San Isidro on June 24, 1934 (OC 261).

8. Anita: Ana Solana, who ran a publishing house called Editorial Escuela Española that focused on Christian education. She went to India as a missionary, but got sick and returned to Madrid to resume work as a publisher.

forgot that *poor lady* who, in India, had the same thing on her mind as I did . . . serving God. In fact, I'll tell you when I prayed for her.

Since, in La Trapa, not a minute is wasted—not during intervals, and not even while moving from one place to the next—upon leaving the church, after the examination of conscience, on my way to the refectory, I'd devote that time to the missions . . . We'd leave church in a line and walk through the cloister, very slowly, with our hoods up, all the way to the refectory. Since we were walking in silence, each of us would pray whatever he liked . . . As I said, I devoted that time to the missions. I'd think of God's goodness in giving me the food my body needed . . . I'd thank Him for the peace of my convent and, at the same time, I'd ask Him not to forget the missionaries who sometimes don't have anything to eat, much less a convent. It is the Trappist's obligation to pray in silence for those who are in the world winning souls for Christ; I saw myself as under that obligation . . . and every day, absolutely every day, during the six or seven minutes we'd take walking from the choir to the refectory, I'd pray for Anita.

This shows you that in La Trapa, you are in communication with God from the moment you wake up to when you fall asleep . . . Every monk has his particular devotions, and the silence helps so much . . . I remember a priest in Ávila who, one time, I think I already told you this, was arguing with me at Father Justo's[9] house. He was saying that monks' silence was absurd, and that this business of not talking was so stupid, and so on and so forth . . . I've thought of that priest so many times . . . If only he knew that the most beautiful thing there is in La Trapa is the silence . . . But what does the world know of that?

All right, I'm finishing this letter, I think this is enough for today. Write me back if you feel like it. The other day Casio[10] wrote a very nice letter to Papá; greet them for me. As usual, all my love to you and Aunt María from your nephew and brother,

Rafael

9. Fr. Justo: Father Justo Sánchez Muñoz (see #5, n. 19).
10. Casio: A friend of Leopoldo Barón and María Osorio.

38. Dedication of a Holy Card[1] of Saint Thérèse of the Child Jesus to Ramón Vallaure[2]

Oviedo, July 7, 1934

If we have something to learn from all the saints . . . when it comes to Saint Thérèse of Lisieux, we ought especially to imitate her joy amid suffering. How beautiful it is to have one's heart torn open for love of Jesus, to suffer bitterness, to carry the weight of a great cross, and yet, all the while, to show a bright face and a friendly smile so as not to disturb the peace of one's neighbor with our troubles . . . Tell them only to our good Jesus, and suffer them joyfully. Carry the cross with a joyful heart, and if tears should come to our eyes, let us ask forgiveness of God for our weakness on the cross, and ask forgiveness of our brothers, too.

Brother María Rafael Arnaiz

1. Holy card: a small picture, usually of Jesus, Mary, a biblical scene, or a saint, produced for devotional use. Some holy cards come with prayers printed on the back, while others are left blank so that a handwritten message can be added.
2. Ramón, the younger brother of Rafael's close friend Juan Vallaure (see #9, n. 5), later entered the monastery at San Isidro. Rafael did not include the date; it was later added by Ramón.

39. To Fr. Marcelo León

Oviedo, July 22, 1934

My dear Father Master,

This letter, naturally, is addressed to you, but it is a reply to the kind letters I received from Fr. Francisco[1] and my co-novices.[2] If I haven't answered them earlier, as I should have, it's because I've been waiting for the doctor's permission, which I now have, to announce that I will be visiting on the first of August, name day of our dear Father Abbot.[3]

I am, thank God, almost completely well. I hardly have any "sugar" anymore, but I'm continuing the "insulin" treatments and diet . . . The doctor told me that I can absolutely go spend three days at my monastery, so I'll leave here on the 31st on the express train, and I'll be at La Trapa the 1st, 2nd, and 3rd. He'll give me a note that explains what I can eat, which is almost everything. I'll bring the injection so that Fr. Vicente[4] can give it to me. Afterwards it's just a matter of two or three more months, though to me they seem like centuries, during which I will return to the monastic diet on a trial basis, so that later I can pick up my life where I left off, alongside the Tabernacle at La Trapa and my good brothers.

According to the doctor I'll have to be under observation for a while, but I am sure that I can count on your charity to arrange that.

If only you could see, Father, how disoriented I am in the world! . . . I would return to La Trapa even as a gardener, eating the leftovers that are given to the poor . . . But such extremes are not necessary.

1. Father Francisco Díez Martínez (1907–1954), the sub-master of novices.
2. My co-novices: Brothers Isidro David Ortega, Bernardo Michelena, and Damián Yáñez Neira.
3. August 1 is the feast of two saints connected with Fr. Felix Alonso García's name: Saint Felix of Girona and Saint Alphonsus Liguori.
4. Fr. Vicente Pardo Feliú, the monastery infirmarian.

When I left the infirmary to come back here, I thought that God would either bring me to heaven or make me healthy so I could keep being a Trappist . . . It seems that God has opted for the latter. He must know better than we do what is good for us, and even in adversity, we must continue to give Him thanks for everything, especially me. Our good God treats me in such a way that I can do nothing but sink down to the ground, prostrate myself at His feet, and exclaim: "Lord, who am I that you should care for me,[5] the least of the Trappists, the creature who has never returned unto God all His benefits, and yet whom, in Your infinite goodness, you take by the hand and guide through the world? And if it is You, O Lord, who put obstacles before me, it is also You who take them away, so that your children might not stumble."

But I know that it's not on account of my merits, for when I examine my conscience, I know I don't have any. It's the other way around . . . Everything we receive from God is on account of the merits of the Christ who died on a cross, and we receive them through Mary's intercession.

And what more can God give than a vocation? Oh, my dear co-novices, you don't know what you have, nor will you ever be able to give God sufficient thanks for such a great blessing; I didn't know what I had either, until I had to return to the world. If I thought the world was crazy or disturbed before going to La Trapa, now I feel as though God has abandoned it, that He has left people all alone, for in their suicidal pride, they shout, "We don't need God . . ." And society is unhinged, focusing on *everything* except what is actually important, and I'm telling you, honestly, seeing people be so blind, it makes me sad and makes me want to shout at them . . . "Where are you going?! Fools or lunatics . . . You are crucifying Jesus, that man from Nazareth who commanded us to love one another[6] . . . Can't you see that you are going down a terrible path . . . that life is very short and we have to use it well, for God's Judgment draws near?" But it's useless; in the world no one talks of God and His Judgment . . . It's all envy, earthly ambitions, and uncontrolled passions. Seeing this sad spectacle, how could I not give thanks to God for my vocation? . . . How could I not yearn for my corner of La Trapa? . . .

5. Ps 8:5.
6. John 13:34; 15:17; 1 John 3:11.

No, Brother Isidro, it is not, as you said in your letter, unusual or surprising that I should try to advance, as you say, and scorn what the world offers me, yearning for the beans at La Trapa . . . I see it as perfectly natural and logical. The world pays me in currency that holds no value in the eyes of God . . . You can buy the world with money, but not heaven. Therefore, just as you dispose of a counterfeit duro that can't buy you anything, so also you ought to dispose of everything that serves no purpose except to get through life pleasantly . . . but that's all. Truth be told, life is a very little thing . . . it's nothing really. For us Christians, our life is not here on earth; let us leave behind, then, those who are content with less, and instead go store up good treasure for ourselves in heaven[7] with the only currency that has any value . . . And that currency is sacrifice, mortification, prayer—in a word, the life of a Trappist.

It's not, therefore, that I am advancing or retreating, it's simply . . . utterly logical, for, as Brother Bernardo tells me, peeling potatoes for love of God is better than all the luxuries the world could give me.

I'd love to be able to put some texts in Latin here for Father Francisco, to respond in kind to his letter, but it just so happens that I still don't know any. What I will tell him is this: Father Francisco, I prayed the novena to Saint Thérèse in union with you, and I hope that she will make me well.

You can't imagine how grateful I was for your letters, and how much consolation I received from them. I read them over many times, giving thanks to God for the true affection rooted in love for God and charity that they exuded. In truth, I don't deserve any of that; but it's also true that if we Trappist monks do not put into practice the Gospel precept, *love one another*,[8] who will? We seek perfection in the world, and that is the only perfection there is.

When will Brother Damián profess?[9]

In brief . . . there are so many things I'd tell you and ask you, but I can't express it all in a letter. I am counting the days until I am able to come spend three nights at the monastery.

---

7. See Matt 6:19-21.

8. John 13:34; 15:17; 1 John 3:11.

9. Brother Damián Yáñez Neira made his first profession of vows on July 25, 1934 (see #20, n. 4).

Keep praying to Our Lady the Blessed Virgin for me, just as I am, so that we might be able to resume my novitiate, and that instead of going around in a car, living the high life, I might be able to keep trying to light and snuff out candles without making any mistakes and operating the organ bellows when the power is out[10] . . . At the end of the day, that's my place.

I am always thinking of my life in the monastery, and I still don't know if I am dreaming. Who could have told me, as those trains passed by at such high speed while we were out among the vines, that I'd have to use them again? . . . But what do we human beings know of what might happen to us? And when you surrender yourself to God without reserve, you have to be open to anything.

Tell the oblates and Fr. Amadeo[11] that they'll see the "tall novice" in just a few days, God willing.

Father Master, give my regards to Rev. Father Abbot. Commending myself to your prayers, and looking forward to seeing you very soon, your brother in Jesus and Mary,

Brother María Rafael
✠
O.C.R.[12]

10. See #34, n. 8.

11. Fr. Amadeo: Father Amadeo Pérez García (1908–2008) was responsible for the young oblates, children being raised and schooled in the monastery (see #7, n. 13).

12. O.C.R.: Short for Orden Cisterciense Reformada, lit. "Reformed Cistercian Order," a name that is no longer in common usage. The official abbreviation for the Trappists is O.C.S.O., for the Order of the Cistercians of the Strict Observance.

40. *To María Osorio*

Oviedo, July 23, 1934

My dearest Aunt María,

Counting on your promise that you'd write me back, I'm writing to you, even though in reality I have nothing to tell you that you don't already know.

Uncle Polín will have already told you how I'm doing, and I can assure you I'm getting better every day.

On the 31ˢᵗ I'm leaving for Venta de Baños on the express train. I'll be there for just *three* days, the 1ˢᵗ, 2ⁿᵈ, and 3ʳᵈ of August . . . I don't have the doctor's permission to be away any longer. If I did, I'd have come to pay your family a visit[1] . . . but I don't want to take advantage.

I need these days at La Trapa with my dear brothers as I need to eat . . . And it seems that God, in His goodness, has granted them to me in order to give me a light rest. It's not that I deserve it, but Jesus knows very well how far His creatures can go, and at opportune moments He always holds out His hand. If, for a moment, it seems as though He has left us all alone . . . it's not so; for when we most feel that we are alone, that is when God is nearest to us, keeping close watch. If He puts obstacles in our path, He removes them Himself . . . There's nothing to do but let Him work.

The first day of August is the name day of our good Father Abbot,[2] and he'll be pleased to see me that day, if I do say so myself.

The other day the doctor told me that I'll be able to resume my novitiate in just a few months . . . I won't dare to say that I ardently desire it, since it is because of an excess of *personal desires* that I find myself at home . . . I imagine you know what I mean . . . but the lesson has been beneficial to me.

---

1. Despite what Rafael says here, he did in fact go to Ávila to see his aunt and uncle, after spending eight days at La Trapa (OC 272).

2. See #39, n. 3.

I now understand very well the rather narrow way that Saint John of the Cross points out to us, the one that is between two others. Those two, he says, are prayer, contemplation, spiritual consolations, earthly gifts, spiritual gifts, etc. . . . But between those two ways is the one I am talking about, and on that one is simply nothing. . . nothing. . . nothing. . .[3]

How difficult it is, Aunt María, to reach that. And for those of us who are just starting out, how easy it is to get it wrong, and how many times we want to find God where He is not to be found! And when we believe we have found Him, we find only ourselves . . . but we need not lose heart. God permits all things for the good of one's soul; without knowing failure, one cannot savor success. And one cannot approach God without having first relinquished *everything* and being left with *nothing*, as Saint John of the Cross says.[4]

But anyway, I'm not telling you anything new, and may God forgive me for wanting to address such exalted things; I can't even crawl yet, and here I am already wanting to fly . . . That has been my sin, and it continues to be . . . But if you only knew, Jesus is so good to me that He forgives me everything and understands me. After all, all children falsely believe that before they have even reached their father's knees, they are already strong enough to handle his saber and put on his spurs. Meanwhile the father looks on lovingly, and the bravado of his children makes him laugh, knowing that if he were not watching them from behind, who knows what would happen to his darlings . . . The same thing must happen to God with me. When He saw me take up arms with such exuberance, it must have made Him laugh, and He said to me, "To become a general, first you must be a soldier. And before you can become a soldier, I have to

3. Here Rafael is describing the "mount of perfection" as envisioned in the treatise by Saint John of the Cross, The Ascent of Mount Carmel. The work begins with a visual representation showing three ways up the mount: two labeled "the way of the imperfect spirit," and one in the middle, labeled "the way of Mount Carmel, the perfect spirit." The two imperfect ways begin by seeking the "goods of heaven" and the "goods of earth" respectively, while the perfect way begins by seeking "nothing"; it is the only one that reaches the perfection to be found at the mount's peak (see SJC 110–11).

4. As Saint John of the Cross wrote to Sr. Magdalena del Espíritu Santo, the nun to whom he had addressed the "mount of perfection," "To possess God in all, you should possess nothing in all" (SJC 752).

take your measurements and see if you'll do . . ." And that's what He is doing with me, and I can promise you, Aunt María, that I'm standing on my tippy-toes and raising my head up high, but I just barely measure up.

Pardon my simile. I don't know how to express myself any other way, and if I'm telling you all this, it's because I have so much inside me and no one to share it with. And since you, in your great charity, listen to me, I'm pouring my heart out.

Before, finding myself so alone, I was greatly saddened. Now I'm growing accustomed to it. In La Trapa, sufferings and joys alike are for God alone, and He is the one whom we ought to seek out as our only confidant.

But for some reason, you two are the exception, and if God offers me this consolation, I'm not going to reject it . . . I'm not seeking it out. He is offering it to me through you, and affection, when it goes far beyond earthly things, is pleasing in the eyes of God. The only pleasure that we, His true children, can experience is to speak of Him; and our great joy is to find souls whom God finds pleasing. For here on earth it is so difficult to find creatures of His who, forgetting everything—dealings, affairs, laughter, tears—lift their hearts and think of nothing but God, who sing to Him, gaze at Him, worship Him; whose earthly life is a continual *hosanna*!

What does it matter if we are above or below, close to God or far from Him; let us turn our gaze toward Him and join together to praise Him, some in monastic life, others at the missions, others in the world, some this way and others that way . . . what does it matter? . . . He fills it all, and if we look around at one another, we are wasting time . . . Sometimes a creature is very beautiful, but the sight of it distracts us from the Creator.

We ought to go on with our gaze fixed on Him, whether we are among saints or among sinners . . . We are nothing; we are worth nothing and we are good for nothing when we are distracted and don't take notice of the Lord. So let's not waste time. If we please the Lord with a little sacrifice, with a prayer or an act of love, then we can say that at least we've been good for something, which is giving Him greater glory . . . That ought to be our only occupation and our only desire.

I won't ask about your concerns because I already know they are going poorly . . . Jesus loves you so much!! Most people don't see it this way, but it doesn't escape me: you have the greatest fortune in the family. It seems paradoxical, doesn't it? . . . But you also know it's true. If there's one thing you have that's worth anything, it's not your titles, or your money, or anything else the world aspires to . . . The best thing of all, the thing of which, to a certain extent, you can be proud, is your poverty . . . God loves you so much, Aunt María. Jesus does not do such things for anyone but His chosen ones; with that you can be pleased.

Well, I have nothing else to tell you; my life is very simple. In the morning I go to receive Communion; afterwards I have breakfast and I go to a quiet beach near Cabo de Peñas; I sunbathe, make sketches, and praise God as I look at the sea. After eating, I sleep for a bit, take a walk, make my visit to the Most Blessed Sacrament, have dinner, say the Rosary, and go to sleep . . . That's it.

Today I went to El Musel, which is the port of Gijón.[5] I go there sometimes to watch the fishing. I saw a spectacle that's always impressive, but it left me a little sad, which was a German passenger ship departing for the high seas . . . It was a lovely evening and the sea was calm; it would have been around eight o'clock; the lighthouses of the nearby ports began to illuminate . . .

I was at the end of the quay, listening to that noise so characteristic of ports with their cranes and ship sirens and churning oars. Suddenly, pilot boats surrounded the ship, requesting passage for the colossus; one could hear the creak of the chains weighing anchor, and above all that noise, the deep, powerful siren of the ship as it advanced slowly toward the port's exit . . .

As it crossed out and around the breakwater, the boat's lights came on and the orchestra on the poop deck played a foxtrot. The travelers looked scornfully upon the humble fishermen who in their old, dirty barges were getting their nets in order or returning from the open sea after a thirteen- or fourteen-hour work day. The fishermen, in their turn, watched the gigantic ship approach, all strength and lights and music . . . that floating hotel where brothers and sisters in God are separated into first-, second-, and third-class passengers . . .

I'm telling you, Aunt María, it's made me think, for the world is nothing but that . . . a big ship that heads out to sea confident in its own power and strength, when at the slightest breeze all that power would be sunk for good.

5. Gijón: The largest city in Asturias, just north of where Rafael's family lived in Oviedo.

On the ship, as in the world, people numb themselves by making the jazz band play, and for them life seems to drift by pleasantly . . . but behind all that, such bitterness, such falsehood in everything, such ambition repressed and such passion released . . .

I don't know if my brother Trappists were praying the *Salve* to the Virgin at that same time . . . but the truth is, that music coming from the ship . . . saddened me greatly, and later, when I went into the church and saw the Tabernacle so alone, with just four old ladies and me . . . believe me, my prayer was to put all humanity in God's hands and to intercede for them all . . . the ones on the boat, those fellow creatures of mine, who were dancing on the deck so calmly and confidently, without thinking about how God, if He wanted, needed nothing more than a whim to make all that power disappear under the waves . . . What sorrow, my God, what sorrow . . . and the Tabernacle all alone.

So many times, there at La Trapa, getting up at two in the morning and going to choir, and laying myself at the feet of Jesus, I offered up my exhaustion and the cold for the sake of humanity . . . and I thought: "Lord, what I'm offering You is such a little thing, but these days there are so many souls, creatures of Yours who, since they do not know You, may perhaps be offending You . . . Forgive them, Lord . . . if I could stop some people from drifting away from You . . . I'd be so pleased . . ." And I believe that God heard me, for the cold and the exhaustion became almost pleasant to me.

I should like to see the whole world prostrate itself before the tabernacle, before the cross, and instead of that, what do I see? Why am I explaining any of this to you? . . . You already know all this quite well . . . We Christians are largely responsible if we don't do anything for the conversion of the world; we can all contribute something.

Don't let anything I'm saying shock you. My departure from La Trapa has made me see humanity in a whole new light . . . that is, now I see people as my brothers and sisters who do not know their Father . . . I have more of a Trappist mindset, and the Trappist judges charitably . . . that's all.

Well, a good deal of nonsense and foolishness occur to me, none of it relevant. I'm writing down everything that occurs to me, and there are things that shouldn't occur to me, but you, who know me, will be able to handle it . . . Don't pay me any mind, because if my actions corresponded to my words, "that would be a different story," as they say, but unfortunately that's not the case.

Tell Uncle Polín that I'll do his cover[6] when I get back from La Trapa. By the way, I'll see my brother Fernandito while I'm there. When he heard that I'd be there for three days, he wanted to come see me . . . Is it true what they say, that one fool makes many?

Tell Uncle Polín also that his friend Pedro[7] decided to start praying the Little Office of the Blessed Virgin.[8] I'm very happy for him . . . but I'm even happier for Our Lady, who now has one more devotee. If only you knew what devotion she receives at La Trapa, it's rather marvelous. There's not a single Trappist who isn't a loving son of our Mother . . . Just one detail: when they brought in the statue that Granda[9] made, Reverend Father strictly prohibited kissing it because it was going to end up without any paint on it at all.

The first words the porter said to me when I got to the guesthouse were "Now, not to worry. Anything that occurs to you, tell it to the Virgin Mary, for in my twenty-something years as a Trappist, she has never refused me anything." [10] And the man said it with such devotion, and spoke about Our Lady with such great faith, that from the very first day, she indeed never refused me anything.

I remember those first few days, I had to control myself somewhat in the refectory, because the iron plate and oxhorn spoon weren't to my liking . . . And so, before going in, I'd pray a *Salve* to my Mother asking Her to help me . . . and very calmly. When I'd go out to work in the fields, one hand on my hoe and the other on my rosary, frost could fall and it wouldn't matter anymore . . . If only you could see what care we took in the novitiate with the May flowers . . . it was interrupted by my illness.[11]

---

6. Rafael painted the covers for various books that his uncle translated from French (see #6, n. 1). It is unclear to which of them he is referring here.

7. Pedro: Their mutual friend, Pedro Sánchez del Río; see #37.

8. Little Office of the Blessed Virgin: A liturgical devotion; see #24, n. 1

9. Granda: A liturgical art firm based in Madrid, founded in 1891 by Fr. Félix Granda y Buylla. The monastery had commissioned a statue of the Assumption for their main altar from the company in 1926.

10. When Rafael entered the monastery in January 1934, the monastery porter was Brother Justo García Hidalgo (1893–1980).

11. According to Br. Damián, the novices gathered wildflowers as they worked, and Rafael would arrange them before a statue of Our Lady, to whom the month of May is

How gentle and sweet it is to devote oneself to Mary. It is the one consolation in La Trapa, to know that Mary is protecting us. And last, the *Salve* at dusk, before heading to the dormitory; they are the Trappist's last words at the end of the day . . . and with that he sleeps soundly, knowing that if he were to die that night, the Virgin would come for him and present him to Her Son . . . If you knew how well you sleep knowing that, even if your bed is hard . . . With bodies that are tired and sometimes in pain, but with hearts trusting in Our Lady and calm faces, there is not a single Trappist who cannot get to sleep. Later, when Vigils begin in the choir, the Trappist's first words are also *Ave Maria*.

If you knew how ashamed I felt at having gone so long without a true devotion to Our Lady. It's not enough to pray the Little Office, or the Rosary, or half a million novenas . . . You have to love Her very much . . . so much. You have to tell Her everything, trust Her with everything; she is a true Mother . . . And it seems to me—and this is just what I think, so don't give it a second thought—that the more love one has for the Virgin, without even realizing it, the more love we have for God. That is, our love for God grows in proportion to the love we cultivate for the Blessed Virgin[12] . . . and that's only natural. How are we going to love a Mother and not Her Son? Impossible. And what won't we receive from God if we ask it of Him through Mary's intercession? . . . Nothing . . . Jesus' first miracle was at the Virgin's request, and I imagine Mary's face as She looked at Jesus and told him, "They have no wine."[13] It's one of the miracles that resonates most with me because Mary takes part.

Well, I'm going on too long, and I'm preaching to the choir, but if I don't talk to you about God and the Virgin, what do you want me to talk to you about? I don't know anything else, and I'm not interested in anything else, and let's not take up something less important just for the sake of leaving the weighty stuff behind, don't you agree?

---

traditionally devoted. They stopped when Rafael started experiencing symptoms in mid-May (OC 280).

12. While this formulation is Rafael's, the practice of growing in love for God through Marian devotion is a broad tradition in the church. The most prominent advocate of drawing close "to Jesus through Mary" is Saint Louis de Montfort (1673–1716), whose True Devotion to Mary is a popular guide to Marian consecration. See Louis-Marie Grignion de Montfort, *True Devotion to Mary* (Charlotte, NC: Saint Benedict Press), 2010.

13. John 2:1-3.

I'm going to finish this letter. I don't think you'll complain about the length, but even though I want to tell you so many things, since they're nothing of any interest, I don't want to distract you any longer . . . When I'm back in the novitiate, I'll write you and tell you things about La Trapa, which I suppose will interest you. For now, let it be enough to know that your nephew, Brother Rafael, never forgets you in his prayers, and that I don't ask God to fix anything for you, because He'll know how best to handle it. And since the interests of humankind are nearly always in opposition to the interests of God, when everything seems like chaos with no possible resolution in sight, that's when everything is at its best . . . And what more can you ask than to live by alms? We have to atone for the blood poured out by Christ somehow, and if it's not in this world, it'll be in the next. And when the Lord offers a trial on earth, we must give Him infinite thanks, and the true, worthy trials are the ones He sends us, not the ones we seek out . . .

To that end, I'm going to tell you something trivial that astonished me one day at La Trapa.

In the early days of my novitiate, as is rather natural, I felt a real thirst for humiliation and mortification . . . I wanted to perform penances, so I asked them of Father Master . . . and I went all the way up to Father Abbot. Naturally, they laughed at my candor . . . and afterwards I understood what I told you earlier. I thought I was seeking God, but what I was doing was seeking myself . . . we all fall into that . . .

But you'll see. In the refectory, when the whole community is eating in silence, listening to the reading of the Martyrology,[14] whenever a monk makes a noise—he drops a piece of cutlery or spills his water or something similar—that is, whenever he disturbs the silence or calls attention to himself, he has to get up and go to the middle of the refectory. Then he must fully prostrate himself on the ground in front of all his brothers and ask Father Abbot's forgiveness, and remain there until he is sent back to his place.

This is always very embarrassing, and I've seen little old men with white hair go scarlet when a similar mishap befalls them . . .

Anyway, I too desired to prostrate myself in front of the whole community in the refectory, but it just so happened that I didn't make any noise, nor did I drop anything. So I spent a few days with the strong temptation

14. Martyrology: The Roman Martyrology lists the saints and beatified who are commemorated each day.

to throw something, as if out of carelessness, and thereby make a noise
and go to the middle of the refectory . . . As you can see, this was all
very poorly done. It was clear that the spirit of evil desired to be at work
in me. The end was a mortification but the means was a lie; assessing the
situation rightly, even the mortification itself was a lie, for it gratified a
desire of mine and there was even vanity in it . . .

This went on for a few days . . . how totally absurd. Anyway, I wasn't
at peace . . . I told Father Master what was going on and he told me to be
careful not to do anything that would disturb the silence in the refectory
. . . that to do so would be very bad . . . And so then I turned to the Virgin
and told Her about it one day before going in to eat. When we were in choir,
I explained my predicament to Her, and since the mortifications I sought
out were imperfect because they were according to my desires, I asked Her
to send me some, and I'd leave it be . . . I thought it best that way.

Well believe me, after asking the Virgin for that . . . We got to the
refectory, and as the reader paused, when there was even greater silence
. . . I got tangled up somehow in my cape, dropped my water, made a
ruckus, nearly spilled all over the brother next to me . . . and finished by
dropping the little crystal glass we use to drink right on the stony floor
. . . Between the rules and the noise and my failings, the only thing I
managed to pick up, in my embarrassment, was a handle that had landed
on the pile of shattered glass on the floor.

Didn't you want to go prostrate yourself? So go do it, now that you
weren't expecting it, time to see what you'll do . . . I wished the ground
would swallow me whole. My vision started dancing around, I flushed
deep red, I did what I was supposed to . . . and I did it poorly and hast-
ily. Ever since that day, I take exquisite pains at the table. When I am eating, I gather up my cape very carefully, and I never asked the Virgin for
mortifications ever again. That's no good. Don't ask for anything, because
without asking for it and when you least expect it, you'll be dished up a
whole plateful, and it'll put you in a daze for a good while. I speak from
experience and it's plain to see.

There's something better than cilices and disciplines,[15] and that is conforming *entirely* to the will of God and asking nothing of Him, and desiring

15. Cilices and disciplines: Instruments of physical penance. A cilice is a spiked metal
garter worn on the arm or leg; Rafael had used it occasionally as a layman but was not

nothing. Often, in thinking about those words *ask and it will be given you*,[16] and how needy we are, even as I would ask things of God . . . I'd say to myself, "Lord, I ask *nothing* of you . . . but enclosed in that dry 'nothing' is everything that You can give me, which I cannot quite understand, for you give me so much that my imagination cannot encompass it . . . May my will be Your will; my desires, Your desires; my interests, those of Jesus; my loves, those of Jesus. I want nothing that You do not want. If I do not please You, destroy me and annihilate me. As you can see, Lord, I ask nothing of You, and yet . . . I ask you for everything."

Nevertheless, Aunt María, after all that, I go and draw close to the Virgin and, like a spoiled child, I ask my Mother for candy behind my Father's back.

But anyway, you don't need me to explain all that. You can understand this letter and all its gibberish perfectly, right? And if something in it seems wrong to you, tell me; I've made so many mistakes, what's one more . . . And what does it matter if our judgments and opinions are wrong . . . ? At the end of the day, we are human. But the one thing about which we must be totally sure is our love for God . . . One who has true love for God has everything . . . this love even feeds you, unless you think that irreverent of me to say.

Well, write me back if you have time. Do you still visit the dying? How is Pili doing? Are you finally going to Pedrosillo[17] with your father and the dog? . . . Let's see if you overcome your father . . . I'll help you from here, but don't make him pray too much . . . or else he might end up in La Trapa. Greet him for me. Hugs to everyone, and whatever else you want from your nephew and brother in Jesus and Mary,

Rafael

---

permitted to do so in the monastery. A discipline is a small whip made of rope; in Rafael's community, its use on Fridays, especially in Lent, was largely symbolic and would not have caused physical harm.

16. See Matt 7:7-8; Mark 11:24; Luke 11:9-10.

17. Pedrosillo: The family estate outside Ávila.

41. To Fernanda Torres

Ávila, August 9, 1934

My dearest grandmother,

Just a quick note to tell you that I went to La Trapa for eight days, and that my health continues to improve prodigiously, thanks to the Virgin, who wants me back in my beloved monastery for good . . . There, I was treated like the community's spoiled child. They all desire my return, especially my superiors. In that, I clearly see the will of God, which even in the midst of my illness remains providential and necessary for me. God ordains all things for His greater glory.

Today I'm going to Oviedo to continue treatment. From there, I'll write you at greater length, though you know that regardless, I think of you and Aunt María often, for you are always in my prayers. That is all your Trappist grandson can do, as he remains Brother María Rafael in the eyes of God and men . . . With all the love you know your grandson has for you,

Rafael

42. To Fr. Marcelo León

Oviedo, August 11, 1934

My dear Father Master,

Just a quick note to let you know I've arrived safely at home. I spent a day in Ávila, where I surprised my aunt and uncle, and now I'm back at my parents' house to continue my recovery plan.

I was with the doctor today, and he found me perfectly well. Starting today, I will only take one injection per day rather than the two I was taking before . . . That's all the news when it comes to my health.

When it comes to my spirit . . . what can I say, Father? Just that I am obeying God's will, and not merely with resignation, but with joy, for my desires are His desires. If He has temporarily separated me from my beloved brothers, He must know why He is doing it . . . Of course, my spirit is in the choir singing to God and the Virgin, while my body is here among men and women, dealing with them all, busying myself with the things that keep them busy. The only difference is that I do it all mechanically and indifferently, for I belong to God, my purpose is God, and He is the only one who can satisfy me completely . . . everything else is completely unnecessary to me, I don't need it at all . . . But since in the world, sadly, people occupy themselves with just about everything but Him, my antagonism toward it is very evident and obvious . . . God is giving me this cross, and I bless it, for if, as Job says, *we receive the good at the hand of God*, shall we not also *receive the bad*?[1]

Everything comes to us from Him: health and illness, temporal goods, misfortunes and setbacks in this life . . . He has arranged everything, absolutely everything, with perfection. If creatures ever rebel against what God commands us, we commit a sin, for everything is necessary, everything is well made; laughter and tears are both necessary. Everything can profit us and our greater perfection, so long as we look with the spirit of

1. Job 2:10.

faith and see God at work in everything, and remain as children in the Father's hands. Where shall we go all on our own?

As I find myself once more in the world, sick, separated from the monastery, in this situation . . . I can see that I needed it, that the lesson I'm learning is very useful. My heart is still so tethered to creatures, and God wants me to free it so that I can give it to Him alone.

Father, on the day I left the monastery, I was standing in the back during the Office of None, now dressed as a layman, and while the monks chanted, looking at them and finding myself uprooted from the choir, I shed such bitter tears . . . I bade everyone farewell in my heart, since I could no longer give them a hug . . . After drying my eyes, I realized that those tears would have been more pleasing to God if, rather than looking at my brothers in religion whom I love so much, I had instead looked more at the tabernacle . . . Don't you agree? . . . Ultimately, it is sadder to leave the house of God than to separate oneself from humanity . . . but we do not govern our own hearts, and mine has always made me suffer . . . since God wants me to be better and more perfect, it is clear that this trial He has sent me, however difficult, is necessary . . .

Pray for me then, Father, asking Our Lady to help me profit from this. For it is true that it is beautiful to love one's neighbor, but God comes first, then creatures. The two go together . . . but God first, God always, and God alone. Of course, I'm not trying to root out those feelings entirely, but rather God merely wants me to perfect them. That is why He carries me around like a toy, leaving pieces of my heart all over the place. How great God is, Father Marcelo, and how well He does everything!! He loves me so much, and I love Him so poorly in return! His providence is infinite, and we ought to surrender ourselves to it without reserve . . . He wants me at home now for a few months; all right, then, I'll be here as long as He wants.

Father Master, the day you see me again in the novitiate, you will have yourself a novice who is a bit better than the one you had before, one with a greater desire to love God and the Virgin, one who is trying to return the blessings he receives from Jesus. If he were ever to shed tears in his room, or on his Father Master's knees, they would not be tears of affection or love for humanity, but rather tears of sorrow for the sins of his past life as well as those of the world. For now that I am in it, and I can see it a bit more clearly, it is terribly sad to see people who forget about Christ and adore nothing more than a golden calf,[2] their passions unleashed, without a care for the blood that Jesus shed on the cross.

Forgive me, Father, that I am telling you so many things, and perhaps they are unbecoming. But in your charity, you will be able to handle them. I am a man who is suffering . . . and nothing more, so if I utter some nonsense, perhaps that is why.

Tell Fr. Vicente[3] that one of these days I'll send him the books I promised; I'll never be able to repay him all the kindness he has shown me. I'll write Fr. Francisco[4] and the novices soon, if you give me permission to do so, for though I am in the world, I consider myself your son through obedience, and I should not like to impose upon you. But if only you knew, Father—the letters I receive from La Trapa do me such good! For me they are the real injections . . . The flesh needs insulin injections, but the spirit needs these even more.

I have nothing to tell you, even though I want to use this letter to pour out everything that is in my heart, for the things there are many and much.

Give my best to Father Teófilo[5] and Father Buenaventura[6] and Brother Tescelino[7] . . . Well, to everyone. Let them pray to the Blessed Virgin that I might come back soon.

I'm going to start working on a painting of Saint Bernard,[8] we'll see how it turns out.

Give my kind regards to Reverend Father Abbot. I ask your blessing as your novice, which I remain until you say otherwise,

Brother María Rafael
OCSO[9]

2. Exod 32:4.

3. Fr. Vicente: the infirmarian at San Isidro (see #35, n. 7).

4. Fr. Francisco: the sub-master of novices, who assisted Fr. Marcelo León with their formation (see #33, n. 6).

5. Father Teófilo: Rafael's confessor, Fr. Teófilo Sandoval Fernández (see #35, n. 5).

6. Father Buenaventura: Fr. Buenaventura Ramos Caballero (1903–1971), who served as the monastery porter from 1931 until 1940, when he was elected abbot (OC 73).

7. Br. Tescelino Arribas Jimeno (1912–1992) assisted Fr. Vicente Pardo as second infirmarian. He left the monastery during the Spanish Civil War, reverting to his baptismal name, Toribio Luis (OC 292).

8. Saint Bernard: Saint Bernard of Clairvaux, a doctor of the church who was an influential leader in the early years of the Cistercian reform.

9. OCSO: Order of Cistercians of the Strict Observance

43. To Leopoldo Barón

Oviedo, August 12, 1934

Dearest Uncle Polín,

Just as I promised, I'm sending you the letters that my mother sent me at La Trapa for you to read . . . though it's not particularly important that you read them. It's more important that you praise God in doing so, for when you encounter a soul as generous and great as my mother's, you cannot help but extol the Creator from the depths of your own.

Since she does not know I am sending them to you, please don't send them back to me. They are rather bulky and she may suspect . . . just give them to me when you see me next.

You will see a mother in these letters, and a heroic Christian one at that, one who is so generous with God that when her Trappist son would read them in some corner of the novitiate over in La Trapa, they would make him cry. At the same time, they would make him bless God for having given him such a mother, a mother who not only sacrificed her son to God, but who also helped him to carry his cross and offer his sacrifice, giving him the strength to do so.

How greatly prized in the eyes of God are such quiet souls who drink every last drop[1] resignedly, silently, and even joyfully. What myriad generous acts they can offer to God—even playing the piano . . . don't you think?

As I observed my parents' greatness of soul and the glory they were giving to God in those days, I forgot my own suffering and hardships. What could my own actions merit compared to my parents' sublime generosity? . . . I am not the one who showed merit or gave glory to God . . . no, I am nothing at all. I am merely an implement in the hands of God, who is using me to carry out the work He is doing, and as Saint Thérèse says, what merit can a simple brush have in the ensemble required to create a

---

1. See Matt 26:39: *Father, if it is possible, let this cup pass from me; yet not what I want, but what you want.*

painting?[2] . . . God, the Painter; creation, His painting; and when He needs to add certain details to make it perfect, the great Painter will make use of any little old paintbrush He wants.

Don't think me excessively modest, because I'm not, but when you—perhaps out of great affection for me—think me a bit heroic . . . there's no such heroism . . . Let's be clear about that, as all things ought to be among true children of God. Take a look around me, and you'll see there are such great and beautiful souls here, which need only a brushstroke here and there to make them perfect . . . and that is God's work. He asks me to help, and I do (but understand that correctly: God doesn't need anyone) . . . But now that I've explained myself, in my own way, I think you'll understand what I'm saying . . .

Take a careful look at every detail . . . think on it a little, and you'll see how admirable God is, how everything is good and necessary: a Trappist's exhaustion and cold, a mother's tears . . . And let's not stop and ask ourselves who is giving God more glory, that's for small-minded people. Let it be enough for us to know that all of us put together are the work necessary for His glory. As you very well know, a painting needs light tones and darker ones, bright colors and more muted ones; it's a matter of not clashing with the whole . . . But the world does not generally see this, and in the present case, it only managed to see a man who, leaving the world, shut himself away in order to spend his life wearing sackcloth and gripping a hoe. Some thoughtless souls nearly raised him to the altars[3] . . . But that man in La Trapa, with the help of divine light, stopped to think and meditate, and he saw clearly that he was not doing anything special. Rather, he saw that what was truly beautiful in the eyes of God was those tears shed by a mother and father who, with their hearts torn to pieces, offered up their son for God's service . . . That is what God wanted, that is what He came looking for, and that is what is admirable: that through one soul's *voluntary* sacrifice, others might be sanctified through another sacrifice that is even more beautiful for their not having

---

2. "If an artist's canvas could but think and speak, surely it would never complain of being touched and re-touched by the brush, nor would it feel envious thereof, knowing that all its beauty is due to the artist alone. . . . I am the little brush that Jesus has chosen to paint His likeness" (Thérèse of Lisieux, *Story of a Soul*, 235).

3. Raised him to the altars: that is, canonized him.

sought it, a sacrifice that was given and offered to them by God . . . Isn't God a great artist, Uncle Polín?

I don't know if I am explaining myself well, but I think you will understand me perfectly. One day, not too long from now, we human beings will see the truth of everything I have just told you: that neither you nor I nor anyone else has merits to present before God, that we are nothing more than instruments with louder or softer roles in the symphony of creation, that on our own we are nothing and deserve nothing, that the only merits flow from Jesus on the cross, and in comparison everything else is but grains of sand scattered in the ocean.

It's just as I told you in the other letter: we contemplate ourselves too much, and each other, and we hardly look at God . . . He is all, and He fills all. When we see a creature and find it pleasing, we ought not to exclaim, "Oh, what a beautiful soul, how it shines!" Instead, we ought to contemplate God within it, and nothing more. We know that souls—which are not to be called holy, but merely in a state of grace—are reflections of God's grace . . . And so, rather than stopping to look at the sun's reflection on the water, let's look up directly at the sun, don't you think?

Well, I'm writing you everything I think of, so perhaps I might utter some irrelevant nonsense, but in your charity you will be able to forgive me. For even silly things said for love of God are necessary, and I think that if we had true love for Him, we wouldn't even know how to speak reasonably, and we'd even go crazy. After all, isn't that exactly what the saints were, souls madly in love?

My father couldn't go to Santander because Aunt Petra[4] is very sick; she may not last longer than a few days. She is going peacefully, but it's been six days since she was able to eat anything, and yesterday she couldn't even drink a spoonful of water. How difficult it is to leave behind one's body . . . it's terrible.

How will she present herself before God so soon? Ask the Lord to show her mercy. She has already received all the sacraments, and there's nothing left to do but wait. When will it be our turn?

In a short six months, I've seen four people depart. I'm telling you, it's nothing to take lightly. I've been at death's door myself, and now I almost

---

4. Petra Sánchez de la Campa y Tasquer, Rafael's great-aunt, who died in August 1934 (#2, n. 6) (OC 296).

consider it natural. I pity all these people who think they are going to live here on earth forever. Such ambition, so many concerns, and not a thought for how all this is brief and passing away . . . Well, nothing to be done about that . . . You told me once that the world is not a great big Trapa, but rather it's the other way around.

Antonio[5] asks me if you received the pipe stems.

Now I only take one daily injection instead of two . . . Everything is on the right track.

I'm going to start working on a painting of Saint Bernard[6] for the novitiate; we'll see how it turns out. I'll remember Brother Bernardo[7] in my prayers while I'm painting it, and if it turns out well, I'll send you a photo.

Greet the Poor Clares[8] for me, and ask them to pray to Our Lady for me, that God's will might be done in my life, however difficult it might be for me to find myself away from the novitiate . . . but what does it matter?

The other day Fernandito[9] wrote me with all the details of the three days he spent at La Trapa. He said being there is so good that it hurt to leave, for in that quiet and solitude, you are with God, and being with God, you are no longer alone (his words), and that when he saw the monks' devotion as they sang the *Salve*, he wept . . . Blessed be God for everything, Uncle Polín.

Give Aunt María a big hug for me. I bid you farewell the same way the novices do before going up to receive the Lord: we embrace one another and say *pax tecum*, peace be with you, my brother.

Rafael

5. Antonio: Probably a servant in the Arnaiz-Barón household (see #10, n. 9).

6. Saint Bernard: Saint Bernard of Clairvaux (see #42, n. 8).

7. Brother Bernardo: This is one of Rafael's nicknames for his uncle Leopoldo (OC 523). He once used this term for him in a letter (see #87, n. 2).

8. Poor Clares: The Poor Clares, named for their founder, Saint Clare of Assisi, are the cloistered women's branch of the Franciscan Order. Leopoldo and María often visited the Poor Clare monastery in Ávila, where the abbess, Sor Pilar García (1882–1957), was a friend of Rafael's.

9. Fernandito: Rafael's younger brother, Luis Fernando.

44. To W. Marino del Hierro[1]

Oviedo, August 15, 1934
Feast of the Ascension[2] of the Virgin

My brother in Christ,

This letter may perhaps strike you as inappropriate and presumptuous. You and I do not know each other, and thus I beg you to forgive my impertinence. However, all I know of you is that you recently came to know Jesus, and you are now suffering . . . That is enough for me. In any case, I will fill you in on who I am and why I am writing you.

In the world, my name is Rafael Arnaiz Barón. But I have a very beautiful nickname that I wouldn't trade for anything. To my first name, Rafael, the Abbot of San Isidro in Venta de Baños recently added the "Brother María" that is typical of the Trappists. Therefore, I am Brother M. Rafael, Trappist novice. Perhaps that's enough for you to know who I am, but I'll explain anyway.

On January 15, 1934, I entered the community and spent four months on what felt like the threshold of heaven. Then God, who does all things well, even the crosses He sends us at opportune times, desired that I come down with an illness that would oblige me to leave the monastery temporarily, and so I did . . .

I was very close to death . . . and for the past three months I have been home convalescing from a deadly fit of "diabetes." The Blessed Virgin provided for me, and I was fortunate enough to return to La Trapa recently . . . I was there for eight days, and, naturally, I stayed in the infirmary, though I participated in community life. There I saw Br. Tescelino, who is a close friend of yours, and he spoke about you. He explained the situation,

---

1. As Rafael recounts in this letter, he was not personally acquainted with W. Marino del Hierro before writing him. They were put in touch by their mutual friend, Br. Tescelino Arribas, whom Rafael knew from the infirmary at San Isidro (see #42, n. 7).

2. Rafael's error; it is the feast of the Assumption.

and that it was impossible for him to write you because the rules at La Trapa do not permit it, and he said, "Br. Rafael, since you are going to be away from the monastery for a few months, why don't you get in touch with my friend Marino? He needs like-minded friends to help him in his tribulation," he said of you. "He suffers greatly, and since I cannot write him, you ought to."

That's all, Marino, my friend—if you'll permit me to give you that title. I consented gladly to Br. Tescelino's directive, and if my prayers for you and my letters give you some consolation . . . I'll consider myself well paid.

In the world, nobody understands the feelings of affection rooted in charity and love for one's neighbor to be found in the hearts of Jesus' children.

See . . . you and I do not even know each other, and nevertheless we are very close to one another. You are suffering . . . and so am I. Finding myself at home, separated from my Trappist brothers, is a great trial that has caused me to shed many tears.

It is, then, a most obvious truth that those who truly love God also love one another.

I should like to wipe away your tears; I can tell they are truly bitter from your letters that Br. Tescelino gave me to read.

But do not lose heart in the battle; God has placed you in it . . . One cannot overcome if one does not fight . . . I speak from experience, because three years passed between the first moment I stepped into La Trapa and my decision to take the habit . . . and there was a little bit of everything.

You will suffer many attacks from the spirit of evil, who is God's enemy. When he sees a soul like yours, which wants to surrender itself entirely to God with generosity and without reserve, he redoubles his hostile efforts.

You will be tempted to despair. You will believe that God has abandoned you. You will even lose, or think you have lost, your faith . . . Is it not so? As you can see, I do not know you, and yet I can guess your moral battles rather easily.

And yet it must be a great consolation to know that you are not alone in the struggle . . . that people who desire the salvation of humanity are praying to God for you. Some do it in La Trapa, others in the world, but we all kneel down before the tabernacle, for God is the same God over all the earth, and we pray to the good Jesus for our brother Marino.

Is it not beautiful, the great miracle that is love for one's neighbor?

How we love one another, we disciples of the One who died on a Cross . . . ! For us there is neither caste nor social class nor distance nor language. There is nothing but love of God . . . that is what unites us to one another so wonderfully, and the union becomes perfect when suffering is added to that.

God loves you very much when He makes you suffer in this way . . . It is proof of the affection He has for you, and if your conversion to God is sincere, as it clearly is, you must be prepared to carry your cross.

If only you knew how easy it is to do so, when you truly love Him! He carried His cross up to Calvary for the sake of us sinners . . . and we must pay Him back somehow, right?

I too was a sinner before going to La Trapa . . . and I can promise you that tears are purifying. Suffer with pleasure . . . suffer with faith, and when you believe God has left you, that is when He is closest to you.

You will not obtain your family's conversion with human reasoning either, for it is rather weak. You cannot realize any such endeavor. That is God's business . . . Let's allow Him to do it, for perhaps because of your merits, without your even realizing it . . . in the long run, God is the one who will bring about the transformation.

God often has need of the conversion of one soul for the salvation of many . . . And it matters not what environment surrounds them. The Christian martyrs of the early church needed the circus and its beasts in order to suffer for Christ and gain heaven . . . [3]

Now, in the middle of the twentieth century, we no longer need beasts, for it is enough just to live in the world . . . in this world where the material has overpowered the spiritual, where God is forgotten as if He did not exist . . . Humanity is dominated by unleashed passions and the hatreds of men. No . . . we no longer need the beasts of Nero's circus; it is enough to offer God the sacrifice of living among people who seem to hate God, and who blaspheme His name.

And so, when we see creatures who are distant from the Gospel and do not put its teachings into practice . . . we true Christians ought to

---

3. The circus and its beasts: Under the Roman Empire, early Christians were martyred as a form of entertainment in large open areas called circuses. Rafael later alludes specifically to the circus of Nero, a site of martyrdom upon which Saint Peter's Basilica was built.

extend our bonds of friendship, helping one another in mutual, fraternal affection, consoling one another in our sorrows . . . and, in a word, loving one another as Christ taught us.

Take heart, then, my friend Marino . . . You are fighting, but you are not fighting alone. Friends of yours, people you have never even met, are helping you with great strength.

Now that you know the reason for my letter, I hope you understand my reasons for writing it . . . If you think it indiscreet, tear it up and forget it . . . I am not asking you to reply, for I have no right to do so . . . I merely offer you my loyal, impartial friendship, and whatever else you might need of me. That is all I can offer you: support as you navigate doubts and uncertainties, prayers that you might continue down the path on which you have set out . . . I make this offer in all sincerity, as it should be between brothers in Christ.

With nothing further to add, an affectionate farewell from your friend

Rafael Arnaiz

C/O Argüelles 39, no. 3 – Oviedo.

If you write me, address me by my full name to avoid confusion with my father.

45. To W. Marino del Hierro

Oviedo, August 20, 1934
Feast of Saint Bernard

My dear friend and brother in Christ,

I received your letter, for which I thank you very much, and through which I was able to glimpse your emotional state . . . and it does not surprise me in the least. What you are going through is rather natural; the world is against you, and as they say, you need to "swim against the current." A time comes when it seems that you are not strong enough to do so, and you stop, and the water pulls you under, and you lose in two minutes the distance it had taken an hour for you to swim . . . is it not so? Pardon my simile, but I do not know how else to express this, and I am sure that you will understand me.

It is so difficult to contend with absolutely everyone. Eventually we find ourselves in low spirits, and we start to think, "Maybe *they* are the ones who are right? . . . Perhaps *I* am in the wrong? . . ." We suffer . . . and as we suffer, as we find ourselves alone, perhaps we also shed tears . . . but it does not matter, for those tears are pleasing to God . . . Nor does it matter if one should lose ground, or fall time and again . . . The important thing is to get back up again and start over.

The spiritual life, the life of the Christian, is exactly that . . . we are always beginners . . . We never attain total peace, nor do we cease to offend God, at least until we leave this earth behind in death. The important thing is to reach the end . . . how often we fall is nothing to lose sleep over. In fact, it is necessary to fall, because this helps us to see our own smallness and our wretchedness, and to understand that we can never be at ease. For our passions shall never be subdued until death, and our entire lives are merely a struggle against them . . . As Jesus said, *the kingdom of God suffers violence*,[1] and when we truly love God, that violence is what we must overcome.

---

1. See Matt 11:12; Luke 16:16.

Anyway . . . what could I possibly tell you, poor wretch that I am? You ask me for wise advice . . . advice I can give you, but as for wisdom, God knows quite well that I can offer no such thing. Rather, all I can offer is my sincerest hope that you will benefit from it, and that it might console you.

In your letter, you made excessive mention of not being educated or cultured or lettered, and modesty is a good thing . . . but I myself am no Seneca, or any other Greek sage. Whatever education I have, if it does not help me get closer to God, it does not serve me well; in fact, it is useless to me . . . I was in my second year of studying to become an architect, and as soon as I realized that knowing mathematics and designing buildings would not get me to heaven, I left, taking up the hoe and potato peeler at La Trapa.

And so I left behind the false science for the true one[2] . . . In the world, people base their worth on what they know or the money they have, but God sees things differently . . . God looks at our hearts, not our minds. Therefore, do not worry if you are not a learned man, as Saint Teresa said[3] . . . it is not at all necessary, and certainly not in order to communicate with me, since I am not one either. I should not like you to see me as a person who knows a great deal or very little, to be looked up to or looked down at . . . it's all the same. We are all brothers in God's eyes, and all the more so in our case.

I am very sorry that I cannot come see you . . . but who knows. I have family in Burgos, and it is very possible that our paths will cross there someday . . . anyway, let's not make plans. God will arrange whatever is best.

Do not be afraid of telling me whatever you wish in full confidence. Of course you can count on my discretion, and if you find some relief in writing to me, do it. Though I repeat once again, the help I can offer is so meager and my prayers are so weak and poor, because I am in the same fight, believe me, and swimming against the current, like you . . . The world is rather evil, and wants nothing to do with God's friends.

2. When Rafael speaks of the kind of knowledge he came to learn at the monastery, he uses the word science (*ciencia*). The importance of science was on the rise in Spain, as the country was trying to follow the model of more industrialized countries in Europe. But Rafael was dissatisfied with that kind of knowledge. The monastery is a school where Christ is the teacher of the true science. Its method is the monastic discipline.

3. "If these learned men do not practice prayer their learning is of little help" (Saint Teresa of Ávila, *The Book of Her Life* [13.16], in *The Collected Works of Saint Teresa of Ávila*, 3 vols., trans. Kieran Kavanaugh and Otilio Rodríguez [Washington, DC: ICS Publications, 1976], 1:94).

In your letter, you told me that you are no longer going to Mass or receiving Communion . . . well, all I can tell you, and I speak from experience, is that when you are in the middle of a battle and you throw your weapons on the ground . . . For God's sake, Marino, my friend, do not lay yours down . . . Holy Mass and Communion are indispensable . . . and besides, it is so easy to go.

If you feel no fervor—it doesn't matter. If you are weak and lukewarm—it doesn't matter . . . To receive the Lord, it is enough just to be in the state of grace . . . If you fall—it doesn't matter, you get back up. If you fall again, and again, and a hundred . . . no, a thousand times over—it doesn't matter. You get back up as many times as you fall. For what merit would we have if we did not? . . .

I remember one time I got into an argument with a friend because he told me that he did not receive Communion because he found himself unworthy, because he was a great sinner . . . My friend had faith and yet he still thought that way . . . What a shame! It took a lot for me to convince him that Jesus came down here and died on a cross precisely to seek out sinners, that is, the *sheep that find themselves outside the fold,*[4] and that if we wait until we are holy before drawing close to God . . . there would be no Blessed Sacrament.

Take heart, Marino, my friend. Draw close to God and tell Him everything on your mind . . . tell Him that you do nothing but offend Him . . . tell Him that you want to love Him but you don't know how, that doubts torment you. Tell Him to forgive you, cover yourself with ashes, and hide your face in shame . . . but talk to Him . . . you don't need devotionals or prayers. You'll see, God will console you . . .

So many times, so many, I have been through exactly what you are going through . . . and I drew close to God who is so good, and I told Him everything. Then when I left church, the world seemed completely different to me; I knew that I was a wretch and a sinner, but I knew that God loved me, a sinner, warts and all . . . God had heard me; my prayer had been unfeeling, for I wanted to love Him and did not know how . . . but God looked at me and saw only a worthy desire, and I looked at Him and saw a Father who forgives all his son's faults and all his sins, no matter how horrible they might be . . .

4. See John 10:16.

Is not all this consoling?. . . Is it not true that if we are not good, it is because we do not want to be?. . . What does it matter if the world laughs?. . . Let them laugh. Someday, in the Valley of Jehoshaphat,[5] where we shall all be judged, we shall see laughter turned into tears, and the tears of sinners shall be turned into eternal joy.[6]

Cry, Marino, my friend . . . cry as much as you want, for not a single tear is wasted when God is the cause.

Regarding your doubts toward the faith, and the belief that nothing exists, have no fear . . . this is all part of the purification of your spirit . . . All the great converts went through the same thing. . . and *blessed are those who have not seen and yet have come to believe.*[7]

Thank you so much for the photographs. I'll return them in my next letter, along with some of my own so that you can see what I look like . . . although I am a very different person now from who I was a year before entering the convent.

I am waiting on a letter from La Trapa, and I still do not know if Br. Tescelino knows that I got in touch with you . . . If you write him, send him my regards.

There are so many things I'd tell you, if I knew how to express them in a letter . . . Let us be satisfied with writing for now, but who knows . . . God uses all manner of things to console us, and so we can say nothing as to whether we might meet face to face someday.

I hope that in the next letter I receive from you, you will tell me that you have put things right with God, and that you have gone to Communion . . . Will you do this? From here, I am asking the Blessed Virgin to help you with all this . . . and I believe that She will hear my prayer.

Think on your brothers, the Trappists, who carry out their sacrificial life for the salvation of souls, and how Br. Tescelino is helping you from there . . . Anyway, I wanted to share all the faith and confidence I have in God with you . . . but these things cannot be communicated in words, let alone in words as poor as mine . . . But good will makes up for whatever is lacking in reason and conversation, right?

---

5. Joel 3:2: *I will gather all the nations and bring them down to the valley of Jehoshaphat, and I will enter into judgment with them there.*

6. See Luke 6:21, 25; Rev 21:4.

7. John 20:29.

Marino, my friend: how great God is!! . . . How well He does everything, even when, with our weak human reason, we do not understand Him.

In this admirable symphony of creation, no detail is missing. When you believe that God has abandoned you or does not exist . . . lift your eyes to heaven, and do not look around at your fellow creatures, but rather recognize your littleness before the Creator and exclaim . . . "Who am I, a miserable creature, to desire to understand God? Why does my reason insist on grasping at what it cannot fathom?"

Let us close our eyes and, alone with our consciences and without letting in any noise from this world, let us prostrate ourselves before the great Lord, whose mysteries we cannot understand with our human reason . . . precisely because we are humans and He is . . . God.

Well, perhaps I digress. Forgive me. It is just that for a Trappist, his whole life is reduced to a single word, God, and there is nothing outside of Him . . . The Trappist wants everyone to love God and to live in Him, and for all the nations to prostrate themselves before the altar . . . That is why he gets worked up when he speaks of God . . . Forgive me, but I want your heart to beat in unison with my own, for it to raise its voice above the misfortunes and sorrows and doubts, all the miseries and sins of this world, and let out an immense clamor of love for God . . . Someday, if God wills it, at La Trapa, you and I shall be in even closer communion . . . I certainly hope so . . .

What you must do is not be discouraged, and trust in Him, because He will put everything right. And then perhaps one day you will be able to see "my Trapa," as you said in your letter, and call it your own too.

I do not wish to exhaust you any longer. Once more, I shall remind you that you can count on my discretion regarding everything you write me, and that you may see me as a true brother in whom to confide your sorrows.

Do you have a confessor? . . . Once you are settled somewhere, it is essential.

This is all for now; peace be with your spirit. An affectionate greeting from your friend and brother in Jesus and Mary,

Rafael Arnaiz Barón

C/O Argüelles, 39 – no. 3 – Oviedo

46. To W. Marino del Hierro

Oviedo, September 2, 1934

My dear brother in Christ,

I received your letter with great joy, for in it I can see God's immense grace with respect to your soul, without you even realizing how much.

I was in Burgos a few days ago with my father, who had some business to deal with there, and the other day I was in Santander, but for just a few hours. If I had known your address, I would have gladly come by to greet you . . . Another time.

Do not overanalyze my letters, because sometimes my ideas are a bit mixed up and you might glean something I did not mean to say . . . Just see good will in them.

Tell me when you are going to Burgos. I have good friends there who might be able to help you with anything you might need, and it's possible that I might go and spend some time there myself. Perhaps we'll end up there at the same time, and we could talk there, because really . . . it's so hard to express what one feels in a letter . . . don't you think? . . .

All I can say is that when I am with the Lord in Communion, I remember you and ask Him to give you enough strength and grace to bear your bitter sorrows. I do not ask Him to take them away from you, for when He sends them it is because He believes them necessary for our salvation and sanctification, and it is evidently true that we are not tested beyond what we can bear . . . Even those anxieties of suicide, when it seems like everything goes dark and the eyes of the soul cannot see God's light . . . those thoughts, I mean . . . they'd be dangerous in someone else . . . but not in you. Even though I don't know you quite well enough to say so, I think I can say that God is helping you through very effectively.

How beautiful faith is! . . . When it seems that a dark veil has been lowered over our eyes, we can know without a doubt that God is on the other side of it . . . What does it matter if we can see Him or not? What matters is knowing that He is there. *Blessed are those who have not seen and yet have come to believe.*[1]

But it's not enough to believe . . . we must love. And by your letters, my friend Marino, I can plainly see that you love Him . . . but we must do even more than this . . . We must love Him above all things. And how hard that is! Only the saints achieved that, but then, the saints were human beings like us . . . Why, then, should we not achieve that too? What one person does with the grace of God, another can do too, with that same grace of God . . . This must be our one and only, unchanging aspiration. Once we have achieved it, we shall have neither sorrows nor joys, nor shall we be here nor there . . . it will all be the same to us, for *everything* will be God, and we shall love Him more than we do anyone else, and our very being and feeling shall all disappear before Him.

Let us not seek the consolation of men, when God alone can satisfy us entirely. Our sorrows shall disappear, for when we cease to think of ourselves, we shall be less selfish, and our heart, body, and lips will all speak only one word . . . God.

But unfortunately that is not how we are. We are not saints, far from it; we worry about ourselves too much. We want a God who will comfort us and make our lives easy, and when God tests us a bit, we rebel against Him, not understanding that what God wants from us is not discipline and mortifications we choose ourselves, but rather for us to do His will even when it is difficult. And the more difficult it is, the more tears we shed, the better . . .

Marino, do not despair, my friend. When your sorrows make you cry, and the bitter grief of this life upsets you greatly, think about how it is not worth it to shed even a single tear over not being happy on this earth . . . Try not to think about yourself, for we are mere maggots, made of clay and full of misery . . . Treat your body austerely, and pay no mind to the suffering of your spirit . . . Think of nothing but God, and as you say so well in your letter, "only You and everything for You" . . .

If the ground falls out from under you, then it falls. If humanity treats you worse than a dog . . . what does it matter? Do you deserve better? . . . If you have neither health nor wellbeing, but instead only sorrows,

1. John 20:29.

and you do nothing but cry . . . what does all that matter when you have God? . . .

And you'll say to me, "What about my past life? And all my horrible sins?" And I say to you . . . your past life *is past*, and your sins have been forgiven you, and if it's true that you have truly found God, your joy at knowing Him should be greater than your sorrow for having gone so long not knowing Him. And if it is good to cry for your sins and your ingratitude, it is also *necessary* to sing songs of joy at discovering, knowing, and loving a God like ours.

As such, forget yourself. Your time on this earth is short; your tears will not last forever, and above all your afflictions are God and the Blessed Virgin, who watch over you.

What else can I say to you? . . . Nothing. Someday soon, when we are at rest in the Lord, we shall see that all these activities and worries that kept us busy down here below were natural and human, because we are people after all, but seen rightly, none of it was worth thinking about, and all the time we spent thinking about ourselves was time wasted, time that we should have devoted to God.

Pardon my sermon, I might be a bit annoying, but you'll forgive me. And if my letters offer you any consolation, however little, then I will continue to send them as long it is in my power to do so.

Keep going to Communion often, and don't stop praying the Holy Rosary to the Blessed Virgin, and praying for me from time to time. I need your prayers a lot, because it's true what they say, it's one thing to preach and another thing to practice.

Don't let anything or anyone discourage you, and open up your heart, as I suppose you already have, to your confessor and spiritual director, but above all, remember what I said in my last letter . . . everything you experience, everything you think: tell the Lord about it. And when you are tempted, turn to the Virgin, for Our Lady will never desert you.

I am returning the photos you sent me, and sending one of my own (I couldn't find any more). It's from last year, when I served in Madrid, so I am in uniform as a "sapper-engineer."[2]

2. Rafael served in the Regiment of Sappers and Miners, or combat engineers (see #34, n. 2).

Has Br. Tescelino written to you?

When you write him, give him my regards. Don't stop writing me as much as you want and about whatever you wish, for in me you have a brother in Jesus and Mary. A big hug,

Rafael Arnaiz

I have taken the liberty of keeping one of the photos you sent. I have some negatives on hand to develop, which I will then send you.

47. To Fr. Vicente Pardo Feliú[1]

Oviedo, September 3, 1934

Dear Fr. Vicente,

I should have written you days ago to send you the books I promised. Forgive the delay, which was due to my being away from Oviedo; besides, I had to order the books from Madrid, because they were not available here.

Mr. Laredo, my doctor,[2] would gladly lend you whatever you need, but I thought it preferable for the books to belong to the infirmary's library, so I've bought them instead. Sound good to you? . . . Well, whether it sounds good to you or not, it's done.

You'll receive three thick volumes in the mail, chock full of horrible illnesses, and in a few days, another one that hasn't arrived yet: *Caring for the Mentally Ill* by Valenciano.[3] The doctor told me that it's specifically addressed to nurses, and should interest an infirmarian. Along with that, I'm also sending you Father Laburu's Lenten conferences.[4] Tell me if you find them useful and if these are the ones you had wanted to read, and I beg you to tell me if you need anything else, whatever it may be. My father and I are both entirely at your service . . . and above all, I cannot easily forget my good Father Infirmarian.

Regarding my illness, I'll tell you that I'm continuing to improve at a rapid pace. I've been taking two and a half units of insulin, which is hardly any at all, and starting today I won't take anything at all; my sugar

---

1. Fr. Vicente Pardo Feliú: the infirmarian at San Isidro (see #35, n. 7).

2. Mr. Laredo: The Arnaiz-Barón family doctor, until his death in the Spanish Civil War (OC 315).

3. Luis Valenciano Gayá, *La asistencia al enfermo mental* (Madrid: Publ. de Archivos de Neurobiología, 1933). This manual was specifically addressed to psychiatric nurses.

4. Father José Antonio Laburu Olascoaga, S.J. (1887–1972) was a psychologist, Jesuit priest, and author of both religious and medical texts. The book Rafael cites here is *¿Jesucristo es Dios? conferencias cuaresmales* (Madrid: Ediciones «Fax», 1933).

levels have dropped to zero, and soon I'll start that starch diet. Everything is going exactly as you told me it would, though I can't wait to put my novice's cape back on. It shall be when God wishes, though I continue to beg the Virgin to make me healthy soon; I suppose you pray for this too from time to time.

I imagine that Father Marcelo will have received a letter from me,[5] and if you see him, give him my regards and tell him I'll write him again one of these days. My father wants some Masses said for the soul of an elderly aunt of mine who passed away a few days ago.[6]

Give Br. Tescelino a hug for me, my affectionate greetings to Reverend Father Abbot, and all my love to you as your brother who asks your blessing,

Rafael

C/O Argüelles 39, no. 3 – Oviedo

5. This would be the letter of August 11, 1934, #42.

6. Rafael's great-aunt, Petra Sánchez de la Campa Tasquer (see #43, n. 4).

48. To Fr. Francisco Díez Martínez[1]

Oviedo, September 15, 1934

My dear Fr. Francisco,

I received your card, for which I greatly thank you. You cannot imagine the consolation I receive in knowing that people who are so beloved to me, as all of you are, remember their poor brother Rafael, who might need some bodily care, but needs your prayers all the more.

You spoke of my constancy in my vocation, and I'll tell you this, Father Francisco: my vocation is increasingly steadfast and sure, and with every day that goes by I am more and more convinced that my place is in La Trapa . . . I think of nothing else, and if I long for health, it is so that I might return to my beloved Trapa. I can assure you that my confidence in God is such that I am *sure* that I will once more take up my honorable office as an altar server, which I liked so much.[2]

I am getting better every day, and according to the doctor, I am now cured of my diabetes. For many days now I haven't been taking any medication at all, and now the only thing I am focused on is getting used to the monastic diet again, little by little . . . The other day I ate a great big plate of white beans, and when I did the analysis afterwards, there wasn't any sugar in my urine at all. On Monday I'll repeat this test, and at first it'll just be once a week, but then twice a week, and so on, slowly by slowly getting my body back to its normal state . . . Have no doubt that it will, for the Blessed Virgin's help is very effective.

Please keep praying to Saint Thérèse for your novice, that I will return to you soon, and leave the world behind for good. It is full of dangers that, even as God upholds me, I cannot dismiss—and great ones indeed.

---

1. Fr. Francisco Díez Martínez was the sub-master, or assistant to the master of novices, at San Isidro.

2. Altar server: see #33.

If you could see how much I miss the silence of La Trapa! That silence among men, that silence that draws us so close to God . . . ! Here, it is the opposite . . . they talk a lot about everything but speak very little of God; nothing to be done about that, and I offer it all to Him. When I was in La Trapa, I offered Him my silence and all the austerities of the Rule;[3] here in the world, I offer Him my secular life and my interactions with people and all the consequences thereof. . . That's how God wants it, so that's how it should be. But I promise you, what I'm offering Him now is much harder for me than the entire Rule of Saint Benedict observed with maximum severity.

I can't tell you anything happening here that would interest you. On the contrary, it's as if you and I lived on different planets. What happens on mine cannot interest you, but everything that happens on yours interests me greatly.

I am and continue to be Trappist, though not on the outside; on the inside I've got a habit on and everything . . . How I long to put it back on and never take it off again. May I be buried in it, so that one day, when God calls me forth to His presence, I can present myself to Him wearing the monastic cowl. That is my only goal, my only aspiration; and as you can see, it is a rather simple one.

Many people, upon learning of my firm decision to return to La Trapa, some admire me for it and others think I'm crazy . . . But God, who knows all things, correctly sees that neither is correct. I am neither a hero, as many people think I am, nor a man who has lost his mind . . . But rather, all that is happening is that I have simply put my hand to the plow . . . and I don't want to look back.[4] And if I were to turn back now that recovery is in sight, I could never be forgiven . . . nor could I even think to do such a thing.

I know I must take up the fight once more, and perhaps with even greater intensity than before . . . I know that very bitter days lie ahead for me . . . I know that the cross lies ahead . . . But what about God? . . . And my salvation? . . . I am not going to stop following the call of the

3. The Rule: The Rule of Saint Benedict (see #7, n. 2).

4. Luke 9:62: *Jesus said to him, "No one who puts a hand to the plow and looks back is fit for the kingdom of God."*

One who died for us sinners . . . All that is what people don't understand, but I don't care. There is a barrier between the world and my soul . . . In that barrier, darkness reigns . . . Oh, Father Francisco, there are so many things I'd like to tell you about what is happening in my soul, but I don't know how to express them . . . But you, a Trappist, can understand me perfectly without needing me to explain anything.

Anyway . . . let everyone follow their own path . . . but mine is clear.

The other day I sent Father Vicente a letter and five books, I don't know if he'll have received them by now.[5] Ask him, just in case you need to file a claim with the post office. I have nothing else in particular to tell you.

I'll write to my beloved co-novices another day; give them my regards. The same to Reverend Father Abbot and Father Master.[6] A big hug from your novice, who entrusts himself to your prayers,

Brother M. Rafael

I'm sending you two photos I have. I took them before I entered La Trapa, so I have a mustache, which I don't now, but I imagine it's all the same to you. In these photos I was in the tallest building in Madrid, and I took them just days before leaving the Spanish capital forever.

I also promised a few to Fr. Buenaventura,[7] and I'll send him some another day, along with a long letter. Please tell him so for me (if it is permitted).

---

5. Father Vicente: the infirmarian at San Isidro. Rafael is referring to the letter of September 3, 1934 (see #47).

6. Reverend Father Abbot and Father Master: Dom Félix Alonso García (see #5) and Fr. Marcelo León (see #12, n. 3).

7. Fr. Buenaventura Ramos Caballero (see #42, n. 6).

49. *To Rosa Calvo*[1]

Oviedo, September 15, 1934

My dear Aunt Rosa,

For a long time now, I've been thinking of writing you. Now that I happen to be away from my beloved monastery, I have taken up my pen to write you just a quick note, telling you that I have not forgotten about my dear Rosica, whom I imagine, as always, praising God every time she presses a stamp onto a lottery ticket.

First of all, I'll give you the news about Merceditas, whose health, thank God, continues to improve, however slowly . . . She is eating well, though not enthusiastically. According to the doctor, it'll all be easily resolved.

As for the other one . . . the novice, I'll say that he's almost entirely recovered; he can eat everything again, and he's off the medication. I think he'll be back in his white habit soon, returning to his life at La Trapa.

Dear Aunt Rosa, if you knew how much I desire it . . . Sometimes I think having such a strong desire is not very perfect of me . . . but once you have tasted the sweetness and gentleness of the Lord, nothing else pleases you . . . Is it not so? If only you knew how much He loves me . . . This illness He sent me is proof of it. Both when I was at death's door and now that I have a new lease on life, I have never ceased to give Him thanks for everything.

There are so many things I'd tell you about La Trapa if I were in Toro . . . In Toro, where my greatest pleasure was to talk of pious things at the lottery, remember? . . . From time to time, before the tabernacle at La Trapa, I'd think of the administrator there, in that lottery building painted yellow on the outside, with very few *pesetas* inside . . . but a whole lot of love for God.

---

1. Rosa Calvo was a family friend and a lottery administrator in Toro (see #8, n. 1).

You see how everything finds its way, even when it seems impossible, but nothing is impossible for God.[2] Do you remember that dandy little boy who came to Toro one day with his uncle Polín? Well, even though you might imagine me in white sackcloth with a shaved head, I'm still that same little boy, and I suspect I haven't changed much to you.

I don't know if we'll see each other one of these days . . . God knows. But someday, in heaven, at the Virgin's side, we'll resume our chats about God. What are earthly things to us, right? Despite being separated by distance, we are united in the tabernacle, for Jesus in the Blessed Sacrament is the same in La Colegiata of Toro[3] as He is in La Trapa of Venta de Baños. Don't forget to pray for me before Him from time to time . . . I do the same for you . . . That He might send you sorrows and afflictions . . . disillusionment . . . in a word, that He might send you your cross . . . As you can see, I love you in the Trappist style: if love for God unites us creatures, carrying the cross the Lord carried unites us to Him, which is what should matter to us . . . And when we suffer everything with love, charity, and joy . . . then what more could we desire or ask for? Nothing, Aunt Rosa . . . nothing. If we were as we ought to be, we wouldn't ask Him even for that . . . It would all be cut away, leaving only the fulfillment of His divine will.

Well, pardon my sermon. Despite being away from my convent, my inner Trappist almost always comes out, even when I don't mean for it to.

I'm sending you two photos of myself from before I went to La Trapa. I'm sending you them not because my humble personage holds any interest for you, but rather so that you can put them in your books, and whenever you come across them you can say this to the Lord: "Lord, you see this ridiculous-looking man with that mustache, who left everything behind to follow you up to the summit of Calvary? Well, I won't tell you to listen to him, because he doesn't deserve it. But Lord, do pity him from time to time." If you were to say that to the Lord just once, Aunt Rosa, I'd be happy with that.

2. Luke 1:37.

3. La Colegiata: La Colegiata Santa María la Mayor ("the Collegiate Church of Saint Mary the Great") is a twelfth-century church in Toro, a few blocks from where Rosa Calvo worked at the lottery.

I won't tell you to write me, because I know your eyes cause you a lot of trouble . . . You don't owe me a thing, and I've only written you because I felt inspired to, that's all.

Tell my grandmother and Aunt María that I'll write them another day and give them the latest news about Merceditas . . . That poor girl, the Lord loves her very much too . . . but then, whom does He not love? . . . It seems impossible that we should remain in the dark about that, and go about our lives occupied and busy with so many things, and all the while we have forgotten about such a good God.

I'm telling you: after spending time at a Trappist monastery, where everything is centered around Jesus and Our Lady, in community life with men who have forgotten the world and its miseries, whose only occupation is to become saints . . . After adjusting to their way of life, fighting alongside them on the harsh path of the Rule of Saint Benedict (well, that bit about its being "harsh" is just an expression, I didn't think it was that hard) . . . As I've told you, after realizing that in a Trappist monastery absolutely everything is focused on the greater glory of God . . . After all this, realizing that the world is so indifferent to the Master's concerns . . . It makes me sad, Aunt Rosa, to see people be so blind.

But there's nothing to be done about that . . . I don't think people are bad. I love them all, and I suffer to see humanity suffer when the cure for all their sorrows is so near . . . All they have to do is look up a bit. How many tears would dry and how many sorrows would be consoled when they see Jesus . . . but instead, all we see is . . . people's hatred for one another, all of them or nearly all of them busy with wicked and petty matters, never lifting their eyes to God. It is as if He did not exist to them, and as if He were not going to judge them someday . . . How sad! Must one be a Trappist to understand this? No . . . one need not be a Trappist to shed tears for all humanity . . . Perhaps the Trappist sees it all more clearly, as I do now . . . But just a bit of divine light is enough to make the scales fall from your eyes, and make you realize that great darkness reigns over this world . . . You see that, right, Aunt Rosa? . . . Anyway, I don't know why I'm telling you all this . . . Maybe because I carry it all deep inside me, and if it's true that we love God, it must make us sad to see that so many people don't even know Him.

That is the apostolate of the Trappist, to pray for those who do not pray, and to love God because they do not love Him; if anyone tells you that religious are selfish, that all they think about is their own salvation . . .

you tell them that you know a Trappist who asks for nothing for himself in prayer, and who has dedicated his life to God in order to make reparation for all the offenses that people commit against Him.

Well, Aunt Rosa, I don't want to annoy you. May God so desire to take me back to La Trapa soon, so that I can take up my plow again, and there, in silence, without the world noticing, keep praying for everyone, and for that lottery administrator in Toro, that *poor woman* you know, with the white hair and the bad eyesight and quite a few years behind her and . . . with quite a bit of love for God, I think.

All my love, your brother,[4]

Rafael

4. That is, "your brother in Christ." Though Rafael affectionately called Rosa Calvo his aunt, the two were not related.

50. To W. Marino del Hierro

Oviedo, September 18, 1934

My dear friend and brother Marino,

When I received your last letter, it was impossible for me to write you back at Santander without your address, so I sent a card to your house asking after your address in Burgos.

Now that I have it, I'm writing you, although in truth I have little to tell you that you do not already know, but if my letters cheer you up, then blessed be God, who uses an insignificant thing like me to cheer up that heart of yours that evidently suffers so much.

You told me in your letter that you do not repay the grace God gives you, even though you know Jesus loves you, and that you don't reciprocate that love either . . . And now, Marino, my friend, I ask you . . . who among creatures truly returns unto God all His benefits? What soul loves God with all its might and in the same measure that God loves us? . . . We human beings are so stingy that we find it difficult to love God even a little bit.

But don't you worry, one thing is certain: wanting to love God is loving Him. And it's also true that if it is a special *grace* to know that God loves us . . . it is just as much a grace from God to recognize our own misery and weakness, how often we fall and fall again into sin . . .

Last, it's a grace from God to know, as you know quite well, that God loves you very much, even if you don't reciprocate . . . that God loves you despite all your failings, despite your sins, despite you not loving Him back . . . You know all that perfectly well, it's evident from your letters . . . and all that, Marino, my friend, is a very great grace from God.

You asked me to give you an honest answer on this matter . . . and I am nobody, and I hardly have any experience, but I dare to speak to you this way because this is how I think . . . perhaps I am wrong, but who isn't wrong from time to time?

The other day, after going to Confession . . . I usually read the seven penitential psalms,[1] which I recommend you do as well, and when I got to Psalm 51, I thought of my brother Marino . . . The verse says: *The sacrifice acceptable to God is a broken spirit; a broken and contrite heart, O God, you will not despise* . . .[2] King David's words are so beautiful, and so consoling . . . !

As such, what is most pleasing to God is not any great penance or arduous austerity . . . or even ecstasies of divine love . . . What is most pleasing to God is a contrite heart . . . and from your letters, my brother Marino, I can tell that you have one.

Therefore, do not desire to do great things, and envy no one; perhaps someone you think is closer to God than you are . . . is in fact further away. Sometimes appearances can be deceiving, and you'll say, "I wish I were like so-and-so . . . they *really* love God . . ." but then, as I said, that's not at all the case.

Be content to be what you are . . . of course wanting to love God more is a great virtue, but falling into despair and despondency when we do not get where we want to go is not virtue . . .

Leave it all to God, then, and He will take care of leading you wherever He pleases. Meanwhile, I envy your "spirit of compunction" . . . Weep for your sins, consider yourself the most vile and despicable of men, and be ashamed of your misery and all your weaknesses before God; for in considering yourself despicable, and humbling your heart before Jesus, have no doubt that you are offering the most pleasing of sacrifices, as King David says.

Forgive me for resorting to citing sacred texts. On my own I know nothing, but we can always find balm for our wounds in the Sacred Scriptures . . . I read them often, and when we read the divine Word there, it seems as if everything quiets down, and we have greater peace of spirit . . . Don't stop reading them, and very often; don't ever stop. If we had true faith, that would be the only book we'd ever have close at hand.

---

1. The seven penitential psalms: Pss 6, 32, 38, 51, 102, 130, and 143 are often prayed together as an expression of repentance.
2. Ps 51:17.

On the one hand, I'm glad that Br. Tescelino is with you, though on the other I feel bad for him, because I know what it is to leave La Trapa, even if only for a few days . . . Give him a big hug for me, and I hope we will be reunited in our monastery soon . . . whenever God wants.

You said in your letter that you want to be in Burgos already, because there you will devote yourself to thinking about God more frequently . . . I'll pray that it be so.

Now you will be able to devote yourself to talking about God very frequently. That's what Br. Tescelino is for, and I imagine he's quite good at it . . . I'd enjoy receiving a letter from him so much . . . You could say I hardly know him, for we've only spoken a couple of times . . . But it's as if I knew him my whole life, because he's a Trappist, and something unites us Trappists to one another . . . I'm sure Brother can explain it to you.

I hope your appendicitis operation goes well. It's not dangerous, and I trust that the Lord will make it turn out well.

I have nothing else to tell you, my friend Marino. Write me when you'd like, for I always receive your letters with true joy . . . Talk to me about God, about the Blessed Virgin . . . it is so sweet and so consoling to talk about Him . . . always Him.

I continue to get much better from my illness. It's slow and steady, but my recovery, relying on Mary's protection as I always do, is a sure thing . . . I have no desire for health except insofar as it will allow me to return to my beloved Trapa forever, and I know that God wants me there . . . This illness He sent me, though it may seem to be the opposite, is proof of that, because if I had a vocation before . . . now it has grown even stronger. When the Lord provides a vocation like mine, even if He places obstacles in its path, He always provides a way to keep moving forward. All one must do is never lose faith in Him, and obey His holy will.

I don't know when I'll be in Burgos . . . When are you going to do your military service? What about Br. Tescelino?

If you need anything, I have an uncle there, one of my mother's brothers. He is very good and very Christian, and he lives in Burgos, and I do not doubt he would assist you with anything you needed. His name is Álvaro Barón and he lives at Aparicio Ruiz 18; I don't remember which floor.

Take heart, then, my friend Marino, and don't let anything or anyone discourage you . . . God sees you, God loves you, and God will help you with everything. . . . Pray a lot to the Virgin, for it is through that Blessed Lady's intercession that we receive all that we have. It is rare that I do not remember you at Holy Communion . . . I hope you pray for me too, because I need it a lot. . . more than most.

I'm sending you a photo I found from before I entered La Trapa. I'm wearing street clothes, and I'm at the top of the Capitol Cinema Building in Madrid, on the terrace.[3] If you send me one back, send me a small one, so I can keep it in a book . . . I like to keep photos in my devotionals . . . I'd be grateful.

That is all; I await your reply. A big hug from your friend and brother in Christ,

Rafael

---

3. Capitol Cinema Building: Also known as the Carrión Building, the Capitol Cinema is across the street from the boarding house where Rafael lived on Plaza de Callao in Madrid (see #9, n. 1).

51. The Trappist's Apologia[1]

Oviedo, September 19, 1934

God before all else.

With the aid of the Blessed Virgin, to whom I commend myself before beginning this notebook, and with the help of the Holy Spirit, who I hope will enlighten me and prevent me from falling into any error contrary to the Holy, Roman, Catholic, and Apostolic Faith.

I am writing for two reasons: first, because I believe that writing and thinking about the things of God greatly profits my soul, and delights my spirit, which rejoices at the mention of God, and second, because I have time at my disposal, and so I ought to use it in a way that serves the greater glory of God.

If someone should read these lines someday, I ask the reader only for great charity . . . Do not take them for doctrine or teachings, for I attempt no such thing. I write only what I think, what comes to mind, and in a simple way, with no literary aims . . . In these pages I am studying my own soul and my impressions, with no determined plan or set order . . . As such, I repeat, if some curious person should read them (as I will ensure that no one does), I ask for nothing more than that . . . *charity*; that is, a benevolent spirit and understanding. If at any point these pages bring a smile to the reader's lips, may that reader see here only a person who says what he is feeling, even if he might say foolish things sometimes.

I am a Trappist, and I feel, see, and think like a Trappist . . . Trappists are nothing out of the ordinary . . . not exceptional or strange in the least. Trappists are above all human beings just like anyone else, created by God like anyone else . . . Each has their own misfortunes and weaknesses, a

---

1. This title is not original to the manuscript, but was added by Rafael's confessor and biographer, Fr. Teófilo Sandoval Fernández. Rafael wrote this manuscript between September 19 and October 5, 1934 (OC 329).

body to contend with and a soul to save . . . That's all . . . God demands of them a few things that are simple and *pleasant* to carry out here on earth.

First among them is that the Trappist ought not desire anything but what God desires. He must be the Trappist's only occupation, only desire, only love and occupation . . . Trappists must be filled with the Spirit of God, and all their actions in this life must be oriented toward Him alone and His greater glory, and done in His name.

Apparently, the Trappist's occupation is quite simple. It requires no great study or preparation. No exceptional qualities are needed, contrary to popular belief. No need to force it, or cause any harm to oneself . . . One need only "love God above all things,"[2] and that is so pleasant, so sweet, that one might say that the Trappist's occupation on earth is the most *pleasant* of all occupations, the most *divine*, the most *useful* if I can employ such a word . . . When people ask me, "Tell me, what do you do in La Trapa?" . . . Many times I have wanted to answer, "Well, it's pretty simple . . . love God and let ourselves be loved by Him, that's all . . ." But the Trappist's occupation in the monastery goes unnoticed by the world, because the world is too busy with other things to understand that . . . The world looks at a Trappist and just sees someone who doesn't bathe and doesn't eat anything but bread and beans and doesn't ever talk . . . And of course, seen from that perspective alone, it is *odd*.

The other day I came across an old schoolmate of mine, a good kid and a good Christian. Naturally, we started talking about La Trapa, and I told him that when I was entirely recovered I'd be going back there, returning to my monastery . . . Well, without trying to offend me, far be it from him to do such a thing, he did call me selfish and half suicidal, and on top of all that, dirty. It didn't offend me, because I understand that he is in the world . . . and that's how the world is, it sees only what is external, what is counter to its own ways: an indulgent, comfortable life, eating well, talking and singing and listening to music, washing and bathing . . . In short, whatever pertains to the body . . . Meanwhile, for a Trappist, the body is just a bit of clay not worth paying any attention to . . . it gets in their way, so they treat it poorly and master it . . . What does the body matter?! . . . But the soul, on the other hand, they make sure to keep spotless and sparkling, free of the mud of human appetites, utterly tranquil . . . resting in God and singing to the

<hr />

2. See Deut 6:5; Matt 22:37; Mark 12:30; Luke 10:27.

Virgin . . . and the world doesn't see that because it cannot, because it doesn't care, because . . . that's how it is . . . it's the world.

It is plain to see, then, that love for God is incompatible with the spirit of the world. As such, when I hear it said that serving God in the cloister is the same as serving Him in the world, I cannot help but smile, because I can clearly see that the world is an enemy of God. You can't make a deal with an enemy of God, no matter how trivial, or grant any concession, because if you concede just this one thing, soon enough it'll be two, and then three, and then all of a sudden we're completely overtaken.

The spirit of the world creeps in everywhere. Without even realizing it, it infiltrates families and dominates society, judgments and opinions, ideas, even the way we see God . . . It even gets into convents. Thus, its characteristic subtlety is what makes it dangerous.

One often sees very holy people nevertheless ruled, in part, by the world . . . it can even be seen in sermons and in preaching, in laity and religious alike . . . and those who let themselves be influenced by it . . . don't even realize it.

No, serving God in the cloister is not the same as serving Him in the world . . . Serving Him in the world is much harder. Hence the immediate question: "Am I a coward? . . . I am fleeing from it." Maybe it's cowardice, but I figure when we come across an enormous boulder that stands in our way, it's a mark of good sense to jump over it rather than waste time and energy trying to get it out of the way with drills or crowbars . . . It's better, and more *certain*, to put yourself in God's hands, get a running start, and jump on over, rather than to fight the obstacle tooth and nail. We run the risk of destroying our hands and ending up getting hurt in the process.

Another thing: when they tell me that you can be saved here just as you can be saved there . . . of course your soul can be saved anyplace, because God's help is everywhere, and so long as we desire to serve Him with all our strength, place and position and circumstance are all irrelevant.

But I say that if the young man who drew near to Jesus to follow Him had not been frightened away by needing to "jump" over his parents and his fortune, and had made the decision and had the courage to jump . . . surely Jesus would not have been so sad.[3] And so, if some people think

3. See Matt 19:19-22; Mark 10:17-22; Luke 18:18-23.

it is cowardice to leave behind the world and all its creatures to follow Jesus, sometimes it is also cowardice, and a much greater one, to lack the courage to jump.

On the other hand, I know from experience that renouncing everything is no easy thing . . . I understand the doubts of that young man who did not follow Jesus because he was rich very well . . . surely he was not happy with all his wealth after the answer he received from Jesus of Nazareth. Who knows if his wealth later became an obstacle to his salvation . . . When he found himself without the strength to leave it all behind, his distress must have been terrible . . . When He saw that this young man would not give his heart over to Him fully, all because of a fistful of wretched, ephemeral riches, the Lord's smile must have been very bitter.

Do not judge, therefore, O world! someone who, for the love of God and the salvation of his soul, is leaving you behind and abandoning you . . . What do you have to offer? . . . Misery, lies, vanities, everything false and fleeting. Meanwhile, what does He have to give me? Oh, you don't understand what our good Jesus gives me . . . Jesus gives me *everything*, for He gives me His Heart, and He counts me among His guests at the great banquet; therefore, let me follow Him . . . and don't get in my way, because I'll jump over you as many times as I have to . . . and if God doesn't give me the strength to jump, I'll fight you with my own hands and feet . . . You are God's enemy, and thus you are also mine.

God has taken me out of my Trapa in order to have me fight against you . . . and so I will fight; God commands it, and so it shall be.

You've beaten me from time to time, but I am not discouraged; defeat makes triumph sweeter . . . I am weak and miserable, but I have a champion on my side who is not on yours: the Blessed Virgin Mary . . . At Her side, I will advance as far as God wishes me to go, and while you could defeat me, you don't stand a chance against Her . . . She is invincible. She will thwart your worldly spirit, and everything you offer me fades away, becoming insignificant when the Blessed Virgin Mary turns Her gaze toward me . . . and I know that She loves me very much.

But, in short . . . what is the world and what are its dangers? The English writer, Father Faber, defines it admirably in his book *The Creator and the Creature* and truly, profoundly, impresses upon his reader's soul what the world really is:

There is a hell already upon the earth; there is something which is excommunicated from God's smile. It is not altogether matter, nor yet altogether spirit. It is not man only, nor Satan only, nor is it exactly sin. It is an infection, an inspiration, an atmosphere, a life, a colouring matter, a pageantry, a fashion, a taste, a witchery, an impersonal but a very recognizable system. None of these names suit it, and yet all of them suit it. Scripture calls it, "The World." God's mercy does not enter into it. . . .

We are living in it, breathing it, acting under its influences, being cheated by its appearances, and unwarily admitting its principles. . . .

It has its gentle voice, its winning manners, its insinuating address, its aspect of beauty and attraction. . . . It can be dignified as well. It can call to order sin which is not respectable. It can propound wise maxims of public decency, and inspire wholesome regulations of police. . . .

Or there again it is, with high principles on its lips, discussing the religious vocation of some youth, and praising God and sanctity, while it urges discreet delay, and less self-trust.[4]

Thus Father Faber speaks in his book, in his chapter on the world . . . There is a lot to savor in what he says, but still, there comes a point where I am no longer in agreement with him. When he talks about how we true Christians ought to view the world, he says there are two ways of looking at it. The first is in a somber fashion: everything is bad and sinful, it's all dangerous, everything is sad and condemned . . . He talks about a funeral on a wet day as a representation of the state of those who look at the world this way.[5]

The other view is the exact opposite. He calls Saint Bernard the prophet of the first view, and Saint Francis de Sales the prophet of the second, and he supposes that monks are gloomy and dark, lacking for joy . . . He considers that way of thinking about the world necessary to be a contemplative

---

4. Frederick William Faber, *The Creator and the Creature; Or the Wonders of Divine Love* (London: T. Richardson and Son, 1857), 372–73.

5. "Let us live as ancient monarchs lived, in daily fear of poison in every dish. A funeral on a wet day in a disconsolate churchyard, this is the type of the minds who take this view" (Faber, *The Creator*, 391).

. . . and that the monk encloses himself in the cloister in order to think horrible thoughts about the world, in which he sees nothing but misery, danger, sin, and condemnation . . . and the way I see it (though who am I to weigh in), I don't think that's the case, at least it's not for me.

I see creation as very beautiful; I delight in the souls of those who love God . . . Life is not sad when you have God . . . The sun is shining, and I enjoy flowers and birds and children. *Everything* is a reason to praise God: stars, nighttime, fields covered in light. In a Trappist monastery, you delight in all such things, because they all bring you closer to God . . . While it is true that the monk weeps for the sins of men, he also sings the wondrous deeds of the Creator.

The monk is joyful and happy to see the goodness of God reflected in His creatures, to taste the mercy and love of Jesus . . . He thanks Him for having removed him from a world full of danger and sin, it is true, but that is not all there is in the world. There is also pure affection in the world, and holy joys . . . It's not all desolation and misery, for there are smiles among tears, and despite their thorns, flowers are quite beautiful.

When the monk retires to the cloister, it is in order to praise God more easily, without distractions . . . The psalter and silence help him to do that. He thinks of those who are miserable on earth, and of those who are happy, begging mercy for all.

When I decided to go to La Trapa, it wasn't out of fear of the world, or because I was sad to realize that all it could give me was lies and deceit. My eyes hadn't been opened, first of all, because in order to have one's eyes opened, they must first be shut, and the world had never pulled the wool over mine. And secondly, my life had just hardly begun—I don't think twenty-one years constitute enough experience for me to have emphatically proclaimed in a resounding voice, "I'm off to the cloister, for I am disillusioned with life, and so with sorrowful countenance I retire to monastic solitude to weep for my sins . . ." No, none of that.

My life was in full bloom, and it held me in its embrace, and God spoiled me . . . The world didn't pull the wool over my eyes because it couldn't. I saw clearly, because I had God on my side; I'm joyful by nature, and I was happy . . . I enjoyed music, and nature; I hardly had time to get to know the world . . . I saw it up close, but that's it. That was all, and nevertheless, I went off to La Trapa. Why? According to the world,

I had no reason to go, because the world believes . . . Well, the world believes many things that are false, because I didn't need to change who I am and become a gloomy person in order to be a good Trappist, nor do I need to change now. But the joy of jazz is very different from the joy of a conscience in which God reigns . . .

I traded in my desires and interest in being a good architect one day for a desire to obtain a position in heaven loving God. Seeing that my body, with all its cares, was just a bit of clay not worth paying any attention to, I concentrated instead on my soul, which is immortal. And last, since I saw clearly that God loved me so much more than I loved Him in return, I decided to give myself to Him, body and soul, so that, with my corporal and spiritual sacrifices, I might save myself and save others.

That is the whole reason, plain and simple, that I went to La Trapa: love for God, not fear, as Father Faber thought. Of course, Father Faber was speaking about contemplative life generally, and even though if you think about it, his book is right, I am here to confirm that as far as I am concerned, the exception to the rule is clear enough.

Even so, it's so difficult to express the feelings I have about the world, now that I am in it after having been a Trappist . . . They are so varied and so diverse, and there are so many different things that give me reasons to meditate . . . I've been away from my monastery for a few months now . . . I see, I observe, and I keep quiet, but in my soul and spirit, which got rather sensitive on me quite some time ago, these feelings are constantly being rekindled . . . And often, without wanting to, I find myself comparing my life as a Cistercian novice to the life that surrounds me now . . . It is so different!! Different in every way: in how people work, think, and express themselves; people's interests are not the same; it seems as though God is far away . . . At least it seems as though He is to me, even though that may not be the case.

It's not that God has grown distant, but rather that people are so busy with their small-minded interests that they slowly come to forget about Him. God, for them, is a *thing* of little consequence . . . what a shame.

Today I left the house just when it started to get dark . . . I walked the main streets of the city, and, a bit agitated by the hubbub of the crowds, the cars, and the lights, I went where my soul needed to go . . . to the house of God . . . It was nearly empty. One old lady was muttering prayers before a poorly lit altar, another group of women was whispering next to a confessional, and the Lord, the God of Creation, the Judge of the living and the dead, was in the tabernacle, forgotten by humanity . . . This made me feel ashamed, for I am a man, and thus a sinner, and even though I want to atone for the tabernacle's abandonment, I cannot . . . It is enough that God should do me the favor of admitting me into His presence . . . What can I do? . . . Woe is me, if all I do for such a good Father is show myself a bad son!

My prayer was so weak and bland that I didn't know if God would hear it . . . In any case, I didn't stop offering it on that account.

In peace, and in silence, as time went on, my soul abandoned itself in God. I saw, passing before me, all the miseries and misfortunes of humanity, every hatred and every fight, and I thought that if God, who hides Himself in a piece of bread, were not so abandoned, then people would be happier, but they don't want to be . . .

In that moment, I was sad, why not admit it? Perhaps my feelings were influenced by the grey afternoon of this humid city; perhaps it was my soul, upon seeing my sins and those of my brothers and sisters . . . I don't have the words for it, but the solitude of God's temple accentuated my sadness . . . I remembered the chanting of the psalms in La Trapa; I saw my brother monks, singing before God, and I saw myself separated from them, and alone . . . I saw how weak and limp my love for God was . . . I want to be holy, but I can't.

When I left the church, it was night. I didn't want to walk toward the city center, so I headed for the neighborhoods on the outskirts . . . There, I saw the usual: material and moral poverty . . . Occasionally, the dirty, dark houses provided a glimpse into the poorly lit rooms inside, the smell of dust and dampness, disheveled women screeching at the children playing in the ditch . . . dirty, poorly lit streets . . . as for shops, just houses where only the essentials are sold . . . bread and sandals. From time to time, a tavern, emitting the scent of tobacco, wine, and cheap food. All this under a cloudy, starless sky . . .

This is the people, the poor people, among whom hunger is an everyday reality. The residents of the city center don't want to come here, because they find poverty bothersome. There, they have luxury stores, and houses with doormen and elevators; there are dazzling advertisements on the theaters, and their shiny, clean cars can glide over the asphalt without getting filled up with mud or running into children playing in the ditch.

And, nevertheless, the poor and the rich alike are children of God; all have the same weaknesses and the same sins . . . but someday, when God judges, what surprises we'll be in for!! The desperation of the hungry can be justified, but the selfishness of those who have money but are annoyed by the poor, that cannot be forgiven.

If the upper class forgets God, why are we surprised when the lower class rebels? . . . There's no need to go to the poor and preach patience and resignation to them. Rather, one must go to the rich and tell them that if they are unjust and do not give of what they have, then the wrath of God shall fall upon them.

As I walked through these neighborhoods, I was struck by many thoughts of indignation and shame. The further God is banished from society, the more misery there will be, and if, in a place that calls itself Christian, people hate one another on the basis of class or self-interest and separate themselves into rich and poor neighborhoods, what will happen when God's name is cursed by both one and the other? . . . If the idea of God is taken from the poor, they have nothing else left; their desperation is justifiable, their hatred for the rich is natural, their desire for revolution and anarchy is logical. And if the idea of God is a nuisance to the rich, and they do not heed the precepts of the Gospel and the teachings of Jesus . . . then they shouldn't complain. If their selfishness hinders them from drawing near to the poor, they should not be surprised when the latter plan to take what they have by force.

Looking around at today's society, what Christian soul is not pained to see it in such a state? . . . When I think on how all social conflicts and differences would be smoothed out if we turned our gaze slightly toward that God who was so abandoned in the church I just visited . . . When I think, looking at the spectacle that humanity presents, on how hatred and envy, selfishness and lies, would all disappear if we gazed at God . . . When I see such an easy solution for human beings to be happy, but they are blind or crazy and don't want to see it . . . then I cannot help but exclaim, "Lord . . . Lord, look on Your suffering people . . . Human beings are not evil, Lord . . . but if You abandon them, Lord, who can survive?[6]

6. Ps 76:7.

. . . What can we do all on our own? Nothing, absolutely nothing . . . If You were to turn Your gaze away from the world for just a single moment, the world would be thrown into chaos . . . Forgive us, Lord."

Ever since I left my monastery, I hear nothing but noise . . . The only music that doesn't bother me is prayer . . . But you hear very little of that in the world . . . Everything else is noise. A lot of people ask me about the silence of La Trapa, and I don't know how to answer them, because the silence of La Trapa is not silence . . . it is a sublime symphony that the world doesn't understand . . . It is a silence that says, "Don't make noise, brother, I'm talking to God . . ."

It is a silence of the body, so as to let the soul rejoice in the contemplation of God. It is not the silence of someone who has nothing to say; rather, it is the silence of someone who holds many things inside, and even very beautiful things, but keeps quiet so that words, which are always clumsy, don't spoil their conversation with God.

It is a silence that makes us humble, that makes us resigned; for when we have some difficulty, silence makes it so that we tell only Jesus about it, so that He might take care of it in silence too, without anyone else realizing it . . .

Silence is necessary for prayer. With silence, it is difficult to lack charity; with silence, we show greater gratitude for a brother's love and affection than we would with words . . . In short, silence is everything in contemplative life.

As such, now that I am in the world, everything that is not silence seems like noise to me, and sometimes even useless. A Trappist only opens his mouth to sing to God . . . and here in the world it's the opposite, when you want to talk about God, everyone shuts up.

I imagine all humanity in a great valley . . . immense and full of sunlight. Every human being is in it, and they are coming and going, moving and shouting . . . God is atop a mountain, from which He reigns over the valley, which is more immense than the sea . . . The men and women who are in the valley see the summit of the mountain where God is, but they do not see Him . . .

From the immense multitude, which is all humanity, there arises a thunderous clamor that reaches the peak of the mountain where God is . . . This clamor is people's conversations, their music mixed with war cries, sighs of sorrow and shrieks of joy, the echo of drums, the whistling of factories, electric motors, shouts from plazas and circuses, millions and millions of discussions, conversations, lectures, cinemas, and theaters; all this uproar, capable of driving anyone other than God insane, reaches the mountain's peak . . . but there it stops; God does not hear it . . . He scorns all this noise; it offends Him, and He does not hear it . . . So what is He listening to? Why doesn't God clear out the whole crowd of people with one breath, since all they do is make an intolerable commotion? . . . It seems that something is stopping God . . . He is listening contentedly to something. Is it a whisper? No . . . you can hardly hear it . . . So what is it? . . .

We start to look carefully at all the people in the valley, and we see some who aren't shouting, or arguing, or running, or striking blows with a hammer . . . What are they doing? It seems as though they aren't doing anything. . . They are on their knees in silence . . . The others look at them and are surprised; sometimes they bother them as they pass, or they make fun of them, or they avoid them entirely . . . But they remain on their knees and they remain in silence . . . So then we go and ask them, "What are you doing? Why don't you join us, in progress, in civilization?" . . . And then they say to us, "Quiet, brother, don't make noise while I'm talking to God . . ."

What would happen to the world without prayer . . . if the one thing that pleased God, the one thing that stopped Him from doing away with humanity, were to disappear? Why is the world surprised, then, that some people, full of good will, should devote themselves to kneeling on the ground and lift their hearts to God? Does the world think they are useless? The world calls them selfish and crazy and says that they're wasting their time . . . but it's not so; those who devote themselves to prayer are the only people who know how to use time well . . . Talking to other people and arguing over trivialities with them . . . that's the real waste of time . . . Someday they'll see.

The uneducated, simple little lay brother praying Hail Marys[7] silently in his convent is contributing more to "world peace" than all the speeches

---

7. Before Vatican II, lay brothers were obligated to pray a certain number of Our Fathers and Hail Marys every day in lieu of praying the Divine Office with the monks (OC 343; also see #7, n. 13).

ever delivered by the members of the League of Nations since its foundation.[8] That sounds like an exaggeration, but it's the absolute truth, and I
am convinced of it . . . Someday, and someday soon, we shall undeniably
see it. When I see good Catholic people who dismiss prayer as a secondary
concern—when it is quite the opposite, it is the primary concern—I feel
like saying so many things to them . . . but I keep quiet. Martha, too, kept
quiet at Jesus' feet when Mary told her she wasn't doing anything useful[9]
. . . But the Divine Master answered on her behalf, saying that she had
chosen the better part . . . That is, that she was more pleasing to Him.

It's not that I think that those who work for God's glory in the world
aren't doing anything . . . not at all. What I mean is that if they don't
have a prayer life . . . it's all a waste of time . . . It's good to preach and
to move about, but if they don't kneel down from time to time and pray
to God in silence, they run the risk that all their efforts will get mixed up
with the world's efforts, and thus all they are doing is making noise . . .
Noise that does not reach God and, as such, a waste of time.

These things I'm writing down as they occur to me might not be deep
thoughts or have any wit to them . . . far be it from me to imagine that
they do. What I do want them to be is a faithful reflection of what I think
. . . of my way of feeling and seeing things.

When I take up my pen, and I think for a moment beforehand about
what I'm going to say, realizing that all I think about is talking about
God and always about God . . . I feel so small that I feel like shutting
my notebook and leaving the pages blank, for surely they'd speak more
eloquently of the greatness of God, His immensity, His infinite power,
and His eternal love . . . than I could using my clumsy words. But on the
other hand, since I'm not writing this for other people to read, but rather
writing in order to dialogue, or rather monologue . . . to open my heart,
to speak to God as if He were the one to whom I am writing.

My writings are at the same time reflections to myself and prayers to
God. My impressions of what my eyes see in the world where I am, seen

8. The League of Nations: An international organization dedicated to world peace active
from 1920 to 1946. It was a precursor to the United Nations.

9. Rafael mixes up their names; Mary was at Jesus' feet when Martha approached them.
See Luke 10:38-42.

through the prism of God . . . I cannot see it in any other way, nor do I wish to . . . If a landscape impresses me, it is because I see God in it, and the colors and wind and sun are all His works . . . Let us praise Him, then.

I also see God in His creatures, that is, in human beings and in irrational beings alike, in the greatness of souls, to praise Him, and in the misery of bodies, to implore Him . . . I also see God in the activities of life, and I relate everything back to Him . . . An action has no value unto itself if it is not directed toward some end; the action will be good if its end is good, and bad if its end is bad. And it is good when its end is God, and bad when it's the opposite. And since God is all that concerns me, when I analyze an action, an impression of my feelings, or an event that affects me, I look for God first; I analyze my ideas, hoping to come across Him there, and I direct my actions in such a way that, through them, they will take me toward Him . . . And this is so easy!! . . . Even eating, laughing, talking . . . all the actions we do in our everyday lives, all of them, we can direct toward this end . . . and thus it happens that, doing everything for God, everything is good; and in the most insignificant matters in life, we can lift our hearts to Him and entrust it all to Him.

But Lord . . . You know that, even though this is my desire, so many times I forget that You exist, and I act as if You could not see me . . . Many times, at the end of the day, I have spoken as if not in Your presence and busied myself with a thousand chores that, though not bad, have lost their value because I have not offered them to You . . .

Lord, if You are *everything*, how is it possible that I could forget You, even for a moment? . . . Oh, Lord! If it were only forgetting You, that would be one thing, but offending You? . . . Let us draw a veil over this; the past is in the past, but admit me into Your presence. I wish I had the tears of King David, who upon entering into Your presence remembered his sins, anguish seized his chest, and he wept so much that he could not find rest in his bed.[10]

Lord, give me a good look and You'll see—even though I do not deserve Your attention—You can see that even though I am busy with a thousand

---

10. David said to Nathan, "I have sinned against the Lord" . . . David therefore pleaded with God for the child; David fasted, and went in and lay all night on the ground (2 Sam 12:13, 16).

things and necessities, my spirit is in You. And if I get distracted, and creatures take me away from You for even a moment, remember that I am weak, and that my heart is human, and that I am a man full of imperfections. My desire is to see You in everything that surrounds me, to think of nothing more than Your infinite love for me, and to have You present always, when I sleep and when I wake, when I laugh and when I cry. May everything be directed toward Your ends, and may I lack everything but You, for in having You, I have everything.

There is only one thing that makes me suffer in this world . . . and that is the forgetfulness of creatures toward their Creator . . . Knowing Him and having a relationship with Him, it greatly saddens me to see people's ingratitude. I can forgive all the sins, and I try to make amends for them . . . but forgetfulness and ingratitude? How can I not feel pain, looking at children who forget their Father, who do not love Him . . . who do not know Him?

I very much understand the outbursts of those saints who shouted the name of Christ through the streets and plazas, and I don't know how they didn't go crazy when they realized that people weren't listening to them . . . I very much understand why Saint Francis preached to the fish and the birds.

What a shame, Lord, what a shame . . . and I can't do anything about it!

There is one thing that causes me alarm, and makes me suffer greatly . . . and that is my excessive sensitivity. Anything can bring me joy, but any mishap can make me cry; this demonstrates how far behind I am when it comes to virtue.

One time, a brother struck a very personal nerve with me, without meaning to, and I cried bitterly. At first, I thought my tears were because I was humiliated; later, upon reconsideration, I realized that they were also imbued with some pride. I am like a very finely tuned guitar, whose strings vibrate at the slightest twitch in the air or the slightest graze . . . I should make myself stronger; souls that have truly been entrusted to God do not cry when somebody offends them . . . Did they not scourge Christ?

What I can guarantee is that I never hold onto resentment toward anyone, nor do I seek amends for myself . . . And I am much sorrier for a brother's lack of charity toward me than I am offended on my own behalf. We should model ourselves after Jesus, who asked forgiveness for His enemies as they crucified Him[11] . . . Only a God does such a thing, and that God is Jesus Christ . . . Meanwhile we despicable sinners suffer when we are humiliated and cry when we are offended, and it should be entirely the other way around. We should rejoice when someone scourges or injures us, whether they mean to or not.

But such things cannot be helped, and if they can be helped somehow, it is with virtue . . . But when you don't have that, tears are very human.

But, Lord, what do I deserve? . . . I deserve to be scorned and shunned by others, You know that quite well . . . and it terrifies me to think that the world's high regard for me should give You cause to think that I have been well rewarded here on earth, and meanwhile in Your eyes, I should be presented as I really am, which the world does not know . . . As such, Lord, make the world despise me so that all my great sins might be forgotten in Your eyes . . . Do this for me, Lord, and I promise not to cry anymore.[12]

---

11. Luke 23:34.
12. Rafael continued this manuscript on October 25, 1934 (see #56).

52. To W. Marino del Hierro

Oviedo, September 29, 1934

My dear friend and brother Marino,

I received your letter, and it greatly consoled me to learn that you were receiving Communion every day. Even though you say you don't feel any devotion, don't worry, because it's God who bestows that, and God who takes it away when He pleases . . . and we aren't going to give up just because we don't have it.

As long as you keep walking down the path of perfection, you will en-counter many unexpected things. At the beginning, God helps us super-naturally, He opens our eyes, He shows us the true light, and He shows us the way; sometimes He even consoles us, and spoils us like the little children that we are . . . But there comes a time when it seems as if He is hiding . . . the eyes of our souls see nothing, we experience dryness in prayer, ev-erything wearies and bores us, perhaps we think that God is abandoning us . . . but it's not so. Jesus never lets go of our hand . . . but He does test us.

Oh, how easy virtue would be, my friend Marino, if whenever we ad-dressed God, we felt *profound* devotion! At first, God grants us that, but as we grow stronger in the faith, God hides himself away sometimes, and as we grow in virtue, sometimes God also shows Himself to us in all His splendor. But perhaps it takes years to get there, or even a lifetime . . .

We see this frequently in reading the lives of the saints. Saint Teresa her-self tells us that she went many years without knowing what devotion is.[1]

But we should not be discouraged on that account. This happens to me often, but I don't ask God for anything . . . I don't even deserve to feel

---

1. "These labors [perseverance in prayer] take their toll. Being myself one who endured them for many years . . . I know they are extraordinary. . . . Conceal from your eyes the thought about why He gives devotion to one after such a few days and not to me after so many years. Let us believe that all is for our own greater good" (Saint Teresa of Ávila, *The Book of Her Life* 11.11–12, in *Collected Works*, trans. Kieran Kavanaugh and Otilio Rodrí-guez [Washington, DC: ICS Publications, 1976], 1:82–83).

devotion . . . it's enough just that He admits me into His presence . . . Besides, I think it was Saint Bernard (I don't remember exactly) who said, "Brothers, don't ask for consolation or revelations in prayer, for on the Mount of Olives, Jesus did not ask for these, but rather sweated blood."[2]

Take courage, then, my friend Marino. If it is meritorious to act rightly toward God when we feel devotion and enthusiasm for spiritual things, it is much more so when, in desolation and indifference, we nevertheless act as if we truly saw God tangibly in everything that surrounds us.

Regarding reading and meditation, I'll just say that it's a question of habit . . . It often strikes us as overly sentimental, we find it fruitless, it bores and wearies us . . . so we redouble our efforts, ask the Virgin Mary for perseverance and light, and thus little by little we start getting used to it, and then later we even come to find that we miss it when we don't do it.

It's very useful before going to sleep and when getting up . . . I recommend reading half a chapter before you go to sleep, or a whole one, or a few verses; whatever you think . . . it's always better to read only a little, in order not to overburden the imagination, which is not beneficial . . . And afterwards we simply fall asleep thinking about what we have read, and in the morning, we read it again in order to have it present throughout the day . . . to reflect on it, draw conclusions, set goals, or simply remember it fondly . . . As you can see, it's rather easy, especially for someone who doesn't have much time and is busy with a thousand things.

But if you knew how little effort is needed to think of God and the Virgin while you walk, while you bathe, while you get dressed, while you eat, and even while you're talking . . . you need only resolve to do it.

Regarding reading, do what I tell you and you'll see how well it'll go . . . Take it upon yourself as penance; don't other people discipline themselves? . . . So five minutes before going to sleep and five minutes before getting up, who doesn't have time for that?

Anyway, I'm giving you advice that I suppose you don't need, because you know all this already. Forgive my candor, it's all in good faith. If you knew, my friend Marino, how much I care about you continuing onward and not letting anything or anyone discourage you . . .

2. The source for this quotation is unknown; it refers to Jesus' agony in the garden (see Luke 22:39-46).

Knowing that you listen to me charitably, that you enjoy my letters and that they motivate you to love God . . . in all these things, you have more than repaid me. It's so difficult to come to love when there's no self-interest or favors involved, or without even knowing each other . . . and between you and me, there's none of that, there's only God . . . that God who fills all things, who makes people love each other with a pure and disinterested love, who draws close to us and unites us, so that we suffer if our brother suffers, and we rejoice when he rejoices . . . The world is so far from what it really is to love God, and to love one's neighbor. Is it not so, brother?

And so, when I see that you reciprocate what I am giving you and what I am offering you, which is an open heart and my sincere friendship, I cannot help but praise God with all my strength and all my soul. Don't perceive any modesty in me, for there isn't any, and don't thank me for anything either . . . I do what I ought and what I can. If I could communicate to you all my confidence in God, I would do just that.

That is what one must have: confidence, so much confidence in Jesus, who can do all things, and who does not abandon us . . . What we must do is abandon ourselves in Him, with our bodies and souls, with all our weakness and misery and little virtue. If we do this, we have nothing to fear.

Don't be in a rush to draw close to God, because even though you imagine that He is far away, perhaps that's not true. On the other hand, we despicable sinners are not the ones who draw close to God, but rather Jesus is the one who draws close to us, though we don't deserve it . . .

Let's have confidence and faith, and not be afraid of our sins, which we have only to weep over; they don't stop Jesus from loving us . . . that Jesus of Nazareth who ate with tax collectors and sinners, giving great scandal to the Pharisees . . . For us sinners He came down into the world and died on the cross, and the angels in heaven rejoice more over one lost sheep who returns to the flock than all those who are already in the fold.[3]

Be completely assured that, on the day you decided to follow Jesus on the way to Calvary, the Blessed Virgin and all the saints of heaven celebrated with rejoicing and sang the *Gloria* in honor of the Creator. And have you ever thought about turning back? . . . Please, Marino, my friend, don't make Mary sad, and don't think about any such thing.

3. See Luke 15:1-10.

That you'll come across hurdles and obstacles on your path is evident, who doesn't? . . . But commend yourself to Her, and jump over them bravely. . . This life is very short, and when you least expect it, you shall have your reward . . . you'll find yourself *face to face* with the God who is hidden from you now, and there will be no more tears or desolation . . . Use this time well, then; life, as I'm telling you, is a mere breath, and eternity. . . is very long.

Is it possible that Br. Tescelino is going to write me? I was so happy the other day when you told me in your letter that he would. If only you knew, I need the encouragement of my brothers so much too . . . and sometimes I feel so alone!

I await Br. Tescelino's letter with joyful eagerness. I won't say that he's very good, because perhaps he'll read this letter and that would offend his modesty . . . but you know better than I do that he is, for God's will has been such that I hardly know him.

I don't have anything else in particular to tell you. I sent him a card at his house—Calle del General Salinas 20, no. 3 (if I remember correctly), but it doesn't matter; I just sent him a few lines asking for his address in Burgos.

One last thing. . . in your letter, at the end, you asked me for forgiveness a thousand times over . . . Forgiveness? A thousand times over? . . . For what? In any case I . . . for God's sake, don't be ridiculous. And now I'm the one asking for your forgiveness a thousand times over.

I'd also greatly desire to spend some time talking with you . . . but let's wait, everything will take its course.

Without further ado, give Br. Tescelino a big hug for me. Your brother in Jesus and Mary, who truly loves you,

Rafael

P.S. If you have time, don't stop writing back, because I always look forward to your letters happily. Even if you think it's the other way round, they also encourage me to serve and love God . . . Don't you remember the story about Captain Araña, who "boarded everybody else and then got left behind on the shore"?[4] I imagine I don't have to explain any further.

---

4. Captain Araña: In Spanish, this saying is invoked when someone is left behind at the last second, especially on a project of their own undertaking.

53. *To Fernanda Torres*

Oviedo, September 30, 1934

My dearest *abuelita*,

Perhaps you'll be surprised to receive this letter, and upon seeing the signature of your grandson Rafael, you think . . . "but Lord, I haven't the faintest idea who this grandson might be . . . " But if you dig into your memory a bit, perhaps you'll realize and exclaim . . . "Could it be?! . . . For my grandson to write me is a strange, unexpected event . . . " But, nevertheless, it's true.

I already know what you're thinking . . . that I'm ungrateful, a bad person, that I don't love you, that you're just an old woman who is useless to me, that I don't see you as important, that the distance between us has made me forget about you . . . You know, all those delightful things that you say in your letters.

Well, *abuelita* . . . that's all wrong, and none of it is true. I won't try to make excuses for not having written you earlier . . . because honestly I have no excuse, but in any case I am absolutely sure that you aren't holding a grudge against me, and that you forgive my offense . . . We all have many faults, and this is one of mine . . . not writing to my dear grandmother, who loves me more than I deserve.

But look . . . when I offend God, which unfortunately is often . . . later I feel great shame, and since I have no excuse for having offended Him . . . I calmly tell him, "Lord, here I am . . . do you forgive me?" And Jesus, who is so good, forgives me; and while my sins are ever before me, that I might weep over them and see my weakness in them, I am sure that God forgets them . . . So, *abuela*, do the same thing. Forget my tardiness in writing you, and this will make you a better person, a better Christian . . . and a better grandmother, don't you think? At the end of the day, what do you expect from a grandson like me?

Merceditas continues to recover, thank God, albeit slowly. She is eating well and is staying in bed, and the doctors say that things are wrapping up to their satisfaction . . . Now she's starting what they call "ultraviolet light baths."[1] Though the nights are really hard on her, poor thing—on her and her mother—she is content. On her name day,[2] she received the Lord, and He is the one who must cure her.

As for me, I'm also doing much better. I don't take insulin anymore, I've fattened up, and now I can see myself going back to my monastery in just a few months.

One of these days I'll write to my good Father Master[3] to ask his permission to go and make a retreat with the community for eight days . . . I am already rejoicing just at the thought that, even if only for a few days, I'll be able to put on my Trappist habit . . . I'm telling you, it's the only way I'm comfortable.

If you knew how much they love me there, and how much I love those humble little monks . . . They are so good! I know that they'll be very happy to see me in choir again, singing to God . . . That is the only happiness here on earth: to join spiritually with the angels in heaven, intoning the *Gloria* in the Creator's honor. Don't you be surprised, then, that I should have such a strong desire to continue being a Trappist . . . Who cares about the body and its discomforts and austerity when the soul is in God?

I assure you, I notice none of that—not the cold, or my exhaustion, or anything else—when I'm in choir . . . And how true it is what our Father Saint Bernard said regarding Cistercian monks: he saw the angels in choir, helping the monks sing the psalmody.[4]

And look, *abuelita*, when I was there, with the Tabernacle so close by and the Virgin looking at me, I thought of you often.

---

1. Ultraviolet light baths: While his sister Merceditas's condition is unclear from Rafael's description, at the time, phototherapy (the medical use of ultraviolet irradiation) was a cutting-edge treatment for tuberculosis, among other diseases. See Rik Roelandts, "The History of Phototherapy: Something New under the Sun?" *Journal of the American Academy of Dermatology* 46, no. 6 (June 2002): 926–30.

2. Name day: September 24, the feast of Our Lady of Mercy ("Nuestra Señora de las Mercedes").

3. Father Master: Father Marcelo León (see #17).

4. See Conrad of Eberbach, *The Great Beginning of Cîteaux*, trans. Benedicta Ward and Paul Savage, ed. E. Rozanne Elder, CF 72 (Collegeville, MN: Cistercian Publications, 2012), 132–33.

What does it matter if I didn't write you? Is writing necessary in order for me to love you? . . . Of course it's a very human consolation to receive even a few lines from loved ones. But looking at it from a more noble perspective, you'll see that writing is not *necessary*, just as it isn't necessary to shout prayers to love God and know that we are loved by Him . . . don't think that your grandson has forgotten you because he fails to send you a couple of poorly arranged sentences that cannot express my affection accurately.

In La Trapa, we have silence. If only you knew how much that silence, which the world assumes is so gloomy, helps us to understand one another . . . Words are always clumsy, while silence can be rather expressive . . . There, we love one another deeply and truly; our love for God unites us in spirit, while our bodies are united by the Rule, by penance, and sometimes by suffering . . . As for the heart, ours is also very united . . . in silence we tell it . . . If you knew how beautiful it is to be a Trappist!!!

There are so many things I'd tell you if only I knew how to write . . . but there's no need. You, too, understand me even when I don't say anything. I suffered so much the day I had to leave, but when I go back, the monastery won't be big enough to contain all my joy . . . and I know *without a doubt* that I am to die in La Trapa.

My vocation is ever stronger, you could almost say it has grown . . . and as God is giving it to me, He will also give me the means to fulfill it, have no doubt. Right now I am not healthy enough to follow the diet: well that's easy enough, He'll give me health. I might be a wretched sinner, but would I ever fail to have confidence in God? . . . Never.

It was necessary for me to leave the monastery . . . I was too happy . . . God threatened me with death (if it's possible that God can threaten) in order to obligate me to go out once more into the world . . . This trial is very hard; I've been away for four months, and I am still a Trappist . . . He took me away, so He will lead me back . . . He knows what He is doing; we, with our weak reason and human way of thinking, cannot fathom God's mysteries toward His creatures . . . Let's let Him do things, and have confidence in Him. Right, *abuelita*?

The other day I received a letter from Father Master . . . so caring and good with me as he always is . . . For him I am still his novice, Brother María Rafael . . . The will of God is in the will of my superiors, so if for my superiors, the Abbot and Father Master, I am still Brother María Rafael, then that is who I shall also be to the world . . . even if the world is against it. To me, the voice of my Father Abbot is the voice of God, and if he awaits me, then God awaits me too.

I was so grateful, to the depths of my novice's soul, for the letter you wrote me at La Trapa following my entrance, and were I not a son of obedience, I would have written you back. If I write you back now it's not because you asked or pressured me to, but just for its own sake. I never do things out of obligation. While I was there, I only ever answered letters from my mother, and only on my Father Master's orders—that is, not on his orders, but with his permission, which is different.

I haven't heard a word from Uncle Polín . . . but he knows there's no need. Anyway, I'll write him one of these days.

I know Aunt Rosa received my letter. Poor thing, I love her very much, even though she doesn't realize it.

I don't have anything else to tell you, and as you can see, I've said rather little, and you knew it all already.

There's nothing I can say about the world that would interest you and that I would know about. Your poor grandson only cares about God and the Virgin Mary . . . that's what I know. At times, I get very annoying, I know, and you'll be able to forgive me. But look, I think what I'm saying to you about thinking about God and relating everything back to Him isn't exclusive to Trappists . . . It's common to all Christians, don't you think? . . .

We think that devotion, penance, and talking about spiritual things is the domain of vowed religious, but that's not true . . . This life is so short, as you well know, being near the end of it. When we present ourselves before God, He will make demands of us all—according to what He has given us, of course. And then we will see how much time we have foolishly wasted on trivial things and worldly interests.

Before I went to La Trapa, when I thought about the monks of Venta de Baños, I used to say . . . "Well, those men martyr their bodies, devote themselves to prayer, and think of nothing but God . . . What an admirable life . . . But," I thought, "they're Trappists, it's natural that they should conduct themselves this way . . . I'm not a Trappist . . . But," I thought, "we'll be judged by the same God, the duration of their lives is like mine in that it will be over soon, and then what?. . . . Am I not a child of God too?. . . And yet they love Him and I do not . . . There's no reason for things to be this way . . . I have to put these few days here on earth to good use . . . I have to love God much, and I have to weep for my sins and those of my brothers and sisters in humanity who do not love Him . . ." And I kept thinking, and thinking. . . and one fine day, I went to La Trapa.

Now that I am in the world, I see that everybody else thinks the way I used to before, and when they see me in the church often, they say, "Well, that's only natural, of course, he's a Trappist . . ." I don't go to the cinema or the theater, and they say the same thing: "Of course, since he's a Trappist he can't, he shouldn't go, that's only logical . . . That's no place for a monk . . ." What's more, since I've started smoking again, some people have been scandalized, and at the very least they're thinking I've lost my vocation . . . That's how the world is. But watching it happen, I just think . . . "Well, don't we have the same God, me and you and that guy over there? . . . Didn't Jesus die for all of us? . . . Isn't He in the Tabernacle waiting for all of us? . . . So why do so few of us go and keep Him company?. . ." I sincerely believe, *abuela*, that the world has lost its mind . . . and is on its way to losing its heart, which would be even worse.

What does it matter if we are Trappists, or soldiers, or poor or rich, or tall or short, or men or women? We should all have the same love for God. It won't be enough to say, one day, in front of Jesus, "Lord, I loved you, but since I had to go to the barracks every day, well, of course a soldier shouldn't be distracted with something else . . ." And the farmer, busy with his oxen, doesn't have time either, and the intellectual doesn't care about "monkish nonsense," and so on and so forth, everybody makes excuses.[5]

That's it, without a doubt: either the Trappists are completely insane, or everybody else has a suicide pact . . . It scares me, and makes me feel pity for them, believe me. Either we are Christians or we aren't; one either loves God or doesn't; as Jesus says, *whoever is not with me is against me*.[6] And elsewhere He adds that He will spit those who are lukewarm out of

5. See Luke 14:15-24.
6. Matt 12:30.

His mouth.[7] So, as you can see, this isn't just hot air. The words of Sacred Scripture are clear and decisive.

So, *abuelita*, don't be surprised that I don't care about anything but God and His glory . . . What I really want is for everyone, all humanity and all people without exception, to turn their gaze upward a bit and contemplate God who is looking down at us . . . and who will judge us . . . Let's not waste time, for there is so little left . . . this is just as true for you as it is for me. I've been an inch from death and I wasn't afraid . . . I was joyful, even. God did not will it, so may it be when He wills; sooner or later, it's all the same to me . . . And meanwhile, let us love life, for God gives it to us, so we must love it, even with its sufferings and sorrows. Let us praise Him without ceasing and at all times.

True, you are getting on in years, but what does that matter? You see the sun and sky and flowers, which are all God's creatures and proclaim His glory. You have a tabernacle nearby where you can talk to Jesus, so that He can console you in everything. You have a grandson who loves you very much (even if you don't believe it), who prayed and will pray for you in a choir of Cistercian monks . . . In a word, you have God and the Virgin's protection. What more could you ask for? Don't tell me you need something, because you have it *all*.

Well, pardon my sermon, *abuelita*, but "well, seeing as I'm a Trappist . . ."

Give a big hug to Aunt María for me. With all my love, the oldest and littlest of your grandchildren,

Rafael

7. See Rev 3:16.

54. To Fr. Marcelo León

Oviedo, October 2, 1934

My dear Father Master,

I received your lovely letter, which moved me greatly as always . . . I can't help it. Anytime you all say a kind word or do me a courtesy that I don't deserve, it produces a great joy in me. I take such joy in hearing you call me "Brother María Rafael" and "dear novice" that only God in heaven can know how much I appreciated your lovely letter.

I am still much better, and I'm very strong now. According to the doctor, I've been making a surprising recovery from this illness, although I'm going slowly and not rushing because that could lead to setbacks. That's all the news I can give you regarding my body.

Regarding my soul, what can I say that you don't already know or can't imagine on your own? . . . I've been away from my beloved Trapa for four months now, and I can assure you that I think of nothing but the choir, my habit, my little space in the dormitory, my brothers, the chocolate factory . . . all of it . . . all those things that drew me so close to God and made me so happy.

Finding myself separated from you and from the tabernacle of La Trapa, I have been made to live in the world as a prisoner, out of place . . . I don't think I'd ever get used to it, and if it weren't for the absolute confidence I have that God is to bring me back to the monastery, and the knowledge that I am doing His will, I'd find my life impossible . . . But I believe that nothing is impossible when you truly love God, and we know that the Blessed Virgin guides us.

Now, dear Father, I am going to ask one thing of you and Reverend Father Abbot, and it is simply to come visit you for a few days. On October 23, the community's retreat begins . . . and I . . . I know I have no right, because I do not belong to the community, but even if only for eight days, I could stay in the infirmary, and I'd bring my habit with me, which I never leave behind.

Tell me, Father, if that would be appropriate, or if you think the community does not approve of my demand, or any other reason you observe; tell me, and in everything I will obey those who are still my superiors. But if you could see how much I need this . . . Those days of rest would be of great benefit to my soul, which, while it has grown accustomed to suffering, is still not yet what it ought to be . . . And if you were to look me in the eyes right now, surely you'd grant me permission.

With true eagerness, I await your letter, in which you will tell me what you have decided.

You can imagine what those days would mean to me . . . I am so out of it that, despite having been in the world for quite a while now, it seems as though it was just yesterday that I took off that novice's cape under which I was so at ease.

I don't wish to trouble you any further, for I have no right to that either. I simply look to your charity, and thus I beg you to treat me with charity; as you can see, what I'm asking for is rather small, yet for me it would be great.

If you receive this letter tomorrow, October 3, don't forget to pray to Saint Thérèse for me[1] . . . She too suffered greatly before finding herself in Carmel definitively, but she prayed to God so much that she saw her desires fulfilled.

Greet Father Francisco[2] and the novices for me; may they not forget their brother, whose body may be far away, but whose heart and soul are still there, in the choir and at the foot of the tabernacle and of the Virgin.

Give my respectful regards to Father Abbot, and all my affection to you, my dear Father Master, in Jesus and Mary. Asking your blessing, your novice,

Brother María Rafael[3]

1. Until 1969, Saint Thérèse of Lisieux was celebrated on October 3. Her feast day is now October 1.

2. Fr. Francisco Díez Martínez was the sub-master, or assistant master of novices.

3. While Fr. Marcelo's response has not been preserved, Rafael did not make a visit to the monastery because of the outbreak of the Revolution of 1934 in Asturias on October 5 (see #55).

55. *To Rafael Arnaiz Sánchez de la Campa*

Burgos, October 24, 1934[1]
Feast of Saint Raphael[2]

Missus est Angelus Domini, sanctus Raphaël a Deo ad Tobiam, et salu-
tavit eum, et dixit: Gaudium sit tibi semper.[3]
That is precisely what I wish for you, dear father. Though this letter
may arrive late, I don't think you'll mind once you learn that today, at
communion, your son asked God to give his father the same thing that
the angel Raphael wished for Tobit when he greeted him and said, "May
joy be with you always."

I have nothing more to say to you, except that I'm doing well now that
I'm not hearing gunshots or seeing ruins, and now that I've discussed the
events that occurred in Oviedo so many times, I don't know what I'm
talking about anymore.

Tomorrow I'm going to eat at Aunt Malén's house;[4] it's delightfully
sunny out; I don't have any sugar in my blood; and that's all.

How is Merceditas doing? . . . Has Laredo seen her yet?[5] Tell me all
the news, but don't give me the gruesome details.

I suppose Fernando is in Madrid already.

1. On October 5, 1934, a revolutionary uprising led by miners' unions began in Asturias. After the violence ceased in Oviedo, where Rafael was staying with his parents, he went
to stay at the Burgos residence of his aunt and uncle, Pepita Conde Merino and Álvaro
Barón Torres (OC 363).

2. Until 1969, the feast of Saint Raphael was observed on October 24. He is now commemorated alongside Saints Michael and Gabriel on September 29.

3. "Saint Raphael, the Angel of the Lord, was sent by God to Tobit, who greeted him;
and the angel answered, 'May joy be with you always.'" From the liturgy for the feast of
Saint Raphael, taken from Tobit 3:17 and 5:10 (OC 363).

4. Aunt Malén: Magdalena Bohigas, Rafael's paternal great-aunt.

5. Laredo: The Arnaiz-Barón family doctor.

I ran into my Br. Tescelino here, the Trappist, who is doing his service at the hospital. As you can imagine, I have a great time with him.[6]

The military hospital is full of injured people from all over, and there are a few from Asturias.

With nothing else to tell you, hugs to all of you from your son,

Rafael
U.H.P.[7]
R.I.P.

---

6. Br. Tescelino Arribas Jimeno left the monastery on November 6, 1933, to complete his compulsory military service as a medic. He returned on November 28, 1934 (OC 364).

7. U.H.P.: The initials for the Unión de Hermanos Proletarios (lit. "United Proletarian Brethren"), the name adopted by the revolutionary alliance in Asturias.

56. Literary Notes[1]

Burgos, October 25, 1934

Now that a few days have gone by since the terrifying catastrophe in Oviedo,[2] and with a more peaceful spirit and calmer nerves, I shall attempt to continue my interrupted writings.

I won't attempt a summary of the events of those nine days of anarcho-communism that we residents of Oviedo suffered through . . . It was so terrifying that I remember nothing but the apartment building, where it seemed as though we were all going crazy; the unrelenting thunder of machine guns, rifles, and dynamite; enormous fires that lit up the sky with an intense glow the color of blood; and revolutionaries constantly threatening us with their rifles and pistols.

In those days, I saw the hatred of men unleashed. Across Spain, and chiefly in Asturias, under the pretext of renewing society, lifting up workers, and suppressing capitalism, they have committed the most horrifying atrocities.

Those days horrified my spirit. I never thought that human beings could kill one another and destroy with such rage.

1. This manuscript, the continuation of "The Trappist's Apologia" (#51), was untitled. Literary Notes is the title added by Rafael's confessor and biographer, Fr. Teófilo Sandoval Fernández.

2. The terrifying catastrophe in Oviedo: That is, the Revolution of 1934 (see #55). During this violence, the Dominican chapel where Rafael attended daily Adoration was burned, and six seminarians were killed (OC 366). They were beatified in 2019 as Blessed Ángel Cuartas Cristóbal and companions.

57. To Mercedes Barón Torres

Burgos, November 12, 1934

My dearest mother,

I have just received your letter, and while I've been thinking of writing you for a few days now, I'll get to it without further ado.

I'm doing very well, thanks be to God, and I'm very happy . . . I heard from Jesús Martínez, who was in Oviedo, that Merceditas continues to get better. Uncle Polín isn't coming to Burgos, but rather going to Toro with Uncle Álvaro to settle his affairs there.[1] The other day he signed the bill of sale for Pedrosillo,[2] so now that he has that money, he is going to Toro immediately to settle all his debts there. I'll take advantage of the trip, naturally, to give my grandmother a hug . . . The other day she wrote me, saying that if I didn't come, she'd come see me no matter where I am . . . Poor thing . . . Even though I don't like Toro at all, as you know, she certainly deserves what little happiness I can give her.

We are leaving today, which is Monday . . . Uncle Álvaro and I will meet Uncle Polín in Valladolid and continue on to Toro, and, God willing, on Saturday I'll be back in Burgos. Then, I'll be able to tell you when I'm leaving for Oviedo, because it seems to me that as far as rest goes . . . I've already had nearly a month of it, and that's enough, don't you think?

I don't think I'll need you to send me any money for the trip, because Uncle Álvaro told me that Papá still has to charge the tenant at La Cartuja, and when I get back from Toro I'll charge him, so you see, I'll come home fattened up and with more money . . . Stupendous. He should have a tenant in every province in Spain.

---

1. Uncle Polín and Uncle Álvaro: Leopoldo and Álvaro Barón Torres, Rafael's maternal uncles.

2. Pedrosillo: Leopoldo Barón and María Osorio's estate near Ávila.

I don't have anything else to tell you. As for my life here, you can imagine . . . Absolute tranquility in every way, and delighted by how caring my aunt and uncle are toward me, which I don't deserve.

Of course, I have no idea what happened to the money Papá gave me quite a few days ago now . . . nothing to be done about that . . . It rolls away, that's why it's round . . . Clearly, I can't be helped. Now I'm undertaking this trip to Toro on sweet credit . . . Anyway, blessed be the tenant at La Cartuja.

Well, my dearest mother, give Merceditas a big hug for me, and tell her that I'm going to bring her a huge present . . . thanks to the tenant at La Cartuja . . . yes, again with the tenant.

That's all for today. May the Blessed Virgin guide us all. All my love, your son, who is always thinking of you,

Rafael

Uncle Álvaro and Aunt Pepita send you lots of hugs.[3]

---

3. Uncle Álvaro and Aunt Pepita: Rafael's maternal uncle, Álvaro Barón Torres, and Pepita Conde Merino, his wife. Rafael was staying with them in Burgos at the time.

58. To Leopoldo Arnaiz Barón

Toro, November 14, 1934[1]

Dear Leopoldo,

Just a quick note to say that tomorrow I'll offer my communion for you, since it's your name day.[2] Tell Papá that I'll be in Burgos on Saturday,[3] and from there I'll tell you when I'll be arriving in Oviedo.

Fernando told me in a letter that his examinations are on Monday; is Papá going to Madrid? How is Merceditas doing?

I'm doing well, everyone is doing well. Without further ado, a big hug from your brother,

Rafael

The whole family sends you kisses.

1. Rafael wrote this postcard to his brother Leopoldo from Toro.
2. Name day: The feast of Saint Leopold is celebrated on November 15.
3. Saturday: That is, November 17.

59. *To Rafael Arnaiz Sánchez de la Campa and Mercedes Barón Torres*

Burgos, November 19, 1934

My dearest parents,

Today, which is Monday, I'm already back from Toro; I got here on Saturday, just as Uncle Álvaro had expected.

Mariano Sáiz, the tenant at La Cartuja, was given notice, and we expect him to come by and pay the rent today, which is 500 pesetas. From that, I'll pay Uncle Álvaro what I owe, which is around 160, and then I'll bring the rest with me to Oviedo. I found my grandmother and Aunt María well in Toro. Uncle Polín's affairs are not yet entirely settled . . . Anyway, I'll explain it all in person.

I'm doing very well; I've been following my diet, although even with sugar substitutes and following Laredo's advice, on the days I had a little more, Uncle Álvaro gave me ten units of insulin . . . Nothing to be done about that . . . these things happen when you're sick, but since I'm always on top of these matters, I don't want to have any setbacks.

I'll go directly to Santander, as you said, and if I can stop at La Trapa for a day, I will; Fr. Marcelo wrote me to ask what we'd been through at home,[1] and I'd like to say hello to him and explain to him in person how my illness is going. In Santander, I'll go to the Hotel México, where I'll wait for you to come looking for me, as you said in your letter.

I expect to leave here on Wednesday, so that if I stop in Venta de Baños, I'll be in Santander on Thursday night; so on Friday you could drive over in the morning (on Friday) to come find me. Does that sound good to you?[2] If I'm not there that day because of some delay or other, I'll just

---

1. Fr. Marcelo: Fr. Marcelo León, master of novices. Rafael alludes here to the events of the Revolution of 1934 in Oviedo (see #55).

2. The dates of Rafael's trip were Wednesday, November 21, through Friday, November 23 (OC 372).

telegraph you when I get to the hotel; so don't do anything until you receive a telegram from me in Santander, although as I said I'll try to be there Thursday night.

I don't have anything else to report.

I got a letter from Fernando that he'll be taking his examinations on Monday, or rather, he'll start his examinations, because it seems like they go on for a long time.

I've tried to telephone you a few times, but they said your telephone isn't working. My aunt and uncle are doing well; Aunt Pepita has a sore that is bothering her quite a bit.

All my love, your Trappist, and may the Lord and the Blessed Virgin guide us all,

Rafael

If for any reason you cannot go to Santander or you don't agree with my plan, let me know by telephone before I head out.

60. Dedication of a Holy Card
to Fr. Buenaventura Ramos Caballero[1]

La Trapa, November 21, 1934

Father Buenaventura,

I can offer you nothing, because I have nothing; you, on the other hand, who are close to the tabernacle, please remember this brother of yours who is still out there fighting against the world. While I know that Mary has not abandoned me, I still very much need the prayers of my brother Trappists, at whose side I find myself always, if not physically then at least spiritually.

Asking your blessing, your brother in Jesus and Mary,

Brother María Rafael, OCSO[2]

---

1. Fr. Buenaventura Ramos Caballero: The porter at San Isidro (see #42, n. 6). The card is undated but was probably written during Rafael's visit to La Trapa on November 21, 1934 (OC 374).

2. OCSO: Order of Cistercians of the Strict Observance, or Trappists.

61. To Fr. Marcelo León

Oviedo, February 21, 1935

My dear Father Master,

Honestly, I don't know how to start this letter . . . I want to apologize for my silence, though God knows very well that I have no excuse as far as you are concerned.

What I can promise you is that I have taken up my pen many times, and I've put it down just as many. Why? . . . I don't know. Perhaps you've thought me lazy or negligent, and that I've forgotten about my dear brother novices and my beloved Trapa, as you put it in your letter. Not at all, Father Master, quite the contrary. While it pains me that you should think so, that is how it looked. Though I've owed my brothers a letter, my moral state and mood has been such that, as I'm telling you, I haven't been able to write, and I've preferred just to cry a bit without anybody finding out. But now I don't want to let more time go by without writing you and giving you an update about my life.

First of all, I should tell you that I've had a fairly serious nervous breakdown. And why is that? I don't know, Father, because of everything and nothing at all . . . I spent Christmastime at home with my parents and brothers and sister again, and it brought back so many memories for me, and I'd be lying if I said I haven't been suffering; blessed be God who wills it thus. I find myself so far from my monastery, which I long for more ardently with each passing day. For me, that is my life, and I see that time is passing, but I don't see what God wants from me . . . Sometimes I think that, truly, I don't deserve to be a son of the Cistercian Order, that I've been dreaming too loftily for such a lowly person, that God has chastened and punished me . . . Perhaps I committed the sin of pride, and I assure you, Father, I'm certainly being purified of it . . . Perhaps less than I deserve.

When I think on my Trapa, and find myself in the world, it makes me want to cry, and being separated from my brother novices saddens me beyond consolation. Perhaps you understand why I haven't written them; since I know they love me, why should I disturb their peace with my wailing and whining? . . . I'm not happy because I don't deserve to be happy . . . But it's not that I should like to be happy here on earth, no; it's not that. What I want is to be better than what I am . . . When I went to La Trapa, I wanted to be holy . . . you know perfectly well that such was my aspiration. That's why, Father, as I've said, it seems to me that I committed the sin of pride, and God humbled me; may He be blessed.

Now I see that I am wretched and weak, so miserly with His love; sometimes sad, sometimes dejected. I am not at all obedient to His divine will, and holiness consists of that, and I am so far from it.

I thought I'd begun to be good, but I haven't at all. I am where I was before, and perhaps even more despicable now. I don't deserve your affection, let alone that you should be thinking of me . . .

But what nonsense I'm spouting, when it's precisely the thought that there are souls in La Trapa who are praying to the Most Blessed Virgin for me that sustains me in my trials. Sometimes I think I'm alone, totally abandoned, left out in the hurricane that is the world, and thinking of you all gives me the courage and strength to keep fighting.

I so enjoyed my visit from Rev. Fr. Abbot and Fr. Buenaventura![3] I was so grateful to them! . . . Every reminder that comes from the monastery is a balm to me.

The greatest work of charity that the novices did was to write me; they don't know how much that means to me, and if I wanted to explain it to them somehow, I wouldn't know how.

Forgive me, Father, but please see to my situation and, in your charity, pray to our Mother for one of Her sons, a brother of yours in religion who is suffering. Pray not that he cease to suffer, but rather that his tears be beneficial to him and that they be helpful to him in some way; for I believe that suffering is useless if one forgets Christ's Calvary and the Sorrows of His Most Holy Mother, don't you?

As for my illness, I'll say that I am getting better, albeit very slowly. For the time being, I can't yet say when my return will be, but according to the doctor, my recovery is a sure thing because I don't have any injuries whatso-

---

3. Dom Félix Alonso García, abbot, and Fr. Buenaventura Ramos Caballero, porter, respectively.

ever. What I won't be able to do is consume excessive starch. They measure out the food I need to eat every day now, and I follow a very strict diet.

I've only seen the aspirant[4] you mentioned once, when he came to see me. Seeing him so happy about his entrance into the Order stirred up something within me called envy. He said he'd come again, and the other day he came by the house, but I wasn't there.

As for José Fernández Sierra, I don't know him, because the one I talked with a few times was a different man, nothing to do with this one. I don't know if he has written to you.

I've asked around about the former, and his address is Mr. Victoriano Banciella's residence, Truébano, Buenavista, Oviedo. Buenavista is a neighborhood two miles from Oviedo, and it is divided up as well, and one of the divisions is Truébano, but it's all under Oviedo. I think all your letters will arrive using these directions.

In any case, I'll try to look for him and give him the letter you sent me.

I don't have anything else to tell you, although many things come to mind; and I would like to bare my entire soul on these pages, so that you might understand me clearly and pray to God for me. I don't doubt that you will, just as the novices and the community are.

Give my regards to Reverend Father Abbot. With affection, your brother in Jesus and Mary,

Br. María Rafael

4. Aspirant: Someone seeking admission to religious life is called an aspirant until he or she formally enters.

62. *To Rafael Arnaiz Sánchez de la Campa*

Torrelodones, September 24, 1935[1]

J-H-S[2]

My dearest father,

I've been thinking of writing you for days now . . . but you know me, paper and pen (or pencil in this case, forgive the lack of respect) have never been friends of mine . . . but I don't want to put it off any longer.

Today, the name day of both Mercedes,[3] you've left the aforementioned rather dismayed when you told them over the phone that you didn't think the trip to Ávila was a good idea. And so your son Rafael, behind their back, is begging you to write them a letter telling them the exact opposite, that is . . . that you think it's absolutely splendid, that you'd had the same idea, that it's totally logical, that *you see it their way*; you know, *seeing another's way* is the eleventh commandment . . . In short, tell them what you think . . . but try to calm their spirits.

When we got back from Villasandino[4] they were quiet and pensive, in a bad mood, naturally . . . Being at the house was too much for us to handle, and we started to badmouth Bienvenida, because what else were we going to do? Your daughter didn't want to go to El Escorial, nor to

---

1. After his sister Merceditas was diagnosed with a life-threatening case of peritonitis, Rafael accompanied her and their mother Mercedes as they sought medical treatment in Madrid. While there, the three stayed in nearby Torrelodones (VE 205–6).

2. J-H-S: A common Christogram, or abbreviated version of the name of Christ. JHS, sometimes also spelled IHS, is derived from the first three letters of the name of Jesus in Greek.

3. September 24 is the feast of Our Lady of Mercy (Nuestra Señora de las Mercedes), and thus the name day of both Rafael's mother and his sister.

4. Villasandino: A town outside Burgos where the Arnaiz-Barón family owned a house (OC 381).

Villalba, which is so lovely;[5] things were getting ugly . . . She said she'd put on weight, that she was strong enough now, that she wanted the rain back in Oviedo, that she wanted to see Mino[6] . . . and so we kept bad-mouthing Bienvenida, and when we got back from the country nobody gave us one (a "*bienvenida*," that is).[7]

Well then, Rafael, get the car, let's go to the circus . . . The next day, Rafael, get the car again, let's go to the movies . . . Well, things continued to get ugly, because the girl didn't want to go toward Puerto, but if we went toward Madrid we wouldn't be able to stay in Las Rozas . . . anyway, you get it.

We went to see Hernando,[8] and as you already know, he said there's no way she can go back to Asturias until later . . . Moaning and groaning . . . So movies again, and more movies, nothing else to be done. It's the only thing this poor Trappist can think of to console his sister. Hernando looked at her through rays while the German took snapshots. He said she's cured, and what's left will go away in this final phase, but the worst thing she could do is go to Oviedo, and until November she must remain on the Meseta.[9] That's what science says. Alas! There's no other way.

We argued about it and landed on . . . nothing, because whenever you argue with two women you don't land anywhere . . . But anyway, the point is we argued about it: Torrelodones or Villasandino. Torrelodones was all Madrid's cinemas and Bienvenida's dirty looks, poor thing, but what else were we going to do? Movies every day, or at least, an excuse to go to Madrid.

Well then, off to Villasandino, to suffer through the cold, the three of us all alone with Fr. Juan[10] . . . But anyway, we were decided; after all, a month goes quickly.

5. El Escorial is a historical royal residence and monastery outside Madrid. Collado Villalba is a small town just north of Torrelodones.

6. Mino: Short for Maximino, an unidentified acquaintance of the Arnaiz-Barón family (OC 382).

7. Bienvenida means "welcome" in Spanish, although it also appears to be the name of the unidentified woman whom Merceditas and Rafael were criticizing.

8. Hernando: A radiologist who attended to Merceditas (OC 382).

9. Meseta: The Meseta Central (lit. "Central Plateau") are the highlands of central Spain, separated from Asturias in the north by the Cantabrian Mountains.

10. Fr. Juan: Juan Martínez Barbero, the parish priest at Villasandino.

Mercedes *could not care less*; what she wants is the Oviedo rain and to use an umbrella again, and so on . . . and so on. Mamá speaks, argues, and makes plans, gracious under pressure like a glider pilot . . . I go off to see Almenas.[11] We go to bed at nine. Ramón[12] keeps at the fuel pump and Father[13] taps away at the typewriter, getting very close to the keys and using just one finger . . . he makes me nervous.

We head to Ávila and spend the night at Uncle Polín's house. We attend the consecration of Bp. Santos.[14] It is a moving ceremony. I thought of you a lot, you would have liked it. There's an indescribable enthusiasm about the new bishop, who is a holy man, adored by the people of Ávila.

Mercedes is delighted with Dolores[15] and her other cousins. I—forgive me for speaking of myself, as for quite some time now my preferences ought not to figure into the family's plans at all—I do what I ought and what I can, and nothing more. That's how God wants it . . . so all right. As I've said, I'm happy with it too. Ávila means so much to me, and I feel affection for it. For one thing, my aunt and uncle, who love me so much; then there's the peace of the hometown of Saint Teresa, whom I see around every corner. My soul rejoices spiritually so much in Ávila, I don't know why . . . Mamá remembers Villasandino . . . the dusty road, the cold house, and the three of us with Fr. Juan in the afternoon. And without telling *anybody*, after Holy Mass, she goes off to see about a boarding house for eight pesetas a night and whether we might spend the remaining month of our time in Castile there.

When she comes back to the house and tells us about it, everyone bursts with excitement . . . The month of October is so nice here, it's sunny, sure it'll be cold here too, but you notice it less with people around. The girl loves the idea, and it doesn't strike me as absurd, so we go see the boarding house. We don't like it . . . We look at other accommodations, and at last,

11. Almenas: José María de Palacio y Abárzuza, Count of Las Almenas, who owned the Palace of Canto del Pico in Torrelodones.

12. Ramón: A domestic servant who worked for the Arnaiz-Barón family at Torrelodones.

13. Father: Referred to only as the "parish priest" of Torrelodones, his name is unknown.

14. Bp. Santos: Santos Moro Briz (1888–1980) was ordained bishop of Ávila on September 22, 1935.

15. Dolores: Dolores Barón y Osorio Moscoso, the eldest daughter of Rafael's aunt and uncle, María Osorio and Leopoldo Barón.

we see some rooms at the Hotel Inglés. There's lots of light, and a terrace for Mercedes to sunbathe on. It's 12.50 a night, but for the whole month they let us have it for 11 a night, full room and board.

We are all very pleased, the ghost of Villasandino has disappeared, and Mercedes is excited about her cousins. So, do you see it their way now? . . . I think so. I don't want to influence you, but I'm telling it as I see it, and if I must tell you the truth, the idea of Villasandino scared me a little. Not for my own sake, God knows, because I want for nothing when I have Him in the tabernacle . . . But Mercedes has been sick for many months now,[16] and we miss you all very much.

That's all. As far as news, I'll say that Enrique Ortiz fought a young bull the other day . . . and broke a few of his ribs in the process. He is still complaining about his chest, but he's out of danger now, though it was very grave indeed. After all, he is fifty years old. Uncle Polín thinks the business with the tenant is all taken care of, he's off to Toro now . . . I'm getting the carbon buildup out of the car. And that's about it . . . They already took the piano, and on September 30 we're going to Ávila. Mercedes continues to put on weight; I think since you last saw her, it's been four and a half pounds, I'm not sure.[17]

Don't stop writing, that's why I'm writing you. Forgive your son for being a nuisance, all I want is for everyone to be happy.

Don't worry about money. First, if you consider the matter correctly before God, you'll see you have more than you deserve, and to complain is to offend Him; and second, when it runs out, it runs out . . . What do you want it for? The Lord and the Virgin watch over all of us, and won't abandon us.

Sending you a hug to share with my brothers, because everything is better when shared. See you soon. Your son,

Rafael

16. Merceditas had been sick since at least September 1934, when her illness is first mentioned in Rafael's letters (see #49).

17. Both Merceditas and Rafael painstakingly tracked their weight when they fell sick, as a way of measuring their physical strength. During their respective illnesses, they noted increases in weight as signs of improvement.

63. To Leopoldo Barón

My dearest Uncle Polín,

I suppose today that whole collection of papers, cards, flyers, and such that they had at the Parents' Association will have gone out.

Yesterday I went at four, and between a grandfather and a son (this nephew of yours) we did what we could. There were quite a few people there at seven in the evening. We put lodging prices in the bulletins (which we had to take out of their envelopes and put back in) . . . Fr. Herrera is staying with the Sisters of Mary Reparatrix. We got permission from the bishop and the governor . . . the man with the litigation, I don't remember his name, did two reports . . . Anyway, everything is moving forward . . . They spent quite a few *pesetas* on stamps and such . . . As for things here, don't worry, everyone's very happy.

I don't need to tell you that I think of you very often, and I ask the Virgin at my Trapa to enlighten you . . . I assure you that with Her at your side, you don't need lawyers or attorneys, and I'm sure She has heard me; She loves me very much and never refuses me anything. All you have to do is talk, argue, and deal with men . . . If you suffer, all the better; God sees your intentions, and they alone are enough. He'll do the rest.

Today I went to see Sor Pilar,[2] and, after an hour and a half with her, I placed myself at Jesus' feet to give Him thanks, because truly I do not deserve the consolations my good Jesus gives me. Who am I, Lord?

Anyway, Uncle Polín, just remember what I told you that one time . . . We come across many thorns in this world . . . but there are flowers

1. This undated letter was sent alongside one from Rafael's aunt, María Osorio, to her husband Leopoldo. He was away from the family's home in Ávila on business in Toro (OC 388).

2. Sor Pilar: Sor Pilar García, abbess of the Poor Clares at Ávila and a spiritual advisor to Rafael (see #43, n. 8).

too. Sometimes they're very tiny and you can hardly see them, but if you look for them, you'll find them . . . And then . . . how can we not give thanks to the Lord for His kindness toward us?

Take heart, Uncle Polín, because I am *sure* that even in the midst of all your suffering and sorrows, God will give you some consolation; you'll always have something to cheer you up . . . Some act of affection, or some fruit borne of your suffering . . . and if you get none of that, all the better, for as Sor Pilar told me so energetically this morning, "The greatest consolation is to have none at all."

Uncle Polín, forgive your nephew, who am I to give you consolation or relief? But since you know me by now, I want you to realize that I'm not trying to do that . . . Anyway, I've made a mess of it! . . . "*Sursum corda*!!!"[3]

I'm taking advantage of Aunt María's letter to send you this little note . . . Take from it nothing but my affection for you, as you know I truly have. Your nephew,

Rafael

Give my grandmother and Aunt María a million hugs for me.

3. *Sursum corda*: "Lift up your hearts," the first line of the preface to the Eucharistic Prayer in the Mass.

IV. Shaped in His Hands

A Path of Oblation

64. *To Dom Félix Alonso García*

Ávila, October 9, 1935

J-H-S

Reverend and dear Father Abbot,

I have offered many prayers to the Most Blessed Virgin before beginning this letter, and spent a lot of time consulting Jesus by the tabernacle . . . The time has come for me to decide to open my heart to my superiors at once, in order to tell them my decision and the journey my soul has made.

Reverend Father, I want you to understand my words, which, though clumsy, are sincere; and for you to be merciful toward me. And so, I have asked God for this.

Reverend Father, I've been away from my beloved Trapa for nearly a year and a half now, and if only you knew, Reverend Father, how great a work the Lord has done in me! . . . And how grateful I am to Him for the trial that He is making me endure . . . I've often thought about how unworthy I am, that Jesus should care for me, but how could He not? . . . Do I not care for Him? God is so good, and He knows what He is doing, and sometimes He uses the least and most miserable of all earthly things in order to make known His majesty.

When I requested that you admit me into the community two years ago, writing from this same Ávila, my desire was good and holy; I was searching for God, and God gave Himself to me so freely . . . I suffered, but when it's for His sake, it's not suffering . . . I had hopes and dreams, I wanted to be holy, I thought with delight about the choir, about being a real monk someday . . . There was so much happening within me, Reverend Father . . . I was searching for God, but I was also searching for His creatures, and I was searching for myself; and God wants me all to Himself . . . My vocation was from God, and is of God, but it needed to be purified, its rough edges needed smoothing. I gave myself to the Lord generously, but I still wasn't giving Him *everything*; I gave Him my body, my soul, my career, my family . . . but I still held on to one thing: my dreams and desires, my hopes of being a Trappist and making my vows and singing the Mass. That kept me going at La Trapa, but God wants more, He always wants more. I needed to be transformed. He wanted His love alone to be enough for me.

With a novice's zeal, I offered Him . . . I offered Him something, but I didn't know what. I thought I didn't have anything left to give Him, that my life was the one thing I had left, and that He already knew it was His.

Reverend Father, I have nothing else to tell you; God sent me a trial, and at first I thought it meant that God didn't love me, that His will was different, but He doesn't ask for our opinion or explain Himself when He sends us something that's good for us. Weak creatures, what do you know of God's designs! He'll handle doing the work without consulting us. All we have to do is let ourselves be shaped in His hands, and hold still, very still; later, the time and light He has sent us will allow us to see His work clearly, and then we will give Him infinite thanks for His loving care.

How many tears must be shed before one is willing to kiss the cross! First we ask for a cross, and then we cry when it is given to us; but once we are on it, how happy we are to find ourselves at Christ's side . . . Though He is a God, He died on the cross for us; so if we truly love Him, the cross ought to be and must be our delight. Isn't that so?

Forgive me, Reverend Father, I've gone astray from where I should be; I'll return to the purpose of my letter.

I was at the monastery about a year ago, and I shared how I was feeling at the time with Fr. Marcelo and with Your Reverence.[1] I asked Fr. Marcelo if it would be possible for me to one day enter as an oblate,[2] because of the diet I have to follow; he said yes, and Your Reverence told me to wait . . . I have waited, for the will of my superiors is the will of God . . . I have waited a year, which seemed like a century to me. The Most Blessed Virgin has upheld me in my vocation; the Lord has given me to understand that the world is not my place, that He wants me beside the tabernacle—and, Reverend Father, to the tabernacle I wish to go.

Once more, then, I ask the community to admit this poor man, who neither wants nor desires anything more than to dwell in the house of God.

---

1. Rafael spoke with the abbot alongside Fr. Marcelo León, master of novices, on the visit of November 21, 1934 (OC 392).

2. Oblate: A lay member of a monastery who does not take vows and observes a modified schedule (see #7, n. 13).

I don't deserve to be a monk . . . Singing Holy Mass . . . Lord, if I am to see you so soon, what does it matter? . . . The vows . . . do I not love God with all my strength? Then what do vows matter? None of that prevents me from being at His side, dedicating my silence among men to Him, and loving Him quietly and humbly in the simplicity of the oblature.[3] Saint Benedict admitted oblates, and some of them became saints. Why should I not be among them? . . . Of my own strength I cannot, but with Jesus and Mary at my side, I can do all things. When I fall, They will help me.

Your Reverence will speak of the humiliation this entails, the fact of being nothing and no one. But am I someone now? As for humiliation, I don't believe I will feel that way, because in order for a soul to be humbled it must first be up high and then be brought low, and I don't think I have to be brought low at all. Quite the contrary, the real humiliation is when a creature is exalted in the eyes of men, because when that person stands before God, so wretched and wicked in His divine eyes while so extolled by men . . . then he will know true humiliation.

Forgive me, and be merciful to me, Reverend Father—but surely the miter that the Lord has placed in your hands is more of a humiliation than being assigned the lowest place in a Trappist monastery. Did God not humble Himself? That can indeed be called humiliation, but when it comes to us? That word does not apply to us, insignificant dust that we are. Look what I'm saying, my good Father Abbot! Take all this as the ramblings of someone madly in love with God . . . and if I fail to show you the respect I owe you, forgive me; but I want you to know everything I am thinking and how I am feeling about it, and when I sat down to write, I promised to expose my soul completely.

There are so many things I'd say to you, if only I knew how to write. It gives me such joy to think of how God loves me, the path down which He is guiding me, the undeserved light He gives me . . . But of course, I have God, and God has hold of me; what more could I desire? I spoke to you of the cross before, but with Him I no longer have one. My sorrows and the tears I poured out for Him have turned into peace and calm. I have the Lord; let me live beside His tabernacle, eating the crumbs that

---

3. Oblature: The status of being an oblate (comparable to "the novitiate" for the status of being a novice).

fall from the convent's table, and I'll be happy . . . happy in my nothing, and joyous in my Everything, who is Jesus.

Your Reverence, do you see the work of God now? He has accomplished the greatest and most admirable work in me, a creature of His who—and I don't say this with insincerity or false modesty—has nothing and deserves nothing; I have only sins to offer such a good God . . . I possess neither virtue nor knowledge, but I do know what I am . . . and God knows it too. I might be able to fool human beings, but I can't fool Him.

Tell me, Reverend Father, if my vocation is not from God. Enlighten me if I am deceived; have no mercy. Jesus made use of a harsh blow to make me see clearly before. But if Your Reverence goes before God and considers my situation, you will see a man who, despite everything, is still thinking of his Trapa.

It has been two years (or it will be two in January) since I entered the novitiate. Even so, perhaps not in the eyes of men, but certainly in the eyes of God, I have not ceased for even a moment to be Brother Rafael, Cistercian novice. I assure you that, even if I were to spend the rest of my life in the world, in spirit I would continue to be a Trappist. I carry it deep within me, and the Virgin of La Trapa is always at my side. I am sure that She wants me there, and She wants me to inhabit the humility of which She is an example to us.

I fear only one thing, and that is to fail to be a good example to the community in the observance of the holy Rule, but God wishes to take even that from me, which is a great consolation. Of course, being despised and being no one is a consolation too, and a much greater one, but that is out of my hands and I am not seeking it either.

The other day, a very holy nun[4] whom I went to consult about my decision told me that the Lord would give me so much more this way than if I continued to be a choir novice.[5] I also recall what Your Reverence told me when I entered the monastery, that God would repay me even in this world for the sacrifice I was making . . . Anyway, as God well knows, I don't follow God for any of that now . . . I love God just because, and

---

4. Sor Pilar García, abbess of the Poor Clares at Ávila (see #3, n. 8).

5. Choir novice: When Rafael first entered the monastery, he was called a choir novice because he was in formation to become a choir monk, as distinct from a lay brother.

that's it. Even though I love God very little, my love isn't mercenary. I know that He loves me, and that is enough for me.

It is a very great mortification to follow the Rule and observe the fasts, but perhaps it is an even greater one to have to take an indulgence.[6]

I still haven't brought up my health, and well, it is the least of my concerns. I'm doing about the same, I carry on with my normal life other than when it comes to food. I could follow the Rule for many years, even. Diabetes is simply a matter of a particular type of diet: switching out some foods for others, maybe taking indulgences . . . Medication by way of injections from time to time, and that's it.

If what I am attempting were absurd on a practical level, I wouldn't have even dared to propose it to Your Reverence. I am merely holding onto Fr. Marcelo's words: that there are many cases like mine, or very similar to mine, in many of the monasteries in France.

If a donation is necessary in order to avoid burdening the community, I don't think my father would refuse me, but they don't know anything yet. I'm waiting for your reply before talking to them; I don't think they'd have or raise any objections.

In any case, I will wait for Your Reverence to decide and give me your answer about what I ought to do, or if I should come speak to you in person. Everything else can wait until afterwards. It's all in Mary's hands.

In Madrid, I went to see a doctor who is well known in this field, and he told me that I have a light form of pancreatic diabetes that would eventually correct itself, but in the meantime I should not consume excessive starch or sugar. I just have to be careful. I wouldn't have any trouble following this diet in the monastery, whether in the refectory or in the infirmary, it's all the same to me, or in the guesthouse, if Your Reverence so instructs. Ultimately, when we go up to receive the Lord at Communion, He doesn't ask us if we have eaten this or that. He is the same for everyone in the community, isn't that so? He won't love me any less than Br. Damián or Br. Bernardo[7] because they eat bread and beans while I eat milk and eggs. God has arranged it thus, so He must know best. When we are all reunited in His presence, and the day is coming soon, such

6. Indulgence: A reprieve from the usual monastic fare at mealtimes (see #31, #33 n. 2).

7. Br. Damián, Br. Bernardo: Rafael's co-novices when he first entered the monastery; see #28, n. 3.

small differences will fade away. They are merely human differences, and we must dispense with all that is human, not just in heaven but also here on earth. For if we view everything supernaturally, everything brings us to God: both the rigorous fast of the one who can observe it, and the care taken by the one who is sick, amid all his miseries. Thus I return to my theme, Reverend Father: we who have God have everything. What does the rest of it matter?

I'm not writing to Fr. Marcelo because I know that he's sick and is not in the novitiate.[8] Please give him my kind regards, and the same to the whole community. My regards also to my confessor, Fr. Teófilo, who is often in my thoughts, for I have found myself so alone on so many occasions, and in such doubt, that I've had much to offer God, although it is all rather little.

Of course, I've also consulted souls who are very much of God, and they have enlightened me quite a bit. For most of the time that I've been away from La Trapa, however, I have been face to face only with God, and even that was only when He did not hide Himself from me. May He be blessed, for I certainly deserved that; my sins have not been few.

If only you knew, Reverend Father, how much the Virgin has helped me! She lifted me up when I fell, upheld me over all the threats I have faced in my vocation, and consoled me when I found myself struggling against the world, which is so clingy . . . Whether I'd been good, bad, or something in between, at seven in the evening when I united myself to my brothers in choir and prayed the *Salve* to her, I felt a seeming consolation at the thought of the Virgin uniting me to La Trapa; She was protecting us all, gazing upon us all, both the Trappists in their monastery and me wherever I found myself. What would become of us were it not for Her?

Forgive me, Reverend Father, this letter is going on too long . . . this is an outlet for me. It's so difficult to speak of love for God and the Virgin in the world.

Tell Br. Ramón[9] to pray for me, and that I think of him often. He has very much been on my mind, because he suffered, just as I did, in leaving

8. Fr. Marcelo León died on October 1, 1935 (OC 396). He had been succeeded as master of novices by Fr. José Olmedo Arrieta on July 7, 1935 (OC 397).

9. Ramón Vallaure Fernández-Peña (1914–1996), the younger brother of Rafael's close friend Juan Vallaure (see #9, n. 5). Ramón entered the novitiate at San Isidro on July 22, 1935 (OC 398).

it all behind, and that is very difficult . . . His prayers must be very pleasing to the Lord.

There are so many things I'd like to ask you to tell all my brothers, Fr. Francisco, Buenaventura, Br. Tescelino[10] . . . everyone. They'll think I forgot, but souls who love one another for God's sake never forget, and in loving each other they love God. Loving Him in His creatures is a great consolation, and it takes nothing away from His glory; at least, if I am not mistaken.

Answer me, Reverend Father, I beg you for the sake of charity; it will bring consolation to my soul to learn that I may still, however unworthily, begin my name with the "Brother María" of the Cistercians.

Your Reverence can expect an oblate who wants only to give glory to God, to love Him, and to serve Him; a soul who wants nothing, and surrenders to Him even the desire to be professed, for He asks him to. And believe me, I surrender not with any violence to myself, but with pleasure and joy.

I will try to be a holy oblate with the aid of heaven, the counsel of my good superiors, and the help of my community, whom I ask to remember me in their prayers.

Humbly asking your blessing, your novice in Jesus and Mary,

Brother María Rafael
✢*O.C.R.*[11]

P.S. For the full month of October, I will be with my mother and my sister at the Hotel Inglés in Ávila, from which I will go directly to Oviedo. I ask that you send your reply to my aunt and uncle's house, since I do not want my mother to learn of my plans until the latest possible moment. The address is: Duke of Maqueda, San Juan de la Cruz, 4 – Ávila.

10. For Fr. Francisco, see #33, n. 6; #42, n. 4; for Fr. Buenaventura and Br. Tescelino, see #42, n. 7.

11. O.C.R.: "Orden Cisterciense Reformada," or Order of Reformed Cistercians (see #39, n. 12).

65. To Leopoldo Barón

Ávila, October 1935[1]

My dearest Uncle Polín,

When Aunt María writes you, your nephew cannot be far behind . . . Just as well, with so little time left. As you know, we leave on Monday. Don't rush over here, let's not force what's not meant to be. If I can give you a hug, fine. If not, that's fine too, what does it matter? . . . That's what the Rafael in my head says, but as for the real one—poor Rafa, he loves his aunt and uncle so much!

Yesterday we went to Madrid. Aunt María didn't want to come . . . but she came. I'm telling you, Uncle Polín, between the Lord's kindness toward me and the charity of those He places in my path, I don't know what to do with myself. What is the Lord's desire?

Today Aunt María, my mother, and I went to the Shrine of Our Lady of Sonsoles[2] . . . We spent a long time there praying the Holy Rosary. Then, at the feet of Our Lady, I thought about many things, one of which was a poor man who was off in Toro trying to collect some pesetas . . . Perhaps it is the Lord who wants to collect from you, rather than you collecting from men.

I am praying to the Virgin that you will be generous and not mess around. You hear me, Uncle Polín? . . . Anyway, I don't mean to give you advice (too many cooks already). You know better than I do, there's so much that I don't need to say to you . . . just remember who all this is coming from, and be merciful to me.

Aunt María asked me to tell you to write to Mr. Luis.

---

1. This letter is undated.

2. Shrine of Our Lady of Sonsoles: A shrine and hermitage in Ávila dedicated to Mary. The name Sonsoles derives from a local devotion to Saint Zoilus (San Zoilo), an early Christian said to have been martyred by the Romans at Córdoba, Spain.

Pilar[3] has a fever tonight, but don't worry, she's gotten better over the past few days while she's been in bed . . . God is watching over all of us.

I don't have anything else to say. Give my grandmother and Aunt María and "little Ropi" lots of hugs for me.[4] As always, your brother and nephew, more the former than the latter,

Br. M. Rafael

3. Pilar: Pilar Barón y Osorio Moscoso, Rafael's cousin and Leopoldo's daughter.

4. Rafael's maternal grandmother, Fernanda Torres Erro; his aunt, María Josefa Barón Torres; and friend, Rosa "Ropi" Calvo, all lived in Toro, where Leopoldo was visiting.

66. *To Leopoldo Barón*

Ávila, October 1935[1]

My dearest brother in the Lord, Uncle Polín,

Today I went sightseeing with Juan Vallaure and Arraiza,[2] who came here to spend the day with me. I'm a bit tired, because even though they love me very much, I can promise you that I got used to something so. . . different that even the good ones tire me out somewhat . . . Everything is for God.

We leave on Monday, God willing; as to our return . . . we are all in God's hands, and that's a very good thing, don't you think?

When I get to Oviedo I'll write you and Aunt María a very, very long letter. Right now I can't put anything into words; I'm rather out of it. I haven't been able to go make my visit[3] or anything . . . I think the Lord stirs up our spirits just so that we might truly come to know what it is to be at peace.

I am very pleased. I see God at work in someone whom I love dearly . . . It's an extraordinary thing . . . Uncle Polín, if we could truly see, we wouldn't know what to do with ourselves. What have we done? What does the Lord want? I don't know what I'm talking about, may God forgive me, and may you as well.

May the peace of the Lord be with you. Your nephew,

Br. M. Rafael

1. This letter is undated.

2. Juan Vallaure, Rafael's close friend, and Eugenio Arraiza Vilella, their mutual friend and classmate at the Higher Technical School of Architecture of Madrid (OC 401).

3. Make my visit: that is, make an hour of Eucharistic Adoration, which Rafael called his daily "visit with the Lord."

67. Dedication of a Holy Card to Dolores Barón Osorio[1]

Ávila, October 25, 1935

Dolores,

All I can tell you about the Virgin Mary is this: in the world and in La Trapa and wherever I find myself, the Virgin has helped me in some way . . . in a way only She knows how.

You don't have to be a saint to love her very much. Just do it, and you'll find that the thorns you come across on your path soften with Mary's help, and perhaps even become flowers.

No, Dolores, you don't have to be a saint to love Her, the consolation and refuge of sinners.

I assure you that with a little love for God and lots for the Virgin, even here on earth you'll have everything your Trappist cousin hopes for you. Whenever he comes to mind, I beg you, pray to Her for him.

Brother María Rafael O.C.R.

1. Dolores Barón Osorio was Rafael's cousin, the daughter of Leopoldo Barón and María Osorio.

68. *Dedication of a Holy Card to María Osorio*

Ávila, October 27, 1935[1]
Feast of Christ the King[2]

J.H.S.

After giving it a good deal of thought, I'll pray for *nothing* for you, and I'll say nothing to you either, my dearest aunt María. That way, I'm praying for *everything*, and saying everything to you too.

Souls who love one another in God have need of silence . . . let us be silent, then, so that you in the world and I in my monastery might both let ourselves be filled with the love for Jesus that unites us so closely.

Everything is passing away, consolations, afflictions, sorrows, and joys alike, but love for God, our only reason for living, remains. Love flickering out or fully aflame. Love in silence or love out loud. Love in peacetime or love in wartime. What does it matter? As He wishes, but may our lives on earth be nothing more than that: Love!!

May that love for God be all that remains when our souls are united before the tabernacle. God, who sees all things and understands us, will unite us even closer the more we love Him. That is my prayer. Your brother in Jesus,

Rafael

1. The holy card in question featured Saint Teresa of Ávila and Saint Thérèse of Lisieux. María Osorio later gave it to her friend Lilí Álvarez, a prominent tennis player and journalist (OC 404).

2. At the time, the feast of Christ the King was celebrated on the last Sunday of October.

69. To Dom Félix Alonso García

Oviedo, November 7, 1935

J.H.S.

My dear and Reverend Father,

I am writing you from Oviedo, where I arrived a few days ago with my family. The object of my letter is simply to inform Your Reverence and fill you in on the details of how the Lord is clearing the way for me, after facing so many obstacles in my vocation . . . obstacles that I now see were necessary. May the Lord be blessed for all of it.

The other day, after asking Our Lady, the Virgin Mary, for her help, I spoke to my father. Clearly and in detail, I told him of my plans and the conditions under which Your Reverence charitably admitted me into the monastery once more. He found our reasoning very fair and prudent, and even though I had more or less been counting on that, I continue to praise God for everything and for my father's generosity toward me.

He told me that not only would he not stand in my way, but that he would now and forever try to help me morally and spiritually for the sake of my happiness, which he clearly sees is within my monastery.

He found it very fair that he should provide a donation in order to avoid burdening the community. As to the amount, I told him that it would be best for him to speak with Your Reverence about it when we come to the monastery . . . It would be better in person, don't you think? He told me he'd do as Your Reverence sees fit.

As for the timing, all we've decided so far is that I'll spend Christmastime at home. My brother Fernando will be coming from Belgium, and if I can give them the consolation of spending Christmas all together . . . I should. That's what Your Reverence advised me to do, and I believe generosity deserves to be repaid with generosity, and I can do nothing else.

Therefore, the latest I'll arrive at La Trapa would be approximately January 15, the same date on which I entered two years ago.

If I may, Reverend Father, I must tell you how pleased I am. I don't know how to thank the Lord for such a blessing. I'd be an absolute fool not to become holy now . . . but the Lord will help me.

My good Christian father sends his regards (my mother doesn't know anything yet); give mine to the whole community. Awaiting Your Reverence's blessing, your novice,

Brother María Rafael
O.C.R.

C/O Argüelles 39, no. 3, Oviedo.

70. *To María Osorio*

Oviedo, November 8, 1935

J-H-S

My dearest aunt and sister in the Lord, María,

Your letter was such a consolation to me. If I hadn't gone to bed so late last night, you'd have already received my letter and it would have crossed paths with yours, as you predicted.

I want to tell you so many things! How sorrowful I was to see you cry in Ávila when we left . . . ! And that I should be the cause! May it all serve Him.

Nothing you said about the consolation and peace you received from the Lord upon reading Saint John of the Cross surprises me in the least. I experienced the same thing. . . The day before, at Sonsoles, we read, "I will not gather flowers, nor fear wild beasts . . ."[1] Well, I spent the whole ride home with that on my mind, with Mary's help . . . I saw places, people, and panoramas pass by; gripping the steering wheel tightly, and yes, very much wanting to cry, I kept going down the highway without stopping. . .

I had just left behind in Ávila many of the flowers that Saint John of the Cross speaks of . . . The Lord asks me to keep going and not stop. What am I to do? What I always do: look up, up high . . . and keep going and not stop . . . You ought to do the same. The Virgin is gazing upon you and God is helping you; don't be concerned with crying or laughing, what's the difference? Clay is clay, we can't change what we are. The important thing is that this clay be given back to God, so may He do as He pleases with it, and may *everything* bring us toward Him.

How difficult it is not to gather flowers! But how easy it is, too . . . Once the initial break has been made, God draws us in such a way, with

---

1. From the third stanza of the *Spiritual Canticle*: "Seeking my Love / I will head for the mountains and for watersides, / I will not gather flowers, / nor fear wild beasts; / I will go beyond strong men and frontiers" (SJC 471).

such gentleness, that it's no struggle at all . . . What difference does it make to cry? . . . Cry as much as you can; laugh and rejoice as much as you can, what does it matter! You're the one who is doing the laughing and crying. . . and you're nobody, you're nothing. . . And believe me, dearest sister—you won't mind if I call you that?—believe me, when you realize that . . . when you become detached from everything, including *your own self*, only then will you see: everything that happens to us is completely inconsequential. Neither suffering nor rejoicing will draw our gaze . . . Then we shall be able to see God better . . . Let's not look at ourselves so much . . . and if we do look at ourselves, and scrutinize ourselves, let it be in order to seek out the God hidden within us.

The other day, even amid my affliction and sorrow, there were moments in which I forgot everything and delighted in God right there in the middle of the highway. Everything was passing by so quickly! . . . Everything was so small, even me, so insignificant in God's eyes . . . I was in such a rush to see Him . . . I didn't know what I was doing. "I will not gather flowers," I thought . . . What flowers? Have I gathered any flowers? No . . . I can't stop, there's no need to make an effort, I don't need to stop . . . even if I wanted to, *God wouldn't let me.* This happens to you too, right?

What a joy, Lord! Send me whatever You want, be it flowers or thorns. What difference does it make to me? . . . I mustn't stop to look at anything, because I have enough to look at in You. You fill us in such a way, You love us in such a way, that everything disappears before You and we amount to nothing . . . !

What a joy it is, Lord, to be able to see You and not have to see ourselves! . . . What's the difference between flowers and thorns if You are the one who gives them, who brings them to us and takes them away? We do nothing, for nothing is all we know how to do; You do everything . . . If we speak of the cross, it is so that we might complain selfishly; if we seek consolation, we seek it in ourselves; if we want to love You, we do it wickedly and don't even know it . . .

What a joy it is, Lord, to think that You do everything for us! . . . And so it is all great and beautiful.

Lord, I cannot stop, because when I stop it is only in order to seek myself, and I find nothing in myself that is worth the effort . . . I must

continue moving toward You. What do I care about flowers? What do
I care about thorns? I have You, I have Your love, I have everything . . .
What a joy to find oneself in nothing, with nothing.

Alongside these thoughts, the journey to Oviedo continued . . . I
left many things by the side of the road, but I didn't want them. God was
waiting for me on the horizon, so I couldn't stop, nor did I want to.

It's so difficult to detach yourself . . . but once you are detached, it's
easier to fly. Afterwards, I prayed Hail Marys, that God might help you
the way He was helping me.

We arrived in Oviedo at six-thirty. We ate in León and got through the
trip perfectly, without anyone getting carsick.

Today I'm staying at home alone. My parents and my brother and sister
went to Infiesto.[2] I have time now to collect my thoughts for you, so I will.

You say that I've done you a great deal of good . . . if you say so, I
believe you. Sometimes the Lord uses the lowest of the low to realize His
work. You've asked me to help you become holy . . . I read what you
write me, I look up at God, and it seems to me that He is smiling . . .
Either you are very humble, or I am crazy . . . Either way, the Lord knows
best. And if you tell me straightforwardly that I can help you . . . then
I'll straightforwardly respond that everything I am and everything that
is in my power is yours already . . . I united myself to your prayers . . .
and what's more, I've offered so many things to the Lord that I need not
write you a thing in order for you to get where He wants you to go . . .
and don't you stop on the way.

You think of me often? . . . If that helps you to turn to God, it's a good
thing. I think of you too, and how when we were sitting in the car, you
asked me to talk to you about God. I was a bit taken aback by that, but
later on I realized I wasn't the one speaking . . . you already know that;
what I said had the same effect on me that it did on you . . . Talk about
God! . . . talk and talk . . . until I had to fall silent, you remember? I
will always remember that. I see nothing bad in it. If a creature is useful
in getting us to God, why would we be rid of it? . . . Whether through
presence or through memory . . . it's all useful. We are like children still,
and the sweets and candies that the Father gives us make us love Him

---

2. Infiesto: a town east of Oviedo. The siblings Rafael mentions here are Leopoldo and
Mercedes; his brother Luis Fernando was studying in Belgium at the time (OC 409).

more. The day is coming when we will love Him without needing any gift in return. Maybe it's already here.

Tell me whatever you want and in whatever manner you please. I understand you, and while I am not worthy of your expectations, your letters will be read, answered, and destroyed. Do the same with mine. What do we need papers for? I am writing you in confidence.[3] And keep only what suits you from what you read here, and ignore the rest of it. Pay no mind to anything but my intentions, which are, of course, honorable. I asked the Lord and Mary for light before sitting down to write, and if They guide me in great things then surely They guide me in little ones too. Although I haven't done anything great yet, at least not what people consider great. Rather, everything in me is little. I just wish my love were great . . . but you know very well that I don't have room.

Anyway, pay me no mind. I'm just talking nonsense and being mad . . . you know what I mean?

When we got to Oviedo, all I could think about was looking for an opportunity to talk to my Christian father, and I asked the Virgin for one . . . I couldn't calm down, I was uneasy. My secret[4] wouldn't let me rest. On Tuesday morning,[5] I asked the Lord what I should do. He gave me to understand that I should take this step that very day, and that He would be with me.

Indeed, my father and I went to make our visit to the Lord that afternoon . . . I held on to Our Lady tightly, and when we left the church, I told him everything, as gently and clearly as possible . . . Just a few minutes later, I was kneeling at the Virgin's feet, giving thanks. I still am, I'm telling you . . . How great God is, my dear sister! How He loves us! If only you knew . . . My father was so *thrilled*. He told me that he only wanted me to be happy, that he wanted me to become holy so that I could make him holy, that God loved us so much, that he thought everything that was being asked of him[6] was great and very reasonable and very fair, and that he would always help me.

3. In fact Rafael destroyed María's correspondence, but she did not destroy his (OC 410).

4. My secret: That is, that he had been re-admitted to La Trapa.

5. Tuesday: November 5.

6. Rafael was re-admitted to the monastery on the condition that his father would make a regular donation to provide for his care (OC 411).

In short, his was a generosity that only Christ's charity could provide. He said I should go whenever I wanted, and all he asked of me was to help him from the monastery, that he might place himself in God's hands in everything and for any reason. He said he had surrendered his will to that of God, and that he wanted me to become very holy, for my sake and for his.

What do you think? How could I not love God, how could I not drown myself in Him?! I thought I'd go mad with joy. I love Him so much!. . . What did I do, oh God of mine? What are sorrows and tears worth, if we get results like these in exchange?

God heard me then, and He is listening to me now, I know it, I can tell. I don't know what to do with myself, I'm a wreck, as you'd say. . . I knew God loved me, but I didn't know it was this much!. . . Love Him dearly, Aunt María, and maybe between the two of us we can do something. . . I don't know, I feel so helpless, so small, I just don't know . . .

Love Him dearly, make up for what is lacking in me . . . I want to be surrounded only by souls who love God dearly . . . then I'd be calmer . . . Love him dearly, Aunt María, I beg you. If only you knew . . . you wouldn't cry, you wouldn't laugh, you wouldn't be able to do anything but love. But when the Lord gives us this nervousness and exhaustion that we go through for His sake . . . He must know why He is doing it.

I wish I could be quiet and not write any more, but I can't. You don't mind if I tell you that I love God very much, right? Forgive me, and destroy this letter . . . I don't know if I am doing the right thing. . .

I can't have the peace you wish for me as long as I go on like this . . . What I wish for you is . . . just that, lots of love for Jesus . . . that Jesus who does nothing but give and give, who gives even though He gets nothing in return . . . What sorrow! What joy! Do you know what I mean? I want to go crazy.

Anyway, I don't know what I'm talking about anymore.

Yesterday I wrote Father Abbot. Three times I tore up the letter and started over. I'll go after Christmas; generosity deserves to be repaid with generosity, right? . . . My mother still doesn't know anything; my father and I agree that she shouldn't be told until the last possible minute, what good would it do? . . . My mother and sister keep making plans, but I've asked my father not to make me go back to Ávila . . . He understood, and he told me that if Mamá and Mercedes go to Ávila, I'll go to La Trapa. What do you think?

We can still write each other in these coming months, and write about God; He takes care of everything, while we . . . we have nothing to do. Remember? . . . You're so good to me. It gives me such joy to think that in this world, I truly have a little sister whom I can help and be helped by in this endeavor to love God like giants—even though we are children, and very small ones at that . . . But we can do anything with His help . . . doesn't that make you happy?

You, of course, have helped me more than you know . . . When we're in heaven, you'll see.

There are so many things I'd say to you . . . Don't stop writing me. In doing so, you are performing a great work of mercy, even though I am not alone . . . the Lord is present with me at all times, and with Him, I want for nothing.

Write me all the same, though, won't you? . . . Take heart, my dear sister. You are very little now, but with Him, you can do anything . . . You aren't totally detached from the world yet. You still live in it, but that doesn't matter; you'll manage it sooner or later, I hope. God loves you so much, and He wants you to give Him everything.

You've asked me for a spark or two . . . do you know what you're asking? . . . I'll stay quiet and not say anything, because there's no need. Just know that your brother, Br. M. Rafael, doesn't want to share what you think he has in excess . . . rather, he asks the Lord to give you the love I am unworthy to possess . . . May a lively flame burn within you, and thus with your love for God you can return to Him all the love He has for me . . . How selfish I am! Don't you think?

Don't you go thinking that the things you tell me are "silly" or "simple-minded." Maybe to someone else they would be, but not me. I can't tell you anything you don't already know, either. Brilliance is not to be expected of either of us . . . But the Lord sees it all, and that is enough for us. If our simplemindedness leads us to God . . . then may it be blessed. Loving God is so easy!

It consoles me so greatly to know that you have wept at the Virgin's feet . . . Isn't it true that She consoles us? Don't you love Her more now? . . . I know you don't forget to say the *Salve*. Who knows what your tears have earned for me . . . perhaps many things . . . I'm telling you, I count on the Virgin for everything, and there's nothing She could do to surprise me . . . Love her dearly, nothing we do for Her is ever enough . . . If only you knew how much She loves us Trappists!!

I'm so happy to know your prayer schedule. I'll make sure to ask Her to help you, and rather than helping you from above, I'll be giving you a lift from below, helping you climb . . . Anyway, Aunt María—that is, "my dear sister," isn't that what we agreed on—I don't want to mix in anything human, as you'd say, with this letter . . . but I didn't take my weakness into account, and it is very great indeed . . . I want to finish up, but I don't know. I love you so much! . . . And I love you in God and with God in such a way that I don't know what else to say to you.

Forgive this poor man and pray for him . . . Don't love me, because I'm just a creature . . . And if you knew me well, scorn is all you'd have for me . . . I say that nearly in tears. God knows it. I don't know when we'll see each other next, but of course, when you do see me, I'll be wearing my Cistercian hood[7] . . . We need not grow apart on that account. Quite the contrary: without seeing one another, we'll still continue down the same path, a path of humble, quiet love that leads to God. We'll meet again in Him.

I wanted this letter to go out today, but I had a friend over . . . I ran out of time, so it wasn't possible.

I can't yet tell you what exact hours I keep in the house of God, because right now I'm always going with my father and I adjust my schedule to his . . . If you could see what joy it brings me to see him at Mass and Communion, and not to miss a single day of the Little Office of the Blessed Virgin . . . In any case, I'm there more or less at the same hour that you are . . . and some other time, God willing, I'll tell you everything in greater detail. For today, be content to know that I send my *little* sister all my great love, with everything that I am. Your brother in Jesus,

Brother María Rafael

---

7. Rafael implies here that he wouldn't return to Ávila before re-entering La Trapa, but he did in fact make one final visit (OC 414).

71. To María Osorio

Oviedo, November 11, 1935

J-H-S

My dearest sister,

I left so much out the other day . . . despite my letter's length, it didn't really tell you anything at all. Truth be told, we have far too few words to express so many things, and so we aren't at all up to the task . . . Though I think words are unnecessary between us. Don't you agree?

Today or tomorrow, I expect a letter from you full of "silly and simple-minded things"[1] . . . If only you knew how many times I read your letter! . . . Your encouragement gives me such strength to stay the course . . . How good is the Lord! How straight are His paths! . . . It seems that He is just waiting for us to come into difficulty, in order to lend us a hand and give us aid . . . You see it that way too, don't you?

You know . . . I think the Lord heard your prayer. Your charity is not in vain . . . I am so at peace, and my restlessness has quieted down a bit . . . Or at least, I've been able to channel it . . . How are you doing? Surely you love Our Lady more now, isn't that so? I've helped you, haven't I? Tell me everything; it does me so much good.

Speaking of Mary, in your letter you told me that you'd been at her feet, and that you didn't forget to pray the *Salve*. Both are very good things . . . but amount to little. I must scold you here. Forgive me, but we did decide that I'm not your nephew but rather your brother; in that spirit, I'll say that if you talked about the Virgin more in your letters . . . they'd be better. Please, little sister, don't take this as a lecture. When I began to love Mary, I decided not to write anything to anyone without mentioning the Virgin at least once . . . And I've since acquired the custom of first entrusting myself to Her whenever I write. Then, I always look for

---

1. Silly and simpleminded things: presumably quoting María's characterization of her own letters, as implied in #70.

an opening in my ideas to mention Her for whatever reason. Then, when I finish, I give thanks to Her for everything, especially for allowing me to dare to . . . anyway, you understand.

Think of how much the Virgin loves you! . . . You'll be answerable for that before Jesus, Her divine Son. Anything done for Her amounts to little.

I allow myself to say such things to you because I promised to help you. Please don't take this as presumptuousness on my part, but rather charity toward you. Know that I just want you to love Her very much, because then God will love you more, and you will love Him more. Saint Bernard says that we receive *everything* through Mary's mediation,[2] and it's true.

How could we not become saints, my God, when You help us with so many souls of yours on earth, and you help us with Mary from heaven? Will we ever give You something in return? . . . I think so . . . We're going to try now, aren't we? You'll see, it'll be good . . . With the Most Blessed Virgin we can go anywhere . . . don't you forget it. Ask Her for this grace, and I'll ask Her to give it to you too, and you'll see that She listens to me. She loves me very much; my vocation is Hers, and I owe it to Her.

What a fool I am, my God . . . you must be laughing at me, my dearest sister, but I don't mind. I am determined that you should love Our Lady very much, because I see that as your first step toward becoming a saint . . . and since you have a long way to go, that is the quickest way to <u>begin</u> to love God . . . loving His Mother very much. Do you see some other way? Tell me honestly, just as I'm telling you . . . Point out my faults, or those you've observed in me; I'll do the same with you.

As we ascend, we have to be whittled down quite a bit in some ways, and grow in others, which are necessary for us to ascend the mount of perfection.[3] Sometimes, we can't come to know ourselves well enough on our own. If we only see perfection and virtue in others, and we tell them so, then we practice a *false charity*; at least, that's how I see it . . . And as

---

2. "Let us honor Mary, then, . . . with all the affections of our hearts and all our prayers, because that is the wish of him who desires us to possess all things through Mary" (Bernard of Clairvaux, "Sermon for the Nativity of the Blessed Virgin Mary," in *Sermons for the Autumn Season*, trans. Irene Edmonds, CF 54 (Collegeville, MN: Cistercian Publications, 2016), 74.

3. Mount of perfection: Saint John of the Cross's image of the path toward holiness (see #40, n. 3).

for you and me, we are so little, so wicked and wretched; with all that God has given us, it's truly a shame that we aren't saints yet.

How is possible to live this way, my God? How is it possible to resist such grace, such consolation, and such light and clarity as You give us? We must be very wretched indeed, when in order to receive just a little love from us, You have to give us infinite love . . . What patience You have, Lord. For others, a mere fraction of what You give us would have sufficed in order for them to surrender themselves to You entirely . . . And yet despite our resistance to Your grace, despite our resistance to Your love, You don't give up on us. You insist on continuing Your work and trying to win a bit of our love . . . How blind and bumbling we are! We are weighed down with so much muck and mire that keeps us from flying toward You!

But it's never too late, my God; what we've taken so long to give You . . . we are going to give to You now entirely. Isn't that right, Aunt María? . . . What little things we are! And yet how God loves us. We'll never know how much. In the meantime, let's do what we can. The Lord is content with so little.

Today I asked the Lord if I should write you all these things . . . and I believe He has given me to understand that if He can do something in someone's soul by means of our actions . . . we ought to be generous and offer ourselves up for the task, rather than hiding our lamp *under a bushel basket*[4] . . . And truly, my dear sister, the Lord has given me so much light . . . that I don't know what to do with it. If I could send it to you somehow . . . I am so content *in spite of everything*! The Lord is so good to me! . . . Aunt María, I am afraid . . . I don't know what is happening to me.

Anyway, I don't want to talk about me. What would be the point? . . . I will tell you that I am still doing well when it comes to my health . . . I take care of myself more now. My body is not my own, but God's, and if I wish to use it in His service, it must be as healthy as possible, although that is the least of my concerns. I am counting the days . . . Everything is as usual here.

Has Uncle Polín returned from Toro yet? Even if it embarrasses you, do keep me informed as to your affairs, which I consider my own. How

4. Matt 5:15; Mark 4:21; Luke 8:16; 11:33.

is Pili doing?[5] . . . I think of you all so often, and of you in particular . . . God is so great. Consider what He permits . . . He must know why.

The gift of the holy card you sent me was a very godly gift indeed. How good you are! I don't have anything to send you back, since the *Salve* I promised you isn't ready. I don't know if you'll understand it. The holy card I sent you was no trouble at all. Fr. Vicente,[6] a Trappist, gave it to me when I left the monastery, so that I wouldn't forget about Our Mother. Now that I'm going back . . . perhaps you'll find it useful . . . When I was very sick, I cried at that holy card very often, remembering La Trapa . . . Nothing to be done about such weaknesses . . . God permits them, and who is without them?

I'll write you more often in the coming days, it gives me great consolation . . . That is a weakness too.

Anyway, I'll leave you now. I don't have time for anything today . . . another day I'll tell you about my life at home and what I'm up to, so that we can align our prayer schedules. That's enough for today; don't stop writing back, even if it's just a quick note. You will write back, won't you?

All my love, your brother,

Brother María Rafael

5. Pili: Rafael's cousin and María's daughter, Pilar Barón y Osorio.

6. Fr. Vicente: Fr. Vicente Pardo Feliú, the infirmarian at San Isidro (see #35, n. 7).

72. *To María Osorio*

Oviedo, November 16, 1935

J-H-S

My dearest sister,

First of all, I must say that as to "taking advantage" of writing me again . . . How could you say that! . . . Truly, I forgive you, because you don't know what you are saying. Now I'm the one who doesn't know what to say. . . It's very *beautiful* what's happening to you . . . I understand you perfectly, and I praise God for it.

I received your letter this morning. I was waiting for the mail to arrive at noon so that I could then go make my visit to the Lord . . . I read it with all the charity you need not ask of me . . . And after seeing in it your soul, which is so transparent to me, I went to see God at the Handmaids' convent.[1] On the one hand, I was very sad; I am human. On the other, I was very content . . . Overall, a bit overwhelmed by the *work of God* . . . I don't know what I said to Him. I talked to Him about you, and thinking of you, I prayed, though not for very long. . . a friend of mine was waiting for me. He "doesn't know what is happening to him," so perhaps he has a vocation. I didn't seek him out, but rather he sought me out, and if I can do something . . . Well, God will do it, just as He does everything. We are but His instruments . . .

Later, thinking of your letter, I hardly spoke to Him . . . I knew that you were suffering . . . I saw you at the foot of the cross on Calvary, all alone . . . on a stormy night, and the holy wood without Jesus . . . I saw you suffering. Do you remember what I drew that one night on a piece of paper when I saw you cry? . . . How good it is to be at the foot of the

---

1. Handmaids: The Handmaids of the Sacred Heart of Jesus (Latin: Ancillae Cordis Iesu; Spanish: Esclavas del Sagrado Corazón de Jesús) were founded in Madrid in 1877 by Saint Rafaela Maria Porras y Ayllón and have an educational mission. Their building in Oviedo was ceded to the Diocese of Oviedo in 2007; it now serves as a perpetual adoration chapel.

Lord's cross, when He is looking at us . . . The hard thing is to stay on
the cross when Christ disappears before our eyes and the cross remains,
all dry and black and bloody . . . And neither Saint John nor the holy
women nor Mary is on Calvary . . . We are all alone in darkness with the
cross. We neither know how to pray nor do we hear God, *nothing* . . .
all we know is suffering . . . we look for Christ . . . and He is not there.

What does that matter to us? . . . Is that not what the Lord wants?
. . . Well then! . . .

Take heart, my dear sister; Jesus is on the other side of everything that
you can't see. He is looking at you, He sees you crying for Him, and your
tears wash away many things. How happy you will be! Mary did nothing
but look at the Lord. What merit would she have had if the Lord had
been there, and saw her, and spoke to her, and consoled her . . . ? There's
no need for any of <u>that</u>.

Love God without seeing Him or feeling Him, although I know how
hard it is not to feel Him, especially when one truly loves Him . . . And
then you *feel Him without feeling Him.* Does that make sense? You believe
yourself far from Him, but that's not true . . . You tell me of His justice, how
He is punishing you . . . My poor sister . . . you are far from that. It's not
that you don't deserve that . . . but rather that if the Lord were to allow His
justice and punishment to fall upon us . . . who would survive?[2] No, there
is no such punishment; His goodness toward you, on the other hand . . .
Think about it, and you'll see: He loves you so! . . . He is cutting away your
imperfections with the gentlest of chisels; He is *emptying* you out so that
He might enter . . . don't you see? Without a doubt, this process requires
tears, and many of them; but if they are His work, blessed be those tears . . .

Let Him work, suffer . . . but love Him while you suffer. Love Him
dearly through the darkness, despite the storm in which the Lord has
seemingly placed you, despite not being able to see Him. Love the naked
wood of the cross . . . Your tears will dry, your suffering will pass, the
night will come to an end. Such joy! . . . But love never ends.[3] It grows
and expands, and when the Lord allows a small ray of light to reach us
. . . we love and thank Him for it all the more. Is that not so, my dear

2. Ps 130:3.
3. 1 Cor 13:8.

little sister? Haven't you noticed that?. . . When it seems your suffering is at its worst, and God reveals something of Himself. . . What happens then?. . . Then it's as though water is "boiling" inside me, even if it's just for a moment.[4] When the cross returns, and it is bare once more . . . may that be blessed too!

Cry, cry as hard as you can, and suffer . . . but do so at the foot of the cross, and love God while you suffer. Such happiness! How God loves you . . . you'll see, someday very soon. . . What do you care about anything else? You have God's love. Even if you can't feel it, He is doing His work . . . let Him.

You also say that you're selfish to write me about your life and your sorrows . . . Didn't we come to an agreement that I am your brother? Don't worry about that. The Lord has placed me in your path, He must have done so for a reason . . . If I can be of help to you, then I will . . . It is a consolation given to me by the Lord, and a great one at that . . . No, it is not selfish to bring up your suffering to *me*. I'm nobody, I'm nothing, perhaps I'm just a stepping stone that God has placed in front of you to help you keep going. Whether you need material support or human consolation . . . so be it. That's how the Lord has arranged things. If only you knew how much I've needed, how much I still need . . . As the Lord guides us . . . not a single detail is missing.

Your confidence in me does me so much good . . . I know (and I say this before God, who is watching us) I don't deserve it. But I accept it gladly. We understand each other so well, don't we, sister? When I am back at my monastery, you'll see, I'll be able to help you so much.

It's natural that you should talk about yourself when you write me, for God is your life and God is within you. When you talk to me about Him, of course you have to tell me whether you love Him, and how, and how much . . . When you want to talk to me about Him, the same thing happens: the love that He has *for you*, how He treats you, how He spoils you. So, it's only natural that you should talk about yourself when you talk about Him . . . Moreover, and this is what really matters, when you tell me of your sorrows, it's not in order to receive any *human* consolation from me, but rather to hear me speak of God. Isn't that so?. . . So that

4. Quotation marks in the original.

I can relate your suffering and your joy alike to God, and go seek Him out, and tell you, "don't cry, sister, don't cry. God is with you . . . Suffer silently, and in that silence, love the God you cannot see . . . the God who may be hiding, but who loves you all the same."

There are so many things I'd say to you if only I knew how. You must be content with reading not my words, but my intentions.

I've just had to stop because Aunt Regina[5] came by, and I was the only one home. How different is her conversation from . . . Anyway, God makes us each a little different . . . But really, I wouldn't want to see you acting like such worldly creatures . . . You ought to thank the Lord very much for the state in which you find yourself.

I'm so pleased by what you said about the Virgin Mary; there can be no doubt that She is holding you by the hand. You'll see, you'll come to love Her dearly so quickly. It cannot be otherwise. You'll start to notice the effects . . . Loving Mary is so sweet. I didn't even know what devotion to the Virgin was before . . . but in La Trapa they taught me to love Her very much, and ever since then, I've wanted everyone to know and revere Her . . . Don't be surprised, then, at what I said to you in my other letter . . . Perhaps it wasn't the right moment, and it wasn't my intention to teach you a lesson, but you must regard what I have to say as coming from the poor Trappist that I am. After all, the life of a Cistercian monk is nothing but God and the Virgin; that is what he lives and breathes . . . So what else is he going to talk about, right?

Besides, I perceived an opening in you where love for Mary could enter in, while the world is generally so *closed off* to anything to do with God. I see so much indifference that when I come across a soul like yours, so ready and willing to become holy . . . I feel a wild urge to speak to you about God and the Virgin, and fill you up with . . . well, with what I may not even have myself. But then, that's the least of my concerns . . . If only you knew how much this consoles me . . . I would consider all my sacrifices, and even the occasional bitterness of finding myself completely alone in the world, completely worth it for having met a single soul (as I now have) for whom I can do some good in these matters. If you haven't yet experienced this consolation, you will someday, God willing.

---

5. Aunt Regina: Regina González-Tablas Otálora, who was married to Rafael's maternal uncle, Alfonso Barón Torres.

I have such a great treasure, my dear sister . . . I should like to shout for joy and tell all of creation . . . "Bless the Lord . . . love the Lord . . . He is so good, He is so great . . . He is God." And instead, I have to keep quiet . . . quiet, always quiet, and love Him alone in silence. Do you understand? The world doesn't see, it's blind, and God needs love, so much love. I can't give Him enough, I'm small, I'm going crazy trying. I wish the world would love Him, but the world is His enemy.

Lord, what a great torture this is! I see this, but I cannot fix it . . . I am so small and insignificant. The love I have for You overwhelms me. I wish my family and friends, all of them, would love You very much, so that I could rest a little . . . But the world, which is so busy with its concerns and affairs and discussions, takes me for a madman . . .

Lord, what should I do? Love, love . . . I can't. The world spurns this treasure of mine, which is Your love. This makes me suffer, because You are suffering.

And then here you come, my dear little sister, a beggar for love . . . and you want me—of all people, me—to talk to you about God . . . It's enough to make one go crazy. How could I not talk to you? Of course I will . . . even though I have no words. I jump with joy as I see that your soul, like mine, wants nothing and yearns for nothing but love of God . . . That's when I don't know what to do or say. I can't even talk to you about the cross, or suffering, or anything at all, not about you, not about me. Love moves my pen, and the paper feels too small for it. I have no words. I get so worked up, sometimes I don't even know what I'm saying, but I pour my heart out, I can't help it . . .

What does it all matter? We're so little and insignificant. We obsess over the most irrelevant details . . . Love for God!!! There is no path, no route, no peak, no valley; it all disappears; love for God floods it all. Do you know what that means? Do you understand? Forgive me, I can't resist anymore, I'm weak and wretched and unprepared . . . I don't know what I am saying. When the water boils over, I have to let it.

Forgive me, again. I don't know if the same thing happens to you. Sometimes when I talked to you in the past—remember?—I'd get worked up a bit. The same thing happens when I write, I can't help it . . . I have to stop and light a cigarette. I don't know if that's the right thing to do. As you can see, I'm completely honest with you, too . . . But with this pen, I feel completely powerless to tell you everything I'd like to, and send you what I'd like to . . . Anyway, God sees, and you don't need me to explain. But this morning, when I saw that sentence in your letter where you said it was "just for me," I saw that clearly the same thing happens to you . . . Blessed be God, that He should permit such things in creatures as wretched as we are.

What I don't know is how we can live or reflect or think or do anything useful. Either we are foolish or we are oblivious. God forgive us.

It doesn't matter to me if you lack consolation or experience dryness or if your path goes one way or the other . . . It doesn't matter to me if you are suffering or rejoicing . . . What does matter to me is that *all this*, which is *nothing*, helps you to love Jesus as He was at Gethsemane, the Jesus of Nazareth who called mourners blessed.[6] What matters is that you follow Him wherever He goes, and that you see only the love with which He looks at you and draws you . . . Sometimes we are in the wheatfields of Judea, listening to Him speak on a calm afternoon; sometimes we follow Him into the courts of the temple and listen to Him there, awestruck. Sometimes we are on the Mount of Olives, wanting to help Him a little, wiping away His tears of blood . . . that is true suffering . . . We poor creatures know nothing of that.

Sometimes we walk the Way of Sorrows; sometimes He is on the cross, and we are at the Virgin's side . . .

But always with Jesus, at every moment, without giving any thought as to what we are to eat or drink or what we are to wear,[7] forgetting ourselves completely. Always with Him . . . Following Him quietly, without even the expectation that He will turn to look at us . . . Do we deserve that at all? . . . How good such a life is! If only you knew! Beggars for His love . . . when we follow in His footsteps with devotion, we forget about everything else, I promise you. There is nothing left on earth that could distract us.

How sad it is to see people remain indifferent when they see Jesus and his whole retinue of disciples pass by . . . How joyful the apostles and friends of Jesus must have been each time someone saw clearly, gave up everything, joined them, and followed the man of Nazareth. All He was asking for was a little bit of love.

6. Matt 5:4.
7. Matt 6:25.

Shall we go follow Him, my dear sister? . . . He sees our intentions. He looks at us, smiles, and helps us . . . We have nothing to fear. Let's go be the last in that retinue roving the lands of Judea. We'll keep quiet, but we'll be nourished with an immense, enormous love for Jesus. . . He doesn't even need us to speak, or for us to get up close so He can see us, or great deeds, or anything that would call attention to ourselves . . . Yes, let's go be the last of Jesus' friends, but the ones who love Him the most.

What does it matter if we don't hear Him or see Him, if we know He is close to us *one way or the other*?

We shall accompany the Virgin, and speak to Her of Her Son. We'll tell Her how much we love Him . . . so if people don't pay Him any mind, She needn't worry, we'll give Him all the love that is lacking in the rest of humanity, and if we had to give our lives for Jesus a hundred times over, we'd do it . . . We'll give Mary so much consolation, won't we? . . . With the tenderness of children toward such a good Mother . . . And what will She say to us then? . . .

Look, once I start writing like this, I never stop. I have a whole world inside me, and it is so vast, so great, you can't even imagine . . . And yet it is so simple . . . It consists of nothing more than a very great love for Jesus and infinite tenderness for Mary. What more could I desire?

You have one too, you just don't know it. Your whole life is Jesus, although you haven't realized it yet, and that's why you are suffering . . . When you realize this . . . you'll see how good it is. Someday, I'm sure, you'll say, "How blind I was when I suffered for *my* sake rather than *His*." You'll get there, just let Him work.

There are so many things I wanted to share with you in this letter, and I don't know if I'll manage any of them. I wanted to send you consolation from God, but if there's human consolation here, take that too. Why not? . . . To me, you are my very beloved sister, to whom I owe so many things—in heaven, you'll see. The Lord used you and Uncle Polín to plant a seed in me, and it has taken a long time to grow . . . and I don't know whether it'll produce flowers or thorns, but either way, it comes from God.

If only I could repay you some of what I owe . . . I'll always remember our chats at Pedrosillo.[8] I'd tell you one trifle after another, and with such

---

8. Pedrosillo: María Osorio and Leopoldo Barón's former estate outside of Ávila.

charity, that you'd help me to see the Lord. I learned so much from you. It's not that we are doing the opposite now, because even if you don't realize it, you are still doing me just as much good now as you did then. I never suspected that I was going to be able to pay you back. Blessed be God who permits such things.

As for me, I don't have anything new to tell you. My life just takes me from home to church, and from church back home, and always at different times, depending on my father's schedule. He takes great consolation in being with me; he doesn't even go to the cinema, or the theater, or the club. . . . He and I are more spiritually united now than ever before. How great is the work of God.

The other day I went to see my former confessor. He told me that my plan was absurd,[9] and that God seemed to have abandoned me. Those were his words . . . So I haven't gone back to see him. What he said didn't rattle me or trouble me in the least . . . I didn't make anything of it . . . God alone is enough for me. I've gotten used to that over the past two years . . . That's what the Lord wanted of me. May His will be done.

Fernando will be coming over from Belgium, Papá has written him about it. He wants us all together for Christmas this year.

My mother still doesn't know anything, nor will she, until the last possible moment. That's the charitable thing to do, even if she suspects it.

Leopoldo already knows too. The other day he told me he was very happy to learn of it, because it made him sad to see me suffer, even though I didn't say anything . . . He knows it's the only place for me, and that God doesn't want me to be in the world.

That's all I can tell you. I go in and out; on some days there are embers, on others there are sparks, and then some days there's nothing at all. But I'm more at peace now. The Lord has helped me see that I don't need to do anything . . . I just rest in Him and in Mary, that's all.

I hope you give me *good* news in your next letter. But if not, I don't mind. Unburden yourself, speak of God however you wish, and honestly . . . that's what I do with you . . . If you're weak and miserable, well, who isn't? If you *don't know what to do with yourself,* that's no surprise to me. If you suffer, that's fine. If you laugh, that's fine too. Just speak to me of Jesus and the Virgin, and you'll see, *everything shall pass.*

---

9. That is, Rafael's plan to re-enter the monastery.

Don't laugh at my letter, which I'm sure is somewhat naive and doesn't tell you anything you don't already know.

You say the "little things" keep you going. . . Well, that's exactly what I write you. What more could you expect from me? . . . Sometimes I wonder, and I'll say, "Lord, I don't understand it, but You must know . . . I do absolutely nothing, but it's as if I am doing something. What could it be?" . . . But I don't care. I assure you that I am not lacking in humility in these matters, because I know the Lord often uses the littlest things to realize His works. I can fool you, but I can't fool God.

I feel so bad that Uncle Polín isn't with you.[10] Today was his name day and I didn't write him. I have no excuse. If only you knew how often I think of him. God loves him so much!

You'll say I'm getting tiresome with all this talk about loving God . . . Forgive me, I don't know how to talk about anything else.

I'll leave you now. I didn't realize, but it's two in the morning, and I need to sleep a bit so that I can get up in the morning to receive the Lord. How fortunate we are! Don't you think? We don't appreciate it enough . . . To think that tomorrow I'll be with Him and I'll be able to talk to Him about all this . . . I'll explain your situation to Him . . . I'll tell Him to do with you as He wills. Well, maybe I won't say anything at all . . . He'll do all the talking.

Tomorrow, when I get back from Communion, I'll keep writing you. Right now, I'll just pray a *Salve* and three Hail Marys, and I'll fall asleep thinking about how I'll be with the Lord in the morning, and about my sister María's little soul, which I must help to love God and the Virgin . . . Longing to see you at peace in your tribulation, and hoping that your next letter will say, "You know, dear Rafa, it's true: love for God fills me in such a way that it is no longer I who live in me.[11] I neither suffer nor rejoice, because loving, just loving, is enough for me . . . My dear brother, I have no other work, 'now that my every act is love.' "[12] That's what I hope your letter will be like. Will it? . . . Meanwhile, don't worry if it isn't. You

---

10. Uncle Polín: María's husband, Leopoldo Barón Torres, was still in Toro on business. As Rafael indicates, the feast of Saint Leopold is celebrated on November 15.

11. *It is no longer I who live, but it is Christ who lives in me* (Gal 2:20).

12. From the *Spiritual Canticle*: "I no longer tend the herd, / nor have I any other work / now that my every act is love" (SJC 475).

know what Saint John of the Cross says: "He who knows nothing of pain knows nothing of love."[13]

My dearest sister, I've picked up my pen once more in order to continue this letter, which I don't want to go on too much longer. If I allowed myself to keep going, I'd never finish.

I've just received the Lord. I went to Mass at eight o'clock with my father . . . I was thinking of you. I don't have anything else to say. How dull, right? But look, you have to understand, words are so clumsy. You know that it's when we are quiet that we speak the most . . . How sweet the Lord is! Isn't he? How He draws us, and the way He does it.

Look, it is so good to be at the door to the Cenacle,[14] and to watch Him give the bread to each of His disciples . . . and there are always a few crumbs left over for you. Isn't that right? . . . He gives them to you, and they fill you up just so . . . How good is Jesus! With a tender gaze, He commands you to draw near, tell Him everything, let Him console you . . . You see His immense love for you . . . *Everything* disappears, the disciples, even your own self . . . He fills it all . . . How good is Jesus! Then there are no more sorrows or joys, and we don't know what to say . . . we can't speak. We stay there, lost in His embrace, and then He speaks to the soul with such great gentleness . . . My dearest little sister, how good is Jesus! And He loves us so . . . I'm telling you, it's enough to make you melt . . . Does this happen to you too?

Leave it to Him, and you'll see . . . I promise you, in one true Communion we'd receive enough to last us the rest of our lives, if only we knew how to make one . . . But instead, we are so wretched. What a tragedy! But let us not lose heart, even amid dryness . . . again, how good is Jesus!

---

13. "He who knows nothing of pains / in this valley of sorrows / nothing knows of good things / nor has tasted of love, / since pains are the garment of lovers" (trans. Lynda Nicholson in Gerald Brenan, *St. John of the Cross: His Life and Poetry* [Cambridge: Cambridge University Press, 1973], 41). Long thought to be Saint John of the Cross, the author of this short poem has recently been identified as his contemporary and fellow Carmelite, Pedro de San Angelo (Lucinio Ruano and Crisógono de Jesús Sacramentado, *Vida y obras de San Juan de la Cruz* [Madrid: Editorial Católica, 1974], 154).

14. Cenacle: The "upper room" where the Last Supper took place.

Why do I speak to you like this? I don't know. I have this great tenderness . . . I want to be able to share it with you . . . I want to send you *everything* the Lord gives me so generously; I ask Him to share it for me.

I don't know how to keep going, I can't. Forgive me, little sister . . . but you understand, right? All I can say is that you were with me at the door to the Cenacle . . . and He gave you a crumb or two also, isn't that right?

What else do you want me to tell you? You aren't alone, no, it just seems that way to you. And don't you envy me for being able to have a novice master or a confessor . . . Today, I'm telling you, I don't need them and neither do you. What could creatures give us that would be better than what God gives us? Nothing . . . absolutely nothing . . .

Look, tomorrow you're going to do something . . . when you approach the altar for Communion, tell the Lord what you're going through. Tell Him just as you've told me, simply and candidly . . . Ask Him to be your confessor, your spiritual father, your dear friend, and tell Him how alone you feel, and how you need Him for everything. Tell Him all this with humility and simplicity; speak just as you are. Tell Him your suffering in great detail, not so that He will take it away from you, no . . . but rather in order to pour out your heart to Him . . . Your sorrows are His sorrows. You want to be His, so start there, by giving Him and telling Him everything . . . Tell Him that I sent you, and sit on Jesus' knees, and let your tears soak His humble tunic. You'll see, the Lord will listen to you, I'm sure of it. Afterward, you'll be transformed, and so happy . . . and if you experience some weakness during the day, it won't matter. You'll remind the Lord about everything you offered Him that morning . . . You'll ask Him for scraps from His table.[15] And how could He fail to give them to you?

You'll see, my dear sister, you'll see. This will be so good for you. If it doesn't work for you, tell me, but I'm sure that your soul will be filled with such great peace . . . You'll do work around your house with holy joy . . . You'll see the Lord everywhere, finding Him among the pots and pans and even helping you make the beds . . . Nothing in your surroundings will matter to you at all. You won't suffer on account of the sorrows He sends you . . . you'll suffer because you find yourself still in exile, far from Him

15. Matt 15:27.

and from being able to enjoy Him completely. But perhaps you won't even suffer because of that, for after all, you are doing His will . . .

Will you do this tomorrow at Communion? . . . You don't need any preparation, or prayers, or anything like that. He is waiting for you, and He already knows what you're like. He wants you to ask Him for this.

If you don't see Him, don't worry. He is listening to you either way. I'll unite myself to you at the holy altar on the 18th, because today is the 16th, and this letter will get to you tomorrow, which is the 17th.[16]

You'll see how well things will go with you and the Lord. I am praying to His Most Holy Mother for this. Perhaps you've already done this, and I'm just talking nonsense over here, but that's all I can do.

The way I see it, your spiritual problems are simple enough to be resolved by simplicity . . . That's how I resolve mine. But neither of us is complicated. Essentially, we are like children, and very little ones at that. But I think we are very spoiled, and we misbehave quite a bit . . . Well, may it all serve God and the Virgin.

Now I'm going to get the car out, because after we eat, I have to give my father a ride to Infiesto. Afterwards, I'll take this letter to the post office, and then I'll go see our friend Jesus.

So, I'll leave it there for today. Don't stop writing this poor brother of yours, telling him every last one of your "little things." Don't doubt that if I could relieve you of a few splinters of your cross, even at the expense of what I love most, I would do it. For now, I settle for being able to send you this tiny ray of light, however dim, to scatter your darkness, and a few sparks of love for God, too.

All my love and affection, your beloved brother,

Brother María Rafael
O.C.R.

Don't you worry about your punctuation. I understand you perfectly . . . that's not important at all. I don't know how this letter went either; whether it's well written or not, the Virgin dictated it to me.

---

16. Rafael mixes up the dates. He finished the letter on November 17, not November 16 (OC 477).

73. *To María Osorio*

Oviedo, November 18, 1935

J-H-S

My dearest sister in the Lord,

Making the most of the silence in the house, since everyone else has gone to bed, I've decided to begin this response to your letter of November 17. I'm surprised that you didn't get my letter. I wrote you a very long letter, nine pages front and back . . . I guess you'll get it today. Anyway, I did receive yours and answered it in the one I just mentioned. If it is not in your possession, do go and claim it.

What do you want me to say, dear little sister? Your situation pains me greatly, as does that of Uncle Polín. Of course I see God's *benevolent* hand in everything . . . but it's as you said, we are so human and so insignificant that we always think we are on the edge of ruin. May Mary never permit it!

I offered Holy Communion for you today. I'll do the same tomorrow. I don't know how to ask the Lord for anything, but He understands me. Believe me when I say that I asked Him to take your suffering from you and give it to me, or at the very least, that He split it between us . . . Poor and miserable man that I am, will I be able to do you this service? . . . It is harder to see a loved one suffer and not be able to do anything about it than it is to suffer oneself.

You want me to talk about myself the way you do . . . What do you want me to say about myself? Leave me be, don't worry about it. Intercede for what you can, and as best you can. It's enough for me to know that you are helping me that way. I wouldn't know how to describe my interior life to you . . . with everything that happens to me, I don't know how to do anything but thank the Lord and love Him more and more every day . . . Seeing you suffer, and not knowing how to fix it, and realizing I am powerless to do so . . . it's a thorn in my side. On the other hand, I do envy your way of seeing things . . . and the great love with which you carry the Lord's cross . . .

"Help me, brother!" These cries echo in your letters, and when they reach me, they leave me in such a state that only God understands . . . I turn to Him and I ask Him, "But how, Lord? What can I do? What should I say to my sister, whom I love so much, when she asks me for help in carrying her cross? . . . If only I could help . . . but I cannot."

I wish I were big and strong so I could lift you up and help you and encourage you . . . so I could be your big brother, and you could lean on me like the little child you say you are, and I could help you with everything . . . Poor man that I am, I want nothing more than to be to you what you've asked me to be . . . But I am so weak and small! . . . I say all this to the Lord . . . and it seems that He consoles me . . . It's such a paradox, that creatures should place their trust in me! No matter. I trust in God . . .

Pay me no mind, these are just things that came to mind . . . I'm a bit fired up. I may be small, but with the Lord on my side, I am strong.

Count on my help and consider me your older brother; don't be afraid. My prayers are weak, but maybe they can do a lot . . . Your faith can do anything.

I've just thought of something very similar, although completely different, which is what happened with Merceditas[1] when she was so sick. The poor girl was in such a state, it was painful to see . . . Her eyes were protruding and they stared and stared at me . . . She could not have suffered any worse from the pain. She was twisting and turning in her mother's arms, and without being able to speak, her eyes begged me for help, they begged me to pray to the Virgin to put an end to the suffering that was making her cry out and lose consciousness. Oh, how my poor sister suffered!! . . . In those moments, I saw that she was dying, that she was slipping away . . . And she looked at me in such a way . . . if you could have seen her . . . it was as if she was saying, "But Rafael, what are you doing? Aren't you going to pray to the Virgin for me?" . . . So then I ran like crazy to the tabernacle, and offered *my sister's prayer* to the Virgin, since my own was worthless . . . I felt so ashamed! Am I making sense?

I asked the Lord to send me all that pain . . . that He'd make me suffer, and let my sister rest, either in this life or the next . . . Watching someone suffer is terrible. I find it harder to watch someone suffer than to suffer myself . . . But the Lord knows what He is doing.

Now it's not Merceditas who is looking at me in anguish and trusting in my prayers to the Virgin . . . It's another beloved sister of mine, who is

---

1. Merceditas: Rafael's younger sister, Mercedes Arnaiz Barón (see #53, n. 1; #87, n. 5 for her illness).

suffering in a very different way . . . she embraces the cross and, weeping, awaits assistance, putting her trust in me . . . It's terrible, what you're asking me. You don't know what I am . . . but it doesn't matter. Just as I did back then, as I'll never forget, I also place this sister's prayers at the feet of the Virgin . . . I'll tell Her of your sorrows, but I'll hide myself away, I'll conceal myself, because what can I do? Am I making sense?

I don't know if you'll approve of all this, but I can't help but tell you about it. I take the confidence you have in this poor creature—who doesn't deserve anything, let alone your confidence—and I turn it over to the Virgin . . . She is watching over us . . . and She is smiling, I am sure of it. But at the same time, you give me so much consolation that I always await your letters eagerly; I wait for the mail every day too. Is that a weakness? I don't know. If it is, God permits it. And if you experience the same thing, and if my letters bring you consolation too, then bless them for it. Don't you agree?

Love one another as I have loved you.[2] What a great consolation it is to know that we are loved by Christ and in Christ, especially when we are in desolation, and the Lord gives us a sign of His love . . . and in your case, the sign is clear.

How great God is, little sister! In me, the Lord has given you a brother; and in you, He has given me a soul to help, so that I can practice the charity that Jesus taught us . . . If only you knew how pleased I am to do so! If only you knew *everything* that I put into my letters! . . . I think you do know, because if you didn't, they'd be of no use to you at all . . . I put all the love I have for you in these letters . . . but I also put lots of love for God in them. He guides my pen, and I wouldn't be able to write without Him . . .

It's not my words or ideas or affection that I want to reach your soul, nor anything else that belongs to me . . . I want to nourish your poor heart, so hungry for God, with the God who stirs me, who makes me tremble. I want the consolation of God and the Virgin to reach you in my letters . . . To be able to share with you the <u>intense</u> peace of Jesus of Nazareth that so fills me. Do I manage to do any of this? I think so. If not, it's a waste of time. Answer me about this specifically.

I imagine I don't need to tell you to read me charitably, and to keep all this to yourself, because you're the only one I'm writing it for . . . Believe

2. John 13:34; 15:17; 1 John 3:11.

me, I hardly recognize myself; I've never written to anybody this much. You know I've always been a lazy writer.

I don't think this moment is definitive for your interior life, as you said in your letter, because I am sure that you have a greater devotion to the Most Blessed Virgin now, and She will help you in your "little agony." Love for the Virgin is capable of so much, if only you knew! . . . When I was in mine—well, I don't know if it was like yours. When I was going through, let's say, a difficult time after leaving La Trapa . . . when I thought that the world had crushed me, and I had been defeated, and I thought I was not going to be able to resist it, and I even thought I was condemned . . . I don't know, anyway, when I underwent my own "little agony," I turned to the Virgin of La Trapa. It was in that Virgin in whom I'd rest when I went to bed in the monastery's uncomfortable dormitory, exhausted from the day . . . I remembered that She still loved me, and was still listening to me in my tribulation . . . If only you knew, that was the only consolation I've had in the nearly two years I've been like this . . . my Virgin of La Trapa . . . How many times, when nobody could see me, I'd talk to Her about my plans, my desires . . . I'd talk to Her about Her Son, Jesus . . . What a great consolation it is to have the Virgin!

And you won't lack for that consolation . . . and forgive me if what I'm saying sounds childish or sentimental to you, and if you think this is a bad idea, don't do it . . . but what I like to do is talk to the Virgin out loud, as if She were at my side. Now that you spend a lot of time alone, when nobody can hear you, talk to the Virgin about your situation . . . You'll see, She'll listen . . . You know when I do it? When I'm in the car, driving alone . . . For charity's sake, don't laugh, but I've given Our Lady many an earful . . . and I think She listens to me.

Anyway . . . I'm talking such nonsense, but since you did say I should trust you and pour my heart out to you . . . and since you know and understand me by now, I don't mind.

I'm going to leave it there until tomorrow because it's getting late . . . I won't forget about communion.

Today, November 19, I'm continuing this letter that was interrupted last night. I've just received the Lord. Oh, if only you'd seen me, I kept my feet very much on the ground today; I had so many things to tell Him . . . Just those little things that fill this life of ours . . . but there, walking in the midst of all those little things, is the Lord . . . I left church so content. I believe that He will hear us. Don't you?

Don't you worry, little sister. Jesus is so good! I told Him so many things . . . I told Him that I can't do anything . . . and He gave me to understand that I shouldn't worry, that He doesn't want anything from me except love, companionship, and prayer, that with Her I can do anything, and that I should trust in Him . . . because He will do it all . . . How good is Jesus! I left church content because even in the midst of my weaknesses, the Lord does not abandon me. How can I repay Him? . . .

Well, I don't want to go on like this, because you already know where I'd end up and how, and in all my letters I say the exactly same thing in exactly the same way . . . Forgive me, but you understand me by now.

It's true, your situation is difficult . . . But have faith and believe . . . When you leave things to the Lord, He doesn't do them halfway. He either brings everything to an end quickly, or He resolves things . . . What does it matter, if it is what He wills? Didn't you say that you love Him very much? . . . Don't you grasp the crucifix in your sleep? . . . Don't you know that He is looking at you from the cross, and *your agony alleviates His*? So, then, if you truly love Him, if you love Him with all your soul, then what is your agony to *you* if it allows you to serve the Lord *better than ever before*? . . . Have you ever thought about that?

Take courage, my dear sister. Do not desire that your suffering be alleviated, but don't desire that it be increased, either. Desire nothing.

Easier said than done, right?! . . . But if we want to be saints, that's exactly what we have to do. From your letters, I can see that you are determined to do whatever it takes. It consoles me so much to see you in such a frame of mind . . . You'll see, with Mary's help we can go wherever God wants to take us, even if we have to shed tears of blood, as Jesus did in the garden.

You say that your prayer is nothing more than an immersion in your own humility, and that humility is what you are praying for . . . What more could you want in prayer? Be calm, and realize that *you* cannot do anything else, and in that *littleness* in which you find yourself is a great love for God. Could there be any doubt of that?

There are so many things I'd say if I were sitting next to you . . . I'm so clumsy in writing!

Did you make your communion the way I told you to in my letter? How did it go? . . . Write me at great length about it, even if it takes you a few days. Don't worry about the wording.

After reading your letters a few times, I use a red pencil to mark out the parts I think I can reply to. I don't know if what I have to say will be exactly right or if it's appropriate, just that the Holy Spirit is guiding me. As you know, I'm also all alone and without spiritual direction, but I share what little experience I have of myself with you, plainly and simply. As such, just keep whatever you find useful. Everything else is just the rambling of someone madly in love with God, who doesn't always know what he's talking about . . . and just tells you everything he thinks.

One of these days I'm going to go to Covadonga[3] and offer a special prayer to the Virgin, that She might guide you, and Uncle Polín over in Toro; I've noticed he needs it . . . I can't do anything else. If it was up to me, I assure you . . . Well, I won't assure you of what you already know.

I'm sending you a few stamps because I think the next letter you write me will be too heavy.

I'll leave it there for today. I'll write you at greater length another day . . . I should have so much to tell you, but nothing's coming to mind at the moment, I'm a bit out of it. My poor little sister! I'm of such little use to you! The truth is, I'm completely useless.

Did you receive the little "sparks" I sent you the other day? I won't stop sending them, as many as I can. That's why I write you, and as long as I remain in the world (physically at least), I'll keep writing you, if you find it useful. Keep it up on your part, too. I know you will.

To sum it up, my dear little sister: take heart and love God . . . love God so much . . . love God alone, and stay under the Virgin's mantle . . . and then, come whatever storms and squalls that may. Come whatever God wills.

All my affection, your *older brother*,

Brother María Rafael
O.C.R.

Ever since I was readmitted into La Trapa, I sign my name with the "Brother María" attached; it is a huge consolation to me. How great God is! Right, sister?

---

3. Covadonga: the Holy Cave of Our Lady of Covadonga is the site of a Marian apparition and shrine in Covadonga, Asturias.

74. *To Leopoldo Barón*

Oviedo, November 22, 1935
Feast of Saint Lucy[1]

J-H-S

My dearest brother in the Lord, Uncle Polín,

I don't know what you'll think of my silence, but I've been thinking of you so much throughout this difficult time of yours . . . and I knew what you were going through and how you were suffering . . . What could this poor man possibly say to you? Nothing. I just kept quiet, and without the comfort of being able to tell you so, I prayed very much to the Virgin for you and your situation. Now, things are different. I know that you've leased the estate, so at least there's light at the end of the tunnel. I'm sure that you can rest now. How good God is! Isn't He?

Now I can write you again, and praise the Lord with you, as I am sure you already are . . . I have been. If only you knew how happy I am that things are looking up for you. Your affairs are my own; I can't help it.

It pained me greatly to leave Ávila. Not on my own account, as God well knows . . . but on account of leaving Aunt María all alone in your absence. I'm telling you, it was such a hard moment. I write her very often now, because apparently, she says that my letters do her quite a lot of good . . . What else can I do, right? . . . She has been so good to me, and I need her help, too!

I imagine that Aunt María will already have told you that I've obtained my father's permission . . . If I started telling you the details, I'd never stop. My father is so good, and he loves me so much! If only you knew!

I'll go to La Trapa after Christmas; he'll come with me, and will speak with my good Father Abbot in person. My father thought it was <u>all</u> very reasonable and very fair, and he has seen God at work in *all* of it . . . When

---

1. November 22 is the feast of Saint Cecilia, not Saint Lucy. Both saints are third-century virgin martyrs from Sicily.

I told him, the first thing he said in reply was that he had made a complete surrender to God . . . That as for the sacrifice he had made in surrendering me to God, he was happy to make it again, because he only wanted one thing . . . for me to become very holy, so that I could make him holy . . . That for his part, he'd help me with everything, because he only wanted me to be happy, and he could clearly see that I did not belong in the world . . . And that not only was he not sorrowful or upset about it, but he was incredibly joyful and utterly grateful to God: both because the Lord had called me so insistently, and because he could see that my vocation is so sure.

In short, he said so many things that I didn't know what to do but throw myself at the feet of the Virgin and give thanks . . . and I wanted to respond to God with so much love . . . I thought I was going crazy.[2]

Mamá doesn't know anything . . . she suspects, but in the meantime . . . she's happy.

I could've left already, and I'd be there by now if I had, but my father's generosity and his truly *holy* (it's not enough to say *Christian*) conduct have won me over. When I asked him what he thought about me spending this last Christmas at home, his face lit up, and he was clearly very pleased. Did I do the right thing? I don't know. But if I can put those around me at ease, make them happy, cheer them up, and bring them closer to God, even if it were at the cost of shedding my own blood . . . trust me, I'm not afraid of making sacrifices. What do I care? I have God so deep inside me . . . so deep, I can tell. I wonder at it, and I don't know what to do, except love Him dearly, so dearly. Uncle Polín, you don't even know. I don't know how to do anything else!

I don't know when I'll see you next, because Mamá and her little girl are thinking of going to Ávila . . . and Papá has promised that he won't ask me to accompany them, because I want to go to Venta de Baños directly from Oviedo[3] . . . That seems only natural, right? . . . It would be really hard for me otherwise, and I think it would be unnecessary . . . If only I didn't love you all so much! You don't even know . . . And if only I were *strong*, but I am so weak!

---

2. Rafael summarized his conversation with his father in similar terms in a letter to María Osorio (#70).

3. Despite what Rafael says here (see also #70), he did end up accompanying his mother Mercedes and his sister Merceditas to Ávila to see Leopoldo and María one more time before re-entering the monastery (OC 414).

For now, I'm satisfied just to be able to write, and to be writing you . . . If only you knew how much consolation it brings me . . . And then . . . nothing; I want to live the hidden, humble life of my Trapa, where, forgotten by men, I can surrender myself to God completely . . . Now that I'm surrendering for good, don't you think twice about your nephew . . . just pray for him. The more the Lord coddles me, the more help I need in order to respond to His grace . . . Sometimes I feel so alone and so small . . . What can I do, Lord? I wish I could sink away and disappear.

Forgive me, brother, for telling you all this . . . but God is my life, and I don't know how to talk about anything else . . . When I thought about writing you, I didn't dare; I wouldn't have known what to say . . . because I understand you perfectly, and I knew that I couldn't alleviate your suffering. From far away, I was praying for you. Now that the storm is going to pass, as I said, I'm willing to tell you how things are with me. Though I won't tell you about my sorrows or my joys . . . because I have neither one nor the other. I don't know if I'm making sense. I have God . . . I don't know how to explain. May your charity make up for that.

There's no need for you to write me, because even without you reminding me, I know just how connected to my life you are . . . Someday you'll know it too.

I wish you were already back in Ávila with Aunt María.[4] She has been suffering a great deal too . . . and believe me, it's not that I want to see your cross taken from you, because it is the *one* treasure you both have. But from time to time, I do pray to God and to His Blessed Mother, and I ask that my little sacrifices, and the one the Lord is preparing for me right now most of all, be of use . . . in some way. That's all I can do, but I do it gladly. The Lord and the Virgin help me. Knowing that from my corner of La Trapa, without anybody even realizing, I can even sanctify my father—that is enough for me.

I'm counting the days . . . I can't tell you anything else. I want to tell you so many things, but I don't know . . . *You don't need me to*, right?

Give my grandmother and Aunt María a million hugs for me . . . Don't forget little Ropi either. All my great affection, your brother,

Brother María Rafael
O.C.R.

4. Leopoldo was on business in Toro at the time.

75. *To María Osorio*

Oviedo, November 22, 1935
Feast of Saint Lucy[1]

J-H-S

My dearest sister,

Today, November 22, at eight-thirty at night, I am sitting down to respond to your letter, for which I don't know how to thank you. Before I went to the house of the Lord, I wrote to Uncle Polín in Toro; I suppose he'll still be there when my letter arrives . . . Now, after spending some time with Our Lady, I've come back home . . . Nobody is around; I have silence, and I have your letter before me; so, commending myself to the Virgin, I ask you to lend me your ears.

First of all, I'll say that tomorrow, which is Saturday, I shall indeed offer Communion for your intentions, and I'll ask the Lord to give you light . . . or I won't ask Him anything at all, for as you know . . . There's no need. Perhaps you, *as far as I can tell*, won't need to say much to Him either . . . you'll see. It's just a matter of uniting ourselves to the Lord, so that whatever one fails to do, the other will make up for. Are we agreed? . . . Tomorrow, when I return from Communion, I'll tell you what I ended up telling Him.

You said you don't know how to repay me . . . Repay me? You don't owe me anything, but you do owe Jesus.

You say that Jesus is behind me . . . Of course He is, and in front of me, and on all sides . . . and if you pay a little attention, you'll see Him in every creature, and all over the place too . . . and you shall be in Him, and He in you . . . Do you remember what I said about the sea? . . . Just today I was in Gijón,[2] and looking out at that great big sea . . . I thought of God . . . and then I thought: How tiny the sea is! . . . The sea has

---

1. November 22 is the feast of Saint Cecilia, not Saint Lucy (see #74, n. 1).
2. Gijón: A port city north of Oviedo that Rafael often visited; see #40, n. 5.

limits, a surface, a depth, but God doesn't . . . God is limitless, and when we truly immerse ourselves in Him . . . then we don't see anything, we see Him in all things, it's all Him . . . How great He is! Isn't He?

You say that Jesus is behind me . . . yes, indeed He is, little sister. He is within me . . . but He is also within you. You seek Him, don't you? Don't you see Him? Don't be afraid of falling. There's nothing we can't endure. Don't you go thinking that it's all over when one of those moments comes . . . No, that's what we think, and that's what we'd *like* . . . but no, it's just not true. We must drink the whole chalice and *not stop*, whether to taste its bitterness or to enjoy its sweetness[3] . . . We can endure anything; don't you see that it's the Lord who does it all? . . .

Forgive me for always saying the same thing in all my letters . . . But there's nothing to do . . . Poor birds! All they know how to do is chirp, and chirp the same thing over and over again!

Of course, it's only natural that you should say, like David, "How long, O Lord?"[4] . . . Well, as long as He wants. But it's terrible to live like that, isn't it? To be so far away . . . when the Lord could lift us up instantly with a single look, and put an end to this life that is one continuous sigh for His love . . . This life in which there is no rest when thinking of Him . . . The heart trembles and shakes and remains restless; either the Lord must seize it once and for all, or He must widen it so that it can survive . . .

Living this way . . . it's so awful, isn't it? But at the same time, how sweet it is to find your heart all torn to pieces by love of God. In our more selfish moments, we exclaim, "How long, O Lord?" We want to stop suffering; we want to love *fully* and *at once*; we want to be free of our bodies and fly toward God . . . We don't know what we are saying, and in our madness, we let out these cries of love for God . . . in such a state, that if it weren't for God sustaining us . . . by our nature we could not survive. When we feel that urge, that desire to fly forth from our own souls, when we see how small our hearts are and realize that we can't take everything the Lord is giving us . . . that's when we feel that "how long, O Lord?" that you put in your letter. If our love is *pure*, it will pass. But that *pure love*

---

3. Matt 26:27.
4. Ps 12:1-2.

is so difficult to come by! We muddle it with so much selfishness! . . . That cry is much more about us than it is about God.

I don't know if I'm making sense; I'm expressing myself so poorly. But when we essentially have so much love for God that we can't take it anymore, that's when we won't even need to ask the Lord to take us away . . . He'll take us without our needing to say anything. Meanwhile, in such moments of discouragement, as we realize how wretched we are . . . as we look at our souls, which yearn to belong to God but are weighed down with worldly burdens . . . as we see our hearts suffering from love for God, and sometimes from love for creatures too . . . and as we find ourselves still trapped in these bodies and in this life, of course it is only natural that we should shout with our entire soul, *How long, O Lord, will You hide Your face from me?*[5]

But then, later, serenity comes . . . peace . . . the intense peace of Christ, in which we see that as long as God keeps us here . . . I don't know exactly, but it means that He still wants something more from us . . . Our mission is not yet complete; we still have to wait, and wait with faith, patience, and above all, joy. Yes, with true joy. That is what He wants.

Listen, sometimes I feel a holy *joie de vivre* . . . And you know why? Because I live for God and in God. When I feel sorrow, it is because I have offended Him or failed to return His love; so then, realizing my own misery, I do want the Lord to take me away.

Anyway, I think one day we talked about this, and we came to this conclusion: in the ebb and flow between soul and body, and between body and soul, sometimes we wish for a thousand deaths, while other times we wish for a thousand lives, if only to use them to make some reparation for offenses against God and to make creatures love Him. Anyway, you know what I mean . . . But let's allow the Lord to do what He wants with us. Let's not ask Him for anything at all . . . let's just keep chirping like those little birds, and keep loving God very much . . . Are we still here on earth? Well then, let's do so here on earth.

It's one thing to love life, and it's another to *conform in a holy way* to the life given to us by the Lord for His service. Don't you think?

5. Ps 13:1.

You're very right to say that the one who has begun to give is, indeed, the one who has begun to love. I can't add anything to that; I wouldn't know how to put it into words . . .

You talk of starting heaven early, and wanting the world to be on fire. Listen, I'd rather not discuss this subject. You know me by now, I'd just talk nonsense. I'll keep quiet. Have pity on this poor man who, I assure you, suffers greatly because of this. Do you understand?

My soul is a burning volcano about to erupt. I can't go on like this, Lord, I can't . . . I have this urge to lock myself away in the monastery, so that among men's silence, I can let God hear this clamor I carry around inside me, these cries that *won't stop coming out* . . . Have mercy, sister. You say that my letters are on fire, but I assure you, on the inside, I . . . Oh, the Lord is too great for a soul as small as mine.

I don't know if I'm doing the right thing in sharing all this with you . . . Destroy my letters. I start out slowly, but I end up not even realizing what I'm saying . . . But I suffer greatly, above all because I can't quite manage to break through.[6] Am I making sense?

I want to give so much to the Lord, but I can't do anything. He fills me and fills me, I can tell, it's perfectly clear.

I want to go beyond myself . . . but something is holding me back, something is restraining me, I don't know what is happening to me. Sometimes I want to cry, I'm so weak! But the Lord gives me such special treatment . . . I can only rest at night, clutching my crucifix, when I fall asleep thinking of Him . . . at the foot of the cross, not knowing what to do . . .

Forgive me for pouring my heart out like this, but I want to love Him so much . . . I want to come undone . . . I don't know . . . Thinking of God puts me in a daze.

My family is here now, so I have to calm down, and talk and eat and chat with somebody or other . . . So yes, I do say, "how long, O Lord?" . . . But I assure you, the hope of soon finding myself at the foot of the tabernacle and under Mary's mantle forever . . . that gives me the strength

---

6. In the original, here Rafael uses the same verb (*romper*, to break or tear) that Saint John of the Cross uses to describe the mystical encounter between God and the soul: "if it be your will, / tear through the veil of this sweet encounter" (*acaba ya si quieres,* / *¡rompe la tela de este dulce encuentro!*). See SJC 639.

to get through anything. The thought of the silence that awaits me, and the concert that my Jesus and I are going to put on in La Trapa, is enough to make me forget so many other things . . . How good is Jesus, my dear sister! How He loves me! What can poor little me do?

Right now it's midnight. We had dinner and prayed the Holy Rosary, then I listened to the radio for a bit and finished my Little Office of the Blessed Virgin. With Her help, I'll continue writing.

My dear sister, I so wish that the opening I'd hoped to fill with love for God would grow wider.[7] It would be bad if I couldn't do it . . . But I'm nothing. God will do it, have no doubt. But look, careful what you wish for . . . because in another letter, you told me that you could only chew a little at a time . . . Don't let what happened to me happen to you: I can only chew a little bit too, and when the Lord bites off too much for me . . . anyway.

Well, let's leave ourselves in His hands. I'm sending you what you asked for, and I do so sincerely; do make good use of it. When I pour out my heart to you, I am entrusting to you a treasure of mine and placing it in your hands, and that treasure is love for God. Perhaps you alone understand it, and you are the only person in the world to whom I speak this way . . . and I do so because I see that it might do you some good . . . But my love for God has always been hidden from the eyes of others. It's just that people in general don't understand all this. Besides, this intense inner life I have with God shouldn't be marred by the spotlight . . . But it's different for you. You love God just as I do; you share that longing and zeal that won't let you alone. We have come to understand one another very well, and we've seen *God at work* in one another . . . We've praised Him for everything together, haven't we? . . . So, then, I'll also tell you this: place the confidence I have with you at the feet of the Virgin. Will you do this?

I won't ask the Lord to relieve you of *anything* . . . I'll ask the Lord to make you able to respond to Him with absolute generosity; I'm sure you will be.

My dear sister, <u>you</u> are no bother at all when you ask me for help. God's the bother . . . because I don't understand why He has chosen <u>me</u> to be

7. See #72: "I perceived an opening in you where love for Mary could enter in . . ."

able to help you . . . But have no fear, that's nothing more than temptations to humility talking, and I'm already on the other side of them. I
assure you, from the bottom of my heart, that I am at peace in this regard,
very much so. I do whatever God inspires in me, and when I realized that
I am indeed sending you some measure of peace and love for the Lord
. . . how could I not be at peace about it? Or rather, pleased to serve as
a conduit or a bridge. (Remember that?) How good is the Lord, my dear
little sister! How good it would be to find many other souls like yours and
hear them say the very same thing.

Tonight, from Friday to Saturday, I'll do a Holy Hour with you. Since
I'm afraid I won't wake up at two o'clock, because it's already getting very
late, what I'll do is just not go to bed.

My whole family is already in bed, and I'm the only one up. Soon my
brother Trappists will get up too, in order to praise the Lord. They help
me so much. Tomorrow, Saturday, over there in La Trapa, so many prayers
will rise up to God on my behalf . . . Truly, this is a consolation that the
world does not understand . . .

This matter of loving one's neighbor for God's sake and out of charity
. . . it fills the heart with such consolation . . . But the children of this
world have their amusements, such different pleasures, and they cannot
understand this . . . What a pity! . . . What a dull life they lead, where
everything is external, everything is superficial . . . they settle for so little.

Don't be discouraged that your love for the Virgin is "unformed" at the
moment, as you said. You'll see, that dryness will pass, and you won't be
able to do anything without Our Mother at your side . . . It's all a matter
of waiting, and waiting faithfully.

The same thing happens to me: when I take up my pen to write you, I
can't put it back down . . . There's so much I wish to tell you. The worst
thing is when sometimes I can't think of anything to say at all, and so I
end up writing these hilarious letters in fits and starts, and sometimes I
just write awkwardly, putting down whatever comes to mind . . . But
time flies, and I fill page after page. It's almost meditative for me, because
talking about God and His works among His creatures is the only thing
in this life that holds any interest for me. If I'm not going to talk about
Him, I'd rather stay silent. You are kind enough to listen to me, so I direct
it all at you; I don't do anything halfway.

Tonight in prayer, I am going to meditate on the words of Saint John of the Cross: "Now I occupy my soul" . . . Honestly, with that alone, I have enough to consider for many days, because I have been doing so for many days already. When I place myself before the Lord, I feel such great consolation in pondering that verse, and I still have not come to understand it completely . . . but no matter, for I have no other work, "now that my every act is love"[8] . . . Oh, if only that were true! . . . But the day will come when I live solely on love for God, it will come.

I've been thinking of Anita[9] a lot these days, I don't know why. Have you heard anything about her?

Right now it's one o'clock; at one-thirty, I'm going to stop writing, because if I wait until two, it'll be really hard for me to get up tomorrow. All we can do is struggle against these bodies of ours, so replete with weakness . . . I do take care of myself a bit now, but not very much.

I'm so sorry that Uncle Polín isn't quite doing well . . . But then, nothing to be done about that. As I've said, I did write to him this afternoon, and I imagine he'll receive the letter in Toro.

My father hasn't known what to do with himself around me these past few days. May God repay him. He understands that I am in an internal struggle, and even though I don't reveal anything that's going on inside me, sometimes I do have to make an effort not to . . . I'm so weak, my dear sister! I have no endurance whatsoever. And what's more, I've become extraordinarily sensitive . . . if only you could see me with your letters. The first thing I do, after reading them over once, is run straight to the tabernacle. There, I tell the Lord everything you tell me . . . I ask Him for the strength for it all, and I have to cling to Him through it all . . . From time to time, I have my own agonies too, but they're very short. I hardly have time to stop to think about them, because that would be to stop to think about myself . . . Today, when I was with the Virgin, I left church so content . . . She is so good! Truly, I don't know what to do with myself.

---

8. From stanza 28 of the *Spiritual Canticle*: "Now I occupy my soul / and all my energy in his service; / I no longer tend the herd, / nor have I any other work / now that my every act is love" (SJC 475).

9. Ana Solana, a friend of Rafael's (see #37, n. 8).

I am counting the days . . . and time is getting slower and slower on me . . . But at other times it goes so fast, I don't know . . . In the days ahead, I'll need your help so much. Didn't you tell me to ask you for it when I needed it? . . . I'll keep you informed of the steps I'm taking toward the monastery. But I still have, or rather, the Lord still has, a lot of rough edges to smooth out . . . And I am waiting for the cross. I don't know what it'll be like, but I am waiting for it . . . May the Lord send me whatever He pleases . . . There's nothing to do but let Him work.

I'll leave it there for now. I'll continue my letter tomorrow, after I come back from receiving the Lord.

Today, November 23, I continue.

I went to bed at two-thirty last night and got up at eight-fifteen this morning; I'm a bit sleepy.

I can't think of anything to say, even though I have so much inside me . . . At communion, I united myself to your intention, just as you said to do. All I can say is that Jesus is very good to me . . . As usual.

I want this letter to go out today, but I don't know when it will arrive, because I heard that the Pajares Pass[10] is closed, so the trains aren't running.

Forgive me, I'm so boring today. I don't know what's going on with me . . . But sometimes I'm in such a state that I can't converse or think or do anything at all . . . And the same thing happens to me in prayer . . . As you can see, sometimes the volcano appears dormant and makes no noise at all . . . so from a *human* perspective, it's as if I am somewhat at rest. I don't know if I'm making sense. Anyway, I'm so sorry that I don't know how to express myself.

Tomorrow at noon I'm going to make my visit to the Lord, so that, in His presence and without knowing what to say to Him, I can have recourse to those words of Saint John of the Cross and tell Him, Lord, "I no longer tend the herd, nor have I any other work . . ." Lord, You are everything to me. I seek neither myself nor creatures . . . You are everything, Lord. I can no longer do anything, I can't think or speak, "now that my every act is love . . ." Oh, Lord! You are so great, and You love me so much. You offer me so much consolation, and I make such poor use of it.

---

10. Pajares Pass: A pass in the Cantabrian Mountains that links Rafael's home province of Asturias with the rest of mainland Spain.

Listen, my dear sister. Yesterday, when I arrived at church, the sermon wasn't over yet. It was a Jesuit priest, whom I know very well, and he said a few things that left me a bit. . . I don't know exactly. . . He was talking about the active life, and the consolation of being an apostle, and being able to someday present oneself before the Lord alongside all the souls one had helped. He said something about selfish souls who only care about their own holiness, and who hide themselves away from others' sight in order not to be bothered. . . He said a lot of things, and it made me think . . . I don't like what he said. I don't know why, but I was a bit perturbed.

This is the same priest who told me that God had abandoned me, after he'd asked me if I was going to come back to Los Luises and catechesis, and I told him *absolutely not.*[11]

But, Lord, if I just can't. . . If I get distracted around other people . . . and thus I lose out on being with God. . . If all I want to do is love . . . why won't they just let me?. . . Am I doing something wrong?. . . According to this priest, yes. According to him, only those who keep busy like Martha give glory to God.[12] Am I wrong? Am I being selfish? Lord, Lord. . . enlighten me; this conflict is pressuring me from all sides . . . The men of the world call me crazy, and the man of God does too . . . just in a different way.

My dear sister, now do you see how lonely I am? I have no one to help me, except for Mary, my dear Mother . . . After hearing the preacher's words, I threw myself at Her feet. Completely withdrawn, not even hearing the noise that people made as they left the church, I once more told Our Lady what I've told her so many times: "Mary, my Mother, you already know what I'm going through . . . I only want to do one thing, and that is love God . . . and only that, even though the world is calling me, even though from a *human* perspective people think I'm useless and wasting my time. Mother, tell your Son all this . . . place me at His feet, and tell Him that I don't know how to do anything else, now that my every act is love . . . Tell Him that I didn't know if that was for the best or not, but I couldn't do anything else."

---

11. This priest was Rafael's former confessor (see #72). Los Luises was a confraternity of university students of which Rafael had been a founding member (see #5, n. 13).

12. See Luke 10:40.

I am confident that the Virgin heard me, because She filled me with peace and joy . . . above all, at knowing that the world was against me, and that everything God was giving me was hidden, completely hidden, from its sight.

Afterwards, when I read Saint John of the Cross and saw what he has to say about this, I was so consoled and so grateful to God . . . Make sure to read stanza XXIX and the commentary.[13]

Anyway, my dearest sister, I don't mean to annoy you with all this, although I'm just doing what you asked me to, which is telling you my heart's desires . . . expressing my love for God (which is inexpressible), and returning your confidence by pouring out my heart to you completely.

You've asked me what I get out of your letters; the answer is, a great deal of consolation . . . Oh little sister, you are so good to me! The Lord will repay you! . . . I couldn't possibly complain of being alone, no, not at all. Besides, even if I were, it would be for such a short time, right? As long as our bodies are on earth and our hearts are in heaven, everything will be a struggle . . . but a divine struggle in which Mary fights on our side, and the Nazarene always emerges triumphant . . . that blessed Jesus without whom we cannot live. Isn't that so?

I'll expect your reply on Monday or Tuesday.

How are things going with the Nazareth House?[14]

I'll leave it there again for now, because I'm off to the Salesian church.[15] There's nobody there now, so it's a good time . . . Talk to you soon.

My dearest sister, it's now one-thirty, and I am going to leave you here, because I'm going to go sleep for a bit, and then back to church again, and

---

13. Here, Rafael directs his aunt to read Stanza 29 of the *Spiritual Canticle*: "If, then, I am no longer / seen or found on the common, / you will say that I am lost; / that, stricken by love, / I lost myself, and was found" (SJC 475). See SJC 586–90 for Saint John's commentary on this stanza.

14. Nazareth House: An orphanage of which María was a significant patron (OC 456; see also #85, n. 9, and #87, n. 6).

15. The Church of the Sacred Heart of Jesus (Iglesia del Sagrado Corazón de Jesús) in Oviedo was formerly part of the Monastery of the Visitation of Holy Mary (Monasterio de la Visitación de Santa María). Members of the Order of the Visitation, founded by Saints Francis de Sales and Jane de Chantal in 1610, are sometimes referred to as the "Salesian Sisters" (Las Salesas) after their co-founder. When the Order left Oviedo during the Spanish Civil War, the church was used as a field hospital before ultimately becoming a Jesuit parish in 1941.

I want this letter to go out today. Besides, I can't write anything during the day; somebody leaves, then somebody else comes in, and everyone must be attended to. I have more peace and quiet at night, even if it does mean I sleep less.

All yours, your poor brother who loves you too much,

Brother María Rafael
O.C.R.

Let's see if it's true about the fire . . . Whether the logs are big or small, all that matters is that they burn, and that they never burn out . . . Sending *the usual* . . . receive it through Mary's hands.

76. To María Osorio

Oviedo, November 26, 1935

J-H-S

My dearest sister,

I don't know how to begin. Today, your letter was something I don't know how to begin to thank God for, let alone you . . . May He bless you.

I'll just say that for the past few days, I've been meditating on this reading from the Office of Sext: *Bear one another's burdens, and in this way you will fulfill the law of Christ.*[1]

What a consolation, isn't it? What are we doing? I don't know exactly, but this morning, I saw a very sweet and very Christian charity in your letter . . . You want to help and console me, and assist me in carrying my cross, as my "Cyrenian"[2] . . . Blessed be the love of creatures that does such things . . . Blessed be the Lord who gives us a heart that, sure, makes us suffer sometimes. But in exchange, that heart lets us experience such pure and natural delight when we encounter souls who love us, the way you showed me in your letter that you do . . . My dear sister, you are an angel sent to me by the Lord when I most needed you . . . I hope you don't mind me saying so, but that's how I see it.

Right now, as I begin writing you, I've just returned from the Handmaids' convent; it's six-thirty.[3] There, before the Lord, and with your letter in my pocket, I nearly wept for joy . . . How greatly You love me, O Lord! . . . If only you could see how happy I am, little sister . . . As are you. Isn't that so?

---

1. Gal 6:2. The Office of Sext, named for its traditional recitation at the "sixth hour" (noon), is one of the canonical hours of the Liturgy of the Hours.

2. Cyrenian: A reference to Simon of Cyrene, who helped Jesus carry the cross (see Luke 23:26).

3. Handmaids: see #72, n. 1.

Listen, I went to tell Jesus everything, as I always do when I receive a letter from you . . . First I made an act of thanksgiving; He treats me better than I deserve; anyway, no need to repeat the usual. Then, meditating in His presence on some of the things you told me, which you asked me not to be angry about . . . blessed be God, I'm not angry, and you have nothing to be sorry for . . . you might think so, you might think *that's how I am*, well . . . I told the Lord about this and we *laughed* together for a bit . . . In all honesty, that's what happened. Jesus gave me to understand that it's all the same to Him, and that as far as He and His Mother are concerned, it's pretty much a draw . . . no matter what you may think about me . . .

You really are such a poor thing, my dear sister. You make me laugh, I almost envy your naïveté. You can tell me anything . . . God knows everything, and besides, I tell Him all about it later . . .

When I did that this afternoon, I was suddenly filled with great joy as I realized that the Lord was listening to me and that He was smiling along with me . . . And I didn't do this, because I remembered the people praying around me, but if they hadn't been there, I'd have broken out laughing like a fool, I'm telling you . . .

Then I was quietened, and that somewhat inopportune joy was transformed into such a great peace . . . If only you knew, sister, how good God is . . . I forgot everything, I forgot myself, I forgot you . . . everything. Jesus loves me so . . . my dear sister, love God dearly . . . if only you knew. Anyway.

Then I realized that there was still a poor old lady sitting next to me in church, and she started coughing excessively. At first I was annoyed . . . and then I was so ashamed at having been annoyed that I took that poor woman by the hand and presented her to the Virgin. I asked Our Lady to help her . . . and her cough stopped. Then I focused on praying for her. I started with the little old woman sitting next to me, and I ended up putting every single one of the faithful praying in that church under the Virgin's mantle . . . Sometimes I experience these sudden fits . . . and I honestly have to work at keeping still; anyway, you get the idea.

I stayed at church until they ~~through~~ threw me out (I always forget how to spell that word, forgive my shortcomings). When I left, I was so delighted to have been with Jesus that I had an urge to hug the sacristan. Oh little sister, I am so happy! Jesus loves me so! . . .

You do have to forgive me for telling you all this, but I want you to participate in my joys just as much as . . . I was going to say "in my sorrows" . . . but well, leave my sorrows be. They don't last long; the Lord doesn't let me stop to think about them. He doesn't want me to be selfish. And if my previous letters have been tinged with sadness, do forgive me . . . I'm still so miserable.

In your letter you said that, given how much love we have for God, we must be joyful. When I read that, I could not help but bless the Lord with that holy joy of knowing we are His . . . of finding ourselves almost ablaze with Him . . . Sadness and worry begone . . . God and God alone . . . I'm telling you, if we always saw it that way, our life would be almost heaven on earth . . . it would all come down to loving God and knowing we are loved by Him . . . What a concert we'd put on! Wouldn't we? In unison with the angels and the saints and Mary! . . . Then indeed we would not be able to keep still in prayer, and those fits would occur with such frequency that at some point . . . Oh, Lord! How long must You keep me here in search of You, looking for You, loudly calling out Your name . . . without giving my heart rest or repose? . . . And seeing how our misery prevents us from rejoicing in You once and for all?

How selfish we are, Lord! Do with me what You will, pay me no mind. I don't deserve Your love. But Lord, those words aren't coming from my heart. My heart does beg Your love, and asks You to take it at once . . . and either stretch it out, or make it stop beating . . . Lord, this is no life . . . my Life is in You, and sometimes You seem so far away! Oh, my Lord and my God![4]

Look, my dear sister, I only have one thing to offer today . . . God . . . so that's what I'm sending you.

I want this letter to go out today. It's seven-thirty, and the mail goes out at eight-thirty. Even if it's just a quick note, I didn't want you to spend tomorrow without receiving what I'd wanted to send your way.

My next letter will be longer, and I'll tell you what I'm going to do during the sacred time of Advent. Tonight I'll start writing you, and answering your letter more thoroughly. I do indeed see our good Mother in it . . . I can see how much you love her already . . .

How good you are, little sister. May God repay you.

4. John 20:28.

Don't think about me going to La Trapa . . . what's that to you? I'll always be the same to you. Don't you think so?

I can't say anything else for today. There's *something inside me* that won't let me. Sending my greatest affection, your poor crazy brother,

Brother María Rafael, O.C.R.
Forgive him!!!

P.S. I'm sending you a letter I received from my monastery.[5] It doesn't say anything, but it says so much to me . . . How good Jesus is . . . Everything is a consolation.

---

5. This letter has not been preserved (OC 460).

77. To María Osorio

Oviedo, November 27, 1935

J-H-S

My dear sister,

The clock has just struck midnight in London; we heard it over the radio. Everybody has gone to bed, and I'm sitting down to start writing you a long letter, because the one I wrote you this afternoon didn't say anything at all. I was in such a rush to make it in time for the mail to go out that I left out everything important.

But when I pick up my pen and there's silence, as there is now, that's when the party really gets going. . . I'm calm and collected, I gaze toward the Virgin, I commend myself to Her, and time starts flying.

Don't you fret about me losing hours of sleep at night so that I can write. . . I make up for it with the *siesta*. It's just that nobody is around to bother me at night, and I need silence, if only you knew how much I lack it . . . I understand very well that my cousins' commotion doesn't always let you collect yourself. . . But that *noise* is almost better . . . than another kind of *noise* to which you must pay attention . . . for fear of lacking in charity. Am I making sense? . . . Don't you worry about this. Look, you might have a lot of noise around the house, but you have your solitude . . . For His sake, don't even think about crying over a little thing like that.

At home, I have to pay attention to *everything*. . . I have to talk, and laugh, and say something back. If I keep quiet, my father immediately asks me if I'm sad . . . This morning I told him I'm never quiet . . . I'm just thinking about other things that take me away from the conversation. So often, and without meaning to, I just can't think of anything to say, and I keep quiet. . . This morning I was so delighted with your letter . . . that I didn't say anything to them, I needed the silence . . . and right away my father thought that I was sad, when in fact it's exactly the opposite, I was more cheerful and upbeat than a guitar.

And so, after enduring a whole day with so little silence in it, when nighttime falls and I've said my prayers, I take up my pen and prepare for you to listen to what I have to say. And knowing, *as I know*, that you receive my letters joyfully, and that you don't mind it when I tell you everything that comes to mind, even if it's nonsense . . . knowing this, I feel such great consolation in talking to you that I feel that I don't have enough paper, and the words write themselves. But sometimes I have so much to tell you, and so much to share with you, and so much love for you . . . that I can't get anything out at all, and I get all mixed up . . . But you don't mind, right? Now, I'll calmly prepare to respond to your letter.

What you said about not having risen to certain heights, etc. . . . I have nothing to add; I said what I had to say in my previous letter . . . Not only am I not angry with you, but in fact you've really made me laugh quite a bit . . . Of course, you've decided to be my *little sister* . . . and that is what you shall become. I don't need to say anything more, because you say that you understand me, both what I say and what I don't . . . Blessed be God! Isn't that so? I understand you perfectly too, and essentially, God makes that possible in order to console us . . . He is so good, isn't He? . . . You know what I've noticed? . . . Ever since I decided not to stop and gather "flowers"[1] . . . God showers me with them . . . What about you? It's as if He does nothing else but send them, I don't know what to do. Anyway, I'm going to keep responding to your letter, because otherwise . . .

You said that you commended yourself to the Virgin before writing me; I can tell. You can be satisfied that I received *everything* you wanted me to . . . See, little sister? The Virgin listens to you. She never fails, and if you do everything in this manner, you'll see how well things will turn out for you.

I'm also very pleased because I can see how much you love Her . . . How good our dear Mother is! Do you remember when I joked that you and I were going to hold a competition for Her love? . . . Well, from our correspondence, it seems that it's underway . . . That ought to make Our Lady laugh, don't you think?

---

1. "Seeking my Love / I will head for the mountains and for watersides, / I will not gather flowers, / nor fear wild beasts; / I will go beyond strong men and frontiers" (SJC 471). See #70 for Rafael and María's earlier discussion of this poem.

Take heart, little sister, and carry on with Mary. If I could get you to love Her dearly . . . such great consolation would accompany me to La Trapa. And when I get there, and have Her so close by, I'll tell Her, "Virgin Mary, You are everything in my monastic life . . . I love You so much. I am nothing, but I am leaving behind one soul in this world who is very close to You too . . . Listen, my little sister loves You very much too . . . Listen to her, and see that she is a poor beggar who can do nothing on her own. Virgin Mary, I'm not bringing all my love for You with me to La Trapa . . . I *left behind* a little bit in the world . . . I left it for You in a soul that needed it. Now, Mary, there's only one thing left to do . . . You have to make that little *bit* I've left behind grow more and more each day . . . Don't leave her like this, Mother. Make use of my little offerings and sacrifices . . . I'm coming to La Trapa in order to love You, for the sake of those who don't know You . . . What a shame! But look, I have the tremendous, enormous consolation of having helped one soul love You more . . . I am sure of it. Blessed Virgin Mary, protect us both."

Shall I say that to Mary, my dear sister? I think so . . .

I'm so pleased that you speak of the Virgin in your letters. This is the greatest joy you could give me. I'm a bit mad when it comes to the Virgin; forgive me. But look, it's just that I haven't ever been able to talk to anyone else like this before, you know? Only ever to Her. But now, seeing your willing soul . . . and moreover, I'll be honest, seeing how far you have come . . . it consoles me greatly . . . Mary is so sweet. If only you knew how much She loves us Trappists!

When I sent you that holy card with the *Salve*, I knew it would do you a great deal of good.[2] The card itself is worthless . . . but it's Mary. It was already quite worn, but don't worry if it gets faded or frayed. May your poor heart encounter in the Most Blessed Virgin the tenderness of a mother, of a sister—that is what really matters. May you speak to Her with total honesty; talk of Her divine Son; ask Her for anything; and have confidence in Her. Then you'll see, things will go well for you. I'll pray to Her for this intention now, and I always will; I'll never forget, don't you worry. I do this for Her, and also for you.

---

2. See #71.

You'll say I'm being a bit tiresome, that I'm always going on about the same things. . . . I'm sorry. Or rather, I'm not sorry at all. . . . I'm perfectly happy to be such a bother. When it comes to the Virgin, I could keep on writing for ages, and I'd always be saying the same thing. . . . But I know you don't really mind. As such, don't worry if you *forget that you love Her* from time to time. . . . Such moments of weakness come and go quickly. In my littleness, I will help you greatly before Her. You'll see, you'll win Her love. . . . I promise you, soon you'll never forget about Her. Anyway, I'm going to move on to something else, because if not, I'll keep on about this forever.

So what if you can't take any more? Well, don't worry. I can't say anything on that subject; I'll just say, that's what you think . . . So what if you have a little soul? . . . What do you know? What do you care if your soul is little or great? Look, my dear sister, don't focus on the vessel's volume, or whether or not the water is overflowing . . . Focus on the water's purity, its freshness, its clarity . . . Look and see whether the water filling you has anything in it that might cloud it . . . make sure it is clear and transparent, but don't worry about the amount. For some, a single, shining, clear dewdrop is enough; others need a torrent, still others a waterfall . . . What's it to you? Am I making sense? I don't know how to put this into words.

Of course, in such a state, a soul can never be satisfied . . . but God cannot give us all that we ask for. If He did . . . poor us! It's as if we wanted to fit the whole sea into a glass of water . . . But the day is coming . . . Listen, little sister: grab hold of your crucifix and love Jesus with *all* your strength. Don't worry about anything else. He will do whatever you cannot do. What poor little things we are! And how great Jesus is!

You told me about your prayer, about remaining in silence before God . . . I understand. Neither desire nor ask for anything more. If only I could talk to you about this! But it's so hard in writing, even though I know what you're describing . . . How good it is to pray like that! Isn't it? God fills the soul with such gentleness . . . Lord, Lord! What have we done? What will we do with ourselves, sister?

Anyway, let us be quiet, these noisy words are a hindrance . . . I don't know what to tell you, but if you see the work of God in me . . . I see many things in you too . . . I bless God for all of it.

I'll leave it there until tomorrow, when I will continue, God willing.

It's seven-thirty in the evening. Now that I seemingly have some time, I'll continue.

If only you knew, my dear sister, how tired I am sometimes . . . Not physically, mind you . . . God never ceases to be continually present to me . . . That is my only consolation. But dealing with creatures grows ever more tiresome . . . That happens to you too, doesn't it?

When the weather's good and I can, I take the car out on my own, drive a few kilometers from Oviedo, and stop at an overlook on the highway that affords a splendid view. Sometimes I read Saint John of the Cross, other times I ponder what I've already read . . . and thinking of God, I spend a good deal of time there. Then, at twelve-thirty, I go make my visit to the Lord.

Today I wasn't able to do that; I had to take my father to Infiesto. We left after Holy Mass, and came back at one o'clock.

My life is completely disorganized . . . I pray in fits and starts. Today I made five visits.[3] You won't believe me, but I don't have time for anything. May it all serve Him.

I spend all day singing Saint John of the Cross's verses to the Lord . . . If only you knew how much consolation that saint gives me; what I've told you is the least of it. I always carry him around in a little compartment in the car . . . As I walk, I do nothing but ask the valleys and mountains, and the creatures I encounter on the way, and humans and animals, and the earth and the sky, if they have seen my Beloved,[4] "him I love most."[5] This thought gives me wings; I am always so moved inside.

"I don't know how I endure, not living where I live . . ."[6]

I spend all day in a daze.

---

3. That is, visits to the Blessed Sacrament.

4. *Have you seen him whom my soul loves?* (Song 3:3).

5. From the *Spiritual Canticle*: "Shepherds, you who go / up through the sheepfolds to the hill, / if by chance you see / him I love most, / tell him I am sick, I suffer, and I die" (SJC 471).

6. "How do you endure / O life, not living where you live, / and being brought near death / by the arrows you receive / from that which you conceive of your Beloved?" (SJC 472).

Oh, dear sister, how happy I am! How hidden is my Jesus . . . how anxiously I beg Him to "reveal his presence" to me, even if I cannot bear it and "the vision of his beauty be my death" . . . [7]

Such a great love for God for such a little soul, as you would say. How good the Lord is! How I desire silence and recollection, so as to quietly love God forever . . . forever, without distractions or noise, in the humility of my Trappist oblate's habit . . . ! How happy I will be, with or without a cross, but always with Jesus . . . Now I don't know what I'm on about.

There is so much I want to say to you . . . I want to tell you about me, and I am telling you about God. I want to open my heart to you, and in it, I find only God. I want to send you so many different things in my letters . . . and all I can send you is love for God . . .

Don't you believe that I'm flying, not at all. I'm just drifting . . . trailing close to the ground, while my heart and even my eyes are fixed on that sweet, calm Jesus of Nazareth, who is looking at me, waiting for me, loving me more than I'll ever know . . . What am I to do? I don't know. Be astonished, get confused, kiss the ground . . . go mad with joy . . . Since I can't *shout* all this at the world, I *shout it at you* from the very depths of my soul.

My dear sister, don't look at me, don't think about me . . . look to Jesus, think of Jesus . . . love Jesus. And you'll see, then you won't be able to separate yourself from Him, and the world will seem all too small for His love. Does it not fit inside you? . . . Lord, make her burst immediately . . . My poor sister, she doesn't have enough room yet for so much love for God . . . Poor thing, she has a treasure but doesn't know what to do with it . . . Is it weighing you down? How good it is to be crushed beneath such a weight . . . The weight of an immense love for God, with a heart torn to pieces from all that *silent shouting*. If only you knew how much that hurts . . . But how sweet and tender it is to suffer for love . . .

Jesus, I don't know what I'm on about, don't pay me any mind.

But other than when I was napping, I've been like this all day . . . Now, you are permitting me to unburden myself with you . . . so I am calmer.

7. "Reveal your presence / and may the vision of your beauty be my death" (SJC 473).

My soul is so full!! I don't know what is happening to me. As a rule, I am filled with such peace and joy . . . and a mad desire to be holy . . . I'm not satisfied with little either, I feel the same way you do . . . To the greatest heights!. . . Though I do not expect things too great for me, nor is my heart proud, as David says.[8] It's just that in my littleness, I can do nothing, but with God, I can do all things, and with Mary's help, I can do even more . . . You'll see how, with those two things, and without relying on *ourselves* for *anything at all*, we'll become saints . . .

We need to hurry up, little sister. Seeing *how much we already have*, we have a huge *responsibility* in God's eyes. I worry about this sometimes . . . it would be terrible not to respond as we ought, wouldn't it?

Anyway, we'll help each other, won't we? . . . I tell you everything so that you can pray to the Lord for me. But I don't want to be selfish . . . I'm more concerned with your affairs than my own, even when it comes to material things . . . My poor sister, you must be having such a hard time with all the gossip and stories going around . . .

I've been thinking a lot about your trip to Madrid, and you've been very much on my mind, but how good it is to have something to suffer through . . . I don't wish to take anything away from you, but I am *at your side* through *all of it*. That's the most I can do; will that suffice? It's a small thing, but look, I'm doing it for Christ, as He commands us. You'll see, everything will be resolved . . . and resolved well.

I still haven't received a letter from Uncle Polín . . . If only you knew how much I am thinking of him.

The day before yesterday, I received a letter from my grandmother . . . Poor thing, she loves me so . . . She begs me to write her, for charity's sake; of course, I must . . . I've realized that, as long as I am in this world, the mission entrusted to me by the Lord is to help others love Him . . . I have offered myself to Him for this task, and I believe He has accepted me. As you can see, the Lord is bringing about a marvelous change in my family, I think.

As I give up everything, I make my renunciation with great joy, knowing that I can help my Christian father in doing so . . . I am capable of

8. *O Lord, my heart is not lifted up, my eyes are not raised too high; I do not occupy myself with things too great and too marvelous for me* (Ps 131:1).

doing anything that might get a brother of mine in this world to do a single act of love for God . . . This is not arrogance; I say this with an open heart, and this is exactly how I feel . . . as God well knows.

Nobody at home is surprised that you are writing me or that I write you back . . . Several times, my mother has asked me what you were talking about . . . and I told her the truth . . . I told her that you placed great confidence in me and were telling me your *spiritual difficulties*, and that, returning that confidence and *doing what I could*, I was replying in order to help you love God . . . They thought that was perfectly reasonable.

One day Leopoldo asked me if I was translating *Don Quixote* into Greek . . . They've never seen me write this much.

Don't worry about that, then. All this is for my eyes only, and I leave it all at the Virgin's feet.

Don't hesitate to write me, even when I'm back at La Trapa . . . if you ever need me . . . (what am I thinking, who am I to be needed) . . . Anyway, you know what I mean . . . Don't think that La Trapa is some abyss or fortress . . . In La Trapa there is enough charity for both the brothers on the inside and the brethren on the outside; be assured of that . . . Don't let that thought discourage you. Quite the contrary—if I were to remain in the world, you might still worry that life would take me here or there . . . But in La Trapa, you know exactly where I am . . . and what I'm doing: I'll be at the Virgin's feet, always, at all times. You can come see me and tell me about your life . . . I will speak to you about God, and I'll always encourage you to be holy. You will have that consolation . . . and I will not.

You'll always have a brother . . . and a Trappist brother at that . . . A brother who can't offer you what a brother in the worldly sense can (and I don't mean your brothers, whom you've never really had) . . . You'll always have a brother, a true brother, in Christ, and through Christ; and he'll always love you with the greatest affection . . .

Everything is compatible with being a Trappist, and now that I love God more, I love my parents and brothers and sisters *more* and *better*. Only God understands such mysteries of the heart . . . What more do you want, little sister? . . . I can't offer you much, for I am no one, I am nothing . . . But accept this humbly, thank the Virgin for it, and pray for me; if only you knew, I need it now more than ever . . . My soul wants to fly, but this body . . . This body gives me so much to do.

A battle awaits me . . . A battle of a month or more, because I won't be able to go until at least mid-January . . . and even if I don't want that, God permits it, and I'd be lying if I told you that renouncing everything anew was only somewhat difficult for me . . . I already know what La Trapa is. Even though I'll be given some reprieve as a sick person . . . if only you knew, bodies and matter hold us back so much, while the world clings so tightly . . . giving up so many joys, even very good and proper ones, is hard. And sometimes the evil spirit pressures me, and while he never takes away the peace God gives me . . . I can tell you that he makes me suffer.

Of course, I wouldn't trade that small hardship for all the world's glories . . . but I am weak, a creature of flesh and blood, with a heart and soul, and parents and siblings, and very dear friends, and such holy affections . . . I have to leap over all that in order to embrace the blessed cross, where Jesus is waiting for me . . . That leap is hard for me to make, but when I look over to the other side, and I see Mary with open arms alongside Her Son Jesus, who is looking at me and calling me with such love . . . I assure you, I forget everything else . . . No need to pity me, I don't want to make you sad . . . I'm not . . . I'd do it all a thousand times over if God asked me to. What do my tears matter? They are human tears, the tears of the *old self*[9] . . . They don't deserve my attention, let alone yours . . . I am so happy to be able to offer the Lord some of what He has given me.

I am so grateful for the help and consolation that you offer me . . . You are so good to me, may God reward you . . . I can see God in this. He is helping me in an extraordinary way . . . but He has made a sweet gesture . . . in offering me a soul like yours, you, who amid your own sufferings are willing to lend me a hand . . . Well, dear sister to my soul, I'll take it. You are indeed helping me, much more than you realize . . . Anyway, only God knows what my heart feels, and I would tell you . . . but since you understand even my silence, I'll keep quiet and not say anything at all.

What did your siblings have to say in Madrid? When is Uncle Polín coming back? Tell me everything, if that would console you. As you can see, that's exactly what I do with you.

---

9. *You have stripped off the old self with its practices and have clothed yourselves with the new self, which is being renewed in knowledge according to the image of its creator* (Col 3:9-10). See also Rom 6:6.

I'll leave it there for now, because it's time for dinner. I'll keep going after everyone has gone to bed. Talk to you later, my dear sister.

All right, listen, it's eleven-thirty now and I don't have much time, because tomorrow my parents and I are going to go to Covadonga[10] for Mass, and I'll have to get up early, at six. I'll need to shave, then go get the car, and then it's eighty kilometers[11] . . . It takes two hours from here. I promised you I'd go to Covadonga one of these days, so I am . . . My parents think it's just some whim of mine . . . and tonight at dinner we decided to go . . . I'm very pleased. You'll see, everything will be resolved . . . The Virgin, or *La Santina* as they call her here, will make it so.

Merceditas and my mother have just gone to bed; my father and Leopoldo are listening to a concert in Germany . . . I can hear the notes of the piano clearly from here . . . If only you knew how deficient I find music now, having enjoyed it so much before . . . My God, what will heaven be like! . . . We'll know soon, won't we? Don't you worry about anything. Everything is passing away . . . You'll see, there, we'll be with our Jesus for *real*. . . Sometimes I get so impatient . . . I can't help it . . . We are sojourners on this earth,[12] and our Beloved is taking so long to arrive.

Oh, my dear little sister, if only I could put into words what I feel in such moments . . . How great God is! If only you could see how He has transformed me . . . I no longer recognize myself. My God, what do You want from me? . . . I have nothing left to give You, I've already given You everything . . . Lord, don't leave me like this; take me at once, and for good . . . Lord, silence me, for my heart will not let me rest even a moment as long as it is boiling over.

Oh, sister, I envy your peaceful prayer, your tranquil gaze toward God, your silence before Him . . . I can't have any of that. I understand it, but sometimes I just can't . . . Listen, if I look at Him, I melt . . . I can't, I can't take it. If I contemplate His love for me, something pierces me, I don't know what . . . I can't put it into words . . .

---

10. The Holy Cave of Our Lady of Covadonga is the site of a Marian apparition and shrine in Covadonga, Asturias (see #73, n. 4). Our Lady of Covadonga is also known as "La Santina," her Asturian-language nickname.

11. Eighty kilometers is approximately fifty miles.

12. Ps 119:19.

I want to cry out. . . . Am I making sense?. . . What a poor little thing I am. Lord, Lord, forgive Your servant, who knows not what he is saying.[13]

You forgive me too, my sister; have mercy on me. I've gone mad. I never knew before what it was to love God. . . It is so sweet, it's incomprehensible, it's terrible . . . It makes one wish one's heart would stop beating, and at the same time, one desires ever more and more. I don't know, one ends up totally perplexed. . . Anyway, may the Virgin come to my aid.

You've asked how I will prepare to await the arrival of the Child Jesus. I don't know, I'm overwhelmed. . . I'll wait, that's all . . . And if that's not enough? I know . . . I'll wait with great love, I'll wait with faith . . . I'll wait impatiently, and sometimes peacefully. . . I don't know, I'll just wait . . . That's all I could do last year.

Starting this coming Sunday, I'm going to put together a life plan in order to be more focused. I don't want to let even a minute go to waste. When I have ten minutes free, I'll go to the tabernacle, and there, close to Jesus and the Virgin . . . I'll wait. I'll tell you what I end up doing and how, so that together, we can focus entirely on that.

The world, meanwhile, is busy with its own affairs. May it leave us in peace by the tabernacle . . . You, gaze at Him with that peace, if you have it, speak to Him in silence, gaze at Him and wait. I'll try to do the same . . . if I can, that is. Sometimes I get impatient . . .

Of course, it is a season of penance and recollection. I can't say anything regarding the former . . . The Lord will instruct me, and I don't dare promise anything yet. I don't want to repeat what happened last year, when I was in La Trapa and I asked for the disciplines[14] we used there . . . and either I lost them or they took them away from me. I dare not ask.

But anyway, since I don't keep secrets from you, I'll tell you all about it . . . I don't know if that's a mistake, but since we agreed that you'd tear up my letters . . . You will, won't you? One day Uncle Polín scolded me because he said that I needed to be more simple . . . That's fine, but everything I tell you is for your good; maybe somebody else would laugh it off . . . I don't mind being laughed at, but I do mind if God is caught in the crossfire . . . Am I making sense?

13. Luke 23:34.
14. Disciplines: instruments of physical penance; see #40, n. 15.

Well, it's twelve o'clock now. Time to pray the *Angelus* to the Virgin, then the *Salve* and three Hail Marys; then I'll place myself at the feet of the crucified Jesus, and in holy peace, I'll try to fall asleep. Tomorrow I'll tell you what I did in Covadonga.

November 28

My dear sister, I'll now take a few moments to finish this letter so it can go out today . . . I don't have much time; my father and I are leaving shortly to make our visit to the Lord.

This morning we left at seven, and we came back to eat at a quarter past two. I can't put it into words . . . it's best if you just imagine it. I think everything is going to be all right now . . . I placed you at the feet of Our Lady of Covadonga . . . When I received the Lord . . . I could hardly say anything to Him, even though I'd been preparing for our conversation the whole way there, which is a two-hour trip . . . but no matter.

I have so many things I want to tell you . . . but if I do, this letter is going to go on too long . . . Don't pay attention to the number of things I'm telling you, or the messy order I tell them in . . . But with you, I don't worry about that, or bother to organize my ideas. I just write whatever comes to me.

Today is Thursday, I won't write you again until Sunday . . . I have to write my grandmother, and Brother María Jesús, a young brother of mine who is away from the monastery, and Almenas, who wrote me this morning[15] . . . As you can see, it's as if I were somebody important. But in all honesty, if I can bring little rays of light and God's love to souls through my letters, I'll spend the rest of my life with a pen in my hand.

I'll expect your letter on Sunday, or before. Will it arrive by then? . . . I don't want to rush you, you do enough, and you've already done enough as it is. I deserve nothing, I assure you. Write me on your own time, calmly, whenever you like.

This morning my father got very emotional at Communion, and he was crying. May God bless him; pray for him . . . The Lord will repay you, and so will I, however I can . . .

---

15. My grandmother: Fernanda Torres. Brother María Jesús: Jesús Sandoval, oblate at San Isidro from March 1932 to August 1935. Almenas, see #62, n. 13.

My parents and I were alone in the Holy Cave . . . We were deep in recollection. How good the Lord is! I prayed two *Salves* to the Virgin, one for you and one for me. I believe that She heard me; I am so content, little sister. Mary loves me so much. Now, especially when I pray the *Salve*, I pause at the words, "and after this our exile, show unto us the blessed fruit of thy womb, Jesus." Will Mary "show us Jesus"? Yes, She will; you'll see. We'll receive Him through Her, and thanks to Mary, this Christmas we'll have Him in the world, so very close to us.

That's all, my dear little sister. May the Lord bless you . . . Receive all my love, and anything else you wish; I send you all that I can, which is *the usual*, along with my great affection. Your brother,

Brother María Rafael, O.C.R.

78. To María Osorio

Oviedo, December 1, 1935
First Sunday of Advent

J-H-S
Prepare the way of the Lord: make His paths straight.[1]
My dear little sister,

I received your letter the other day. I'll say the same thing you did: the more you feel, the less you can put it into words.

Out of everything you said, there's just one thing I'm going to respond to . . . because as far as I can tell, either I haven't explained myself properly, or I haven't quite gotten this right . . . nevertheless, I understand you.

You said that I don't understand the joy you feel at "immersing yourself in your littleness." Listen, every soul is a mystery that only God can penetrate . . . He alone can understand us completely . . . But sometimes He allows creatures a great consolation . . . which is seeing the many different ways that He uses to draw souls.

Seeing Him *at work* in creatures' hearts . . . the consolation (human though it may be) of knowing you are being helped and understood . . . being encouraged . . . Anyway, what can I say? . . . I'll say this: I don't merely understand the joy you are feeling . . . in fact, I *don't think of you any other way.* Don't you remember how we talked about this on various occasions? . . . Moreover, I envy your simplicity of heart in seeing yourself this way.

I ask the Virgin Mary to enlighten us both, so that I might explain myself well and you might understand me.

Yesterday, while I was praying the Rosary to Mary, I was distracted without meaning to be, and I was thinking about you and what you said to me . . . Many things came to mind . . . Now I've forgotten them all, I'm a mess . . . Believe me, I think less and less by the day . . . I thought

---

1. Matt 3:3; see also Isa 40:3; Mark 1:3; Luke 3:4.

about writing them all down for you that night, but I couldn't . . . I'll try to do it now (it's twelve o'clock).

My dear sister, you can indeed be pleased at how little you seem before God . . . Your joy is that of one who knows she is protected by a good God . . . It gives you great peace to *know* that you *cannot do anything*, and that He is the one who does everything, isn't that right? . . . I can't explain it; of course, you know better than I do, but I do understand it . . . *Your nothingness is your consolation, your littleness is your joy*, because feeling little makes you feel more coddled by God . . . and that's not easy to explain, it's something you feel, that's all . . . You won't deny that this is a consolation, and one of the greatest there is . . . God gives great sweetness to the soul . . . when that soul, finding itself alone and little and wretched, seeing how small and humble it is, submerges itself in God, and then God fills it . . . There is nothing more to do . . . poor us!

My sister, I can see that this is your path . . . humility before God and men . . . A hidden and simple life . . . and being the littlest of all the souls who love Christ, but loving Him as no one has ever loved Him before. Isn't that right? . . .

Yes, I know what you're going through, and I understand. Your soul rejoices in its littleness, because that way, as I said, you feel more coddled by Jesus. By putting yourself last, you find great consolation . . . It's only natural, what more can you do? . . . if you can't do anything at all . . . You are weak, you are wretched, you want to love Jesus and you don't know how . . . and none of that discourages you. On the contrary, finding yourself in such a state, you understand that a heart like yours, so full of human senti-ments . . . cannot aspire to anything . . . to anything more than finding yourself last among God's creatures . . . humbling yourself in His presence, considering yourself little in His eyes, and immersing yourself in Him. This fills you with an intense joy . . . I don't know how to explain it, but I think I understand you . . . Tell me honestly if I'm mistaken.

Anyway (look, read me charitably), knowing how you are . . . I believe that you are capable of even more. We decided not to "gather flowers."[2] Finding that your *nothingness* is your *consolation* . . . don't stop and think about yourself.

---

2. A reference to Saint John of the Cross; see #70, n. 1, and #77, n. 1.

If it makes you happy to realize how little you are before God, that's all well and good. But it seems to me—and forgive me, I'm nobody—that it would be more perfect not to be happy about this . . . Do you understand what I mean?

It would be better if you dispensed with yourself entirely . . . The less you look at yourself, the better you'll see God. Don't you agree? . . . May the Lord grant you true humility . . . but once you've felt it, keep moving forward. Don't stop to consider your humility, for that would be to stop and consider yourself . . . Don't stop to consider your littleness, for that would be to stop and consider yourself . . . Keep moving forward. Climb toward the Lord, and when you are with Him, you'll see, you'll essentially *feel that you are nothing* . . . you'll love Him without *realizing* it . . . Then He will truly fill us completely . . . We'll disappear, and He will be *all*.

Do you understand what I'm saying, my dear sister? Don't listen to everything I'm saying, this is just how I see it . . . and in my previous letters, I may not have explained myself well. I just want you to be very holy, very much in God, very exalted, even though you're always saying over and over again that you're nothing, that you can't do anything, that you're little, that you're the last among all . . .

I don't care. Despite all that . . . dispense with that *consolation* of seeing yourself in this way . . . Don't look at yourself. Look at Jesus on the Cross, look at God who loves you, whatever you may be . . . Don't measure your own love, for it is *yours* . . . Measure out the love God has for you, and let yourself be astonished. Don't look back at your own heart and search it again, because all that is *yours* too, and you're wasting time; you won't find anything, or you'll just find consolation, and as for those . . . let's leave them behind . . . Search the Heart of God, which is unfathomable. Submerge yourself in Him, and do not look at or search out anything else.

If you toss a grain of salt into the sea, it disappears, because the salt dissolves into the water, and thus the sea and the grain of salt become one. But if rather than a very tiny grain of salt, you toss in a grain of sand instead . . . the grain of sand will keep being little, and it will be in the sea . . . but it won't dissolve . . . I don't know if I am putting this well . . .

But let's try to be little grains of salt who are dissolved in God, and thus disappear . . . rather than little grains of sand who either sink to the bottom or end up on shore. Don't tell me that you can't . . . All you have to do is let it be done to you . . . let yourself be dissolved.

Don't you go thinking—well, I already know you don't think this—
don't you go thinking that I've already achieved this . . . Not at all; I am
a dark grain of sand, for I did the same thing you did, I stopped to think
about myself a great deal . . . now I have seen the light, and I don't want
to remain stopped any longer.

Before, when I placed myself in the presence of God, I saw myself just as
you said: little, insignificant, hardly daring to lift my gaze . . . I asked the
Lord for humility and self-disgust; I was astonished by my insignificance
before God; I saw what little love I had for Him . . . I asked Him to fill
me, engulf me, and in His infinite goodness, overlook my wretchedness
. . . This consoled me, God coddled me . . . In La Trapa, I considered
myself the least and most wretched of the monks, and I thanked the Lord
for His kindness . . . and seeing myself this way gave me a quiet consolation: I knew I was beloved of God, despite loving Him so little . . . but
what more could I, such a poor creature, the least of all, possibly do? . . .

Now, dear little sister, I still feel the same way, but I see that it's for the
best. All that isn't necessary to love God and unite yourself to His Heart
. . . It's best for us to dispense with ourselves, so that we can climb toward
Him . . . because otherwise, we'll always be stuck thinking about our own
humility . . . *Without ceasing* to be humble, without ceasing to be little,
let us climb toward Him, so that He can do it all . . .

I don't know if I'm talking nonsense . . . I just write what I feel . . . But if
at the beginning of our dialogue with God, we are the ones who speak, there
does come a moment when we must fall silent . . . and let the Lord speak,
and if we do speak, we cease to speak of ourselves . . . for the same humility
we had at the beginning now *prevents* us from focusing on ourselves.

I do indeed understand the joy of your littleness . . . my dear sister.
I do indeed understand how your insignificance before God could be a
consolation to your soul . . . But I'll say that while you ought not to stop
feeling little and weak, you shouldn't stop to think about it too much,
because that would be stopping to think about a creature, yourself, and
since you are worthless . . . Just leave it be, and instead of your littleness,
consider God's greatness. Instead of your wretchedness, consider God's
virtues . . . Instead of your little love for the Lord, consider the immense,
magnificent love He has for you.

If you consider yourself, even if it's to weep over your ingratitude or your
sins or your wretchedness . . . Let us not gather flowers. Don't you agree?

Everything I'm saying to you right now, I'm also saying to myself. This isn't a sermon or a lesson I'm trying to give you; God forbid . . . These are simply some written reflections I'm sending you in case they can be useful to you in some way. Don't take it to mean anything else. Perhaps it would be best if you didn't even take me into consideration at all, because I haven't consulted anyone about this, nor do I have any relevant experience, nor am I being guided by anything except a great desire to love God the best way I can . . . the least human way possible . . . To love Him and deny myself. To love Him as nobody else has ever loved Him before.

Maybe I'm talking nonsense . . . Forgive me, I'm not trying to lay down any doctrine here . . . I'm telling you right now, I am small and I can't do anything . . . other than desire to love God.

May the Most Blessed Virgin come to my aid. During my Rosary the other day, She was the one who delighted me with these thoughts and inspired me to share them with you . . . You know how I am. On the one hand, I don't want consolations, and on the other hand, I am seeking them by confiding in you . . . Anyway, God sees all.

I'll just say that I pray the Lord sanctifies you through your littleness.

There was so much to respond to in your letter, which I will do another day. I wouldn't know how to respond today. I'll just say that I've already started preparing for December 8 . . . I'll tell you what we're going to offer the Most Blessed Virgin very soon.[3]

I haven't written my grandmother yet . . . I'm more focused now . . . Your letters are my only occupation during this liturgical season . . . but they have provided me with meditation, both in receiving your letters and in answering them . . . so long as we use them to discuss the love of God. Don't you agree? . . . And you help me so much through your letters! May God reward you.

I very much unite myself to you during your prayer times. I pray at approximately the same times you do, and every morning from eleven o'clock onward; today I prayed from twelve to one o'clock . . . But at seven I always remember you when I pray the *Salve.*

There were so many things I wanted to tell you, but I don't know . . .

---

3. December 8 is the feast of the Immaculate Conception.

After reading over this letter . . . well, I don't know what you're going to think . . . But you have to be completely honest with me . . . in case I am mistaken.

Forgive your poor brother, who sends you all his affection, along with his love for God and Mary,

Brother María Rafael
O.C.R.

As for all your affairs . . . of course, I hold them very close . . . God knows, but I have great confidence . . . You'll see, little sister, the Virgin will fix everything . . . Don't worry.

My next letter will be longer.

79. Notes Written by Rafael in His Copy of the Little Office of the Blessed Virgin Mary[1]

Most Blessed Virgin Mary: When the Lord places the words of David[2] in my mouth, bring them to heaven pure and unblemished, not sullied by my unclean lips, which are not worthy to speak them. Ensure that my prayer is answered. . . I offer it to You so that You might present it to the Lord. . . Purify my intention. . . pardon my faults. . . and thus, as my feeble praise passes through Your most pure hands, You will miraculously transform it into the purest of songs to delight Jesus, and He will deign to hear me.

I hope for everything through You. . . for who am I to dare to ask for anything? But if You intercede for me. . . then there's nothing I won't dare to ask for.

And how could You not hear my prayer, knowing how much Your poor Trappist loves You so?

Oh sweet Virgin Mary! Pray for me, and for all sinners like me. Don't forget, Mother, that I am Your son, though I am the littlest.

Brother María Rafael O.C.R.[3]

Lord, Your servant is waiting![4]

Wait for me, Virgin Mary. Humble yourself before the Virgin . . . Consider the sins you have committed as you prayed the Office; ask for the grace to pray it better tomorrow than you did today. Ask that She perceive neither your words nor your composure, but rather the heart of Her poor servant Rafael, who, while a sinner, has left it at the feet of his Mother Mary, so that through Her intercession She might bring it to Jesus.[5]

---

1. These annotations date roughly to the second half of 1935 (OC 482). For the Little Office, see #24, n. 1.

2. The Little Office is comprised of the Psalms, traditionally ascribed to King David.

3. This prayer was written inside the front cover.

4. See 1 Sam 3:10 and Luke 2:29. This line was written on the page before Compline, or Night Prayer.

5. This prayer was written on the page after Compline.

80. *Dedication of a Little Office to his Mother, Mercedes Barón Torres*[1]

Oviedo, December 2, 1935

My dearest mother,

There is only one thing I'd like you to put into your prayer of the Office: love for Mary. Don't worry about anything else. She will make up for whatever is lacking . . . She will present both your tears and your joys to Jesus . . .

She will gather up your praise for God, and will see nothing in you but great tenderness toward Herself. Don't worry if your song to the Lord is not as lofty as you'd like it to be. Mary will be the one to present it to Him, and that is enough for Him to be pleased to accept it.

My dearest mother, those of us who are little and weak need help to make our prayer pure . . . and Mary does just that . . . the Virgin looks on us from heaven and sees our faults and our flaws, but at the same time, seeing our love, She does away with all that, presenting our feeble petitions zealously before God.

Love the Virgin dearly, and that will help you love God. That is my prayer as the littlest among Her children, and the oldest among yours,

Brother María Rafael, O.C.R.

---

1. Rafael wrote this dedication in his mother's copy of the Little Office of the Blessed Virgin Mary (see #24, n. 1).

81. To María Osorio

Oviedo, December 4, 1935

J-H-S

My dearest sister,

I'll hardly have time to write you today, because I have to go to Gijón[1] this afternoon, and I have to go to the doctor shortly, and then I'll go make my visit[2] . . . Anyway, making the most of every minute, I shall begin to answer your letter now.

I don't know where to begin . . . There is so much inside me . . . Well, first of all, I'll tell you that what you said about the Virgin did indeed make me laugh . . . If only I knew; but look, all the contradictions I share with you aren't for everybody . . . Besides, that would be very difficult, although if it were to make someone love the Virgin more . . . I don't know, maybe I could do something . . . And I did have this thought: when I'm in La Trapa, I'll suggest this to Father Abbot, and surely he'll permit me to write. At La Trapa, at Mary's feet, taking my time, I'll write to the Virgin about everything that occurs to me that would be worth reading . . . I'll send you the drafts, and if you think it's good, it can be published under the name "a Cistercian, a son of Mary," that's all.

That way I'll achieve two things at once: I'll be able to keep helping you, and I'll also be able to make known the glories of Mary, which is an obligation of all Trappists. What do you think?

Despite all this, the idea does make me laugh . . . but no matter, I'll be the littlest of Mary's sons . . . but when it comes to Her, there's nothing I won't do. Although it's precisely when I want to write to the Virgin that I can't think of anything to say. I assure you, nothing can be expected of me, I know myself well enough on this subject . . .

---

1. Gijón: A port city near Rafael's hometown of Asturias.
2. Visit: That is, Rafael's daily hour of Adoration.

Anyway, Father Abbot will laugh when I tell him, "Look, Reverend Father, I know I can't write to my family, but let me write to Our Lady . . ." And then, during my free time, I'll set about writing to the Virgin in the form of letters, or whatever She inspires me to do, and if they let me, I'll send them to you; you can edit them and do whatever you want with them . . .

If only there were something I could really do for Mary . . . If only you knew, I owe Her everything . . . my vocation, and my health, be it poor or excellent, I tend to it for God's sake and for Mary's . . . And listen, many years ago, before I went off to La Trapa, I fell into a certain sin, and the Most Blessed Virgin was the only reason I didn't hit rock bottom. She rescued me miraculously from the place I was in . . . And it's not that She revealed Herself to me somehow . . . no. But when I saw how much further I could have fallen, and how close I was to doing so, and the extraordinary way that the Lord held me back, I *understood*, without knowing why, but I *felt* somehow, that it was the Most Blessed Virgin who had done this . . . Then later, in La Trapa, She showered me with graces, some of which I've already shared with you . . . In short, Our Lady has influenced my spiritual life in a very special way, and I wouldn't even deserve to breathe if I weren't grateful.

I have to go now. Talk to you later!

Today, December 5, I continue . . . I'm a bit frustrated, because listen, yesterday after I stopped writing you, I couldn't get anything done. I spent the whole morning at the doctor's, then I went to Gijón with my father . . . Essentially, I didn't pray at all . . . You won't believe it, but I don't have time to do anything. I wanted you to get this letter today . . . But that wasn't possible . . . Nothing to be done about that . . . I wanted to answer your letter point by point, but I don't know. In your letter, I see the Most Blessed Virgin, who is guiding you. I have nothing more to say.

As for what you plan to do every day, I don't think you need to change a thing . . . Such questions you ask me! When I received your letter, I went to go see a Carmelite priest to ask him for one, because I left the one I used to have at La Trapa[3] . . . He's going to give it to me today, and I'll do the same thing at the same times as you . . . and I'll offer it all up

3. Here, Rafael is most likely referring to an instrument of physical penance (OC 487).

so that the Most Blessed Virgin uses it for whatever is *needed*. I believe some of it will come your way.

Don't you worry about me . . . I am completely happy, I assure you . . . If I talked of my sacrifice in my most recent letters, I was just being selfish . . . There's no such sacrifice, and now I'm ashamed of having said that to you . . . How ungenerous I am . . . blessed be God . . . Anyway, He knows better than I do what is going on inside me . . . and in my struggle, which I cannot deny, I almost realize . . . He is helping me so much.

The other day, the devil disturbed me. It was terribly cold and rainy, a fearful night . . . When I climbed into my soft bed, in my warm room, not at all hungry, smoking my cigarette . . . I was afraid of what awaits me . . . It's so different there . . . my nature often rebels . . . I fly unto Mary and everything else passes away. God permits such temptations, but I assure you, they are few and far between . . .

Don't worry about whether or not they cause me to suffer . . . I am very happy, but nevertheless, I am counting the days and the hours. On other occasions, like when I was home last, time flew incredibly rapidly . . . I don't know, it all blurs together . . . But in the middle of all that is Jesus, my Jesus of Nazareth, and I forget everything else . . . I don't want to think about myself . . . May God reward your great charity toward me in wanting to alleviate some of what I am going through . . . I receive that *desire* of yours, I place it at the feet of Jesus, and that is of enormous help to me . . . I am so lonely, I don't know how to thank you for the encouragement you give me in your letters . . . Anyway: God alone.

You were right about what you said in your letter about the consolation I'll have at La Trapa, and how my brothers will help me . . . I don't know what I'd said in my letter. Don't pay me any mind, sometimes I don't even know what I'm talking about.

Lord, Lord, how could I be so selfish!

Forgive me, dear sister. You still don't know me completely, and perhaps you're the one who has the wrong idea about me . . . It doesn't matter. God sees all.

On December 8, God willing, we will renew our offering to the Lord of all that we are and all that we have . . . We'll offer Him once more the flowers along our paths . . .

I'm sending you this drawing of mine so that you remember.[4] It's worthless, it's not as good as I'd like it to be . . . but it summarizes this whole period of time, at least as far as I'm concerned . . . Let us keep moving forward, without turning our heads to the side, totally stripped of everything, not looking at ourselves. With our eyes fixed on the cross . . . the path is so short, isn't it? Who cares about anything else?

Yes, little sister, yes, let's hurry up and become saints. Let's prepare ourselves so that when the Bridegroom arrives, our lamps will be lit[5] . . . Let's not focus on anything else.

I'm getting a shrine ready for Jesus, and I don't know what it's going to look like yet, but I do know that I'm preparing it with *impatient love* . . . My Jesus is taking so long to arrive . . . ! This wait is so long! . . . But for the one who truly loves, waiting is so sweet. Isn't it?

What a great consolation, Lord; oh, how I love You, and how You love me . . . How shameful it is to fear everything that sacrifice represents, when You, O Lord, came into this world naked, cold, helpless, and per-secuted . . . how shameful . . . and I, meanwhile . . . How I love You, O Lord. I won't know what to say to You this Christmas, I won't be able to . . . I'll have to be quiet.

Little sister, will we truly receive Him well? Look, He is capable of coming down here just for us, that's how much He loves us . . . How good is Jesus . . . What a shame that the world doesn't know it. Will we make up for all the love that the world lacks? . . . Let us pray to Mary for exactly this . . . Let us help the Virgin in the stable . . .

Oh, little sister, how many things we could do! How dull we are, how pitiable . . . Our longing is so strong, while we are so little . . . God . . . Jesus, Mary, do we know what we are saying? . . . No. We have merely an idea, and we don't know how to love, not even a little. How pitiable we are . . .

Little Jesus . . . Child Jesus, I love you so! Permit me to spend this Christmastide curled up in a little corner of the stable. There, quiet,

4. On the front of the holy card that Rafael sent María, he drew a forest scene and inscribed the words of Saint John of the Cross: "Seeking my Love / I will head for the mountains and for watersides, / I will not gather flowers, / nor fear wild beasts; / I will go beyond strong men and frontiers" (SJC 471); see #70, n. 1. On the back, he wrote her a note; see #83.

5. See the parable of the ten virgins, Matt 25:1-3.

without the noise of drums or tambourines, I'll sing you sweet, tender carols from the bottom of my poor heart, all covered in wounds and misery . . . but during this time of Advent, You'll fix it up . . . You'll see, Jesus, I'm going to be so good . . . we won't let the world notice, but I'm going to love You so much more.

I want to have such affection for You . . . You are so good, and You love me so much, just as . . . just as I am . . . I don't understand it, good Jesus . . . It doesn't matter, I don't know how I am, it doesn't matter. I know that You are coming down from heaven to Mary's womb, and that You are coming in order to accompany me during my life on this earth . . . In order to console me, heal me, help me present myself to the Father . . . How good You are, my Jesus . . . The Virgin loves You so; see how She lulls You to sleep in Her arms, and how Her heart burns with love of You . . .

Lord, permit me to place my poor soul and feeble heart alongside those of Mary . . . may She impart to me Her tenderness and immense affection for You . . . I don't know what I am asking. I'm crazy . . . I want to love You so much, my good Child . . . Allow me to prepare the way for You . . . I want to clear away the pebbles and mud that Your divine feet are to tread . . . I want You to find in me what You cannot find among men, who offend You with their sins, who do not know You . . . whom You call, but who do not listen . . . I want my heart to be your stable . . . What madness. Lord, forgive me . . . Just let me stay in the corner . . . for I don't know what I am saying, nor what I am asking . . . I want to love You so! . . .

How pitiable I am, dear sister . . . don't pay me any mind. Jesus gives us so much that we'd go crazy trying to pay Him back, don't you think?

It's twelve o'clock now. I'm going to pray the *Angelus*, and then I'm going to pray until one o'clock. Then I'll continue writing for a little bit.

I just got back from my visit with the Lord at the Handmaids' convent.[6] I went to tell Him everything I've been telling you in this letter . . . Time flew.

I dedicated the holy card I'm sending to you before I left the house, and afterwards, when I was walking through the streets, I was absorbed

---

6. Handmaids: See #72, n. 1.

in thought about what I'd written . . . and I didn't take anything else in. "Love . . . love," I repeated. I went to church to see God . . . "Love . . . love . . ." propelled me there. I had an urge to go to the tabernacle . . . and I went.

I'll stop here; they just gave me your letter . . . I don't know what to do . . . Well, yes I do: I'm going to pray a *Salve* to Mary, and *humbly* tell my father about this. I'll do it for love of God and you two.

The Virgin loves you both very much, don't worry; my father will do whatever he can . . . Now, permit me to say a few words to Uncle Polín. Your letter may have been "material," as you said, but it was just as useful to me as the rest . . . You did very well in placing this confidence in me . . . That's how things should be between brother and sister.

Now I'm off to scold Uncle Polín on my father's behalf.

All my love, your brother,

Brother María Rafael

82. To Leopoldo Barón

Oviedo, December 5, 1935

J-H-S

Dearest Uncle Polín,

I've taken away Aunt María's title of "aunt," and now I call her my "sister" . . . with your permission, I'll do the same to you . . . It may not be as respectful, but when I call you my "brother" too, apparently I come to love you more . . . Will you accept? . . . Well then, my dearest brother, I received your letter . . . since you didn't say anything to me, I don't have anything to respond to.

I gave the letter to my father to read. He and I are now closer than ever, and I have a greater confidence with him . . . It upset him, because he is very worried about all your affairs, and he told me to tell you that you're a fool. But as you know, he's always . . . well, he regards you exactly as he should, and in that sense he regrets that you didn't write him sooner, telling him all this and explaining everything . . . because even if he can't solve everything for you, at least he could have sent something your way. And above all, as a brother, he would have sent you some comfort.

Write to him, brother. He deserves it. You ought to place your confidence in my father; don't think of it as a humiliation . . . You already know, and I say this on my father's behalf, that you don't need to knock on our door, it's always open to you . . .

I knew your situation then, just as I do now, and if I didn't say anything to him before, well . . . it's also because I know his situation. But look, everything can be resolved if we have charity toward one another.

He told me that he'd absolutely send you a thousand pesetas in the next day or two . . . He wants to send you more, but he doesn't have any more than that, especially now, at year's end . . . Well, write him yourself, don't be childish.

I've been thinking of you so much during your stay in Toro. I don't know what you've learned there, but if you haven't learned to love God more . . . you haven't done anything at all.

With all my affection, and in the Most Blessed Virgin Mary, your brother,

Brother María Rafael
O.C.R.

P.S. We haven't said anything to my mother . . . My father doesn't want to . . . You know how she is . . . He said he wants to handle this mess on his own . . . and we should hide *everything* from Mamá for now . . . Her soul deserves some rest . . . don't you think? . . . Besides, if she could do anything . . . All this will do is overwhelm her, and you know how she is . . . so very like my grandmother.

83. Dedication of a Holy Card to María Osorio[7]

Oviedo, December 5, 1935

J-H-S

Onward . . .

Onward . . .

Onward . . ., without turning our gaze,
with our eyes on the cross of Christ, and our hearts aflame with Love.
Onward, without turning our gaze . . . Love won't let us stop . . .
Don't look at the flowers, or the beasts, or even the path . . . Look at nothing but God's Love awaiting us on the cross, and behind that cross, Mary.
Onward . . .

Onward . . . with no other light or guide than

Love . . .

Love . . .

Love . . .

Brother María Rafael, O.C.R.

---

7. Text of the image: "Seeking my Love / I will head for the mountains and for watersides, / I will not gather flowers, / nor fear wild beasts; / I will go beyond strong men and frontiers" (SJC 471). Image: LPM 213.

BUSCANDO MIS AMORES,
IRE POR ESOS MONTES Y RIBERAS
NI COGERE LAS FLORES,
NI TEMERE LAS FIERAS,
Y PASARE LOS FUERTES Y
FRONTERAS.

(San Juan de la Cruz)

84. To María Osorio

Oviedo, December 7, 1935

J-H-S

My dearest sister,

I thought about writing you this afternoon, but I didn't have the opportunity. Now that it's eleven o'clock at night, I'll begin.

I suppose you'll have received my last letter, which I thought would be longer, but since I wanted it to go out that same day, and besides I couldn't think of anything to say . . . I can't remember if I even said goodbye . . . If only you knew how upset I am over what is happening to you, and not being able to fix it . . . God has tied my hands . . . and evidently that's for the best, because being able to help would be too much of a consolation for me.

Today I went to go see the Lord and pray for you. When I left the church, my father very mysteriously approached me, gave me a thousand pesetas, and said . . . "Take this, don't tell anybody, and send it to your aunt and uncle. As you know, this is all I can do for now . . ." I kissed his hand, and I happily sent them your way after lunch.

I know it's not enough, but don't focus on the amount, but rather on the affection and intention behind it . . . I assure you, my father is very sorry for what you're going through. Well, *sursum corda*.[1] You'll see, everything will be resolved . . . I see the Virgin's hand in it, and surely She will not abandon you. Now you'll have your "daily bread" for a while, and nothing more. But what about God? Do you believe He will leave you? Nonsense. I am confident that He will not; be at peace.

You'll say yes, well, all that's very well and good . . . but. Well, my dear sister, there's no "but" about it. I don't say that just to comfort you . . . but because I truly feel that way, and since I can't send you any material

---

1. *Sursum corda*: "Lift up your hearts" (see #63, n. 3).

support to ease the situation, I am sending you . . . well, you already know what. If only you knew, I have so much confidence in God!

You say that your horizons are narrowing . . . What does that matter? The horizon of earthly things . . . that's a small and limited horizon . . . Don't go drowning in it . . . Look, on the holy card I sent you (if I can call it that), the Cross is not on the horizon, but rather *much higher up*. Am I making sense? . . . So look at the Cross, look at Jesus hanging on it . . . Don't let earthly things overwhelm you. Your horizons aren't important . . . Jump over the horizon . . . and if it seems that everything is narrowing, don't believe it. The good Jesus will always make an opening for you, wherever you see Him . . . You'll see His attentive care, His love. You'll see Mary, and even amid the darkest storms this world can bring, if you lift your eyes to Mary . . . you'll find something there. Isn't that so, little sister?

Don't worry; you'll see, everything will be resolved. I am sure of it.

The clock just struck midnight. It is now December 8, the Virgin's feast day. I hope you both have a very happy day. I'm sure you won't forget to pray for my poor soul at communion . . . I promise, I won't forget to pray for yours . . . I'm going to dedicate the whole day to the Virgin Mary as best as I can. I don't know how I'll manage, because I'm totally inept, but anyway . . . the Lord sees me. I won't worry about anything else.

I'm glad that you understood my letter. I'm telling you, after I read it, I thought about starting it over . . . But then I thought about it some more, and I just sent it. As I've told you before, I write down everything that comes to mind, and I don't censor myself . . . I do so in the name of the Virgin; may She be the one who guides me.

I'm so pleased that Uncle Polín is with you in Ávila again. I can assure you, I didn't want him to stay in Toro much longer . . . No longer than necessary . . . That wasn't good for anyone . . . For that, you need to be holy . . . Anyway, such trials are sent by the Lord . . . So then, may they come.

He promised to write me; I hope he will. I have so little time left in the world . . . and when I go back to La Trapa, I'll just have one little thorn left piercing me, and that's you two . . . Of course, I am not leaving you in a good financial situation, but I carry with me the consolation of having done what I could . . . above all, of your having a greater devotion to

the Virgin . . . That almost worries me even more . . . Blessed be God,
I'm growing so tiresome.

I'm laughing right now . . . I figure you'll laugh too, in a few years'
time, thinking about your poor little brother and how he couldn't talk
about anything else . . . I must have uttered so much nonsense in these
letters these past few months, talking to you about God and Mary . . .
but I can't help it. I don't know if this will just be a passing phase . . . I
don't think so. But these letters have been helping me so much, especially
during this time, when I desperately need it.

Did you like what I wrote on the back, from Saint John of the Cross?[2]
. . . You already knew that passage, didn't you?

I want to make another one for Uncle Polín one of these days, but I
don't know if I'll manage . . . He's very . . . very difficult to please.

Listen, what I want to send you in this letter is a great deal of joy . . .
So much joy, in order to love God amid everything that is happening to
you . . . Besides, no one can be sad today . . . Of course, there must be
great joy in heaven today . . . Who must be there? . . . All the genera-
tions of angels singing to Mary . . . Mary looking at the Son . . . The
Father looking at Mary, being glorified in Her, loving Himself in loving
the Virgin . . . The Holy Spirit . . .

Well, I've gotten myself into a bit of a mess. But anyway, all of heaven
is celebrating, and in the middle is Our Lady, who doesn't forget about us
little maggots who are still stuck on earth just because She is in heavenly
glory . . . . Everything is to be joyous in heaven today; Mary will very
lovingly hear everything we ask of Her.

Oh, little sister! How is it possible that, knowing this is not our homeland, we still remain worried that our horizons are shrinking? . . . How
is it possible that, looking up at heaven just a little bit, we remember only
that we are still here on earth? . . .

Blessed be God, who has not yet called us to participate in heaven's
festival of love for the Virgin . . . But Lord, tarry not . . . even if you
find us selfish, even if you know that it would be more perfect for us not
to desire anything at all . . . But Lord, how is it possible not to want to
be in heaven already, with body and soul and everything else, at once . . .

2. See #83.

to be where we will see You . . . where we won't sin . . . where we will praise the Father, Son, and Holy Spirit, and adore the Most Blessed Virgin Mary . . . where we won't be separated from Her ever again? . . . And you still keep us down here, *where everything is an obstacle to enjoying You.*

But anyway, it doesn't matter . . . we'll just act as if we were already there, and God had sent us back down here for just a little longer. We'll make heaven here on earth . . . glory within our own hearts . . . Make room for the Virgin and Jesus and the saints there . . . We'll unite ourselves to the angels . . . We'll sing just like them . . . We'll celebrate too . . . We'll jump for joy at the mere thought of the glory given to God by the Immaculate Virgin.

How could we keep from rejoicing? . . . We're just here for a short time, I'm sure of it . . . Let's make use of every moment. Let's love God dearly . . . love Mary dearly . . . look to heaven . . . sing . . . go crazy . . .

Forgive me . . . I always do this, I always end up talking nonsense . . . And this topic, it's no wonder.

Tell me what you did for the Virgin today, on this feast of the Immaculate Conception.

Today we'll have Uncle Alfonso and Aunt Regina over for dinner . . . Of course I won't have any time to write, except for a little bit in the morning. It's one o'clock now, so I'm going to leave it here . . . My brothers will be up in less than an hour,[3] and I want to help them a bit, and I want them to help me . . . am I making sense?

Today is no ordinary day. Since, in my Trapa, feasts are celebrated differently than they are in the world . . . and I am a Trappist who is in the world, what I'll do is unite myself to the Trappists during the night . . . and spend the day in the world . . . Although I think I'll be united to them during the day too . . . in choir, at the Hours . . . and even though I'll be talking and laughing . . . I'll be united to their silence, too . . .

Don't you go thinking that it's somewhat difficult for me to pay attention to everything while my spirit is so far away . . . It doesn't matter, She is helping me . . . What do I care? I won't be able to sing her solemn

---

3. My brothers: That is, the Trappists at San Isidro de Dueñas, who would rise at 1:00 a.m. on feast days (OC 498).

Vespers, but I'll listen to Uncle Alfonso's jokes, and in return . . . I'll make some of my own.

Oh, dear little sister! How pleasant it is to love Mary, nothing is difficult with Her . . . Everything turns out well, everything is easy, even being holy. I believe that if we decide on something, and we tell Her about it, She will do it for us.

When I go to communion in the morning, I'm going to tell Jesus that we want to be very good, and that we're counting on the Immaculate Virgin to make it happen.

Anyway, I'll leave it there for tonight . . . Now I'm going to tell the Lord to help us all tomorrow morning, so that we can do something for Mary's glory.

It's now eleven o'clock in the morning. I went to the eight o'clock Mass with my father to take communion. Afterwards, my father and I went to the cathedral for the Papal Blessing.[4]

Shortly, I'll go mail this letter, and then I'll make my Visit[5] . . . And then, I don't know what will become of me. As I mentioned, we have a family gathering.

I'm expecting a letter from Ávila today. Will I get one?

My mother is leaving messages over the telephone . . . My cousins are arriving now.[6] I'll have to leave you for today . . . I'm surrounded by noise. *Sursum corda.* All for Mary.

Give Uncle Polín a big hug for me. All my affection, your brother, who also longs to send you all the affection he has for the Virgin.

Brother María Rafael, O.C.R.

4. Papal Blessing: Bishops may impart a blessing on behalf of the pope three times a year on important feast days, such as, in this case, the Solemnity of the Immaculate Conception.

5. Visit: i.e., to the Blessed Sacrament.

6. My cousins: The five children of Alfonso Barón Torres and Regina González-Tablas: Álvaro, Fernando, José María, Teresa, and Amelia (OC 499).

85. To María Osorio

Oviedo, December 10, 1935

J-H-S

My dearest sister,

With the help of Jesus and Mary, I will begin this letter.

I'll start by saying that I go through the same thing you do . . . I never know where to begin when telling you everything within me . . . We'll go point by point . . . I have your letter in front of me, fully marked up in red pencil.[1]

Right now it's midnight . . . I can't find another time to write . . . I'm telling you, I spend all day busy with a thousand different things . . . Today, for example, in the morning I have to accompany my mother to the prison in order to visit a prisoner who wrote her, asking for her help . . . I'm sure something can be done for him . . . Then I have to go to the Carmelite monastery[2] . . . I might have to go to Infiesto with my father, then later I have my Visit with the Lord . . . Anyway, you can see that I don't have any time. That's why I'm more able to collect myself at these late hours.

Look, sister, when you said in your letter that you'd simply follow whatever I told you to do . . . Honestly, I don't know what to do . . . You've put me in a tight spot. It's one thing for me to share with you all the reflections that come to mind . . . but please don't take them literally . . . even though you say that you think I am very much walking in the truth . . . keep in mind who I am . . . And now I am not looking at myself, but rather you are the one who should look at me . . . I am telling you this

---

1. "After reading your letters a few times, I use a red pencil to mark out the parts I think I can reply to" (#73).

2. The Monastery of Our Lady of Carmel (Monasterio de Nuestra Santísima Madre del Carmen), a community of Carmelite nuns, was then located at the intersection of Calle Muñoz Degraín and Calle Sacramento, Oviedo. The community relocated to Barrio Toleo, Oviedo, in 1980 (Carolina G. Menéndez, "Sabores monacales" [*La Nueva España* Aug. 26, 2012]).

as I see it . . . Pay me the *appropriate amount* of attention. Remember, I have no experience; don't go thinking otherwise.

I'm a little afraid of what you said about simply following my advice . . . Nothing like this has ever happened to me before. I only ever wanted to influence you in one matter: loving God and Mary more . . . When it comes to that, absolutely . . . But when it comes to telling you what is most perfect! . . . Maybe I could tell you, but you shouldn't heed my answer without first consulting someone else about it . . . Remember, little sister, who is telling you all this! No, this is not false modesty . . . All I'm doing is telling you everything that comes to mind . . . but always from my limited perspective . . . I am sharing my reflections and meditations with you, that's all, and since I love God very much, I want you to love Him . . . perhaps the ways we love Him will be different . . . but I believe that when it comes to love for God, we should all be equal, for its expressions are the same, and so too the feelings it inspires. Don't you think so? Well, I don't want to go on too long about this.

Now what I'm going to do is *forgive you*. Listen, I'm laughing about this . . . you poor thing. Let's see if you pay me any mind now . . . don't you ever put the phrase "forgive me" in one of your letters ever again . . . I've been a bad example for you in this regard, saying it to you too . . . but I think there's no need. Don't you agree? What do I have to forgive you for? Because you're suffering and you tell me about it? . . . Why should you feel bad for sharing your hardships with me? On the contrary, you should greatly rejoice, if indeed you find consolation in me . . . You poor little thing, what do I have to forgive you for? On the contrary, you give me so much consolation.

Those who are *truly* brothers and sisters, listen carefully, those who *truly* are . . . don't notice such things. We ought to place our confidence in God, but we are still on this earth, and the desire to leave creatures behind isn't meant to be . . . Don't go thinking that you're mixing in anything human here, because *everything* can be *divinized* . . . suffering and joy alike. Everything, absolutely everything, can point us to God . . . and for the one who lives according to His holy law, everything he does, thinks, says, and experiences—he does, thinks, says, and experiences for God and in God.

Look, I'm going to be direct: if I didn't love God, I wouldn't care very much about whether or not you loved Him, or whether you were suffering on this or that account . . . *I'd just be yet another relative.* I don't know if I'm talking nonsense, but since I love you with God's love and for His sake . . . unselfishly, in the love of Christ . . . everything you tell me, all your human and material affairs, point me to God and are placed in Him. I want nothing more than to help you, *with whatever you might need.* If I had economic resources, and could tell you in a worldly way, "Take it, Aunt María, don't worry . . ." To the world, that would be the human thing to do . . . but for us, it would be different . . . It would go like this: "Take it, sister, in the name of Jesus through Mary." See how everything can be transformed in the name of Jesus and through His love?

Besides, it would be another thing if you were to deceive me . . . and why would you? Besides, you aren't deceiving me, because as long as we are on this earth, everything will be a struggle . . . A struggle between matter and spirit . . . Right now, that struggle is coming to a head in both of us, each in our own way . . . You said to me, "Everything is closing in on me, I have to suffer humiliations and I resist them . . . I am suffering in the dark, and earthly things are tormenting me . . ." And in my own way, I say just the same thing to you. But both of us help each other to raise our eyes to Mary, we encourage each other to be holy, to struggle faithfully and confidently, to place ourselves at the Virgin's feet . . . to cease thinking of ourselves.

Listen, let's do this: everything you see in my letters that you think is "human," you can make it holy . . . Or rather, "de-humanize" it . . . I'll do the same thing.

It's all the same to me. Tell me everything, and unburden yourself . . . It's as if you had a bundle of heavy, useless things that are weighing you down, and you give them to your brother so you can rest . . . I'm sure you'll be more calm once you've written me . . . you'll love the Lord more . . .

I don't know how to express everything that I'm feeling. Maybe that's very "human" of me, but God loves me just like this . . . In one of your letters, you told me that you wanted to be a saint, but a human saint; I understood. So understand what I'm saying now.

So everything I send you that is "creaturely," return it to me in God and in love of God. I'll do the same . . . Do you remember the reading at Sext?[3] Little sister, don't be silly. If we were already saints, our correspondence

---

3. *Bear one another's burdens, and in this way you will fulfill the law of Christ* (Gal 6:2). For Sext, see #76, n. 1.

wouldn't be necessary. It's very beautiful to want to leave creatures behind and be left with God alone, but it's also beautiful to bring creatures with us, whether to help them or to help ourselves.

Look, in La Trapa, we love another in this way . . . We love one another in Christ, and with the charity of Christ . . . I'm going to give you an example. If one brother sees that another brother is struggling *materially* with work, and helps him, he has performed an act that is *material* in the eyes of men, but divine in the eyes of God.

I remember this one little old man there, almost incapacitated by age, who was in charge of the produce[4] . . . One afternoon he was assigned the task of bringing some baskets of potatoes up from the ground floor, where the kitchen is, to the pantry on the second floor . . .

He took a very long time with each basket . . . He was sweating and panting, he couldn't do it . . . An oblate happened to pass by, he must have been about twelve years old . . . and without saying anything, he took the old man's basket and started running up the stairs, after having had to fight the brother for it a bit, because he didn't want to let go . . . The brother went back to try to carry up another basket, and the little oblate came back to try to get the old brother to rest and take it up himself . . .

Then the novices arrived, and we realized what was going on. Between the four of us and the oblates who accompanied us, even though it wasn't time for work, we took all the potatoes up to the pantry for the brother . . . The old brother rejoiced at the novices' charity, and we finished in five minutes what it would have taken him an hour and a half of exhausting effort to do . . . He laughed at the racket we made going up and down the stairs, until he nearly cried . . . That's La Trapa for you.

Every bit of that is human, even the old man's laughter and tears . . . Yes, it's all human, for we do have hearts . . . but God sees charity, He sees His love, for everything is done for Him in La Trapa . . . No one expects a reward, because even though the joy of the poor old man was

4. Brother Pacomio Hernández Sevillano (1859–1936) was in charge of the pantry at San Isidro de Dueñas (OC 503).

reward enough . . . even if it weren't, we'd still do the same thing . . . To do otherwise would be selfish. We would be like *whitewashed tombs.*[5]

I don't know if I'm making sense, I think I am . . . And so, I'll say that if I could help you carry your "baskets of potatoes" . . . I absolutely would . . . Tell me how many there are, and how heavy. Tell me if you're getting tired, and I'll lend you a hand from here . . . It's only natural, don't you think?

No, don't you go thinking that selfishness . . . is just honesty . . . Just as the old brother neither hid his exhaustion nor possessed self-love (and I am not implying that you do), so too you should not be ashamed or afraid to tell me everything you are going through, everything that comes to mind . . . your sorrows, your difficulties . . . Everything that you think is "human," but that you can't leave behind—because for one thing, you're not yet holy enough for that, and besides, you're still here on earth, where God has us surrounded with misery and weakness . . . but that's for the best . . .

There's no need to be afraid. Love for Jesus of Nazareth does all things, and bears all things . . . Rest, as you said, and tell me everything. If in doing so you receive some human consolation . . . *it's not.* When a consolation is received *in the name of God and Mary*, even if it comes through the most vile of all earthly creatures, that consolation comes from God. Don't reject it, accept it, and please, dear sister, don't you ever ask for my forgiveness again . . . I won't ask for yours either. I also rest when I take up my pen and, in one way or another, tell you all my business, my miseries, my love for God.

I don't know if I'm doing a good or a bad thing by making you a participant in the insights that the Lord gives me . . . Of course, there are many of them, and if I could make you holy, even if I were to stay down here below . . .

How great God is, sister! I've said it so many times, and I'll never get tired of repeating it . . . I'm so pleased that your suffering and your "little agonies" make you cry out to Him, cry out to Him with "loving cries"

---

5. *Woe to you, scribes and Pharisees, hypocrites! For you are like whitewashed tombs, which on the outside look beautiful, but inside they are full of the bones of the dead and of all kinds of filth* (Matt 23:27).

. . . Suffering brings so much delight when one suffers for Christ . . .
The Blessed Cross is our only treasure. I don't want to take it away from
you. If I did, I wouldn't love you very well.

You asked what happened to me in my last letter . . . I don't know. I
barely remember what I said in it. To be honest, I don't remember *at all.*

Don't go looking for what isn't there. It's true that sometimes I lose my
train of thought and I don't know what I'm saying, but when I sit down
to write you, I collect myself, I think a lot about Jesus, and I want to tell
you so many things, but I can't.

He absorbs me. I start out talking about Him, and I end up talking to
Him . . . I start wanting to send you *everything*, and since *everything* is quite
a lot, I don't know what happens to me, and so sometimes, I write things I
didn't plan to . . . and what I did plan to write, I *cannot.* I don't know if I'm
making sense. It's so difficult to put it into words . . . I have to be careful,
and if I start talking about the love of God, the love He has for me, the love I
have for Him, I get the urge to say . . . God, love, God . . . etc . . . and fill
my letter with these words: "Love for God." . . . Do you know what that is?

Yes, little sister, yes, I've gone mad . . . Don't pay me any mind, but if
I let myself get carried away, I'd start a letter . . . and when it occurred to
me to talk about God . . . then I'd finish it. Am I making sense? But then
I wouldn't be writing you, I'd just be sending you a couple of pages full of
the word "love," scribbled loudly, and I wouldn't even be able to sign it. Can
you see how much I need to go back to La Trapa? . . . The only thing that's
keeping me calm is knowing that I'll be there soon, and when I am, then I'll
be able to shout . . . Nobody knows what a Trappist's silence really is . . .
especially that of a Trappist who's madly in love with God and the Virgin.

There are so many things I could say . . . so many, but when I come to
one of these moments in my letters, I can't say anything at all . . . believe me,
it's not that I'm very godly or anything . . . don't you go thinking something
that isn't true . . . It's just that I want to send you everything within me,
and I'm powerless to do so . . . I can't write, I don't know how . . . I get
worked up, and then I fall silent . . . How great God is, sister. I don't know
how we can live like this . . . So many impediments, Lord, so many obstacles
between us and enjoyment of You . . . The Bridegroom is long delayed.[6]

6. Matt 25:5.

While the soul remains imprisoned in the body, everything is a struggle, and we are so weak, so feeble. Blessed be the Lord . . . how great the Lord is. My life has not yet begun . . . I have an idea about what love for God should be . . . and I don't understand how anyone who has loved the Lord has been able to survive . . . Either the Lord sustained the saints, or they never loved God. Don't you think?

Anyway, sister, don't pay me any mind. Just love God as best you know how and as best you can . . . If only you knew . . . yes, you do know what love for God is. You'll see, then nothing in the world will matter at all to you, not even suffering . . . Love God and *nothing* else . . . That's what I'm saying in my letters, in all of them . . . Don't read anything else into them . . . Look, it's just as I said, I start out writing you, and I always end up at Jesus' feet.

Oh, dear sister, how great is that Jesus of Nazareth . . . May He forgive me, not you.

Do you know what time it is? It's three o'clock in the morning! . . . Now I do have to leave you for now . . . I'll continue in the morning. Blessed be God, how mad I am!

Today, December 11, I am continuing. I want to finish today, so that you receive this tomorrow. Today I received your letter . . . and . . . well, nothing. God alone, as you said.

Don't you go thinking that I'm going to stop writing you . . . Sometimes I'll go on longer, and other times I'll be shorter . . . what does that matter? And don't think that I have to force myself to write you, not at all. I'm not losing sleep over it either, because I always take a *siesta* . . . So don't you worry about that.

What I want is for *you* not to force yourself to write, which you ought not to do, especially when my grandmother and Aunt María are there . . . I'll keep writing you, but even though you are the last consolation that the Lord is offering me in the world before I go back to La Trapa . . . I want to be generous . . . That is, even if you don't write me . . . and even if I never hear from you again this side of heaven, I need not cease to offer what little I can for my part.

Don't wish to clear thorns from my path, as you said you do . . . Then what would I have left to offer the Lord?

Since you asked after my health, I'll just say that I'm in the doctor's hands for now. I told him about my situation and what I'm planning to do . . . He thought it was fine . . . He put me on a very strict diet and told me that for now I need to have a blood sugar level of zero, and then later, in the monastery, my nutrition plan there will probably be enough . . . I'm not worried about my health at all, praise God. My mother says I've gained weight since I started my diet . . . and it's possible.

I'm so grateful to you for everything, sister. You're so good to me, and if it didn't bother you, I'd say that over and over again . . . May the Lord and Mary reward you for it.

In your letter, you mentioned a silly thought of yours in regard to what my parents might think . . . Well, what my father might think, since my mother doesn't know anything . . . Well, sister, may God forgive you for being silly . . . since I don't need to forgive you for anything you say to me.

Do you know what I saw in your letter today? I saw that your soul loves God very much. If only you knew how much that consoles me. He is doing this. May He be blessed . . . Someday you'll come to *love Him as you desire to* . . . and then . . . that's when you'll need to remember me . . . I, poor soul, am no longer the one who is helping you . . . He is, He who makes use of anything and everything to accomplish His works . . . What are we? . . .

In your letter, I see a desire to fly to God . . . Waiting to embrace the Bridegroom is taking too long . . . Fly, sister, fly. Look not to us creatures who, as you said, *pass away* while only He remains . . . Run, hurry, don't worry about whether your heart is suffering as you leave bits and pieces of it scattered in the world . . . The world, and creatures, have nothing to give you . . . God alone.

Rise up, rise up, dear little sister. Don't worry about your brother who helped you that one time, in his own way, as the Lord instructed him to do . . . Very soon I won't be able to do anything for you at all, *materially* speaking.

In my corner of La Trapa, I'll pray to the Lord, I'll pray to the Virgin in silence . . . Pray for me too, that the Lord might accept my offering . . . That's what "oblate" means . . . "offering" . . . I offer myself to Him as I am, whether good or bad, in good health or out of it; I offer Him my life, my body, my soul, my heart, everything . . . absolutely everything.

I have offered myself for everyone: for my parents, my brothers and sisters, missionaries, priests . . . those who are suffering, and those who offend Him . . .

May He make of me what He wills. Pray that the Lord accepts me . . . That is the only way I'll be able to help you when I am in my monastery . . .

Don't worry about me . . . Fly to the Lord . . . Rise up into the embrace of that Love for whom you suffer and struggle . . . Think of nothing but Him . . . and you'll see, the wait won't seem long at all.

I don't want your gratitude . . . it ought *not* be directed at me, understand? . . . He's the one who does it all.

May the Lord be your only light . . . and may that light never be darkened by any shadow . . . or any other soul, no matter how good it may be . . . When you look to heaven, may you see that God who loves you so much, who never needs an excuse or misses an occasion to show Himself to you, even amid the dark night of the soul . . . What does it matter how?

When you look to heaven, may you see God and only God . . . His love . . . There are so many things I want to tell you! I don't know how, I'm not expressing myself well . . . But as for that nephew of yours, that brother . . . who passed through like a faint shadow and helped you grow closer to God . . . leave him behind, don't suffer on his account. That is his vocation . . . to desire to be forgotten by the world and by creatures . . . in order to offer himself to God in the silence and humility of an oblate's habit . . .

He wants to be an offering to God, but without the world taking any notice of him . . . To be a faint shadow who passed through life loving God dearly and quietly . . . To help every soul in the world love God, without their even realizing it . . . Am I making sense? I don't want anything for myself, I desire nothing . . . May the Lord accept me, my renunciation, my sacrifices . . . Pray to Him for this, my dear sister. Perhaps my intentions are not as pure as they ought to be . . . may Mary sanctify them. And if you ever think of me, may it be in order to keep offering me to the Lord . . . and to tell Him, "Look, Jesus, I have a brother over there in La Trapa . . . He's worthless and very little, but despite how little his heart is, he lives for You alone, and he has no other mission than to love You as much as he can, and to *offer*[7] even his own blood, so that everyone else might love You too . . . Accept him, Lord. He offers himself through the Most Blessed Virgin Mary . . ."

---

7. Rafael's emphasis; note his observation above that oblate means offering.

Will you do this, sister? In doing so, you'd accomplish two things: offering a soul to God, and helping me. That's no small feat.

Anyway, I don't want to go on . . . I'll just say that: fly, and if you fall, it doesn't matter. Mary is at your side; with Her, you have nothing to fear. Fly to that God whom you *ought* to love madly, without thinking of yourself or anyone else . . . helpless to do anything but love.

Anyway, dear sister, I don't want this letter to go on any longer. Tell Uncle Polín that I'm waiting on his letter; keep me updated about your affairs. How are the children at the orphanage doing?[8] When is my grandmother coming to Ávila?

Fernando is leaving Belgium on the 20th to spend Christmas at home.

Anyway, don't you worry about a thing! . . . Make room for heaven within your soul, and during this season, place the Child Jesus in Mary's arms there . . . and quietly sing Him carols . . . Don't worry about anything external . . . Do you not have Jesus in your heart? Then so what? . . . But take note: don't *drop hints* about your interior life, or allow your *detachment* from everything to *show through* . . . It's quite easy to lack charity this way . . . I don't know if I'm making sense . . . Be a saint, but a saint who is present in everything: one who talks, laughs, consoles others . . . Shut yourself away inside with that Jesus you love so much. But . . . I think you understand what I'm saying: invite others to participate in what you have . . . Embark upon everything with charity toward all, even if sometimes you have to strain yourself.

I think I know you in this regard, don't I? . . . Look, this is very important for you; you're a mother . . . am I making sense?

If only you knew how pleasing this is to Jesus . . . To dwell in Him deeply, so deeply within yourself, but at the same time, to externally display . . . humility, charity, tender care for one's neighbor, for all . . . To know how to console, to know how to take care of things, to act in a way that brings creatures to God, not to hide your lamp under a bushel basket[9] . . . To maintain holy joy at all times. To be with God in your heart, praying Hail Marys to the Virgin, but at the same time, not to shut yourself

---

8. María was a benefactor of an orphanage called Nazareth House (OC 456; see also #75, n. 14, and #87, n. 6).

9. Matt 5:15; Mark 4:21; Luke 8:16; 11:33.

away so much that the world *notices* . . . Am I making sense? . . . I'll say it again . . . *given your character*, you could easily lack charity this way . . .

Do you mind that I'm saying this to you? . . . Look, all I want is your good and your perfection . . . and this Christmas, you could do great things . . .

How good God is, to provide the circumstances that allow you to carry out what I'm saying . . . Do you think I'm wrong? Respond to this and tell me if you've understood it.

Sometimes this has happened to me, where when the internal clashes with the external . . . I fail. Sometimes it's a gesture . . . a word . . . a *silence* . . . I've fallen into this many times, and I repent of it . . . We mustn't be this way. We must be saints . . . but human ones, as you said, and in your case, a holy wife, mother, and daughter . . . Am I making sense? . . . I am saying all this because I know you.

Focus on God, and engage with him . . . but focus on God's creatures, and engage with them too . . . If you have to strain yourself at first, don't worry . . . Eventually, it will all come easily to you, because you'll do it in the name of Jesus . . . You'll see, you'll see, this Christmas is going to be great for you. I'll help you as much as I can . . . Don't worry, everything will turn out fine.

Anyway, I won't say anything more . . . "forgive me," that's the last time I'll say that to you . . . But I might actually need your forgiveness for this letter. Read it charitably, because I don't know what's in it . . . I repeated so many things, then I contradicted myself . . . Anyway, sometimes I don't know what I'm talking about, but you understand me, and that's enough for me.

I have lots of other things to tell you, and to respond to, but I'll do that another day.

Give Uncle Polín a great big hug for me, and another one for you, as "human" as you'd like, but a very big one regardless. Your brother, who loves you dearly,

Brother María Rafael
O.C.R.

86. *To María Osorio*

Oviedo, December 15, 1935

J-H-S

My dearest sister,

It's very late at night, but I don't want to put off starting this letter, even though it's going to be short, because I want to make sure it goes out tomorrow. I haven't answered Uncle Polín's letter . . . but I haven't painted the holy card for him yet, and it takes time.

Listen, I read your letter with simplicity, as you asked. Even though I wanted to laugh at some things . . . I don't know what to tell you. You might think that you are nobody, and you don't deserve my attention, and I shouldn't worry . . . but it's not so . . . You are a soul belonging to God. However good and holy you may or may not be . . . you belong to God. Isn't that so? . . .

When you ask me (blessed be God) . . . when you ask me for advice or help . . . when you tell me about your setbacks, your love, your longings, and your misery, it's not you I see . . . I see neither you, María . . . nor my beloved little sister. I don't see a creature, believe me . . . Now, I see only *a soul that belongs to God*, and that's how I want to treat you: as one *belonging to God*. That's how I want to help you: as one belonging to God . . . But at the same time, if only you knew what a spot you've put me in! . . . Or rather, God has . . . I've offered myself to Him so that I might help souls to get to heaven, *as best I can* . . . I believe that the best way I can do that is by offering . . . a bit of silence. Nevertheless, the Lord has placed in my path a soul, your soul, whom I look at, and He asks me to give her help and advice. He asks *me* . . . Blessed be God, I am nothing, I am nobody, I have no experience, I am without learning, as Saint Teresa said.[1] I say this without false modesty. The Virgin knows it . . .

---

1. "For I am without learning . . . without instruction from a learned man or from any other person . . ." (Saint Teresa of Ávila, *The Book of Her Life* 10.7, in STA 1:77).

I see my path as such a simple one . . . absolute love for God, and silence among men.

In your letter, I saw nothing but that one doubt you pointed out. I read between the lines and understand everything that's going on with you . . . You told me to place you under the Virgin's mantle . . . and trust me, that's exactly what I did at the Carmelite chapel this morning.

Could I possibly give you an explanation? I don't know. If Fr. Torres[2] couldn't answer you . . . I'm sure to do a poor job of it. I ask Our Lady for Her help, that you might understand me.

Listen, my dear little sister. When I left La Trapa, the same thing happened to me that's happening to you . . . I was leaving a supernatural world in order to enter into a material world . . . and when I say a material world, I include even my parents' and my family's affection in that. I don't know if I'm making sense . . . *Everything* would startle me. God was my interior life, and people were my exterior life.

I was leaving my Trapa where, I don't need to tell you, God was both inside and out. And when I had to leave, I flailed about like a fish out of water . . . I <u>know what you are suffering</u>, but listen, in the love for God and the interior life I had before . . . there was so much imperfection, and the Lord wanted to perfect me in that regard . . . I know what you are going through. You think that in order to *immerse yourself in God*, you have to *forget* that you are among creatures . . . and that's not so.

You think that your interior life is in *conflict* with your exterior life . . . and believe me, that conflict exists *now*, but have no doubt that the Virgin will put it right. These are simply trials sent by the Lord, and they're difficult, but they pass.

What would have become of me, if that had not happened? Since my only source of experience with this is my own soul, that's what I'm writing you about . . . You can see if my own case is useful to you in some way with your own situation . . . I can do nothing more.

So anyway, I struggled with that for a long time. If I gave myself fully to my life with God, in God . . . when I came home . . . I would even be in a bad mood after taking communion, because I'd have to have breakfast

---

2. Father Alfonso Torres Fernández, S.J. (1879–1943), María's confessor at the time (OC 514).

and then talk about this or that, I even lacked charity . . . I wanted recollection, and I wanted *others* to collect themselves, so that they could *help me* . . .

Perhaps I'd be coming back from church, thinking about God, longing for my Trapa, and one of my brothers would pester me with something or other . . . I'd want to give him a rude answer . . . and sometimes I actually would . . . On the inside, everything annoyed me . . .

Other times, I'd find myself all alone, isolated, helpless . . . The world was going its own way, and I was disoriented. I wanted to place my life <u>entirely</u> in God, and I couldn't . . . I thought I had to make a Trapa within my own home . . . and as in the monastery, after receiving the Lord, nobody should talk and everything should help me remain in prayer . . . Such suffering that causes! And sometimes even tears . . . How wrong I was . . . and how wrong I think you are, my dear little sister . . . what doubt can remain that you can give yourself *entirely* to God, and also remain in the world, without letting the world notice *at all*?

I know well the sins you are falling into. God permits them, but you'll see, you'll change.

The Lord made me see, though it took some tears . . . He made me see that I was wrong . . . That I could love Him very much and maintain an intense life in God, but at the same time, I could dwell among creatures with true joy . . . I could invite others to participate in what I carried inside me . . . I could hide God away inside me first . . . but then not hide myself away. Am I making sense? Sometimes it requires effort . . . but then, the Virgin makes everything possible.

Now I'm more loving toward my parents, and I'm more charitable toward my brothers and sister . . . There's no other way about it. This is what God wants, and if He wanted me to continue like this forever, without going back to La Trapa . . . what do I care, so long as I have His love? Don't you agree?

If only you could see how much joy that thought gives me. Nothing matters to me . . . Wherever I go, there He is . . .

I'd like to spend every hour talking of Him, or not talking at all. But that's not possible . . . it is His will that it not be . . . I'm satisfied with just talking to Him alone, and treating the world as something secondary—but when done for the sake of His love, all is well, little sister. If only you could see.

Tomorrow, after Holy Mass, I have to go to the mechanic, to get something or other fixed in the car . . . but I'll do it with true joy. I'll see God among the screws and oil . . . I'll think about the mechanics around me, who may not know God, so I'll pray for them . . . I do know Him, and I'll have Him there at my side, talking about everything with everybody with great cheer, because that's what the Lord wants . . . I'll practice patience, charity, love of neighbor . . . But don't you get the idea that all this will be work. As I said, I do everything with joy . . . how could I not? I have God within me, I receive Him in the morning, He accompanies me all day . . . The struggle has disappeared, nothing annoys me anymore . . . Why?

Before, I wanted everybody to observe silence. I wanted everybody to see God. When the Lord's name was mentioned, I wanted even the trams to stop. It was a very special way of loving God, but it was also a very special way of loving myself (I don't know if I'm making sense!), for in my external recollection, I was seeking only myself.

This is no longer the case, thanks be to God and the Virgin. If one of my brothers needs me for something other than God, I do it in God's name . . . and so I do two things at once . . . but one thing above all: fulfill His holy will.

Take heart, little sister. You can fly, I'm sure of it. Pay the world no mind. Make a tabernacle within your own heart, place the Lord there . . . and what more do you want? You are the temple for that tabernacle . . . You are the temple where God is hidden. Open your doors, don't hide Him away . . . I know how sometimes those humble little chapels look like they're going to collapse from all the bad weather . . . so don't worry if from time to time you have to repair the roof or the bell tower . . . Everything made of clay and matter will wear and tear, and sometimes it'll fall, but it doesn't matter. Everything can be fixed.

Your path is that "little footpath," and you don't need to do great things . . . But who's to say that the lay brother wasn't flying high? Who's to say that while he carried his jug in one hand, his other hand wasn't holding God's?[3]

---

3. "It was afternoon already, and the clouds / were illumined with the sun's rays / when the good lay brother, carrying his jug, / went walking along the little footpath, blessing God" (José María Pemán, "Ballad of the Lay Brother's Doubts" ("Balada de las dudas del lego"), in *Poesía: nueva antología, 1917–1959* [Madrid: Escelicer, 1959], 67; trans. CA).

I no longer see your doubt anywhere. Perfect your interior life, and you'll see, your exterior life won't disturb your peace, but quite the contrary . . .

You'll see, then your temper will go away. And you'll see, when you come back from communion all recollected, only to go back to your house chores, after having been in contemplation and having spoken with Our Lady, you'll be filled with joy (and even *joie de vivre*) from every direction . . . You'll see, you'll come to love everyone more and better.

The thought that God loves you will give you wings . . . That thought alone must be enough for you . . . You'll move through the world, and the world won't take notice . . . And if *now* you allow creatures to see rudeness in you, rather than patience; impatience, rather than charity; and agitation where there should be serenity and sweetness . . . then go ahead and doubt, little sister, doubt away. (Maybe I'm being too hard on you . . .) But either you lack humility, or the devil is in your way.

Don't worry, it will all pass. You'll see, the evil spirit will shrink away when the Virgin comes to your aid . . . Don't doubt as you give yourself fully to God . . . If only you knew how much He loves you!

What *you'd prefer* is to fly, not to come down to earth . . . but you can do so much good right where you are.

You spoke of your character . . . Well that's easy enough. Ask Mary to reform you, and there you go. If you fall from time to time? . . . Well all right, who doesn't fall? Get up and carry on . . . Anything but getting discouraged . . . God loves you the way you are, despite everything.

It seems impossible that you should think such things. I can almost guess your thoughts. I know what you'll think when you get this letter. But look, Saint Teresa would go into ecstasy in the morning, and then go deal with people in the afternoon, handling all the material things that would come up. Isn't that so?

In short, my dear little sister, there are so many things I'd tell you if only I knew how . . . but I can't. I just want to send you the very great peace that belongs to those who know we are beloved by God, despite knowing just how miserable and ungenerous we are.

I want to send you the sweetness of character and heart that belongs to the one who truly loves God. Follow your path, but with the peace of Christ. That's all I can say for today . . . It's getting very late.

I was so grateful for the gift of the holy card. Tell Dolores it's very well written[4] . . . If only you could see what delight such little things bring to my soul. Sometimes I think this sensitivity of mine doesn't serve me well . . . But anyway, as always . . . God wants it that way. May He repay your kindness.

Well, little sister, I'll leave it there for today. It's already the 16th now that it's one in the morning. I've just come back from the doctor's house, and he thought I was doing much better. He reduced my dose of insulin, and he told me he'd get me down to zero very soon . . .

I'm very pleased. But something's missing today . . . I couldn't go to communion. My father didn't wake me up, and I had a pretty bad night . . . I don't know why . . . but on the days I don't receive the Lord, I'm all disoriented, as though I'm missing something, something that's everything to me. Anyway, blessed be the Lord.

I don't know if I've quite gotten it all right in this letter, but listen, I'll say it again: take from it what suits you, and leave the rest. I never want to be the reason that you get all mixed up, despite my best intentions. Do you understand? I'll write you a longer letter another day.

Uncle Polín told me he'd seen you crying over one of my letters . . . *don't be silly.*

With all my great affection, your brother,

Brother María Rafael, O.C.R.

Meanwhile, let's get the stable ready for the Child Jesus.

4. Dolores: Dolores Barón Osorio, Rafael's cousin and María's daughter.

87. To Leopoldo Barón[1]

Oviedo, December 16, 1935

J-H-S

So as not to be outdone by you, I'll say: "Brother Rafael begs Brother Bernardo to have charity, that he might hear him."[2]

My dearest brother in the Lord,

I received your letter, and now I'm sitting down to write you . . . and I have nothing to say. If I were to talk about myself, what for? . . . And if

1. According to OC 523, Rafael began this letter with a Christmas-themed sketch. These two sketches can be found in LPM 183.

2. "Brother Bernardo" was one of Rafael's nicknames for his uncle Leopoldo; clearly it was an inside joke between them.

I were to talk about God and the Virgin, I don't know. It's almost better to remain silent; but since I don't want to do that, I'm sending you this note, though it be poorly written, so that with it you might receive the *Te Deum* (on my holy card).[3] The *Te Deum* of life, as you would say.

You might think it looks sad, but it's not . . . Whenever I paint, what happens is that after adding and adding to it, the paintings always turn out like that . . . a bit gray.

But look . . . for a Trappist, *joie de vivre* consists of the sure hope of death . . . and when we contemplate the crosses in the cemetery that mark the places where our brothers are at rest . . . it brings us great joy . . . An intense joy at knowing they are in heaven already and thinking about the fact that we will be with them one day . . . Our entire science consists of knowing how to wait.

Then, my dear brother, then indeed is there *joie de vivre* . . . There is happiness in the waiting, and in the suffering as one waits . . .

Don't think of my poor drawing as something sad, then . . . It's not at all. It might strike you as paradoxical, but it's the happiest thing I've been able to do . . . It is a joy to think that everything comes to an end, a holy joy to think that we are foreigners on this earth . . . To think that we are to die very soon, so that we can see God and Our Lady, brings true delight to the monk's heart . . .

You know the whole Rule, or nearly all of it. You've visited the monastery. You're very close to the Cistercian spirit . . . But what you haven't seen is that in La Trapa, the Trappist's most sublime moment, his *Te Deum* moment . . . is the moment of his death . . . Am I making sense? . . . Meanwhile, waiting is his life . . . Waiting with faith, with love, with holy peace . . . That is the only *joie de vivre* . . . to burn with love for God, and to know that our God is waiting for us.

What does it matter if you're suffering or rejoicing? You have God, don't you? . . . Who are you, meanwhile? Don't worry about yourself, poor thing. You don't even *know* how to suffer, you aren't *capable* of rejoicing . . . Let God take you over, and then you will have neither suffering

---

3. *Te Deum*: a hymn of thanksgiving, then prayed at the conclusion of Matins (the earliest Hour of the day) on Sundays and feast days. Today, it is prayed at the conclusion of the Office of Readings. For the holy card Rafael painted for his uncle, see p. 334. The inscription reads "knowing how to wait" ("saber esperar"). Image source: LPM 215.

nor joy . . . you will have peace . . . Your heart will be still and rooted in God, and waiting will be your life . . . and waiting serenely, without being impatient or afraid . . . That is life, that is the only *joie de vivre* . . .

Anyway, dear brother, don't pay me any mind. I'm just a poor Trappist who's a bit mad.

You say that sometimes you regret speaking . . . Maybe, but listen . . . that's because you don't know how to speak about God. If you did know how, you'd shout, and you'd speak of nothing else . . .

God, the only reason for our lives. How could we not speak about Him? . . . But we don't know how. When we realize how little we are, and how big He is, we fall silent, and it seems that we speak more by our silence . . . Anyway, I don't know what I'm talking about. You already understand. I want to talk to you about God, and I fall silent too. You don't need me to say a thing.

I would like to write you a long letter, but I'm going to leave it there . . . I wish I could pour my whole soul into it, but since I can't, I'll be satisfied with just sending you my holy card. When you look at it, remember your nephew, your brother, who made it for you with all his love. And if you don't like it, send it back with your comments, and I'll make you another one.

Everything in your letter gave me great consolation . . . I'd never want to take your cross away from you, and believe me, I don't pity you . . . quite the opposite . . . You'll see, we're going to have such a *Te Deum* to sing together, you amidst all your Toro business, me at La Trapa . . . What does it all matter? Don't you think? . . . If only you knew how happy I am. The Virgin loves me so much.

Tomorrow I'm going to write to my grandmother . . . Please tell her not to worry, she'll never go without.

As for my mother and Merceditas's journey, I have nothing to tell you . . . My mother suspects, but she doesn't yet know.[4] The coming days will be a bit . . . Anyway, when Merceditas's return to Castile comes up[5] . . . we fall silent. My mother is saddened by the thought of just the two of them going now . . . I understand that, and I assure you, it breaks my heart.

---

4. My mother suspects: that is, Rafael's plan to re-enter La Trapa after Christmas.

5. Both Rafael and his mother had accompanied Merceditas on her previous long-term stay in Madrid (Castile) for medical treatment (see #62, n. 3). However, this time, Rafael had opted not to join them but had not stated that his decision was because he was returning to La Trapa.

Lord . . . Lord, make me generous and give me strength . . . You ask so much of me, and I want to give You so much . . . It's everything, and even that everything is so little and so full of imperfection . . . He will know how to put it right . . . Let us place ourselves in His hands, and in those of the Virgin.

I have nothing more to tell you . . . I'm truly sorry that the orphanage is closing.[6] There is no faith anymore . . . People look to human beings for everything. It's sad that Nazareth House is closing precisely when it ought to be even more of a Nazareth House . . . now, in this season when we commemorate the home, the very thing these children lack. With just a little effort from everyone, maybe we could give those little angels the joy of finding themselves absolutely coddled by Christ's love . . . for the love of the Christ Child . . . What a shame . . . I'd been thinking of them during this season . . . I'd grown rather fond of them . . . I promise you, when Aunt María told me in her last letter, it caused me great sorrow . . . But there's no faith anymore, brother . . . Besides, the way I see it, if those children come and go like that, as if they were at school, they could get lost. Don't you think?

I think the people from the government didn't understand the spirit of the enterprise . . . Anyway, who am I to have an opinion . . . but don't be discouraged . . . Well, I already know.

Tell Aunt María to be good, and I'll write her back one of these days . . . I'm telling you, I don't even recognize myself these days, I'm using up so much ink and paper.

I know you don't need me to write, but I'll write you again before I leave . . . even if you think it's a bad idea.[7] It can't be helped, we'll always be what we are to each other. My desire is *God alone* . . . but what am I going to do, brother? . . . I don't need you to write me either . . . Do what you want, but I don't want to say one way or the other, just in case, because if we decide one way . . . the Lord might go the other way. Am I making sense?

6. Nazareth House, an orphanage of which María Osorio was a prominent sponsor (see #75, n. 14).

7. No further letters from Rafael to his uncle before his return to La Trapa have been preserved.

Well, that's all. I know I needn't ask, but please do remember to pray to the Virgin sometime, not to ask Her to take anything away from us here at home, but rather to help us all.

With all my great affection, your brother, the future Cistercian oblate,

Brother María Rafael, O.C.R.[8]

In a few days, I'll send you something you'll like . . . And no, it's not turrón.[9]

8. Underneath his signature, Rafael included a drawing with the phrase "Gloria in excelsis Deo" (Luke 2:14). See OC 527.

9. Turrón: a type of nougat, traditionally eaten in Spain at Christmastime.

88. *To Fernanda Torres*

Oviedo, December 17, 1935

J-H-S

My dearest grandmother,

It's past time I answer your letter. First of all, I should say that you don't need to ask me for what you asked . . . Rest assured that my poor prayers are headed your way, and that you have a grandson who has offered himself to the Lord for the sake of all in the silence of my Trapa. Believe me, if by my sacrifices I could alleviate some of the difficulties of your final years, I would do so gladly . . . I offer them all to Our Lady, so that She might do what She wills . . . I can do nothing more.

I'm so grateful that you've been thinking of your grandson during this time, which is going to be somewhat sorrowful, and that you're praying, not for me . . . but rather for my parents . . . Ultimately, I suffer gladly for God's sake; for Him, I'd do what I'm doing now a million times over . . . and I assure you, that when you do everything for Him . . . there is no difficulty or sorrow that you cannot endure, and even the tears shed along the way become the treasure with which we shall someday present ourselves before Him . . . Don't you go longing to wipe my tears away, because I'm telling you . . . I am completely happy.

In your letter, you asked me to pour out my soul to you . . . How difficult it is, *abuelita* . . . I wouldn't know how, in such a short space, being as incoherent as I am . . . But I'll just say that my life is my vocation, and my vocation comes down to this alone: love for God. With that, I've said it all . . .

I assure you, my return to La Trapa is nothing but that: love for God.

Over these past two years, the Lord has been perfecting my vocation, without me even realizing it until now . . . and all I can do is thank Him from the depths of my soul for the gentleness with which He has treated me. It was my very great fortune to have had to leave my monastery . . . Now I know much more deeply what a Cistercian vocation is worth . . . Blessed be the Lord for everything!

334 The Collected Works

Don't you worry, *abuela*, because your days are coming to an end. Have confidence in the absolute certainty that they will come to a good one. You, poor creature, can do nothing; all you can do is wait . . . And the thought that you are getting close now must be a deep consolation to you . . . You should think of nothing but that, but not on account of your age. What does age matter?! I am 24 years old, and seen rightly, we have the same amount of time left, considering that eternity comes afterward . . . Your days are a mere speck of dust that will dissolve into infinity; don't focus on that speck, but rather immerse yourself in that infinity, which is God.

Why should you be afraid? . . . Have confidence that the Lord loves you, and if you have lived your life according to God's law, that is the law by which you must be judged, and that law is not severe. It doesn't demand great things. It comes down to just a little bit of love . . .

It doesn't consist of austerity or fasting or disciplines or suffering or sorrow . . . None of that is of any use if you don't have love for God . . . Practice that during these final years, and you'll see how holy you become . . . You don't need a whole lifetime for that, a mere minute is enough, and you still have time . . . Don't you worry, *abuelita*, I'll be helping you from La Trapa. You'll see.

I wholeheartedly accept the gift you sent me, which is your love . . . I don't deserve it, I know, but I'll take it with me to La Trapa. There, I'll place it at the feet of the Virgin, alongside that of my parents.

I almost have nothing left to say. Don't measure my love by this letter's length . . . Look at my intentions instead, and be charitable and understanding. I would like to tell you so many things, but what for? I don't know if we'll see each other again. I think we will . . . but whatever the Lord wants. We are in His hands.

Don't worry about material things . . . You will want for nothing, you can be assured of that.

Give Aunt María a very big hug for me.[1] With all my great affection, your grandson, who is always thinking of you,

Brother María Rafael, O.C.S.O.

From the bottom of my heart, I wish you a Christmas very close to God.

---

1. Aunt María: María Josefa Barón Torres, Fernanda's daughter, who lived with her in Toro.

*Samples of Rafael's art
before his entrance into the monastery*

An exaggerated portrait in watercolor (LPM 41).

A playful line drawing (LPM 63).

One of a series of sketches in pen and watercolor
commissioned by his mother, portraying costume designs
for a theater performance she directed (LPM 44).

Covers commissioned for his uncle's books

A cover for *Él* (LPM 224).

Ora et labora

A cover for *Del campo de batalla a la Trapa: El hermano Gabriel*
(LPM 224).

Holy Cards

INCOLA EGO ·SUM IN TERRA . PS.CXVIII~V. 19.

"I am a stranger and pilgrim on earth" (see #207; LPM 225).

"All the earth worships you" (see #207; LPM 225).

OMNIS TERRA ADORET TE . PS.LXV. V.4

VIAM VERITATIS ELEGI. PS.CXVIII. V.30

"I have chosen the way of truth"
(see #207; LPM 219).

BUSCANDO MIS AMORES,
IRÉ POR ESOS MONTES Y RIBERAS
NI COGERÉ LAS ·FLORES,
NI TEMERÉ LAS FIERAS,
Y PASARÉ LOS FUERTES Y
FRONTERAS.

(San Juan de la Cruz)

Holy card with the text, "I will not gather flowers, / nor fear wild beasts; / I will go beyond strong men and frontiers" (see #83; LPM 213).

Holy card with the text, "The tranquil night / at the time of the rising dawn, / silent music, / sounding solitude, / the supper that refreshes, and deepens love" (text: SJC 474; image: LPM 211).

La noche sosegada
En par de los levantes del aurora
La música callada
La soledad sonora
La cena que recrea y enamora.

The Holy Face of Jesus (1937). Painted as a mural above the staircase at his parents' residence in Villasandino (LPM 175).

89. To María Osorio

Oviedo, December 20, 1935

J-H-S

My dearest sister,

Did you get my letter? I expect yours tomorrow. I thought it would get here today, but it didn't.

I don't have anything to tell you right now, I can't think of anything . . . These past few days have been somewhat rough . . . Well, very rough. I'm not complaining, because it's my own fault, but sometimes it makes me sad that I am the way I am . . . If only you knew, little sister. What the Lord gives me, I don't reciprocate. He has legitimate grievances against me, I know . . . And nevertheless I do nothing to fix it . . .

For a few days now, I don't know what has been going on with me . . . Every morning, I go to receive the Lord with most ardent desire. I go in order to ask His forgiveness and to tell Him that I love Him and that I'll never separate myself from Him . . . Well, believe me, the minute I leave church, I forget about all that *entirely*. I'm a fool for the rest of the day, I pray badly, I get tired, and then when this time of night comes (it's half past midnight), I go to my room and do my examen . . . and it greatly saddens me to realize that I *don't reciprocate*. I promise to love Him more tomorrow . . . I go to sleep with the consolation of knowing that I'll have Him close to me again the next morning, in just a few hours . . . He'll be with me, and I'll tell Him about my infidelity and sorrows and weakness . . . and every day I fall asleep in that peace . . .

But look, I <u>know</u> that if I reciprocated all God's gifts and little hints, I'd be a saint already . . . I see a very long road ahead . . . I'm at the beginning, and I contribute nothing for my part . . . It's sad, but true. Any obstacle appears . . . and I stumble . . .

Anyway, I've often heard Uncle Polín say that "we must love our own weaknesses," and it's not that I love mine, exactly . . . but I recognize them, and they make me practice humility before God . . . We are nothing,

sister . . . such children we are. What would we do without Jesus? . . .
I tell Him that every morning . . . and it's not that I get upset, but He
knows that if He leaves me on my own . . . where would I go?

Lord, Lord, look what You are doing to Your servant. But if only you
knew, I'm so *distracted*, it pains me so. I have such a strong desire to be
back at La Trapa already.

No one and nothing is coming to my aid, and these are truly days of
trial. I can only rely on the Virgin Mary. I think of Her always, but sometimes I fall into *human* concerns, and I find myself alone. As I said, I'm
not complaining, God and Mary forbid . . . I'm just telling you about it,
and that brings me consolation . . . But I am truly a wretch . . . I should
so like to love God . . . Lord, I don't know. Either I don't want to, or . . .
Oh, if only I reciprocated what You give me.

Anyway, I don't want to fill this letter up with lamentations. It shouldn't
be like that. But of course, you think I'm a different kind of person than I
am. You have to remember, dear little sister, who you're dealing with . . .
Well, I won't say any more because you wouldn't believe me, and you'd
think maybe it's false humility . . . But the Lord knows it all, and that's
enough for me.

Did Uncle Polín like the holy card I sent him?

I wrote to my grandmother the day before yesterday. What is she going
to do? Will she finally go to Ávila? . . . How is your business? And what
about you? Has your grumpiness gone away? So many things, sister . . .
there are so many things I'd ask you and tell you.

I only have a very few days left now at home, very few days left dealing
with the world . . . And if only you could see this, God is permitting it,
but now I'm suddenly interested in all of it twice as much. I don't know
what's happening to me . . . I'm acting as if I were never actually going
to leave . . . On the other hand, I don't care about any of this, I'm eager
to have silence again and leave it all behind. I want to fly, and everything
is holding me down . . .

Oh, sister, if only you knew what a difficult struggle this is . . . How
long it's taking for these days to pass . . . but they're getting shorter and
shorter . . .

My mother and sister think (they aren't sure yet) that they'll go to
Portugal on the 8th, apparently that's the cheap option, and then they'll

go to Madrid. They also want to go to Zaragoza to visit the Virgin . . .
They don't have a set plan yet, but I don't know if I should leave before
or after. What's best? I ask not for my own sake, but for my mother's . . .
She still doesn't know anything, but since she's very worried about me,
I'm going to tell her . . . Maybe tomorrow.

My father and Leopoldo want to come to Venta de Baños[1] . . . Fernando arrives on Saturday.[2]

I'm in a daze . . . I didn't think it was all going to be this hard. But I'm
not complaining . . . if the Lord wants to prolong this struggle, even if it
means I'll be in constant agony . . . may God be blessed.

Listen, I didn't want to make you sad . . . I shouldn't tell you about
any of these troubles of mine . . . But have pity, sister . . . If only I were a
saint! . . . All this is an escape, a chance to unburden myself . . . I'm very
low to the ground today . . . I'm a man just like any other . . . and when
I see myself like this, it pains me to think about the trust you've placed in
this creature . . . I don't deserve it, and it puts me to shame.

For the world, what I am going to do is such a lovely gesture . . .
Heroics are just delightful when performed with a smile . . . But look,
I'm telling you all this so that you can see me for what I really am, and
despise me . . . Behind that façade, sometimes there are very bitter tears
. . . crosses that the world doesn't know about, and I don't carry them
well, dragging them around . . . Underneath the surface there's nothing
but misery, foul misery . . . What a shame! I don't know how I could be
like this . . .

There are so many things I would say, but I'm afraid of scandalizing
you. But underneath that gesture of going to La Trapa, which the world
thinks I'm doing with extraordinary pleasure and purely for love of God,
there's a man—me, all too refined, averse to the cilice and horribly repulsed by the discipline[3] . . . I carry around this material being, which
is in rebellion . . .

---

1. Venta de Baños: the town where the Monastery of San Isidro de Dueñas was located.

2. Saturday: that is, December 21, 1935. As Rafael implies here, his father and his brother
Leopoldo both accompanied him when he made his second entrance into La Trapa on
January 11, 1936.

3. Cilice and discipline: Instruments of physical penance (see #40, n. 15).

Oh, little sister, sometimes it puts me to shame to call you that . . . You don't know what I am, you don't know me . . . Suffering terrifies me, when it should be quite the opposite. I should love the cross, I should rejoice in it . . . but as I stumble over these thorns . . . Lord, Lord, I don't know what I am saying . . .

You told me not to ask your forgiveness ever again, but look, I can't help it. You love me, and I don't deserve that. You don't know what I'm really like . . . I don't deserve the good opinion of any creature, I'm telling you that right now, hand on heart . . . God knows it, and so do I. I'm going to La Trapa to be holy, but I'm not holy yet. I don't want to deceive the world, I don't want to deceive you . . . I can't convince the world, but you understand me, although maybe you don't understand me right now, and you think I'm exaggerating . . . but I'm not.

If only you knew, if I were as I ought to be, and I loved the Lord as He deserves . . . I wouldn't think about myself at all, I wouldn't struggle at all. But my love for God, which is great, has to struggle against myself . . . am I making sense? I'm a wretch and I don't know how I even dare to talk about God . . . but the Lord is so good! Isn't He? That is the only consolation I have . . . that and Mary.

Today I'm looking at myself too much. I'm always telling you to do the opposite, and instead of preaching by example . . . look at how I'm acting . . . But have pity on me . . . When you've been struggling for many days . . . I won't say any more, just that your last letter inspired me to tell you everything. I fear only one thing, which I'll tell you honestly, and that is the possibility of scandalizing you . . . But I'll consider this all quite proper if it has made it possible for you to know me more deeply. If sinking to the bottom of my soul helps you see what's really there . . . misery and cowardice . . . Don't look for anything else.

Right now it's eight o'clock at night. I've just finished reading your letter. All day I was in Infiesto[4] and I wasn't able to finish . . . I was about to tear up everything I'd already written, I'm telling you . . . but I thought better of it, and you can be the one to rip it up . . . Listen, that's just what came out yesterday . . . You have to understand, and when I start to look inward . . . I don't know what to do with myself . . . and everything

---

4. Infiesto: a town east of Oviedo.

causes me shame. Today I'm doing well . . . very well. Your letter gave me deep consolation. You're the only one who talks to me about God . . . You think you aren't doing anything, but you're wrong. You're a very good example to me, *despite your wretchedness*, and you're teaching me how to suffer. Blessed be the Virgin Mary.

You said that we'll spend Christmas rejoicing and suffering . . . I don't know. I'm a bit out of it. Believe me, I don't know how to carry on a conversation, I don't know what I'm saying or doing, or what's happening to me. Sometimes everything just gets so overwhelming . . .

But look, despite everything I said to you before, I have peace . . . I don't understand it . . . But I am content, and this "understanding while not understanding" fills me with joy.[5]

See? We all have our ups and downs . . . and we must thank the Lord that we do not lack for suffering.

How great the Lord is, little sister. He loves us so much, how happy I am . . . I'm more cheerful today, if only you could see. Nevertheless, I have one affliction . . . I saw my mother crying . . . I don't know if I'm making sense, I'm just writing non sequiturs.

Well, I'm going to stop thinking about what's going on with me . . . and . . . let us love the Lord, let us look to Mary. Let us unite ourselves to the angels in heaven who are singing of His imminent arrival on earth . . . Everything passes . . . let us wait, are you agreed? And let us wait with joy . . . What a great consolation it is to have God . . . How selfish of us to fail to appreciate that . . . I have such a desire to be in La Trapa again . . . to throw myself entirely into the arms of the Virgin, and there, without anyone taking notice . . .

Don't you go thinking that you're a "nuisance" I need to be patient with. Bless the Lord, such things you say. You don't know how much encouragement I get from writing you . . . Truly, it is a gift from the Lord, that right now, when He *knew* that I was going to need it, He gave me a reason . . . an occasion to express the movements of my soul. Whether

5. "I entered into unknowing / and there I remained unknowing / transcending all knowledge. . . . I was so [over]whelmed, / so absorbed and withdrawn / that my senses were left / deprived of all their sensing, / and my spirit was given / an understanding while not understanding / transcending all knowledge" (Saint John of the Cross, "Stanzas Concerning an Ecstasy Experienced in High Contemplation," in SJC 53).

they are movements of intense love, or sometimes desolation . . . expressing them to another soul who understands me gives me so much peace . . . The day is coming, and it is coming soon, when the silence will be absolute, and then, perhaps, the love of God will enter into me more fully.

So, then, you don't need to worry about me. I've done what I could, I've shared with you what I could . . . my love for God, my joy when I have it, my affection for the Virgin, my great tenderness toward Our Lady, who consoles and guides me . . .

The only thing I don't want to share with you is my cross . . . leave my sorrows to me. Even if I gave you a bad impression at the beginning of this letter, please forgive me. Who doesn't have moments of discouragement? . . . So you know me better now, and more deeply, but those moments pass quickly. The Lord *doesn't let me* stop and stare at myself for too long . . . He *knows* that it just makes me feel bad, even though it's necessary sometimes . . . He wants us to be humble, and this is one of the ways He does that . . .

Don't you see, little sister, how great the Lord is? . . . At the same time that He shows us our misery and weakness, He also gives us . . . such a great love! . . . What a great consolation this is . . .

When we reach eternal glory, we will love the Lord, from Mary's arms . . . But until then? . . . Well, nothing, it's very easy. We'll just love Him from our littleness, from this "one night in a bad inn," as the Saint said,[6] referring to this life in which everything is an obstacle to our delight in God . . . our own selves being the primary obstacle . . .

Take heart, little sister, and pay me no mind. Go beyond the created being, go beyond yourself, and love God . . . Believe me, the mere thought of that gives me wings . . .

God! . . . God! . . . There is nothing but that . . . there's no cross, no delight, no creature . . . The creature cannot endure, but God alone can . . .

---

6. "If it is hard for a self-indulgent person . . . to spend one night in a bad inn, what do you think that sad soul will feel at being in this kind of inn forever, without end? Let us not desire delights, daughters; we are well-off here; the bad inn lasts for only a night" (Saint Teresa of Ávila, *The Way of Perfection*, trans. Kieran Kavanaugh [Washington, DC: ICS Publications, 2013], 442).

Pay me no mind, please forgive me . . . just hear these cries of a soul who is surrounded by sins and obstacles, as many joyful ones as sad . . . It's as if I were deep in a well, with the water up to my neck, cold and half dead. What does it matter? But from those depths, I cry out with all my soul . . . "God, God, Mary . . ." And then, believe me, what's the difference if you find yourself in the murky blackness of the darkness of that well or on the sunny plain? . . . In either place, the soul knows only one thing, and that is to cry out . . . "God, God, Christ . . . how long You delay!"

Suffering and rejoicing are the least of our concerns. Whether we are suffering or rejoicing doesn't matter at all. Ultimately, that's about us. No . . . Lord, You alone are our life. You alone should be our only reason for living . . . You alone . . . not us, not at all.

Little sister . . . what depths, what a flood! . . . To love God . . . Do you know what that is? . . . No, you don't. It makes one go mad, you don't know what to say . . .

To love God . . . what a disgrace, Lord, I should be silent . . . I don't know, I'm a fool . . . But even so, Lord, I love You madly and utterly foolishly, perhaps even without realizing it . . . I don't want to realize it. What would be the point? . . . I want to love You just because. Why are You doing this to me, Lord? . . . Why do You treat me like this? . . . I don't know, I've gone mad.

Forgive me, little sister. The Lord is great, He is greater than all other gods, and He treats this brother of yours with such . . . If only you knew, I have such an urge to go hide.

Well, it's passed now. This letter will be full of nonsense when it reaches you . . . I don't mind.

I'm so happy that Uncle Polín was pleased with my holy card . . . If only you knew, I painted it with so much affection.

I'm going to do a drawing of Saint Francis of Assisi for my father next, he's the patron saint of the Forest Engineers . . . He's very excited about it. He is so good.

What you said about leaving on the 15th, well, I don't know. I think I'll leave sooner than that, but once my mother and sister have left, it's going to be very difficult for me to stay home . . . I shouldn't keep pushing it . . . that would be tempting God, and I don't know my own strength. Please understand me. But look, since I'll be going by car . . . who knows.

Anyway, I won't promise anything. The Lord will tell me what to do. But maybe on the way I'll decide to come by and give you and Uncle Polín a hug[7] . . . Do you think that would be a bad idea? It's of no importance, but I'll do whatever you tell me to do. But don't you go thinking that would be goodbye . . . Anyway, I'll leave it there. We're off to dinner . . . I'll continue later.

My dearest sister, now I have peace and quiet, so I'm going to continue answering your letter.

I'm glad my letters don't get you all mixed up . . . you don't know how glad. They're so messy . . . but it's true, where clarity is lacking, your good will makes up for it. Indeed, you don't need to contribute anything on your part, just your good will and intention, as you said, right? . . . Because that alone is *enough* . . .

Besides, everything is so simple, so clear, so easy . . . What's bad is when we not only fail to contribute our good intentions, but we in fact contribute obstacles . . . That's the worst. But letting you be . . . you don't need to do anything, and nobody needs to point you down any particular path, or tell you how to act . . . The way I see it, love is the only science you need, and nothing else . . . *Love on the inside and humility on the outside*, and nothing else. And that's plenty. We think that we need to do great things in order to be holy . . . and no. We don't even need to draw any attention to ourselves.

You shouldn't care that *right now* you don't know or see what you're meant to do . . . You'll see, Our Lady will enlighten you, and in addition to Her help, *your own failings* will instruct you . . . They are the only teachers I've ever had . . . If only you knew how well you learn while weeping . . . and we'll never stop failing, nor will we ever stop learning. So don't you worry . . . Right now you have only one task, one occupation: loving God . . . the best you can, the best you know how, but always loving Him. Let's see if that heart of yours is finally set alight . . . Then you won't have any questions left to ask . . . and you'll *know* what you're meant to do . . . Then *you'll see* that there is only one path, a great broad path, a path that never narrows or curves . . . A path that leads to the widest of horizons . . . God . . . See how easy that is?

7. As Rafael implies here, he did end up passing through Ávila to see his aunt and uncle before his re-entrance into La Trapa.

How innocent you are, I was going to say simple . . . it's as if I were to say to you, "Little sister, I love God so much! He is my only life and my only treasure . . . I love Him so much, so much that I don't know what to do. What should I do?" . . . And you'd reply laughing . . . "Well don't do *anything* at all. What more could you do?" . . . "But if I am meant to do something, I don't see it. I don't see any path, all I see is how much I want to love Him . . . and love Him truly . . ." And then you'll say, "And?! What else is it that you want to see? . . . Do you want to look for complications? Your whole interior life comes down to this: loving God, and loving Him more and more . . . Why are you looking for a path where there isn't one? . . . Are there paths in the sea?"

How innocent you are, little sister. I envy you . . . What more help could you want other than God and Mary? . . . Maybe you haven't realized.

See how easy it is? . . . Your interior life: loving God . . . and as for your life in the world? . . . If I were a terrible preacher, I'd scowl and tell you . . . penance, prayer, mortification of the senses, etc . . . And sure, that's all well and good . . . but I think it's easier than all that: *All you have to do is humbly obey the dictates of the love for God that you carry within you* . . . I don't know if I'm explaining myself well, but you'll see.

If you love God, you must love creatures; they are His work, His image . . . And so, you have charity.

If you love God, and you love Him *completely*, you won't love yourself; you'll consider yourself so despicable that you won't think about yourself at all; while loving God, you cannot care about anything that concerns yourself . . . so, you have humility. If you love God, how could you not be humble? I can't see any other way.

If you love God . . . then you have prayer, even if you don't think you do . . . You don't need to rack your brain to pray, right? . . . What does your prayer consist of? Well, one act of love for God after another . . . until one day, all those separate acts of love are transformed into one, and then you truly will be set alight. Then, as I said, you'll have no questions left to ask.

I won't go on, but you understand what I'm saying, don't you? *Everything* comes from love for God . . . You'll see, if you perfect that love which is your only interior life . . . nothing else is of any importance. That same love will make you humble, penitential, charitable . . . It'll make you holy. . . . holy for love's sake. . . . Holy entirely and exclusively for love's sake. . .

See, little sister, how easy that is? . . . You don't have to do anything but obey the dictates of your own poor heart, which is more or less alight. It doesn't matter if you fall. . . . It doesn't matter if you're discouraged . . . The miracle of love can do all things. . . . Everything will become easy for you . . . delight, suffering, and even *waiting*.

Look, everything I'm saying here, I don't know if it's what's best for you, but it's what's easiest. It's not complicated, and you'll see, it produces results . . . Ask Our Lady for the love She has for Her Son . . . That's how the Virgin was able to endure everything, that's how She was able to witness Her Son's death: for love's sake, and that alone . . . That's how our Mother was able to suffer what she suffered. That's how She was able to be separated from Him . . . For love's sake, She was humble; for love's sake, She was the holiest of women . . . Ask Our Lady for some of that love . . . and you'll see.

Yes, little sister, give yourself over completely, and don't you go thinking that your exterior life will suffer as a result, no . . . quite the contrary . . . How beautiful it will be for you to do your tasks around the house for God's sake. To speak and laugh for God's sake, to love your children for God's sake . . . And if God *floods* you, some of that flood will reach those around you . . . Be generous, and don't put any obstacles in their way . . . May your life be a continuous act of love for Jesus . . . I'll pray to the Virgin for this intention. She will hear me, I'm certain. Isn't it true that there's no possible complication this way? Answer me honestly.

I wanted this letter to go out today, but it wasn't possible. I'll leave it there for now, it's getting late. I'll finish it tomorrow, although I won't have any time to write at all.

For tonight, then, receive all your little brother's affection.

Today, Saturday the 21st, I continue, even though I don't have anything to say . . .

We're all eager for Fernando to arrive today from Belgium . . . I don't know how long he'll be here, but around fifteen days or so.

You didn't say anything in your letter about how you're getting along . . . Are you afraid to worry me? . . . I'm so stupid, every day I wait for the mailman . . .

Now I'm going to eat and then pray, because this morning I didn't get to pray, I just received the Lord and heard holy Mass . . .

By God, little sister, don't forget to pray for me in the coming days, just look at how I'm doing. If you go and see Sor Pilar,[8] tell her that I'm very much thinking of their community this Christmas, won't you?

Well, that's all for now. I no longer have the peace and quiet I need in this house to write you. I want this letter to reach you tomorrow (Sunday),[9] so I'll end it here.

How is Pilar doing?[10] I remember everything about that house . . . I can't help it. Blessed be the Most Holy Virgin. I ask Her to guide my letter, and by means of Her, may you receive all that I wish to send you through it. It's so much, dear little sister! . . . I don't know, I can't say anything more.

Brother María Rafael, O.C.S.O.

8. Sor Pilar: Sor Pilar García, the abbess of the Poor Clare monastery in Ávila and a friend and spiritual mentor of Rafael's (see #43, n. 8).

9. Sunday: That is, December 22, 1935.

10. Pilar: Pilar Barón Osorio, María's daughter and Rafael's cousin, who was sick at the time.

90. *To María Osorio*

Oviedo, December 24, 1935

J-H-S

My dearest sister,

I don't know what to say about your last two letters . . . There's so much to say, but I don't have time (*materially* speaking). Right now it's one-thirty, and we're about to eat. Later, at three o'clock, we're going to go to Avilés,[1] and we'll get back at six, and then the mail goes out at eight. Despite all that, I don't want you to spend tomorrow, Christmas Day, without a note from me, even if it doesn't say anything.

I'll take my time answering both your letters later. For now, let's not think about *our concerns* . . . Let us look at God in the stable.

If only you knew how impatient I am for tonight to arrive . . . I haven't thought of anything else all day . . . I don't know if it's because of your prayers, but the Most Blessed Virgin is helping me in a very *special* way . . . What a joy, little sister, to have a God like ours. Isn't it? . . .

I can't say anything today . . . All I know how to do is wait . . . How great is the Lord, little sister!!!! In just a few hours, we will have that God, become a Child . . . and we will have Him with us . . . I am so happy! . . .

When you receive this letter, the Lord will already be in the world. What will we do? Adore Him, and weep for joy. He is coming for you and me, He is searching for us, He is looking at us. The Virgin Mary is offering Him to us . . . How tender the divine Mother is . . .

I don't know what to tell you, I can't think of anything . . . I want to be in heaven, intoning the *Gloria* with the angels and saints. My body is here . . . my soul is very far away . . . Oh, little sister! There are so many things we are going to say to the Child tonight . . . Rather than frankincense and myrrh, we will offer Him our whole heart, without reservation . . .

---

1. Avilés: A prominent town in Asturias, north of Oviedo.

That's what you have done, right? I'll unite myself to your intentions . . .
How happy, how joyful we will be! The Lord loves us and accepts us . . .

Anyway, there's nothing I can tell you, I don't know . . . We'll know
neither how to rejoice nor how to suffer, we'll come to nothing . . . The
mystery of the Nativity fills everything.

Here we are all very worried about Pilarcita[2] . . . Blessed be the Lord!
Such things He does. We don't know it, but despite the fact that He has
seemingly unleashed pain and the cross upon humanity . . . How gentle
these become when we *see* that the Lord is the one who is doing it! . . .
I don't know what to say to you . . . everything else disappears when we
look at Him . . . isn't that so?

Listen, in La Trapa there was a novice who had just three words written
down. He kept them above his desk, so that he could see them and read
them constantly . . . That gave him great consolation. The words that surely
made my brother *fly* were these: "What about Him?" Enough said, right?

In conclusion, I'll just say that I've seen so much charity and tenderness in your letters, that all I can do is thank the Most Blessed Virgin for
that . . . and you too, my poor sister. I am so sorry for involving you in
my suffering at times . . . since I have so little of it, while the consolation
the Lord sends me is so great . . . that really I am very selfish. Pay me no
mind. Everything will pass . . . and if it doesn't, that's all the same to me
. . . I want neither to suffer nor to stop suffering. I don't want anything
. . . I want to love that Jesus who is coming soon . . . to love God, to
love the Virgin . . . I don't know, I don't want anything.

They're calling me to come eat. At six o'clock, I'll keep going for a few
more minutes.

It's now seven o'clock and we just got back from Avilés. I don't have
time to say anything more except that I'm sending you all the love you
could ask for, and as much as I could hope to send.

May you have a very holy Christmas with Uncle Polín and my cousins.
Sending my great love to all of you, and as for you . . .

Brother María Rafael, O.C.S.O.

---

2. Pilarcita: María's daughter and Rafael's cousin, Pilar Barón Osorio, who was sick at
the time.

91. Dedication of a Holy Card to Br. Jesús Sandoval[1]

Christmas 1935

May this little memento help you to remember your dear brother before the Virgin . . . I'll do the same. Our prayers thus united will ensure that our good Mother helps us to achieve our desire, which is to be able to live and die as Trappists.

When you are discouraged, look to Mary, and you'll see, She will ensure that your tears blossom into flowers that can be offered to Jesus.

In this holy card, I send all my love as your brother,

Brother María Rafael, O.C.S.O.

1. Br. Jesús Sandoval was an oblate at San Isidro de Dueñas.

92. To María Osorio

Oviedo, December 26, 1935

J-H-S

My dearest little sister,

I'm beginning this letter in the waiting room at the dentist's office . . . I came to make sure my teeth are clean when I bring them to La Trapa.

I'll remember yesterday, Christmas Day, all my life. On the one hand, it was very hard to leave the Christ Child after Communion. I told my mother that I was finally leaving, and under what circumstances . . . You can imagine, I don't need to tell you . . . The Most Blessed Virgin helped me. Everything will be as the Lord commands.

Of course, I'll pass through Ávila . . . I'm not relying on my own strength for anything. I have God, and if He had abandoned me, I don't know what would have become of me, quite some time ago . . . I am very pleased because *I* am not doing anything.

I wanted to write you yesterday, Christmas Day, but we stayed up until two in the morning talking about La Trapa . . . My mother is calm; she has a generosity that elevates her in the eyes of God . . . but she is a mother, and even though she sees that I am happy, I know that she cries when I'm not looking.

We still haven't set a date, but I'll leave before my mother and Merceditas do. Fernando is leaving for Leuven again on January 7.[1] My mother and sister still don't know where they are going, and my father and Leopoldo will stay here. On a human level, it is sad that a family that loves each other so much should be separated in four different places . . . My parents have so much to offer God . . . It is all for God.

I've just come back to the house. It's eight-thirty, and I just spent a moment with the Christ Child at the Carmelite chapel.

---

1. Rafael's mother and sister were heading to Castile for his sister's medical treatment. His brother Fernando was returning to Leuven, Belgium, where he attended university.

All I can do is think about that house in Ávila . . . I consider it my own home!! . . . If only you could see, I've prayed for all of you so much before Jesus . . . He must hear me.

Today we went to Salinas to look at the sea[2] . . . How great is God, little sister! How beautiful His works! I see Him everywhere I look. I'm so happy. I love Him so much . . . Jesus loves me so much. When will I become convinced of it? . . . We creatures are so forgetful . . . What a pity! . . . Anyway, Mary will make it happen.

I don't know what to say . . . I don't know what to tell you. I seem to be empty, and nevertheless, if I were with you, I'd say so many things . . . or maybe nothing at all . . . I know that you are suffering, and that makes me fall silent . . . What else can I do? The Lord is so great . . . He'll do what I don't know how to do, what I can't do . . .

I want to send you little rays of light and love for Jesus. I don't know if they are reaching you. I think they are . . . I'm sending them by way of Our Lady . . . Maybe they're very weak, but I put all I can into them.

I love you because you are suffering, and you are suffering for God, that God who is mine . . .

How often I have offered myself to the Lord for the sake of all the souls who are suffering for Him . . . I find myself so united to all the pain in this world . . . If only I could relieve any of it . . . But I don't need to relieve you of anything . . . you are going in the right direction. Even though I am suffering with you . . . I don't mind. That's the best thing you could do.

I don't know what to say. I understand you. You abhor the world, I know, but doesn't the world you carry within you make up for that somewhat? My poor, dear little sister . . . You told me about how the struggle is what matters most, according to Saint Teresa,[3] so I'll say the same thing, and I say this to myself also . . . let us struggle against whatever we must, however we must.

I've had to interrupt my letter again. I'll continue now with greater peace and quiet. It's almost twelve o'clock. I have your last two letters in front of me, and I don't know where to begin. All I can tell you is that they have achieved what you set out to do; may God reward you.

---

2. Salinas: A beach town north of Oviedo.

3. "Do not stop on the road but, like the strong, fight even to death in the search, for you are not here for any other reason than to fight" (Saint Teresa of Ávila, *The Way of Perfection*, chap. 20 par. 2, in *The Collected Works of Saint Teresa of Ávila*, trans. Kieran Kavanaugh and Otilio Rodríguez [Washington, DC: ICS Publications, 1989], 2:114).

Look, little sister, we ought never to complain. I won't anymore . . .
You are very right when you say that I am leaving the world, which does
not provide for the needs of the heart . . . the world, which is nothing
in comparison to what the Lord is giving me. You are right, but if I were a
saint, none of that would matter to me. Since I am not yet one, by the grace
of God, don't be surprised that you found my last letter to be a little bit
like me . . . I have a heart that suffers greatly when I see suffering around
me, and it is full of love for my parents and brothers and sister, whom it
has to leave behind . . . But look, pay me no mind.

You can't imagine how much consolation you gave me in your letters
when you said that I've been somewhat useful to you, and that I truly
understand you . . . When a soul loves God, I assure you, you don't need
a degree to understand another soul that loves Him too . . . No, it doesn't
need any at all. It's a most natural thing. You love the Lord very much,
right? Well, so do I, and that's enough for us to be able to understand one
another . . . What difference does the place or location make? The world
is a very big place, it's enormous . . . When we look at God's greatness in
His creation . . . we are so little! But when we look at Love, and nothing
but Love . . . then the world seems very little . . . Everything disappears,
and the soul expands . . . it flies to God, for there is no room for it here.
If on the way it encounters another soul going through the same thing,
what a consolation that is. Don't you think? . . .

How little everything is. The work of God is great and marvelous, but
God Himself is infinitely more great and marvelous . . .

Don't look at your surroundings, don't focus on your suffering . . .
it's all *little*, it's pathetic, it doesn't matter at all . . . Don't look at your
consolation and joy either, they too are *little* and unimportant . . . Your
soul is the work of God . . . but God is even greater than that . . . Don't
stop, little sister. Keep going without fear, despite your tears, your worries,
your misery, your consolations . . . Keep going . . . God and nothing else.

Some days I'm very happy, I don't know what is going on with me . . .
Well, I do know . . . I know nothing except that God loves me, that's
enough for me . . . Other days, when I see my parents and brothers and
sister, I want to cry . . . Everything intensifies, and without wanting
to, I start worrying. But neither my joy nor my sadness matters to me. I
absolutely could not care less. I have to go beyond myself in order to get
to God. I make an act of love for Him, and everything passes . . . It's

necessary. How little everything is. I don't want to look at myself, I don't want to suffer or rejoice, it's all the same to me, I assure you . . . I want only to love God. I want only to give myself over to Him, so much so that even my very breath belongs to Him.

Listen, little sister, I can tell you're somewhat overwhelmed. I have been too . . . You sent me encouragement, and bless you for that, because you sent it in the name of Christ's love. I want to send you some right back . . . but don't you go explaining what exactly that encouragement *consists* of.

When someone is fighting, you encourage them with shouts. When someone is languishing and dying, you encourage them with medicine that rouses them . . . But when someone is suffering for the love of God . . . or *just* suffering, how do you encourage them? You don't, because in that very suffering . . . is everything they need. And if that suffering does not appear all on its *own*, but rather accompanied by the love of God . . . Then what more could you want, you happy mortal who are experiencing this?

I can't give you relief, and I don't want to . . . If you enter into agony for Christ's sake . . . Christ Himself will wipe away your tears and carry your cross for you. I don't know if I'm making sense, but I understand this very clearly.

You'll say that your suffering is *human* and so you need *human* help to withstand it. But I say to you . . . sanctify it with love for God and in God, and then . . . listen, little sister, you either understand me or you don't, but there are no words . . . But I can see from your letter that this is what's happening to you. As you receive this *joy of suffering*, you write me *crying* as you tell me your sorrows. At the same time, your soul is in a *special* state . . . and it possesses a special joy because it finds itself in such a state . . . Seeing all this, I understand you, and I am amazed that the same thing is happening to me.

Do you see now that you don't need me to encourage you? What for? Don't you see that God is working in your soul? Don't you see God's tenderness in your tears and woes? Don't you see God's greatness in your suffering? And isn't it true that you *thank* the Lord from the bottom of your heart for the way that He treats you, even if it makes you cry on a *human* level? . . . Yes, little sister, yes, all of humanity suffers, but there are so few who *know how* to suffer . . .

The one who lacks God needs consolation . . . but the one who loves God doesn't care for it.

What a joy it is, Lord, to love You like this . . . even if the world is falling apart, even if our hearts are shattered, even if our bodies suffer martyrdom . . . What does it all matter? So long as You love us and we love You . . . *everything* else disappears. How great the Lord is, little sister . . . how great. Love Him deeply, never grow tired of Him . . . Love Him in suffering and in joy alike. There is no other science, no other virtue, no other path. Don't you agree?

When I told my mother about Pilar and your worries, she started to cry . . . And as I read your letter, I felt great pain as I thought about your worries and those of Uncle Polín, but I looked to the Lord . . . and I saw that His goodness is eternal . . . and that His works among creatures are of infinite greatness.

My poor brother and sister, if I could send you some of what I have within me . . . But then, you already have it too. All I can do is what you do for me, and that is to send you the consolation of knowing that, united to you in the Lord and in Mary, *everything* is done for His love, and we wait in the peace of Love.

I only have a few days left in the world . . . And they are the most difficult ones yet. The Most Blessed Virgin is my strength.

I'll keep writing you, even if my letters turn out a bit messy, but I won't ask you for charity again . . . don't be angry, but sometimes I don't know what I'm saying, and I almost do everything mechanically . . . I'm very weak, little sister.

Now I'm going to leave you again, because it's getting very late.

December 27

I've just received your letter. It seems this letter is already getting too long to be able to answer yours.

I'm so sorry about what's happening with Uncle Polín . . . May it all be for God. As I told you earlier, I'll go to Ávila. My father, my brother, and I will spend the night there, and then in the morning we'll go to Venta de Baños . . . Don't say a word to my grandmother. You understand.

And now I'm going to close this letter so that it gets to you tomorrow, and tonight I'll write you another note . . .

All my affection, your brother, who is very much united to you,

Rafael

93. *To María Osorio*

Oviedo, December 27, 1935

J-H-S

My dearest little sister,

I begin this letter in the name of Jesus and Mary, just as I promised in my last letter. It's eight o'clock at night, and I just got back from the Carmelite chapel . . . Nobody else is home right now.

First, I'll fill you in on some of the little things, and what's going on at home . . . Then tonight, when everybody goes to bed, I'll talk to you about God . . . Everything is necessary, right?

Today I saw my doctor, and he said I was doing much better . . . Surely tomorrow I can reduce my dose of insulin . . . God is so good. I am much stronger . . . Thanks to my very strict nutrition plan, which I never make exceptions to . . . I do what I can for my recovery, because if I'm going to serve God in La Trapa, I'm going to need my health . . . I do it all in His name . . . My good Jesus knows very well that it's all for Him . . . I'm very happy.

My parents are very calm . . . My father more so than my mother . . . I told them that Father Abbot was going to have me study for ordination, and naturally, they're very pleased about that . . . I understand that it would be a great consolation to them to have a son who is a priest . . . Even if he's an oblate, that doesn't matter to them . . . They just want me to be happy, which they know I am at the tabernacle's side . . . We are all very happy . . . It seems that the Virgin is at work in this house . . .

My father is more devout every day . . . He never misses even a day of Holy Communion and Mass . . . I don't know where he is right now, but since I went to the doctor's, I couldn't go with him to make our daily visit to the Lord.

On Christmas Eve, we all went to Midnight Mass at the Adoratrices[1] . . . If only you could have seen it. The nuns do everything with such

---

1. Adoratrices: the Adorers Handmaids of the Blessed Sacrament and of Charity (Adoratrices Esclavas del Santísimo Sacramento y de la Caridad), known as the Adoratrices, were

fervor . . . We heard all three Masses . . . and during the last two I was able to spend quite a bit of time with the Christ Child . . . I understand that it pains you to have to leave Him . . . You have to offer Him that . . . It was very hard for me to leave Him too . . . even if we don't make noise at home . . . we do eat right afterwards, and it's so good to be with Mother and Child at the little stable in Bethlehem, isn't it?

But don't let it trouble you. Remember when I was in Ávila and I told you that when you left after Communion . . . or after a Visit, anytime you had to leave the temple, you didn't have to leave your heart at the tabernacle? Rather, I said, it's better to ask the Lord to come with you . . . Remember that? It often pains me to have to leave behind my prayer of thanksgiving after receiving Communion . . . but since I can't spend hours and hours in church with the Lord, that's what I do . . . I ask the Lord to come with me, and He does, little sister . . . have no doubt.

How fortunate you are that both Uncle Polín and Pilar are bedridden . . . Take this to heart: the Lord has put them there entirely so that you might have an occasion to practice the charity that He is asking of you, so that you might love Him by taking care of your loved ones . . . Everything that is happening around you—the Lord is doing all that for you, didn't you know? Don't put obstacles in His path, little sister! . . . Look up high, so you won't get dizzy. If a chasm suddenly opens up underneath your feet, and the world starts falling apart, but your eyes are still fixed on God . . . then what's it to you? . . . But if you look down into that chasm, you run the risk of getting dizzy . . . and falling in.

I don't know if I led you toward the Child Jesus or not, but when I was with Him I did talk to Him about you. I don't remember what I said to Him . . .

When you write me, don't stop updating me on how Uncle Polín is doing. We'll see if the Lord wants me to say goodbye at his bedside again, just as I did two years ago. Well, things are different now.

I can't wait for these days to be over already, if only you knew . . . I don't intend to say goodbye to anybody.

---

founded in Spain by Saint María Micaela Desmaisieres in 1856 to run women's shelters. Their house in Oviedo, located at the foot of Monte Naranco, was destroyed in October 1937 during the Spanish Civil War (see Foto Delespro, *Barrio de las Adoratrices destruido* [Delegación del Estado para Prensa y Propaganda, 1937], photo 40); see #72, n. 1.

I haven't told Mamá anything about my grandmother, just that they're going to Ávila one of these days, but I imagine that Mamá will send them something . . . She shouldn't worry so much . . . Everything will be resolved, and everyone will do what they can . . . Her old age is quite sad. May it all serve God.

I suppose my mother and sister will go to Burgos. For now they've canceled their trip to Lisbon. It turned out to be too expensive and too far. They'll be away for a few months, and they'll start in Burgos, but they haven't decided anything yet. It's very hard for them to leave home, but Merceditas needs it . . .

If only you knew how often we think of Pilar . . . But don't worry, the Lord will fix everything . . . Remember, everything is for <u>your</u> sake. You ought to be so happy, He loves you so much, you don't even know.

I was so sorry not to be able to write you at length on Christmas Eve . . . But if what few words I did write were useful to you at all . . . blessed be the Lord.

Tell Uncle Polín that one of these days I'll send him what I promised.

You asked me if I regret having given myself over to God entirely . . . You say such things, sister . . . I have nothing to say to that.

I've just picked up my pen again. It's midnight (my best hour, as always). My father and brothers haven't gone to bed yet, they're listening to the radio.

In your letter, you asked me to talk about love for God . . . well, little sister, I don't know . . . I assure you, I don't know how to talk to you about God . . . What do you want me to say? . . . I know that it is the one thing that can satisfy you, the only thing in my letters that could be of any interest to you . . . But I'm going to confess something very strange to you . . . as I said, whenever I want to talk about God, I can't think of anything to say. When I think about Him, I am stupefied . . . I don't know how to explain it . . . but the truth is I can't think of anything to say.

I just wish I could transfer my entire soul onto paper. When I see how paltry my words are, I become overwhelmed . . . such little things, for so great a purpose . . . But anyway, if you've ever received a spark or two, it's been without my knowledge . . . Or rather, I do know about it, but . . . I don't know how to explain myself. It's easy for me to get excited when I write you about God, because I know that I'm not speaking into the void, because I know that you understand me. I know that you receive this love I have for God—which whether it be great or small, is true . . . Don't you laugh at me, or act all *surprised* . . . it's only natural, the way I can pour out my soul to you . . . it happens on its own. These suppressed shouts reach God; yes, I do believe they reach Jesus . . .

You alone know so many things about me and God, so many things that the world would laugh at if they found out. The world doesn't know what it is to love God, it just doesn't, it has no clue . . . but you do. That fills me with joy, and consoles me more than you know.

In La Trapa, in silence with my brothers . . . all my affection for God, all the love contained in my soul, will rise up to God in silence and through Our Lady's intercession. But it has been Jesus' desire in these last few days to show me clearly that there are souls in this world who may not be in a convent, but they too suffer and rejoice and want nothing more than to love . . . to love God, to melt, to sink ever more deeply into love for God, which is the only reason in the world to exist. How great is the Lord, little sister; look at how He treats us, and you won't even be able to breathe.

Today was a day very much spent *in the world*, very much as a creature . . . I see nothing but creatures who don't know God. It causes me great sorrow. It's all useless conversations, worldly business, material interests . . . nothing about God, nothing about Jesus, nothing about the newborn Child who offers us love in exchange for love. The world doesn't understand these feast days. There's nothing but noise and festivities . . . but human festivities. Nobody is thinking about Mary's anguish, Joseph's tenderness, the Christ Child calling out to humankind from the humble stable with His little arms wide open . . . It pains me. I see Him. As poor and miserable as I am, I want to make up for all the love I don't see in others. It makes me so sad . . .

On the other hand, it fills me with joy. For what have I done, that God should give me a heart that, despite all its faults, can hold a bit of love, a bit of that love that Jesus is so sweetly asking for?

For me, everything is a cause for rejoicing and suffering . . . and when I find myself like this . . . alone . . . alone with my love for God . . . I receive a letter from a creature, from a soul who is a child of God just like me, and amid her hardships and sorrows, she says to me, "Brother, speak to me of God's love . . . write me what you know of God. I ask nothing more, I want nothing more."

What a great consolation, little sister! A consolation only known to those who truly live the intense love for God that makes them say crazy things, and whose souls, no matter how much they want to express, don't know what to say, and fall silent!! . . . What can I say? I can just keep quiet, not knowing what to say . . . So much has been written about love for God . . . so much. The saints have put all their science into their books, and I can't find anything in them that satisfies me. It's all fragments, vague reflections of what love for God truly is . . . And if the saints haven't known what to say . . . then what will we poor souls do?

Oh, little sister! Such things you ask for. You almost cause me to suffer. I can see what you need, I can see how you're doing. I understand that your soul is only asking for love, and knows only how to love . . . and you come asking me, poor man that I am . . . a miserable creature, you ask me for light in order to love Jesus of Nazareth, who just in these past few days came into our world, begging for exactly what you're asking for . . . love.

My poor little sister, look who you've wound up with. God is so good! How happily I go to La Trapa . . . ! I love You so much, Lord, I am so happy, the world doesn't know . . . Sometimes I want to jump up and down, I'm telling you, little sister . . . I'm crazy, I don't know what's happening to me . . . Might that be love for God?

Oh my God, how the angels must be delighting in You in heaven . . . To think that I'll be with them soon, it makes me feel something that essentially makes me forget everything . . . If only you knew, sometimes I laugh inside when I see the pained faces of some people when they learn I'm going to La Trapa . . . They can't conceive of it. They think I've gone mad. It makes me want to shout, "You dimwits, can't you see that I just love Jesus so much? Can't you see that it's God? You don't know what it is to love God! Don't you pity me, don't you cry, don't you go worrying, even if I were to die . . . I'd do it a thousand times over again if I had a thousand lives to live."

How great is the Lord, little sister. What things He does!

Laugh and jump for joy with me. We'll sing carols at the stable, and you'll see, the Child Jesus will laugh too, and He'll reach out to us with His little arms . . . What a joy! The Virgin will laugh too, and the patriarch, Saint Joseph, will look at us. What jubilation we'll bring! . . . The shepherds, the wise men, the stars, and the sky, all will laugh, all will sing. It is Jesus who has been born . . . We'll sing too . . . Leave all your sorrows at the Child's feet, all your worries and joys too, leave everything there . . . and free of it all, with your arms relieved of their burden and your heart clear of its obstacles . . . look at Jesus, little sister. He asks nothing of you. He wants only for you to love Him a little, show Him a little tenderness . . .

Let us sing with all creation, the animals and plants . . . Jesus is laughing, and so is Mary. Let's help our Blessed Mother forget Her woe when She was abandoned by others, when She and Joseph did not find shelter . . . Let's help Mary forget Her sorrows. Let us love Her Son, don't let Him get cold . . . Let's not make noise, He's sleeping . . . it's Jesus, the blessed Child . . . He was just born and He loves us already, He knows us already. . . . His pale little face is already smiling . . . What great tenderness, sister! Let us keep quiet, for Jesus is sleeping, and He is sleeping in our arms . . . ! What a joy! How sweet His breathing is . . . ! Mary is looking at us. She is not afraid to leave Him with us, because She knows that we love Him, and that we are cradling Him in our arms with tremendous affection . . . How sweet this Child is! And this Child Jesus is God . . . He is our God.

Oh, dear sister, what a great joy it is to have a God like ours.

Forget everything. Let nothing worry you. Sing carols, but sing them in your heart, without anyone else being able to overhear . . . you'll see, it'll be good. This newborn Child loves you so much! Don't tell Him about your sorrows, leave those for you . . . just give Him love, nothing but love. You'll see, He'll laugh and give you hugs, and the Virgin will help you . . . Love, love, that's what Jesus wants.

Well, I'll leave it there for now because it's getting very late. I'm going to fall asleep thinking about everything I just said to you . . . Blessed be God, how happy I am.

December 28

I have nothing but reasons to praise God. It is noon on a splendid day. I took the car out alone, stopped at an overlook, and thinking of God, being reminded of you, I delight in writing.

How great You are, Lord, in Your works! . . . You have made all this for me . . . the earth, the sky, the birds, such peace in the air! . . . Lord, if people saw You in creation, if they looked up occasionally at the sky You created, I'm sure that they would be better people . . . It's impossible to be a bad person while loving the countryside, the sea, the works of Your hands. Lord, if people loved You, how happy the world would be. How great You are, Lord!

My dear little sister, right now I lack the words to share with you this peace I have . . . With all my heart, I wish the same for you. When I think of God for any reason . . . I am so utterly flooded that death would seem small by comparison.

Why, Lord, are You keeping me here? Everything speaks to me of what You are, everything points me toward You, but it is all a weak reflection of Your goodness and love. It is all the work of Your hands, and that is why I love the whole world . . . but all that . . . it's not You . . . Lord, pay me no mind, understand that sometimes my soul asks for things . . . Lord, silence is best . . . Love and silence.

Sunday, December 29

Yesterday I left this abruptly. I didn't know what to say, and I started to walk along the highway. I wanted to keep writing last night . . . but I was with my father and brothers until very late . . . I can't wait for these days to be over . . . I'm somewhat uncomfortable at home . . . Every time my mother looks at me, she gets sad, I can tell, even though she doesn't say anything. Yesterday I told my father that I didn't want to delay my departure. As soon as I've finished with the dentist, I'm going to decide. I'd been thinking January 8 . . . we'll see.

Pray for me, little sister. This *slow goodbye* to everything . . . is somewhat hard on me, and sometimes I sin against patience, it can't be helped.

I won't write you very much today, because I want this letter to go out today.

I don't know how you'll interpret these messy letters of mine, but you'll have to manage it. It's all ups and downs, and until I find myself with a bit of silence again and the troubled waters of my soul are made still, that's all I will be able to do.

For today, then, I'll leave you, until next time. Through the Virgin Mary, receive all my affection as your brother,

Brother María Rafael, O.C.S.O.

94. To María Osorio

Oviedo, December 29, 1935

J-H-S

My dearest sister in the Lord,

I am beginning another letter now that it is evening. As you can see, this'll sound more like a diary than anything else.

This afternoon, I thought about you a lot while I was at prayer. I went to the Dominican chapel at seven, because they keep it open until nine.

When I left the house, I was a bit sad, because I was going alone. It was entertainment time, and I felt like a stranger in the crowd. Everyone was busy with the cinema and theater, and meanwhile, the Lord was waiting all alone in the tabernacle . . . It caused me great sorrow. The world doesn't know that Jesus is among us . . . it doesn't know that Christ is in the tabernacle and does nothing but wait for His children to come over for a little while to be with Him . . . even if it's just for a minute. What a shame, little sister. What a shame.

I saw that the Lord was alone in the tabernacle, and I found myself alone too as I went to keep Him company.

But then suddenly everything changed. It was as if the angels were guiding me through the streets . . . they encouraged me and told me not to worry, that it was in prayerful recollection that I could be pleasing to God . . . and that I should be very happy, because it was God and Mary who were calling me . . . that I should leave these creatures be, and that there was no comparison between what the Lord was going to give me at His side and what the world was so eagerly searching for—diversion, delight for the senses, etc.

If only you could have seen it. I was so encouraged by this that I started to cross through the streets without even realizing it. I united myself to the angels and told them, "You're right, God is so good, I am so happy."

I spent an hour at church, most of it with Our Lady . . . If only you knew, little sister, how much She loves me. I thought of you. I was deep in recollection. It had been a long time since I had been like that. Tomorrow I'm going to go back at the same time. It's Our Lady of the Rosary. She's holding the Child Jesus in her arms, and She's in a side chapel that's very well cared for by the confraternity.[1]

By the way, during my last few moments there, a girl went up to the altar on her knees, and when she reached it, she held out her arms in a cross, and I heard her crying as she looked up at the Virgin. I nearly cried too. She must have had a very great sorrow that she was bringing before Our Lady. I was greatly edified, and I also prayed that the Virgin would hear her . . . I believe that She will. If only you knew, the Virgin is so good. There is no sorrow She will not sweeten, and no joy She will not sanctify . . .

I'm telling you, if we always turned to Mary, things would be different for us. She has always been helpful to me, in so many things; I owe nearly everything to her, including my vocation. Loving Mary is so sweet! . . . You'll see, the Virgin will resolve your concerns for you, I'm sure of it. Look, you have to come help me by Her side. Two heads are better than one, don't you think?

In your last letter, you mentioned that you were experiencing some nervousness, perhaps of a physical origin. I don't know about that, but look, don't deceive yourself . . . Can you not master yourself? I think you can, give it a try, once, twice . . . twenty times. You'll see, it'll pass . . .

A year ago, one of my confessors told me the same thing. He said I had a nervous imbalance because of the Revolution.[2] Maybe, but I never believed it . . . I would enter a church and not be able to stay there, it would make me too anxious. Everything irritated me. One time I went to confession crying because I *couldn't* make my examination of conscience, and I felt like such a sinner.

Do you know what convinced me there was no such physical disorder? Well it's very simple: that would only happen with things concerning God and religion, while I never got agitated about *anything else*. Try to follow this. For example: if I had to perform an act of patience or charity toward my neighbor, I could not do it . . . everything irritated me on the inside,

---

1. Confraternity: An association of laypeople, often under the patronage of a particular saint or title of Jesus or Mary (in this case, Our Lady of the Rosary).

2. During the Revolution of 1934, Rafael witnessed a great deal of violence and destruction in Oviedo (see #55, n. 1, and #56, n. 10).

and nothing came out right. On the other hand, if it was an action that was pleasing or flattering to me in some way . . . then I could be normal . . . That is, I was normal and ordinary when it came to the things of this world and its diversions, but on the other hand, I had this stupid nervous anxiety when it came to the things of God. No, my confessor was wrong, I could tell right away. He said that it was because of my illness, having to leave the monastery, my sister, those nine days of fires and looting, etc. Well, sure, that's all true, but in that case I would have gone <u>entirely</u> crazy, not just *partially* . . . right?

It passed, just as everything passes, even the temptations that God permits to go as far as they do . . . Don't pay me any mind, but I think you possess a great ability to endure suffering (well, you don't possess it, it has been given to you) . . . Consider what is happening to you carefully, and don't let the same thing happen to you that happened to me.

Well, don't take that too literally . . . Pay me no mind. The Lord deals with our souls according to our needs, which are not all the same. But sometimes we use one thing as a pretext to fall into something else entirely, and we shouldn't do that . . . Instead, turn to Our Lady, so that She can tell you what you ought to do. I'm sure you'll recover your usual composure, despite it all.

The clock has just struck twelve, so I'm going to leave it there, because I'm a bit sleepy. I'll continue tomorrow, Monday, when I'm expecting a letter from you . . . Now that I'm thinking about it, if I can, I'll make my Visit from three to four o'clock on Friday at a solitary tabernacle, and then again at night, from two to three o'clock, at home. Will you do the same? I'm not going to pray for anything or say anything, I'm just going to *be* there, so you can be the one to choose our intention. Are we agreed?

Until tomorrow, little sister, God willing.

December 30

I just came back from being with the Lord . . . I have nothing new to say. It's eight o'clock at night. I received your letter, along with that of Uncle Polín. You can't imagine how much they've cheered me up . . . You are both so good to me! I don't deserve any of it. Truly, not at all worth the effort.

I don't know if I'll be able to write tonight because I have to draw . . . I've got it all prepared now. As I said, it's a Saint Francis of Assisi, patron of the Forest Engineers[3] . . . My father is very excited and wants it to turn out well. It's going to be one of my last drawings, at least at home . . . In La Trapa, who knows. It's all the same to me.

I agree with everything you said in your letter . . . Don't worry about what you choose to discuss with me. You are writing me, and you write about yourself . . . that's only natural, we always let out whatever we're carrying inside, and you shouldn't try to force yourself to talk about something else. Even though you're saying it all to a mere creature, I won't share what you say here with anyone but God. Be at peace, little sister. I am too, and I don't worry about this.

I've just taken up my pen again. I'm telling you, I can't get ten minutes in a row. It's twelve o'clock. I drew for a while . . . and before going to bed . . . I thought, I'm going to write a bit . . .

Just one thing: Don't get too excited about my stay in Ávila. I'm going to try to have us leave Oviedo very early . . . If possible, at dawn . . . The worst thing about it is the question of Holy Mass . . . I don't know, we'll see. On the other hand, my mother . . . Anyway, it'll all be very quick, most likely we won't be able to talk at all. Offer it up to the Lord . . . Don't you think we've talked plenty already? . . . Oh poor little sister, one can never exhaust the subject of God, isn't that so? But don't you worry. The souls of those who love God are forever united, and often, words tarnish feelings . . .

Be generous, my dear sister. What's it to us, so long as the silence we offer serves God? You'll see, one day, when you come to La Trapa . . . we won't even be able to speak. Or maybe we'll talk each other's ears off, who knows! . . . Let us do each day's work and nothing more . . . Today I can write you, so I write you. Tomorrow I can see you, so I'll see you. After that . . . well, is that up to us? . . . Everything is so fleeting.

I'm so glad about your state of mind . . . Don't let the storms and squalls trouble you. You have Mary, don't you? . . . Of course, it would be easier to lead a calm life, never offending God, a life without complications as you'd say . . . But do you have any now? . . . Is loving God that complicated? . . . Please, little sister. How could we lead *calm* lives, possessing what we possess? . . . It would be impossible . . . We can't let our love for God sit still . . . More, always . . . always more. We must never

---

3. See the image at the end of this letter, which Rafael painted in watercolor for his father.

abandon the fight, even if it's difficult . . . The day will come when we can truly possess that still, calm love . . . But on that day, we'll be in heaven. In the meantime, let's not seek out calmness. Let's never stop. Let's keep moving forward, fighting against ourselves in order to banish that "self" who does us so much harm . . .

Let us love God more and more, always . . . Let us not settle for less. And if one day we catch fire . . . isn't that what we are looking for? . . . We're going to follow Jesus, we're going to follow in His footsteps . . . and Jesus didn't rest . . . even after His death, they thrust a spear into His side.

I know what you'll say, because I know you . . . "But if only a little bit is enough for me . . . but if I'm satisfied with just a crumb . . ." Yes, little sister, yes. At first, a crumb is enough. But soon, the whole loaf won't fill you up . . . Don't put obstacles in the Lord's way. Let Him work . . . Don't you go thinking it's arrogant or lacking humility to court His love . . . and to court His love in abundance, in excess, until it undoes you completely . . . The other way is easier, more comfortable, perhaps more comforting.

But let's not seek out comfort . . . We'll have it in the end. Meanwhile, let's be generous . . . Let us open our hearts to God without reservation, without holding anything back. Between God and Mary, may He do what He wishes with us . . . If suffering, then suffering; if rejoicing, then rejoicing. What's it to us? . . . God is great and we are nothing.

Don't you worry. You'll see, the day I give you a hug and head off to La Trapa, there won't be any tears . . . we don't suffer. Why? We'll proclaim that *sursum corda* I like so much, and you'll see how joyfully you respond[4] . . . "Yes, brother, yes, go in peace . . . My heart has been lifted up to the Lord . . ." And that's all. Then, if our eyes of flesh saw with the eyes of faith, we'd see all the choirs of angels singing to the Lord with great rejoicing upon seeing that here on earth, despite all its misery, there are still a few hearts that belong to God alone. And Our Lady will rejoice, and She will help us so much that we'll almost physically feel it. You'll see.

Well, that's all for now. I'm going to bed. I don't want to keep my head in the clouds like a fool . . . Like I said before, let us do each day's work and nothing more, and all through the Virgin Mary, always.

---

4. *Sursum corda*: "Lift up your hearts"; in the Mass, it prompts the response "We lift them up to the Lord" (see #63, n. 3).

I'll barely have time to write you even a quick note tomorrow, and besides, if I do manage to write one I'd like it to be addressed to Uncle Polín. So, be satisfied with what your little brother is sending you for today, which is all his love,

Brother María Rafael, O.C.S.O.

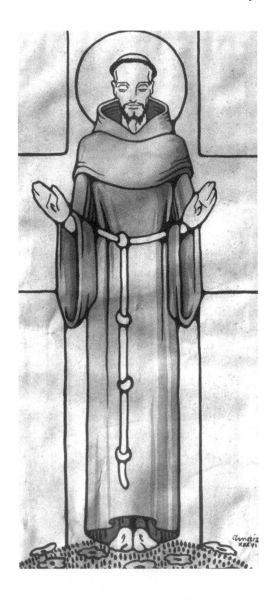

95. To Fr. José Olmedo[1]

Oviedo, January 3, 1936

J-H-S

My dear Father Master,

At last, the day approaches when I will return to my beloved Trapa once more. We still have not set the date, but it will be approximately after Epiphany. In any case, I'll give you a few days' notice.

For now, I merely request that you inform me as to what I should bring in terms of clothing . . . I remember what I brought last time, but not in detail.

I wanted to ask if I can bring books that I use for prayer and meditation . . . It would be about three or four, but I can also go without them. It is up to you.

I would also appreciate it if you could ask Br. Ramón which books he asked his brother Juan for when they saw each other a few days ago.[2] His family has asked me to inquire if he needs anything else, so that I can bring it for him.

As for my "papers" or documents, everything is already at the monastery.

I have nothing else to tell you, dear Father . . . just that I am counting the days until I am back in the community. I just ask you to tell the novices, and I ask this of you as well, to remember my poor self in prayer in the coming days, for I am battling many things right now . . . and truly, I need it. Although I can assure you that the Virgin Mary is helping me . . . in the way only She knows how.

---

1. Father José Olmedo Arrieta (1892–1967) replaced Fr. Marcelo León as master of novices at San Isidro on July 7, 1935, after the latter had fallen ill. Unlike his predecessor, Olmedo did not have any particular affection for Rafael and was not in favor of his re-admission into La Trapa (OC 569).

2. Br. Ramón Vallaure Fernández-Peña was a novice at La Trapa (see #38, n. 2), and his brother Juan was Rafael's close friend (see #9, n. 5).

Give Father Abbot and the whole community my regards, and those of my parents. Counting on your blessing and your prayers, your novice,

Brother María Rafael
O.C.S.O.

96. To W. Marino del Hierro[1]

Oviedo, January 3, 1936

My dear friend and brother Marino,

What must you think of me? . . . I am ashamed to write you, but you must forgive me. This year has been such that it would've been impossible for me to have anything to say to you . . . I've picked up my pen to write you a few times . . . but I couldn't. Maybe you won't understand . . . but I haven't even written to La Trapa.

Now things are different, and I'm only writing you to say goodbye . . . around January 8 or 10, I'll be returning to the monastery . . . Of course, I'm thrilled . . . Toribio sends his regards . . . I'm not completely recovered yet, and I have to keep following my diet . . . I'll carry on with it there, and I'll never leave again . . . if we ever meet, blessed be God, and if not, I'll see you in heaven.

Forgive this poor soul who has behaved so poorly toward you, but nevertheless begs the Virgin to help you with whatever you need . . . I won't forget.

I have nothing more to say . . . as you can see, it's rather little.

A big hug from your good friend and brother in Jesus and Mary,

Br. M. Rafael

1. W. Marino del Hierro was an acquaintance of Rafael's by way of their mutual friend Toribio Luis Arribas. Under his religious name, Brother Tescelino, Arribas was the assistant infirmarian at San Isidro during Rafael's first stay at La Trapa (see #44, n. 1).

97. To María Osorio

Oviedo, January 3, 1936

J-H-S

My dearest little sister,

I received your letter, and you have no idea how pleased I am that Pilar is doing better. Of course, it's a long road . . . but the Lord will resolve everything . . . you'll see.

Yesterday I sent Uncle Polín some photographs of La Trapa.[1] Juan took them, he's the novice Ramón's brother. Even though they aren't worth anything, I thought Uncle Polín would like them.

Today is Friday, and I went out to take a walk. It's eleven in the morning, and even if it ends up just being a quick note, I'm writing you so that this letter can go out today. I have nothing new to tell you . . . This afternoon I'll go to the Salesian church,[2] and from there, I'll help you however I can.

Today I wrote to Father Master to firm up the details of my departure . . . I'm a bit impatient, it can't be helped, but I'm telling you, I consider myself the happiest man on earth . . . Yesterday, when I left after spending time with Our Lady, I was half mad as I left the church . . . Although I'm telling you, my prayer is very strange . . . I don't know how to pray. Time just flies by while I think about La Trapa, and think about how the Lord is waiting for me . . . and how Mary is waiting for me, and how the angels are waiting for me in the choir there, and honestly not knowing how to thank the Lord for all His benefits[3] . . . I begin to feel such a great joy, and I don't know what to do.

---

1. If Rafael included a letter with the photographs he sent his uncle, it has not been preserved.

2. The Church of the Sacred Heart of Jesus (see note on the Salesian church in #75, n. 15).

3. *Bless the Lord, O my soul, and do not forget all his benefits* (Ps 103:2).

At home everyone is very calm and content. Nothing is difficult for the Lord. I can assure you that He is the one doing everything.

Listen, little sister, I'm very glad that you're getting your usual peace back, a little at a time. Of course, I think they're temptations. Ask Our Lady to help you, and you'll see, everything will pass.

Listen, I'm going to leave it there for now. I'm writing from inside the car, it's splendidly sunny out . . . and extraordinarily peaceful. I'm going to take a walk along the road. Later, at twelve o'clock, I'll make my Visit. After I get back from prayer, I'll continue writing for a bit this afternoon. Then I'll go to the dentist. Then I'll go back to the Dominican chapel for some more prayer time. Then tonight, at two o'clock, I'll come to your assistance again . . . My God, how boring I am.

I just came home and got your letter . . . may God reward you for everything. . . you poor thing, I'm still laughing. . . blessed be God.

Look, in accordance with today's intention, I'll do as you said . . . As for what I'd like for dinner, I'll tell you soon. Don't lose your patience on me, but I'll tell you in detail, even down to the wine . . . You're so funny. God reward your generosity.

My family's coming home now. Talk to you soon.

January 4

My dearest sister,

Today, January 4, I'll continue. Yesterday it was impossible for me to string even two sentences together. I felt really bad, because I wanted you to get this letter today.

I did everything just as I said before, although my nighttime Holy Hour turned into a holy half hour. It turned out that I didn't go to bed, so by two-thirty, I physically could not stay awake. Anyway, I do what I can.

I have so many things I'd like to write you, plus everything you asked about . . . but I'm telling you, I'm getting more scatterbrained by the day . . . Nothing to be done about that.

Yesterday I was talking with my parents and we agreed that if I finish up with the dentist on Tuesday, I'll leave Wednesday or Thursday.[4]

---

4. Ultimately, Rafael left Oviedo on Thursday, January 9, with his father and brother Leopoldo.

Fernando is leaving for Leuven on Monday, January 6. What's happening is that we're all really feeling our impending separation . . . so we're *all* getting antsy for things to get back to normal. I'm going to write you yet another letter; I don't know what for, but anyway, you understand, right?

I'm *impossible* these days, whether I'm up or down, though generally I'm always down. Our Lady permits this, may She be blessed. She wants me to absorb everything, and She has heightened my sensitivity. I'm wound tighter than a guitar. You'll be able to forgive me, won't you?

It's very hard for me to leave home, but on the other hand, I long to. Anyway, God alone.

Oh, little sister, I can't think of anything to say . . . God and God alone . . . I don't know . . . the world is so clingy.

Anyway, just reply to me one last time . . . just to this letter, if it can be called that. But don't write me after that, because we might miss each other, and I wouldn't receive it either here or there, and I don't want your letters to *get lost*, do you understand? But mine are another matter, I'll keep telling you everything until the very last minute, even if you already know it all.

Is my grandmother in Ávila? I thought about writing Uncle Polín, but I didn't. Tell him so . . . I'll see him in a few days.

Well, don't you worry on my account. I'm a bit selfish, and not at all generous. God wills it thus, or at least He permits it. I seem empty, don't I?

Well, I have nothing else to tell you. Help me a little before Our Lady of the Rosary. I go to be with Her every afternoon, and if only you knew how much She encourages and helps me . . .

I can't say anything more. I'm sending you so many things in this letter, just not with words, which aren't coming to me today. It doesn't matter, it's all the same.

I'll tell you what I want for dinner soon.

A very big hug from your brother,

Brother María Rafael, O.C.S.O.

98. *To María Osorio*

Oviedo, January 4, 1936

J-H-S

My dearest little sister,

Just like the other day, I'm starting this letter in the waiting room at the dentist's. Sometimes I have to spend a lot of time waiting, and this way I'm using it well.

I got your letter, and Uncle Polín's. I knew he'd like the photos.

Listen, don't worry about being left all alone, as you said. When you truly want to love and serve God, you are never alone . . . You'll see, He'll arrange things so that you find help, *if you need it*. That is, if according to Him you need it, not according to *you*. Understand? . . . We poor creatures know and understand nothing on that front . . . and we are generally mistaken, believing we see a need when perhaps there isn't one. Don't you think so?

During this time, which we can now say has come to an end, we've helped each other . . . We'll always have, or at least I will, the memory of God's tenderness, which comes to us when we aren't expecting it, and often from whom we least expect it . . . What's that to us? Creatures are nothing more than a means, and God is the end.

So remain calm, don't worry, the Lord never abandons His children, least of all His most beloved children . . . and have no doubt, we are among them . . . and I'm not being presumptuous. I don't think that because of my merits. I'm just utterly convinced that the Lord loves me very much, I don't know why.

It's as I said, the help we've given one another came to us from Him. If He's taking it away from us now, it's because we don't need it anymore . . . When He treats us like this, it's because He has seen that we are frail and weak . . . and since He loves us, He helped us, He used others to give us light for our path . . . He strengthened us on the cross, He stretched our hearts so that we could love Him, He consoled us as He does the weak. What is there left to do now? Nothing, little sister. Don't stop, remember not to "gather flowers" and keep advancing in love. That is what the Lord wanted to show us. Did we learn it? Yes, of course . . . let's go then. During my first few days at La Trapa, they taught me how to use the hoe . . . Once I'd learned how, they left me on my own.

Now it's the same thing. The Lord gave us a lesson. He showed us how to use the tool with which we are to work, and that is love . . . Well then, now let's love, and nothing more. Don't worry about all the details, they're insignificant.

If you ever fail, then the divine Master will once more lovingly attend you, and once more He'll give you what He gave you just now. Don't ask Him; He already knows what you need and when you need it.

Listen, little sister, if you really believe that I've helped you, you're mistaken. I know you don't see it this way . . . but in order to *complete* God's work, you need to move past me, because I am nothing . . . Don't think about me except to pray for me from time to time . . . And if you have affection toward me, take it away from me and give it to God. Don't think I'm being harsh. As a *human* creature, it's hard for me to say that to you . . . but as a Trappist, who is also human, but has a bit more of God's spirit, I beg it of you.

His work must be completed. No longer look to me for consolation that I cannot give you. I'd rather you ask the help of God, whom you love so much . . . Don't expect *anything* from human beings, even the holiest among them, because the more you expect of them . . . the greater your disappointment will eventually be.

Place your hope in God, your consolation in God, and all your love in God. Then you'll see, nothing will be difficult for you, not even loneliness, because being alone with God . . . may in fact be the summit of the mount. Do you know what I mean?[1]

Today I wasn't able to go see the Virgin. I finished up with the dentist at nine, and then I came home. He told me we'd be finished on Monday. We'll see if I can leave here on Tuesday or Wednesday. I'm still waiting for a letter from La Trapa. I'm telling you, sometimes I get a bit nervous. It can't be helped. Sometimes I even start physically shaking.

---

1. Rafael is referring to the "mount of perfection" envisioned by Saint John of the Cross, a text that he and María had discussed before (see #40, n. 3).

Little sister, it's turning out to be so difficult for me to master my poor nature . . . anyway, that's of no importance.

In order to demonstrate that I'm exactly as you want me to be, I'll tell you what we're going to have for dinner: exactly what I have for dinner every day. I don't want to deviate from my diet. Any vegetable, maybe green beans with tomatoes or boiled cabbage; whatever vegetable you want. Then I have a soft-boiled egg, and then either meat or fish, either is fine. A glass of any wine (nothing special), some water, and no bread. Most days I don't eat dessert, what for? And if I do, I have an apple.

As you can see, it's pretty simple. If I weren't sick, just the vegetable and glass of wine would be enough for me, I can assure you. But anyway, it doesn't worry me in the slightest. It's God's will that I can't do that right now, so, very well then . . . I'll humble this poor body by treating it well. Since it already knows exactly how much it deserves, I'll make it blush with shame.

As you can see, you can do penance by eating chicken just as well as you can do it by eating root vegetables . . . It's a matter of doing so with great love for God. Don't you think? You'll do this for me, won't you? Remember who it is you're having over for dinner, just a poor man passing through this world, stopping by in order to be able to continue on his way. Don't you worry about him.

What a poor man I am . . . If only you knew how grateful I am for your gentleness toward me. The Lord gives us such gifts! Isn't it true, little sister, that the cross is gentle? Of course it is. I can't complain. I won't stop to gather flowers, but I will smell them, and I'll thank the Lord for them from the depths of my soul. Not everything is thorns, not everything is tears. It's just that everything is necessary to create harmony in God's works. Everything is so good! Not a single detail is missing . . . and when the Lord grants us the light we need to be able to appreciate them . . . I can assure you, it brings great joy. The Lord made the night, but He added stars . . . if someone is short-sighted, perhaps they just can't see the stars.

May Jesus always grant us light to see, and ears to hear.

January 5

My dear little sister,

It is currently one-thirty in the morning. We all went to our rooms late, because we have to get up at the crack of dawn tomorrow. Fernando is leaving, and we have to go hear Holy Mass beforehand.

I haven't had time to write you even a sentence or two today, and it'll get harder and harder by the day. Still, I won't fail to put down a few words for you today.

My father is somewhat sad . . . Fernando will be the first one to leave. With every passing hour . . . what am I telling you this for? God alone.

I am so happy to see how gentle sorrows become when they are directed toward and focused on God . . . Thanks to Mary, under whose special protection this home rests, we are carrying on with a spirit that must truly be pleasing to God . . .

Pardon my selfishness, sister. What else could I talk to you about right now, other than my parents and brothers and sister? I am neither affectionate nor forthcoming . . . but I can see clearly that God has given me a heart for two things only: first and foremost, in order to love Him, and Him alone . . . and also to suffer. I'm very happy, little sister, as God knows . . . I'm not complaining. It is a special grace that He is working in me. Blessed be God.

I don't know if I have come to love suffering. I don't think so. But on the other hand, I'm telling you, despite my very human tears, I wouldn't trade positions with anyone for anything . . . I am happy, despite all my great weaknesses . . . And the more wretched and less generous I am, the more I love God, and the more motivated I am to follow this path that terrifies me somewhat when I consider it from a human perspective. But then I look at the Virgin, I look at the world, I contemplate God, and all those tears, bitter though they may be, fill me with peace, because they are for Him and they reach Him. And then . . . what can I say? The world seems small to me. I disappear, and God alone remains . . . God, little sister. Do you know who He is? Do you know what He is?

Blessed be He who permits that we creatures lack the words to speak of God and His love, because if we had the words, no matter how lofty they might be, they would shed no light at all. I have nothing to say. Take my meaning . . . I cannot explain anything to you. Who am I, a poor human being, to even try?

I've spoken of God in all my letters to you . . . but I still haven't told you a *thing*, don't you see? You don't need me to try anymore, do you? . . . I've done what I can, and now that I am going to fall silent, I can see that I have done nothing at all . . . I've fumbled for feeble words, made myself *nervous* from time to time, and nothing . . . Well, what I mean is, perhaps what I *have not been able to say* managed to bring you closer to God than all my idle words, which were a creature's words and thus imperfect. But it doesn't matter.

Now, in the silence of my Trapa, you'll understand me better. I won't be able to say anything to you, but whenever you think of me, know that this is always what I'd say to you: "Rise, sister, have no fear . . . love God . . . fly toward Him, rest in Him . . . don't look down, don't look at yourself . . . love God with abandon, for He is already near . . . so little time remains. Let's not waste time on commentary or explanations, leave behind even the writings of the saints . . . they have *nothing* to say . . . *nothing* . . . Forget everything but God . . . God. Oh, little sister! Do you know who He is? . . .

Never mind suffering, never mind rejoicing, what's it to you? . . . God alone suffices.[2] He fills all things, He has to bury us in His love . . .

Lord, Lord, how is it even possible to have a conversation? What could we human beings have to say?

We must be silent, little sister, not because our words might taint what *cannot* be tainted, but rather because unless we are silent, we cannot . . . we do not receive Him, either in our miserable bodies or souls. What more reason do we need? That's why you can't imagine how *thrilled* I am to have to fall silent . . . Only you know, and even if the whole world knew, who cares? . . . I don't.

Rest assured that with whatever strength I have, be it great or little, from the *silence* of my Trapa I am shouting out to you, "Sister, love God! . . . . Let yourself be loved and do nothing more! . . . Oh soul of God who is longing to give yourself over to Him . . . what are you waiting for? Why are you suffering? . . . Why are you crying? . . . Why are you laughing? Don't let any of that rattle you or bother you. Immerse yourself in that Love . . . rise up and fly toward Him, and if you fall . . . what does it matter? You're the one who is falling, and you are nothing. Get back up again, and get back to flying . . . with God you can do anything, all is forgotten" . . . There are no words, little sister. There are no words. There

---

2. From a poem by Saint Teresa of Ávila: "Let nothing trouble you, / Let nothing scare you, / All is fleeting, / God alone is unchanging. / Patience / Everything obtains. / Who possesses God / Nothing wants. / God alone suffices" ("Efficacy of Patience," in *Collected Works*, trans. Kieran Kavanaugh and Otilio Rodríguez [Washington, DC: ICS Publications, 1976], 3:386).

is only one, which is love. And when that love refers to God . . . silence is best. Am I making sense? I have so much going on inside.

I don't know when I'll finish this letter. I wanted it to be my last one, and to include when I'll be coming to Ávila . . . I'll wait, and so will you.

I'll leave it there for now. I'm off to bed. Tomorrow, which is Epiphany, I'll go adore the Child Jesus, and I'll offer Him . . . what I always do . . . Until tomorrow, my dear little sister in Jesus and Mary.

January 6

My dear little sister,

We just saw Fernando off. Poor kid . . . he's going so far away . . . I'm a bit restless today, I'm waiting on a letter from Venta de Baños and I don't know if it'll get here . . . Of course, I am expecting your letter. I don't know what to say . . . I'm very boring. There are days when I feel so worn out . . . I don't know why.

My mother is very sad . . .

Lord, Lord, Your will be done . . . Forgive me, I've only just started and I'm already going to leave you again . . . I'll keep going later.

January 7

Yesterday, my dear sister, I had a very bad day. I spent the whole afternoon with horrible mouth pain . . . I was hardly myself . . . I'm doing better today.

I still can't tell you when exactly I'm coming, because I haven't gotten a letter from La Trapa yet . . . I was expecting it again today, but it didn't arrive. Instead, I got one from you . . . Look, I don't want to make any comments. I'll just say that I very much liked what you said about the Virgin Mary . . . How great the Lord is . . .

Since I don't want this letter to go on any further, I'm going to send it to you today. As soon as I learn the date of my departure, I'll send you a telegram to let you know as soon as I can, just as Uncle Polín asked.

I have nothing more to say . . . With all my great affection, your brother in Jesus and Mary,

Rafael

99. To Fr. José Olmedo

Oviedo, January 7, 1936

My dear Father Master,

Just a quick note to let you know that once I have resolved all my concerns in Oviedo, I await only a letter from you with the instructions I requested before setting off for my Trapa.

Since I fear that my letter most likely has not reached you, I will take the liberty of reminding you that all I wanted to know was what clothes I should bring, and whether I could bring books, and which books Br. Ramón asked for so that I can bring them for him.

I'll be coming by car with my father and brother. I'll stop by Ávila beforehand to say goodbye to my aunt and uncle . . . I can't wait until I'm back in my monastery again for good.

There are so many things I'd like to tell you . . . but why bother? I'll tell you everything when I'm there.

Please pray often to the Virgin for me, and give my regards to Father Abbot. Counting on your blessing, your future novice,

Brother María Rafael, O.C.S.O.

100. Dedication of a Holy Card
to Mercedes Barón Torres

Oviedo, January 9, 1936

J-H-S

My dearest mother,

I am going to La Trapa . . . but I go very happily, because I go "seeking my Love," as the poem by Saint John of the Cross says.[1]

What more can I say?

I long to remain somewhat hidden from others . . . but for you, I'll always be your beloved son, who, at the Virgin Mary's feet, hopes to follow the path described in that poem by Saint John of the Cross. No gathering flowers, and no fearing wild beasts.

May Mary enlighten us, and may Jesus grant us the grace to bring our journey to a happy end. That is my prayer for both of us. Your son, the Trappist,

Brother María Rafael, O.C.R.

---

1. "Seeking my Love / I will head for the mountains and for watersides / I will not gather flowers, / nor fear wild beasts; / I will go beyond strong men and frontiers" (SJC 471) (see #70, n. 1).

101. Dedication of a Holy Card
to Leopoldo Barón Torres[1]

Ávila, January 10, 1936

J-H-S

I wanted to leave so many things for you here . . . but why bother?
. . . I've renounced everything I have . . . as you well know, and it's all
gone up to God.

Turn to Him, and in Him you'll find me . . . I have nothing else to
offer you, for of what use to you is my human affection?

Today, on this red-letter day, I have nothing to say to you, and nothing to leave here for you. Our Lady will do it on my behalf, as only She
knows how.

God alone!

Brother María Rafael

1. During his visit to Ávila on his way back to La Trapa, Rafael wrote this dedication to
his uncle on the back of the holy card he'd painted for him, "Knowing How to Wait" (OC
5; see #87 and accompanying image).

V. The Circus Clown

The Last One in the Community

102. *To Rafael Arnaiz Sánchez de la Campa*

La Trapa, January 14, 1936

J-H-S Ave Maria
My dearest father,

Reverend Father Abbot gave me permission to write you because I need my things for drawing. I'm very happy and doing very well . . . For now they don't let me participate completely in all the community activities; Reverend Father wants me to take it slowly. I eat and sleep in the infirmary, and during work hours, I help the infirmarian. There are so many things I would tell you, but that's not the purpose of this letter . . . I'll tell you everything later.

Did you arrive safely in Oviedo? How are Mamá and Merceditas? Of course, I don't know if you are in Oviedo or Burgos . . .

Well, the situation is that Reverend Father has asked me to take on a line drawing, so if you don't mind, I need you to send me a few things I have back home. Here's the list:

By registered mail, and tied simply with a string, a finished wood panel, which I believe is on top of the white armoire.

A long straightedge.

A 50-centimeter or 40-centimeter ruler.

A triangular scale ruler, in its cardboard case (green).

A set square.

A ruling pen and a compass.

Two no. 2 pencils, Harmaout brand, or however you spell it.[1]

Two no. 1 pencils: "   "   "   "

A box of thumbtacks and three or four nib pens with their penholder.

Whatever watercolor brushes you can find, and the watercolor palette, and the white porcelain jars, however many there are.

---

1. Koh-i-Noor Hardtmuth is a Czech brand of writing implements and other art materials.

A bottle of India ink, and an inkstick of it as well.

Whatman paper, fine-grained, three sheets or so.

Canson paper, a bit of that . . . well, just take however much of it you think is appropriate from the office, and leave it at that.

I'm so sorry to have to bother you with such a nuisance . . . but there's nothing to be done about that. If I'd known, I'd have brought all that instead of the oil paints.

But look, the rulers, the wood panel, and paper can all be sent registered together, and everything else can just go in a shoebox stuffed with newspaper.

Right now it's six-thirty in the evening, but since they don't let me get up until three-thirty, I'm not sleepy at all.

They gave me a novice's habit, the same one I had before . . . I'm very happy. I'm confident that just by being obedient, I can be completely happy, and with Mary's help, become holy. What more could I ask for?

I'm sure you're all calm and content by now . . . From here, I ask the Lord to make it so.

Well, my dearest father, I'll leave it there for now. I'll write you at greater length another time.

If you're still with my mother . . . what do you want me to say? . . . And if you're just with Leopoldo . . . well, nothing to say to him either. This poor Trappist has so much to send you that it is all reduced to nothing.

Your son, who loves you very much,

Brother María Rafael, O.C.S.O.

103. *To Rafael Arnaiz Sánchez de la Campa*

La Trapa, February 9, 1936

J-H-S Ave Maria

My dearest father,

I'm sure you've been waiting for a letter from me for a while now . . . But look, obedience is what it is, and that is what rules my actions. I'm writing you today because Reverend Father ordered me to tell you, or rather to inform you, about the state of my health, which thanks be to God is very good . . . I am very happy in my cloak and scapular.

When I had just arrived at the monastery, my blood sugar levels rose somewhat, thanks to the days that the Lord had just kindly allowed to pass, if you know what I mean . . . Now my levels are much lower, and on one occasion they even went down to zero . . . I can tell you that I honestly don't concern *myself* with my illness at all. In his charity, Brother Tescelino, the infirmarian, makes up for that . . . He gives me insulin, takes care of me, checks my levels every eight days, weighs me, etc . . . I've gained weight, by the way.

Anyway, I won't say any more about my health, which is the least of my concerns.

Now, time for a bit of news: I start studying Latin tomorrow . . . Up until now, my only work tool has been the broom, because they haven't let me use the hoe . . . but Father Master told me that tomorrow I can go out into the fields with the novices for work time in the afternoon, and I'll do my studies in the morning. They still won't let me get up at two o'clock either, but rather at three-thirty. I will never be able to thank God, first of all, and then my superiors, enough for the charity with which I am being treated . . . Honestly, it often makes me feel embarrassed . . . In truth, I don't even deserve . . . Anyway, pay me no mind.

I received all the supplies you sent me.[1] Happily, I finished what Reverend Father had asked me to do, which was a landscape of the monastery

---

1. See #102, in which Rafael requested various art supplies.

for some postcards . . . I also painted Saint Bernard, but I ended up giving him a bit of a smirk . . . I don't like it.[2]

Anyway, my dearest father, I don't have anything in particular to tell you . . . My life carries on with total tranquility in prayer, at work, and in silence. Now study will intervene, too . . . Everything for God, and with His help . . . what more could I require to be happy? I assure you that I am indeed happy . . . not in the way that the world understands happiness, because for the religious, happiness is found in the cross, for which the world has no love. But look, that's what we're for, right?

Now Spain has asked for our prayers, sacrifices, and penances; we offer them all with pleasure . . . It's not all about political campaigning.[3] Everyone must do what they can . . . and what a Trappist can do is remain in the presence of God, whether to deter His wrath or beg His mercy . . . What a beautiful purpose we have, isn't it? Nobody knows what that means.

Don't think that I've forgotten about you. I think of you all very often. I am determined to help my parents and brothers and sister to . . . well, you can guess . . . Sometimes my prayers go to Oviedo, other times they head for Burgos, and still others for Belgium[4] . . . It's as I said before, all must do what they can, and I can do nothing else.

Look, since it may bring you comfort, I'll tell you that I think of you every day, especially when I pass by the image of Our Lady of Carmel, to whom I know *abuela* Luisa[5] was very devoted, as are you. So anyway, every day, even if it's just a Hail Mary, know that you will be remembered before Our Lady of Carmel as long as I live. I ask Her to enlighten you, to give you faith, to make you holy in the midst of the world, and to help you bear whatever sorrows you might have.

If only you knew, my dear father. All this is so brief, and it's going by so quickly . . . If only I could make everyone see that *there is need of only one thing*,[6] and that everything else . . . Well, what can I say that you don't

---

2. For the postcard image, see p. 389; for Saint Bernard, see p. 395.

3. The Spanish government held a general election on February 16 and 23, 1936.

4. Rafael's father and brother Leopoldo were at home in Oviedo, while his mother Mercedes and sister Merceditas were visiting Burgos. His brother Luis Fernando was studying in Belgium.

5. Luisa Sánchez de la Campa, Rafael's paternal grandmother.

6. Luke 10:42.

already know?...Your Trappist son has nothing to say to you. He will surely not make his vows in the eyes of men, but with each passing day, he grows more Trappist in the eyes of God. What does it matter? It's a question of knowing how to make use of this life, in one way or another. But always with love for God, and seeing ourselves for what we are: pilgrims on this earth. *Our citizenship is in heaven*[7]... Everything else is fleeting. Isn't that so?

Well, I don't want to preach, I'm not ordained yet.

I'm telling you, at 24 years old, Latin's going to be much harder than scrubbing and sweeping. Nothing to be done about that. In chapter today, Reverend Father spoke to us about obedience, and it is clear that he who obeys his superior does the will of God.

Well...I haven't heard a thing about my mother and sister...I suppose they're in Burgos, doing well and being happy. Since I'm not going to write two letters, send this one to my dearest mother. It's for both of you.

Now I'm going to ask you for a favor... Reverend Father Abbot didn't want me to, but I insisted, and he gave me permission to ask you this. He says he doesn't want to take advantage of you, and his civility forbade it, but I'm your son and I don't see anything bad about asking.

It's about Brother Tescelino, the infirmarian I mentioned earlier. The lymph nodes in his neck are swollen, and they've recommended ultraviolet or quartz light, or whatever it's called. They're finding it impossible to get it for him, so I mentioned that you could lend us the lamp we have at home for as long as necessary. You'd be doing a work of mercy, because with the cold these days, Brother is getting worse, and he really needs it. If you come, please bring it, if you haven't sold it already, and when his sessions are finished, you can come get it again, simple as that. Don't you think I did the right thing in asking you? When a friar or monk needs something, first he asks God, and then he asks human beings... Hence "the lips of a friar," as they say[8]... But I'm not just some friar to you, right? I'm your son.

Anyway, I also told Reverend Father that you'd certainly come for Holy Week. He told me that even though you'd wanted to come during Lent,

7. Phil 3:20.

8. In Spanish, the phrase "he's got the lips of a friar" (*le ha hecho la boca un fraile*) refers to someone who is constantly begging for things.

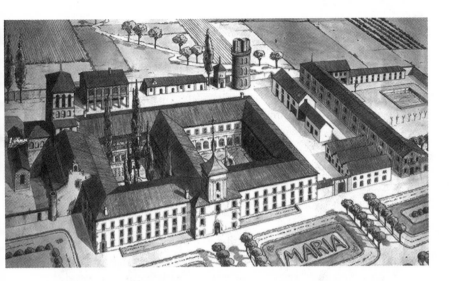

and even though we aren't receiving visitors, since it's you, you would be able to see me[9]. . . . Yet another favor to be thankful for, right? As you can see, the doors of this monastery will always be open to you . . . and I'm very glad about that . . . At first, you don't want to see anyone . . . you're looking for peace, and we can be a bit selfish. That is, listen, you always have to be careful at first, because our nature is weak, and exposing it can lead to trouble. But as time goes by, you come to understand that with God's help you can do all things. As for myself, I can tell you that if I could bring some glory to God in this way, even if I had to visit with people every single day . . . You can come whenever you like.

Today a priest came by, one whom I met in Toro, a former Jesuit, Fr. Joaquín Redín . . . I assisted him at Holy Mass, and then I spent a few minutes with him at the guesthouse. . . . So I lost about half an hour of my day, and I had to pause writing this letter, even though I honestly don't have anything else to tell you. But you know me, when I start writing, I don't know when to stop.

9. Rafael's father stayed at La Trapa from April 9–11, 1936 (Holy Thursday through Holy Saturday). Rafael's mother joined him there on April 11 (Holy Saturday). See OC 600.

If you write me, please do so before Holy Lent, because Reverend Father hasn't told me if he'd give me any letters then.

Have you heard from Fernando? I can assure you that while nothing in the world holds any interest for me, my family certainly does. I came here with the ambition of becoming a saint (woe is me) . . . but I want to be a very human saint (not that I think there are saints who aren't). Just a few words are enough for a good listener, even if those words are a rushed mess. It doesn't matter.

It's true, my dearest father, love for God does not exclude love for creatures. It's a matter of purifying that love and making it holy, and believe me, now I love you all more and better than I did before. I don't know if I'm making sense.

Anyway, I'm going to ask Father Master for more paper because I'm running out. He gave me two more sheets, but I don't know if I'll have enough time to fill them. . . fill them up with words upon words . . . I don't know what I'm saying. I'm doing what I always do, just writing whatever comes to mind in the moment, whether or not it flows from what came before. If I can't be familiar with my parents, who can I be familiar with? I have more free time today, since it's Sunday, and I'm using it to write you.

In a little bit, we'll go down to choir for None, the hour at which our Lord died. Afterwards, all the lay brothers have catechism. By the way, after catechism class the other day (Saint Alberic's feast day),[10] a very holy novice[11] sang to us, both because of obedience and in honor of our patron (Saint Alberic is the patron of lay brothers). Guess what he was singing? That's right, *fandanguillos*.[12]

And he did a very good job indeed. First he looked at the Virgin, and then at Father Master, and he cleared his throat, and with mournful sighs, he burst into song. We had such a good time with that novice . . . If only you knew, he's such a kind soul.

---

10. At the time, Saint Alberic of Cîteaux, one of the founders of the Cistercian Order, was celebrated on January 26. Now all three Cistercian founders are celebrated on that day: Saints Robert of Molesme, Alberic of Cîteaux, and Stephen Harding.

11. Brother Doroteo Martín Renedo (1907–1985); see OC 602.

12. A fandango is a type of Spanish folk song, in addition to a type of dance. A fandanguillo or "little fandango" is a subgenre generally distinguished by its 3/8 time signature.

In fact, sometimes I feel like singing "María de la O," [13] but since we're never alone here, I haven't been able to. Besides, it wouldn't be very edifying for us to sing. Anyway, perhaps these are all weaknesses of ours, but I assure you that the Virgin loves us Trappists very much, weaknesses and all.

How's the Fiat? And what about the Chevrolet, did you sell it already? As you can see, I keep an eye on everything.

We've just finished our catechism class. Now we have an interval,[14] and then Vespers. Then another interval, and then prayer in community for fifteen minutes. Then dinner, and after dinner, another interval which I use for the following: I clear the refectory plates out of the infirmary, sweep up the crumbs, and close the windows. Then I get the lamp ready for the Blessed Sacrament, which we bring up to the infirmary chapel every day to prevent sacrilege, as has been happening nearby.[15] Then I make a short visit to the Virgin, and then it's off to chapter for the recitation of Compline. Then choir, the *Salve*, Father Abbot's blessing, and then, in the peace and grace of God, to bed.

Nearly a month has gone by since I've arrived, and I've hardly noticed. You don't notice time passing here; everything seems so quick.

Tell the Vallaures that Ramón is doing very well and he's very happy . . . and nothing else in particular.[16] Tell me if you know anything about Uncle Polín's situation.

Anyway, my dearest father, I want to put my whole soul into this letter, I want to share everything I am feeling with you . . . What can I tell you about my life that you don't already know? On the outside, my life is the Rule, followed more or less perfectly as a sick person, and on the inside,

13. A flamenco song first recorded by Estrellita Castro in 1935. The title comes from the chorus: "María de la O / what an unhappy gypsy girl you are / even though you've got it all" (OC 602).

14. Intervals: In the monastic schedule, any time not officially assigned to work or prayer is referred to as an interval. Monks and nuns may use this free time as they see fit.

15. In December 1935, Bishop (now Saint) Manuel González García of Palencia ordered the diocese's parishes and monasteries to remove the Blessed Sacrament from their chapels at night for safekeeping in living quarters. This order was in response to a spate of sacrileges committed at night in the area, including desecration of the Eucharist during thefts (OC 603).

16. Br. Ramón Vallaure was a novice at La Trapa (see #64, n. 9), and his brother Juan was Rafael's close friend (#9, n. 5).

my life is God . . . and I wish He were alone, but sometimes creatures sneak in there too . . . nothing to be done about that . . . Or rather, let us praise God for all of it.

He loves us like this . . . weak, wretched, and sometimes very sinful . . . What can be expected of us feeble creatures? . . . I assure you that I will fall into temptations, I will not achieve my goals, and I will not recip-rocate God's goodness toward me . . . but nothing should discourage us . . . On the contrary, the more we come to know what we are, the less we will expect of ourselves, the more we will despise ourselves, and the more we will turn to God . . . With Him we can do all things. Isn't that so?

Anyway, don't listen to me. Pay attention only to my letter's intention, and disregard its words, which are always a bit clumsy, and mine all the more so.

How is Merceditas doing? I imagine she's very happy in Burgos with Uncle Álvaro,[17] who I'm sure is as loving toward her as he always is . . . Tell her that if she's not grumpy anymore, and if they let me, one of these days I'll write her a letter or homily or spiritual talk with jokes and sto-ries. There's a little bit of everything in my writings . . . Blessed be God, a leopard can't change its spots . . . Anyway, my superiors know me by now, and since they have to read these letters, they might as well realize what I am. I'm not embarrassed.

I'll change and improve. The Lord and the Virgin will make it happen. In the meantime, be satisfied with what I am and what I'm like.

Now I'm going to make my visit to the Lord, and then go to Vespers, and then I'll finish up here.

Now we've just come back to the novitiate, after having received Bene-diction with the Most Blessed Sacrament and prayed Vespers. It's a quarter to four, and it's almost dark here . . . These past few days, or rather this whole month, it hasn't stopped raining, and it even rained a little today.

Well, my dearest father, I hardly have anything else to tell you. Pray for me sometime. Pray for my perseverance, and above all, pray that I might be able to reciprocate the enormous graces God gives me. The great respon-

---

17. Rafael's maternal uncle Álvaro Barón Torres and his wife Pepita Conde Merino lived in Burgos.

sibility I have in God's eyes scares me a little sometimes. I am accountable to Him for so many things.

Just like the first time I came here, I imagine you're hearing all sorts of ridiculous things about me . . . Pay them no mind. The world's mottos and maxims are incompatible with the spirit of God. Where people see madness, stupidity, and folly, perhaps Jesus does not . . . and He is the one to whom we must give an account. So then, let us focus on that and that alone. Thank the Lord endlessly that you have a son in La Trapa, in the "school for the Lord's service," as our father Saint Benedict says.[18] What more could you want for me?

I don't want to get tiresome, so I'll leave it there for now, until next time. You can't complain that I write you short letters. But I know you like it when I write, and it feels like rather too little, since I have to pay you back somehow for all I owe you . . . which is everything.

Anyway, forgive your son for . . . I don't know, whatever needs forgiving, there's always something. Give Leopoldo a big hug for me, and send one Fernandillo's way too.[19] Send this letter to my mother. As for you, all my love, your Trappist son,

Brother María Rafael, O.C.S.O.

P.S. My dearest mother,

Everything I said to my father was also for you, so I don't have anything else to say. If you're in Burgos, give my aunt and uncle a hug for me. I'm praying to the Most Blessed Virgin for you all very much; do the same for me.

Does Mercedes have a dog now? If you come to Venta de Baños don't leave it behind, of course . . . And if it's big, that's even better.

Well, I think we've all gone mad . . . I keep thinking of silly things to say. In truth, I'm a very unserious Trappist, especially when it comes to my little sister Mercedes . . . but you'll see, I'm going to come up with a rather beautiful sermon to preach at her when she comes here . . . it'll

18. "Therefore we intend to establish a school for the Lord's service" (RB Prol. 45).

19. Rafael's brother Leopoldo was at home in Oviedo with their father, while his brother Fernando ("Fernandillo") was away at school in Leuven, Belgium.

start with Latin and everything, and end by wishing her eternal glory . . . But of course, when you're dealing with a girl who loves mutts so much . . . what can you expect? Nothing, absolutely nothing. Her stern, terrible Trappist brother might as well go about correcting her . . .

My dear sister, I can hear you saying it now, "Well, I never! Who does that boy think he is? . . . That's the last thing I needed, you coming around here to chat . . . I'm going to go buy a dozen dogs right now." Well, Mercedes . . . no matter what I say, you'll do the opposite, just to be contrary . . .

Anyway, pay me no mind. Be good. Don't make your mother angry. Offer a prayer to the Virgin sometime for your brother . . . Are you still making your meditation?

With hugs for both of you,

Br. M. Rafael

104. To Rafael Arnaiz Sánchez de la Campa

La Trapa, February 18, 1936

J-H-S Ave Maria
My dearest father,

Father Master gave me your letter today. I understand your unease, but I don't think it's quite that bad.[1] Of course, Reverend Father Abbot gave me permission to write you a quick note, due to the *exceptional circumstances* we're living through.

What can I say? . . . Nothing. Don't worry, and to tell you the truth, I don't know anything about what's going on . . . That's what my superiors are for, and rumors are all that reach us in community . . . but from what Reverend Father told me, I don't think there's any reason to fear for now.

I don't know, you're in the world, you know better than I do. But don't worry about me. Revolutions can't touch us Trappists . . . Our treasure is God, our life is God, and fortunately, they can't take God away from us, whether through laws or at the price of our blood . . .

Be calm. Why worry? Everything is a great mercy from God, and humanity cannot go further than He permits them to . . . I promise you that we are all calm. We are still singing to the Lord in choir as always, and, as always, praying only that His will be done.

Reverend Father Abbot told me to thank you for your offer,[2] which he doesn't think he'll need to take you up on . . . If laws persecute us for being disciples of Christ, they'll persecute us just as much there as they

---

1. In the Spanish general elections of February 16, 1936, the left-wing coalition (Frente Popular, or Popular Front) won a majority of the seats in the legislature. The coalition included many politicians who espoused anticlerical policies and, in some cases, anticlerical violence.

2. Rafael's father had offered the monks refuge in his home, should they have needed to flee the monastery because of anticlerical violence.

will here, and wherever we go; for we will always follow the divine Master, and the more persecuted we are, the better.

Anyway, I don't have anything else to say . . . Turn your gaze to heaven, and you'll see, *everything* is merely God's mercy. I suppose you'll get a letter from Father Abbot letting you know we received the lamp.

I don't write unless they tell me to . . . I have to submit to the Rule, and as you know, when you enter religious life, things aren't the same as they are in the world. So don't worry about your son, who may naturally be sad about the situation in Spain, but on a personal level . . . he is so calm . . . God alone suffices[3] . . . besides, you'll see, the Virgin will help us all.

If we're going to fear something, let's fear God's judgment, because that of human beings is of no importance.

Farewell, with a great big hug for you and the same to my mother, brother, and sister, from your son,

Brother María Rafael, O.C.S.O.

---

3. From a poem by Saint Teresa of Ávila: "Let nothing trouble you, / Let nothing scare you, / All is fleeting, / God alone is unchanging. / Patience / Everything obtains. / Who possesses God / Nothing wants. / God alone suffices" ("Efficacy of Patience," STA 3:386).

105. To María Osorio

La Trapa, February 23, 1936

Ave Maria

My dearest sister in the Lord,

The other day, Father Master gave me a letter from you so that I might answer it. Today I'm doing that, although I don't know where to begin.

First of all, I should tell you that my superiors gave me permission to answer you *this one time*[1] . . . I am a child of obedience now, and neither my actions nor my will is at my own disposal any longer . . . That's the first thing the Lord asks of those who give themselves over to Him . . . But look, don't worry. When you get a letter from me, it'll be because God, by means of my superiors, has arranged it thus. And when you don't get one from me . . . see that as an act of God's will, too.

In your charity, please don't compare me to Saint Bernard; the abbot of Clairvaux was an advisor to kings and popes, while I occupy the last place among the oblates of San Isidro . . . do you understand?

Besides, what else can I do? As you know, I came to La Trapa in order to be forgotten by others, as much as possible, and to remain in silence before the tabernacle . . . That is the only way I can help you . . . and perhaps more than you know. In the world, I did whatever I wanted, I sought out the consolation that my soul demanded, and my actions were for the sake of God's glory, but I was always guided by my own will and my own way of seeing things.

Now it's different, I can't do whatever I want . . . well honestly, I don't want anything, but you know what I mean. My renunciation is not yet as perfect as it ought to be, but my desire is to give myself over to Jesus in all

---

1. Rafael and María had thought they would be able to continue their correspondence when he returned to La Trapa, but it was not permitted. Since this was the only time Rafael ever wrote his aunt from the monastery again, it is clear this letter truly was the exception to the rule (OC 608).

things, and I can clearly see that obedience is the way to do that . . . If only you knew, it's not difficult when you truly see the Lord's will in even the most minor details. Anyway, it is all a great mercy.

If only you could see how much I've changed in a month . . . I am so grateful to the Lord for everything He is doing in me; I don't know what to do with myself . . . What I can say is that when I came here, I was full of desires . . . and now, I don't have any left. I see God's hand so clearly in everything, and from the bottom of my heart, I bless Him in the midst of my illness and all my sacrifices, which aren't sacrifices anymore, though they were at first . . .

If only you knew, it's so pleasant and sweet to be in God's hands . . .

Oh, sister, don't you worry, don't you cry or get upset over temporary troubles. Even if they never ended, and we had to remain on the cross until the end of the world . . . Jesus is so good and He loves us so much!

Don't be afraid of being alone . . . you should never say that, because those who love Christ are never alone, you know that perfectly well . . . I'd like to comfort you, but I don't know, this poor Trappist doesn't have much to offer.

I wish I could fly around the world and shout to every creature that they should love God, and yet that same God has bound me to His tabernacle, so that all the shouts I'd like to let loose in the world might be transformed into loving silence for His ears only . . .

See, sister? I can't do anything . . . All I can do is pray, with faith and love, and live out Christ's words *"amare et pati,"* "to love and to suffer."[2] I no longer want anything but God, and His will shall be mine.

I wish this letter would inspire you to put yourself completely and totally in God's hands . . . and with feeling. Then you'd see, peace and tranquility would come upon you, even in the midst of weakness and misery . . . When it does, we will desire nothing, and we won't even look for consolation from creatures, who can offer so little! . . . We can waste precious time that way.

This brings to mind two ideas from Anita's letter,[3] which you showed me when I visited . . . They gave me food for thought, and I've been

---

2. This phrase, *amare et pati,* is not drawn from the Gospel. It is unclear if Rafael is quoting the words of Christ to a specific saint here.

3. Ana Solana, a friend of Rafael's (see #37, n. 8).

reflecting on them a lot recently. They stuck with me, and I've come to understand one of them very clearly.

The first one went like this: "Seek out whatever is least palatable, even when it comes to love for God," or something like that. Well, little sister, I think I said something to you about this, but I think it's best not to seek out anything at all. The Lord will give us whatever He thinks apt, *according to our need*. What do we know of what we need? . . . We think we need one thing, but actually we need another. We seek out consolation when the Lord wants us on the cross, and we seek out the cross when we can't handle it . . . Let us neither desire, nor seek, nor ask for anything . . . let us simply love God, and place ourselves in His hands like little children. I don't see any other way, sister, and this one is so easy!

Look, I can just say that for me, I came to La Trapa looking for one thing, and the Lord in His infinite goodness and mercy gave me something else . . . When we want a certain cross, it's not the right one, because it's ours. We should love God's cross, the cross God gives us. Am I making sense? We deceive ourselves so often on this front.

That's why I'll say it again: let the Lord work . . . He'll send you consolation and feed you with sweet nourishment when you need it, and He'll send you a cross and spiritual dryness and even send your soul into agony whenever you need that . . . and He knows what you need better than you do . . . So, you'll see, even in the midst of everything and everyone, we can have peace.

One of the other things Anita's letter said, if I remember correctly, is that she "rejoiced" (or something like that) in her "uselessness." Truly, my dear sister, it is a great thing, a tremendous mercy from God, to realize that you are useless and to be humiliated because you are of no use whatsoever, because you can't follow the Rule, because you're sick.

If only you knew how grateful I am to the Lord on that account. He has shown me my own self-love with such gentleness, and helped me see my many imperfections. It was necessary for the Lord to put me in this situation in order for my eyes to be properly opened, and for my desires to be uprooted, even my desire to be a Trappist; for me to abandon myself in His hands, and love Him more and more every day, as I realize that He alone can satisfy my soul . . .

I needed my illness to show me that I was still attached to the world, to creatures, to my aches and pains and weaknesses. Living off alms and charity, holding God's hand tight . . . What a great mercy, Lord! I was so blind!

At first, it made me sad to take my meals in the infirmary, apart from my brothers. Now, from the bottom of my heart, I bless God. Whenever it seems to us that He is treating us harshly . . . we are so mistaken. The more He wounds us, the more He loves us . . . don't you think so?

So yes, if some priest or another wants to pray for my health . . . fine, if that's what's best, then at least I won't be as useless to the community as I am now . . . But for myself, I'll just say that not only do I not pray for my health, but in fact I "rejoice in my uselessness," which has helped me to gain knowledge of myself, to uproot so much of my self-love, and to praise God.[4]

Everything in the world is nothing. God alone can satisfy us. Let us not seek out creatures, because in them we'll find . . . just that, creatures. And what else? Nothing! . . . Creatures come and go, and if you take a liking to them, sooner or later the Lord will make you see that they are nothing, and then the hopes you'd had for them will disappear, and that will help you grow closer to God. He will permeate everything. You will see Him in everything, and even your weaknesses themselves will help you love Him, because despite every one of them, He loves you.

Do not let yourself be troubled by poverty, or illness, or the world's disregard for you . . . all of it will help you attain what the Lord has prepared for you . . . do not just accept it all, but love it, for as Saint Francis de Sales says, "The virtue of poverty is not in being poor, but in loving one's poverty."[5] I believe that's true of everything. Don't you think?

This is where you find yourself today, because God wishes it. So praise God for being where you are.

Everything is so easy for those who see things this way. We abandon ourselves in God with such peace and joy. We feel such great love when we realize that we are loved by God, in spite of everything, in spite of our ingratitude and lack of generosity. We are loved by God when we are sad,

---

4. See 2 Cor 12:5: *On my own behalf I will not boast, except of my weaknesses.*

5. While not a direct quotation, this is essentially a summary of the saint's teaching on poverty. See Saint Francis de Sales, *Introduction to a Devout Life*, trans. John K. Ryan (New York: Harper & Row, 1966), part III, chaps. 13–15.

when we are joyful, when we are fervent, when we are lukewarm . . .
What a joy it is to know you are entirely loved by God, in spite of it all.

What does it matter where we are? Who cares if we are first or last, so long as the place we have on this earth is the one that the Lord has chosen for us? . . . Let us live it well. Let us love our place on earth, because it is God's will. Let us not concern ourselves with whether it is high or low, whether we are healthy or not, whether we are on land or at sea . . . We're just passing through this place, it's of no importance to eternity, which is our true home . . . eternity with God.

Meanwhile, let us wait, and wait with faith, patience, peace, and love, detached from ourselves, free from our own desires, seeking out neither crosses nor paths. If we are docile, the Lord will point them out to us. He'll show us our path or road, and it's all the same so long as they lead us to Him. And as I said, He'll also give us a cross without our needing to choose one . . . Let us accept it and jump for joy at our undeserved fortune in possessing it. That is what distinguishes us as lovers of Christ. Blessed be the cross that brings us closer to Him.

Anyway, I don't know what more I can say that you don't already know. There are many things I'd say, but I fear I'd be breaking silence.

Don't you worry about me. I'm neither happy nor unhappy . . . I'm with God, and that's enough for me. He'll do whatever's best for me . . . What do I know? When it's time to be glad, let us be so with joy, and when it's time to suffer, let us do that with joy too . . . It's the same Lord on Mount Tabor and Calvary, even though it's easier to find Him on Calvary.[6] Don't you think so?

Today, which is Sunday, when a long line of Trappists approached the tabernacle to receive Christ, one of them was thinking of you. And not for the first time, as you can imagine. What else am I here for?

I see that you've kept up your devotion to Our Lady. I'm so glad to see that you love Her . . . We receive everything through Her . . . I haven't written anything because honestly I don't have time.[7] They've got me studying Latin in the mornings, and in the afternoons I go to work with the novices.

---

6. Mount Tabor is traditionally held to have been the site of the Transfiguration of the Lord, while Calvary was the site of his Passion.

7. See #81, when Rafael proposed a writing project on the theme of Marian devotion.

These days we're peeling onions. I sit down at the foot of the cross to peel them, and by the second or third one, I've cried a whole river of tears, and they aren't all exactly tears of compunction, as you can imagine.

Whenever I do have free time, between the Stations of the Cross, a Holy Rosary for Mary, a bit of spiritual reading, and spending as much time as I can near the tabernacle, my day is over before I know it.

I don't know anything about what's going on in the world, including the elections. We heard from Reverend Father Abbot that the Right lost, and my father was all worked up about it when he wrote me. But here, we're just doing what we always do, praying for Spain, but knowing nothing about it. If something happens, our superiors will tell us. I trust in the Virgin so much . . . There's no need to worry. Human beings can only go so far as God allows.

Right now the important thing is doing a bit of penance for Holy Lent.

They don't let me get up at two o'clock yet; I get up at three-thirty. At first this sacrifice of getting up so late was very hard for me, because I'm almost sleeping more now than I did in the world, but it's like I told you before: if there's one thing that's going to make me holy, it's obedience . . . I'll just say that it's thanks to obedience that I'm putting on weight.

Don't worry, the Lord will send someone to help you with everything, since I can only help you from my place near the tabernacle . . . so I'll ask Him and Mary to do what's best. Sound good? Don't worry, everything is so brief, it's all passing away. If only the world realized that!

When you write Anita (if you know where she is), give her my regards, you can fill in the rest. I don't know why, but she is often on my mind.

As for me . . . well, don't write me for now. Would I even be able to answer whatever you have to ask me? . . . What do you have the tabernacle for, then? And the Virgin?

Take heart, little sister. This life is full of little sacrifices, but just because they're little doesn't mean they aren't hard . . . That's what we little souls can offer the Lord. He doesn't want me to do it all; you've got to help me with some of it, all right? And even if I won't write you again because of obedience, I won't say I have as much love as Saint Bernard did, but I do have some. Someday you'll realize that. You're going to think I'm not being very humble, aren't you? But it's true.

Well, I'd like to end this letter with what I've already told you. Forgive me for being so tiresome, but until we put ourselves completely in God's hands, we won't have achieved anything at all.

But may we surrender ourselves joyfully, truly confident that the Lord will find our souls utterly indifferent to sorrow and joy alike . . . But may that indifference never become apathy, or something even worse. Do you know what I mean? May we surrender ourselves for love of Jesus, and may love be our guide, rather than the selfishness of an easy path.

May we love with joy, be glad with joy, and suffer with joy. May we see the world for what it is, may we see God in every creature and go beyond them, disappearing from our very selves, annihilating that *I* that is such an obstacle to us. Then we will be at peace, wanting only what God wants and loving whatever He sends us . . . forgive me, but I think between that and a bit of love for the Virgin, we will become saints. But if not, well then, we'll get as far as we get with the help of Christ Jesus.

Wishing you His peace, your brother, who remembers you at the Tabernacle,

Brother María Rafael, O.C.S.O.

P.S. Do me the favor, or rather the kindness, of not showing me "respect" as you put it. And don't worry about the cold either, or tobacco, or anything else . . . What is all that compared to what the Lord gives me? Besides, I don't see it as a mortification, believe me. But even if it were, isn't it all for the love of Jesus? Then so what? Besides, don't forget, we have Our Lady with us here.

106. To Leopoldo Barón

La Trapa, April 17, 1936[1]

J-H-S Ave Maria
My dearest brother in Jesus and Mary,

I suppose you won't be expecting a letter from me, because first of all, I don't have any news for you, or anything to say that you don't already know. However, at Easter we generally write our families, and since my parents were just here, they gave me permission to write you and wish you a happy Easter. What do you think?

Both my parents were here on Holy Saturday, and my father was here the two previous days to attend the holy Office throughout Holy Week. I was so pleased that he came, because this is the best place to spend these days in recollection. He enjoyed it very much, and left utterly pleased with La Trapa, as did my mother. They could tell that this is all so different from what the world thinks it is. Above all, they loved the peace and tranquility that the Trappists have, in the midst of the hatred that apparently dominates Spain. Even though we don't hear about anything here, we do nevertheless receive bits and pieces of news from our superiors, and as far as I can tell, the world is falling more and more under the power of darkness with each passing day.

Everything is a great mercy. Don't you think so?

Don't laugh if I ask you how things are going with your situation . . . You'll say "what's it to you" . . . well you're mistaken. I'm the same person here as I was there. Do you remember that nephew of yours who came with you to Toro, talking about God in between conversations about notaries and tenants? . . . Well he hasn't changed . . . he's just got a hood now. And he's got those notaries and tenants at something of a distance, while he's a bit closer to God, or at least, he's in His house . . . and that's something.

---

1. From #106 through #159, Rafael is twenty-five years old.

Since I wrote Aunt María last time, it's your turn now, but I'm honestly telling you I can't think of anything to say that you would find interesting. You already know what kind of life we Trappists lead. And as for me, I'll just say that the Lord and the Virgin Mary have been helping me in such a way, and still are, that you could say I'm not doing anything at all.

Besides, what about creatures could still hold interest for you? And I say "still" because I imagine that you're on the true path, which is God and Him alone, and as Kempis says, "Whatever is not God is nothing, and as nothing we ought to reckon it."[2]

As such, why talk to you about La Trapa? Why tell you about the state of my health? If the subject is not God and God alone, this letter . . . is a waste of time, because everything else is creaturely and thus vain . . .

Believe me, brother, I've changed my ways of thinking and feeling so much . . . If you come here someday, I'll explain, if it's worth explaining. Today, I'll just tell you that I'm happy, not because I'm in La Trapa, nor on account of the peace in the air here or the silence of monastic life . . . That's all well and good, but it's not enough to satisfy the heart of someone who is in love with God . . .

It is, and for me it has been, necessary to dispense with everything else, in order to be able to breathe a little bit . . .

Believe me, brother, all created things bring us toward God, but they are not God. People can bring us toward Him sometimes . . . Perhaps our desires, when they are holy, can too. But as long as our hearts are not empty and solitary, the vastness of God cannot enter in. If only you knew . . . I won't say that I'm completely detached from everything yet, but I can breathe a bit better . . . What about you?

Anyway, pay me no mind. I'm a bit mad, but I wish I could spread my madness to you.

I don't know how you're doing right now, or what your situation is like, but look, however you're doing, it doesn't matter. Everything passes, and with time, it will become clear just how brief it all is. It feels like just yesterday we were hunting turtledoves at Pedrosillo,[3] remember? Although in truth it's not worth remembering . . .

2. Thomas à Kempis, *The Imitation of Christ*, trans. Ronald Knox and Michael Oakley (New York: Sheed and Ward, 1960), 131 (III.31.3).

3. Pedrosillo: Leopoldo Barón and María Osorio's former estate outside of Ávila.

God is so great! When we consider Him, why should we remember what happened in the past or let ourselves be troubled by what is to come? If we have Him right now, what more could we desire?

If we truly had faith, if we truly loved God . . . and God alone . . . Oh, dear Uncle Polín, the soul gets lost so easily when thinking about Jesus' love . . . it's best to be silent, don't you think? What can I possibly say to you, poor Trappist oblate that I am? Here in my silence among men, I have so many things to say to my God . . . but what could I have to say to human beings?

Since you know me by now, and you know many of my soul's inner workings, this letter won't surprise you . . . but believe me, sometimes I am greatly saddened when I think about those who don't love God . . . and I know you aren't one of them, right? . . . Anyway, I won't say anything to you at all. What for? Besides, not everything I want to say is coming out right. I sat down to write you because I wanted to send you the Trappist *pax tecum*, but I ended up with just the intention of doing so.[4] Words truly are helpless. The more we have inside, the less comes out. The best thing to do is keep silent . . . So then, I'll send you my silence. Perhaps you'll understand me a bit better that way.

Have you thought about coming here? Look, don't come to see me . . . Wow, I'm being so pretentious! . . . You know what I mean. That is, don't come for La Trapa, but rather for the God of La Trapa. I'll say it again, creatures are good in that they come from God, but God is even better . . . Believe me, I've wasted so much time, and now that I've found what I was looking for, I want to . . . well, I don't want anything . . . love God and God alone, and pay your nephew no mind, and don't think about him at all, except to commend him to Our Lady. Everything else is nothing at all.

Father Master asked me to ask you about Ana Mozo, because I told him that she wanted to enter religious life, and he's decided to look into whether it's possible and where. I am not intervening in this situation except by asking the Virgin to help her. Tell her that for me, and tell her that if her vocation is from God, she'll encounter difficulties sooner or later. So let her neither be afraid, nor put her hand to the plow and look back.[5] Between her good desire and heaven's aid, everything will work out.

---

4. See #43.

5. *Jesus said to him, "No one who puts a hand to the plow and looks back is fit for the kingdom of God"* (Luke 9:62).

I'm writing you little by little, because we don't have much time and I get more of it by taking it away from other things. Don't you go thinking there's time to waste around here.

Now, since I'm doing much better, Reverend Father has given me permission to go down for Matins at night. Before, I was getting up at three-thirty. If my health stays the same, they'll move me to the novices' shared dormitory soon. Then, the only thing I'll be doing separately from the community will be my meals.

I assure you it's all the same to me, because being Trappist isn't about the exterior things, right? And holding tight to God's hand is the greatest happiness on earth . . . I've now realized that my illness is my treasure in this world . . . How great God is, brother! How well He arranges things, how He goes about His work! . . . There's nothing to do but let Him carry you. Trust me, it's easy, and when you come to have no desires at all except those of God, that's when it's all done . . . there's nothing to do but wait.

Do you remember my holy card?[6] Listen, often, when I visit the cemetery in the evenings, I think about it and what I wrote you on the back . . . and I think of you, and pray that the Lord we love will give you that science, which is the only necessary one: the science to love and wait in hope . . .

If only you know how good it is to live like this . . . it doesn't matter where you are, or what position you find yourself in. Don't envy me for being in a monastery. What I have here, you have where you are too. In the monastery, La Trapa and the Trappists are the least important thing . . . what really matters, the only thing that matters, is the tabernacle, in which God's greatness and grandeur is hidden . . . and you have that too. You can set up your Trapa next to any tabernacle on earth.

Let us not live for exterior things, brother. It's all vanity, and it will pass away soon. Let us have the courage to live in Christ and Him alone . . . are we agreed?

Let us hide ourselves away with Jesus, in the mystery of the Blessed Sacrament: let us live with our hearts by the tabernacle, and our bodies . . . well, who cares where they are? May the Lord use them as He pleases. Who cares where we are? Any place we might seek out is a good place to love God. Moreover, seeing as it's transitory and we are mere sojourners on this earth, why worry?

---

6. See #87 for the image and #101 for the inscription.

Listen, one time, when I had just arrived, the devil tormented me in various ways; the Lord permitted it . . . It's only natural, I am weak, and a mere man, not yet entirely given over to interior things. Anyway, what am I telling you this for . . . Well, I turned to Kempis, and I found this sentence: "Why stand gaping here? This is no place for you to settle down."[7] Truly, my dear brother, we are such fools. We pay so little heed to what the Lord told us, *there is need of only one thing.*[8]

Anyway, I'm not telling you anything new, as you can see, and what I do want to send your way, you may already have. Since I know some of the inner workings of your heart too, today . . . this morning, and before this letter goes out, at the Virgin Mary's feet, after receiving the Lord, I prayed for you. I asked for many things on your behalf, but one above all . . . and that is detachment from everything and everyone, so that the Lord might flood you, and in forgetting all created things, you might think of no one but your Creator, and your soul might find the peace that only Christ may bestow.

That, my dearest brother, is what I wish for you . . . because it's so good to live like this! Believe me, if there's one joy to be savored in this life, it's knowing you are loved by God.

Answer me if you want, though you know quite well it's not necessary . . . you know what I mean. I'd write you at greater length if I had time just for me, and if they'd give me more paper, but here we must put our own desires to one side. That's what religious life is, detaching from oneself in all things.

There are so many things I'd ask you to tell Aunt María! But I'll be silent. I'll just repeat what I've told her many times before, which is that our truest conversations take place at the foot of the tabernacle. We can do more in silent prayer than with the noise of all the words we could imagine. Be confident of this . . . your Trappist nephew tells Jesus and Mary everything he'd like to say to his aunt and uncle. It's better that way, don't you think?

There are also many things I'd ask you, but I don't need to. I'm sure you can guess, and if you write me back, you'll know what I'm interested in hearing.

7. The passage continues, "Heaven is your destination, and you should look upon this earthly scene only as a transit-camp" (Thomas à Kempis, *The Imitation of Christ*, 61, II.1.4).
8. Luke 10:42.

Poor Brother Rafael, he'll always be the same. They say the habit doesn't make the monk. Well, as for me, no matter how much of a monk I am, despite my hood, I'll always be your nephew . . . You know, the slightly wacky one who used to twirl around by the radio, and then go visit nuns . . .

Trust me, you don't have to change in order to become a good Trappist. God merely asks us to be simple on the outside, and loving on the inside . . . See how easy that is? "From surly-hooded monks, Lord, deliver us," as Saint Teresa used to say.[9] And in reality, how easy and simple are God's true paths when you walk them in a spirit of confidence, with a free heart fixed on Him.

When complications arise, it's because we don't go to God with utter suspicion of ourselves and true confidence in Him . . . It's because we look at ourselves too much, and we seek out our own preferences and desires more than what God really wants from us . . . But my dear brother, if we put our many obstacles to one side, and looked up at the cross and called out to Mary . . . I'm not saying we'd have God immediately . . . well, I don't know, but we'd have Him soon.

Take heart, brother. I'll help you as much as I can from here. Let's see if we can manage not just joy, but the "skill of jubilation," as Saint Augustine said.[10]

Well, that's enough *citations* from me, I don't want you to call me a tiresome pedant. That's all for today. Forgive everything I said if you don't agree. My regards to Aunt María and my cousins, and as for you . . . blessed be God, I can't think of a single thing

Brother María Rafael

9. Rafael is playing on a saying commonly attributed to Saint Teresa, "From sour-faced saints, Lord, deliver us."

10. In his commentary on Ps 33:3, Saint Augustine writes, "Sing unto Him a new song; sing unto Him a song of the grace of faith. Sing skilfully unto Him with jubilation; sing skillfully unto Him with rejoicing" (*Expositions on the Psalms*, trans. J. E. Tweed, in Nicene and Post-Nicene Fathers, ed. Philip Schaff [Buffalo, NY: Christian Literature Publishing Co., 1888], 33:3).

107. Dedication of a Holy Card to Leopoldo Barón

La Trapa, June 14, 1936

Brother,

Whether in the cloister or in the world, whether in peace or at war, only one thing matters: loving God. All science and all virtue are found there.

In loving God, you will be happy in this life, you will always know peace, and one day, you'll die happy.

Here at La Trapa, your brother is praying to the Most Blessed Virgin, that She might enlighten you and guide you along the wide path of love for Jesus.

Everything else . . . believe me, it's nothing. It comes and goes . . . and as Saint Teresa said, "God alone suffices, who possesses God nothing wants."[1]

Don't forget about your brother.

Brother María Rafael

---

1. From a poem by Saint Teresa of Ávila: "Let nothing trouble you, / Let nothing scare you, / All is fleeting, / God alone is unchanging. / Patience / Everything obtains. / Who possesses God / Nothing wants. / God alone suffices" ("Efficacy of Patience," STA 3:386).

108. Meditations of a Trappist[1]

I live without living in myself,
And in such a way I hope,
I die because I do not die.
—Saint Teresa of Ávila[2]

How Great God Is![3]

La Trapa, July 12, 1936

With the help of the Virgin Mary, to whom I dedicate these ramblings, meditations, monologues, impressions, etc., since you could really call them anything, I begin this notebook, in which I hope to expel something of the excessive verbiage that the Lord has given me.

It's true, with a pen in my hands, not a moment goes by when I can't think of something to say or talk about . . . . Perhaps that's a fault of mine . . . I don't know. What I know for certain is that God asks me to remain silent among His creatures, and I do so with pleasure. Seen rightly, of course, it's not the sacrifice the world thinks it is, because keeping your mouth closed puts your heart to rest, and it allows you to speak to Him . . . He offers Himself to me in the tabernacle, where He remains day and night solely to attend to my every request . . . He comes to my soul through Communion in order to sustain me in my monastic life. He

1. Rafael drew the image of the kneeling monk for the cover of the notebook he titled Meditations of a Trappist. The quotation from Saint Teresa was inscribed on the inside front cover as an epigraph. See manuscript photographs in Juan Antonio Martínez Camino, *Mi Rafael* (Bilbao: Desclée de Brouwer, 2003), 242–44. Image source: LPM 239.

2. Saint Teresa of Ávila, "Aspirations toward Eternal Life," in STA 3:375.

3. While Rafael did divide Meditations of a Trappist into individual entries or "meditations," he left them untitled. His mother, Mercedes Barón, gave them titles when she prepared his writings for publication in 1947 (Juan Antonio Martínez Camino, *Mi Rafael* [Bilbao: Desclée de Brouwer, 2003], 242).

listens to me in my silent prayer . . . And last, He gives me blank paper and . . . allows me to write.

"How great God is!"

When the monk looks out at the external world that surrounds him and contemplates the wonders of creation, if truly in love with Him, that is what his heart must first exclaim.

"How great God is!"

Thus he exclaims once more when, closing his eyes to all created things, all external things, he refocuses his sight on his own soul, seeks Him out within his own heart, and withdraws into silence.

"How great God is!"

That is the Trappist's only and constant meditation as he follows the Rule in silence, whether he follows it well or poorly. At the end of the day, he is a man, and an imperfect one at that, but it doesn't matter . . . What can be expected of such rough clay? . . . It doesn't matter. Even among his weakness and misery, "how great God is!" Even when his eyes are still heavy with sleep as he sings in the choir . . .

"How great God is!" when the law of his life, which is God's law, calls him to go to work and he bends down over the earth, hunched over and sweating.

"How great God is!" . . . when in the silence of the cloisters, he waits faithfully with a peaceful face for the Lord to call him . . .

"How great God is!" . . .

And when at last the sun is going down and the day is coming to an end, that Trappist brings his day to a close by prostrating himself before the Virgin Mary and placing his day's work at Her feet. "How great God is!"

Honestly, with that said, I could finish my writing right here. What else could I add?

I wanted to begin at the end . . . but in the spiritual life, the interior life, there are no beginnings or endings . . . there is only God, and after any reflection one always looks at oneself in one way or another and realizes how little we are, how trivial and insignificant . . . we are nothing compared to Him. The soul is left merely with an impression that is so difficult to explain . . . An impression of God's vastness, His greatness . . . A feeling that makes words fall short, that makes the soul wish it couldn't see itself anymore, wish it could disappear, no longer be or exist, just God's greatness . . . Anyway, I'm getting lost.

109. Meditations of a Trappist
Knowing How to Wait

La Trapa, July 12, 1936

In La Trapa, we Trappists have a consolation that is little known in the world . . . Here in the house of God, away from all that hustle and bustle, we can clearly see how short everything is as time passes . . . The world knows it too, but it's different.

When the world talks about how quickly life passes, it does so with a hint of sadness. It laments how short-lived everything is . . . People often live in the past, and what good does it do them? . . . They don't change their ways. They just use whatever time they have left to keep searching for the things they didn't find in the life they've already lived. Then their final years come, and then they become even more aware of their nostalgia for the past and how short-lived everything is . . . Old age is so sad, according to the world.

In La Trapa, monks don't care about the past . . . They just have the great consolation of knowing that whatever remains of this life will pass, too. What more is there to do, then, but wait? And they wait with such joy and peace, certain of what is to come.

What peace it brings to the soul to think that neither human beings nor world events can hinder the coming of what awaits us . . . With each passing day, we are a step closer to the beginning of our true lives. What the world sees as the end is what the monk sees as the beginning. Everything comes, everything goes . . . only God remains.

110. Meditations of a Trappist
A Worldly Youth

La Trapa, July 19, 1936

Ave Maria

It is seven in the morning on a bright July day. Through the vines covering the novitiate window, sunlight is streaming in, if somewhat weakly . . . A multitude of birds is singing among the stalks of wheat, and from time to time, a partridge's harsh tune pierces through their concert.

Silence reigns in the monastery, as always, and the monks all devote themselves to occupying the free time permitted to them by the Rule in a holy way, between breakfast and the conventual Mass.

Entrusting myself to my Mother, Mary, I have taken up my pen and notebook, and alternating my gaze between the sun as it passes through the leaves on the vines and the crucifix I have before me, I have decided to write for a little while.

It is so difficult to put a Trappist's impression of La Trapa into words.

Some years ago now, a worldly youth stopped by this abbey,[1] his head full of . . . Well, I don't know what was in that man's head. He spent a few days staying with these good monks, and since he was a lover of music, color, and anything with an element of art about it, he was deeply moved when he heard them sing the psalmody in choir . . . He was touched by the silence of these men who live a good life away from the world. He delighted in the ineffable as he saw white-clad men working in spring-clad fields, full of flowers in bloom. With the sweat of their brow and the calluses of their hands, they were helping one another provide for their bodies as long as they were to remain in exile, while at the same time they were working to earn their rest in their true Homeland.

---

1. Rafael's first visit to La Trapa took place on September 23, 1930, a visit he described in #5. Here, he is probably describing his second visit, for a retreat beginning on June 26, 1932.

When that worldly young man saw what he saw, his soul underwent a change, and perhaps the Lord God of the Trappists made use of the perception of his senses to make him think.

And the young man thought.

Today, he's just another Trappist in the choir, another worker in the field, and a man who, desiring to forget the world, seeks out silence among creatures and peace with God.

He saw art in that scene at the abbey years ago, an occasion for delight . . . Everything played a part in making an impression on him . . . the austere monks dressed in white; their silence; the sometimes deep ring of the large bell, and the cheerful jingle of the little bell; the cloisters flooded with sunlight; the long line of monastery residents crossing fields of wheat as they returned from work.

That young man thought, God made use of all these external things in order to help His divine light penetrate that somewhat starry-eyed soul.

How great is the Lord's mercy!

Some years passed, and the man traded his worldly clothes for a Cistercian monk's habit. He exchanged his old ways as a man of the world for the simple Rule handed down to us by our father Saint Benedict.

He changed the course of his life. Leaving to one side the world's torturous paths that lead to well-being, fortune, and perhaps even glory, he left behind his career. He directed his steps and thoughts toward the way that leads to eternal life, the way followed then and now by those who love God.

Everything underwent a transformation, and so that he was left with nothing from before, his way of feeling began to change, too.

Now, he is no longer a spectator, but an integral part of the scene that he had admired those years ago, and to the great surprise of his soul, he has come to realize that one thing was missing among the impressions made upon his senses . . . a feeling for God was missing from the scene.

That beauty touched him deeply, but even in those external things, he had not yet seen God. Now, it's different . . . Now that Trappist, who was once that young, restless dreamer . . . doesn't care so much about the bells or birds, or even the sun. Now, with Mary's help, he has come to see that the most important thing in a monastery is God.

He no longer sings the praises of art made by creatures, but by God. He is no longer all that moved by the colors of the field, except insofar as he sees their Creator in them.

Now he has come to understand that all external things are vanity. . .
That whatever touches only the senses is smoke, and like smoke, it too
disappears without a trace . . . Flowers wither, the cheerful springtime
sun turns pale and sad in winter, the birds of the sky hide away, and the
emerald-green fields lose their color.

Everything passes. . . Man grows old and, at last, dies. Behold the one
and only truth: God alone remains.

All that worldly young man's thoughts as he contemplated La Trapa
have now been transformed into just one thing, something he didn't have
before: God. Who cares about the color of the habit? Who cares if the bells
sound high or low? For our purposes, what does it matter if it's winter or
summer? Let us dispense with all external things, and let only God and
pure faith make an impression on us.

This is why it is so difficult for a Trappist to write about his impressions of La Trapa.

Visitors from the world can find sufficient cause in these Cistercian
abbeys to meditate, think, and reflect, and if their soul is somewhat artistic, they'll enjoy the silence and peace of the monastery, but make no
mistake, God isn't in all that. Rather, one must dispense with all that in
order to encounter God.

Now, as he contemplates the tranquil skies of Castile, that Trappist
sees in them the grandeur of God. His soul is immersed in the goodness
of the Creator. Lifting his heart up above the things of earth, letting go
of his senses, and seeing the vanity of it all, he exclaims, "Lord, You are
admirable in Your creatures. You reveal Yourself to my soul by means of
them, but You do not allow me to remain fixed on them. The sky, the earth,
and all that dwell in them are beautiful, but they are not You, and I want
to reach You by means of everything and everyone."

And as for that Trappist all dressed in white, working and sweating
in the Castilian countryside under his wide straw hat and the blazing
summer sun, surrounded by flowers, or perhaps by thorns . . . he notices
none of it, not the sun, not the sky, neither the heat nor the cold. No, he
has eyes for nothing but God. And if ever the sound of the monastery bell
reaches his ears, without lifting his gaze from the ground, he offers up a
prayer to God, who, humbly hidden in the church tabernacle, awaits and
anticipates him. God is waiting for that Trappist to finish his work and

come into His presence, showing Him the fruit of his labor, which has nothing to do with the number of hours spent working, or whether he worked in the vineyard or the orchard, or using a hoe or a rake. Rather, it is about the inward intention, hidden from the eyes of men, with which that Trappist worked.

God alone should occupy the soul. Peace is not the result of silence, or the cloister cypresses, or birdsong. . . For the Trappist, peace is God, and there is nothing in La Trapa of any value but Him.

It is now nine in the morning. The sun, still streaming in through the window from in between the vines, has moved a few centimeters. The birds are still singing. The silence of the monastery is interrupted only by the sound of the organ, where a priest is practicing for Mass. All of this is very beautiful, very poetic . . . but this poor Trappist oblate is going to dispense with it, put away his pen, close his notebook, and before they ring the bell for Holy Mass, he will go and spend a few minutes at the threshold of the tabernacle. Closing the eyes of his body, and also those of his soul, he will say . . . "Lord, You alone . . . You alone remain . . . There is nothing under the sun that satisfies the heart of man but You."

And my heart is thirsting for You, and it seeks You as deer do flowing streams, as David says.[2] Everything outside of You is darkness.

Help me, O Virgin Mary, to obtain the only thing that can satisfy my soul . . . and that is Christ Jesus. May it be so.

---

2. *As a deer longs for flowing streams, so my soul longs for you, O God. My soul thirsts for God, the living God* (Ps 42:1-2b).

111. Meditations of a Trappist
What Will Happen in Spain?[1]

La Trapa, July 19, 1936[2]

The same day.

I'd hardly put down my pen and gone down to the chapel when, while we were in choir waiting for Mass to begin, there was a stir among the monks . . . Just one priest came out to say Mass rather than the usual three . . . The bells didn't ring, and we spoke the Office[3] . . . When we left the chapel, we learned only that there's a revolution in Spain, that you can see soldiers on the road, and that there's talk of an uprising . . . I know nothing more. Just that we can't hear any trains . . . it looks as though there's a strike on.

We are in God's hands. What will happen in Spain? . . . I don't know anything. No news reaches us novices.

---

1. The Spanish Civil War officially began July 17, 1936, with a military uprising led by General Francisco Franco against the government of the Second Spanish Republic. Broadly speaking, the war was a conflict between the right-wing Nationalists and the left-wing Republicans; on a practical level, each side consisted of a complex ideological alliance that varied by region. For an overview of the conflict's origins, politics, and course, see Paul Preston, *The Spanish Civil War: Reaction, Revolution, and Revenge*, revised and expanded ed. (New York: W. W. Norton, 2007); or Helen Graham, *The Spanish Civil War: A Very Short Introduction* (New York: Oxford University Press, 2005). Franco declared victory for the Nationalists on April 1, 1939, and ruled as dictator of Spain until his death in 1975.

2. On July 18, 1936, Rafael's father and brother Leopoldo left their family home in Oviedo to join his mother Mercedes and sister Merceditas in Burgos. The four of them planned to flee to Lisbon, Portugal, but ultimately rode out the war in Villasandino, a small town outside Burgos. Rafael's brother Luis Fernando was studying in Belgium when the war broke out, though he later returned to Spain to serve in the Nationalist-allied military (OC 638).

3. We spoke the Office: That is, rather than singing it.

There's something of a disturbance among the priests and brothers. Anyway, God alone. Perhaps they're just fears, and fears that are coming from the world, but no matter how indifferent one may be to what comes from the world . . . when you realize that we are surrounded by hostile towns with people who hate us . . . you cannot remain unaffected.

These are difficult times, but it doesn't matter. "Whoever possesses God nothing wants."[4] Whatever people might do to us,[5] the most they can take from us is our lives . . . and a Trappist's life isn't worth all that much . . . Nothing, really. As for me, of course, while I have life, I will use it in God's service. When He takes it from me, in one way or another, that's all right. My life is His, and as such, it is at His disposal . . . I can't understand how a monk could fear death.

Oh, what a great joy it would be if I could give my life for Jesus . . . I'm afraid I won't be so lucky. But if the Lord grants that my sojourn should end in martyrdom . . .

Anyway . . . what am I saying. It's best to be content no matter what events God sends us. Whether they belong to peacetime or revolution . . . Nothing happens in this world that He has not foreseen in His infinite goodness, and creatures will not go any further than God allows them to.

Anyway, "God alone suffices,"[6] and we rest in the hands of the Virgin Mary. It's sad not hearing the bells.

4. From a poem by Saint Teresa of Ávila: "Let nothing trouble you, / Let nothing scare you, / All is fleeting, / God alone is unchanging. / Patience / Everything obtains. / Who possesses God / Nothing wants. / God alone suffices" ("Efficacy of Patience," in STA 3:386).

5. In the original, Rafael inserted the word *do* (*hacer*) between the lines as a correction (OC 637).

6. STA 3:386.

112. Meditations of a Trappist
"The Nations Are in an Uproar"[1]

La Trapa, July 24, 1936

Ave Maria

By the grace of God, I've been in the infirmary for a few days. I had a bad reaction to something, and it put me on bedrest for a day.

I'm nearly well now. In these days when Spain is undergoing anxiety, the Lord wanted me to remain in silence and withdrawal, separated from my brother novices. Blessed be God forever.

I still don't know what's going on outside the monastery walls. I know there's a war on, or something like that . . . Last Monday (today is Friday), while I was resting in bed, a bit tired from my fever, I heard two things at once . . . through the door to my room, I heard clearly the sound of the organ and the voices of the monks as they sang the Office of Vespers in choir. At the same time, through the window, I could hear gunshots and the rattling of a machine gun here and there. I could still hear some gunshots yesterday.

The news I'm getting is all mixed up . . . They say there's Communism in Madrid, that there are Fascist armies coming up into Spain from the south . . . I can't hear any trains . . . We heard a few yesterday, but not on the regular schedule . . . In short, everything is confusing.

From the quiet of my room, I raise a prayer to God for all those who are fighting and dying.

It's sad to think about the hatred that dominates humanity . . . among brothers and sisters who share a homeland. There was also talk that they were going to burn us[2] . . . Praise God . . . it wouldn't be a bad thing

---

1. Ps 46:6.

2. According to Rafael's confessor, Fr. Teófilo Sandoval, "On July 19, two large vans of Republican fighters armed with pistols, carbines, and rifles surrounded the monastery,

if they did. As for me, I can say that I am willing, because I know that martyrdom is like baptism, and of course, it would be a very lovely way to enter into heaven.

But for now, that's not how it is. The Trappist's martyrdom is not at the stake or down the barrel of a gun . . . God asks something else of us. God asks us to live this life while we are still separated from Him, and for a little while, we suffer the hardships of the body, the miseries of the spirit, and the weaknesses of the flesh . . . Behold, the true martyrdom of one who loves God and yearns for the peace of eternal life.

The people of this world have gone mad . . . Why are they killing each other? I don't understand it. But I can clearly see that what some want, others do not; what some have, others desire and want to take it from them; some say this, others say that, but everyone wants to be in charge . . . First, they disagree; then they argue; then they hate each other; and finally, they will kill each other . . . Behold, the law that the evil spirit has smuggled into the world, displacing the law of Christ: *love one another.*[3]

I am so happy that I am a Trappist, and at something of a distance from the fight . . . not for selfish reasons, because I don't mind suffering, much less dying. Rather, far from all that infighting, with a tranquil spirit, I can hear shouts of hatred and smell the gunfire, and then lift my eyes to heaven and truly exclaim David's words: *God is our refuge and strength.*[4]

The nations are in an uproar, the kingdoms totter; he utters his voice, the earth melts, but *the Lord of hosts is with us; the God of Jacob is our refuge.*[5]

The one who truly counts on God for everything possesses such joyful confidence in the midst of all the world's disasters. *Therefore we will not fear, though the earth should change, though the mountains shake in the heart of the sea.*[6]

---

threatening the monks. A small group of soldiers came from Palencia to drive them away . . . [The Republicans] had planned to strip the monks naked and burn them alive in the town square of Dueñas, along with the local Teresian Sisters and parish priest, Don Fulgencio, whom they had captured a few days prior" (testimony quoted in OC 637).

3. Matt 19:19; 22:39; Luke 10:25-37; John 13:34-35.

4. Ps 46:1.

5. Ps 46:6-7.

6. Ps 46:2.

The soul stretches upon encountering these words of Psalm 46, upon which I have been meditating these past few days. It pains me to think that so many of my brothers and sisters, alienated from the truth, place their hopes in earthly goals, in passing prosperity, and in power that will not last. Blinded by pride, they don't realize that God is the one moving them about, like puppets in His hands . . . They don't stop to consider that

Surely everyone goes about like a shadow.
Surely for nothing they are in turmoil;
they heap up, and do not know who will gather.[7]

How great is God! And how small and wicked is humanity! How blind they are! There is so much madness in the world! *He who sits in the heavens laughs.*[8] Terrifying words that make one tremble, and are not often meditated upon . . . God's wrath is to be feared, and so too His rage. Someday it will shake the whole earth, on the day when we shall all be judged. But what one's soul cannot understand, and what makes every fiber of one's body tremble, is God's "laugh" as He watches the nations conspire against Him.

"Enough! Acknowledge that I am God. I have dominion over the nations and all the earth."[9]

Anyway, what can this poor Trappist do but silently lament how God's creatures have forgotten Him, lift my heart up above all this misery, make Him my *refuge and strength*, and wait in hope?

Beatus vir, cujus est nomen Domini spes ejus.[10]

7. Ps 39:6.
8. Ps 2:4.
9. Rafael's paraphrase of Ps 46:10: *Be still, and know that I am God! I am exalted among the nations, I am exalted in the earth.*
10. *Happy are those who make the Lord their trust* (Ps 40:4).

113. Meditations of a Trappist
The Circus Clown

La Trapa, July 24, 1936

Once upon a time there was a circus clown who would fall over whenever he entered the ring . . . he'd walk around dragging his huge shoes, and with great effort, he'd manage to smooth out the corner of the rug. Just when he thought he'd got it, he'd trip . . . he'd smooth out the rug again, and fall down . . . he'd sweat . . . His job was just to get a chair out . . . In order to do that, he'd roll up his sleeves, wipe the sweat from his brow with a huge handkerchief, drag the chair into the ring as if pulling an enormous weight, and finally, he'd sit down on it. Everybody would laugh at him for being so proud as he exited, thinking he'd helped the others get their equipment, tools, and rugs ready so that the artists could go about their work.

I know a Trappist who is the "circus clown" of La Trapa. His whole performance consists of "stage business," dragging his feet around and wiping away his sweat.

That poor man makes the angels laugh as they look down from heaven upon the spectacle that is this earth. He might not run the same risks as the other artists do, or make death-defying jumps, or perform feats of strength, or do twists and turns on the trapeze . . . But what does it matter if all he knows how to do is smooth out a rug? With that he earns the angels' applause! . . .

There's just one small difference. That circus clown thought he was doing something, and the praise he received from the audience for his humor made him vain, and he waved to them with satisfaction.

Meanwhile, this Trappist *can't hear* his audience's praise . . . He *plays* the fool, but he doesn't have anybody to wave at, and if they're laughing up in heaven, he can't see it. Besides, since he's no fool, he doesn't really believe that he's doing anything . . . just doing what he can, dragging his feet, wiping the sweat from his brow with a huge bandana.

114. Meditations of a Trappist
Silence

La Trapa, July 25, 1936
Feast of Saint James the Greater, Apostle

Ave Maria

One of the most consoling things in Cistercian monastic life . . . is silence; above all, those particular hours when silence is imposed as obligatory. We need that silence. It is the consolation of the Trappist, the refuge of the afflicted and distressed, the mirth of the joyful, and the happiness of those in love with God.

It is in silence that the monk finds balm for his wounds, and sometimes for his distress . . . It is in monastic silence that the soul who delights in God hides his joys . . .

One loves God better in silence. Suffering is more effective in silence . . . Consolation that creatures cannot give can often be found in silence.

How beautiful and lovely silence is! It is such a great help to the soul that seeks God! . . . And once we have found God, it helps us keep Him there without *profaning* His presence!

Some days, a certain Trappist's soul finds its happiness in maintaining silence.

That Trappist wouldn't trade places with anybody. What the world sees as a penance is heaven on earth for him.

When the hours of the night pass by slowly . . . that same night which the monk uses to pray before God . . . When all of nature is sleeping, and darkness itself invites the soul to prayer and recollection . . . When, during those serene hours, that brother draws close to the altar of God, and receives the Creator of the night into his heart, the God who made those star-studded skies . . . Then, when the soul is surrounded by peace on the outside and flooded with light on the inside, when darkness envelops the monastery and divine splendor illumines the heart . . . that is when silence is necessary.

The sun, as if ashamed to disrupt the peaceful night, slowly peeks out over the horizon . . . A gentle mist hugs each aspect of the landscape . . . Creation begins to awaken; little by little, everything is flooded with light . . . The monastery church has a window above the main altar . . . Light streams through it, and the soft light of dawn both wounds and caresses the statue of the Virgin Mary . . . it reaches the sanctuary and even finds the choir . . . finally, we can read clearly from those enormous books . . .

In the same way that the light God sends to the world each morning floods everything . . . so too is the monk's soul flooded with joy, peace, and gratitude to the Lord who is so good to human beings . . .

Then, when everything comes alive, when the birds disturb the cemetery with their song, when the calm of prayer is exchanged for the tools of manual work . . . When the monk begins his work day, perhaps he is going to suffer . . . then the soul of this man, realizing that life on earth is struggle and that he is still in exile, raises his heart up above everything and asks the help of God, to whom he offers the day's work; he embraces each day's cross; and thinking of the Virgin, he takes refuge in silence . . . in the silence that helps him preserve the prayer of the night . . . And in that silence, he makes an offering to God: sometimes the sweat of his brow, sometimes the cold, but always his work, no matter what it may be.

How beautiful is the silence of a Trappist as he works . . . The soul stretches as it loses itself in God's greatness, manifested in the skies under which the monk is working . . . All of creation is subject to human hands . . . everything sings God's praises . . . the wheat, the flowers, the mountains, and the sky . . . Together, they perform a concert with sublime harmony. Nothing is missing, and nothing is superfluous. Everything God makes is well made . . .

Sometimes the Trappist's soul is on earth, clawing away at clods of dirt, and sometimes it is in heaven, blessing God . . . but it is always in silence . . . although sometimes he interrupts that silence in order to sing to the Virgin . . . or so I hear.

115. Meditations of a Trappist
The Day Goes By

La Trapa, July 25, 1936

The day is going by . . . Holy Mass calls us to choir . . . what can I say? God comes down to console human beings who are still living on the earth.

How could the soul not rejoice, then, upon realizing that it doesn't matter if the work is hard or the body is tired . . . God is with us . . . every day and every hour, though at the most solemn moments of conventual Mass, it does seem that the Lord loves us more . . . When He gathers together all of us brothers, and at the request of a mere man, He comes down from heaven, and in order not to intimidate our nature, He does so under the species of bread and wine so that we might adore Him.

And we monks, prostrating ourselves on the ground, adore Him in silence too . . . How great God is! And when the bell summons us to the refectory, reminding us that the body needs tending to, we take refuge in silence then also, and we hide the humiliation of our physical being there while our souls keep thinking and adoring the God who manifested Himself on the altar . . . How great is God!

In other religious orders, they have this so-called "recreation" . . . Sometimes I wonder, if we Trappists were given time to talk, what would be the point? The Rule is so well arranged. Our greatest recreation is to go without it . . . We don't miss it. It would annoy us to have to break our silence . . . having to talk to one another would be distracting to us . . . Our conversations would disturb God's presence, or at least rob us of our peace, because it is very difficult not to offend God in one's speech, you could almost say it's impossible not to.[1] The Rule does permit us

---

1. "Indeed, so important is silence that permission to speak should seldom be granted even to mature disciples, no matter how good or holy or constructive their talk, because it is written: In a flood of words you will not avoid sin" (Prov 10:19) (RB 6.3-4).

to speak when absolutely necessary, and to one's superiors, etc . . . But recreation? That we are never to have . . . Saint Benedict must have set it up that way for a reason.

Humans are human . . . And even as Trappists, we'll always be human . . . So the silence is a good thing. We came to the monastery in order to seek God, at a distance from people and the world. Let us be quiet, then, and let's not talk to people about the world. The greater our silence, the closer we will be to God, and the further we will be from the world we want to forget.

The monk has sacred reading and prayer for his recreation. What more could he want? In this way, before he knows it, the day goes by . . . Work or study reclaims his attention once again in the afternoon, and when the day comes to an end and the sun starts to go down, the choir calls us back to pray Vespers.

116. Meditations of a Trappist
The Hour of Vespers

La Trapa, July 25, 1936

Vespers . . . afternoon prayer . . . A time of peace and hope, when the soul is at rest, happy to find that another day has gone by.

Vespers marks the end of our work day . . . Everything passes . . . Soon, night will be here again.

Vespers . . . the sun reaches into the chapel obliquely through a window, lighting up the tabernacle . . . it is red . . . its rays are weak, and they come up against the altar gently . . . as if kissing it. Our chanting is solemn . . . and the *Magnificat* to the Most Blessed Virgin is moving.[1]

Vespers . . . afternoon prayer . . . a prayer of rest, if there is rest to be found on this earth. A time when the soul comes to see that everything passes . . . The day's tasks have passed . . . Sorrows, if there were any, have passed; joys have passed . . . the day has passed, and with it, we too are passing, sometimes dragging the cross behind us, other times on the wings of consolation . . .

Everything has passed, and we're another day closer to our end . . . We hardly notice, and already the sun that awoke creation this morning is inviting it to rest now . . . As it starts going down, it makes us think about how everything in the world remains on the path that God has ordained for it, never stopping. Everything stays its course . . . Everything has its purpose . . . Everything has an end, suffering just the same as joy.

Vespers . . . prayer at twilight . . . the prayer in which the soul asks God for the peace of a good end.

The Trappist asks the Lord for the joy of a holy death.

Those moments of great solemnity during the psalmody, with great peace in one's heart, bring such consolation! . . . The hour of Vespers

---

1. Magnificat: the Canticle of Mary (Luke 1:46-55), prayed daily during Vespers.

contains so much joy! What a happy thought, that the day is now spent
. . . and it was spent before the tabernacle of the Lord . . .

The soul is so moved upon having completed another day in the Lord's
service. Our hearts are so grateful for the sublime privilege of having been
able to spend the day singing before the Lord . . .

In such moments, the soul longs to fly up to the glorious heights of
heaven, in order to keep singing there alongside the angels, the saints, the
Virgin . . . The soul wishes the day would never end . . . that Vespers
would go on eternally . . . The soul wants to hold back the sun . . . and
rise up to heaven with a *Gloria Patri*.[2]

Anyway, the ramblings of a mad monk.

But it's true that for me in particular, this is one of the Hours of the
Office that moves me the most.

As I said, everything contributes toward the solemnity of that Hour
. . . How sweet it is to spend a sunset singing in choir! It is a most propi-
tious hour for meditation and prayer! I believe that when Jesus of Nazareth, our divine Redeemer, was on this earth, it was at the hour of twilight
that He would speak to His disciples of heaven and His Father's love as
they walked along the wheat fields of Galilee . . . and He would console
them, promising to remain among humanity until the end of the age.[3]

It must have been at this serene hour when our Lord spoke to them
about how short life is, and how we must place our love in God alone
. . . It must have been this hour when Christ flooded the souls of His
disciples with light, and filled them with supernatural hope . . . How
serene that time spent with Jesus of Nazareth among the wheat fields of
Galilee must have been.

But we are no longer in those biblical times . . . not that it matters.
The same sky that was covering Palestine then, we are seeing right now.
The same sun that shone on Jesus comes up every day. The same words
Christ spoke to His disciples were left to us, written down so that they
might bring us consolation and so that as our souls, like theirs, are filled
with hope at this hour . . . in this time of afternoon prayer . . . we might

2. The Gloria Patri (Glory to the Father) is prayed at the conclusion of each psalm during Vespers.

3. *Remember, I am with you always, to the end of the age* (Matt 28:20).

raise ourselves up above the earth; we see how short-lived everything is and think only of the love of a God so good that He has permitted us to spend the day in His presence. The hymns, psalms, and prayers of this Hour of the Office . . . are infused with love, faith, hope, and charity . . .

Let us know how to collect ourselves in the silence of our hearts, and let us thank the Lord for the joy of knowing that just as the day ends with the Virgin Mary's help,[4] so too will our lives as Trappists . . . Our lives of prayer and sacrifice, silence and love.

How great God is!

---

4. At San Isidro, every Hour of the Divine Office was preceded by the corresponding Hour from the Little Office of the Blessed Virgin Mary. While the Little Office fell out of practice after Vatican II, Trappists still end each Hour with an invocation to Mary.

117. Meditations of a Trappist
How to Be Happy

La Trapa, July 26, 1936

Ave Maria

Yesterday and today, as they are feast days, I've had a lot of free time
. . . and so I can spend it writing down my thoughts, as I have been doing
up to now.

Today is Sunday, and at the moment it is seven in the morning on a
beautiful July day. I have already heard the holy Mass, at which I received
the Lord . . . I heard the word of God at chapter[1] through our Father
Abbot, who spoke to the community about the duties of fraternal correction . . . And then I had breakfast, and afterward I went to pray a *Salve*
to the Immaculate Virgin in the little chapel next to the main altar.

Now I have before me a crucifix made of iron and a portrait of the
Virgin Mary, cut from a newspaper and pasted on cardboard . . . It is an
image of Our Lady of Solitude,[2] which a pious soul sent me in a letter
that included these words: "How can anyone complain of their suffering?"

There is a window on my left, through which the morning breeze
reaches me . . . along with a fly or two.

---

1. Chapter: This refers to a gathering of the entire monastic community, named for the
historic purpose of such meetings: hearing and reflecting on a chapter from the Rule of
Saint Benedict. At San Isidro, the community would gather for such reflection every morning after the hour of Prime (*La vida cisterciense en el monasterio de San Isidro de Dueñas*
[Burgos: Tipografía de «El Monte Carmelo», 1923], 85). The hour of Prime fell out of
practice after Vatican II, and with it, the frequency and purpose of chapter meetings were
modified at many monasteries.

2. Our Lady of Solitude: The devotion to Mary under the title of Our Lady of Solitude,
in commemoration of Mary's solitude on Holy Saturday, is common in Spain. The specific
image Rafael refers to here was of the patroness of the Confraternity of Mena (Congregación
de Mena), an association of lay faithful in Málaga, Spain.

I have two hours ahead of me . . . Two hours of peace and quiet . . . And on top of all that, a heart in love with God . . . and pen and paper . . . I have, then, reasons (except for the flies) to be happy.

Truly, how little it takes to make a Trappist brother happy. If I were in the world, perhaps I would be thinking about some complicated excursion, the more complicated the better . . . I would surely have paced through the house a thousand times in circles, not knowing what outfit to put on. I would have read the newspaper headlines, without absorbing the news. I would have given the piano a smack or two and turned on the radio, and in the end, I would have decided not to do anything, which is the most comfortable choice.

Lord, Lord, what a complicated life they lead in the world . . . How much time I wasted . . . How difficult it is for people to be happy.

Meanwhile here, in the peace of my monastery, how well we live without anything . . . Without newspapers or radios . . . with only one outfit that we never take off, not even to sleep . . . With our Rule that sets our schedule and tells us what we must do, with the assurance that what we are doing is the will of God . . .

How good life is without the complications of the world . . . In silence and in detachment. How many reasons I have to thank God for my vocation . . . my vocation that is based on seeking God in the plainness and simplicity of everything.

How happy the Trappist is—one who is truly Trappist, not just in external things but in internal simplicity.

For those of us who were somewhat complicated in the world . . . Well, I can't explain it, but I have come to understand those words of Jesus: *Unless you become like children.*[3]

How many things the world needs to be happy . . . ! To be happy on their terms . . . and seen from a Trappist perspective, how little they settle for! . . . For not even a million planets loaded with riches would be enough to equal a single act of love for God from the most humble Trappist oblate.

The world says to the monk: you're crazy, leaving everything behind and finding your happiness in nothing. But the monk says to the world:

3. Matt 18:3.

not at all, it's exactly the other way around . . . I have left behind nothing in order to have everything.

The truth is that I have nothing here, neither my own will nor my freedom, but in exchange I have God . . . this God that you cannot give me. In short, there are some things that do not compare.

Question:
Why would God create flies?

Answer:
So that I would put my hood up.

118. *Meditations of a Trappist*

Viaticum

La Trapa, July 27, 1936

Indeed, everything comes and goes. There is a brother in the infirmary who is dying . . . and has known it for a while.[1] We gave him Extreme Unction yesterday . . . If you're not used to seeing it, it's a somewhat moving experience.

Once we finish None in choir, Reverend Father Abbot goes to the sacristy, puts on his vestments, miter, and stole, and takes up the crosier.[2] From there, the procession begins. A priest carries the cross; another carries the holy oils; Reverend Father Abbot follows them, preceded by the crosier-bearer, who yesterday was me; and last, the master of ceremonies . . . the community follows behind in two lines, singing the penitential psalms.

We head for the sick brother's room. Our sick brother joyfully awaits the visit of the Lord, who will come to be with him, after Father Abbot anoints him with the holy oils . . .

The community sings the psalms proper to the occasion as the ceremony proceeds. The bell rings from afar . . . for Viaticum . . . Christ is coming to visit our sick brother . . . Perhaps this is the last time he will receive Him sacramentally . . . The community prostrates themselves as the Lord passes by, and through the hands of his Father Abbot, the sick brother receives true Life and Health . . . What does the rest matter?

I don't know how to write about this . . . All I can do is roughly describe the external ceremony . . . the ceremony and the rubrics laid out

---

1. Brother Gabriel Salevicens Amboz (1873–1936), a lay brother who worked in the laundry at San Isidro for many years (OC 654).

2. The miter (a triangular headdress) and crosier (a pastoral staff) are symbols of authority most commonly associated with bishops, but also used by monastic abbots. Abbesses are also presented with a crosier upon being admitted to their office, though not the miter.

in our Usages[3] . . . But when it comes to the spirit that animates the Trappists . . . the faith of the dying man, who no longer expects anything from this earth . . . the emotion in my soul as I realized that man's end is life's true beginning . . . I don't know how to put any of that into words . . . These things are so huge, and so personal . . . All I can say is that when you see how Trappists prepare to leave this world, your soul feels envy, and you wish you were dying . . .

On the cover of this notebook, I have drawn a Trappist and a cross.[4] The monk is kneeling at the foot of the cross . . . And the cross's shadow darkens his white habit. No comment or explanation needed, I think.

3. The Usages of the Cistercian Order of the Strict Observance govern the daily life of the monastery, including liturgical practices, as Rafael notes here. For the Usages in place at San Isidro during Rafael's time, see *Usos de la Orden de los Cistercienses de la Estrecha Observancia* (Westmalle, Belgium: [General Chapter of 1926], 1928), available in English as *Regulations of the Order of Cistercians of the Strict Observance published by the General Chapter of 1926* (Dublin: M. H. Gill & Sons, 1927).

4. See #108.

119. Meditations of a Trappist
Not Knowing How to Cut Grass

La Trapa, July 29, 1936

Ave Maria

A pause in the morning's work. It's a bright day, but not a hot one, and a fresh breeze ripples through the greenery, bringing forth a whisper from the leaves of the trees. It is seven in the morning. A monk kisses the cross of the rosary he was praying on the way, and then he puts it back in the roomy pockets of his tunic. He crosses himself, and without further ado, he diligently gets to work cutting grass.

Silence . . . the only sound is the slash of the sickle as it cuts through the plants . . . from time to time, a rock goes flying . . . that Trappist doesn't know how to cut grass. An hour goes by.

At a distance, from the monastery tower, a bell rings eight times. A clap is heard, signaling a pause in the work period. The monk obeys, laying the sickle down, wiping the sweat from his brow, and sitting down at the edge of a pathway . . . He looks up at the sky and takes out his rosary. The sky is blue . . . very blue, very clear, not a cloud in it, flooded with light, and as the Trappist holds his rosary, he thinks about how Mary's mantle must be just like that . . . so clear, bright, and blue.

Everything exudes peace . . . It makes one want to die. How great God is! How wonderfully He does things! That poor Trappist loves God so much! . . . And God knows it.

The monk is still holding his rosary, but he hasn't gotten past the first bead . . . Lost in thought about Mary's mantle covering the earth and everyone on it . . . the Trappist got distracted and didn't pray at all . . . How sweet it is to think of Mary!

A clap rings out . . . How the time flies! He puts his rosary away again, crosses himself, and picks the sickle back up. The meadow is full of sunlight, the sky is still blue . . . just like the mantle of the Virgin, who, from Her throne at God's side, is looking down on Her son as he thinks of Her and hunches down over the grass to cut it . . .

All is peace, silence, and prayer in the Trappist's heart. All that can be heard is the sound of the sickle as it cuts the grass, and the occasional rock goes flying . . . That monk doesn't know how to cut grass . . . It doesn't matter. The Virgin looks down at him and smiles at his clumsiness. The Virgin Mary is good that way.

120. Meditations of a Trappist
The Sea in Fair Weather

La Trapa, July 30, 1936

Ave Maria

The Cistercian life is a life of silence. It's no surprise, then, that the Cistercian monk should find inspiration for his meditation in silence or, rather, that silence should be the environment or place in which his spiritual life develops.

Silence is like a sea where all our thoughts are sailing. And just as all kinds of vessels plow through the sea, from little sailboats to proud, majestic ships, so too is the sea of our silence populated with little white-sailed schooners, or dirty fishing boats that spew out a ton of smoke, or, sometimes, a passenger ship plowing serenely and majestically through the waters.

The life of silence is very much like a sea in fair weather with calm waters. A soul in silence is like a sea undisturbed by even the slightest breeze.

Thoughts of God sail around the silent soul, and with greater silence comes greater peace and serenity, and a greater capacity for remaining in the Lord's presence.

The Trappist loves his silence as a sailor loves the sea.

But not everything in this life is peace. A pilot must often struggle against stormy seas . . . The waters are not always still, and sometimes they grow weary of being calm, and they roar and foam with fury, beating against the shore as if it were the cause of its ill temper. Similarly, when souls are at rest in God, their peace will be disturbed when they break silence.

When the monk breaks his silence, without even meaning to, he speaks of the world, of his tastes and pleasures . . . of himself . . . The sea is troubled now . . . Oh, if only he would speak of God alone . . . but even so . . . it is so hard not to offend God with one's tongue.

Let us Cistercian monks be quiet, then . . . We came to the monastery in order to seek God in the silence of our souls . . . so let us be quiet, and not stir up the waters of our memories, our passions, our own self-love.

Let us be quiet, both when the divine Jesus has consoled us and when we are alone with our cross.

Let us be quiet, and keep our silence, for in it we shall find our treasure, if we know how to seek Him.

So, then, let us love silence, as a sailor loves the sea.

Let us distance ourselves from the shore . . . and put out into the deep[1] . . . When we can no longer see land, and the horizon blends into the sky, let us lift our eyes to the heights where God dwells; then we shall see that our peace in this world grows in the same measure as our silence, and it shall be complete only when it is as great as the seas over all the earth.

The Virgin Mary, the Star who guides sailors, will guide us and give us light when we enter into the night of our solitude.

The life of a Cistercian monk is . . . love for God, love for Mary, and silence among men.

1. See Luke 5:4.

121. Meditations of a Trappist
"How Great Is the Mercy of God!"

La Trapa, August 1, 1936

Ave Maria

How great is the mercy of God! The heart stretches as it contemplates divine mercy. Man is nothing . . . perhaps worse than nothing. His life on earth is of no importance, unfathomably so.

God is infinite . . . The human mind cannot comprehend His existence from all eternity.

Behold the two, man and God. Two different beings, infinitely so . . . It would be a sin of pride even to attempt to compare them . . . God, who exceeds the heavens, the mere idea of whom drives man's soul mad; man . . . misery, sin, littleness . . . an invisible atom in space.

How great is the mercy of God!

The soul of this man, who approached God in communion today, cannot put that mercy into words. How great is the mercy of God!

The heart of this poor Trappist, who, unable to understand it, stunned with admiration, had God within him today . . . doesn't know what to say.

How great is the mercy of God! He repeats this exclamation slowly but does not come to understand it . . . His soul loses itself in the greatness of the Creator, who deigns to come down among creatures . . .

In the mysterious, silent hours of the night, the Trappist meditates upon the mysteries of his religion . . . the mysteries of a God who, being God, became man, and not satisfied with that, hides Himself in the humility of a tabernacle to be our consolation on this earth.

The monk also hides himself from the eyes of the world in order to be with his God, and in these tranquil hours spent in His presence, the Trappist finds that the austerity of his life is abundantly rewarded . . . In exchange for his monastic silence, sweet conversations with Jesus . . . for his sacrifice and crucifixion to the world, the treasures of supernatural graces.

"How great is the mercy of God!" he slowly repeats along the monastery cloisters, while dawn's first light seeps in through the windows, little by little, announcing the sunrise . . . And the new day dawns as if answering the birds' call, and as if the joy of the light were itself a response to the exclamation of that Trappist, whose heart never tires of singing the mercies and greatness of the absolute Master of all creation.

122. Meditations of a Trappist
The Tower Bells

La Trapa, August 2, 1936

Ave Maria

It's two in the morning. . . . A brother lights a candle in the chapel and another in the cloister. The community wakes up . . . The only sound to be heard is that of the monks' habits rustling as they hurry from the dormitories to chapel.

The choir fills up with white shadows who silently kneel in their places. The Trappist leaves sleep behind in order to praise God, who is waiting for him in the tabernacle.

A few brief minutes go by. The last one has finally arrived . . . In every community there's a monk who arrives last . . . Someone has to, and the last monk is just as necessary as the first.

The clock repeats the hour . . . it's two o'clock. A brother rises from his place and slowly goes over to ring the tower bell. It is a solemn moment . . . Men inform heaven that they are about to begin chanting, and ask God to listen to them . . . Their first words will be for the Virgin Mary.

The tower bell rings out low . . . Its sound flows through the valley and over the fields, and jumps from star to star until it reaches Jesus and Mary in heaven. The bell's final toll has not yet come when, at the superior's signal, all the Trappists prostrate themselves, and their bowed foreheads nearly touch the ground. A voice is heard uttering the first words said in the monastery, those that the angel spoke to the Virgin: *Ave Maria, gratia plena, Dominus tecum.*[1]

And the choir responds, *Benedicta tu in mulieribus et benedictus fructus ventris tui.*[2] And up in heaven, Mary hears them.

---

1. That is, "Hail Mary, full of grace, the Lord is with you."
2. "Blessed are you among women, and blessed is the fruit of your womb."

I believe that the humble prayer of that Trappist who lifts up his heart to God in the silence of the night while his eyes are still heavy with sleep must be pleasing to Mary.

And thus Matins begin in La Trapa, with the ring of a bell, prostration on the floor, and an appeal to the Virgin.

123. Meditations of a Trappist

Spain Is at War

La Trapa, August 2, 1936

J-H-S

We are in an age of revolution, a time of bloody war among brothers and sisters who belong to the same nation.

The news that reaches the monastery from the world has introduced a note of sadness into our conventual peace. Spain is at war. Our brothers and sisters out there in the world are killing each other. Some are God's enemies, and others fight under the banner of Christ. All battle beneath the gaze of the King of the world . . . Everything was prepared by the Master and Lord of humanity. No one will go further than He allows them to.

Here in this Trappist monastery there are souls who are offering themselves to God for the sake of peace in Spain. These souls, at a distance from political battles, beg God for peace among brothers and sisters, victory for Christ's followers, and forgiveness for God's enemies.

Everything that Spain is going through is a test of divine mercy. Impiety reigned among evil people in broad daylight; apathy and lukewarmness overpowered good people, and immorality and paganism seeped in on all sides.

Spain needed to be shaken up . . . It needed to be made clean . . . It needed to react . . . It even needs martyrs to die for it. And God's mercy is permitting a war to break out.

Perhaps entire cities will be destroyed. Perhaps Spaniards will die by the thousands . . . Perhaps this will be the material ruin of the nation. It won't matter . . . if as a result, Christians are purified of their sins, immorality is at least somewhat banished from their ways, and Spain is spiritually elevated.

God deals with the peoples as they deserve, and if He sends war and desolation to some in punishment for their sins, He scourges others with suffering to remind them that He exists, and to show them their own ingratitude, in order to shake them out of their indifference.

Spain, which has given so much glory to Christ's church, a home to saints, a land that is exceptional for its Catholicism, is asleep. With this war, God is giving it a wake-up call. Will it respond?

The Trappists of Venta de Baños are praying to the Virgin Mary for Spain. May Our Lady of the Pillar of Zaragoza[1] turn Spain back to the faith . . . But if victory does not make us better people . . . then it would be preferable not to be victorious. If martyrs are needed, let there be martyrs; anything but continued offense to God. But that won't happen . . . the Virgin is watching over the Spanish people, and the Heart of Jesus will not abandon us.

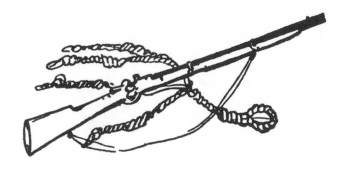

Today, August 2, 1936, the whole community is keeping vigil before the Most Blessed Sacrament to pray for peace, to pray for those who are dying, to make reparation for many sins, and so that He might conform us all to His divine will.[2] And God must hear us . . . because God is very good.

1. The title of Our Lady of the Pillar (La Virgen del Pilar) refers to the apparition of Mary to Saint James while he was preaching in Zaragoza, now part of Spain and home to her major shrine.

2. The Bishop of Palencia, now Saint Manuel González García, in consultation with the abbot of San Isidro, Dom Félix Alonso García, had the community increase their penances and offer time spent in Adoration for the intention of a triumph over atheism and anti-clericalism (OC 665–66).

Of course, our fasting, prayer, and use of the discipline[3] is not enough . . . All that is a drop in the bucket . . . The death of every human being would not be enough to atone for a single mortal sin . . . an infinite offense against the Infinite One.

But we should not let despondency fester in our hearts . . . When we beg God for mercy and forgiveness, we do so as David did, *secundum multitudinem miserationum tuarum*.[4] That is, it is not on account of our own merits, but rather because of the abundance and greatness of His mercy that He will remove our sins and those of the whole world. God is so great! Humanity has gone so mad!

---

3. Cilices and disciplines: Instruments of physical penance (see #40, n. 15).
4. *According to our abundant mercy* (Ps 51:1).

124. Meditations of a Trappist
"Life Is a Struggle"

La Trapa, August 3, 1936

Ave Maria

Five o'clock in the morning. A Trappist has just received communion. What does he have to say? What is he thinking about? Perhaps his soul is in a daze. . .he has just done something so sublime. . .But no, unfortunately, although he'd like to go mad every time he receives his God, that's not what happens. . . He's still a man on earth, not an angel in heaven, and as such, what can be expected of him? *The spirit indeed is willing, but the flesh is weak.*[1]

He bears with his body as God instructs him. His soul would like to fly unto realms of light, but his eyelids are heavy with sleep. . . they close . . . and they remind him that life is a struggle, and a struggle against darkness.

It is truly a humiliation to have to live. It is truly a humiliation to be subject to the body, which so often conquers us, and which we could not do without, even if we wanted to.

It is truly a humiliation not to be able to receive God somewhere else. Rather, it must be here, within us, within our misery, within our souls bound to physical form. . . to a physical form that holds us back, as when our eyelids, heavy with sleep, want to close. . .

Lord Jesus, forgive that poor Trappist oblate. . . Don't measure his love for You by what he does or says to You, because he often fails to say or do anything. His will is different from his actions. His soul is merely able to recognize that it deserves nothing. If you, Lord, were to put us under scrutiny, who could withstand it?[2]

---

1. Matt 26:41.
2. Rafael's paraphrase of Ps 130:3, *If you, O Lord, should mark iniquities, Lord, who could stand?*

That poor Cistercian oblate, who falls asleep in choir without meaning to . . . That poor little brother, who wants to fly, but finds himself with clipped wings, bound to his body and its miseries.

Let it be enough for you to walk in the humble way that the Lord has marked out for you, and may your very weaknesses help you to learn to love God . . . who loves you just as you are, frail and weak, eyelids heavy with sleep.

125. Meditations of a Trappist
Tying Sheaves

La Trapa, August 3, 1936

Today we went out to tie sheaves of wheat . . . It was fairly hot out, and our work location was a few kilometers from the monastery.

It's one thing to eat bread . . . and another thing entirely to trudge through wheatfields in August . . . Our habits are so thick! . . . If we were in white pants and shirts then maybe it would be all right . . . that is, in the shade, cooling off with a drink.

All that nonsense about the "sun" . . . and the "fields of golden grain" . . . and the "humble reaper," etc.[1] . . . etc. . . . It's lovely when Gabriel y Galán[2] is writing poems about it, to be read under the shade of a thick black poplar . . .

But enough . . . enough already with the "fields of golden grain." Still, it's a good thing that this business of wheat and sheaves is all very biblical,[3] . . . and it's always a consolation.

Of course, this sweaty, dusty Trappist isn't complaining . . . Quite the contrary, he thanks the Lord profusely, and offers Him these little tasks . . . At the end of the day, he is merely complying with the law imposed upon him, and he does so with joy and true peace.

---

1. The "fields of golden grain" and "humble reaper" are tropes of pastoral poetry. Despite citing a different poet, Rafael appears to be drawing specifically from neoclassical poet Juan Meléndez Valdés (1754–1817), whose pastoral romance "The Reapers" includes the following chorus: "Reapers, to the fields of grain! / For the golden morning / has already opened her rosy gates / to the sun rising from the east" (Juan Meléndez Valdés, "Romance XV: Los segadores," in *Poesías* [Madrid: Imprenta Real, 1820], 2:70–71).

2. José María Gabriel y Galán (1870–1905) was a Spanish poet whose works are known for their pastoral themes and Catholic perspective.

3. The motif of sheaves of wheat is prominent throughout the Bible; see, e.g., Gen 37; Lev 23; Ruth 2; Pss 126, 129; Matt 13.

On the other hand, he is so grateful when it's time to return to the monastery . . . to the house of God, who awaits us in the tabernacle, where we will tell Him all about what we just finished doing outside . . .

Everything passes, cold and heat, and the day is coming when our work will be finished . . . In heaven, there's no need to tie sheaves . . . because there isn't any wheat up there.

126. Meditations of a Trappist
No News from the World

La Trapa, August 4, 1936

Ave Maria

We still don't have any news from the world . . . How faraway that word sounds, "the world" . . . What, are we Trappists no longer part of it? Yes, we are, but thanks be to God, our cloister protects us from its many spiritual dangers. We live in the world, but at a great distance from it.

But now, Spain being in the condition it's in, we Spanish monks cannot remain unaffected . . . If we have no desire to learn anything about the world when it's happy and enjoying itself . . . now that it's suffering and there's a war on, we want to know everything and help everyone . . . Monks are not so selfish as people think.

Nevertheless, we don't know anything . . . for better or for worse. We just keep praying to God for the sake of our beloved country.

127. Meditations of a Trappist
On Our Way to Work[1]

La Trapa, August 5, 1936

Ave Maria

In just a few minutes, it'll be six-thirty in the morning. . . One must make the most of one's time. A Trappist oblate's first duty is to Mary. . . So he turns to Her, and kneels before Her altar for the few moments at his disposal before the Rule sends him off to work.

At the altar, he venerates the Immaculate . . . She has a little chapel next to the main altar, and is very often visited by those devoted to the Virgin. He kneels upon the first steps and gazes up at the statue, which looks back at Her son from Her little alcove.

"Our Lady, I'm off to work . . . come with me," he says to her . . . "Our Lady, help me . . . help me morally and physically. May my work be acceptable to God . . . Accompany me as I leave the monastery. Don't abandon your poor oblate at this moment, which may be when he needs you the most . . ."

On the steps of the altar, the man keeps praying to Mary . . . and I think that up in heaven, the Virgin is listening to him . . . listening, and looking after him.

It's time to go to work . . . a *Salve*, a bit of holy water for the sign of the cross, and then we're quickly off to the speaking room.[2] There, we put on our black-and-white-striped aprons and wait silently in a line for the superior to tell us what our task is.

1. Although Rafael's mother provided the title for most of the essays in Meditations of a Trappist, Rafael titled this one himself (see #108, n. 3).
2. Speaking room: A designated room in a monastery where speech is permitted. At San Isidro, the speaking room was used for brief audiences with superiors and for the daily distribution of work (OC 671).

Father Master arrives. One by one, he tells us our tasks . . . Today, we're off to the fields. We put on our straw hats and our clogs . . . Those are heavy, and pretty hard. Mine are fairly big. I call them my "luggage."

The monastery's iron gate opens, and a line of Trappists heads out to work in the fields. Father Master leads them, while Father Submaster follows behind the group, or in his absence, the most senior novice.[3] The only sound to be heard is that of our clogs, scraping against stones with their thick nails as we walk.

Man is observing one of God's laws . . . work . . . A punishment imposed because of the fall of Adam,[4] a punishment that many rebel against and, in doing so, offend God . . . But for the Trappist, everything is made gentle and pleasant because he relies on heaven's aid . . . which never fails.

No matter how hard the day's work may be, God is the one who directs it . . . and the Virgin is the one who helps, encourages, and consoles us.

Of course work is a punishment, but when you truly love the one who imposed it . . . when you see the mercy of the one who is punishing us . . . then you come to see that work is necessary. When the Lord provides for us the means to obey this law on earth, He distinguishes us as His favorite children. Besides, as Saint Francis de Sales says, "Let us make a virtue of necessity."[5]

So there is nothing to fear from working in the fields . . . Let us have compunction for our sins and faults, and let us love the difficult penance that God asks of us . . . and thus, with a rosary in one hand, a hoe in the other, and our hearts fixed on Christ, the line of Trappists goes forth to obey what Saint Benedict laid out for us in our Rule . . . manual labor.

Among them . . . rather, the last among them, is an oblate . . . a soul who wants to become holy, and who also, as a Trappist, wants to offer to God a heart and soul redeemed through work.

3. Father Master: Fr. José Olmedo Arrieta (see #95, n. 1). Father Submaster: Fr. Francisco Díez Martínez (see #48, n. 1).

4. See Gen 3:17, 19.

5. While Rafael attributes this now-common saying to Saint Francis de Sales, it can be found (as *faciat de necessitate virtutem*) in Saint Peter Chrysologus as well as Saint Jerome. See Peter Chrysologus, *Selected Sermons*, vol. 2, trans. William B. Palardy (Washington, DC: Catholic University of America Press, 2004), 171; and Jerome, *Dogmatic and Polemical Works*, trans. John N. Hritzu (Washington, DC: Catholic University of America Press, 1965), 164.

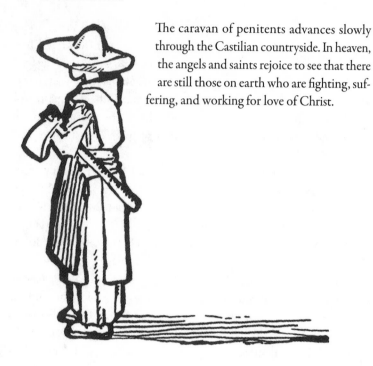

The caravan of penitents advances slowly through the Castilian countryside. In heaven, the angels and saints rejoice to see that there are still those on earth who are fighting, suffering, and working for love of Christ.

128. Meditations of a Trappist
You Don't Just Come and Conquer

La Trapa, August 5, 1936

Ave Maria

Unfortunately, in the religious life, it's not all devotion . . . People change seven times a day, and anything can make them waver . . . At the end of the day, people are people; creatures with bodies and souls, and, therefore, with struggles in which the spirit does not always have the upper hand. God in His mercy permits this, so that we might not boast about ourselves, but learn to humble ourselves as we realize how little we are and turn to Him in everything.

It's true, the Trappist lives more for heaven than earth, but he is still on earth. As long as he is walking through this valley of tears,[1] he has to keep his spirits up so that he doesn't lose heart. Often, that means *doing violence to himself*, and in that he is joyfully obeying another law of Christ, who imposed it upon us that we might gain the kingdom of God.[2]

No . . . the monk's life is not all peace and sweetness. Our souls are not always in the heights of consolation in prayer, or even in contemplation . . . Sometimes the old self reawakens and wages war on us.[3] Our past life with all its memories . . . we can't forget a single blow, even if we want to.

You don't just come and conquer . . . The eternal life for which the soul yearns day in and day out cannot be earned except through surrender, sacrifice, and embracing the cross of Christ . . . That is the only way . . . That is the way followed by religious. Hope keeps them going, faith guides them, and love is their light . . .

---

1. See the *Salve Regina*: "To thee do we send up our sighs, mourning and weeping in this valley of tears."

2. *From the days of John the Baptist until now the kingdom of heaven has suffered violence, and the violent take it by force* (Matt 11:12).

3. See Eph 4:22-24.

458   *The Collected Works*

But when God allows faith to darken, and hope to be lost, and love to grow weak, oh! in that moment . . . when the soul is all alone with its cross, surrounded by darkness, plagued by its own misery and weakness . . . oh! in that moment, one comes to understand the martyrdom of religious life . . . That is when God tries souls, and when heaven's aid and Mary's protection are needed.

How easy it is to love God in consolation, when everything smiles upon us, and our spirits seem to fly . . . ! But those who truly love God don't need any of that. Joy and suffering are all the same to them, and they love God when they are flooded with sunlight just as much as when they are drowning in darkness.

How necessary are the peaks and valleys of spiritual life . . . How great is the mercy of God, who permits even the weaknesses and imperfections of His most beloved children, so that we might come to understand what we are.

Let us keep fighting day after day, without losing heart, whether our souls are ecstatic with love or in the sad human condition of dragging on the ground.

Onward, all for Jesus and always through Mary!!

129. *Meditations of a Trappist*

The Pears in the Grove

La Trapa, August 6, 1936

Ave Maria

Today, Father Master ordered me to gather up the straw and ears of wheat left over on the ground at our work site once the sheaves have been tied.

You do this with a long rake. I don't know what it's called, but it doesn't matter. Armed, then, with my work instrument, I distanced myself from the other novices and went where I'd been told to go.

On my right is wheat that hasn't been reaped yet, crossed by a road, covered in brick-red dust. On my left is a grove full of trees and tall grass, with a great deal of shade and many birds. And above me is the blue sky, which is very clear, not a cloud in it. In my hands, I have the rake, which I use to gather up ears of wheat scattered across the uneven ground.

There's nobody around . . . An absolute silence reigns at this hour in the countryside, interrupted only by a nightingale singing in the grove, while the other birds serve as its choir . . . I start singing too . . . Nobody can hear me here . . . My work is simple, and it doesn't wear me out . . . It doesn't require much effort to rake up stray ears.

Amid all this, I hear the faraway footsteps of a little donkey . . . and I fall silent.

Coming down the road covered in brick-colored dust, there is a good woman wearing a kerchief on her head, carrying a basket, and riding elegantly on the donkey, whose quick little steps make a joyful click-clack . . .

The woman sees me, and as she passes by, she hollers out a thunderous "good morning," perhaps stretching out the "o" in morning too long. And since I can't speak, I thank her for her greeting by raising my hand up to the brim of my hat and doing a very strange gesture with my fingers . . .

It was hot out . . . The sun was doing what the Lord asks it to do in August, which is beat down . . . and today, it was doing that quite well.

The good woman was already a good distance away when she stopped her ride, turned back toward me, and shouted, "If you go down into the grove, my husband will give you a pear". . . . I raised my arm to her once again, and with a joyful click-clack from the little donkey as it stomped along the brick-red road, the charitable woman went away . . .

I looked at the dust rising up . . . then I looked over at the grove where her husband was, and therefore, the pears . . . and last, I looked up at the sky, which was still very blue and clear, and I kept gathering up the ears scattered on the ground with my long rake.

130. *Meditations of a Trappist*
You Alone

La Trapa, August 8, 1936

Ave Maria

God . . . He is the one thing that keeps me going, the only reason for my monastic life . . . For me, God is everything, He is in everything, and I see Him in everything. What interest can creatures hold for me? What interest can I hold for myself? Dwelling on myself just makes me crazy, and it's vanity to busy yourself with things other than God. And nevertheless, how easy it is to forget our true reason for living, and how often we live without any reason at all.

Every minute, hour, day, and year that we have not spent living for God is time wasted.

One can understand and explain why people forget about God in the world, and focus only on living this mortal life well . . . after all, the world is God's enemy. Enough said. But in our life of solitude and silence, we often waste time . . . it is truly a shame, and nevertheless, that's often how it is.

Lord, my God, what do I care for anything that isn't You? What do I get out of focusing on creatures so much? What am I, that I should look at myself so much? Truly, it's all vanity. You alone should occupy my life. You alone should fill my heart . . . You alone should be my only thought.

God, the only reason to live, to exist . . . God should reign over even the air we breathe, the light shed upon us. God, who is the beginning, middle, and end of all things, ought to be all the more so for a Trappist monk . . . who dwells in the house of God, who lives only to praise Him, and who remains in His presence day and night.

He is in everything . . . in choir, in the fields, in our work, He is there when we eat and when we sleep . . . It's all the same, because it all reminds us why we came to the monastery, which was to seek Him in austerity, in silence, in chapel, and in the garden, to seek Him inside ourselves as well as outside.

We should see the Creator in everything that surrounds us, whether it is beautiful and pleasant or ugly and repulsive. . . It is all His work. There is nothing useless under the sun. The times when our souls are flooded with God's light, and it seems that everything is smiling upon us, are just as necessary as when the darkness of desolation overpowers us, and the cloudy skies weigh down on us as if to crush us.

It is a matter of seeing God in everything. . . and not wasting a minute of our lives, not believing that fervor is a sign that everything is going well and that when we lack it God is far away from us. . . May the Virgin free us from that mistake.

May we Trappists be persuaded of the fact that God is with us at every moment. . . May we be rid of any impression that deludes our senses . . . Let's go beyond ourselves, let's get rid of that ego that does us so much harm, and throw ourselves into God's arms, just as we are, with our weaknesses and our virtues, our sins and our miseries. Let us put our souls against His bosom, both when they are laughing and when they are crying. If we truly do this, and we make our lives entirely for Him, and make Him our everything, we will have obtained true peace of heart, we will be closer to heaven than earth, and then . . . what will you care, Brother Rafael, if it's rainy or sunny?[1]

1. The first of the two images below shows a scroll reading "God alone suffices" ("solo Dios basta"), from a poem by Saint Teresa of Ávila (see #107). Image source: LPM, 238. The second, showing the back of a monk in his cowl, was done on the inside back cover of the notebook and served as a conclusion to Meditations of a Trappist (see Juan Antonio Martínez Camino, *Mi Rafael* [Bilbao: Desclée de Brouwer, 2003], 242–44). Image source: LPM, 232.

Solo Dios basta.....

131. To Leopoldo Barón

La Trapa, August 30, 1936

J-H-S
Ave Maria
My dearest brother,

You weren't expecting a letter from me with all this going on, were you? But look, it's Sunday, so I have more time. Therefore, not knowing why and not really having anything to say, I asked Father Master for permission to write you, and so I am. May the Virgin guide my pen so that I might find something useful to say. Perhaps that's a bit daring of me. What help can I offer you, since I have nothing of my own? But look . . . I won't stop wanting to help you however I can on that account. I don't need to tell you what my assistance consists of now.

I'm so far away from what's going on in the world. Believe me, I don't know what to say . . . I know there's a war on, that half of Spain is fighting the other half. I hear terrifying news. I know nothing more . . .

My parents have been here. In the few moments I spent with them, they filled my head with battalions, injuries, deaths, shootings, cities laid waste, hymns that were new to me, and new flags too, war and velocity . . .

I'm telling you, from our perspective here, it would be enough to make one go mad, were it not for our ability to see God's mercy in it. We monks turn to His tabernacle in an effort to make up for what seems to be lacking in the world.

It's so hard for a Trappist to talk about war . . . !

I'm telling you, I can't comprehend what's going on. If I were writing to anyone but you, I'd worry that my letter and these words would strike a discordant note amid all the chaos of the world, in which I imagine you're quite involved . . .

They say you're carrying a rifle around Ávila now. Every visitor we get here does nothing but talk about the war. It seems like everyone is extremely nervous, fearful, zealous, anxious . . . it must be awful. Perhaps all that will make this letter sound strange to you, since I can't offer you any news, but I do want these words to bring you some peace . . . Not the peace that the world gives, which is deceptive, but rather that other peace that the world cannot understand.[1]

I want to give you strength to keep going . . . I don't know how to write or express myself . . . just hear everything I want to say without me having to say it. I don't want to be impertinent by telling you what's going on with me . . . Just know that I have my "front" too, although mine isn't so noisy, and there are no flags or gunshots here. With the Virgin's help, I am fighting for Spain too. Everything is a battle on this earth, but the difference is that the victories won by those who fight at the tabernacle's side will be known only to heaven.

Take heart, my dear brother, and fight faithfully . . . and look, don't tell anybody, but I think there's still a lot of vanity around despite people's enthusiasm . . . They say there's been a big religious uprising, is that true? . . . A lot of military men come through La Trapa, and they all drink wine and shout a lot, but only a few will actually come to chapel and pray a *Salve* to the Virgin.

Look, pay me no mind. Remember, I'm not in the world, and I don't know what's going on . . . I just see the war through the lens of my Trappist spirit, and maybe I'm getting it wrong. It's just that . . . well, I still don't have the words to express myself, but I'm sure you'll understand what I mean.

The soldier's fight in the world is so different from the monk's fight in his monastery! . . . Their weapons are so different! But no matter . . . it's a question of redirecting everything toward God, don't you think? He sees it all, and someday He'll put an end to it all, too.

Let us keep moving forward, dear Uncle Polín . . . . Each of us in the place that God in His infinite goodness has marked out for us . . . Let us love this fight, and not fear to lose our lives in it . . . Let us each love our battle front, despite the occasional defeat. Let us seek out Mary's help and fear nothing . . . What a fool I am, I don't have to tell you any of this . . . You know it all perfectly well.

But look, it's never a bad thing to remember that, even if I am coming off as impertinent. From the silence of my refuge, this poor Trappist oblate

---

1. *Peace I leave with you; my peace I give to you. I do not give to you as the world gives. Do not let your hearts be troubled, and do not let them be afraid* (John 14:27).

remembers those who are struggling and fighting, those who are suffering and dying, since I can't send you strength, weapons, or money, which is what Spain is asking for . . . instead, I send you my poor prayers and the consolation of knowing that, amid the fighting, there are souls lifting their hearts to God . . . God, the one who is organizing and controlling all this child's play . . . because that's what it is, despite the cannons.

If only you knew how time spent in La Trapa changes your way of seeing things! . . . That's why I don't know how to express myself, why I can't open my heart to you . . . Besides, why bother? You know me, and even though God is changing me little by little, I'll always be the same to you.

I don't have anything in particular to tell you . . . I've started study-ing philosophy, because Reverend Father wants me to move forward.[2] Everything's the same here, as if there weren't a war, at least on the outside. But you know we Trappists are public penitents, and we have many obliga-tions now . . . as you can imagine.

My brother Fernando was here the other day. He came back to Spain to join up . . . I saw solid piety in him. He left me feeling edified, and I'm telling you, seeing God at work gave me such a motivating joy. I don't know how to explain it.

Anyway, there are so many things this little monk from Venta de Baños would like to say.

How great God is! . . . Just look at what He does in human beings . . . and despite them! What does it matter if there's a war? . . . What would it matter if the whole world were to collapse and cave in? What does it matter if people don't see God . . . so long as God sees them?

How great God is, Uncle Polín! How great is that God who hides Him-self from the powerful of this earth, and reveals Himself to the lowly! . . . How great is that God who protects the good and, as David says in Psalm 2, laughs at the impious[3] . . . ! Have you ever meditated on God's laugh? It must be terrifying . . . something we ought to fear when the time comes.

Take heart, Uncle Polín . . . let's follow God in spite of it all, in the face of it all . . . . Your little brother is encouraging you and helping you from here. He's no good for shooting guns or fighting in the world, but as

2. That is, move forward with his program of study for ordination.
3. Ps 2:4.

far as his strength allows, especially as a sick person, he wants to contribute to God's work too. For everything is His work, even when we attribute events to human beings in our stupid vanity.

As you can see, I have nothing to say that could be of any interest to you . . . I'm very dull, and more so every day. If I keep on like this, in a few years I'll even have forgotten my name . . . Being cloistered here, everything that reaches us from the world seems shallow and uninteresting . . . even though our memories sometimes wage war on us, the Most Blessed Virgin helps us so much!

And don't think that I feel bad about this, but when my family is here I can't think of anything to say or ask, and what's even more strange is that I immediately forget everything they say. I've gone a bit mad . . . but that's no wonder, given how much Jesus loves me.

Now I am following the community in everything except food, because I can't do that, but it's all the same to me. I can see clearly that Our Lady doesn't care whether I eat potatoes or rabbit . . . She loves me just the same.

If you have some free time at your disposal, put down your rifle and pick up your pen.

What is Aunt María up to? Don't you think I have forgotten about her. You told me she'd come by here, and she didn't . . . but when I learned she wouldn't have been coming alone, I understood and was glad of it. Just so you know how it is.

Tell me what's going on with you and how things are . . . although considering the state of the world, I'm guessing they're going poorly.

Well, I don't have anything else to tell you, and besides, I'm running out of time and paper.

Don't laugh at your nephew's candid tone in writing you. Remember who it's coming from and take it as such.

Give Aunt María a big hug for me . . . Tell her the *Salve* is at 7:45 now, and starting on the 14th, it'll be at 6:45. Tell her to remember that her little brother is here at La Trapa praying to the Most Blessed Virgin for her . . . And you can have whatever you'd like from this poor man, your brother in Jesus and Mary,

Brother María Rafael, O.C.S.O.✝

132. To Rafael Arnaiz Sánchez de la Campa

La Trapa, September 13, 1936

Ave Maria
My dearest father,

I received your letter the other day, and I was very grateful. As you can imagine, I was a little nervous not knowing what Fernando was doing or where he was assigned, although up to a certain point . . . seeing as this war is putting bodies in danger more than souls, the worst thing that could happen to him is getting killed . . . and you can't die more than once, you know.

Well, don't worry if they send him to the front. God is in all things, and we can do nothing but accept His will, and not with resignation but with joy. Often, there is no virtue in resignation, it's more of a necessity . . . I'll stop there, I don't want to bite off more than I can chew.

The other day we hosted General Mola and some bishops, I'm not sure how many.[1] They came here to eat . . . I didn't see any of them, of course . . . Right now we're hosting any number of *requetés* serving in this area.[2]

A plane flew by the other day looking for the Venta de Baños train station, but since all the lights were out, it couldn't find it. For those of us who live our life precisely at night, who are already in full swing at two in the morning, this business of sneaking around in the dark is a bit complicated . . . We seem like ghosts . . . We pray the Office in the lay

1. On September 10, 1936, the monastery hosted the archbishop of Burgos, Manuel de Castro Alonso (1864–1944); the bishop of Segovia, Luciano Pérez Platero (1882–1963); and one of the leaders of the Nationalist coup that kickstarted the war, General Emilio Mola (1887–1937), among other guests (OC 684).

2. *Requetés*: A paramilitary organization associated with the Carlists, a traditionalist and monarchist political movement that formed part of the Nationalist alliance during the war. Approximately half of the thirty *requetés* stationed in Venta de Baños were sent to protect the monastery, keeping watch from the bell tower at night (OC 684).

brothers' chapterhouse, because it's the only place we can all fit and keep the windows closed.

Blessed be God, how long will this all go on.

Our life hasn't changed in the least, so I don't know what to tell you that you wouldn't already know. I know nothing outside of it, and I don't want to.

I have the fortune of not having to listen to the newspaper because I don't eat in the refectory,[3] so my mind doesn't get filled up with lies and absurd contradictions. When you're far away from the world and can't see what's going on with your own eyes, it's best not to know anything.

I'm going to write Fernando a quick note[4] to say, essentially, that I'm praying for everyone and for Spain . . . Now it's up to the Virgin Mary to do with this poor Trappist's prayers as She wills.

---

3. Refectory: the common dining area in a monastery. Traditionally, meals are taken in silence while a monk reads aloud from the Roman Martyrology, Scripture, or lives of the saints. In this case, the monks were listening to a newspaper being read aloud in lieu of their usual spiritual reading.

4. See #133.

Please, don't leave me out of the loop with family news. Tell me as soon as you know anything, especially about Fernando. I have no doubt of success, because even though this seems to be going very slowly, God and the Virgin will surely come to our aid.

Well, my dear father, I don't have anything else to say.

Right now the community is offering extraordinary prayers to God asking for rain in the countryside. Honestly, it's really shocking that it hasn't rained . . . I don't know what God is doing. He must be very busy with political matters and have forgotten all about our vines. Look, I'll never be a formal monk.

Give my mother, brother, and sister lots of hugs for me. As for you, all the love you deserve and more from your son, who is thinking of you, as you know, from a place you know

Br. M. Rafael [5]

5. Rafael included the illustration of a monk's cowl and a gun underneath his signature. Image source: LPM 232.

133. To Luis Fernando Arnaiz Barón

La Trapa, September 13, 1936

Ave Maria
My dearest brother Fernando,

I got a letter from our father the other day giving me an update on you. I'm writing you a reply today, but a short one, because in all honesty I don't have anything to tell you.

Everything continues as usual here, except we don't sing Matins or Lauds in chapel anymore because we have to keep the lights out at two in the morning as a precaution against enemy planes.

I'm so glad you're in the corps of engineers. I'm sure that once you've been trained, they'll have you put what they're teaching you into practice . . . Don't worry about it. Trust the Virgin and do whatever Colonel Pruneda tells you to do.[1]

From La Trapa, your brother is helping you as much as he can, and although his prayers aren't worth much, everyone must do what is in his power. Whenever I pray for Spain, I am praying for you, because these days Spain is to be found in the army, and as far as I'm concerned the army is you, and that's it . . . But don't let it go to your head!

Do keep me apprised of what they have you do. The rest of the family is doing well, I presume, since they're in Burgos.

I don't have anything else to say that could be of any interest to you, and I don't want to make a comment about anything either. What would be the point? Don't you agree? May God help you and help us all . . . Nothing else, not even the war, matters.

---

1. Fernando had not completed his obligatory military service, so he had to start with basic training. Salvador García de Pruneda was a colonel in the corps of engineers at Cuartel de la Montaña in Madrid, where Rafael had completed his own military service also under his command (OC 687; see #10, n. 3, and #34, n. 2).

Give everyone a hug for me. All my love, your brother, who is thinking of you,

Br. M. Rafael O.C.S.O.

Don't forget that you will find everything in the Virgin Mary, as I told you that one time. If you turn to Her, I promise you everything will go well for you . . . Don't forget (and don't call me tiresome).

VI. A Deer That Thirsts

The Interior Trappist

134. To Mercedes Barón[1]

Atlantic Hotel, A Coruña,[2] October 18, 1936

Ave Maria.

¡Viva España! ¡Viva la Virgen del Pilar![3]

My dearest mother,

At this moment, your son Rafael is taking up the pen to give you the news about what's going on here.

As you can imagine, A Coruña was briming over with enthusiasm yesterday after the capture of Oviedo:[4] banners, celebrations, music, flags, cheers for Galicia and the army and the city of Oviedo.

Papá saluted the area commander with the other authorities. Rubio and Echavarri had dinner with the Asturian community, including those of us from Oviedo. I don't know where everybody else is, I guess they haven't gotten up yet.

I celebrated Spain's triumph as best I could, praising in today's Communion the only Commander of all things, the true Defender and Liberator, the Master of the world, Jesus, whose mercy is infinite . . . my dear mother, how great God is!

Now that I am in the world, amid all this commotion of movement and excitement in the frenzy of war, it is so necessary to collect myself a bit in order to see God's mercy and designs in all this. He desires only our good, and though this might seem like a punishment to us, and the horrors of

1. On September 29, 1936, Rafael left the monastery for a second time, having been called up for military service. He reported to Burgos, where he was found medically unfit to serve (VE 305).

2. A Coruña: A port city in Galicia, a province located in the northwestern corner of Spain. In Spanish it is known as La Coruña.

3. "Long live Spain! Long live Our Lady of the Pillar!" Our Lady of the Pillar refers to the apparition of Mary to Saint James while he was preaching in Zaragoza, now part of Spain and home to her major shrine (see #123, n. 1).

4. Oviedo fell to the Nationalist army on October 17, 1936.

war might make us tremble, we must keep seeing the gentle hand of the One who governs humanity's destiny at work.

We are close to seeing what happened in Oviedo, and what's left of our family and our home . . . There's no need to worry. Blessed are those who gave their lives for God and Spain. As for material goods . . . What do you want this poor Trappist-in-training to say that you don't already know? . . . God alone suffices.[5]

I don't want to do bad philosophy about this, but I'm telling you, even when surrounded by debris and corpses, one still can and should praise God and thank Him for His infinite mercy.

I don't know if we'll leave here tomorrow (Monday) or maybe Tuesday . . . First we have to make sure we can get to Oviedo, because there will be difficulties along the way . . . We'll see. We don't want to be imprudent, but I think we could get there today if it weren't for the passports.[6]

I'll tell you this: we've been praising God a great deal, and we also stocked up on ham, cold cuts, oil, cheese, canned goods, chocolate, etc. We'll arrive with a car full of enthusiasm and provisions: everything is necessary.

There is so much joy . . . .But as you can imagine, we're also very impatient. Our joy is further dimmed at times because of all the deaths and firing-squad executions and misfortunes we keep learning about . . . It's frightening. Nothing will be left of Asturias. The tragedy of the war will remain in the souls of all Asturians and all those who love Asturias for many years. Anyway, God above all things, and may Mary come to our aid.

I don't have anything else to tell you. I'm very glad I came. Since my uselessness keeps me from taking up arms to serve my country, at least I can be useful to Papá right now, and who knows . . . When God takes me away from La Trapa, He does so for a reason. As we have seen, I'm meant to be in the world at the least enjoyable times . . . Remember that October?[7]

---

5. From a poem by Saint Teresa of Ávila: "Let nothing trouble you, / Let nothing scare you, / All is fleeting, / God alone is unchanging. / Patience / Everything obtains. / Who possesses God / Nothing wants. / God alone suffices" ("Efficacy of Patience," in STA 3:386).

6. Rafael and his father were ultimately unable to enter Oviedo and rejoined the family in Burgos (OC 693).

7. Rafael alludes to the Revolution of 1934, after his first departure from the monastery (see #55, n. 1).

Anyway, dear mother, I have nothing else to say. Keep calm and wait for news from us, which we will share as soon as we know anything.

Tell Toribio[8] not to forget about his patient Brother Rafael, won't you?

That's all. Hugs and all my affection from your son who, without shouts or flags or music but with all his silent Trappist's heart, lays his "*¡viva España!*" at the feet of Jesus in the tabernacle,

Rafael

---

8. Toribio Luis Arribas was the former Brother Tescelino, who had attended Rafael in the infirmary at San Isidro (see #44, n. 1).

135. To Rafael Arnaiz Sánchez de la Campa and Mercedes Barón

Ávila, November 14, 1936

Ave Maria

My dearest parents,

Just a quick note to let you know I arrived safely in my beloved Ávila, thanks be to God. On the train, I learned that instead of getting to Ávila when I thought I would, I was on track to get there at the lovely hour of three o'clock in the morning—a perfect time to pray Matins, but not to arrive in Ávila. So I decided to get off and stay the night at Medina del Campo and take the tram to Ávila the next morning.

I arrived in Ávila at ten in the morning, to my aunt and uncle's great surprise.[1] Luckily, Aunt María's sisters had left for Valladolid the previous day, so I did end up with a roof over my head. May God reward my aunt and uncle for all their kindness toward me.

The ticket I got in Burgos is good for four days with the option to extend for another eight days, but I don't want to be here that long . . . At the end of the day, my monastery is my monastery, you know?

God is so good to me. Without my even asking for it, He has given me the joy of being with my aunt and uncle again, whom I love so much, and once more staying within these walls of Ávila, which contain so many things for me.

I'm telling you, my dear parents, I'm a poor man. I'll never amount to anything. I still have so much inside me . . . But God, who is very good, and the Virgin Mary do not take into account the fragility of my little

---

1. After going to Ávila to visit his aunt and uncle, Rafael returned to Villasandino, the small town outside Burgos where his family was staying. From there, his brother Leopoldo and sister Mercedes accompanied him to La Trapa, where he re-entered the monastery on December 6, 1936 (OC 695).

soul as it rejoices at the sight of the Sierra de Gredos[2] and these skies that taught me to love God.

I have nothing else to tell you . . . Your Trappist is thinking of you all very much. Hugs from my aunt and uncle, and all my love, your son,

Brother María Rafael

---

2. Sierra de Gredos: a mountain range in central Spain.

136. My Notebook[1]

La Trapa, December 8, 1936
Solemnity of the Immaculate Conception

In the name of the Father, and of the Son, and of the Holy Spirit. Amen.
Ave Maria.

I have a crucifix in La Trapa, and a brother in the world. I begin this
notebook with the former before my eyes and the latter on my mind.

Perhaps my brother Leopoldo will read these words one day, uneven and
messy as they are, but written with heart and soul . . . Often written in
order to console myself in my loneliness . . . Always written at the foot of
the crucifix atop my desk, that He might guide my pen and I might manage
to say something that will reach my reader's heart, even if it's not new or
well put, and after making him reflect, he might grow closer and closer to
God, who cannot be reached through profound study or long conversations with others, but only by gazing simply and steadily upon the crucifix.

If only the world knew how much one learns at the foot of the cross
. . . If only the world knew that all theology, all mysticism and asceti-
cism, even a thousand years' worth of philosophy is completely useless if
one does not meditate and study at the foot of the cross of Christ . . .

If only the world knew that all learning is *useless* and goes *nowhere* unless it is directed toward perfect knowledge of God and self. One reaches
that knowledge by placing oneself before the cross on which God died . . .
At the foot of that cross, and not making noise with words, one comes to
see Infinite Love nailed to its wood . . . At the foot of the cross, one learns
to love Christ, to scorn the world, and to know oneself . . .

---

1. My Notebook is the title given by Rafael's mother, Mercedes Barón, to the reflections
he wrote between December 8, 1936, and February 6, 1937. While Rafael did not give the
notebook itself a title, he did structure it into chapters to which he appended his own titles.
My Notebook also includes 17 drawings and a dedication to Rafael's younger brother,
Leopoldo Barón, indicating that he did conceive of it as a coherent work with a specific
intended reader (VE 356).

If the world knew any of that, it would be less crazy. People wouldn't waste their time—the <u>only</u> time they have—on vain arguments, often full of pride, that lead to anything but God.

Look, brother: talk, argue, and study all you want, but if your soul is truly searching for God, always do your talking, arguing, and studying at the foot of the Lord's cross. There, argument falls silent before Christ's blood; there, speech grows humble and serene; there, study points us toward horizons so cloudless they dissolve into infinity.

Listen to me, I'm writing this for you . . . In the nothingness and simplicity of the cross, you will find the solution to difficult problems to solve. Nothing is difficult for the spirit that travels by way of the great valley of humility, and humility is born at the feet of a God nailed to the gallows.

I don't know anything, or at least, I know very little. But what I do know, I have learned there. You'll see, as you read these pages, if you have the patience to do so, that I'm not saying anything in particular. Look at what these pages really contain, which is a soul that wants to love God, and wants everyone else to love Him too.

If only you knew—it's so easy!

You'll find a bit of everything in this notebook: faults and virtues, anguish and joy. Between the lines, you'll read about sunny days and cloudy ones, moments of calm and storms . . . but a soul is all of that and much more. All of it is a necessary part of the rhythm of life, both materially and spiritually speaking, and since material matters don't change much in La Trapa, it's the interior life that develops in this way, moved by unfathomable forces . . . A Trappist who *doesn't waste his time* can't help but very often marvel at the work God is doing in his soul . . . In his interior life, he comes across nooks and crannies that are unfamiliar to him at first glance, but in silence and prayer, light is shed upon them.

You'll read many things here that you already know, which might be annoying. There will be a little bit of everything except literary quality and perfection, but it doesn't matter, so long as there's simplicity and good intentions. And believe me, those you will find.

I ask you only one thing, which I already said, and that is to read these pages in the same place your Trappist brother wrote them, namely, invoking the Virgin Mary's aid and sitting at the foot of the cross of Jesus.

137. *My Notebook*

"As a Deer Longs for Flowing Streams . . ."[1]

La Trapa, December 9, 1936

Longing for eternal life . . . Longing to fly unto true life. The longings of a soul subject to the body, wailing to see God.

It is a great suffering to live when all that remains in life is the hope of dying . . . the hope of death . . . the hope of an end, so that we might begin . . . Living is hard, but the hope that everything will come to an end does make it all easier.

Longings for eternal life flutter about the choir in our church, even when the monastery is enveloped by the darkness of night.

The clock strikes four-thirty . . . The cold is deeply piercing, so deep. The body shivers slightly from time to time. It doesn't matter . . . noon will come, and the sun with it, and there will be heat and light, and the joy of its radiance will spread to the body of the man who is now shivering in the church's choir.

The soul is cold too . . . In one of its nooks and crannies, a little flame is burning . . . a weak little spark of love for God. The soul sees it and strains to fan the flame that, weak though it may be, is shining forth in complete darkness. The soul is suffering from its desire to love God . . . its desire to be with Christ . . . It is pointless to try to fly when weighed down by chains, and to the soul, life is a cold chain indeed.

Longing to die, yearning to be free and to love God. It's cold here on earth . . . Cold with the chill of mortal life . . . the chill of a pilgrim with no house or home traversing an empty, impassable desert.[2]

The soul aches to be free already from the flesh that holds it captive and torments it . . . it's all a struggle, fought in the silence of the church . . . The spirit that wants to fly, and the flesh it's dragging around. The

---

1. *As a deer longs for flowing streams, so my soul longs for you, O God* (Ps 42:1).
2. See Ps 62:2.

soul weeps for not yet being able to see God, while sleepy eyelids fall shut after trying to stay awake.

Lord, Lord . . . the lips whisper . . . *as a deer longs for flowing streams*, as a thirsty fawn sniffs the air in search of something to quench its thirst, so too my soul pines with thirst for life . . . Eternal life, a life of space and light, a life in which the little spark I carry around inside me will grow, ignite, and, at the sight of Your face, shine brighter than the sun.

Lord, Lord, *as a deer longs for flowing streams*, so too does my soul.

Outside the monastery, the sun is wrestling with what's left of night . . . Everything comes and goes. Frost and snow will pass, each day and year will pass, tonight will pass and day will break . . . It's all a matter of knowing how to wait, and in the end, up there, when our lives are over, our souls will quench their thirst at the one true stream, which is God.

Great is divine mercy when it grants the soul a certain condition in which everything inspires it to lift its heart high above all created and earthly things. When the soul is in pain because it cannot see God, what does it care about the world? When the spirit loses itself in reflection on eternity, what could it possibly care about the short, limited span of its own life? When the heart yearns for its homeland in heaven and union with the Eternal One, how could it not be indifferent toward this valley of tears in which it is exiled for a short time?

In moments like that, everything recedes and disappears . . . You forget about the world, which is so wicked and small . . . You forget about people, who are so caught up in their ambitions, fights, and miseries . . . The soul is suffering because it remains on earth, so naturally, it doesn't make sense for it to be attached to anything but heaven and God. It is bewildered that it ever sought out a position in this passing, unimportant place. It is amazed that there are people who love God and nevertheless argue and worry about the place they currently occupy in this world, or the one they are to occupy.

How small everything seems when you're dizzy with love for God! How small the whole world and its centuries upon centuries seem when you're waiting impatiently for eternity! How petty people's earthly ambitions look!

Who cares about health? . . . Who cares about being here or there . . . being loved or despised, being rich or poor . . . It's all nothing to the soul that truly lives more for the hope of heaven than for earthly realities.

That soul truly understands these verses from Saint Teresa:

I live without living in myself,
and in such a way I hope,
I die because I do not die.[3]

These desires of Teresa's must have been so strong for them to make her die.

Woe is me. This unhappy Trappist is suffering too, but from just a little spark of the great bonfire in Teresa's heart . . . In my littleness, I too desire eternal life . . . that life "without living in myself," that death "because I do not die."

How great is God's mercy to put a soul in a state like that . . . One comes to no longer feel the cold, or one's sleepiness. The spirit loses itself in God's immensity, in His infinite Love. The soul is ecstatic at the mere thought of the supernatural world that awaits us at the end of our lives, a world in which there will be no sorrows or tears and our only occupation will be delighting in God without ever being able to offend Him again.

3. Saint Teresa of Ávila, "Aspirations toward Eternal Life," trans. Adrian J. Cooney (STA 3:375).

Such longing for Christ!! How can one not long for Him? How is it possible to love this life, which separates us from God? One might think it is more proper for angels to ache for eternal life, rather than human beings . . . but this is a mistake. The more human you are, the more human your feelings, the more you'll weep for life and long for death, and all the more urgently.

A deer that thirsts . . . is an animal pursued by hunters . . . It thirsts because it is constantly running through the mountains, cliffs, and brush. It searches frantically for the hidden stream where it knows it will find rest for its weary being and water to quench its longing. A deer that thirsts is a deer on the run.

So too is the soul in search of God's streams a suffering soul . . . Like a deer, a human being who is eager for immortal life is pursued by mortal dangers: stalked by hunters, afflicted with miseries, troubled by passions.

A soul that longs for heaven is a soul that knows its own weaknesses. A person in search of Christ's streams is a person who thirsts, and thirst is human, not angelic.

The Lord well knows that when I feel my weakest, when I struggle most with the materiality that weighs me down, when my heart is at the mercy of so many things, and when my soul is suffering a pain more human than divine, that is when, kneeling before the tabernacle in the silence of the night, I wail and weep like the deer that thirsts . . .

That is when I come to see that in Christ alone can rest be found . . . That is when we realize that the love we have for Him is weak and frail . . . a spark that hardly burns . . . We see our nothingness and littleness, we see our selfishness, and we see that the world with its hunters, snares, and swindles is pursuing us and pushing us to zealously seek out something that is not a lie or deception, something that is true love and perfect happiness, the one thing that can satisfy our thirst . . . Christ.

At that moment, when the soul catches a faraway glimpse of its resting place, when in the midst of utter darkness it comes to understand that up there in heaven, its little flame of love for God will become a dazzling lamp . . . At that moment, when the soul sees how small everything is, and how great God is . . . When it realizes that what it is experiencing is thirst . . . thirst for divine love, and the pain of going on living, and a desire for eternal life . . . At that moment, but not before, is when its suffering comes to an end, its agony becomes sweet, and everything vanishes: the world and its people, darkness and sunlight . . . everything in creation, everything in existence fades away, leaving only a soul looking up at his God, sometimes laughing, sometimes crying, but always sighing the same song . . . "Lord, Lord, as a deer longs for flowing streams . . ."

The church bell rings out slow and deep. The early morning chill is deeply piercing, so deep, but it doesn't matter. It's a passing chill, a momentary one . . . merely lifelong, and life is an instant in eternity, an instant hardly worth our attention.

138. My Notebook
Solitude

La Trapa, December 11, 1936

Solitude . . . that word brings so many things forth in my soul. It's so difficult to express the joy of solitude when it has caused you to shed so many tears in the past.

Nevertheless, how joyful it is to be alone with God . . . Such great peace prevails when we are alone . . . when God and the soul are alone. How different are the world's ways from those of Christ. The world seeks itself, and finds itself. The soul that does not look for God looks instead for other souls, and if it does not find them, it weeps for its loneliness . . . weeping sorrowful tears that embitter the heart and do not bring consolation.

But the heart that seeks Christ loves its solitude from everything and everyone, for it is in that very solitude that Jesus reveals Himself. It is in that solitude that He seeks souls. He leads them into that solitude, sometimes by means of sorrows and sacrifices.

God is selfish, and He doesn't let His friends seek any consolation outside of Himself . . . At the beginning, He pacifies them with consolation from other human beings, but there comes a time when human beings have nothing more to give, and what little they can offer cannot satisfy the soul . . . Tears may come, or disappointment, or heartbreak . . . but what does that matter? God is the one who is doing it. It's a question of perseverance, and if the soul perseveres, it will find itself alone . . . God's infinite mercy!!

Alone is exactly where God wants the soul. It's so hard to get up that little hill and leave behind all those hopes and affections. Sometimes it feels like leaving behind pieces of your soul . . . Oh, Lord! It's so hard sometimes to accompany You into the solitude of spirit and body where You want to take us! Day after day, Jesus accomplishes His work in the hearts of His friends . . . Little by little, sometimes gently, sometimes all at once, he goes about stripping away the many things that bind the soul to the earth and its creatures . . .

Let Him do it . . . He is the master of everything. And indeed, if God wants us for Himself, we can't stop Him from leading us into solitude, where He shall speak to our hearts, as Hosea says.[1] How great God is! How wonderfully He does things!

What was difficult for us at first and made us shed so many tears . . . that blessed solitude with Christ . . . becomes our greatest consolation on this earth!

In that solitude, the soul delights in the great consolation of knowing it is alone with God. In that solitude, it loves Jesus with all its strength, it laughs with Him and weeps with Him . . . What more could one want? . . . What could human beings have to offer? . . . Solitude is a divine school where one comes to know God and learns to stop expecting things from the world.

Blessed is the solitude that draws us closer to God and helps us detach ourselves from creatures. In it, we learn to accompany first Jesus on the cross, and then Mary, whose soul was more in heaven than on earth, and who reveals to us Her own loneliness in the wake of Her Son's death and invites us to accompany Her in it.

How great is the mercy of God!!

How deceived we were when we believed that solitude was a cross. How deeply blind we were to look for God in human consolation. It is true that when He wills it, He reveals Himself to us in a thousand different ways . . . but it's also true that when this is by means of a consolation, it will always be like looking at a foggy landscape. Yes, it's true, God is there, but He is behind the fog . . . behind our senses, our feelings, our delusions . . . behind all those creatures we seek out first.

God reveals Himself to the soul through all these things, and essentially His image appears unfocused, hazy, imprecise . . . A foggy landscape . . . The landscape is there, but the fog makes it blurry, and all you can see at first is the fog.

God is in everything, but not everything is God. Souls who are accustomed to seeing the Creator in the smallest details of creation, in the

1. See Hos 2:14.

wonders of nature, in the harmony of the introit to the Mass,[2] or in a human heart doubtlessly delight in God, and God often makes use of such things to awaken a sleeping soul.

There is no doubt that such a soul sees God, but it does so imperfectly, because before arriving at the landscape itself, its gaze has stopped to linger upon the fog. . . whether that be in the form of an insect, or the sun, or a piece of music, or the magnificence of someone's heart.

One comes to see so clearly that it is in solitude that one can truly encounter God. How great is His mercy, that He should help us leap over created things and place us in an immense plain without rocks or trees or sky or stars . . . An unending plain without any colors, without any human beings, without anything that could distract the soul from God.

This is the infinite goodness of the Eternal One, who without any merit on our part leads us into the realm of solitude in order to speak to our hearts there.

This is the infinite patience of God, who, day after day and night after night, remains in pursuit of souls, despite our faults, despite our ingratitude and selfishness, despite the obstacles we constantly put between us, despite how often we hide from Him, hiding not from His wrath but rather . . . I'm ashamed to say . . . from His grace.

My soul stretches when I meditate upon those divine poems by Saint John of the Cross, who says in one of them,

> She lived in solitude,
> and now in solitude has built her nest.[3]

The mystical Doctor, in his commentary on the poem, says that the soul was already living in solitude when God, pleased with that solitude, built the nest in her.[4] The Carmelite clearly had a generous soul, since he went looking for God in solitude; mine is not at all like that, for I do just the opposite. The Most High takes my hand and leads my soul from place to place, and often kicking and screaming against my will.

---

2. Introit: the entrance antiphon at the beginning of the Mass.

3. *Spiritual Canticle* stanza 35 (SJC 476). She refers to the soul, figured as a dove.

4. See commentary on stanza 35 of the *Spiritual Canticle* in SJC 607–9.

God's mercy is everlasting! What have I done to deserve such treatment from You?

But that's all over now. I will be generous. I will be docile. Wherever you lead me, I will love what You love, even life itself, if that is Your wish.

I will lose myself in solitude of spirit and body so that, as the poem said, we might build a nest of divine love within it, and there may You speak to me, instruct me, and guide me so that I don't get lost and go astray as I make my way through this world.

Lead me, Lord, down the path of solitude. It is a sure path, trod by no one else. With You for my guide, what is there to fear?

In the monastery of San Isidro, there is a little monk . . . no, even less than that, there is a simple oblate who is walking in the way of monastic life, his heart driven mad with joy in his solitude. His lips are sealed with silence, but nevertheless they are always whispering some prayer or song. Right now, they bear the poem of that monk from Fontiveros, Teresa's brother:[5]

> She lived in solitude,
> and now in solitude has built her nest;
> and in solitude he guides her,
> he alone, who also bears
> in solitude the wound of love.[6]

5. Saint John of the Cross, born in Fontiveros, Spain, was the co-reformer of the Carmelite Order with Saint Teresa of Ávila.

6. *Spiritual Canticle,* stanza 35, in SJC 476.

139. My Notebook
The Antics of the Turnips[1]

La Trapa, December 12, 1936

Three in the afternoon on a rainy December day. It's time to work, but since it's Saturday and very cold, we aren't going out into the fields. We're going to work in the warehouse where we wash lentils, peel potatoes, chop collard greens, etc. We call it the "laboratory."[2] There is a long table there, with some benches, a window, and a crucifix up above.

It's a melancholy day. The clouds are rather gloomy, and the winds somewhat strong. A few drops of water begrudgingly lap at the window-panes. Pervading it all is a chill befitting the country and the times.

Truth be told, other than the chill—which I can feel in my frozen feet and frigid hands—you could almost say I've imagined all this, since I've hardly even looked out the window. The afternoon that faces me today is murky, and everything seems murky to me. Something is disturbing my silence, and it seems as if some little devils are determined to aggravate me with what I'd call memories . . . Waiting with patience.

A knife has been placed in my hands, and a basket in front of me, full of some kind of big white carrots that turn out to be turnips. I had never seen them raw, they're so big . . . and so cold . . . Well, nothing to be done about that! All we can do is peel them.

Time passes slowly, and my knife does too, moving between their skin and flesh, leaving the turnips perfectly peeled.

The little devils continue to wage war on me. To think that I left my house to come here in this cold and peel these stupid turnips!! It is a truly

1. The title of this meditation was first translated this way by Fr. Edmund Waldstein, O.Cist.
2. Laboratory: The name for this monastic workspace is derived from *labor* (Lat). Keeping in mind the familiar phrase *ora et labora* ("pray and work"), the laboratory where the monks work can be thought of as the counterpart to an oratory, where they pray.

ridiculous thing, this business of peeling turnips with the seriousness of a magistrate in mourning.

A tiny, shrewd devil infiltrates me, and from deep within it reminds me subtly of my house, my family, and my freedom . . . which I left behind in order to lock myself in here with these lentils, potatoes, collard greens, and turnips.

It's a melancholy day . . . I'm not looking out the window, but I can guess as much. My hands are chapped red as the little devils; my feet are frozen solid . . . And my soul? Lord, perhaps my soul is suffering a little. But it doesn't matter . . . let us take refuge in silence.

Time kept on going, along with my thoughts, the turnips, and the cold; then suddenly, quick as the wind, a powerful light pierced my soul . . . A divine light, lasting but a moment . . . Someone saying to me, "What are you doing?!" What do you mean, what am I doing? Good Lord!! . . . What a question! Peeling turnips . . . peeling turnips! . . . "But why?" . . . And my heart, leaping, gave a wild answer: I'm peeling turnips for love . . . for love of Jesus Christ.

Now, there's nothing I could say to make anyone understand this clearly, but I can say that somewhere inside, deep inside my soul, a very great peace took the place of the turmoil that had been there before. All I can say is: just thinking about the fact that in this world we can make the smallest actions into acts of love for God . . . that closing or opening our eyes in His name can earn us a place in heaven . . . that peeling a few turnips for true love of God can give Him as much glory, and give us as many merits, as the conquest of the Indies; thinking that only through His mercy do I have the great fortune to suffer something for His sake . . . it fills the soul with such joy that if I had let myself be carried away by my interior impulses at that moment, I would have started flinging turnips in the air, trying to communicate the joy of my heart to these poor root vegetables . . . I would have made a miraculous show of juggling the turnips with my knife and apron.

I laughed at those little red devils until I cried, and frightened by my change in attitude, they hid among the sacks of chickpeas and a basket of cabbage that was sitting there.

What do I have to complain about? Why should I be sad over what is a cause for joy alone? To what more can a soul aspire than to suffer a bit for a crucified God?

We are nothing, and we are worth nothing; one moment we'll be overwhelmed by temptation, and then the next we'll be flying on the wings of consolation at the smallest touch of divine love.

When work started, clouds of sadness covered the sky. My soul was in pain at finding itself on the cross; everything weighed it down: the Rule . . . work . . . silence . . . the absence of the sun on such a sad, grey, cold day. The wind rattling the windowpanes, the rain, the mud . . . the absence of the sun. The world . . . so far away, so far . . . and all the while I was peeling turnips without thinking about God at all.

But everything passes, including temptation . . . Time has passed, it is already time to rest, there is light again, and I don't care anymore if the day is cold or cloudy or windy or sunny. All I care about is peeling my turnips, peaceful, happy, and content, contemplating the Virgin, blessing God.

What does a moment's regret matter, an instant's worth of suffering? All I can say is that there is no sorrow that will not be repaid, if not in this life then in the next, and in reality, so little is asked of us in order to gain heaven. Perhaps it is easier in La Trapa than it is out in the world—but not because of this or that state of life, for in the world they have the same means of offering something to God. It's just that the world is distracting, and a great deal goes to waste.

People are the same there as they are here; our ability to suffer and to love is the same; wherever we go, we shall carry a cross.

May we be able to make the most of our time . . . May we be able to love that blessed cross that the Lord places in our path, whatever it may be, no matter what.

Let us make the most of the little things in our everyday life, our ordinary life . . . There is no need to do great things to become great saints. Making the little things great is enough.

In the world, people waste many opportunities, but the world is distracting . . . It is worth just as much to love God by speaking as it is to love Him in Trappist silence; it is a matter of doing something for Him . . . keeping Him in mind . . . Location, place, occupation are irrelevant.

God can make me just as holy through peeling potatoes as through governing an empire.

What a shame that the world is so distracted . . . because I have seen that people are not evil . . . and that *everyone* suffers, but they don't know how to suffer . . .

If they would lift their eyes a little to look beyond the frivolity, beyond that layer of false joy with which the world hides its tears, beyond their ignorance of who God is, if they were to lift their eyes up above . . . surely what happened to that monk with the turnips would happen to them too . . . many tears would be wiped away, many sorrows would become sweet, and many crosses would be embraced as offerings to Christ.

When work ended, I placed myself in prayer at the foot of Jesus, dead on the cross . . . there, at his heels, I left a basket of clean, peeled turnips . . . I had nothing else to offer him, but anything offered with one's whole heart is enough for God, be it turnips or empires.

The next time I peel root vegetables again, whatever they may be, even if they are cold and frozen, I ask that Mary not allow those little red devils to get near me and afflict me. Rather, I ask her to send me angels from heaven, so that as I peel, they might carry the work of my hands in theirs, and place red carrots at the feet of the Virgin Mary; at the feet of Jesus, white turnips, and potatoes and onions, and cabbage and lettuce . . .

Anyhow, if I live in La Trapa for many years, I will turn heaven into a kind of vegetable market . . . and when the Lord calls me and says to me, "that's enough peeling, drop the knife and apron and come enjoy the fruits of your labor" . . . when I see myself in heaven among God and the saints, and so many vegetables . . . my Lord Jesus, I cannot help but laugh.

- AVE MARIA -

140. My Notebook
Hidden . . .

La Trapa, December 14, 1936

One of the joys, or rather, consolations of the monastic life is being hidden away from the world's gaze. Those who delight in meditating on the life of Christ will understand this.

In order to devote yourself to a certain art . . . or to grow in science, the spirit requires solitude and isolation, it needs recollection and silence. Now for the soul in love with God, for the soul that no longer has eyes for any art or science but the life of Jesus, for the soul that has uncovered hidden treasure on this earth, silence is not enough, nor is recollection in solitude. For such a soul, it is necessary to hide away from everyone, to hide away with Christ, to seek out a little patch of earth where the world's profane gaze cannot reach it, and to be alone there with its God.

The king's secret is sullied and tarnished when made known.[1] The king's secret must be hidden away so that no one else can see it. Many believe that the secret consists of divine messages and supernatural consolations . . . but the king's secret, the thing we envy the saints for, is often simply a cross.

Let us not hide our light under a bushel basket, Jesus tells us in the Gospel.[2] Let us make God's wonders known. Let us share the abundance of graces that God freely showers upon us with our brothers' and sisters' hearts. Let us proclaim our faith to the whole world, filling it with shouts of delight that we should have a God this good. Let us never tire of preaching His gospel and telling anyone who will listen that Christ died for love of humankind, nailed to a tree . . . That He died for me, for you, for that person

---

1. See Tob 12:7.
2. See Matt 5:15; Mark 4:21; Luke 8:16; 11:33.

over there . . . And if we truly love Him, let us not hide Him away . . . let us not hide under a bushel basket the light that could enlighten others.

However, blessed Jesus, let us carry that divine secret within ourselves, without letting anybody else notice it . . . The secret that You give to the souls who love You most . . . That little share in your cross, in your thirst, in your crown of thorns.

Let us hide our tears, pain, and grief away in the farthest reaches of the earth . . . Let us not fill the world with sorrowful wailing or let anybody else share in even the smallest aspect of our afflictions.

Let us be selfish with our suffering and generous with our joy. Let us be the happiness of those around us, and not mar our surroundings with gloomy expressions whenever God sends us some trial or another.

Let us hide ourselves away so that we can be with Jesus on the cross. Let us not seek relief for our suffering in creaturely consolation, for to do so would be to do two things that, while not bad, are not perfect. First, we would be trading God for something that is not God—for consolation that does not come from Him is not His, and if He does not want to give it to us, and we go looking for it outside of Him, we will lose Him, and often we will also lose the merit of our suffering. Second, we would be acting out of selfishness, or at least out of a desire to ease our burdens by sharing them with others, and all we would get out of it is a false, fictitious relief. If you've got a toothache, your tooth will keep hurting whether you mention it or not.

In short, this is almost always an act of selfishness. It also betrays a lack of humility by giving importance to your own concerns, as if they were important because they're about you. If you instead ask nothing of creatures and turn to God in everything, you will come to love the cross, but you'll be alone with that cross, unseen . . . your cross will be hidden with God, far away from human beings.

Let us hide away our life, if our life is sorrow.

Let us hide away our suffering, if suffering causes us pain.

Let us hide ourselves away with Christ, so that He might be the only person with whom we share that which seen properly is His alone: the secret of the cross.

Meditating upon His life, passion, and death, let us learn once and for all that there is only one way to reach Him . . . the way of the holy cross.

141. My Notebook
Freedom

La Trapa, December 15, 1936

Some days, planes fly over the monastery, rushing through the sky at impressive speeds. Their noisy motors terrify the little birds who have made their nests in the cypress trees of our cemetery.

There is a paved road in front of the monastery that crosses our grounds. Cars and trucks pass by at all hours. The sight of the monastery is of no interest whatsoever to them.

One of the most important railroads in the country also comes through our fields. The trains pass by so close to the abbey walls that when they go fast enough, they shake all the walls of the building and our church.

So much for the outside.

Inside, there are a hundred men or so who don't care about all that movement.

They say all that is "freedom." And they say the opposite, that is, a monk in his cloister, is "enclosed."

But anyone who meditates upon this for a little while will see how deceived the world is about what it calls freedom, and see that true freedom is often enclosed within the four walls of a monastery. Physical freedom is no freedom at all; in carnal man, it is subject to flesh and passions, while in spiritual man, it is subject to the spirit.

Spiritual freedom is not true freedom either, for as long as it lives within the body, it is a prisoner and cannot fly free.

Where, then, is freedom to be found?

It is in the heart of the one who loves no one and nothing but God. It is in the soul attached to neither spiritual nor material things, but only to God.

It is in the soul that does not subject itself to the selfish ego. It is in the soul that soars above its own thoughts, its own feelings, its own suffering and rejoicing.

Freedom is in the soul whose only reason for existence is God, whose life is God and nothing but God.

The human spirit is little, it is limited, it is subject to a thousand variations, ups and downs, periods of depression, disappointments, etc., and a body . . . a body that is so weak!

Freedom, then, is to be found in God, and in the soul that truly transcends everything, builds its life in Him, and thus can say that it enjoys freedom . . . insofar as it can, still being in the world.

Those who love anything other than God and things that represent Him indirectly (such as love of neighbor, love for the saints, and love for the Most Blessed Virgin, for example), those who fix their hearts on things outside of God . . . do not know what it is to enjoy freedom, even if they cross the Spanish skies in airplanes and travel the whole world in high-speed trains.

Loving God!! . . . Living for eternal things! Rejoicing in the enclosure of body and spirit so that the soul might fly unto God and lose itself in the infinite beauty of the Eternal One! Flying to the realm of the supernatural on the wings of divine love! Behold, this is freedom.

Nevertheless, let us not be deceived . . . the soul is still longing for something else, the word for which I do not know . . . It is not freedom, exactly. It's something more.

Let us be consoled, those of us who still sojourn upon this earth. Let us be consoled by our hope. Let us be encouraged to know that God is waiting for us, and that He is coming soon.

This evening, a man, imprisoned at his place in choir, asked God for freedom. The man was longing for freedom, not to travel the world, because neither this world nor all created things would be enough for him . . . He was longing for the freedom to be released from his bodily flesh in order to be able to fly unto the Heart of God.

Crouching in the darkness of the church, he looked up at the tabernacle where the Resurrection and the Life was dwelling.[1] The Lord helped him see that freedom was within his reach. That freedom on this earth is a heart united to Him, and that a soul free from everything and fixed upon God wants for nothing.

1. John 11:25.

But the man remained kneeling at Jesus' feet, loving the will of the Eternal One, enjoying the freedom of his heart to love God . . . and yet still begging Him for that other freedom, beyond this world, for which he yearns all day long.

Meanwhile, people are flitting and flying above the monastery and across its fields . . . people who say they enjoy freedoms . . . how foolish and deceived they are!

Once upon a time I too was out there in the world, driving the roads of Spain, excited to get the speedometer up to 120 kilometers per hour[2] . . . How stupid I was! When I realized that I was running out of horizon, I was disappointed, like everyone else who enjoys earthly freedom . . . for the earth is a small place, and you run out of it very quickly.

People are surrounded by small, limited horizons . . . and for souls that thirst for horizons that go on forever . . . earthly ones won't do . . . they're drowning in them. The world isn't big enough for such souls, who will only find what they are looking for in the greatness and depths of God.

You "free" men who roam the earth! I do not envy your life in the world. Enclosed in this monastery at the foot of the crucifix, I have infinite freedom, I have heaven . . . I have God.

What a great fortune it is to possess a heart in love with Him! How widely the soul stretches at the thought of the love between God and His poor little creature!

How far away the world seems! . . . And how small! . . . How fragile physical life is . . . How short is the time we have to live this life; and how long it feels when life is waiting for you on the other side of death, when you desire true freedom, when you realize your own misery, your own nothingness, your own inability to love God!

Saint John of the Cross, a saint in whom I so often find thoughts that were seemingly written just for me, was able to express the agony of living on this earth separate from God, in a poem that reads,[3]

---

2. The equivalent of 75 miles per hour.

3. Saint John of the Cross did not write this poem, "The Soul Longs to Be with Christ" ("Ansía el alma estar con Cristo"); its author is unknown. It was briefly attributed to John of the Cross after its discovery at Convento del Carmen in Pastrana, Spain, in the late 19th century. See "Poesías de nuestro Padre San Juan de la Cruz que no están en sus obras," ed. PP. Carmelitas Descalzos in *S. Juan de la Cruz: Revista Carmelitano-Teresiana* 1, no. 1 (November 1, 1890): 311–12.

O fleeting, wearisome life,
if only I were free of you already!
O stifling tomb,
when will I be released
from you, into the arms of my Beloved?

O God, who will be at last
all aflame with the fire of Your holy love?
Woe is me! Who could ever
leave behind all created things
and be transformed with You in glory?

What more could I add to Saint John's words?[4]

Poor Brother Rafael! God has wounded you, but not yet killed you. Wait on . . . wait on with the sweet serenity of a certain hope. Remain still, nailed to your place at the foot of the tabernacle, a prisoner of your God.

Listen to the faraway din of people enjoying their earthly freedom, their short time in this world.

From a distance, listen to their voices, their laughs, their cries, their wars . . . Listen, and meditate for a moment. Meditate upon the infinite God . . . God who created earth and everyone in it, the absolute Master of the skies and all the land, of the rivers and seas, He who, in an instant, just by willing it, just by thinking it, made everything that exists from nothing . . . Meditate briefly upon the life of Christ, and you will see that there are no freedoms, no noise, no voices to be found there. You will see Jesus, obedient and submissive, in calm peace, whose only rule was to do the will of His Father. And finally, contemplate Christ nailed to the Cross . . . How could one talk of freedoms?!

Beata es Maria quae credidisti Domino.

Blessed are You, O Mary, who believed the Lord.[5]

---

4. *¡Oh vida breve y dura, / Quien se viese de ti ya despojado! / ¡Oh estrecha sepultura, / Cuándo seré sacado, / De ti, para mi Esposo deseado! / ¡Oh Dios, y quién se viese / En vuestro santo amor todo abrasado! / ¡Ay de mí! ¡Quién pudiese / Dejar esto criado / Y en gloria ser con Vos ya transformado!*

5. See Luke 1:45.

142. My Notebook

"Raise Your Heads, because Your Redemption Is Drawing Near"[1]

La Trapa, December 22, 1936

Christmas . . . A feast in heaven, a feast in the soul . . . A feast in the home.

There are many ways to celebrate the feast of feasts . . . There are many ways to wait for the God who is to be born among human beings. There are many ways that the world celebrates the event of God's coming.

This is the first time in my twenty-five years that I am not at my parents' house for Christmas. This year I'm going to celebrate in a monastery, in a very different way from other years. I don't know if it will be better or worse, but I do know that there will be more austerity and greater recollection in it.

Christmas . . . It reminds me of so many things . . . That word brings up so many things! There will be a struggle in the coming days between my monastic soul, which seeks only the love of Jesus in silence and solitude, and my sensitive human soul, which has not yet died to human loves. In its weakness, my human soul longs for the warmth of Christmas with my loved ones, in my house, with my parents and brothers and sister . . .

Things are different now. God no longer permits me to indulge in turrón[2] and marzipan and music and cards . . . God is asking something more of me now. He is asking me for something I have already given Him . . . For I have given Him everything, so when the child Jesus calls me forth to adore Him in the stable, I won't know what to bring Him . . . That's what I'll bring Him . . . Nothing.

1. Luke 21:28.
2. Turrón: a type of nougat, traditionally eaten in Spain at Christmastime.

I don't know why, but everything in the past seems far away to me now
. . . So far away, as if it were a dream . . . I remember my happy childhood
as some thing that came and went in my life, like a flash of lightning . . .

Childhood Christmases, seasons of expectation and sweets and the
Three Kings[3] . . . A time that reminds me of the warmth of our home, my
parents' love, almond soup . . . Those days when snow made the world
look like a postcard . . . A time when people become children all over
again, and are moved by the oft-repeated tale of the poor little orphan
shivering in the cold as he looks sadly out at the children of the powerful,
whom he can never reach . . . Who hasn't read that story about the poor
child and the rich child? . . .

Midnight Mass . . . Christmas carols at nuns' convents, cold weather,
and glasses of sherry . . . Presents, letters, and hugs . . .

Celebrating Christmas in the world . . . I don't remember it with sorrow, and it doesn't make me sad to remember it either . . . I just remember
it . . . A thing of the past, never to come again . . . and why should it?
That's always what people say when they've been happy. Meanwhile, the
rainy days of this life, when God is testing us . . . how quickly we forget
about those.

It is a good thing, for God has arranged it thus, that nothing in this
life repeats . . . It is good that pains and sorrows alternate with joys and
happy days . . .

In this life, the soul that has given itself over to God learns neither to
yearn for the past nor to fear the future . . . God is in the present, and
He alone suffices.

Christmastime in La Trapa . . . Joy in the liturgy, hope in the songs we
sing in church, hymns that speak of love and gentleness of heart. Thinking,
in the silence of the temple, about Mary's humility, Joseph's chastity . . .
God's love. The harmonious blend of angels' melodies and shepherds' ballads . . . Christmas in La Trapa . . . Frankincense and myrrh offered up
by souls who quietly live their lives in the divine service[4] . . . the gold of
sacrifices. No loud cheers or external expressions or music or drums . . .

3. Three Kings: the Magi are the traditional gift-bringers in Spain, equivalent to Santa
Claus.
4. "Therefore we intend to establish a school for the Lord's service" (RB Prol. 45).

Christmas in La Trapa. . . . silent adoration. . . . a heart detached from this earth and placed at the feet of Jesus in the stable.

Sweet, serene days. . . . days filled with divine love. . . . a season of calm and peace. A time when the soul flies over the Judean countryside, dreams of eternal glory, and loses itself in contemplation of inscrutable goodness . . . God's love for humanity, His incarnation in Mary, His nakedness and cold humbly hiding a majesty that the skies could not contain.

During this season, the Trappist doesn't want noise and doesn't need a worldly celebration to glorify the newborn child. The parties, the joy, the music, the drumbeat. . . . he carries all that in his heart, which loves Jesus so much, in a joyful silence . . . an inner song. . . . a quiet, silent love.

During this time, he meditates upon the great mysteries of his faith . . . and very, very deep within his soul, he delights in the consolations that the Child Jesus offers him through sacred Scripture. . . . In peace and quiet, he meditates upon the psalms, the hymns, and the whole liturgical arsenal that the church provides for this season.

He contemplates with amazement how *the young woman is with child and shall bear a son, and shall name him Emmanuel,* and how *the uneven ground shall become level and the rough places a plain.*[5]

You don't need to make noise to love God. You won't mind solitude, silence, austerity, penance, or any amount of suffering if you know that *the wilderness and the dry land shall be glad, the desert shall rejoice and blossom; like the crocus it shall blossom abundantly, and rejoice with joy and singing.*[6]

Of course, there will be moments when his heart remembers its worldly affections, those happy days in the past . . . the warmth of hearth and home, amid children's laughter . . . Moments when he remembers what that joy was like, how different it is from the tranquil, pure, holy joy of humble Trappists.

Everything balances out in this world. Everything is necessary, and everything is well arranged. The world's celebration, with marzipan and turrón and wintry landscapes, is necessary, and so is the monk's silence mixed with angels' choirs and shepherds' ballads.

In the perfect harmony of creation, every person and thing follows the path that God has laid out before them.

5. Isa 7:14; 40:4.
6. Isa 35:1-2.

What a joy it is to know we are rooted in His will . . . Whether we end up here or there, what does it matter? Wherever we might go, wherever we are, so long as we don't separate our heart from Jesus' heart, what do we have to fear? What is the world to us? . . . The world is very small, and God is so great that it cannot contain Him . . . But no matter, God has made Himself small in order to save humanity . . . To God, the whole world is a vast temple . . . and the Son has come down into it, and it is in this world that He does the will of His Father.

We are passing through this earth; it is our waiting room, not our resting place. It is a waste of time to look for a place here, or try to make yourself comfortable here . . . Our time here is so short!

God, to whom I owe everything, has often made me think about this, when temptation tries to rob me of my peace by rummaging through my memories . . . by making me remember this or that, mixing up my life at present with the past or the future. God, whose goodness is great, makes me think . . . and sometimes He laughs at me.

Indeed, now that Christmas is approaching, and perhaps my struggles on this front are harder, God is calling me to account. Without letting anyone else overhear, He is saying to me very softly, "What does it matter?" . . . And then I come to see the poverty of this world, the brevity of this life . . . we must make good use of it, we must make haste . . . it doesn't matter where or how . . . We must not waste time talking to people, in search of consolation . . . thinking about our past joys that will never come back again.

And then the soul comes to understand and contemplate the only truth . . . and that truth is Christ. Christ, who transforms the world into a great big stable! Christ, with Joseph and Mary . . . Christ, made human for love of humanity . . . Christ, born among the animals and hay, with no shelter or clothing, in great solitude . . .

And faced with the thought of an incarnate God, faced with the grandeur of His boundlessness, the soul stretches, forgets its sorrows, longs for death, and yearns for delight . . . and the voice of Christ sweetly draws me in, speaks to me of love, and makes me forget all my cares.

Today, at prayer, a little monk was thinking about this. Looking around him, he could not help but close his eyes as he realized that nothing in this world will remain . . . it is all vanity. Leaving behind his feelings and sorrows, he lifted his eyes to heaven and heard his soul cry out clearly . . .

"Brother!. . .Brother!. . .Love Christ!. . .As for everything else. . . what does it matter?"

Prope est jam Dominus; venite adoremus.[7]
QUIS ASCENDET IN MONTEM DOMINI?[8]

---

7. The invitatory antiphon for the Third Week of Advent in the Divine Office: "The Lord is now near; come, let us adore him." This antiphon is recited before the invitatory psalm, which opens the Divine Office for the day.

8. *Who shall climb the mountain of the Lord?* (Ps 24:3). Psalm 24 is sometimes used as the invitatory psalm.

143. *My Notebook*

"*Pax!*"[1]

La Trapa, December 23, 1936

"And on earth, peace to people of good will."[2] These are God's words, and people have forgotten them.

There are only a few days left before the coming of the God of peace . . . and we are at war. For some time now, I've been in the monastery without knowing anything about what is going on in the world . . . I just know that the war goes on with no end in sight. That is up to God alone.

From the peace of my monastery, I often think about those who are fighting and dying at the front. The Prince of Peace is coming for their sake, and for mine, and for the sake of the whole world.

Let us monks be *just a bit* quieter during this time, so that we might prepare ourselves to receive the Savior. Soon, I will be at the feet of the newborn Jesus, and I will ask Him for nothing on my own behalf, because I already have everything. However, I do have brothers in the war . . . Anyway, God already knows that, and the Most Blessed Virgin Mary understands.

REVELABITUR GLORIA DOMINI.[3]

1. *Pax*: the Latin word for *peace*.
2. See Luke 2:14.
3. The Communion antiphon for the vigil of Christmas: *The glory of the Lord shall be revealed* (see Isa 40:5).

144. My Notebook

Meditation

La Trapa, December 27, 1936

It is very cold on earth. The heavens are painted with so many stars that one can only imagine the dark blue canvas of the firmament, which is flooded with darkness.

On earth . . . under one of the smallest stars in our great solar system . . . tonight, marvels are taking place that astonish the angels, and were it not for a divine miracle, all of creation would collapse and the skies would sink into the abyss as they witness what only the mind of God can comprehend . . . the mind of a God who, for love of humanity, humbled Himself to take on mortal flesh and was born of a woman on one of the smallest, coldest stars there is . . . this earth.

The land of Judah . . . humble towns where God's equally humble creatures reside . . . On this land of Judah, a child will take His first steps; this is the One who is later to be crucified, the One who has been given power over heaven and earth, the One who will be called Jesus of Galilee, Christ, the Savior of the world.

It is cold . . . there is ice in human hearts, too. Nobody comes to witness the miracle of God's birth. Out of the whole world, there is just a woman named Mary, a blue-eyed man named Joseph, and a newborn Child. Wrapped in swaddling clothes, He opens His eyes for the first time to the breath of an ox and an ass, resting upon a fistful of hay that Joseph's poverty and Mary's devotion and love have obtained for Him.

The whole world is unconscious with the heavy sleep of flesh . . . It is so cold tonight in the land of Judah . . . The stars that cover the sky are the eyes of the angels as they sing *glory to God in the highest.*[1] This song, composed for God, is overheard by shepherds keeping watch over their flocks. With their childlike souls, they come to adore the newborn Jesus.

---

1. Luke 2:14.

This is our first lesson in God's love. The first favor He sought out in this world was the tender love of Mary, the poverty and chastity of Joseph, and the humility and simplicity of the shepherds . . . This is the scene that the Son of God chose for His first appearance in this world.

Nearly two thousand years separate us from that night, but the miracle of Jesus repeats in our times, too.

Christmas Eve has already come and gone . . . On that day, I too went to adore Jesus the Redeemer . . . it was cold that day, just as it was back then . . . and while my soul lacks the chastity of Joseph and the love of Mary, I offered the Lord my utter poverty in all things, my empty soul. Although I could not sing hymns for Him as the angels did, I tried to sing Him some shepherds' songs . . . the songs of the poor, those who have nothing, the songs of those who can only offer their miseries to God . . . But no matter. When we give Jesus our miseries and weaknesses, so long as we offer them from hearts that are truly in love with Him, He accepts them as if they were virtues . . . Great and vast is the mercy of God.

My mortal flesh cannot hear heaven singing praise, but my soul imagines that today, too, the angels are gazing with astonishment upon the earth just as they did that night, and today, too, they are singing *glory to God in the highest heaven, and on earth peace among those whom he favors!*[2]

2. Luke 2:14.

145. My Notebook

"Laudate Dominum omnes gentes"[1]

La Trapa, December 30, 1936

In just a few minutes, the monastery clock will strike two in the morning. It's one of those things you can't explain, but it happens to everybody in their sleep: almost every day I wake up at more or less the same time, and half asleep, I think . . . "it's going to strike two o'clock . . . God is waiting for you."

Then the silence of the common dormitory[2] is broken by the strident ring of a bell that wakes us up and reminds us that it's time to leave behind our bodily rest; it's time to stay awake and pray.

I'm on my feet in my little room before the bell has even finished ringing, putting my shoes and choir cloak on. Those are the only two items of clothing that we take off to sleep.

The soft rustle of blankets and curtains being drawn back signals that the monks have started their daily lives. All of them, to some extent, have taken up their daily crosses in order to follow Christ.

I'm so tired, Lord! I'm practically still asleep. Nevertheless, the fog of sleep doesn't keep me from mumbling out "Hail Mary Immaculate, conceived without sin."[3] I don't know if the Most Blessed Virgin can hear me . . . but I think so . . . I'm so out of it at that hour! I think of Her almost automatically.

Lord . . . Lord, I'm so tired and it's so cold . . . the temperature in the dormitory must go down to freezing some days, or close to it. The

---

1. *Praise the Lord, all you nations* (Ps 117:1).

2. At the time, the monks of San Isidro slept on straw mattresses separated by partition walls in a common dormitory, and the entrance to each bed was closed with a curtain (OC 731).

3. That is, "Ave María Purísima, sin pecado concebida." This common prayer in Spanish was traditionally used as a greeting, particularly at the beginning of Confession.

hygienists say this is very good for you, and I don't doubt that it is . . . but, well, I think that's a rather low temperature . . . Anyway, that doesn't matter. Let us make use of the moment, whether it's cold or hot. This is no time for stupid reflections, although I do know someone who does so even at the most solemn of moments . . . Let us make use of the night to pray, and let us be glad that God is the one calling to us and waiting for us in the tabernacle.

I quickly realize that I'm a monk and that the bell has rung to call me to pray Matins. It's as I said, for the first minute or so, I don't remember what I am. I just look down and see a bunch of clothing and a man who rose fully dressed from a straw mattress . . . My soul loves the Virgin and reveres Her greatly . . . but that's the reality of life in this valley of tears[4] . . . penance, exhaustion, cold . . . and sometimes back pain.

Nevertheless, even though the evil spirit surrounds us, the Lord, who is very good, does not permit him to get close to us . . . The monks have been called to prayer, and so, in spite of everything and everyone, they go down to the choir to adore God, while perhaps many other souls are offending Him.

As I said, once I've become aware of the situation, there's nothing left to do but joyfully go down the stairs, walk through the cloister, and place myself at the feet of Jesus in the Blessed Sacrament.

Saint Benedict commands us to use these minutes well.[5] It is not advisable to let those first few minutes of the monastic day go to waste . . . They are precious in the eyes of God, who examines the most hidden movements of the heart[6] . . . These minutes ought to be used well because they come first . . . If we truly love God, those first minutes should feel centuries long to us, for the desire to fly into His presence upon rising should make us lament the long walk from the dormitory to the tabernacle.

You poor man, so long as your pilgrimage upon this earth has not yet come to an end, may your weaknesses serve as stepping stones toward loving God. Even if your little love for Him doesn't make you fly across

---

4. See the *Salve Regina* (#5, n. 6)

5. "On hearing the signal for an hour of the divine office, the monk will immediately set aside what he has in hand and go with utmost speed, yet with gravity and without giving occasion for frivolity. Indeed, nothing is to be preferred to the Work of God" (RB 43.1-3).

6. See Jer 17:10; Rom 8:27.

the monastery cloisters, even if your misery is weighing you down and your mortal flesh has you kicking and screaming . . . Don't worry . . . the Infinite One sees your intention . . . and maybe He is smiling as He watches the little monk bumble around the monastery cloisters with his pointy hood up, all cold and tired, but still singing David's psalm to God in his heart: *Laudate Dominum omnes gentes . . . Praise the Lord, all you nations . . . Extol Him, all you peoples.*[7]

And very quickly, muttering that psalm and praising God, those minutes become pearls that the humble monk offers to Jesus.

The silence of the night makes even the littlest of prayers great . . . At this hour, the dew begins to fall upon the ground while creatures are sleeping. The thick darkness pours over the Trappist's hood and weighs upon his shoulders as he is charged to pray for the world . . .

Laudate Dominum omnes gentes. Laudate Dominum omnes populi.[8]

The soul should like to fly throughout the whole world, extolling God's greatness at the top of its lungs . . . The soul wishes it could praise God on behalf of all the creatures who fail to do so . . .

The soul forgets about the body's exhaustion and cold. The body, for its part, is perhaps not entirely rested and is experiencing the harsh, crude aspects of having to stay awake . . . but God can do all things . . . In these moments, God comes to the aid of the soul that longs to praise Him, the soul that in spite of its weaknesses wishes all the nations on earth would adore God.

The path from the dormitory to the choir is short, but so much can happen in those few moments it takes to walk it . . . one can rejoice, one can suffer . . .

How often do the movements of our hearts make us soar on the wings of holy joy! How often do we bless the Lord in these first moments of the day, when we come to understand what a manifest favor He has granted us in allowing us to render Him service!

And still, how often does our rebellious nature also complain and protest. Misery comes calling and reminds us of other miseries. The worldly part of us, which we always carry around inside of us, reminds us of the

7. Ps 117:1-2.
8. *Praise the Lord, all you nations! Extol him, all you peoples!* (Ps 117:1).

world sometimes too . . . The world that doesn't know about or isn't aware of the little things, whether they be little tragedies or great joys, that happen in monasteries . . .

It's not all consolation and devotion. When we find ourselves surrounded by darkness, and in possession of a sensitive human heart and a fleshly body . . . when we find ourselves rather enclosed by our own egos, and very far from God . . . then we are truly suffering.

When we realize how little we are, and see that there's a whole world out there that Christ died for and that world is totally asleep . . . and so few of us are awake . . . sometimes that makes us truly suffer too. God permits this, and grants that it should come to pass.

Two o'clock in the morning . . . Shadows, monks, whispered prayers . . . The chants of Matins. Bells. Silence. Divine love flying around the cloister. Sometimes, pain, a sacrifice in full bloom. "Silent music" and "sounding solitude," as the mystic Saint John of the Cross would say.[9]

Two o'clock in the morning. Peace in souls who walk the earth and yearn for heaven . . . A calm hour, when petitions rise up like incense and reach the Eternal One with no need to shout or make noise . . . the prayers are scented with our penance and silence. The birds are not yet singing, nor are the flowers shining. Everything is darkness . . . The monastery is dominated by what Saint Teresa called the "watching fears of night."[10]

In this environment, an earthly garden exuding heavenly aromas, a heart that is not quite awake yet begins to sing, *Praise the Lord, all you nations! Extol him, all you peoples! For great is his steadfast love toward us, and the faithfulness of the Lord endures forever.*[11]

And who knows? I can't see them, but maybe the angels in heaven are helping that poor man sing as he ponders divine praise in his heart, as full of misery as he is amid the solitude of a night on earth.

---

9. "The tranquil night / at the time of the rising dawn, / silent music, / sounding solitude, / the supper that refreshes, and deepens love" (*Spiritual Canticle* 15, in SJC 473).

10. Rafael's error; these words are also from Saint John of the Cross, not Saint Teresa of Ávila. "Swift-winged birds, / lions, stags, and leaping roes, / mountains, lowlands, and river banks, / waters, winds, and ardors, / watching fears of night" (SJC 474).

11. Ps 117:1-2.

146. My Notebook

Happy New Year!!

La Trapa, January 1, 1937

It is the beginning of January in the year 1937. Today is the same as yesterday, and tomorrow will be the same too. For human beings, anyway, time passes . . . For God, there is no time. God alone endures.

A year . . . Just another year, as the homilist said, a year that is a drop in the bucket of eternity. This past year felt like a mere instant to us. A year has gone by, and we haven't done a thing with it . . . but we are closer to God than we were. That is the only consolation we have upon considering the passage of time, or how we are passing away with it . . . I don't know. I don't want to belabor what has already been said . . . Do we even know what time is? . . . Then why bother?! . . . To some, a year is a lifetime; to others, it's a mere flash of lightning, immeasurably quick . . . It doesn't matter, it's not worth thinking about . . . To me, it's just a number.

We will keep on living. Our bodies will get older. Our hair will fade and fall out. Our whole being will get worn out. What is young today will be old and decrepit tomorrow . . . That's what time is.

You won't be tomorrow what you are today, and you aren't today what you were before. Everything changes. That's what time does, it leaves nothing stable . . . What's the difference between a year and a century or a million centuries? Time is not worth our attention.

There is only one truth, and that is God, for God alone endures. God alone is unchanging. Everything else is like the year that just came to an end . . . lies and vanity that die with time . . . time that is a drop in the bucket of eternity.

Happy New Year . . . well, it will be if we are better people from now on and take less time to hurry toward being perfected in God's love.

But it's not the year that needs to be better . . . We are the ones who need to improve . . . We are the ones who really exist, not this new year . . . That's just a number that lives in our heads . . .

Goodness, look at me, I'm doing economic philosophy now. God help me. And the Most Blessed Virgin too.

Welcome, 1937, whatever you may bring, for God is the one who sends you. What do you have in store for me? It's all the same to me, for the Lord is the one who sends all that, too.

May He help me to serve Him better within your days and weeks . . . May He and Mary protect me as they have in previous years. When you are finished, may I be able to say not what I have said today—that I am closer to God in terms of the time left in my mortal life—but may I truly be able to say that the year 1937 helped me grow closer to God in terms of holiness, perfection, and true love . . . As for the rest, I don't want anything that won't help me do that. Everything else is just wasted time . . . and seen rightly, from the perspective of my conscience, I've already wasted enough of that.

Welcome, 1937, in the name of the Father, and of the Son, and of the Holy Spirit.

147. My Notebook
Just God and Me

La Trapa, January 4, 1937

Silence on the lips, songs in the heart; a soul that lives on love, on dreams and hopes . . . a soul that lives for God. A soul that turns its gaze far away . . . so far from this world, spending this life in silence . . . singing in its heart.

A monastery . . . a Trappist monastery . . . men.

It's just God and me!

The days pass quickly, and life with them . . . We dream about the past and hope for what is to come . . . The soul turns its gaze far away, seeking out true life, which is looking down from above a sea of hopes, and the soul hopes for better things.

A Trappist monastery . . . songs for God. Who cares about human beings? Who cares whether it's foggy or sunny? . . . Who cares about our surroundings? All of that is nothing, and nothingness is not worth our attention.

The soul is looking for what it cannot find here . . . it is searching in the heights for the God it desires. When Christ sends rays of light to a soul . . . what does that soul care for human beings, or whether it's foggy or sunny? . . . The soul sings silently, whispers love, and seeks out consolation in the tranquil, calm, and still peace of someone who no longer has any expectations, never looking back at a world that knows nothing of prayer.

The days pass with serenity amid the gentle calm of a love that waits. The soul understands that nothing in this world can satisfy it . . . Earth is dust, people are nothing, life is short, and everything is so small and fragile and falling apart . . . And the soul is eager to be in heaven already, gazing at the Virgin, contemplating God.

A monastery full of men . . . is a temporary shelter. Penitent monks . . . are migratory birds, singing as they fly. Flowers and thorns. Tears and crosses. Wind and ice. Hymns of joy. Moments of anguish. Bells, incense

. . . Everything that moves, everything that surrounds the soul in this life
. . . It's all so short-lived, here one day and gone the next. The soul has no
interest in anything but Christ. It is not moved by anything but God. It
hides its longings, sorrows, crosses, and love deep within itself.

Everything tires it out now. It no longer seeks in human beings what
they can never give. For this soul there is no heaven or earth, no people
or animals, no world at all, just mortal dust . . . The soul has only one
occupation, and it fills its whole life: yearning greatly for heaven, and
adoring God.

In the monastery, the days go by . . . but what does it matter? . . .
Just God and me.

I am still living on this earth, surrounded by men . . but what does it
matter? Just God and me.

And when I look out at the world, I don't see great things or misery,
I don't see the fog, and I can't make out the sun . . . The whole world is
reduced to a tiny little dot . . . and on that dot there is a monastery . . .
and in that monastery, there's just God and me.

148. My Notebook

*"Wise Men from the East Came to Jerusalem,
Asking, Where Is the One Who Has Been Born,
Whose Star We Have Observed?"*[1]

La Trapa, January 6, 1937

The homage of the Three Kings . . . those who have earthly power are bowing their heads before a baby's humble crib . . . Gold, frankincense, and myrrh: Jesus accepts these earthly presents . . . The divine child accepts these pagan gifts and presents with his newborn smile, underneath which his divine spirit is hiding . . . Gold, frankincense, and myrrh from the East . . .

Anxiety in their hearts. Dusty roads, traveled by night, following a star. "Where is the one who has been born?" This question bursts forth from souls that have been on a long journey through the desert and foreign lands . . . "Where is the one who has been born, whose star we have observed?"

It has been twenty centuries since then . . . and still there are souls who wander the earth as the Wise Men from the East did, and along the way, they are asking, *Have you seen him whom my soul loves?*[2]

And there is still a shining star lighting our way to the humble stable, and it shows us the one for whom we rose and went about the city.[3] It shows us a God who, though Master of all things, has nothing now. The creator of the sun's light and heat is shivering cold . . . The one who came into this world for love of human beings is forgotten by them.

And there are also souls searching for God now, just as there were then . . . Souls who roam the world in search of the mystery within the stable.

1. See Matt 2:1-2.
2. Song 3:3.
3. *I will rise now and go about the city, in the streets and in the squares; I will seek him whom my soul loves* (Song 3:2).

But unfortunately, not all of them find it; not all of them keep their eyes on the star of faith, or dare to start down the paths that lead to God . . . which are humility, renunciation, sacrifice, and almost always the cross.

Today there is a feast in the stable at Bethlehem . . . The wise men have come to adore Him.

Today is also a feast day at La Trapa . . . so we got up at one o'clock this morning and sang to the Lord for many hours.

When I was little, I would be so eager for Epiphany to get here[4] . . . I wouldn't be able to fall asleep because I was too excited about waking up on Epiphany . . . Children are such happy creatures!

It's been years since then . . . turrón, presents, getting excited about the Three Kings . . . Things have changed somewhat . . . I can't eat turrón anymore, I'm sick . . . As for gifts, what greater gift could there be than God? . . . But the excitement . . . I'm still a child when it comes to that! A child excitedly waiting to wake up happy . . . An excitement that fills the nighttime of life with holy joy, and makes for peaceful sleep . . . Someday we'll wake up in the embrace of God and Mary . . . There won't be toys or turrón . . . There will be something so much greater than that.

When, without meaning to, I remembered my childhood in choir tonight, and my home, and Epiphany . . . My white garments got me thinking about something else . . . Like the wise men, I too went in search of the stable . . . I'm not a child anymore, I don't need toys. I hope for much greater things now, and not in this life . . . Worldly hopes are like children's toys: waiting for them makes you happy, but once you get them, it's all just cardboard.

Hoping for heaven . . . is a hope that will last your whole life long and won't let you down in the end. How happy the wise men must have been to return, having seen God! And I will see him too . . . I just have to wait a little while.

Morning will be here soon, and light with it . . . What a joy it will be to wake up! We monks are like children too, all excited for Epiphany.

Remembering my childhood and all those cardboard toys doesn't make me sad . . . No, I don't miss how happy I was then, because now I await

4. In Spain, gifts are opened on the feast of the Epiphany, January 6.

the certain hope of a greater happiness . . . I'm waiting for something I shouldn't just call "happiness," which is too short a word for it.

Today, there is a feast in the stable at Bethlehem.

Today is also a feast day in the choir, where the monks spent all night singing to the Child Jesus while the world was asleep . . . dreaming worldly dreams . . . childish dreams, like short-lived flowers or cardboard toys.

149. My Notebook
A War in the World

La Trapa, January 8, 1937

Spain is at war, and I have a brother in it[1] . . . Some days ago I received a letter from him, in which he discussed exactly what one would think he'd discuss . . . battles, death, gunfire . . . everything that makes up a war. But at the same time, he spoke to me about the Virgin Mary, and what a beautiful thing that is, that someone firing cannons against God's enemies is thinking of Mary.

The war going on in Spain is cruel and bloody, but it is giving a great deal of glory to God . . . I don't know the details of it . . . and I don't want to, because in order to do my duty, which is to pray for peace, I have no need of them. All I know is that people are fighting, suffering, and dying in Spain.

When the choir begins singing the *Magnificat* to the Virgin during the Hour of Vespers, a Cistercian oblate prostrates himself at Mary's feet. There, lifted up by the petitions that all Christendom offers to Mary through that sublime canticle to Her humility, he asks Her for many different things . . . The other day, he told Mary that he had a brother in the war. I'm sure She already knew.

There are certain moments of the day when the Most Blessed Virgin listens to all the petitions offered up by Her children: during the *Magnificat* at Vespers, and during the *Salve Regina* after Compline.

In the peace of our monastic life, many men are praying for peace for those who are at war. For my part, I tell the Lord that since I don't understand His plans . . . He ought to do whatever He wants, and I just offer my prayers and supplications so that He might make use of them, for He knows better than I do what their intention ought to be. Thus I avoid

1. Luis Fernando Arnaiz Barón.

asking for the wrong thing. On the other hand, with the Virgin Mary, I simply tell Her what is going on . . . but it's only so that She won't forget.

Ask and you will receive, Christ said[2] . . . I ask for so many things, but in order to avoid asking for the wrong thing, I ask God for whatever He wants us to ask Him for . . .

Spain is at war . . . I ask God, may it end or may it continue . . . whichever is best. I believe the best thing would be for His will to be done.

Now, then, I'll tell Him this too: "Lord, be careful what You're doing, because I have a brother on the front lines! . . . Virgin Mary, remember that." And I'm sure both Jesus and Mary hear me . . . and I haven't asked them for anything . . . at least I don't think I have. But as you know, monks can be so crafty!

2. John 16:24; see also Matt 7:7.

150. My Notebook

"The Lord Gave, and the Lord Has Taken Away"[1]

La Trapa, January 10, 1937

The life of a sick person . . . A sad thing to those whose happiness depends upon this present life. The life of a sick person . . . Perhaps a hopeless thing, living only to wait for death . . . Blessed are those who wait and see their illness as nothing but God's will.

I've been in the infirmary at La Trapa for a few days now. Naturally, that means I've been separated from community life.

God has ordained, for my greater good and His greater glory, that for a few days I should go without the health that allowed me to enjoy my brothers' company as we worked in the fields and made it possible for me to join them at prayer in choir. Blessed be God, who sends me trials that I have not earned.

Illness . . . separation. Long hours sitting in an armchair, hearing the bells, and directing my intention toward all the community's activities.

As for my illness, why bother talking about it? . . . It's just one of many . . . It just makes me tired . . . and hungry, and very thirsty, and totally lacking in energy . . . Otherwise I am fine. I am very pleased to have such an attractive illness that makes me suffer sometimes.

I was also healthy, once . . . but that was then. Now, thanks be to God, I am sick. When the Lord thinks it necessary, He reminds me of this fact by having me sit in an armchair in the infirmary for a few days and keeping me away from the choir . . . Blessed be God.

He is the one who ordains all things, and He does well in leading me into solitude. Showing me the great void that is nothingness, which is everything outside of Him, He invites me to reflect and obliges me, in my uselessness, to seek His aid. He separates me from everything else in order to unite me more closely to Himself.

1. Job 1:21.

Blessed be God, and blessed be my illness, which is the means He is using to accomplish His designs in me, insignificant as I am.

"How great God is!. . . How vast is his mercy!. . . How little we human beings are!. . ." That's what I think about all day as I sit in my armchair and hear the bells announcing the community's activities.

Sometimes these little sufferings are needed in order to arrive at that spiritual peace, that holy *joie de vivre* as we fulfill our destiny as sick people. We have to give up many little things, but once the soul has come to understand that the only way forward is waiting in God's embrace. . . it willingly and joyfully gives up all that is temporal, all that is changing, all that is not *our own* . . . like health, for example.

At times, I've been sad to find myself in this situation in a monastery where we live in continuous penance. At times, it has been a humiliation for me to be exempted in part from the Rule. . . What a fool I was!. . . My heart contains so much self-love!. . . How stupid, to be sad over not being able to do public penance. One can hide so much pride beneath a fast or a *noisy* discipline![2] . . .

Humiliation! What a poor understanding we have of that word. I have come to realize that in order to be humiliated, one must be *made low* . . . And could I possibly be made any lower? Am I high up in any way?

True humiliation, for a Christian, is being lifted up. I don't find scrubbing floors and toilets humiliating. I'm no longer ashamed of not being able to fast or spending my life watching my energy drain away slowly. . . it wasn't mine to begin with, and now the Lord has taken it away. Does any of that prevent me from loving God?

How easily we fixate on all these external things . . . and how often we fail to love God's will and unite ourselves to it.

Blessed be my illness, which makes me think about God and separates me from human beings.

How great is the Lord, who turns tears into laughter. What seem like evils to us are in fact generally sources of wealth . . . Happy are those who know how to mine them!. . .

Happy are those who see God's hand in everything that happens to them . . . Happy, a thousand times over, are those who love everything the Lord

---

2. Discipline: An instrument of physical penance (see #40, n. 15).

sends them affectionately, even if that means spending my life in an armchair hearing the bells of my monastery call the other monks to penance.

The hours pass by slowly in my cell at the infirmary. In the solitude
and silence of my continuous waiting, there is no sadness or bitterness
or disorder in my soul that could disturb the vast peace of the one who
yearns for God alone.

What is health to me, if I can't have any more than I already do? Who
knows if I would offend God more as a healthy person? . . . I am happy
with what I have. I aspire to nothing but God, and I have Him in the little
cross of my illness.

What do I have to complain about? . . . I see nothing but divine mercy
at work in my life! How can I not love my solitude? . . . The Lord has
placed me in this solitude, and it is here that He is instructing me in the
only science there is: contempt for the world, and the art of loving Him!

So much happiness can be hidden away within the walls of an infirmary! What a joy it is to be able to love God in the uselessness of everything, being incapable of everything oneself! How the soul stretches upon
realizing in recollection that the earth is not its center, and that the body
with all its weaknesses and illnesses and miseries is not where it is truly
meant to live . . . When it comes to see that God alone can satisfy it, and
a mere veil separates it from Him . . . a curtain of smoke, which is this
life, that can be blown away with the slightest breeze!

How the soul grows as it witnesses the mercy of God! *You gave me room
when I was in distress*, as the prophet David says.[3]

How gentle it is to suffer, when one waits in hope.

How sweet it is to wait, when one's heart is calm.

How joyful it is to be calm, when one desires nothing.

The only thing that disturbs the silence of my cell is a desire for God
. . . A prayer bursts forth from my sick lips . . . Saint John of the Cross
composed it . . . It's just a line from one of his poems:

"Tear through the veil of this sweet encounter."[4]

3. Ps 4:1.

4. "O living flame of love / that tenderly wounds my soul / in its deepest center! Since
/ now you are not oppressive, / now consummate! if it be your will: / tear through the veil
of this sweet encounter" (SJC 639).

I believe that's what he says . . . I don't remember . . . it doesn't matter; the Lord knows what I mean. "This sweet encounter!" Is there a more divine name for death? . . . And what separates us from God? . . . Just that veil that we ask him to tear away . . . this life with all its ambitions and wakefulness . . . this all-consuming illness . . . this beating heart.

"Tear through the veil of this sweet encounter." One desires death so tenderly . . . but being intimately conformed to the divine will soothes all things.

The life of a sick person . . . A life of prayer. Restful work in peacefulness and repose. Eyes that gaze far off, dreaming of horizons of light . . . Sometimes I think about the sea.

The life of a sick person . . . is made up of long hours thinking about God, who seems to be taking so long to arrive, and reading books that speak to me about Him. I have the *Revelations* of Saint Gertrude[5] on my table . . . God loved that saint so dearly! And she too was sick nearly her entire life.

Studying . . . philosophy, a thick Latin dictionary . . . papers covered in translations and . . . yes, I can't help it, doodles and scribbles too.

And in this way, sometimes looking at books, sometimes thinking about how good God is, the hours pass by peacefully . . . Days pass . . . My life will pass. As a sick person, I may be separated from the rest of my brothers, but it doesn't matter that I sing, fast, and work in intention alone.

God has placed me here . . . may He be blessed!

I should so like to have not just the message of Job,[6] but his patience too. Even so, I cannot complain, because I don't have friends who come here to bother me, let alone a wife . . . Truly, what a magnificent gift . . . God permitted it, and everything was taken from Job: his home, his livestock, his children, his health, everything *except* his wife, who also came to bother him . . . Truly, I cannot complain.

5. See, e.g., Gertrud the Great of Helfta, *The Herald of God's Loving-Kindness*, 5 vols., trans. Alexandra Barratt, CS 35, 63, 85, 86 (Kalamazoo, MI, and Collegeville, MN: Cistercian Publications, 1991, 1999, 2018, 2020).

6. See Job 2:9-13. After God allowed Satan to test Job's faithfulness to the Lord by sending him the trials Rafael describes in this passage, Job's wife tried to convince him to curse God. He responded, *Shall we receive the good at the hand of God, and not receive the bad?* (Job 2:10). Afterward, three of Job's friends came to sit with him.

Anyway . . . I don't want my clumsy words to perhaps fall short of the hidden mysteries of the Sacred Scriptures.

If God let Job keep his wife in order to test him further . . . and the world fell through the actions of another woman . . . God also praised one creature above all else, and that is Mary, who is a woman, too.

God knows what He is doing in everything that He does. That's why He didn't make me a married man . . . but rather a monk.

I have such stupid thoughts sometimes.

Anyway, there's time for everything in solitude, and so long as I do not offend God, everything is fine. The soul serves God by meditating upon death just as much as it does by thinking joyful thoughts, and just as much as it does when doing anything for His greater glory.

Let us say, then, with Job . . . So I no longer have my health? It doesn't matter . . . *The Lord gave, and the Lord has taken away; blessed be the name of the Lord.*[7]

7. Job 1:21.

151. My Notebook

The View from My Window

La Trapa, January 13, 1937

My cell in the infirmary has a window, naturally, and since I live in this cell, when I'm not looking at anything else, I look through its glass at . . . well, whatever's outside. Today, it's raining quite a bit out there.

When I was free (?) out in the world, it was thrilling to stand among the imposing cliffs looking out over the Cantabrian Sea,[1] gazing at the wide horizon . . . seeing God's wonders.

The view from my window today . . . is much better than the sea.

When I was free, and my body enjoyed fresh air, the sun, and its health, my glycosuria-free[2] legs would take me up over those crags in the snow-capped mountains of Asturias, all covered with goats and chamois[3] . . . My soul rejoiced so greatly at seeing the vastness of God reflected in the depth of the valleys and the steepness of the mountain peaks! . . . How much time have I spent looking out over seas of fog, listening to the solemn silence of nature, in places where people so rarely go?

The view from my window . . . is even more magnificent.

When I was free, and I was longing for horizons, I traveled the plains of Castile. My eyes would soak in the light of its skies, and my soul would be flooded with the peace of its fields, enjoying the austerity of the land-scape, and loving that land, which is my homeland . . . and I blessed God then, too.

The view from my window right now . . . is even greater, even wider . . . it's even better.

1. Cantabrian Sea: the body of water that runs along Spain's northern coast, the south-ern part of the Bay of Biscay.

2. Glycosuria: the presence of glucose in the urine, often leading to dehydration. Usually it is a symptom of diabetes caused by elevated blood-sugar levels.

3. Chamois: a species of goat-antelope native to various European mountain ranges.

My window doesn't look out over the sea . . .
or a valley, or the foothills. From it, I don't see
seas of fog or cliffs or rocks or sunsets . . . From
my window, I see some yellow stones that, along
with some tiles and old wood and manual labor,
have been made to contain the Holy Ark of
God for centuries.

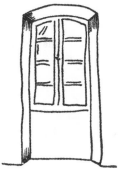

The apse of the church . . . a Romanesque
apse, not that I care about the architecture,
because when I look at it, all I see is a rough
stone carved by men, in order to . . . Marvel, you seas! Quake, you mountains of the
earth! . . . Stop in your tracks, you planets, twirling about in
space! . . . These yellow stones and Castilian tiles . . . are God's house!!

I see some other things from my window too . . . I don't know, I don't
care; grass, trees, sky, a little town[4] . . . who cares!

It's only a few meters from my window to the sanctuary, and spanning
that space, there are just a few fragile, sunbathed stones. What better view
could I want? . . . What in the world could bring more joy to my soul,
or possess more charms?

During the time I spend looking through my window, I <u>see</u> more of
God's magnificence in the humility of His house and the sublime mystery
of His presence among human beings than I see in all the works that came
forth from His hands, made manifest in the world.

How great God is! . . . How infinite is His wisdom! How well He
orders events, always toward His greater glory!

He doesn't need to lead me through the world and show me His wonders in order for my poor soul to lose itself in its nothingness and adore
Him in His magnificent majesty.

He has no need of my liberty, my health, or even the praise I offer as
I contemplate the works of His hands. My profound admiration at the
sight of His sanctuary, humbly hidden among earthly stones and human
clay, is enough for Him.

---

4. This little town is named Tariego de Cerrato. The slightly larger town with which the
monastery is associated, Venta de Baños, is slightly to the northwest of Tariego.

My window doesn't look out over the sea. From it, I can't see wonders of the world, or landscapes that would inspire my soul to dream . . . I have neither horizons nor deep chasms . . . I'm not so crazy that I still want to have what human beings dream about, what I used to call . . . my longing for freedom.

But God who is just, God who is thrice Holy, God who is Infinite, wants me here, keeping still . . . sick, silent, loving my solitude, looking out the window . . .

God clipped my wings . . . I cannot fly.

152. My Notebook
The Wind

La Trapa, January 15, 1937

I've been listening to the wind this morning. It is not yet dawn . . . The last shadows of night are clinging to the scenery and fields, taking refuge among the trees and the corners of the monastery. The wind was blowing furiously, as if hoping to scatter the darkness and rid the sleeping world of gloom.

It whistled through the tower as it brushed against the bells . . . I don't know why, but it reminded me of the dead . . . maybe I was afraid. It was completely dark, silence reigned . . . Sitting in my sick chair, I looked at what I could not see, and I listened to the wind. Moments of calm in the soul . . . and chills, too.

What a black night! How thick the sky is! You cannot see the stars, and all the lights of the stark monastery are out. It all makes you think . . . maybe about the dead.

A rainy day is struggling to dawn . . . The shadows are maintaining their grip, and it seems as though they are moaning . . . Maybe it's just a dream . . . Maybe it's the wind.

I throw on my cloak, looking for a refuge to free me from such dismal thoughts . . . My lips whisper, and my eyes close so as not to see such a sad, dark world.

I wished I would die, so I wouldn't have to hear the wind anymore.

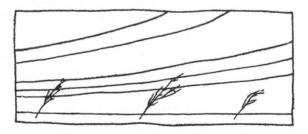

153. My Notebook
My Notebook

La Trapa, January 18, 1937

I still have one consolation left in this world . . . my notebook. I know this is a vanity. I know nobody's interested in my writing. Nobody cares about a dead man's life.

But even so, I keep putting words down on these blank pages . . . words that express laments, or speak of love, or talk of the things of heaven . . . They may be clumsy words, but they speak with a sincere voice.

My notebook! . . . In it, I lay down the sentiments of my soul as it ruminates in silence . . . and divine love . . . and childish fear of the wind.

I don't care if anybody reads it, or if anybody should laugh at its jumble of ideas, mixing trivial things with deep thoughts.

It doesn't matter . . . I'll keep on writing . . . Silence seeks out this kind of relief, a relief that only someone who has experienced it can understand.

What I can say for certain is that a great deal of silence and continual reflection bring about a state of mind that is good for two things. The first is prayer . . . a desire to remain silent and not interrupt the interior peace that leads us to kneel at Christ's feet or Mary's heels, and tell Them about our struggles and ambitions . . . to remain silent among men so as to love God better, and adore Him without distraction.

The second thing that the soul feels is odd, it's the complete opposite . . . A desire to shout out and proclaim to the whole world that what you are *feeling* is God . . . the reason you are *suffering* is God . . . what you are *thinking* is God . . . the reason you are *living* is God . . .

The soul wants to get everyone else to feel, suffer, think, and live in God and for God too . . . But everything stays inside. Everything is reduced to remaining silent and feeling, suffering, and living for God . . . but in silence.

I have two paths . . . prayer in the presence of Jesus, and my notebook.

Sometimes I put my pen down when it doesn't express what I want it to, because it doesn't know how, and it can't. Then I prostrate myself before the tabernacle, and while there, I write, sing, pray, or cry . . . about whatever God tells me to . . . and nobody will ever read it, ever.

Other times, I sit down in front of these blank pages and I fill them up . . . I don't know what with. But sometimes they also help me to pray, because writing about God is a form of prayer too.

But above all, what motivates me is a desire to lead whoever might read this closer to God . . . May they see that God's ways are simple, that His yoke is easy and His burden light.[1] May those who encounter these pages understand that death to the world is birth in God, that within the austerities of a life of silence and solitude is found the sweet joy of a heart whose happiness lies in simplicity and openness, and that while anyone who follows Christ undoubtedly follows Him down the only path, which is the cross . . . I believe it is in loving the cross that all things have been achieved.

Oh, if only my notebook and my sorry ideas could capture these truths that one can only come to understand through silence and *prayer*!!

Whenever I start to write, I ask the Virgin Mary to enlighten me. She will guide me in what I say, but sometimes there's so much I want to say . . . that I end up not saying anything at all.

---

1. Matt 11:30.

My notebook! . . . How often has my pen brought me consolation! . . . How often have I gotten up from my desk and told God out loud what I'd just written down!

I guess nobody will be interested in this, but maybe also this might console somebody. What poor things we human beings are! I feel so incapable of writing clearly, of expressing God's greatness . . . but I am a Trappist. Even when writing, I must observe silence!

154. My Notebook

Meditation on a Passage from Kempis

La Trapa, January 20, 1937

Lord God, I can see that patience is something vitally necessary to me, because this life abounds in circumstances that thwart our happiness. No matter how carefully I endeavour to live in peace, my days must have their share of conflict and sorrow.

That is so, my son; but the kind of peace I want you to aim at is not one in which temptations are not present, or difficulties not felt. The time when you may reckon you have found peace is when you have been harassed by various temptations and put to the proof by much adversity.[1]

Note what this wise man has to say on the topic of peace. How mistaken we can be sometimes, those of us who are seeking the true peace of God. We have such a human concept of what peace is. Our desire for peace can, at times, cover up a great deal of selfishness . . . But often, the peace we seek is not peace according to God . . . but peace according to the world. But God, who is very good, always gives light to hearts that love Him and seek Him with simplicity.

Once upon a time, in a certain monastery, there was a certain novice who was neither particularly pious nor particularly depraved; he consistently obeyed the Rule and didn't bother anyone . . . and that was it, no more, no less.

That novice was happy. He had what he considered to be "so much peace." Nothing in the world held any attraction for him; nobody bothered

---

1. Thomas à Kempis, *The Imitation of Christ*, 3.12, trans. Michael Oakley and Ronald A. Knox (New York: Sheed and Ward, 1960), 102.

him. He loved God in silence, was moved by the birdsong in the cemetery
. . . All that was left for him to do was live "happily ever after," as they
do in fairy tales.

Our Lord loved him then just as much as he does now. He spoiled him,
and laughed at him . . . The angels in heaven laughed at that naïve novice
too, the one who said he had "so much peace" and was happy because the
monks' white cowls were lovely alongside the organ music and monastery
bells . . . Does it get any more naïve than that? He had peace according
to the world . . . but a little bit of God's peace, too.

When the world talks about peace . . . that's what it means. When the
world goes looking for peace . . . that's how it thinks about it . . . silence,
stillness, love without shedding any tears . . . a lot of hidden selfishness.

People seek out that kind of peace in order to *rest*, in order to avoid
suffering. They seek human peace, the *feeling* of peace . . . A peace as
the world imagines it, a sunny cloister with cypress trees and birds in the
background. Peace without temptations or a cross, a life of tossing scornful
smiles to the world while gazing calmly upon God . . .

Indeed, there is peace in all that . . . but it's not true peace. That novice's peace . . . was God's bait.

That novice . . . isn't a novice anymore. God loves him so much . . .
more than he can imagine. God took that novice's health away . . . and
showed him that sometimes bells have cracks in them, so they sound bad
. . . and the sun hides sometimes, and the birds go quiet . . . He changed
the landscape around him, and sent him a cross . . .

God has so much love for that novice who used to sing songs to the
Virgin while he worked in the fields![2]

He doesn't have the energy to work anymore . . . but he's still singing
those songs. Trials and temptations came . . . sometimes the cross weighs
heavy on him. On the one hand, the world; on the other, his solitude . . .
all mixed in with so many miseries and weaknesses . . . and setbacks . . .
But Christ arrives in the midst of it and says, "Here is your peace."

How good God is!

It's true. Today, I wouldn't trade places with the novice I once was. Today,
from the depths of my soul I bless the God who loves me so much, who

---

2. See #37.

shows me why He wants me to be as He is . . . nailed to His cross, kissing
His wounds, accompanying Him in His agony . . . He wants me, with all
my miseries, sins, tears, and joys. He wants me to have the peace Kempis
describes, which is not the saccharine serenity of a sunny cloister . . .

I don't know if I'm making sense, but God knows what I mean . . .

I love Christ the more trials He sends me . . . My soul knows peace
. . . perhaps in the agony; I don't know when I am suffering, because I
suffer for Christ, and I suffer with pleasure. I wouldn't trade places with
anyone, because I have the best thing a Christian could hope for . . . the
cross of Christ deep within my heart.

There's so much I could say about this! There are so many things to
say about God, that God who loves me so much! I so wish I knew how
to express where my peace lies! . . . But I don't know how. My pen is too
clumsy to talk of God. All I can do is poorly describe His little gestures
toward me, which aren't small to me at all, for everything He gives me is
great indeed. And He gives without my even looking for gifts, let alone
deserving them. How great God is!

My soul enjoys the peace of one who no longer hopes for anything
from anyone . . . just God, just the cross of Christ, just the desire to live
united to His will. That is what the soul who is still in this world hopes
for. It waits calmly for these things, *peacefully*, despite the difficult sadness
of not yet being able to see God, the copious tears sometimes shed while
accompanying Him on the cross, and the unrelenting sorrow of realizing
it still has its own will, and therefore the miseries, defects, and sins that
go along with it.

Everything is a struggle, as Kempis says[3] . . . A struggle against oneself, against tribulation and temptation . . . Everything is fighting and
pain, but Jesus is in the midst of it all, nailed to a cross, and He gives the
soul strength to keep going . . . In the midst of the battle that we are
fighting in this world, Jesus is there, with a serene countenance, reminding
us that those who follow Him do not walk in darkness.[4]

---

3. "You will not reach this state without a hard struggle and a certain amount of pain"
(Thomas à Kempis, *Imitation of Christ*, 103).

4. *Whoever follows me will never walk in darkness but will have the light of life* (John
8:12).

It is a great consolation to have a cross . . . There is no greater peace than that which is bestowed by suffering.[5] Those who leave all things behind suffer . . . those who leave all things behind for God's sake rejoice in their suffering.

Those who eagerly await life in heaven, who yearn for Christ at night . . . where can they find peace?

Foolish are those who look at this world and try to find their rest in it . . . they will not find peace. Blessed are those who look for peace in sacrifice, pain, and penitential life.

Blessed are those who look for peace in Jesus' wounds. Only those who renounce themselves and take up their cross daily[6] will find what they are looking for . . . but not on this earth, which sprouts only thistles and thorns . . . it may be true that there are flowers on this earth, too . . . but lovers of Christ cannot be satisfied with earthly flowers.

As such, Lord, patience is indeed "vitally necessary to me" . . . the patience to wait and suffer . . . the patience to find that true peace, which is only to be found in Your cross, and in life's battles . . .

Lord, give me the patience that turns people into saints; give me the patience that is vitally necessary to me, so that I can carry the weight of the tribulations of this life, which feels as though it's going on too long sometimes.

If only the world knew! . . . But the world knows nothing about God.

Here, in the infirmary of a Trappist monastery, there is a man who is very much loved by God . . . and he knows it. He also knows that everything will come to an end very soon. He knows he will only be happy in heaven with Jesus and Mary, and they will not delay. So, what does he have to complain about?

What greater peace could he want? . . . There's a voice inside him that says . . . "Take heart, Brother Rafael, expect nothing from the world and human beings . . . God alone . . . just wait."

5. "The more you withdraw from the comfort you find in anything created, the sweeter and stronger will be the comfort you find in me" (Thomas à Kempis, *Imitation of Christ*, 103).
6. Matt 16:24.

JE*SU*S   NAZARENO

155. *My Notebook*
My Pencil

La Trapa, January 22, 1937

My pencil is running in a thousand directions all over a thick bit of cardboard that the infirmarian found for me.[1] Today, my prayer was at the tip of my pencil, which drew Christ, dead on the cross.

A painter's easel reigns over my cell . . . memories of my student years . . . memories of pleasant hours spent among canvases and paintbrushes. God is so good, to let me <u>still</u> remember what charcoal and erasers are . . . I'm very clumsy, but I can still handle them.

With God in my heart and a pencil in my hand . . . what more could I ask for? . . . How lovely it is to spend time drawing Jesus! I never thought a pencil and a simple piece of cardboard could bring me so much consolation . . . How good God is, that he <u>still</u> lets me enjoy one thing I brought with me from the world . . . my love for painting and drawing.

I had a happy day today, sitting next to the easel, caressing the outline of Christ's figure.

But if I take more time to think about it, it's not the paintbrushes and colors that bring joy into the hours I spend working . . . It's the work itself, the cross that I'm drawing, the cause of my joy . . . It's seeing how my clumsy hands and these crude instruments combine to bring something forth from this rough cardboard . . . something I carry deep inside me . . . that figure, that wood, those nails.

Even so, I always end up saying, "<u>No, that's not it.</u>" But it doesn't matter. Neither I nor the greatest painter of all time could manage to depict <u>that</u> . . . nobody could.

---

1. Brother Domingo García Hidalgo (1882–1948) was the infirmarian assisting Rafael at this time. He replaced Brother Tescelino (Toribio Luis) Arribas, who had been called up to military service along with the other young monks in September 1936.

In the meantime, nobody is stopping me from praying with the tip of my pencil, which, little by little, fills out this image of Christ dead on the cross with great tenderness.

156. My Notebook
Simplicity and Openness

La Trapa, January 25, 1937

One must walk so many tortured paths to arrive at simplicity. Complication is such an uncomfortable thing. . . and we human beings like to complicate everything for ourselves. Often, if we fail to practice virtue, it's because our complicated nature rejects what is simple.

Often, we fail to appreciate the magnificence hidden within an act of simplicity, because we look for greatness in complicated things; we judge the magnificence of things based on their *difficulty*.

Perhaps I'm not expressing myself well, but now I clearly see that what seemed dark and complicated to me before is actually rather simple and straightforward.

Virtue . . . God . . . the interior life, how difficult I thought it was to *live* that! It's not that I'm virtuous now, or that I have a completely clear knowledge of God and spiritual life, but I've realized that you get there without complications or complexities, without clever philosophy, without *technical* challenges.

I've come to see that you reach God in precisely the opposite manner. You come to know Him through simplicity of heart and being uncomplicated. There's nothing difficult about acts of love . . . What's truly difficult is wanting to know God by searching out His mysteries.

The former leads us to God, and the latter does not.

Virtue . . . oh, that's for saints! . . . That's hard to put into practice. Yes, indeed it is . . . but you don't have to get a degree or devote yourself to serious study in order to be virtuous . . . It's enough just to simply *be willing*; sometimes it's a simple act of the *will*.

So, then, why do we lack virtue at times? Because we aren't simple; because we complicate our desires; because everything we want is made difficult by our weak will, which gets carried away by whatever is pleasing, comfortable, and unnecessary, and often by its passions.

We lack virtue not because it is difficult, but because we don't want it.

We lack patience . . . because we don't want it.

We lack temperance . . . because we don't want it.

We lack chastity . . . for the same reason.

We would be saints if we wanted to be . . . it's much harder to become an engineer than it is to become a saint. If only we had faith!

The interior life . . . the spiritual life, a life of prayer. "My God! That must be difficult!" But it's not at all. Get rid of everything in your heart that's in the way, and you'll find God there. That's it.

Often we look for things that aren't there, and on the other hand we'll walk right by a treasure without seeing it. The same thing happens with God. We look for Him in a life of abstraction and reading, which is often more perceptible to the mind than to the heart.

We look for Him in a whole tangled mess of things, and to us, the more complicated they are, the better. And all the while, we are carrying God around inside of us, yet we don't look for Him there.[1]

Collect yourself within . . . gaze upon your nothingness, gaze upon the nothingness of the world, place yourself at the foot of the cross, and if you are simple, you will see God.

Behold, the life of prayer. We don't need to add something that's already there. Rather, we need to get rid of what is in the way. I say "something that's already there" because I assume the soul to be in a state of God's grace, but if God is not present there at times, it's because we don't want that.

We have such a great big heap of interests, distractions, affinities, vain desires, pretensions . . . we have so much of the world inside of us that God is driven away . . . But all we have to do is want Him, and God will fill the soul again in such a way that you'd have to be blind not to see it.

If a soul wants to live according to God's ways . . . it must be rid of everything that is not Him . . . and that is it. It's quite easy.

If we wanted to, and if we asked God with simplicity, we would make great progress in the spiritual life.

1. See John 14:21-23.

If we wanted to be saints, we would be . . . But we're such fools that we don't want to . . . We prefer to waste time on stupid vanities. We'll regret that someday.

But I am very happy, because I have come to see that everything is simple and straightforward . . . and this is within my reach.

May the Most Blessed Virgin Mary come to my aid. Amen.

157. My Notebook

My Heaven on Earth

La Trapa, January 28, 1937

I've turned my cell into my heaven on earth. I don't live alone. My cell is full of people. There are laughter, and songs, and angels frolicking about, fiddling with my papers.

I don't live alone. Christ lives by my sickbed, and Mary's here too . . . There's a little bit of everything in my cell: silence, peace, joy. There's a monk who dreams of heaven, a heaven without pain or weeping, a heaven that isn't like the one he has now, a heaven on earth . . . a heaven with four walls.

My heaven is my cell. There's silence here, and peace, and joy. I live with the saints; Christ keeps me company; I dream of Mary.

158. My Notebook
"Fiat"[1]

La Trapa, February 6, 1937

This is as far as I'll go in my notebook, since obedience obliges me to leave behind my cell in the infirmary, my silence, my life of retreat from the world . . . May God's will be done.

He is taking me away from here . . . He must bring me back to live within these walls once more . . . I'm so sure that I am to die a Trappist! . . . I don't know why . . . but even though it seems as though everything is against me, humanly speaking, it's really not . . . God's infinite goodness and His plans for His creatures are often disguised in ways that seem so strange in the eyes of human beings . . . who need <u>other eyes</u>, not those of the body, to see them.

I've left my home and my family three times. Three times now, I've believed that I was leaving everything behind, but I wasn't. If God grants me the grace and health to do so, I will leave it all behind again, not three or four times . . . but a thousand times over, if necessary.

This is the third time that I am taking off my monastic habit and putting on secular clothing . . . The first time, I was so upset I thought I would die[2] . . . I thought that God was abandoning me.

The second time, I left for the sake of the war[3] . . . I was happy when I left . . . as if I were *going on vacation* . . . The novelty of war, the curiosity of it, a few days of rest from penance, it all sounded good to me . . . I knew that going back to the monastery would be hard for me . . . I could tell that God was testing me.

---

1. *Fiat*: From the Latin version of Mary's words, *Let it be with me according to your word* (Luke 1:38).
2. Rafael left the monastery for the first time on May 25, 1934 (see #35).
3. Rafael left the monastery for the second time on September 29, 1936 (see #134, n. 1).

This is the third time[4] . . . and I see God's hand in it so clearly that it's all the same to me. Suffering is the only treasure that will retain its worth on the last day . . . and wherever you go, you will find the cross, as Thomas à Kempis says.[5]

Now I see that God is neither abandoning me nor testing me . . . rather, God is loving me.

I leave for the world again tomorrow . . . May the Virgin Mary of La Trapa accompany me, and may She bring me back here.

I want to do what God asks of me with simplicity and openness. Behold, an opportunity to put what I said the other day into practice.[6]

There can be no doubt that I am not yet detached from this earth and from human beings . . . It's still hard for me to leave, I still love something that is not God . . . I'm still seeking myself in so many things . . . What a poor man I am! . . .

When will I come to be a little better than this? When will my gaze be fixed more on God and less on the world?

It is sad to still be walking in this valley of exile, where nothing is stable or lasting, and yet our little faith and our selfishness make us think we were going to live here on earth forever.

"Why stand gaping here? This is no place for you to settle down."[7] That sentence is forever etched in my memory . . . and in spite of that, I do stand gaping here, instead of looking up at the one place I ought to be looking.

How good God is! He picks me up, carries me, and tosses me about from one place to the next. Sometimes He makes me cry, sometimes He makes me suffer, sometimes He makes me rejoice and laugh . . . One right after the other.

---

4. Rafael's condition had so deteriorated that the monastery was no longer able to provide sufficient care. Thus, he left La Trapa for the third time on February 7, 1937 (OC 770).

5. "Walk where you will, seek whatever you have a mind to . . . you will always find the cross" (Thomas à Kempis, *Imitation of Christ*, 79).

6. See My Notebook #156.

7. "Why stand gaping here? This is no place for you to settle down. Heaven is your destination, and you should look upon this earthly scene only as a transit-camp" (Thomas à Kempis, *Imitation of Christ*, 61).

How good God is! He only wants what is best for me . . . He knows what He is doing . . . Now that I'm getting used to His way of going about things, I don't even ask Him about it anymore . . . I just let Him lead me, and do whatever He wants, and that's the best thing to do . . . Woe is me. When will I ever learn?

Anyway . . . I think once I've learned, the Lord will leave me in a calm place. May this be a new chance to look not at myself, but at His hand at work.

But I was already *so* happy in my solitude!

FIAT

VII. Foolishness for Christ

In the World Once Again

159. To Leopoldo Barón

Villasandino,[1] March 18, 1937

Ave Maria
My dear brother,

Aunt María left me some space in her letter . . . but I didn't think it would be enough, so I decided to get another sheet of paper. Believe me, I'd decided not to write to *anybody* ever again, but yesterday Aunt María said that your letter made it seem as though you were in low spirits and a little sad . . . That changed my mind. If brothers who truly love one another don't help each other when suffering comes, what kind of charity is that? . . .

I can't say anything, or help you with anything. I know your situation, I know the environment in which God has placed you, and I also know many of your soul's nooks and crannies . . . I understand, and I say nothing, but in my silence, I am with you. The greater your suffering, the more united I am to you. How could it be otherwise, if we truly live the love of Christ? Take heart, my brother. Don't let the little thorns along your path scare you. Our lack of generosity and our selfishness make them look bigger than they are.

What does it matter where you happen to be? What does it matter who surrounds you, or whether you're alone? What does exhaustion, cold, or sickness matter? What does it matter if you live or die? . . .

Oh, Uncle Polín, if only we truly loved God! If only we saw His will in everything that surrounds us! . . . Then we would not suffer, and we'd see the infinite glory of God in our flaws and those of others. Then our life, which is so busy with things of this earth, would instead fly by with the serenity that is bestowed by love of God and love of neighbor.

---

1. Villasandino: A town outside Burgos where the Arnaiz-Barón family owned a house (see #62, n. 6). Rafael convalesced there while staying with his parents and siblings (other than his brother Luis Fernando, who was serving in the military). Other family members came to stay with them as well, including Rafael's aunt, María Osorio. Her husband, Leopoldo Barón, was in Toro when this letter was written.

Listen . . . in one of the letters you wrote me at La Trapa, you said that I never told you anything about myself. To be honest, and this is not false modesty, I consider myself to be of such little concern that nothing about me could be of interest to anyone. But if it might be useful to you on this occasion . . . I will tell you something about me now.

Listen to me, brother. On the path that the Lord is leading me down, this path that only God and I know, I have stumbled many times; I have endured deep, bitter sorrows; I have had to make continual renunciations; I have experienced disappointments, and the Lord has frustrated even the hopes I'd thought holiest. May He be blessed.

Because, well, every part of that was necessary . . . My *solitude* was necessary. The renunciation of my will was necessary. My illness was, and is, necessary.

But why? Because, look: as the Lord has led me from place to place, leaving me without a fixed abode, showing me what I am, and detaching me from His creatures, sometimes gently, other times roughing me up . . . along this whole path, which I see so clearly now, I've come to learn something, and my soul has changed . . . I don't know if this will make sense, but I've learned to love people as they are, and not as I wish they were. My soul—with or without a cross, whether good or bad, wherever it may be, wherever God places it, as God wishes it—has undergone a transformation . . . I can't explain it, I don't have the words . . . but I call it *serenity* . . .

It is a very great peace that allows you to both suffer and rejoice . . . It is knowing you are loved by God, despite our littleness and misery . . . It is the sweet, serene joy of truly abandoning yourself in His hands. It is a silence toward all external things, even though you're fully immersed in the world. It is the happiness of the sick, the lame, the leper, and the sinner who, in spite of everything, followed Jesus of Nazareth throughout the Galilean countryside.[2]

Look, Uncle Polín, my dear brother . . . God takes me by the hand and leads me through a field where there is weeping and war, pain and misery, saints and sinners. He brings me close to the cross and, showing me all this with His gaze, He says . . . "*All this* is mine . . . do not despise it, you whom I love so much . . ." Yes, Uncle Polín, Jesus loves me very much . . .

"I have given you light, so that you might see. I have given you a heart, so you might love Me. I do with you as I please, because you are Mine . . .

---

2. See Matt 2:23; 4:25; Mark 3:7-8; Luke 6:17.

Do not despise this life, since it is all for Me. Love your fellow creatures, for they are Mine. Do not cry as you walk your path, for I am the one who has laid it out before you. Love My cross and follow in My footsteps. Weep with Lazarus and be lenient with the sinner."[3]

Oh, my dear brother, I'm in the weeds now . . . All I can say is that once you have given over your life to Him, everything is God, everything is Jesus . . . suffering is sweet, and silence is pleasant, and all is *serenity* as you wait.

I don't know why I'm telling you all this. Maybe it isn't the right time. But in my prayer, as I kneel under the mantle of the Virgin Mary, from whom we receive all things,[4] I pray for all these things for you.

Yesterday, in particular, I said all this to Her. Seeing Aunt María so sad, whom I cannot bear to see suffering, and thinking of my brother over in Toro, I placed myself at the Virgin's feet and asked Her for *serenity* and *peace*, among other things, for those I love most. Will She hear my prayer? I think so. The Virgin Mary always grants my requests, so long as what I am asking for is good and holy.

Take heart, my dear brother. Your Trappist nephew may not be worth much . . . but who knows? Perhaps, in my silence, I can help you in some way, even if my help isn't very impressive in the eyes of men.

I'll leave it there, because I have nothing else to say.

I'm sending so much your way . . . my prayers, first of all, and after that . . . the great affection of those souls who truly love one another in Jesus and Mary.

Hugs to everyone, and everything you could ask for from your nephew,

Brother María Rafael

✠

When you have Jesus, and Mary, and souls praying for you, you are never alone. Isn't that so?

---

3. See John 11:33-38; Luke 7:50.

4. "Let us honor Mary, then, . . . with all the affections of our hearts and all our prayers, because that is the wish of him who desires us to possess all things through Mary" (Bernard of Clairvaux, "Sermon for the Nativity of the Blessed Virgin Mary," in *Sermons for the Autumn Season*, trans. Irene Edmonds, Cistercian Fathers series 54 [Collegeville, MN: Cistercian Publications, 2016], 74).

160. To María Osorio

Villasandino, May 8, 1937[1]

Ave Maria

My dearest sister,

To be honest, I don't know where to begin this letter, for which you have been waiting so eagerly. I received both of yours; I got the second one yesterday. I was planning on writing you back on Sunday, but since you're in such a hurry, I'll do your bidding today, which is Saturday, instead—with Mary's help.

First of all, I should say that the purpose of this letter is to console neither you nor myself. Rather, I seek only the greater glory of God in trying to use my clumsy words to send you little boosts of encouragement to keep going, some gentleness and peace to help you wait, and a whole lot of serenity, both in your suffering and in your joys.

You asked me so many things that I can't answer in a letter! And so many things are coming to mind right now that I don't know how to put into words!

You asked me to tell you about what's going on with me . . . what for? Neither you nor anyone else should concern yourself with this poor man, who is trying to keep his cross—that is, his only treasure—hidden from his fellow creatures. Instead, I'm trying to share with those around me all the peace, gentleness, and light that the Lord, in his goodness, deigns to send me.

Believe me, I am completely happy. I don't want anything for myself. God gives me everything I need, and more . . . He has generously poured far more into my little heart than it could possibly hold, and when a soul finds itself this full . . . how could it think about suffering? Who would dare fixate on his own sufferings while also having the blood-stained cross

---

1. From #160 to #200, Rafael is twenty-six years old.

of Jesus so deep within? . . . Who could be so selfish as to cry about his own insignificant pain when they enjoy the very real friendship of Jesus, who was executed for me?

Oh, little sister, if we truly loved God, how irrelevant everything else would seem to us . . . not only would our life consist of a renunciation of the world and its creatures, but our detachment would be such that our egos would simply be in our way, for we are nothing but selfishness, misery, weakness, and sin, and all of that hinders us from seeing God's goodness and majesty. All of that gets in the way of us coming to understand His infinite love.

Oh, if only we loved God, how different we would be! We would learn to make our renunciations with such generosity; we would live our lives in the world in such great peace; we would care so little about our suffering and pain; we would be neither bitter with tears nor reliant on the consolation of creatures . . .

Listen, my dearest sister, I don't know what more I could say about myself, and don't think I'm holding out on you . . . Somebody once told me that the surpassing, supreme rule of my life was *deny yourself, take up your cross daily, and follow me.*[2]

That *"deny yourself"* is the work of a soul who wants only to be hidden away, who wants nothing for himself, who longs only for divine love, and who understands that God does not want us to renounce only the world, but to renounce something much more difficult: ourselves. That self-renunciation is a renunciation of something we carry around inside of us, I don't know how to explain it, something that truly hinders us . . . perhaps you'll understand: when you place yourself at the foot of the tabernacle, and look at Jesus, and contemplate His wounds, and cry at His feet, and you realize that in the face of Christ's immense love, <u>you</u> disappear, *your* tears disappear, <u>your</u> entire soul is overwhelmed and becomes like a tiny speck of sand in the vastness of the sea . . .

Then you'll neither suffer nor rejoice, for everything is God. God fills it all. You won't even have *desires.* Then when someone asks you, "What's going on with you? . . . Are you suffering? Why are you crying? What

2. *If any want to become my followers, let them deny themselves and take up their cross daily and follow me* (Luke 9:23).

do you want?" maybe you'll smile and say, "Who, me? Sweet Jesus! I'm nothing, I want nothing, don't ask about me . . . I don't know . . . Talk to me about God instead."

Then you'll see how God fills it all . . . you'll come to realize that you aren't all that concerned with *yourself* anymore. You'll realize that all you want is to invite others into the tenderness that Jesus has placed in your heart. You'll understand your own littleness, and you'll renounce it. Your preferences, your comforts, your desires, and your opinions will all be nothing . . . God alone, nothing but God. A love for God that fills your life, a life that entails renunciation, sacrifice, prayer, and silence . . . that, I believe, is the love that God asks of us.

Don't worry about me . . . I am completely happy . . . not that I've spent a great deal of time making sure of it, mind you.

I ask for nothing, but nevertheless, I accept. Since I am, in spite of it all, a poor man full of misery, I don't know how to thank God for souls like yours who want, as you put it, to help me in some way . . . Blessed be the Most Holy Virgin. She, through whose hands He sends us all things, knows very well that you are a great help to me, of course . . . May She reward your great charity. Believe me, even the shortest little prayer that you offer for your brother's sake . . . it doesn't go to waste . . . You'll see it someday.

How good God is! Don't you think?

I can see every last thing that your little heart feels for me. Sometimes it puts me to shame . . . and other times, well, only God knows. How sweet it is to love one another in the Heart of Jesus, a Heart where there is room for everyone, and yet a Heart so little known.

What a shame that people are so blind . . . They don't know how sweet it is to practice charity as Christ did. Isn't that so, little sister? You know it well . . .

How encouraging it is to be helped and understood . . . How much closer we are to God when someone transcends all these earthly things and just says to us, "What are you looking for in this world? Can't you see it's all nothing? . . . Just press on . . . keep loving Christ. Ascend by way of the path of sacrifice and renunciation, but with a serene gaze, look and see that this is what it is to love God; this is the only way to quench the parched soul's thirst for Christ."

From heaven, the Virgin is gathering up your tears. Your consolation comes from God . . . Keep going, and don't look away, don't stop[3] . . . What a great consolation that is! Isn't it, little sister? If only people understood that! But they don't. What a shame!

The soul stretches as it contemplates the beauty of kindred souls . . . I long so greatly for us to find ourselves reunited in heaven, loving one another fully, flooded with the gentleness of Jesus of Nazareth, who said *love one another*, a command to be fulfilled eternally in heaven. Isn't that a joyful thought? It is to me.

Anyway, sister . . . we have to be better already. We have to hurry up. Life is very short. Brother Tescelino said so the other day. He's been sent to a hospital in Oviedo,[4] which is why he came by the other day to spend the night at our house. If only you knew how good he is . . . and how much we love each other.

We slept in the same room, and we stayed up talking . . . talking about God . . . all through the night until dawn. If only you knew, what a holy soul . . . he loves God and Mary so much; it's a very beautiful thing.

Of course, we both found it consoling. Our conversation ended in tears, as always . . . I don't know why, it's just that God is so good. If only you knew.

He promised to write me and send me his address so that I could talk to him about the Virgin, because according to him I am obliged to do so, and thus we Trappists can keep helping each other while we're away from our monastery.

Anyway, there are so many things I could tell you, but I'll answer your questions now.

I did stop by La Trapa on the way back, but not for long.[5] We stopped in Valladolid to eat, and we were waiting for the shops to open back up, because we had some things to buy.

---

3. See #81, n. 4, and #83.

4. Br. Tescelino (Toribio Luis) Arribas Jimeno was the assistant infirmarian at La Trapa. He was conscripted into the army as a medic during the Spanish Civil War (OC 782).

5. While the date of this trip is unclear, Rafael was in all likelihood on his way back from dropping off his grandmother Fernanda Torres and aunt María Osorio in Toro.

There's quite a commotion at the monastery right now, since they've got a thousand Italians staying there.[6] The necessities of war. I could only see Father Master for a moment. I went to Vespers.

Alvarito Barón went to Burgos.[7] Something to do with his training.

We receive news from Fernando often. He's doing well. Leopoldo hasn't been called up yet. He's waiting very patiently, but he doesn't know anything for sure at the moment.

The orchard is lovely. It makes me think of you, because the weather is splendid right now; we spent all day outside, all at our own tasks, in truly enviable peace.

I spent the morning all by myself and devoted it to Sacred Scripture, in which the word of God always proves to be an inexhaustible mine.

Mass is at seven-thirty, with the May crowning at eight.[8] The whole family goes . . . The Virgin is so good. I've dedicated Mary's month to three people: my brother Fernando, my brother Tescelino . . . and my sister María . . . You'll see how good She is and how well She listens to me.

Well . . . we have dinner at nine, and then we're all in bed by ten or ten-thirty.

I don't go to Burgos at all, because I've got nothing to do there.

I gave your message to Vicenta[9] this morning after Mass, because we're always the last to leave, as you know.

Anyway, now we've got lots of flowers and lots of water. Eutiquio, the gardener, is thrilled with the hose that my father bought. With the motor, it's quite powerful.

As you can see, I'm giving you a lot of details about Villasandino . . . Who would have thought that you'd ever think about this town again?! . . . That's God's way. You had some bad times here, but some good times

---

6. The Monastery of San Isidro de Dueñas lodged several divisions of Italian soldiers, as well as a battalion of Italian volunteers, all serving under the Spanish army (OC 783–84).

7. Alvarito Barón: Rafael's cousin, the son of his maternal uncle Alfonso Barón Torres and his wife Regina González-Tablas.

8. May crowning: the tradition of laying a crown of flowers on a statue of Mary during the month of May, which is dedicated to Marian devotion.

9. Vicenta: the mother of Isidro Dueñas, a tenant of the Arnaiz-Barón family in Villasandino (see #176, n. 8).

too . . . That "Rafa" you used to turn to ("oh, Rafa, Rafa!") is still here, and he can see that you're still a poor little thing. God bless you.

We're finishing up the duck house. It turned out so cute. We're also finishing the bench over by the well, and a little fish pond.

Anyway, my parents and brother and sister are all happy with this simple life . . . and so am I. I can see that the life here is more of a true life, and here is where . . . well, everything is in God's hands.

You don't know how grateful I am to Rosa[10] for the holy card she sent me . . . Be very loving toward her, she's so good. Tell her a great many things for me, and how sorry I was not to see her the other day in Toro. Of all the people I know in Toro, she's among those I love the most.

I'm very pleased that you have a confessor. You'll see, God will help you every step of the way. Listen, just tell him everything. Don't think of him as a man, but rather as the one whom God has sent your way, in order to enlighten you. Trust in his word, and above all, be very obedient in everything he tells you to do, without *judging* it, but rather considering it to be God's will . . . Place yourself humbly under his direction, and you'll see: the more humble and obedient you are, the better things will be for you . . .

If only you knew how happy you made me with this news . . . Open your soul to him, because that's why the Lord places priests on our path. Tell him about your sorrows, your joys, and your loves . . . Talk to him about God and Mary . . . do not be afraid. I won't say anything else, I'll just say it again, and listen well: if you are humble and obedient with your confessor, the Lord will give him light so that he will say only what is advisable and necessary for you to hear.

You'll see. With Mary's help, everything will work out, and you'll have so much peace, inside and out.

I'll say one more thing . . . maybe you'll say I'm meddling . . . but look, when it comes to dealing with the family, with the life I imagine you're all leading at my grandmother's house . . . try *not to do anything in particular*, if you know what I mean.

Independence is a very good thing, but true independence, the true monastic cell, is something we carry within ourselves. Try not to hurt anyone. Don't just be patient, which is the least you can do. Rather, practice a

---

10. Rosa Calvo, a family friend who lived in Toro (see #8, n. 1).

virtue that is very acceptable to God, and that is this: *seek out* those who are imperfect, *love* those who don't appreciate or understand you; make the sweetness with which God fills you available to everyone, and let it be gentle, too. Am I making sense?

Wherever we are, whoever we are, there is always *something* we can do. Try not to *close yourself off* . . . Yes, keep God hidden within you, and keep your periods of silence and prayer, but don't let anybody take notice . . . Don't do anything in particular—not in order to be acceptable to the world, that is, but rather to please God, and to be *useful* to creatures at the same time.

You don't have to tell me a thing. I know you. I know who you are and what you're like. So listen, my dear sister: try not to hurt anyone. Be charitable when you run up against others. Sometimes, with certain kinds of people, *silence* can be more painful than the harshest words . . .

I want to be as straightforward with you as possible . . . Excessive reclusion can come off as contempt, and that's not what Jesus taught us to do.

Jesus sought out the company of the sick and the poor, the company of his friend Lazarus, whom He loved so much. He sought out the souls He was going to redeem with His blood at wedding feasts and the public square alike, surrounding Himself with sinful women.

That's how much Jesus loved people! We have so much to learn from Him!

If I could speak with you in person, there's so much I would say . . . Love for neighbor contains such great treasure. Anyway, I'll be quiet now, I don't know how to write. But listen, my dear sister: don't waste your time on vain arguments with others or passing frivolities. Rather, be utterly charitable toward all. Be understanding; don't judge; be humble and simple. Try to sweeten the lives of those around you . . . Don't close yourself off, and . . . *deny yourself.* With that, I think I've said it all. Perhaps you'll receive it. Either way, I'm nobody. Your confessor will tell you what to do . . . and you'll obey, and that way you'll avoid making any mistakes whatsoever.

I don't think you'll complain about this letter. I've answered both of yours in this one . . . haven't I? Look, don't get antsy about it. Write as often as you like, about whatever you like. I understand all your concerns, and you know I lay them all at the feet of the Most Blessed Virgin.

I don't know when we'll come to Toro. I can say it won't be anytime soon, but later, I honestly promise you we will.

I don't know what to say about the holy card you sent . . . You are so good to me. The Lord will repay your kindness toward me . . . I don't know what to say except thank you. Everything in my life is just giving me reason after reason to try to be better . . . when will I be?

Pray for me a lot—I'm still rather selfish when it comes to that. I'll send you the prayer to the Virgin that you asked for another day. For now, I'll just pray it for you. Is that all right?

Tell my grandmother that Mamá thinks of writing every day . . . Honestly, it can't be helped. Nothing to be done about that.

Do we know anything for certain about your father and brothers?[11] Let me know.

But don't you worry. As I said, this poor monk without vows or a monastery will make up for whatever you may lack in the future. And with this page, I'll finish.

I don't know if I managed to send what I proposed to send you in this letter, but my intention was good, and God can see that . . .

Keep loving God, keep seeking out Mary's protection. Keep very still underneath Her mantle, kneeling at Her feet, and you'll see how much sweetness and peace comes to flood your soul. When you are with Mary, remember your brother Rafael. Do not fear that your life is going to waste, when your heart is truly ablaze with love for God and neighbor. You'll see, even life itself can be sweet when it is a continuous act of love for God, and when you no longer live it, but rather it is Jesus who lives it in you.[12]

Meanwhile, my dearest little sister: silence, prayer, renunciation, and sacrifice, with a smile on your face and peace in your heart . . . that is what love is. Everything else we offer to God is a flower yet to bloom or already faded away.

---

11. María had four siblings: a sister, Soledad; two brothers, Gerardo and Francisco Javier; and a half-brother, Ramón. As devout Catholics and members of the nobility, the family was a target of violence during the Spanish Civil War. All three of María's brothers were killed on November 28, 1936, during the massacre at Paracuellos, the site of many massacres and executions during the war (OC 789). Their father, Francisco de Asís Osorio, survived the war, dying in 1952.

12. Gal 2:20.

All for Jesus, *always* . . . *always*. Remember? Not looking for relief, not holding anything back for ourselves . . . all for Him, as He wishes, and . . . *always*.

Well, that's all for now.

Give Uncle Polín and my grandmother and everybody else lots of hugs for me, especially Rosa. As for you . . . I don't know, ask the Most Blessed Virgin. All I can do is send you the great affection of your brother, who loves you very much,

Brother María Rafael
✠

161. To María Osorio

Villasandino, September 3, 1937

Ave Maria

My dearest sister in the Lord,

I'm not at all surprised to hear that my silence has surprised you. To tell you the truth, I just haven't had anything to tell you. Honestly, even now, as I pick up my pen, I don't know what to say. I didn't want to fill up page after page with empty words that don't convey anything, since he who has nothing has nothing to give. But, not that I need to tell you this, you can believe me when I say that I'm still the same as I always was.

You asked me for news, so I'll share some. Leopoldo didn't receive an official post.[1]

They weren't taking volunteers, so he's here at home now. He's waiting for another medical exam this month, as am I.

Merceditas is the same as before. Right now she's delighted with all the tasks that come with this season.

We receive news of Fernando often, and he says he's doing very well.

Mamá is very busy with her critters; we've got ducks and chickens. We made a great big chicken coop to hold about eighty animals, so between gathering their eggs and feeding them grain, she keeps herself occupied.

My father, now that he doesn't have a car,[2] finds himself needing to go to Burgos even more often. It's not hot anymore, but there were a few days when the poor man would get off the bus with heat exhaustion.

There's been a lot of fruit here, and there still is, but since it was all so neglected and the trees have been left to their whims for so many years, nearly all of it is infested. On the other hand, there's been lots to do in

---

1. Leopoldo Arnaiz Barón had volunteered to serve in the army, but was not called up until July 1938 (OC 790–91).

2. The family car had been requisitioned for military use (OC 791).

the garden, and now we don't know what to do with all these tomatoes and cucumbers.

Anyway, if you could see all this, you wouldn't even recognize it here. Things are getting better, little by little.

I'm the same as before. I don't worry about my blood sugar levels one way or the other. What for?. . . Whatever God wants of me. . . is what will come to pass. It's all rather simple. I don't have anything else to say for now.

With God's help, and the Virgin's protection, you can do anything . . . even be a little good.

Don't expect to find rest *here* . . . why would you? Nothing in your letters surprised me, and all I can say in response is that, indeed, it is very human to get discouraged and want a little rest, even if that's just being back in your home again.[3] Longing for spiritual and material peace is very human, as is distress when in isolation, which can make you cry and suffer.

I'll see to all of it. All I hope for you is to be convinced that this is all a moment's suffering for which, in His time, God will reward you with *what no eye has seen nor ear heard nor the human heart conceived*,[4] and that is eternal *rest* in the Heart of God.

In the meantime . . . poor creatures, projects, ambitions, tears and laughter, hopes of getting from this world and its creatures what they cannot give, looking for a rest from suffering, seeking the consolation of a moment's repose and finding nothing in this life that could possibly satisfy, or even alleviate . . . so many things.

Why am I telling you something you already know? Sometimes silence speaks more eloquently than words. I am ever more convinced that the more words . . . the worse.

Let's not let the little things stop us in our tracks. Let's not stop to talk about our temporary sufferings, even if they go on *forever*, even if they take over our lives . . . let's go a bit further and realize that it's childish to look for rest and shelter by the side of the road when we're just outside the city gates . . . Am I making sense?

3. That is, María and her husband Leopoldo's home in Ávila; they were living in Toro at this time.
4. 1 Cor 2:9.

I know you'll say that you already know all this . . . That I'm not telling you anything new when I say that all suffering comes to an end . . . and we just have to wait a little while.

You'll say that's all true, but those who are weak are always weak, and there are moments when everything closes in on us, and the weight of the world crushes us, and darkness looms over us and keeps us from seeing the nothingness and vanity of it all clearly . . . and what are we to do then? What should we do when our souls are deprived of light, when we see nothing but our own misery, when even our spirits seem to crumble into dirt and mud, when our lips bless the cross . . . but our hearts reject it?

I don't know, dear sister, what to do . . . no consolation can come from human lips . . . no advice could possibly be satisfying. There are no words to express what such a soul is feeling, suffering, or longing for, and as such, neither are there words that could console and help someone in such a state . . . But I, who am no one, will dare say this: when there aren't any words, there is still silence. Right now, I am remembering the Lord's words (I don't remember the citation), when He said He would lead the soul into solitude and speak to her heart there.[5] What more could I say?

I have come to realize that in this world there is something that can bring rest to the soul, and it is a material thing, in a certain sense: solitude and silence . . .

You'll say that's all well and good for a Trappist, but not for everybody; but I'm telling you it is. You can understand *solitude* to mean the absence of desire for anything that creatures might give you . . . To live in the world in solitude with God, despite everything that surrounds us, to keep our hearts free, detached from everything, longing only to be offered to God . . . Solitude in our suffering, too, so that He alone might see it.

And as for silence . . . what can I say? It is the silence of those who love God so much that the mere thought of Him either drives them into the street, shouting like crazy in the public square . . . or draws them into silence. It is the silence of those who have such great expectations of heaven that they disregard everything that is earthly, like people's words and human consolations, as useless . . . And sometimes it is the silence of those who suffer so much, but in order not to fill their surroundings with

5. *Therefore, I will now allure her, and bring her into the wilderness, and speak tenderly to her* (Hos 2:14).

complaints and anxieties, thereby making others sad, keep their sorrows quiet; they only open their lips to console those who are weeping and cheer up those who are sad, never to talk about themselves and their own crosses.

Solitude and silence are essential to create a setting for prayer, and once you have them, you have all that this world has to offer. Even if you were back in your house, even if all your material problems were resolved, even if *everything you wish for* came true, you would have *nothing* if your soul did not dwell in solitude, if your heart were not at prayer . . . If it were, you would consider your suffering to be of no importance.

Anyway, I want to end here because I might be getting lost. I'm getting clumsier and clumsier when it comes to expressing how I feel. If all you want is the consolation of a few poorly scribbled lines from me . . . then in the name of the Most Blessed Virgin, our good Mother, I will send them to you.

I'll tell you what I'm going to do at the proper time. Don't worry about me at all. Just remember me when you are with the Lord, as I do for you.

My mother said to say that they'll send you the records, reducer, blankets, and God knows what else.

Give my grandmother hugs for me, and everyone else, too. And for Uncle Polín, I want to be honest with you—regarding his condition, as you described it in your letter, I'm not worried about his health at all. Since I love him in such a *special* way, it would never occur to me to tell him to take care of himself. First of all, he wouldn't do it, that's for certain. Besides, as a Trappist, I have to say that *all that* is so unimportant that if I saw him drawing near to the City, I'd just give him a few requests to take to the Virgin . . . that's how we Trappists are.

There are so many things I'd ask you to tell him. I'm thinking of you all very often. Give him a big hug for me. All yours, your brother in Jesus and Mary,

Brother María Rafael

Give my regards, among other things, to Rosa.
¡¡VIVA LA VIRGEN DEL PILAR DE ZARAGOZA!![6]

---

6. "Long live Our Lady of the Pillar of Zaragoza!!" The title of "Our Lady of the Pillar" (La Virgen del Pilar) refers to the apparition of Mary to Saint James while he was preaching in Zaragoza, now part of Spain and home to her major shrine.

162. To Leopoldo Barón

Villasandino, September 25, 1937

Ave Maria

May the peace of the Lord be with you.

God alone . . . How difficult it is to understand and live these words, but once you do, even if just for a moment . . . once your soul has realized that it belongs to God, that it is His possession . . . that Jesus dwells within it, despite its wretchedness and weakness . . . once your eyes are opened to the light of faith and hope . . . Once you understand the purpose of life, which is to live for God and for Him alone, there is nothing in the world that can trouble your soul. And those who, possessing nothing, hope for everything, can wait serenely instead of anxiously. A great peace fills the hearts of those who live for God alone, and only those who desire God alone find peace . . .

God alone! How sweet it is to live like this!

My dear brother, I don't know why I have taken up the pen and begun to write . . . Really, I don't know; there's no need and I have nothing to say. There is only one reason, though a very small one, and that reason is a desire of mine (I still have some desires), which is the desire to speak of Him.

Nobody out in the world listens patiently to the crazy thoughts of someone who, upon glimpsing a small fraction of God's greatness, is stupefied . . . someone who, leaving behind the nothingness and vanity of worldly things, feels the urge to shout, "Senseless fools . . . what are you looking for? Make haste! . . . God alone, what else is there but Him?"

How could we possibly occupy ourselves with so many things—laughing, crying, talking, arguing—and meanwhile, God gets nothing?

The world cannot and need not understand the foolishness of a lover of Christ . . . Foolishness, yes, there is no other word for it, the foolishness of the cross,[1] which drives our souls nuts and scrambles our words, which try

---

1. See 1 Cor 1:18.

to say so much and end up saying nothing at all. A foolishness tempered only by the "straitjacket" of conformity to God's will, which makes us quiet down when we want to cry out, which makes us prudent when our souls break loose and want to . . . I don't know . . . which makes our waiting calm, when longing for Christ beats impatiently in our hearts.

Foolishness for Christ . . . naturally, people don't understand it, so it must be hidden away . . . hidden within, deep within, so that only He may see it, and so that no one—if possible, not even we—realize that we are completely consumed by it . . .

Don't pay me any mind. I've already told you the reason behind all these clumsy words. As you can see, it's simple; I've gone crazy, that's all.

You are very busy with many things, which are all very appropriate, very good, and very necessary . . . Perhaps you suffer, perhaps not . . . But, seeing as we've agreed that I'm crazy, I'll tell you this: "So what! What about God?"

And then you'll start to say to yourself a bit, slowly at first, and then very quickly, "God alone . . . God alone . . . God alone," until suddenly you realize that you've gone crazy too, and your heart is overjoyed and you don't know what to do or say, and you laugh a lot, so much, like an idiot, because of how much you love God, and you haven't a care in the world, and when someone says something to you, you'll answer "yes, yes, it's true, you're right," but within yourself, deep within, you'll be saying . . . "God alone, God alone."

And when someone makes you laugh, you'll laugh, and you'll also say, "God alone."

And when someone makes you suffer, you'll suffer, but you'll also say . . . "Well, all right . . . but God alone."

And then one day, you too will take up pen and paper and share all the foolish things that occur to you and you'll send them off wherever you like, or maybe you will lose so many of your marbles that you'll forget how to write at all.

I wouldn't want you to laugh at me, but it's all the same to me. Perhaps all these foolish things I'm writing to you will speak to you in some way. Perhaps they will communicate the state of my soul to you, which I would so like to communicate to the whole world, so that the whole world would love God madly, and not think of anything else, and everyone would be very happy, as I am now, I who have nothing, not even my health, yet have everything . . . everything one can have in this life. I have God deep within my heart and want for nothing. That, believe me, is perfect happiness, a happiness so hidden that of course no one thinks to envy it.

You love God too, don't you? And so perhaps you will enjoy knowing that not everything in the world is arguments and noise and material desires . . .

Since you love God, and want the whole world to love Him, you will be pleased to see that someone else loves Him very much too.

That's why I'm saying all these things to you . . . these things that hardly anyone cares about, or is interested in, and instead people laugh at them or twist my words . . . because only those who have some love for God can understand these things.

What do you see when you look around you? If you really examine it all closely, you'll find that none of it satisfies you completely, not at all. You'll find a great deal of frivolity, perhaps even paganism sprouting from the cracks in a poorly understood Christianity; efforts toward well-being, as if this life were eternal; fights, disputes . . . but very little of God.

If you're looking at yourself, it's best not to say anything. So, then, what's left? . . . God and God alone. He gives what the world and its creatures cannot. Our misery, forgetfulness, and ingratitude are covered with His infinite Mercy. The consolation that people so often deny us when we are in pain can be found in His cross, alone with Him on Calvary. The only Truth can be found in His Gospel, the words of eternal life.[2] And as if that weren't enough, everything else . . . can be found in His Mother Mary.

How joyfully one lives when one has God, and God alone.

How small life's problems prove, for their solution is in . . . God alone.

No, don't tell me what the luminaries of this age have to say about this . . . You know what they say. Why should I repeat it? . . . Didn't we decide that we wanted to be fools? Let's be fools, then, even if the world takes us for senseless idiots . . . Who cares? God sees it all, and there's more senselessness and idiocy in a single so-called luminary than there is in a million souls seized with foolishness for Christ.

Blessed is that foolishness, which makes us live beyond the bonds of this earth, which helps us see the sorrows of our exile through the daz-

2. See John 6:68.

zling lens of hope, the certain hope of a splendid, resplendent day that *will not delay* . . .

Blessed is that foolishness for Christ, which makes us realize how vain and small our suffering is, turning our bitter tears into the sweetest of songs, the pain and heartache of this life into the gentle fetters that bind us to Jesus . . .

Blessed are those who mourn,[3] Jesus said on earth, by the water's edge, and a crowd made up of the sick, the lame, the poor, and sinners followed Him . . . I believe that after turning toward Jesus, their faces, once tear stained from all their weeping, were transformed with joyful laughter, blessing their afflictions and miseries, which united them to Jesus.

And Jesus looked at them with the tenderness that won over the world, and let Himself be loved by the poor, the afflicted, the sick, and sinners . . . And Jesus healed them, and Jesus consoled them . . . and Jesus, that loving Jesus, forgave them.

This scene is repeating itself now. Nothing has changed, except that Jesus is not walking by the Sea of Galilee . . . rather, Jesus is in the tabernacle. There, He receives His friends, consoles them, heals them, and forgives them . . .

What great intimacy Jesus has with those who mourn! Blessed are our tears, sorrows, and illnesses, which are our treasures, all that we possess. They make us draw near to Jesus, since the love we have for Him is so little, so feeble, so weak that it is not enough on its own . . . !

What a great joy it is to realize you are beloved of God! To be counted among His friends, to follow Him step by step in Jerusalem with your eyes fixed on His divine countenance, blessing our own misery for having inspired Jesus to attract our gaze, so that He might reach our hearts, heal us, forgive us . . . and love us enough to die for us on a cross.

Such is foolishness for Christ . . . with eyes fixed on Jesus, one forgets to eat and fails to fear the cold; neither humble poverty nor love of family can hold back lovers of Jesus . . . God alone . . . only Him . . . that is the only thought that holds power over them . . . the miracle of being madly in love.

3. Matt 5:4.

The world and all who dwell in it come and go; people keep thinking about their businesses, the future of their estates, their illnesses. They cling to this earth, where they seek their rest. They suffer when they don't find it here, and weep when they have to leave . . . Those are the real fools, even though the world thinks it's foolish to love poverty, contempt, illness, and the cross.

What is the world, in all its prudence, sense, and rationality, supposed to think of such utter nonsense? I don't bother to argue with it. It's useless and unnecessary.

There was a poor brother at La Trapa who often wept before the cross. The world was saying to him, "You're an idiot, weeping by choice is foolish, you're uselessly wasting your life with all that silence and penance. Why love the cross when life is so beautiful? Freedom is bright, not gloomy!"

But that Trappist kept on weeping and weeping, and his tears were sweet sighs in his heart, placed lovingly at the Virgin's feet. He wouldn't have traded a single one of his tears for all the gold in the world . . . That Trappist wept, but he wept for joy . . . What does the world know of love?

Blessed is foolishness for Christ, which turns tears into pearls and makes us love the cross. That is true joy, the joy of the one who lives for God alone, who trusts in God alone, who hopes in God alone. And it is not a raucous joy; it is the serene joy of a soul who might still live on this earth, but expects nothing from this world. It is the joy of one who lives for Christ and dreams of Mary, and so, my dear brother . . . what do you want me to say? I don't know how to speak, let alone write.

God alone, God alone . . . Seek nothing else, and you'll see: once you find yourself in Jesus' retinue across the fields of Galilee, your soul will be flooded with something I cannot explain.

You'll see, you'll remember neither your sorrows nor your joys, and you won't focus on yourself at all. You'll see, too, how foolishness comes over you. You won't mind walking around in the sun, or sleeping out in the open . . . Jesus is so sweet! It is so good to be in His presence!

If the path proves difficult, or arduous, or long, it won't matter . . . Jesus goes before us. We won't even look where we're going . . . for we have Jesus as our guide. We will be silent when He speaks, and treasure His words in our silence . . .

We'll press on, day or night, drunk with joy, utterly mad with it, not listening to the world or eating or sleeping or anything else. "God alone

. . . God alone," our heart will *bellow*, because our lips cannot part to shout the name of Jesus through the streets and in the public square, to cry out the wonders of God, His greatness, His mercy . . . His love.

And that is how we shall keep our silence as we walk around in this world, which professes to be Christian but does not follow Christ. We will make up for what is lacking in others. We will love Him like nobody else. If anyone asks after your health, or your crosses or consolations, if anyone asks you anything about yourself at all, you can respond, "I don't know. I love Jesus so much that I don't have time to worry about that." That's when you'll have done it . . . your foolishness will be complete.

Oh, blessed Jesus, when will this farce come to an end?! When will the day come when we can leave behind this body and all its afflictions and miseries?! When will we leave behind this world and all its lies?!

How long, O Lord?[4] David said as his soul was bursting. "Must we live in so miserable a life?!" Saint Teresa of Jesus said.[5] What else could we poor sinners say? For even if we have good desires, our works are so weak and feeble . . .

Oh, we can indeed weep and suffer, but not because of our own crosses and sorrows, which are very small indeed, but rather, because we do not love Jesus. We can indeed weep over how ungrateful we are toward Jesus, and how often we forget to turn to Mary . . . Mary. It wasn't enough for God to give us His Son on a cross; He gave us Mary, too. How is it possible, brother, that we aren't better than this?

I don't want to get lost in thought here. There's so much I want to say to you, but I'm so clumsy about it . . . as you can see.

All I can say is that what we can do, with Mary's help, is wait . . . Remember when we used to talk about that? I remember drawing you a Trappist looking straight at a wooden cross driven into the ground upon the place where one of his beloved brothers was at rest.[6]

For the one who hopes, waiting is sweet . . . This thought comes over me often, and everything I have learned from it has helped me whenever I feel as though I've been waiting too long.

---

4. Ps 13:1.
5. Must we live in so dangerous a life?" (STA 1:55).
6. See #87, n. 10.

572 The Collected Works

How sweet it is to wait with closed eyes and an open heart. Neither the body, our soul's prison, nor the world with all its creatures can damage the soul that hopes in God, no matter how harshly they chafe against it. We can conquer and disregard the body, and instead of fearing contact with creatures, love them, even searching them out in order to teach them the science that Christ taught us . . . love.

How sweet it is to wait while doing good . . . How sweet it is to wait with a smile for our brothers and sisters as well as for our enemies . . . How sweet it is to wait when Jesus is the one we are waiting for . . .

How sweet it is to wait while thinking of God and dwelling under Mary's mantle.

But the waiting starts to feel slow and painful when we are afflicted with desires other than God, when our selfishness rejects the cross, when we confuse our longing for God with getting tired of living, *however subtly*. How often we deceive ourselves, thinking something is God that isn't. I don't want to pontificate about the definition of perfection, God forbid. But I do believe that our longing to see God and our impatience in waiting for Him are made perfect in absolute submission to His will, with the serenity of those who desire nothing.

But we are still imperfect, and we cannot help it when our souls cry out to Christ, saying, "Why do you fail to carry off what you have stolen?"[7] as Saint John of the Cross wrote in his canticle, although he came to love Him "with a flame that is consuming and painless."[8]

But I don't want to talk about myself, and I don't want to get involved in your business either . . . It's all of so little importance!

When I picked up my pen, I decided to talk to you about God alone, and now I can't think of anything, maybe because there's so much I want to say, and because I have such an intense desire to share the gentleness and peace that God has placed in my soul with another . . . As you can see, I can't do anything, but my intention is good, even if I don't know how to

7. From Saint John of the Cross, *Spiritual Canticle*: "Why, since you wounded / this heart, don't you heal it? / And why, since you stole it from me, / do you leave it so, / and fail to carry off what you have stolen?" (SJC 45).

8. From Saint John of the Cross, *Spiritual Canticle*: "The breathing of the air, / the song of the sweet nightingale; / the grove and its living beauty / in the serene night, with a flame that is consuming and painless" (SJC 50).

express myself. Perhaps the same thing has happened to you before, and thus you will understand what I mean.

Let nothing trouble you,[9] for He gives so much to the souls of His friends, only to have us shrug off the treasure that is Christ's gentle yoke[10] at every vain disturbance that life provides.

Let nothing trouble you, because everything is nothing. . . God alone. Let us not grow tired of repeating it. If we were to take the intensity of the effort we put into earthly matters and put it into love for God instead . . . things would be different.

Don't go looking for someone to talk to you about Him . . . you'll come away disappointed, and it isn't necessary, because "they cannot tell you what you want to hear."[11] When you hide the love you have for God, it's as though you love Him more . . . does that happen to you, too?

With silence, prayer, and a whole lot of inner madness, we can wait well for what is to come . . . and it will all come.

I don't know what else to say . . . I paused just now, and with my pen in my hand, looking up at this clear blue Castilian sky, I just ended up thinking . . . God alone . . . God alone . . . God alone.

Brother María Rafael

9. From a poem by Saint Teresa of Ávila: "Let nothing trouble you, / Let nothing scare you, / All is fleeting, / God alone is unchanging. / Patience / Everything obtains. / Who possesses God / Nothing wants. / God alone suffices" ("Efficacy of Patience," STA 3:386).

10. See Matt 11:29-30.

11. From Saint John of the Cross, *Spiritual Canticle*: "Do not send me / any more messengers; / they cannot tell me what I want to hear" (SJC 45; translation emended).

163. To Leopoldo Barón

Villasandino, September 26, 1937

How can one possibly talk to people when your heart and soul are full of divine passion? . . . How can you focus on earth when thinking of heaven? . . .

Such are the miracles of God, who robs us of our souls and then lets us keep living on earth . . . Such are the miracles of Christ, who lives in us, and is not afraid of the poverty of the matter that imprisons every soul in love with Him.

Oh spirit, aflame with love . . . where do you live? . . . How can you bear this prison? How can you breathe in the atmosphere of misery and sin in which you are chained?

Divine passion . . . Longing for Christ . . . Hoping for glory and peace . . . How can one live like this? . . . I don't know . . . Such are the miracles of grace and love . . . Dreaming and thinking of heaven, while living on earth . . . With God, love; with other people, worthless words . . .

Longing for eternal life, and labored breath in this world . . .

Peace in the soul that belongs to God, and a struggle against the body, which is ruled by the flesh . . . Such are the miracles of grace and love.

How difficult it is to live among those who do not know God, or love Him, or talk about Him.

Sometimes the soul is taken aback by such ingratitude, such abandonment, and silently weeps for it . . . It is not that you suffer as a human being, but rather it is your heart, which is in love with Christ, which wails when you witness the world's disregard for Jesus . . . How can one live like this? . . . And yet we do live, and talk, and argue . . . and we still think about eating and sleeping . . .

Oh, Lord, how feeble we are! How desperately we need You to uphold us in our great weakness. How could we not lose ourselves in Your greatness, in Your unending mercy, that dwells within us and upholds us!

How could we not be astonished by Your patience toward us! You deign to live among sinners who do not know You or pay You any mind.

You forgive what a human being could not conceive of forgiving.

You forgive our lack of gratitude.

You delight in the children of Adam,[1] even when those children do not love You. Even so, Lord, You do not complain, and You have a smile even for those who nail You to the cross. What an admirable example! We are blind and ruled by our selfishness, those of us who complain that we are still living and have not yet flown unto You . . . We do not know what we are asking . . . such poor, unhappy creatures.

You teach us, and we do not want to learn . . .

They offend You, and You forgive, and we get annoyed.

People forget You, and You lovingly wait, and we get impatient.

You zealously seek out human beings, despite their misery, and whenever we have the slightest inkling of desire for glory . . . the misery of the world and the flesh make us suffer.

Such great fickleness, Lord. How good You are, Lord!

You uphold us, and You channel our fervor . . . You fill the soul with love, and at the same time, You help us to wait.

You dwell in our hearts, which long to fly unto heaven, and You uphold us even as we remain bound to this earth . . . for the time has not yet come . . .

You do it all, Lord.

You sustain us in our weakness and feebleness. If it were not for You, maybe our craziness would result in crazy things . . . but all is well this way, for You wish it.

You want silent love . . . may it be so.

You want us to be patient and in peace as we wait . . . may it be so.

You want renunciation and sacrifice . . . may it be so.

You want us to want nothing . . . well, as You wish.

But listen, Lord, to the soul suffering in love. Do not look at its faults or ingratitude. Do not grant its requests, for its love for you is so great that it does not know what it is asking for . . . Give only Yourself, Lord, and pay it no mind. Steady it in its fickleness, and . . . Blessed be the Most Holy Virgin Mary.

---

1. Prov 8:31.

September 27, 1937

God, always God; the heart never grows tired of Him, nor can the soul ever find peace away from Him.

People have nothing to tell you. You won't find anything in books, either; only in the silence of everything and everyone . . . a silence that not even thoughts dare to disturb, where love and hope are taken in. That silence is the only place it is possible to live. Everything outside of it is just noise, a racket. There is nothing outside of God; peace is to be found in God alone, and God dwells in the souls of His friends, and if we don't seek God in silence and prayer, if we don't keep still . . . we won't find peace, nor will we encounter God.

Only in silence is it possible to live, but not just any silence without words and actions . . . no, it's different, it's very hard to explain . . . It is the silence of one who loves very, very much, and doesn't know what to say or think or want or do . . . God alone, deep within, so very quiet . . . waiting, waiting . . . I don't know . . . the Lord is so good.

Oh poor, suffering soul . . . are you looking for a place to rest? You won't find it in anything or anyone . . . Quiet down a little, look for a place in your soul, some place very hidden and very silent, and put a little love for Jesus there . . . and you'll see: neither pain nor joy will disturb your peace, and even the waiting will become sweet. Jesus in your soul! What can I, poor creature that I am, say?! Why am I bothering with all these vain words that can't possibly express anything?

What a presumption I have made in wanting to talk to you about Him! And even so, I'm not running out of ink, and this paper seems too small and narrow to me. I am bursting with desire to fill up the souls of my brothers and sisters with peace, love for God, and joy. I long to cry out like a madman about all the wonders hidden within the act of humbly surrendering everything into God's hands and the sweetness of a love without shouting, a love that waits . . . I don't know. My desire is too great for me to be able to explain it.

Looking at Jesus makes everything find its place, absolutely everything. Everything else must come to an end, absolutely everything . . . except what I cannot describe.

I have walked through the countryside. I have seen people cultivate their fields, eagerly awaiting their fruits . . . I have seen their struggles and ambitions. I have seen people put too much stock in things that come to an end, suffer because of things that will not last, and vainly focus on this earth as if they were going to settle down here and never die . . .

I have looked up at the blue sky, not a crease or wrinkle in it . . . I have thought about God, who is waiting for us up there . . . His harvest is coming very soon . . . And the Virgin Mary is up there too . . . Why would anyone think about their suffering? Lord . . . how foolish we human beings are.

But let us not pay so much attention to what creatures are doing. Let us look to the Creator instead. Let us forget the miseries of this earth and be merciful so that we can understand others, for sometimes we don't know how to forgive, and we judge without charity.

Nothing is perfect except God.

If we were better, everybody else would be too. I am utterly convinced of this: many of our neighbors' failings and much of the forgetfulness that people show toward God are truly our own fault. I have seen this clearly, and I could say more about that . . . although maybe this one word says it all . . . penance.

If you, who know God, are the way that you are . . . what can you expect of those who do not know Him?

Believe me, we are to blame for many things. Someday we'll realize it, and we'll have to throw ourselves into the arms of divine mercy and beg for Mary's help.

But I don't want to get all gloomy or upset anybody by talking about God's terrible Judgment Day. That's not what I'm trying to do here. Rather, I want to fill these pages with love, so that by talking about the tenderness of loving God, life's many crosses might be made lighter, and perhaps help achieve something I can't quite pin down . . . because I don't know what it is, not that I need to know . . . may my intentions alone, which I believe to be good, suffice.

Isn't it true that you don't hear anyone talking about God anymore? And isn't it true that anything having to do with Him is treated as a secondary concern? And isn't it true that the world cares more about a good harvest than a good communion?

That's why I want to go mad . . . mad for Christ, and tell you with my whole soul, "God alone, brother, God alone."

That's why I wanted to talk to you about what nobody will talk to you about. Something that, once you get past *all those other things*, will lead you to consolation in what is not of this place . . . what is not of this world, or of human beings . . . in God, in our God.

I wish you wouldn't listen to me. Who am I? Nobody . . . just another man, but one who is truly your brother and who, upon seeing clearly the vanity of everything and how good God is toward those who love Him, cannot help but do whatever he can, no matter how little or how poorly, for the sake of someone who he suspects also wants to fly to heaven whenever it feels as though the world is caving in and even good people are starting to tire him out . . . am I right?

Besides, what greater pleasure could we have as we remain in exile than to console and help one another? In doing so, we enjoy a foretaste of the happiness that is eternal life, the brevity of this life, the greatness and grandeur of God, and the beauty of Mary, our Mother . . .

What greater relief could there be in this life than to forget, even if just for a few moments in the day, this earthly life and its troubles; to forget for a moment that we are still human beings, and fly a little through the realms of supernatural life, even if we're just hovering a bit over the floor; to dream of heaven; to lose ourselves in the eternal happiness of a love for God without any veils between us, without sins, without obstacles . . . ? To close our eyes and fix these words in our hearts that I once saw underlined on the monastery wall in chalk . . . "Forever . . . forever . . . forever."

No, I'm not doing anything extra . . . for me, it is a consolation to give up a bit of sleep in order to rest from the day, writing about God in the silence of the night while everyone else is asleep, thinking that the whole world is looking for something they cannot find, something that I, a poor sinner, possess.

How could I not think about those who are suffering? And who isn't suffering from one thing or another? But how few are suffering for God.

And as I put pen to paper, words come out, and they're just human words. But from my heart, desires flow that turn into prayer without even trying, a prayer that intercedes for everyone: for those who are fighting, those who are suffering, those who are blind to everything but the pettiness of this earth and forget God's greatness, those who are working so hard for mere worldly things, those who are being presented before God at this very moment, undergoing the ultimate disappointment, realizing that they left everything, absolutely everything, behind, and saying, "The day was so short. . . I didn't have time. . . and now. . . forever, forever."

And so, don't be surprised that I write you these things; I live my life thinking of heaven, for which I am happily waiting.

Listen, brother, I might be talking a lot of nonsense at this point. It's very late. Sleep weighs heavy on my eyelids. The Trappists get up around this time, and what a consoling thought, that the tabernacle does not lack for humble souls who sing and pray at night while the world sleeps, and sometimes even weep for the sins of humanity.

If only the world knew! But God permits the world to be ignorant!

I am going to bed now, and I'll finish up by telling you what I'm thinking and what I'm going to dream about.

Because it won't be about people or this world . . . I'll think about how everything is nothing, how it's all so short-lived, how life is but an instant, and clutching the crucifix, with a *Salve* to the Most Blessed Virgin, I'll fall asleep whispering. . . "Soon enough . . . forever . . . forever."

Brother María Rafael

Don't write me back, but do send me a postcard letting me know that you've received these pages.

164. To Leopoldo Barón

Villasandino, October 11, 1937

Ave Maria

And David said:

> *I love, you, O Lord, my strength.*
> *The Lord is my rock, my fortress, and my deliverer,*
> *my God, my rock in whom I take refuge,*
> *my shield, and the horn of my salvation, my stronghold.*[1]

What a shame that David didn't get to meet the Most Blessed Virgin! Isn't it? He would have said such lovely things to Her! A heart as great as his would surely have been full of love for Mary . . .

"Mary!" That word expresses so many things . . . If only I knew how to write about it! . . . But then, I'd never stop. Tonight I just want to write you a quick note and pour out my own heart a little, telling you about Our Lady.

Affection for the Virgin is so lovely and consoling. It makes me sad when people don't know Her or don't love Her, even just a little bit . . . ! Even so, my dear brother, what Christian is there, even the most lukewarm of all, who doesn't think of the Virgin Mary at some point in life?

Everyone, every single one of us, carries something inside of us that, second to God, only Mary can understand and console . . . That "something" is creaturely; it is human need, affection, sometimes pain . . . God placed that "something" in our souls, and creatures can never fill it. That way, we have to seek out Mary . . .

Mary, who was a Spouse, a Mother, and a Woman . . . Who could understand, help, console, and strengthen better than Mary? . . . Who could be a greater refuge from our sins and miseries than Mary, the Most Blessed Virgin?

---

1. Ps 18:1-2.

God is so good and so great to offer us Mary's heart as if it were His own! God knows our fearful little hearts so well! He knows our misery well enough to give us a bridge in Mary! The Lord does things so well!

Oh, if only we knew how to love the Virgin, if only we knew what that means to Jesus, how much love we could offer the Virgin . . . we would be better than we are . . . we would be Jesus' favorite children.

I don't know if I'm going to say something that isn't right here; if I do, may She overlook it and may God forgive me. But I don't think we need to be afraid of loving the Virgin too much . . . I think everything we entrust to Mary will reach Jesus multiplied . . . I think in loving Mary, we love God, and it doesn't *take anything away* from Him to do so, quite the contrary.

It's a hard thing to explain. Am I making sense? But listen, when we set our hearts on what He loves most, how is that not loving God?

And how could we not love God when we see that, in His infinite goodness, He has provided a creature like Mary as intercessor between humanity and Himself? She is all gentleness, all peace; She sweetens all our bitter sorrows on this earth, placing a honeyed note of hope within the sinner, the afflicted . . . She is the Mother of those who mourn; She is the navigator's northern star in the night; She is . . . I don't know . . . the Virgin Mary!

How could we not bless God, then, with all our strength, considering His great mercy toward humanity in placing the Most Blessed Virgin Mary between heaven and earth?

Given Mary, how could you not love God!!!

Oh, dear brother, the soul loses itself thinking about this . . . it cannot comprehend it. There's only one thing it can do to keep from going crazy . . . and that's love. Loving so, so much. Living on fire with love for Mary, Mother of God, the Most Blessed Virgin, full of grace. She who helps us in time of affliction, covering us with Her blue mantle. Refuge of sinners. She who is our hope. She who helps us on earth so that She might later give us Her Son Jesus Christ in heaven. She who is blessed and praised by all the choirs of the heavenly hosts. She who . . . lovingly smiles whenever any little monk weeps in La Trapa.

What more can I say? . . . Who am I to praise Mary's beauty? I'm nobody, I know. But it doesn't matter. When I took up my pen, I decided to talk to you about Our Lady and remind you that . . . how presumptuous of me!!! . . . that Mary, our Mother, is in heaven.

I wanted to fill up page upon page . . . even if I fill it with nonsense . . . but you must forgive my roughness. She forgives me, and sees only my intention, just as Jesus does . . . and that is enough for me.

Oh, if only I had David's words, and David's heart! I would have my strength in Jesus, and at the same time . . . I would place my weaknesses in Mary . . . God, my rock in whom I take refuge; Mary, my consolation.

I don't know, I'm getting lost now. My dear brother . . . I'm so insignificant.

You often say, "All for Jesus." Why not add, "All for Jesus, and to Jesus through Mary"?

Yes, my dear brother, "I have placed my hope in God alone," says the great King David[2] . . . Oh, if only he had known the Most Blessed Virgin Mary! Then he would have added, "And that hope is Mary . . ." Don't you think so?

I don't know how everybody else feels when it comes to the Virgin . . . but as for me . . . what can I say? You know how crazy your nephew can get.

As you know, we have so many images of Our Lady at La Trapa that it's as if it were Her house. There, nothing is done without turning to Mary first . . . All vocations come from Her. The Marian atmosphere there is a consolation to every Trappist.

Don't be surprised, then, that I am so devoted to Her, and that I wish everybody else were too . . .

Everything would be so easy if we always turned to Our Lady! She has provided for me so many times. I haven't been as good a son to Her as I ought to have been, but our Mother is so good, and She is willing to forget those many occasions.

Do you remember our time in school? I've heard you talk about Our Lady of Remembrance from time to time[3] . . . She's the best memory you

2. See Ps 62:5.

3. Rafael and Leopoldo both attended Jesuit schools as children, though not at the same time. Our Lady of Remembrance (Nuestra Señora del Recuerdo) is a title of Mary to which the Spanish Jesuits had a special devotion; Rafael recalled learning a hymn to her in #37, n. 3.

have of that time, isn't She? Of course She is. I too am very grateful to the Jesuits for initiating us into Marian devotion at an early age.

Do you remember all the special celebrations during Mary's month? . . . Everyone gathered with their blue-and-white ribbons[4] . . . Those somewhat artless songs we'd sing in the chapel . . . Our well-thumbed books with all their colorful covers, which talked about Saint Stanislaus, Saint Aloysius Gonzaga, Saint John Berchmans[5] . . . all such great devotees of Mary Immaculate . . .

How far away it all seems! Doesn't it? But the Virgin remains, and even though we aren't children anymore (would that we were all still as innocent as we were back then!), Mary hasn't forgotten us . . . She reminds us that we were better once, and She consoles us amid our human misery, continuing to treat us like children . . . and, may She be a thousand times blessed, sometimes . . . sometimes She gives us a special vocation.

You see God's hand in everything . . . can you not also see Mary's hand at work?

Times have changed, and so have our circumstances . . . No more blue-and-white ribbons . . . now it's a Cistercian monastery dedicated to Mary,[6] and the white-robed abbot, Saint Bernard, is teaching us how to sing and make known Her praise.

How great God is! And how sweet is Mary!

What a great joy it is to think that in heaven, when we're there by Her side, we'll sing forever, forever . . . Some of us will sing those sweet school songs, others the *Salve Regina*, still others the solemn, divine *Magnificat* of

---

4. The blue-and-white ribbon, with a medal at one end and a pin at the other, was a symbol of membership in a sodality (association) devoted to Mary. The Jesuits promoted these sodalities at many of their parishes and schools worldwide.

5. Saint Stanislaus Kostka (1550–1568), Saint Aloysius Gonzaga (1568–1591), and Saint John Berchmans (1599–1621) were all Jesuit saints and Marian devotees who died young, hence their position as role models for students at Jesuit schools.

6. "Each community of the Order and all the monks are dedicated to the Blessed Virgin Mary" (*Constitutions and Statutes of the Monks and Nuns of the Cistercian Order of the Strict Observance and Other Legislative Documents* [Rome: Cistercian Order of the Strict Observance, 1990], 5). While the Abbey of San Isidro de Dueñas carries the name of the former Benedictine monastery revived by the current Trappist community, the Order's monasteries are otherwise traditionally named for Mary.

a monastic choir . . . and there will be those who find themselves unable to sing in the face of such beauty as that of Mary . . .

The thought of it makes everything on earth seem like nothing at all, doesn't it?

Oh, Lord! How can one live without loving Mary, without dreaming of heaven? . . . Everything is nothing . . . there is nothing under the sun worth rejoicing about or suffering over. There is only the joy of true hope, and the great pain of not loving enough.

Oh, my dear brother! Surely we'd go mad if we truly loved Mary. By honoring the Virgin, we will love Jesus more. By placing ourselves under Her mantle, we will understand divine mercy better. When we invoke Her name, it's as if everything becomes lighter. When we turn to Her as our intercessor, what will we not receive from Her Son, Jesus?

I don't want to keep harping on. What could I possibly say that you haven't already heard, not just once, but a thousand times before?

But I'm not trying to tell you anything you don't already know. I just wanted to send you a few pages, and for my part, I just wanted one word to reach your heart . . . Mary.

Meanwhile, you can see what I've actually managed to do, which is a whole hodgepodge of things . . . It doesn't matter. I'll consider myself very satisfied with it if, after you've read these lines, you lift up your heart over everything that surrounds you, place it before Our Lady, and pray a Hail Mary for me. You and I would both be better off for it, and I truly need it . . . and She would have another prayer to use as She sees fit . . . You'll do it, won't you?

For my part, I ask the Lord for so many things for you, and I ask Her, too . . .

Brother María Rafael, O.C.S.O.

P.S. I got your postcard.

165. *To Leopoldo Torres*[1]

Villasandino, October 30, 1937

Ave Maria
On the subject of old age . . .

A few days ago, I had the opportunity to read a few pages written by an elderly Christian. In his writing, I could observe the prudence that age bestows, as well as the serene peace of the one who no longer expects anything from this world, because he hopes only in God.

He ended his reflection by saying, "How happy old age is!"

How lovely that exclamation sounds on an old man's lips . . . He ought to thank God so very much for that inner joy, which thrives on the hope of ceasing to live one day . . . the hope of a death that draws near . . . the hope of seeing God.

One cannot live without hope.

Children dream of becoming adults. Adults often put their hope in things that prove disappointing as the years go by, but God often uses these things to draw people to Himself and fill their hearts with the one hope that can truly satisfy the soul, a hope that is ageless . . . the hope of God.

Happy . . . happy, a thousand times over, is an old age marked by white hair and fading eyesight, lived by one who no longer expects anything from this world and smiles with the joy of the inner peace granted by God to His friends.

Happy is the old man who can say, "I almost can't see anymore, but what does it matter? In the light of faith, I can see the glories of God. I almost can't hear anymore, but what does it matter? Are people saying something important? . . . Deep within me, I can hear God's call to prayer, recollection, and holy compunction . . . that's enough for me . . .

---

1. Leopoldo Torres was Rafael's great-uncle, the brother of his grandmother Fernanda. He had written a short reflection on the spiritual dimension of old age at Fernanda's request, and she passed it on to Rafael (OC 822).

My legs can hardly hold me up anymore . . . I'm totally useless . . . but what does it matter if my physical being weighs me down, so long as I have a supernatural life within me that has cherubim's wings and can fly all the way to God? . . . What does it matter if my body is sick, when we can see that the Great Doctor heals our souls of their wounds and past sins with such tenderness? . . . When we can see that it is our hearts that Jesus is asking for, and no matter how many years and illnesses we have endured, we can give Him our hearts in utter sincerity . . . and often, that offering is the heart of a child in the body of an old man, weighed down by his years.

Bodies that hunch over and grow tired of living, souls that love God, eternally young . . . there is no age in the eyes of the Infinite One.

Sad is the old age of those who just weep over memories and live in bitter loneliness.

Joyful are the years of the elderly who only weep over their sins, and live only for the hope of forgiveness, and love the solitude in which they find God and God alone.

Happy are the final years of those Christians who live and breathe for heaven, and see it up close. Passions no longer plague them. They understand the vanity of the things of this earth. They have no interest in wealth or honor. It was all like delicate smoke, scattered by the winds of time; nothing remains of it. They look at things with the serene stillness of those who live more on heaven than on earth . . . Truly happy are the elderly who truly love God.

In one's final years, why wail and weep over what has already come to pass? Is the past better than what awaits you? No . . . your days have come and gone, but your days are nothing at all . . . Your hopes and desires have come and gone . . . if you saw them realized . . . what's left of them? Nothing . . . perhaps some bitterness. Your loved ones have come and gone, and what's left of them? . . . Nothing, just memories, and they too fade away like smoke, lost in space and time.

You look back, and your eyes, weakened over the years, weep over time wasted on vanities that did not satisfy your heart.

But the joy of your final years will be holy indeed if, instead of dreaming about your past, you look toward the eternity that awaits you, where there will no longer be any lies or jealousies or tired eyes or weak, sick, old limbs . . . Holy is the joy of the old man who dreams of God alone, who looks toward death with great tenderness and inner peace . . .

Children are unaware of death . . . The young sometimes seek it out generously, spurred on by desire . . . The old await it serenely, according to God's will . . . *Peace* is a word very often repeated and very little understood . . . Peace in the soul of an elderly Christian . . . The peace of those who calmly hope in divine mercy, and in the infinite goodness of the Crucified One. Old age is truly happy!

I don't know how to put anything into words. I have neither age nor experience, nor even any disappointments. From a young age, Jesus began to show me the way, and I didn't have time to listen to human beings. The Lord didn't let me stop and listen to the world's flattery . . . I'm still young, maybe I haven't even begun to live. But I listen to my elders, I respect them and their white hair when they say, "I lived my life, and it was nothing . . . I have come to the end of the journey and I have learned only one thing: everything is vanity, and God alone suffices."

I listened to the old people who told me, "I was young once too, and the years passed me by before I knew it. I loved the world, and the world gave me nothing. I sought wisdom, and I found it not in war, or in science, or in animals, or in human beings . . . I found it only in the love of God and contempt for the world."

I listened to the wise, I listened to the elderly . . . perhaps that's why my heart has something old about it, and can understand my old uncle's words when he and his white hair, deaf ears, weak legs, and tired eyes cry out with holy joy, "Happy is old age!"

It is not that old age itself is happy. Rather, happiness is in the hearts of those elderly people who, having let go of the things of this world, live and breathe for God alone.

And that can happen in a young person, too.

One need be neither old nor young to love God . . . It is not time that teaches us to be detached from this world. One doesn't need to be a certain age to understand those words in the Gospel, *I am the way and the life*;[2] one need only stop and think about it . . . and sometimes also listen to those who know more than we do . . . to the wise monk in his cell, meditating upon eternal truths . . . to the old man who, at the end of his life, tells us that the world and its creatures are passing away, as is life, and

2. John 14:6.

nothing of it will remain, that it is childish to love vanity, that peace can only be found in Jesus, that the only truth is Christ, that the only treasure is God, and that the only life is God, and God alone.

Now, I'm not saying, "Happy is old age," but rather, "Happy is the one, whether young or old, who has come to understand, who has come to love and live for Christ alone."

Death will come sooner or later . . . what does it matter which? God is not limited by time or space; He is infinite. For Him, there is no age, just hearts who are truly His.

There is nothing left for us to do but wait . . . without looking back, or regretting what happened, or expecting anything from human beings; just happy to obey the will of God, whatever and whenever it may be.

When I write, the Most Blessed Virgin receives my intention. I just wanted this young man's heart to reach your old man's soul, in order to show you that we who love God are united in Him, even if age separates us . . . That it is possible for a child's soul to live in an old man's body, and it is possible for a very old heart to live in a twenty-five-year-old body.

I just wanted to help you see that the elderly are not alone. And when an old man speaks of God and the Virgin, there's always someone listening, someone silently receiving, respecting, and obeying his words. An old man's words are words of wisdom, for there is no greater wisdom than coming to truly love God and detach yourself from the world, whether you do it sooner or later.

Happy are the elderly who speak of God!

Happy are the young who listen to them!

What more can I say? . . . Nothing. All I can do is ask your forgiveness for my boldness for having spoken of what I may know with someone who knows far more than I do about it, but if we young people ought to listen respectfully to our elders . . . our elders ought to be lenient toward our youthful audacity in return . . . that is what is asked of them.

And when your tired eyes read these lines, may you realize that this young Trappist in his solitude understands your elderly Christian heart, for he too has a heart that loves Christ and exclaims, "Happy are those who hope in God!"

May the Virgin Mary be forever blessed!

Brother María Rafael

166. To Toribio Luis (Br. Tescelino) Arribas[1]

Villasandino, November 1, 1937

Ave Maria

My dearest brother in the Lord,

You've truly taken your time in sending me your address. Of course, if you'd done it earlier, I would've written you earlier, even though I wouldn't have had anything in particular to tell you, because you already know about my life. Even so, perhaps I would've sent you the diary I promised, if only I had written it. Although perhaps I wouldn't have sent it to you for the simple reason that I have so, so much boiling over inside me that I find silence to be more appropriate. Isn't that right?

My diary!. . . Woe is me. . . who could possibly be interested in that! A diary of mine! What do you want me to say, my dear brother?. . . The consolation you offer me is very great, in remembering this poor sick man . . . that's what my diary would say . . . sick, useless, nothing. What else do you want to know? Do you perhaps want me to send you a little piece of my cross?. . . You already know about it, why discuss it? May God reward your charity, and may the Virgin Mary bless you.

Don't you worry about Brother Rafael, neither he nor anything that happens to him is of any importance whatsoever. The Lord wants to lead him down this path of insignificance; a path on which he is nothing and is good for nothing, where he seeks only to be forgotten by everyone and to pass through this world without anyone noticing.

Believe me, God alone is my desire. Realizing how empty creatures and earthly things leave the heart, I have learned that happiness does not come from seeing our desires fulfilled.

God alone, brother, God alone . . . That is the only diary I have, the only thing that can be said to satisfy this poor sinner's soul. This poor

1. Br. Tescelino was the second infirmarian at San Isidro, also known by his baptismal name, Toribio Luis. After his conscription into the army, he was serving as a medic at the time of this letter.

soul, in its pride, wanted to fly one day, and God, in His infinite goodness, clipped its wings, humiliated it, and showed it what it was . . . a piece of garbage with a great deal of vanity . . . that's all.

Don't worry about me, honestly . . . I'm embarrassed that you would. Besides, I can't tell you anything that you don't already know. I'll just give you the news you asked for.

I went to Burgos eight days ago.[2] I spent three of them hospitalized at San José. My urine glucose test came back 42/1000, and they declared me completely unfit. The first time they did so, as you know, I was frustrated that I could not serve God and Spain at the front . . . or perhaps take a bullet for them . . . Now, believe me, I couldn't care less, because I've realized that what I want is worth nothing in the eyes of God. The best thing to do is to place yourself in His hands, and nothing more . . . May He make of me, *and you*, whatever He wants. Don't you think so?

I know sometimes it's exhausting to suffer. But so what? . . . It's such a short time. I know that the desire to fly to God and cease to offend Him is strong. But so what? . . . We are so insignificant, and we know so little; the best thing to do is let Him work . . . It's clear that my time has not yet come.

I know the anguish of having to keep kicking and screaming through this life as the world hurts us, our passions afflict our flesh, and creatures make us suffer, is very great at times . . . but what of Him? I'll stop here, perhaps I've said enough.

Jesus lived thirty-three years *knowing* that He was going to die on a cross, and all He asked of His Father was that His will be done.

Christ taught us to suffer, He taught us to keep quiet, He taught us to desire nothing but the Father's will. When will we ever learn?

How selfish we are! . . . How little love we have for God!

Anyway, I don't want to get off topic . . . they sent me home from the hospital, and now I'm here waiting . . . I don't know *what for*.

I wrote to Father Abbot saying that once I'd had my medical exam, I'd return to the monastery. Fr. José[3] wrote me back saying that I could come back whenever I wanted, the doors would always be open to me . . . *but* that I should think it over and not rush, because they don't have an infir-

---

2. The purpose of Rafael's trip to Burgos was to undergo a second medical exam for the military, to assess whether or not he was still unfit for service.

3. Fr. José Olmedo, master of novices.

marian right now, and it would be a shame if the same thing happened to me as before. That's all.

Humanly speaking, this is very prudent, don't you think? But what should I do? Well, look, this is how I'm thinking about it, let's see what you think.

Imagine that you were sick at home, surrounded by care and attention, practically lame, useless . . . in a word, incapable of taking care of yourself. But one day, you see Jesus walk by outside your window . . . You see a crowd of sinners, lepers, the poor and the sick, all following behind Him. You see that Jesus is calling you, and He *offers* you a place in His retinue, and He looks at you with those divine eyes that radiate love, tenderness, and forgiveness, and He tells you, "Why aren't you following Me?" . . . What would you do? Would you tell Him . . . "Lord, I'd follow You if You gave me an infirmarian . . . if You gave me the means to follow You *comfortably*, without endangering my health . . . I'd follow You if I were healthy and strong enough to take care of myself . . ."

No, I'm sure that if you saw the tenderness in Jesus' eyes, you wouldn't say any of that. Rather, you'd get up from your bed without a care in the world, without thinking about yourself at all, and you'd join Jesus' retinue, even if you were the last one . . . you hear, the *last one* . . . and you'd tell Him, "I'm coming, Lord. I don't care about my illness, or death, or eating, or sleeping . . . If You'll have me, I will go. If You want, You can heal me . . . I don't mind if the path that You are leading me down is challenging and rugged and covered in thorns. I don't mind if You want me to die with You on a cross . . ."

I will go, Lord, because You are the one who is leading me. You are the one who promises me an eternal reward. You are the one who forgives, who saves . . . You are the only one who can satisfy my soul.

Begone, warnings about what might happen to me in the future. Begone, human fears. When Jesus of Nazareth is the one who guides you . . . what is there to fear?

Don't you think, brother, that you would have followed Him? And that nothing in the world, or in yourself, would have mattered? Because that's what is happening to me.

I feel Jesus' sweet gaze deep within my soul. I know that nothing in this world can satisfy me, just God alone . . . God alone, God alone . . .

And Jesus is saying to me, "*You can come whenever you want* . . . Don't worry about having the last place. Would I love you any less for that? Perhaps even more."

Don't be jealous, brother, but God loves me very much.

On the other hand, my flesh is weighing me down; the world calls me crazy, senseless . . . I'm getting all kinds of prudent warnings . . . But what's all that compared to just one look from a God like Jesus of Galilee as He offers you a place in heaven and eternal love? Nothing, brother . . . even if it meant suffering until the end of the world, it would never be worth it to stop following Jesus.

I'm going to La Trapa very soon. I can't give you a date yet. My brother Fernando will be coming home from the front in the next couple of days, and I want to spend a few days with him. Then, my father wants to go to Oviedo . . . I don't know what plans he has. I'm sure he'll be getting everything out of the house. As soon as I have an opportunity to tell my parents (who still think I'll be spending the winter with them) that I have nothing left to do here and they should let me leave, I will go.

Believe me, all this is making me suffer greatly. You know where I'm going, and what I'm headed for. But I trust greatly in Mary, our Mother; She will help me, as She always has.

My cross is ever more difficult . . . it weighs ever more heavily on me, but my soul is also ever more filled with that . . . "God alone," who, as I've said, gives me strength. And that is the only account of my life that I could possibly give you.

Take heart, brother, and keep fighting. As you know, one need not be at the front, even if our selfishness would rather have us be there, where . . . perhaps a bullet might . . . Let us be generous. Are we agreed?

Do what they tell you to do, obey, and keep quiet . . . The bullets will come whenever the Lord decides it's the right time.

Am I wrong to say all this? I am ever less sure of myself, and I don't have anyone to ask. If only you knew how relieved I am to tell you all these things . . . You understand me so well. You've been so charitable toward me; only the Lord knows how much gratitude I have in my heart for you.

I'd appreciate it if you could write me back and tell me what you think, even if it's just a quick note.

When one is suffering, the sincere affection of a brother who can offer counsel is so encouraging. It helps us to embrace the cross of Christ, don't you think? . . . What else is love for?

If only I could do the same for you . . . But what good am I? If only I could help you in combat, at your side in the rear guard; if only I could help you with your family . . . I understand it all, even when you don't write about it.

If only I could make this sentiment penetrate your soul: that in God, in Him alone, is life, health . . . everything.

Believe me, brother, finding myself powerless to do anything I desire, the only thing I know how to do is humbly remember you in my prayers before the Most Blessed Virgin . . . I can do nothing more. But here, from His humble tabernacle, the Lord receives the words of your brother Rafael, who is thinking of you.

Do whatever you'd like with the books and all the other things. Let's not talk about it again, I have nothing more to say. My sister doesn't need them at the moment, and if she does, she'll find them elsewhere in Burgos, but I don't think she's all that keen on studying.

How was your family when you saw them last? My mother, in particular, thinks of you often.

How is your health? Any headaches recently? I want to hear everything. Don't you go thinking that I've ceased to be human, I am seemingly more and more so by the day . . . As you can see, everything contributes to an increase in . . . Well, nothing to be done about that.

Please do write me back. I truly need it right now, and welcome any help I can get. Please pray to the Virgin Mary for me especially; you know we can do all things with Her help . . . you'll pray for me, won't you?

I have nothing else to tell you. I know this letter is a total nuisance, forgive me; but please understand me and be merciful toward me as I pour out this soul you know so well. Sending you a big hug in Jesus and Mary,

Brother María Rafael

I was very pleased that Father Abbot gave you Aloysius Gonzaga's name[4] . . . A very kindly saint . . . May he protect you.

¡¡VIVA ESPAÑA!!
Viva Cristo Rey[5]

---

4. Saint Aloysius Gonzaga (1568–1591) was a young Jesuit saint from Italy; his name is translated as "Luis" in Spanish. Before his religious profession, Br. Tescelino went by his baptismal name, Toribio Luis. From Rafael's letter, we may infer that the abbot had given Br. Tescelino permission to revert to his baptismal name while away from the monastery.

5. "Long live Spain!! Long live Christ the King."

167. To Fr. Francisco Díez[1]

Villasandino, November 29, 1937

My dear Father Submaster,

I am taking the opportunity presented by my letter to Father José to add a quick note to you as well and let you know I am thinking of you.

Father Master will have told you of my desire to join up (if I may say so), coming back to the monastery to live among my dear brother Trappists once more. Believe me, Father Francisco, I don't know how to live in the world anymore, and every day I am separated from La Trapa gets longer and longer.

The Lord is testing me greatly with this illness of mine, which picks me up and pulls me to and fro. This spiritual exercise of going back and forth from the world to the monastery is something one must experience in order to understand it.

Truly, I ask God to do with me as He wishes . . . but if only the Lord wished that La Trapa were my only refuge in this life! . . . How happy that would make me! . . . I seek only one thing in this life, to live in the house of God, as David said,[2] and to occupy the last place within it, for that is better than the most glorious and honored place in the world, I think.

Soon, God willing, you will have Brother Rafael under your instruction, so you can resume teaching him those things he always forgets: the order in which candles ought to be lit, how the bowing works in choir, sign language . . . everything . . . everything that I'm missing so much right now in the luxury of my home, so far away from the tabernacle before which monks keep watch day and night.

You'll see, Father Francisco . . . you'll see, I'm going to be much better now, much more obedient. I'm already doing well and have gotten

---

1. Fr. Francisco Díez was the submaster of novices at San Isidro. This letter was sent alongside a letter to Fr. José Olmedo, master of novices, which has not been preserved.
2. See Ps 27:4.

stronger; of course, I'm still keeping up with my injections as always. God wants it this way; may it be so. I offer it up to the Blessed Virgin.

Please commend me to Her at Holy Mass sometime, and tell the novices to remember their brother Rafael in their prayers too . . .

Believe me, I need it. The world clings so tightly! Family! Freedom! . . . But what's any of that compared with what God will give to those who abandon it all? . . . Believe me, Father Francisco, I'd leave it all behind for Jesus not once . . . not twice . . . but a thousand times over. Even so, I'll always need heaven's aid, because I am human. You know how weak I am, how attached to everything . . .

Blessed be God who has sent me this illness that has given me so much trouble, and yet also allows me to truly place myself in His hands and depend purely on His blessed providence.

Some might say, "Poor brother Rafael, he can't make vows . . ." But trust me, it's not like that . . . Happy is this sick, useless oblate who only wants to love God and take up a little corner in a Cistercian monastery; any corner will do.

Anyway, I don't want to go on too long. Greet all the novices for me, and don't let them forget about my request for Our Lady of La Trapa. A big hug, your oblate,

Brother María Rafael

I imagine that you'll have saved my spot at the desk, remember what I said about that? Although I imagine there will be very few of us now; war is war . . . May God watch over our Spain.

168. To Toribio Luis (Br. Tescelino) Arribas

Villasandino, December 1, 1937

Ave Maria

My dear brother Luis (how strange it feels to call you that),

Today I've taken up my pen to write you a few lines that may be the last I send you from the world. The day before yesterday, I wrote to La Trapa to inform them of my next re-entrance into the monastery.[1] I have placed my hope in God and the Virgin that they will reply telling me to come whenever I like. If that is the case, I will go up to the house of God sometime after the eighth of this month, because I'm expecting my father to return from Oviedo soon; he's been there for a few days now.

You might think this is strange, but I want to spend Christmas, the feast of the home, away from my own. I will go and celebrate God's coming quite the opposite of how the world does it . . . You know what my Christmas present will be, eating red cabbage[2] with Fr. P.[3] . . . but we must have something to offer to the Divine Child, mustn't we? . . . At the end of the day, it's such an insignificant little thing.

Besides, so many of our brothers are far away from their home these days, and I don't want to be any exception. That's why I'm eagerly awaiting a reply from La Trapa, so I can go as soon as possible.

In my letter to Fr. José, I told him that not having an infirmarian was no excuse for me not to go. My relapse was God's will, of course, but it was also my own fault, and no one else's . . . my self-love, my desire to do what I cannot and should not do, my refusal to humble myself in the face of my own illness, my capriciousness and disobedience, my inability to see that this is what the Lord wants for me.

---

1. This letter has not been preserved.

2. Red cabbage was the traditional Christmas Eve meal at the monastery (OC 841).

3. Father Pío Martínez (1886–1966) was one of Rafael's companions in the monastery infirmary. He struggled with serious mental health problems and was known to torment Rafael in particular (OC 841–42).

Believe me, I'm a changed man now. My intention now is a deep desire to be obedient in everything, to humble myself before the community, and to take care of my illness as if it were my most precious treasure, because in a certain sense, it is.

You can imagine how difficult that is . . . pampering and caring for this miserable body, this sinful clay that deserves a cilice and contempt instead . . . But it doesn't matter, it won't be for long. Besides, I've realized that true mortification is doing what you don't like or want to do, even if your desires seem good and holy to you.

It is a great consolation to me that my poor letters comfort and encourage you in loving God. That's motivation enough to keep writing you, in addition to being able to unburden myself a bit . . . at the end of the day, I'm a creature like any other. Although, to tell you the truth, I'm not scared of the utter solitude that awaits me, the lack of human consolation, and perhaps even the lack of understanding. It doesn't discourage me at all, quite the contrary . . .

Believe me, brother, it must be so lovely to have nothing but God, to find our help in Him alone, to entrust our lives in His hands alone . . . nothing but Him.

What does it matter if we suffer, if Jesus of Galilee is the one who wipes our tears away with His white tunic?

If only you knew how much I long for silence, to live hidden within God's house . . . to be there, at the foot of the tabernacle, with my heart detached from the world, with one sole occupation: obedience, obedience, just . . . obedience. That would be plenty.

It's so hard for me to put everything in my heart into a letter . . . The Lord has given me so many ups and downs in so few years that at times I am utterly perplexed. But when I serenely contemplate all the wonders He has done in me, despite my resistance to His grace, despite there being nothing in me but selfishness, forgetfulness, and all kinds of sins . . . then my perplexity is transformed into a marvelous light that speaks to me of God's greatness and infinite mercy. Then we forget our own weaknesses, and God alone reigns in our souls. Lord, *what are human beings that you are mindful of them?*[4]

I feel this desire to disappear from the earth, to be swallowed up by the abyss or the sea. There is such greatness in God! Oh, my dear brother, I

4. Ps 8:4.

would say such crazy things to you, if I let my clumsy pen write whatever it wanted.

Talking about God . . . what madness.

In your letter, you told me that the world was doing you harm (I'm sure it is; you're made of flesh, after all) and flattering your passions. It is laying traps in order to ruin your spirit and let luxury, vice, and matter triumph. It's hurting you . . . I know, but we must keep fighting . . . and we will be victorious. That's what the Most Blessed Virgin is for.

But look, what hurts the most and makes me suffer the most is seeing how much people have forgotten about God, seeing creatures aspire to vanity when the ultimate Truth is so near to them, the soul's true peace and sole happiness . . . God. Yes, brother, believe me: that is the greatest danger in living among creatures who don't think about God.

I speak from experience. I know what it is to live an empty day, to feel that contagious lukewarmness that lets us live without suffering or rejoicing or anything else . . . I don't know. I don't have the words for it, but I'm sure you'll understand and are going through the same thing.

You'll say that the same thing can happen in La Trapa. I don't deny it, but there, at least God is on the other side of your loneliness . . . If you suffer there, you suffer only for love of Christ, because nobody is keeping you there but Him. Every tear shed in the house of God is a pearl that adorns the tabernacle. Even if we find ourselves taken over by lukewarmness and a lack of energy sometimes, it doesn't matter. The Lord and the Most Blessed Virgin see our good will as we serve and love them. What more can we do?

Whether we love a lot or a little, as long as it's as much as we can; whether we cry or laugh, it doesn't matter, so long as we remain in silence in the house of God. Everything else is to fail to follow our vocations: yours, as a vowed religious, doing whatever obedience commands you; and mine, as an oblate without vows but still obeying; yours, as an infirmarian, and mine, as infirm; yours, wearing brown, and mine, wearing white.[5] But so what? There is only one thing: God. There is only one occupation: loving God. There is only one habit: the cross of Christ . . . Everything else is secondary and passing away.

---

5. At this time, lay brothers wore an all-brown habit (as distinct from the choir monks, who wore white with a black scapular). Oblates wore the same all-white habit as choir novices, but with a shorter cloak (OC 882).

599 VII. Foolishness for Christ

You, following the Rule, and I, not following it, are doing the same thing because we are obeying the one true Rule, which is His holy will . . . don't you think so?

Yes, brother, I do want to get rid of my cigarettes and stop sleeping in a soft bed, listening to the radio, drinking sherry at eleven, and taking walks in the sun.

Now, I want to do what I don't even like to do . . . but if I really think about it, I don't care about anything anymore, I don't even know what I like. All I desire is to love God; all I want is to serve Him. I see La Trapa, I see a cross, and there I go. That's it.

As for my health, I don't have anything in particular to tell you. I'm on my feet, and that's enough for me at the moment, but I will say that I'm doing better these days. I'm not doing any testing, because why bother? I can observe all the typical symptoms of diabetes in my body without needing a test tube to confirm it.

I'll be asking Father Abbot for his permission to regulate my own dosage of insulin. I will be completely honest with Brother Domingo about the food he needs to give me.[6] I will get over my shame. If I need to eat meat in the middle of chapter, I will ask him for it . . . and that's all I have to say about that.

Since they won't let me go out into the fields, I think I'll make great strides with the broom and sweep the infirmary with the same enthusiasm as if it were the threshold of heaven itself. If at any point I think about crying, and I'm sure I will, I'll collect my tears in a little bottle . . . remember? . . .

But what I will say is that I won't let a single night go by without giving your regards to the Virgin before I sleep . . . you can rest assured of that. Of course, you can free me of this obligation upon your return. Are we agreed?

I don't need to tell you that all this is contingent upon my receiving a response from La Trapa telling me that I can come. I don't think they'll raise any objections, and I think I'll be there for Christmas. If not, I'll write you again, but don't answer me for now . . . If only you knew how hard it is for me to say that . . . I don't need to explain it, but as I'm sure you'll understand, once you get this one, by the time you respond I might

---

6. Brother Domingo García, the acting infirmarian.

already have my hood back on and I wouldn't want to get a letter from you when I'm already back at La Trapa . . . Do you understand?

But of course, it depends on what you need to write. I don't need to say anything else, I'll leave it up to your prudence and discretion. If I don't write you back, it's because I've already left.

For God's sake, brother, keep praying to the Most Blessed Virgin, asking Her to guide me, encourage me, and help me. I'm so insignificant and weak; I need all the help I can get.

As you can see, I'm telling you everything, just as you asked in your letter, but I'm so bad at putting everything that I want to tell you into words. Your charity will make up for what is lacking in me, and when you read this, remember the fight that your brother is putting up against everything that surrounds him, including himself.

My brother Fernando, the kindly lieutenant, was on leave here for a few days. We had a long talk one night, and we agreed that I had to return to my battlefront in order to help him with his.

If only you knew what a consolation it was to realize there are souls like his in the world. How great God is! . . . How well He orders things in creation! . . . How could anyone not love Him, my dear brother . . . how could anyone not love Him!

With such tenderness He touches our hearts . . . With such gentleness He helps us to see His will, He shows us His ways . . . There is such sweetness in the voice of that sweet Jesus of Nazareth when He says, "Follow Me."

What a great desire for eternal life enters the soul that comes to know Jesus! . . . How small everything is, brother . . . how small and unsatisfactory is everything that is not Jesus!

Look, sometimes my weakness makes me suffer . . . I look around me, and I see my freedom and my family's pure affection, and then I see La Trapa with its obscurity and silence; my head is spinning; I can't sleep; I am a human being, I am made of flesh . . . that is what suffering is.

But at the same time, brother, God is merciful and kind. He draws back the veil, and in my darkness, I consider Jesus . . . so sweet and peaceful. He shows me His wounds; He shows me how much He loved the world, and how much He loves me.

Everything is peace in His divine countenance. There is something about Him that makes you forget your sorrows. The soul is flooded with light and longs only to love Jesus . . . You forget about the path and no longer care about all its thorns. Silence and obscurity are no longer anything to fear. Everything around you seems petty, not worth thinking about. Once you've come to understand those words of Jesus, "follow Me" . . . you wish you would die.

That is the struggle, my dear brother . . . . but Jesus triumphs.

I don't know what I'm talking about, I'm just talking nonsense . . . forgive me. It's getting very late, it's almost one in the morning. My family and the servants have been asleep for a while now, and a solemn silence reigns over the whole house . . . Outside, the wind whistles over the eaves and through the trees . . . Perhaps all that nonsense is coming from the silence and the wind? . . .

At the thought of God's greatness, I want to fill page after page with everything that comes to mind.

I wish that same wind would scatter my longing for God over all the earth and plant it in the souls of my brothers and sisters . . . I wish I could fly just like it, and tell every creature . . . "Wake up and look up at the sky! Jesus is there, waiting . . . waiting for your prayers . . . waiting for you to love Him, even if it's just a little bit . . . waiting for you to look to Him in your suffering and pain so that He can help you."

I wish I could fly over the whole world, shouting to all who live in it . . . "God! . . . God! Only Him! . . . What are you searching for? What are you looking at?" This poor, sleepy world knows nothing of God's wonders . . . This poor, silent world is failing to sing a song of love to God . . . This poor soul is lovesick for God and still has to keep on living . . .

I don't know. You're the only one I write to, my dear brother; please forgive my enthusiasm . . . But don't go thinking I've gone mad already, I wish. God willing, you'll catch my desire for madness too . . . I need enclosure . . . La Trapa.

And with that, I'll bid you goodbye. I've already written quite a bit and I don't want to go on too long . . . Don't forget about our Mother; She will reunite us whenever She thinks best . . . She will do it all from heaven, I know it. Nothing is difficult for Our Lady.

Remembering you in Jesus and Mary, and begging you to remember me too, your poor brother, with all my affection,

Brother María Rafael, OCSO

169. To Toribio Luis (Br. Tescelino) Arribas

Villasandino, 1937[1]

I'm jealous of your life in the war . . . your struggles and pain . . . I'm jealous of how much God loves you . . . Yes, my dear brother, God loves you very much and He's showing you that right now. He's showing me that, too, but I return His love so poorly! I am so lacking in merit, if only you knew! What can I say? What can poor Brother Rafael say to your generous soul? Nothing . . . absolutely nothing . . .

Pray for me . . . since I cannot serve our country because of my uselessness, ask the Lord to send me whatever will make me holy . . . because it's so difficult, if only you knew . . . When I see my dear brothers fighting for God and Spain, suffering through this utterly cruel war with such a generous spirit . . . when I see that all of Spain is suffering, and that people are fighting and dying . . . brother, it is so hard to find myself where I am, relegated to a little corner of the world, good for nothing.

May His will be done . . . As you can see, this is my path: a sick oblate . . . useless in time of war.

God above all . . .

Truly, believe me, I do envy you; and at the same time, you can't imagine how much it consoles me to realize that, while I cannot do anything for God or for others, there are souls like yours who are placing your abilities at God's service . . .

. . . Paulino is the servant who sleeps in the house.[2] The books are entirely at your disposal. If there's something you're interested in, that's up to you, but in the study (to the right of the balcony, I believe) there are some thick volumes on the life of Christ and the Old Testament. Anyway, whatever books you want . . . I wish I could see you . . .

---

1. Only copied fragments of this undated letter remain.
2. That is, the Arnaiz-Barón residence in Oviedo, where Arribas was stationed at the time of this letter.

If you don't come by here again, I'll write you a longer letter, but not in your tragic tone, saying you don't think you'll get out of Oviedo alive. May God's will be done, but . . . may He want it otherwise. May we both return to La Trapa and help each other keep our monastic hoods up and persevere until the end . . .

The Most Blessed Virgin is the one who took us out of La Trapa, and She will be the one to return us there unscathed. With such a valuable protector, we have nothing to fear. If we rely on our own feeble strength . . . I don't know about that. But . . .

Don't you think we'll make it with the Virgin's help? Our Mother is so good! Consolation of the afflicted! Refuge of sinners!

Look, I'll say this: everything in our lives, absolutely everything, is in Mary's hands. As such, we need not worry, for She will take care of it all. Put yourself in Her hands, and trust.

I have nothing more to tell you. If you have any use for the affection and love I have for you in God, I'm sending it your way with my whole heart. Meanwhile, I beg you, say a prayer for me. Your unforgettable brother,

Brother María Rafael

VIII. It Is Love . . .

The Ultimate Sacrifice of Praise

170. God and My Soul[1]

La Trapa, December 16, 1937

Ave Maria

After spending a long time (nearly a year) at my parents' house,[2] recovering from an aggravation of my illness, I have returned to La Trapa to continue following my vocation, which is to love God alone, in sacrifice and renunciation, with no Rule but blind obedience to His divine will.

At present, I believe I am following it, obeying the superiors of the Cistercian Abbey of San Isidro de Dueñas without vows and with the status of an oblate.

God asks nothing of me but humble love and a spirit of sacrifice.

Yesterday, when I left my house, my parents, and my brothers and sister, was one of the hardest days of my life.

This is the third time[3] that I have left everything behind in order to follow Jesus, and I believe this time it was truly a miracle from God. By my own strength, I absolutely could not have come back to the infirmary at La Trapa in order to undergo hardships, or bodily hunger because of my illness, or loneliness of the heart because of how far away I find myself from other human beings. God alone . . . God alone . . . God alone. That is my theme . . . that is my only thought.

I am suffering greatly . . . Mary, my Mother, help me.

---

1. God and My Soul: Notes on Conscience (Private) was the title that Rafael gave to a folder where he kept notes written on looseleaf at the instruction of his confessor, Father Teófilo Sandoval, who did not read them until after his death (OC 852). Rafael's mother, Mercedes Barón, added titles to each section upon initial publication (OC 855).

2. Rafael left La Trapa on February 7, 1937, and returned on December 15, 1937 (OC 855).

3. Rafael's mistake; this was his fourth entrance into the monastery, not his third.

I have come for the following reasons:

1. Because I believe that here in the monastery I can better follow my vocation of loving God on the cross and in sacrifice.

2. In order to help my brothers in the fight, because Spain is at war.

3. In order to make use of the rest of the time that God has given me in this life, and make haste in learning to love His cross.

I aspire to the following in this monastery:

1. To conform absolutely and entirely to the will of Jesus.

2. To live only to love and suffer.

3. To be the last in everything, except *obedience*.

May the Most Blessed Virgin Mary take these resolutions into Her divine hands and place them at the feet of Jesus. Today, that is the only thing this poor oblate desires.

171. God and My Soul

Everything I Do Is because of God

La Trapa, December 21, 1937

I must convince myself of one thing: everything I do is because of God. He sends my joys; He provides my tears; I eat and sleep because of Him.

My rule is His will, and His desire is my law; I live because it pleases Him, and I will die when He wants me to. I desire nothing but God.

May my life be a constant *fiat*.

May the Most Blessed Virgin Mary help me and guide me in the short journey of life on earth.

172. God and My Soul
Take It All, Lord!

La Trapa, December 26, 1937

In community life, as long as I fail to master my whole "nervous system," I won't ever really know what it is to mortify myself.

Poor Brother Rafael . . . keep fighting until death; that's his destiny. On the one hand, a desire for heaven; on the other, a human heart. Add it all up . . . you get suffering and the cross.

Poor Brother Rafael, his heart is too sensitive to creaturely things . . . You suffer when you don't find love and charity among human beings . . . You suffer when you see nothing but selfishness. What do you expect of things made of misery and clay? Place your hope in God and leave creatures be . . . you won't find what you're looking for in them.

But what if God hides Himself? . . . How cold it would be in La Trapa then. La Trapa without God . . . is nothing but a bunch of men.

It is Christmastime, and all I have to show for it is profound loneliness . . . A very deep sorrow . . . No one to rest in, sick and weak as I am . . . Oh, Lord, I have such little faith! My God, my God, You are so good . . . Your mercy will pardon my forgetfulness . . . but what I am suffering is so great, Lord, that my weakness alone cannot abide it.

I see nothing but my misery and my worldly soul, of such little faith, and no love at all.

I will go, Lord, as far as You want me to; but give me the strength to do it, and aid in my hour of need . . . Look, Lord, and see what I am.

On Christmas Eve, I gave the Lord, the Child Jesus, the last of what was left of my will. I gave Him even my littlest desires . . . So what is left? . . . Nothing. Not even my desire to die. Now, I am nothing but God's possession. But Lord, what a poor little thing You possess!

Poor Brother Rafael . . . you came to La Trapa to suffer . . . what are you complaining about? . . . I'm not complaining, Lord, but I am

suffering without virtue. Those little tears of *loneliness* on Christmas Eve
. . . Lord, You know all things and see all things . . . and You also forgive
all things.

Fill my heart, Lord . . . Fill it with *that thing* that human beings cannot give me.

My soul dreams of love, of pure and sincere affection. I am a man made
for love, but not to love creatures, but rather You, my God, and to love
them in You . . . I only want to love You. You alone do not *disappoint*.
In You alone are hopes realized.

I left my home . . . I pulled my heart to pieces . . . I emptied my soul
of all worldly desires . . . I embraced your cross. What are You waiting for,
Lord? If what You want is my loneliness, my suffering, and my desolation
. . . take it all, Lord. I ask for nothing.

173. God and My Soul

Perseverance in Prayer

La Trapa, December 29, 1937

An hour at prayer without a single thought of God. I hardly noticed time was passing. The clock struck five and I'd already been on my knees for an hour . . . What about prayer? I don't know . . . I didn't do it. I was thinking about myself, about my personal suffering, about my memories of the world. What about Jesus? What about Mary? Nothing . . . All I have is selfishness, a little bit of faith, and a great deal of pride . . . I think I'm so important! I hold myself in such esteem!

Poor little thing! Insignificant dust in God's eyes! Since you don't know how to pray fruitfully, learn to humble yourself before Him, and then you'll be more humble before others.

Lord, have mercy on me . . . Yes, I am suffering . . . but I wish my suffering weren't so self-centered. Lord, I want to suffer for the sake of your pain on the cross, for the forgetfulness of humanity, for my own sins and those of others . . . for everything, Lord, but not for my own sake . . . What is my significance among all creation? What am I in Your eyes? . . . What does my hidden life represent within infinite eternity? . . . If I could forget myself, it would be better, Lord.

I have nothing but a refined sense of self-love and, I'll say it again, a great deal of selfishness.

With Mary's help, I will try to do better. I will endeavor to turn to You, Virgin Mary, whenever a memory from the world disturbs me, and offer You a *Salve* for the sake of all those in the world who offend You.

Instead of meditating upon my suffering . . . I will meditate upon gratitude, and love God in my misery.

Even when I get distracted and waste time, I will persevere in prayer.

174. God and My Soul

Humility

La Trapa, December 31, 1937

I have realized that the most *practical* virtue in order to have peace in community life is humility.

Humility before God helps us to trust, because humility is self-knowledge, and who can expect anything of themselves once they know themselves well? . . . It would be foolish not to expect *everything* from God instead.

Humility imbues our interactions with others with peace. With humility, there are no arguments or jealousies, and it is impossible to be offended . . . Who could offend nothingness itself?

I earnestly beg Mary to teach me this virtue, of which She is an exemplar . . . so humble before God and others.

"Thy will be done"

175. God and My Soul

My Vow

La Trapa, January 1, 1938
Feast of the Circumcision of the Lord[1]

I made a vow at prayer this morning. I made a *vow to love Jesus always.*

I have realized what my vocation is. I am not a religious . . . I am not a layman . . . I am nothing . . . Blessed be God, I am nothing but a soul in love with Christ. He wants nothing but my love, and He wants it detached from everything and everyone else.

Virgin Mary, help me keep my vow.

To love Jesus in everything, because of everything, always . . . Only love. A humble, generous, detached, mortified love, in silence . . . May my life be nothing but an act of love.

I can clearly see that it is not the will of God for me to make religious vows or follow the Rule of Saint Benedict in everything. Am I to want what God does not?

Jesus has sent me an incurable disease; it is His will that my pride humble itself before the misery of my flesh. God has sent me this illness. Am I not to love everything that Jesus sends me?

I kiss with great tenderness the blessed hand of God, who gives health when He wills it, and takes it away when He pleases.

As Job said, *shall we receive the good at the hand of God, and not receive the bad?*[2] Besides, does any of this keep me from loving Him? . . . No . . . I ought to love Him madly.

A life of love, that is my Rule . . . my vow . . . That is my only reason for living.

---

1. In 1960, the octave of Christmas was renamed the Solemnity of Mary, Mother of God.

2. Job 2:10.

The year 1938 has begun. What has God prepared for me this year? I don't know . . . Perhaps it doesn't matter . . . It's all the same to me, so long as I do not offend Him . . . I am God's. May He do with me as He wills. Today, I offer Him a new year, which I want to dedicate entirely to a life of sacrifice, self-denial, and detachment, guided only by love for Jesus . . . by a very great, very pure love.

My Lord, I want to love You like nobody else. I want to spend this life with my feet barely touching the ground. No stopping to look around at all this misery, no stopping to dwell on any creature. A heart on fire with divine love, upheld by hope.

Lord, I want to look only up at heaven, where You are waiting for me, where Mary and all the saints and angels are, blessing You for all eternity, having spent their lives on earth loving only Your law and observing Your precepts.

Oh, Lord, I want to love you so much! Help me, Mother!

I must love solitude, for God has placed me in it.

I must *obey* blindly, for God is the one who commands me.

I must *mortify* my senses constantly.

I must have *patience* in community life.

I must exercise *humility*.

I must do everything for God and Mary.

176. To Mercedes Barón

La Trapa, January 6, 1938

Ave Maria

My dearest mother,

You ought not be surprised that I haven't written you sooner. You know that religious life comes down to just one word, *obedience*. If I'd asked, I'm sure they would've let me; still, I thought it better to wait to be ordered to write you.

On the other hand, I have absolutely nothing to tell you all. You already know nearly every detail of my life. So what can I possibly tell you?

I will just say that, with a love I do not deserve, I was received into the monastery once again. My shaved head is back under a Cistercian white hood. May the Lord will that I never take it off again, but His will is truly my only Rule, and little by little, I have already gotten used to always doing what I don't want or like to do . . . so now I don't even know what I want or like anymore . . .

God is so good to me. As the days and years go by, I am realizing that God's way of showing His great mercy toward me was sending me this illness; believe me, it is truly my treasure. I am very content, and I am happy. What else do you want me to say? Nothing is difficult when you love God, and everything is easy for the one who lives in trust.

I got the vest you sent, which I've already put on . . . may God reward you. Although I must say that I wasn't cold, even though it was cold out . . . As my father said in his letter, you all know that just as well as I do.

My father tells me, with such innocence, to remember Fernando in my prayers, and you all, and Spain . . . *¡Virgen del Pilar!*[1] Of course, what am I here for? All I feel is . . . unable to use my clumsy words to tell you what

1. Our Lady of the Pillar, a title of Mary from Zaragoza, Spain.

I'm feeling. I regret that I cannot fill the whole world . . . and my family home . . . with what I came to La Trapa to seek: the peace of Christ.

But it doesn't matter. May my good intentions suffice, my dearest mother, to send you that peace I have, which consists only of happily submitting to whatever God sends us . . . God everywhere and in everything.

Don't worry about either of your sons, the soldier or the oblate; each is doing his duty in his own way, as best he can . . . And I believe (and I'm not speaking from vanity here) that both are acceptable to God . . . What more could you want? Besides, you have two other children, of whom you ought not to complain; they are at your side, so praise God in them. As you can see, you have no reason to be upset. The Lord is very good, and does everything well.

I haven't heard anything about Fernando, but I'm not worried about him. I am as sure that Mary is helping him as I am that the sun is out today. It will all come to an end, and a good one at that. It's just a matter of knowing how to wait and trusting in God. What is there beside Him? . . . I haven't been able to find a thing, except misery, of which this life has plenty . . . and yet there are still those who are attached to it.

We Trappists aren't crazy, no . . . it's the world that's gone nuts.

Well, I'm not telling you anything new, but certain ancient truths are our only sustenance in this monastic life . . . Is there anything new under the sun? . . . *Vanity of vanities! All is vanity.*[2] Only love for God can satisfy the soul . . . It's nothing new, but it's the truth.

I hear the tenants have come to see reason . . . Blessed be God, I'm glad to hear it, although I'm sure they'll still put up a fight. Don't worry about it. You must be understanding with them, and then it will be easier for you to forgive. Jesus forgave everything . . . He understands everything.

As you can see . . . they are so attached to this earth that what they say and do isn't all that surprising . . . Perhaps they are suffering. But they'll be the ones who are surprised when one day, not too long from now, they have to leave it all behind . . . and can't take anything with them.

Look, don't let the same thing happen to you; don't live for this earth, but may it live for your sake . . . Anyway, you know how we monks are! What I will say is that while I don't know what it will be like for those who

2. Eccl 1:2.

leave it all behind at the hour of death, I do know what it's like to leave it all behind before you die . . . and it's a little bit difficult. But after that, my dear mother, if only you knew how good life is when you have nothing and are entirely in God's hands.

Poor Isidro . . . and Vicenta and Rupertus "and company"! I think of them from time to time.[3]

Give everyone my regards: Quica and her hens, Eutiquio, Aurea, Carmen, Peché and the oxen, I'm sure they've done a bit of plowing by now; anyway, everyone else too.[4]

Whenever Pepinilla writes to Fernando next, ask him if he got my letter, and tell him I'm here now, so he should write me sometime.[5]

Poor Brother Rafael! Sometimes, in his Trappist silence, he remembers the world . . . but not the world of pleasure and fun, even if it was perfectly licit amusement . . . No, it's good that all of that, all that freedom, is locked away . . . What's harder is the world that cannot be locked away, the world of the flesh, which is in your heart, with all its affections and pure loves. In enclosure, these things do not die, but are rather purified and divinized through enclosure with Christ, even if they can sometimes cause suffering . . .

I don't know what I'm saying, but a mother always understands, right? . . . Even if she's dealing with a poor, crazy little monk whose only desire in this life is to love God very much, and help others to do the same.

"God alone suffices," he exclaims when he gets up, and "God alone suffices," he repeats when he goes to bed.[6]

<hr />

3. Isidro Dueñas and his mother Vicenta Dueñas were tenants of the Arnaiz Barón family at Villasandino (OC 871), while Ruperto Martínez was the majordomo there. Rafael uses the English phrase "and company" in the original.

4. Quica, or Francisca, was married to Eutiquio, the gardener at Villasandino. Aurea and Carmen were servants in the Arnaiz-Barón residence there. The identity of "Peché" is unclear, but presumably he was one of the farm workers there (OC 871).

5. Pepinilla: a nickname for Rafael's younger sister, Mercedes, who wrote letters on behalf of the whole family to their brother Luis Fernando while he was away at the front. Rafael's letter to Fernando has not been not preserved (OC 872).

6. From a poem by Saint Teresa of Ávila: "Let nothing trouble you, / Let nothing scare you, / All is fleeting, / God alone is unchanging. / Patience / Everything obtains. / Who possesses God / Nothing wants. / God alone suffices" ("Efficacy of Patience," in STA 3:386).

And thus the days pass by quickly, almost without realizing it . . . thinking of God, praying to the Virgin Mary, and hoping for divine mercy. That's all. As you can see, it's not much to tell, and yet I've managed to fill up a whole letter with it.

But it's not my words that I wanted to send you, let alone my ideas, which are old as time, and you already know them well . . .

Rather, you already know what I want to send you; it's something I placed at the feet of Jesus in the stable at Bethlehem this Christmas.

This is for my dear father and my brothers and sister, too. The Most Blessed Virgin sees my intention, and I hope you all do too.

These days, while Spain is at war, all I want for you is peace . . . A very great peace at Villasandino, among the frost and the wind, not worrying about creatures' ambitions and miseries, without the impatience that distances us from God and sometimes offends Him . . . I wish you all a very great peace as you hope for the war to end, for Fernando to come back, for the wheat to grow, and for Leopoldo to learn to ride a horse already so he can crisscross the countryside blessing God.

It will all come to pass, don't you worry. In the meantime, I too am waiting in hope, and working my field, which, sadly, is covered in weeds . . . but when you sow and tend in God's name . . . He will provide as He pleases, when He pleases.

I don't know when I'll write again . . . whenever they tell me to. Meanwhile, what's that to you? Do you think I'm going to forget you in my prayers before the tabernacle? No! And that's what counts, my dearest mother. Everything else is just hot air.

Don't forget to pray for me either. If you pray for those fighting for Spain, include me among them, because in my own way, as God permits, I am fighting too.

Hugs for everyone; and for you, all the affection of your son,

Brother María Rafael, OCSO

177. God and My Soul

My Will Is Yours, Lord!

La Trapa, January 6, 1938

This morning, I received great consolation and a lot of peace at Holy Communion. I was deep in recollection for a long time: I saw clearly that only Jesus can satisfy my soul and fill my life.

I wanted to offer something to the Child Jesus . . . something I don't have. I wanted to die in His presence, forgetting everything, just loving Him . . . How good God is!

About three-quarters of an hour had gone by when . . . I don't know, I can't explain it, but a very great anguish filled my spirit. My soul broke out in tears in the novitiate chapel. Lord, I'm such a poor man!

I felt so alone! . . . What happened to my fervor? . . . What happened to my longing for God and my contempt for this world, where did they go? . . . Why did You leave me, Lord? . . . What will I do without You? I was ashamed of myself, to be so weak.

When I did my examen tonight, I came to understand many things that I can't manage to write down.

God is very good to me.

178. *God and My Soul*

"The Greatest Penance Is Community Life"

La Trapa, January 7, 1938

Impatience is one of my greatest faults. Sometimes a brother, without realizing it, will work my nerves into such a state, especially by making certain noises, that if I let my nature take over I'd start screaming.

But I came to La Trapa to mortify myself, and to suffer whatever the Lord wants to send my way.

The greatest penance is community life.[1]

Our Lady, Queen of Heaven, grant me the grace to be docile. Amen.

One of my greatest sorrows is finding myself embracing the cross of Jesus, but not loving it as I ought.

1. This is a statement often attributed to Saint John Berchmans, SJ.

179. God and My Soul

Teach Me, Lord, to Love Your Cross

La Trapa, January 31, 1938

My God . . . My God, teach me to love your cross. Teach me to love absolute solitude, away from everything and everyone. I understand, Lord, that *this* is how You want me, that *this* is the only way that You can win over this heart of mine, so full of worldliness and occupied with vanities.

Thus, in the solitude in which You have placed me, You will show me the vanity in everything; You alone will speak to my heart, and my soul will rejoice in You.

But Lord . . . I suffer greatly when temptation presses in on me and You hide Yourself . . . my anguish weighs so heavily upon me!

"Silence!" You demand . . . Lord, I offer You silence.

"A hidden life!" . . . Lord, may La Trapa be my hiding place.

"Sacrifice!" . . . Lord, what can I say? I gave up everything for You.

"Renunciation!" . . . My will is Yours, Lord.

Lord, what do You want from me?

"Love!!" Oh, Lord, I wish I had that in spades! Lord, I want to love You like nobody else . . . My Jesus, I want to die on fire with love and longing for You. Of what importance is my loneliness among people?

Blessed Jesus, the more I suffer . . . the more I will love You. The greater my pain, the happier I will be. The less consolation I have, the more I will have. The lonelier I am, the greater Your help will be.

I will be everything You want.

I'd like my life to be a single act of love . . . a prolonged sigh of longing for You.

I'd like my poor, sick life to be a flame of love where every last sacrifice, every sorrow, every renunciation, every moment of loneliness are consumed.

I'd like Your life to be my one and only Rule.

Your eucharistic love, my only food.
Your Gospel, my only object of study.
Your love, my only reason for living.
I would rather stop living than live without loving You.
I want to die of love, since I cannot keep living on love alone.
Lord, I'd like to . . . go crazy . . . It's agonizing to live like this.

It is so painful to want to love You and not be able to! It's so sad to have to drag this physical matter around the world, imprisoning my soul, which yearns only for You . . . Oh, Lord, life or death, whatever You want . . . so long as it's for love.

I don't even know what I'm saying, let alone what I want . . . I don't know if I'm suffering or rejoicing . . . let alone what I want or what I'm doing.

Come to my aid, Virgin Mary . . . Be my light in the darkness that surrounds me. Lead me down this path, which I walk alone, guided only by my desire to love Your Son wholeheartedly.

Do not leave me, my Mother. I know I'm nothing, and I'm worthless. Just misery and sin . . . that is all I can offer You, the best I can do, in asking You to hear my prayer.

Mary, I left human beings behind when I came to La Trapa, only to find them here. Help me to follow the counsel of the *Imitation of Christ*, which tells me to seek nothing in creatures, and take refuge in the Heart of Christ.

I don't want anything that isn't God . . . other than Him, all is vanity.

180. *God and My Soul*

"How Good You Are, Lord; You Love Me So Much"

La Trapa, February 5, 1938

The days are passing quickly, as am I. With a pen in my hand, and paper in front of me, I don't know what to do . . . My soul contains so many things that if I were to try to write out everything I'm feeling, I'd never finish!

God, in His infinite goodness, with no need for human words, has been teaching me the science I came here to La Trapa to learn . . . contempt for the world, and the practice of loving Him. It is through much suffering that I am learning.

I am getting used to being permanently enclosed within the monastery. It's been two months since I last enjoyed a bit of fresh air and sunshine . . . Oh, Lord, how hard that is for me! . . . In the world, I so enjoyed singing Your wonders and glories in the countryside . . . My greatest pleasure was to open my eyes wide to gaze upon the sea . . . My soul would be captivated by star-studded skies, and would bless You whenever it heard the earth's silence upon a gentle, tranquil sunset.

All that is over for me . . . the sky, the sun, flowers. Lord, the human part of me . . . which is a lot of me . . . weeps for my lost freedom. But You come and console me . . . Is there anything You would not do for me, blessed Jesus?

Yesterday, when it was time for work, a splendid blue sky surrounded the monastery . . . A bright winter day reigned over the Castilian countryside. Obedience commanded me to wrap chocolates in the factory. I felt deep sorrow . . . I held tight to my crucifix and determined to obey, and You, Lord, made me think. "What greater flower is there than penance?" . . . I wanted to cry, but you can't do that in community.

"You came here to do penance . . . so what are you complaining about, Brother? If only you realized that each tear shed for My love while doing penance in the cloister is a gift that makes all the angels of heaven sing for joy."

"Take heart, Rafael," it seemed like God was saying to me . . . "Everything passes . . ." and blessed Jesus, the sorrow went away . . . I no longer cared about the beautiful day, or anything else earthly . . . I knew that God was helping me, and that God blessed me. As I clumsily worked to wrap chocolates, I envied no one on earth or in heaven, because I was thinking: if the saints in heaven could come down to earth for just a moment, it would be in order to increase the glory of God here, even if it were just with a single Ave Maria on their knees in silence . . . or who knows, wrapping chocolates.

How good You are, Lord! You love me so much! . . . Little by little, I am coming to understand the vanity of everything.

After Vespers, I knelt at the foot of Your tabernacle, and realized that the day had passed, and with it, the blue sky, the shining sun, my sorrows, and my joys . . . Everything passed, and nothing remained.

I understand very well the vanity of loving what is perishable. At the end of the day, all that will be of value is what I suffered for Your love . . . Everything else is a waste of time. Oh, Lord, then we will truly weep that we did not do penance; then we will bless each chocolate we wrapped in the darkness of the factory . . .

How good You are, Lord! You are so sweet when You give consolation . . . but You show us Your true love in our trials and tribulations.

I will not ask You for rest on this earth, Lord. I want to obey Your will until the very end . . . Teach me, just as You have been doing up to now . . . in solitude and distress, in pure faith . . . in the abyss of my nothingness . . . in the arms of the cross. What do I need in order to be happy? Nothing, for I desire nothing.

You know it, Lord. Don't mind my tears, and don't be deterred when I utterly fail to return Your love at times . . . You know what I am and what I'm like.

I won't dare to ask You for sufferings and crosses, for that would be a proud presumption on the part of one so weak . . . but if You send them to me, I will bless them.

I bless Your hand, Lord, and finding myself so poor, useless, and sick, I am filled with this great joy . . . and sometimes I am afraid . . . there are still those who love me, and I have a bed to sleep on . . . The holy man Job blessed You from among the ashes, scraping himself with a potsherd.[1] What do I have to complain about? . . . Oh, Lord, I still am something, and I still have something.

I surrender myself into Your hands, and I lay myself at the feet of the Most Blessed Virgin Mary . . .

Why keep writing? That seems like vanity, too.

May Jesus and Mary forgive me. Amen.

1. Job 2:8.

181. God and My Soul

The Greatest Consolation Is to Have None at All

La Trapa, February 12, 1938

I have often thought that the greatest consolation is to have none at all;[1] I have thought this, and I have experienced it.

If we receive consolation from creatures, it becomes difficult and painful to *return* to desolation. And if we receive consolation from God . . . then how can we go back to living among such misery! Life becomes such an upward climb! It hurts so much to deal with people! It's so painful to have to take care of this miserable body and have to eat and sleep and endure the many weaknesses of the flesh!

From time to time, I have felt my heart quietly beating with love for God . . . Longing for Him, with contempt for the world and for myself.

From time to time, I have felt the great, profound consolation of finding myself alone, having surrendered myself into God's arms. Solitude with God . . . nobody who has not experienced it can understand it, and I don't know how to describe it. All I can say is that it is a consolation one can only experience through suffering . . . and suffering alone . . . and with God, that is true joy.

It is a desire for nothing but suffering. It is a very great longing to live and die ignored by everyone, unknown to the whole world . . . It is a great desire for everything that is God's will . . . It is not wanting anything but Him . . . It is wanting yet not wanting . . . I don't know, I can't explain it . . . only God understands me, but while I may not know the cause, I do know its effects.

Everything in my soul is changing. Now I am indifferent to things that used to make me suffer . . . At the same time, I keep finding more nooks

1. Rafael attributes this phrase to Sor Pilar García of the Poor Clares in Ávila in #63; see also #43, n. 8.

and crannies in my heart that were once hidden, and are now coming out into the light.

First of all, things I used to find humiliating almost make me laugh now. I no longer mind my status as an oblate in the monastery . . . Sometimes I look at others' cowls with a certain envy, but I'd be glad if they gave me an oblate's cloak in place of the novice's cloak I have now.[2] I can see that the last place is the best one. I'm glad to be no one and nothing. I'm delighted with my illness, which has given me cause to suffer physically and morally. In general, I could not care less about cloaks and cowls at all . . . let alone my place, which is the least important thing there is, as far as I'm concerned . . .

My illness . . . what does it matter if I eat alone or in another's company, or whether I have lentils or potatoes? What does it matter if I am hungry or thirsty, whether I live in one way or another?

It's all the same to me. I just want to love God and do His will . . . What else is there? Vanity . . . air . . . people's childish desires.

I used to suffer because I was alone. Blessed is the solitude in which You have placed me, Lord . . . I don't want any creature to talk to me. What can they possibly say that You, on Your cross, don't teach me?

Whenever I doubt, or am uncertain about something, or feel a temptation pressing upon me, or let myself be carried away by some weakness . . . I try to make an act of humility at the foot of your cross, and kissing Your divine blood as it drips from the wounds in Your feet over the wood, I ask for Your protection, help, and counsel . . . and whatever You inspire me to do in that moment, I do it.

Blessed is this solitude, where *You alone* gather up my sorrows and *You alone* receive my tears. For *You alone* is all my fervor, my longing for Your love, my desire to carry a little piece of Your cross.

I'm not complaining about anything anymore, Lord . . . I just want to do Your will, Lord, and in humble obedience, I believe I will.

I aim merely to live a very simple life, nothing extraordinary about it . . . keeping my love for You very hidden from the eyes of others.

---

2. The cowl is proper to solemnly professed monks. Oblates and novices both wore the same all-white habit, but oblates had a shorter cloak than novices. Despite being canonically an oblate, Rafael was given a novice's habit to wear when he returned to the monastery.

Living my life as a sick man in La Trapa with a smile on my lips . . . Doing with simplicity whatever I am ordered to do. Obeying promptly . . . and hiding the little volcano of my heart from everyone, as it hopes to die embracing the cross of Jesus . . . the desire I sometimes have for penances I can't do . . .

I wish I could sleep on the stairs . . . I wish I could eat under Father Abbot's table . . . I wish I could walk around wearing a sack and a rope . . . I wish I could become mute for You, Lord . . . And sometimes I wish I could act the fool, shouting all through the monastery cloisters . . . throwing myself at the monks' feet . . . Lord, I don't know what I would do if they let me . . . perhaps nothing at all.

Oh, who can think about white cowls . . . when my Jesus is *naked* on a cross? . . . Who can think about wanting to be appreciated by others, when my Jesus is forgotten by His friends, jeered and spat upon along the way of sorrows? . . .

Who can think about prudence, when we see Jesus with the cloak and scepter of a *fool*? . . . Lord, Lord, I wish I could be that fool . . . and receive all the laughs and jeers You received . . .

Lord, I wish I could be that fool . . . I don't know what I'm saying . . . poor Trappist oblate, whose life You want to quietly unfold in silence, in obscurity . . . in simplicity . . . May Your will be done, Lord.

But do not delay, Lord! Look at Your servant Rafael. He wants to hurry up and be with You . . . and see Your Most Holy Mother, Mary . . . and sing Your praises with all the angels and saints . . . Oh, Lord! When will I get to stop eating . . . and sleeping . . . and dealing with everyone?

What a beautiful profession I will make on the day of my death! . . . Eternal vows of love! . . . Forever . . . forever.

Who could think about earth and human beings? It's all so fleeting, and little, and pitiable . . . God alone . . . All external things are vanity . . . God alone . . . Time passes, as does the human being . . . God alone.

God alone . . . God alone . . . God alone . . . may He be my life; and may Mary, my good Mother, help me to walk this valley full of miseries. Amen.

182. *God and My Soul*
Living United to Your Cross

La Trapa, February 13, 1938
Septuagesima Sunday

Blessed Jesus, O Lord, how can I express the great tenderness of my soul before the sweetness of Your love?

What have I done, my God, to deserve You treating me like this? One moment my soul is flooded with deep bitterness, and the next, it is filled with joyful delight at the thought of You and what You promise me at journey's end. What have I done, Lord?

Today, at Holy Communion, I felt the consolation of being close to You when it seems that everything else has abandoned me. Lord, I wanted to nail to Your heart the words I say every day: "Lord, do not permit me to be parted from You."[1]

May I remain, Lord, in the shadow of the stark wood of the cross forever. Put my cell and my bed at Your feet . . . There may I find all my delight, Lord, and my rest amid my suffering too . . . Water the ground at Calvary with my tears . . . There, at the foot of the cross, may I pray and examine my conscience . . . "Lord, do not permit me to be parted from You."

What a great joy it is to be able to live at the foot of the cross. There I find Mary, and Saint John, and all those who love You. There is no pain there because, looking up at Your own, Lord, who would dare to suffer?

There everything is forgotten. No one desires joy, no one thinks of suffering . . . Upon seeing Your wounds, Lord, only one thought reigns in the soul . . . love . . . yes, love, to wipe away Your sweat; love, to tend Your wounds; love, to relieve such great and immense pain.

Lord, do not permit me to be parted from You.

---

1. From the Anima Christi prayer, popularly attributed to Saint Ignatius of Loyola.

Let me live at the foot of your cross without thinking of myself, or wanting or desiring anything other than gazing wildly upon the divine blood that is pouring down upon the earth . . .

Let me weep, Lord, but weep for how little I can do for You, and how much I have offended You while I was far away from Your cross . . . Let me weep for the forgetfulness that humanity shows You, even those who are good . . .

Let me live at the foot of Your cross, Lord . . . day and night, at work and at rest, in prayer and study, while eating and sleeping . . . always . . . always.

How far away the world seems when I think of the cross. How quickly the day goes by when I spend it with Jesus on Calvary. How sweet and tranquil it is to suffer in the company of Jesus crucified.

I only came to know the gentleness of Christ's ways such a short time ago, but I have always found consolation in the cross. What little I know, I have learned from the cross . . . I have always done my prayer and meditation at the cross . . . In truth, I don't know a better place, and I'm not going looking for one . . . so stay still, then.

Therefore, Lord, as I consider the divine school of your cross, as I consider that it is only on Calvary, at Mary's side, where I can learn to be better, to love You, and to forget and disregard myself: "Do not permit me to be parted from You."

God is so good to me. I truly don't have the words for it. He *forcibly* removes me from the world. He sends me a cross, and draws me near to His own . . . and so all I have to do is wait, wait with faith and love, wait, embracing His cross.

Oh, if only I had the foolishness of the cross! Oh, if only the world understood the treasure of the cross, how different people would be.

Oh, if only God would not allow me to offend Him—and I always do, whenever I am parted from His cross—how happy I would be then.

Therefore, Lord, clinging to the cross with all my strength, uniting my tears to Your blood, shouting, wailing, howling . . . wanting to go mad . . . mad for Your most holy cross . . . Hear me, O Lord! Listen to my supplications, and do not spurn them . . . With the water pouring from Your side, wash away my great sins, my faults, and my ingratitude; fill my heart with Your divine blood, and give rest to my soul as it unceasingly cries out, "Lord, let me live united to Your cross, and do not permit me to be parted from it."

Virgin Mary, Mother of Sorrows, when you gaze upon Your Son, bleeding on Calvary, let me humbly tend to Your great sorrow, and unworthy though I am, allow me to wipe away Your tears.

183. *To Rafael Arnaiz Sánchez de la Campa*

La Trapa, February 14, 1938

Ave Maria

My dearest father,

I received your letter today, and gave thanks to God, who takes care of me so that I am never wanting for anything.

Yes, I've only got one tube of insulin left, and I was just thinking of asking you for more when you got the jump on me . . . May God reward you. You can send me however much you want, whenever you want; as you know, I take 900–1000 units per month. Just so you don't get confused, I'll lay it out for you:

The tubes with 60 units per cubic centimeter contain 300 units.

The tubes with 40 units per cubic centimeter contain 200 units.

The tubes with 20 units per cubic centimeter contain 100 units.

These are the three dosages I've been using, and of course, a 300-unit tube ends up being cheaper than a 100-unit tube.

As for my health, I've never been better. I've put on quite a bit of weight, at least for someone with this illness, but you don't have to worry about me, I'm treated too well if anything. Reverend Father Abbot doesn't allow me to work very much, or sleep too little, or fast or attend Vigils,[1] and so, of course, receiving so much charity on earth and so much help from heaven, all your son Rafael can do is praise God from the bottom of his heart . . .

May the Lord reward my superiors and my parents for all their patience with me, poor man that I am, good for nothing, relying on everyone for everything.

I got my mother's letter, and Fernando's as well. I'm going to reply to him today.[2]

---

1. Vigils: the first hour of the Divine Office, prayed at two in the morning at San Isidro.

2. This letter to Fernando has not been preserved.

I have nothing else to tell you. Besides, I ought to keep it brief, as has been recommended by the military censor at Valladolid.[3]

I'm sure the land issue is well in hand. Believe me, I remember everything in my prayers. I very much wish you all the holy peace of living in Christ and for Christ in every moment.

Once again, do not worry about my health. If I didn't write you before, it's just because I figured you wouldn't forget about your son. Besides, if I had needed to, the infirmarian would have taken care of it.

When I pray to the Lord for Spain, I always include Uncle Paco and his family.[4]

Oh, if only we saw rightly . . . how little we'd complain about our own matters. Isn't that so, my dear father? Anyway, I don't want to go on too long.

Anything I'd tell you in a long letter, I'll save, and leave it at the tabernacle and at the feet of Mary instead.

A great big hug to all of you. Kissing your generous hands in God's name for all the help you have given me, I remain, your son, who remembers you in prayer,

Brother María Rafael
✝

I'll leave the amount of insulin to your discretion. For the sake of not bothering you with too many packages, just calculate the amount according to when you'll next come here. Besides, since I don't expect to die quite yet, I'll use whatever you send me. If you can find the 300-unit tubes, even better.

3. Valladolid is a city just south of Venta de Baños. Postal censorship was in place throughout the Spanish Civil War.

4. Uncle Paco and his family: Francisco "Paco" Fontanals had married Rafael's aunt, Fernanda Barón Torres, who died in 1926. Fontanals and their four children lived in Madrid (OC 30), which was under siege for the entirety of the Spanish Civil War. He died on March 28, 1939, the last day of the war, as the Nationalist forces took Madrid.

184. God and My Soul
You, Lord, Are My Hope

La Trapa, February 18, 1938

Fortunately, Lord, it is not only my spirit that is suffering! Until I came to La Trapa, I did not know what it was to cry of hunger. My illness is an inexhaustible mine of physical and moral suffering . . . Blessed be Your hand, oh good Jesus . . . I kiss it and adore it both when it strikes me and when it caresses me . . . Blessed be Your will!

Tears of hunger . . . who would have imagined it? And nevertheless, that is the reality. I am suffering so much, Lord! You know I am . . . How often I leave the refectory with tears in my eyes, and place my penance at the foot of Your blessed cross . . . this hunger that my illness produces, and that I will say is very infrequently satisfied here in La Trapa.

I remember my first Lent as a novice.[1] I was so happy to be fasting among the community. Where was the penance in that? . . . What of the *bread of tears* that is pleasing to Jesus?[2]

Back then, all I had was a *vain satisfaction* with the poverty of my nourishment . . . Perhaps from time to time I'd remember what I'd left behind . . . but I didn't experience hunger the way I do now, as my life has become and will remain a continuous Lent . . . lived amid the loneliness of the infirmary.[3]

When I get up from the table after eating, and physical, fleshly, miserable being that I am, go off to cry over the suffering caused by my illness at the foot of the tabernacle . . . oh, if I were an angel, I wouldn't cry! But I am human . . . and very human, as God knows.

---

1. See #33.
2. Ps 80:5.
3. See RB 49.1: "The life of a monk ought to be a continuous Lent."

Lord, help me . . . come to my aid in temptation. Don't leave me, Lord, for what can I do on my own? . . . Where can I bring my pain? Who will listen to my cries?

I am suffering, Lord, You know I am . . . How much further will You prolong this life of mine? It's useless to You and everyone else. Even though, in my generous moments, I wish I could suffer for the whole world, and I offer myself to You for whatever You wish . . . I have so few of those moments . . . the physicality of my flesh and the weakness of my spirit is so great that, as You can see, Lord . . . I so often falter.

I am nothing, and I am worth nothing . . . What can be expected of mud, this weak, sick, miserable clay?

Lord . . . Lord, do not delay . . . Help me. See how my feet stumble when I am alone . . . Look, I don't know how far I will make it. I want to make it to the end, Lord, but looking down at my bloody feet, in so much pain . . . will I persevere? . . . Don't leave me, good Jesus . . . Shelter me, Virgin Mary.

I don't know why I'm writing this! . . . I don't know why! Who wants to read about my weakness and misery? . . . I don't know, I don't even care, but since I don't talk to anyone anymore, it brings me consolation to fill up page after page writing as if I were writing to Jesus Himself . . . Perhaps it's a form of prayer, and He is listening to me.

Sweet solitude, which makes the soul draw closer to Jesus and seek Him alone.

Sweet penance, neglected by human beings, which makes one weep in silence, known only to Jesus.

I am happy, a thousand times over, when at the feet of Christ's cross, I tell Him all my cares, and only Him. I offer Him the profound joy of knowing I am loved by Him. Other times, when I am alone in my tribulation, I give my pained, sorrowful soul over to Him and water the foot of the cross with the tears of my penance . . . and I sing and weep and . . . all I can do is ask for love . . . love so that I can wait . . . love so that I can suffer, love so that I can rejoice . . . And in certain moments, I don't care about anything in the world, not human beings, or animals, or darkness, or the sun . . .

In certain moments, I even forget my hunger . . . I wish I could die embracing the cross of Jesus, kissing His wounds, drowning in His divine blood, forgotten by everyone and everything.

I am happy, a thousand times over, even if, in my weakness, I complain sometimes.

I desire nothing and I want nothing, except to meekly and humbly do God's will. And someday, die embracing His cross, and rise up to Him in the arms of the Most Blessed Virgin Mary. Amen.

185. *God and My Soul*

I Desire Only You and Your Cross

La Trapa, February 23, 1938

Lord Jesus! You are the only one who can console me in my exile among humanity, the only one in whom my soul finds rest. You are my only *teacher*, my only *guide*; be also, Lord, my help and support in times of temptation and weakness.

What did I come here in search of? Was it human beings? No, my God . . . no, it was not . . . I desire only You and Your cross . . . but (there's always a "but") I am still a human being, subject to fickleness, with a vain and capricious heart . . . Lord, I came here in search of You . . . but *I have to live among creatures.* What a great cross that is! . . . While loving You and yearning for You . . . I still have to live among human beings. With every step I take on this earth, I have to come across some misery or weakness or suffering. . . Living on this earth is so hard, Lord!

There was a time when I did go in search of human beings . . . I sought their comfort . . . I sought God in creatures . . . What a vain delusion . . . it caused me so much suffering.

I no longer expect anything of human beings . . . What could they possibly give me? . . . You alone, Lord, are my only hope.

Where are those who love You, my God? I was a fool when I first came to the monastery . . . Reality has opened my eyes . . . You upheld me, Lord, as I fought . . . (and I'm not done fighting yet . . .) When I faced disappointment in this life, I could have gone down another path, the world; but God's mercy upheld me, and upholds me still . . . And what a marvelous feat of Jesus that is!!! My soul expands and delights as my illusions are shattered, enthralled with the reality that *God alone can fill my life.*

<u>Alone</u> in La Trapa, detaching my heart from everything little by little, I am sharing my loneliness with God. What joy! But at the cost of so many tears. Temptation is so difficult sometimes.

The other day, I *realized and understood* something that deeply perturbed my soul . . . How is it possible, my God? I am a human being, and I suffered . . . how could I not? . . . I didn't know whether to weep or throw myself against the wall . . . I couldn't study, I couldn't pray, I couldn't think about anything else . . . My God, my God, where are those who love You? . . . How is it possible to live among human beings? . . . Lord, have mercy on me, the most miserable of all . . . I don't know . . . It's something you can only understand if you have experienced it.

As I walked frantically through the novitiate, not knowing what to do . . . I leaned out through a window, going against both my usual habits and the rules that prohibit this.

The sun was just coming up. A very great peace reigned over nature . . . Everything was just starting to wake up . . . the earth, the sky, the birds . . . Everything, little by little, was gently waking up at God's command . . . Everything obeyed His divine laws, meekly and gently, without complaint or distress: both the light and the darkness, both the blue sky and the hard earth covered in the dew of daybreak . . . "How good God is," I thought . . . "There is peace everywhere, except in the human heart."

And gently, sweetly, God taught me obedience too, using that lovely, peaceful sunrise . . .

A very great peace flooded my soul . . . I started thinking . . . only God is good. Everything is arranged by Him . . . What does it matter to me what people do or say? . . . There should be only one thing to me in this world . . . God . . . God, who arranges everything for my good . . .

God, who makes the sun rise each morning, and melts the frost, and makes the birds sing, and colors the clouds in the sky with a thousand different shades . . .

God, who offers me a little corner of this earth so that I might pray, a little corner where I can wait for what I am waiting for . . . God, who is so good to me . . . God, who speaks to my heart in silence and teaches it, little by little, sometimes through tears and always through the cross, to detach from creatures and seek perfection in Him alone . . . who shows me Mary, and tells me, "Behold, the only perfect creature . . . you will find in Her the love and charity that you do not find among human beings."

What are you complaining about, Brother Rafael?

Love Me, suffer with Me, I am Jesus.

Ah, the Virgin Mary! . . . Behold, the great mercy of God . . . This is how the Lord has been working in my soul: sometimes in desolation, sometimes in consolation, but always for the sake of showing me that I must fix my heart on Him alone, that I must live in Him alone, that I must love, desire, and wait for Him alone . . . in pure faith, without the consolation or help of human creatures.

What joy, O Mother of mine . . . I have so much to be grateful to God for . . . How good Jesus is!

Once I stopped looking up at the sky through the novitiate window . . . I started thinking . . . The Lord brings good out of bad things. If anyone had seen me, they would have thought . . . "There goes a novice wasting time."

Is it wasting time to lovingly adore God? . . . The temptation passed, the perturbation too, and as they did, I stopped thinking about what I'd heard. Uniting myself with God's will in prayer, something I do whenever I remember to do so, I went down to the church to hear Holy Mass. There, at the foot of the tabernacle, I lifted my heart up to God and Mary, Our Most Holy Mother, and I offered it to Him, so that He might *keep purifying it*, and doing with it as He pleases.

How great is the mercy of God! I have come to understand these words so well (I don't remember where I heard them): "I allured her into solitude, and there I spoke to her heart."[1]

Only You, my God, only You.

It is when I have most drawn near to other creatures that I have felt farthest from them, and the farther I am from human beings, the closer I am to God.

1. *Therefore, I will now allure her, and bring her into the wilderness, and speak tenderly to her* (Hos 2:14).

Blessed be the Lord. Any little hint from Him after a temptation or trial fills my soul with great peace.

186. God and My Soul
"I Am the Resurrection and the Life"[1]

La Trapa, February 26, 1938

Blessed be the Lord. Any little hint from Him after a temptation or trial fills my soul with great peace.

A good thought, a random word in a book, a verse from the Gospel is enough to scatter the darkness and fill my soul with light . . . Blessed be God . . . His servant Rafael blesses Him a thousand times over, not knowing how to thank Him for such kindness, wanting only to lose himself in nothingness so that he might glorify the Lord's greatness.

My life is a constant flow of desolations and consolations. My desolations are sad and painful, and sometimes very deep . . . they can be disturbing thoughts, or temptations that cause suffering.

Consolations are the same way, just the opposite . . . unknown inner joys, desires to suffer and love the cross of Jesus . . . they fill my soul with peace and tranquility in the midst of my loneliness and pain, which I wouldn't trade for the world.

Here is a recent example.

The other day, everything seemed *dark* to me. My somber life, *locked up* in the infirmary, no sunshine, no light, or anything else that might help me bear the weight that God has thrown down upon my shoulders . . . Illness, silence, abandonment . . . I don't know. My soul was suffering a great deal. Memories of the world and my freedom overwhelmed me . . . My thoughts were sad and gloomy. I felt no love for God, and I felt forgotten by human beings, with neither faith nor light.

My habit weighed upon me . . . I was cold and sleepy . . . I don't know, it was all piling up. The darkness of the church saddened me . . . I looked up at the tabernacle, and it had nothing to say to me. I felt *dead*

1. John 11:25.

though alive, trapped within the monastery like a dead man in his grave . . . worse than that, because at least there's rest in the grave . . . Anyway, this is what I was thinking about the other day before I went up to receive the Lord in communion.

I was obsessed with this idea of being *buried alive*, it was driving me crazy . . . The devil was determined to make me suffer, using my memories of the world, and light, and freedom . . . and he hinted at *joie de vivre*.

It seemed to me that the monks were souls in pain, that they too were *the living dead*, that they were trapped as in the grave . . .

Anyway, I don't have the words for it . . . At that moment, I wanted to die for real . . . *but in order not to suffer anymore* . . . Afterwards, I realized this was a temptation.

Such was the state of my soul when I went up to receive the Lord. I had just knelt down and was about to ask Jesus to put my spirit to rest when I felt this very great fervor and immense love for Jesus, and completely forgot about everything I'd been thinking about before, because I remembered these words that *I believe* Jesus gave me at that moment: "*I am the Resurrection and the Life.*"

Why attempt to put my soul's consolation into words?! I nearly wept for joy, finding myself at the feet of Jesus, *buried alive*. My hands gripped the crucifix, and my heart longed for death again, but this time *for love of Jesus*, for love of true life and true freedom . . . I wanted to die on my knees, embracing the cross, loving God's will . . . loving my illness, my confinement, my silence, my darkness, my loneliness. Loving my sufferings, which in a moment of light, with a little spark of love for God . . . are so quickly forgotten.

How little everything suddenly seemed to me! . . . How little is the world with all its creatures . . . How insignificant is my life with all its cares, and such childish ones at that . . . How insignificant are human concerns . . . How little is the monastery with all its monks . . . And so everything began to fade away in the light of the infinite goodness of a God who would lean down toward me to say, "Why are you suffering? . . . I am your health . . . I am the Life . . . What are you searching for here?"

Oh, good Jesus . . . if only people knew what it means to love You on the cross! . . . If only they had any idea what it means to renounce everything for Your sake!

What a joy it is to live without a will of one's own.

What a great treasure it is to be no one and nothing. . . to be the very last . . . What a great treasure Jesus' cross is, and how wonderful it is to live in its embrace. No one would ever guess.

Do with me as You will, good Jesus . . . Send me consolation when I need it, and don't worry about my distress and desolation; in them I find my happiness, my love, my . . . I don't know what I'm saying. . . Lord, I want to love Your cross madly . . . do not permit me to be parted from it.

This is my life as a Cistercian oblate . . . to suffer, to endure, and to love with abandon everything that God in His infinite goodness wishes to send me . . . He is the one who is doing it, and if my consolation comes from Him . . . so too does my pain . . . How could we not love the one who does it all for our own good?

How could we not go mad with joy upon realizing that God is the one who sends us our cross? How could we not adore that blessed cross until our dying day, knowing that it is our only health, resurrection, and life?

I don't know . . . if I keep writing, I'll get lost in thought. All I can say is that I have found true happiness in loving the cross of Christ. I am happy, completely happy, more than anyone could ever imagine, when I embrace the bloodstained cross and realize that Jesus loves me despite my misery, my negligence, and my sins, as does Mary. But I am of no importance . . . God alone.

187. *God and My Soul*
I Offered My Life to the Lord

La Trapa, February 27, 1938
Quinquagesima Sunday

Today, I offered the Lord the only thing I had left . . . my life. I laid it down at His feet, so that He might accept it, use it however He wants, and take it away whenever He wants, for whatever he wants . . .

When I left home, I also left behind, of my *own* volition, the care that my illness demands. I came here to embrace a state in which it is impossible to truly care for such a delicate illness. I knew perfectly well what I was getting into.

Even so . . . Poor Brother Rafael! Sometimes, without even realizing it, you suffered in being deprived of so many of your needs . . . you suffered in being deprived of your freedom to remedy the weaknesses of your illness, as you were always able to do back when you were out there in the world.

From the very beginning, you embraced the cross of Christ, but you would falter sometimes.

Other times, you'd realize that you were *knowingly shortening* your life being here at La Trapa, and that it was *the will of God* (not that of human beings) that the weight of your incurable illness would be heavier here than out in the world where *everything* was at your service, and this realization would make you suffer too.

Still other times, you'd suffer just because of your life as a sick person, from which you would *never get relief.*

But all that is over now.

This morning, I offered my life to the Lord. It is no longer my own . . . May He be the one to take care of it, if He wants, because I'm not going to worry about it anymore. I will deal with it, yes, because He's the one who has lent it to me, but . . . that is all.

If He wishes, He will send me the remedies I need. If He does not wish it, I'll be just as content without them. I won't worry about my health at all whatsoever . . . I'll take whatever they give me, do whatever they tell me to do, be obedient in everything.

I'll treat my body as if it were someone else's and seek only God's will. I will love His desires, and they will be my only law. If He wants my life to be long and painful . . . may it be so. If He wants to end it this very night . . . may it be so. Whether it's today or tomorrow or a thousand years from now, my life is His, my body is His, and my health is His for better or worse. He can bear the *responsibility* for whatever happens to me.

I asked the Virgin Mary to intercede for me with Jesus, so that He will accept my offering. What a great joy it would be if God were to accept it! What a joy it would be to die for Jesus . . . and for Jesus to offer my life to the Eternal Father in reparation for the sins of the world, for wars, and unfaithful peoples, and priests, and the pope, and the church!

I don't mind enduring suffering, so long as Jesus accepts my offering. I've already given Him my heart . . . I've given Him my will . . . Now I'm giving Him my life. I no longer have anything left, except to die whenever He wishes.

May His will be done, not mine.

I'm so happy not to have anything left! To not have to go around over-thinking everything, worrying about whether this or that is good or bad for me, about my medication or my diet, or whatever else . . . I'll do whatever they *tell me to do*, but that's it.

May the Lord *tend to* my illness as He pleases. And the less care He sends me, the more needy I am . . . all the better.

Lord, sometimes I wish I could die indigent, abandoned by everyone, on the street or in a public hospital . . . Dying of necessity . . . but I think that's a temptation . . . I don't know. I am in Your hands, and I entrust myself to the Virgin Mary.

I have noticed and realized that I am more fervent and closer to God the hungrier I am and the more my legs give out from under me.

The tears I shed in choir sometimes after collation[1] are very *helpful* to me.

---

1. Collation: a light snack when fasting.

At such moments, I suffer greatly physically and morally, but later, I come to bless God so profoundly.

Truly, I am nothing but misery, inside and out. When night falls, and I realize how tired my body is, how poor and needy my physical being is, how little and insignificant it is . . . And when I consider the childishness and futility behind the agitation of my spirit throughout the day, suffering for such petty reasons . . . And when I see how little the whole world is, even when it's crushing me . . . When I look at all that, and I compare it to the most holy cross of Jesus . . . would anyone dare think about themselves and say that they are suffering?

Oh, human selfishness! . . . You'll cry over an apple, get upset over something your brother said . . . let the memory of a sunny day in the world shake you up . . . and what's making you suffer is mere air and vanity.

Oh, human misery! You look to Christ crucified so little! . . . You suffer and weep for His sake so little! . . .

Humble yourself and eat dirt, Brother Rafael. Stop thinking about anything that's made of clay, anything that is a creature, or has to do with this world, or with you . . . Let your soul be filled with love of Christ. Kiss His wounds and embrace His cross. Dream of Him, think of Him, and fall asleep contemplating Him . . . How good it is to rest at the foot of the gentle cross! How good it is to fall asleep holding the crucifix tight!

How good God is!

188. God and My Soul
"How Long, O Lord?"

La Trapa, March 4, 1938

Blessed be the ever-adored, ever-tranquil, Most Holy Trinity.

Today, I take up my pen in the name of God so that my words, as they are printed upon this blank paper, might give perpetual praise to God, the blessed author of my life, soul, and heart.

I wish the whole universe, with all its planets and stars and countless galaxies, were a vast flat surface upon which I could write the name of God.

I wish my voice could speak with the force of a thousand storms, stronger than the power of the sea, more terrible than a volcano's roar, to say only this: "God."

I wish my heart were as great as the sky, pure as an angel, simple as a dove, so that I could keep God there.

But since all those majestic dreams cannot be realized, Brother Rafael, be satisfied with the little things. Nothingness itself ought to be enough for you who are nothing.

How hypocritical, for me to say I have nothing. . . when I have God! Yes, I do! Why keep it quiet? . . . Why hide it? Why not cry out to the whole world and proclaim God's wonders to every corner of the earth?

Why not say to all the peoples, to everyone who will listen . . . See what I am now? . . . See what I was before? See my misery, dragged through the mud? . . . Well none of it matters. Behold, and be amazed: *in spite of it all*, I have God. . . God is my friend. . . the God who could cast down the sun and make the sea draw back in awe . . . that God loves *me* so dearly that if the whole world had any idea, every creature on earth would go mad and howl with astonishment.

But even all that. . . is nothing in comparison.

God loves me so much that even the angels cannot fathom it.

How great is the mercy of God! That He should love me . . . and be my friend . . . my brother . . . my father, my master . . . when He is God, and I am what I am!

Oh, my Jesus, I don't have enough paper or ink! What can I say?! . . . How could I not go mad? . . . How can I go on living, eating, sleeping, talking, and dealing with everyone? How could I possibly have the composure to think about something the world might consider reasonable when I'm losing my mind thinking about You?

How is any of it possible, Lord?! . . . I know how, You've already explained it to me . . . It's possible through the miracle of grace.

If only the world that is searching for God knew . . . If only those sages who go looking for God in science and endless debate knew . . . If only people knew where to find God . . . how many wars would be prevented . . . how much peace there would be in the world . . . how many souls would be saved.

You senseless fools, you who go looking for God where He is not.

Listen . . . and be astonished. God is in the human heart . . . I know He is. But look, God lives in human hearts when they are detached from everything that is not Him; in the hearts that realize God is knocking at the door, and go around sweeping and cleaning up their lodgings, preparing to welcome the only One who can truly satisfy.

How sweet it is to live like this, alone with God in one's heart. To be filled with God is such great tenderness. How easy it must be to die like this.

It isn't very hard to do what He wants . . . or rather, it's not hard at all for the one who loves His will. Even pain and suffering become peace, because one suffers for the sake of love.

God fills the soul . . . and fills it completely.

There is no room for creatures or the world, there is nothing that can disturb the soul . . . It suffers only at the thought of offending God and losing Him . . .

Bring on the sages asking where God is. God is where no sage, with all their arrogant learning, can reach . . . God is in the detached heart . . . in the silence of prayer, in voluntary sacrifice to pain amid the emptiness of the world and its creatures . . .

God is on the cross, and as long as we fail to love the cross, we will never see or feel Him . . .

May human beings fall silent. All they do is make noise.

Oh, Lord, how happy I am in my solitude . . . I love You so much in my loneliness . . . There is so much I wish I could offer You, but I cannot, because I've already given You *everything* . . . Go ahead and ask me, Lord, but . . . what more can I give?

Do you want my body? You already have it. It's yours. My soul? . . . Lord, what desire does my soul have, other than its longing for You to come and take it? My heart? . . . It is at Mary's feet, weeping with love . . . no longer wanting anything but You.

My will? . . . Is there anything I desire that You do not? Tell me if there is . . . tell me Your will, Lord, and align mine with it . . . I love everything You send me and demand of me, sickness as much as health, here as much as there, this as much as that.

My life? . . . Take it, my Lord God, whenever You wish.

How could I not be happy?!

If only the world and humanity knew. But they'll never find out; they're very busy with all their concerns, hearts full of things that are not God. The world lives for worldly ends; people dream about this life, about everything that is vanity, and so . . . they cannot find true happiness, which is love for God. They may come to understand this, but in order to feel it, you have to live it, and very few will renounce themselves and take up their crosses . . . even among monks . . .

Lord . . . You allow such things . . . Your wisdom must have its reasons. Take me by the hand, and do not let my feet stumble. If You don't . . . who will help me? And if You don't build me up?

Oh, Lord, I love You so! *How long, O Lord?!*[1]

Virgin Mary, tell Jesus that I want to go mad and do crazy things for His love. Tell him . . . to forgive me . . . He will do it, Blessed Mother, if You tell Him to. Amen.

---

1. Ps 13:1.

189. God and My Soul

Jesus Is Where I Belong!

La Trapa, March 7, 1938

The world finds it so easy to judge, and it makes mistakes rather easily, too. To my family, it's the most natural thing in the world that I am here in La Trapa.

My brothers and sister, carried away with affection, want me to be happy. While I was in the world, they saw that I wanted to live and die a Trappist . . . Now that I'm here in the monastery, they say . . . "God help you. You're finally *where you belong*; God willing, may you never have to leave it again . . . You're happy in the monastery. The world isn't the place for you."

These are the sorts of reasons, among others, that my family gives. It makes sense . . . they *don't understand* my vocation.

If only the world knew what a continual martyrdom my life is . . . If only my family knew that *where I belong* isn't La Trapa, or the world, or among any creature, but rather in God, and God crucified . . .

My vocation is to suffer, to suffer in silence for the whole world; to immolate myself with Jesus for the sins of my brothers and sisters, for priests, for missionaries, for the needs of the church, for the sins of the world, and for the needs of my family, whom I do not want to see enjoying earthly abundance but rather very close to God.

Oh, if only the world understood what my vocation to La Trapa is . . . If only they could see the cross behind a peaceful smile; if only they could see the great battles taking place within monastic peace . . . But no, they shouldn't see any of that . . . God alone. It's better that way.

I'm not complaining, I'm not bitter . . . no, it's *the other way round*.

My longing for the cross isn't getting any weaker. My greatest joy is to be unnoticed. I understand my vocation, and I praise God for it by embracing it with my whole heart . . . How sweet it is to suffer for Jesus, just for Him and for His concerns.

The world thinks La Trapa is where I belong. . . .what a contradiction. Jesus is where I belong, His cross is where I belong. . . .I don't care about La Trapa at all. . . .if God were to show me *some other place* where I might *suffer more*, and He asked me to go, I'd walk there blindly.

Sometimes I don't understand myself. I'm absolutely happy in La Trapa, because I'm completely miserable here.

I wouldn't trade my sufferings for all the gold in the world, yet at the same time, I weep over my tribulations and my distress as if I can't go on living with them.

I long for death so that I can stop suffering, yet at times I very much don't want to stop suffering even after I die.

I'm crazy, I've gone mad, I don't know what's happening to me, Sometimes, alone in prayer at the foot of Jesus' cross, at Mary's side, I find repose.

May He come to my aid. Amen.

190. God and My Soul
"Nothing That Comes to an End Is of Great Value"

La Trapa, March 8, 1938

Only God and His will occupy my life. In His infinite mercy, He is *tempering* what was once vehement desire. How great is God's grace as He fills the soul, little by little. The vanity of everything that is human becomes clearer and clearer. At the same time, one becomes convinced that true wisdom, true peace, and true life can only be found in God, who is all that the soul needs, its only love, its sole desire.

I was with Reverend Father Abbot the other day. I went to ask Him to permit me some penance during this holy season of Lent, which he refused. Instead, he told me that he would give me the monastic cowl and black scapular on Easter.[1] How joyful I was, my good Jesus! I wanted to hug Rev. Fr. Abbot . . . he is too good to me.

I've dreamed of wearing the cowl for such a long time now . . . What a joyful thought, that in just a short time, I won't be any different from a real monk (except that I won't be able to wear the crown).[2]

But afterward, when I went to thank the Lord for this blessing, I *clearly* saw that this is vanity in me. I realized that this is an honor that the community is giving me, and that is what *pains* me, more than anything else. Oh, if only he'd given me a lay brother's habit[3] as I'd suggested . . . that would have been something else entirely. But it's all the same to me.

In brown or white, with a cowl or without one, I'm the same in the eyes of God. I don't care one way or the other about external things . . .

---

1. The black scapular and monastic cowl are both proper to solemnly professed monks. Rafael is the only oblate ever to receive either in the history of San Isidro de Dueñas (OC 910).

2. Crown: That is, tonsure, a haircut that leaves only a ring of hair around the head. This style is no longer worn by Trappist monks (OC 910).

3. At the time, lay brothers wore an all-brown habit (OC 910).

I just want to love God, and I do that *interiorly*, without others finding out about it.

Honor or contempt . . . it's all the same to me, Lord. My slightly childish, vain joy over the prospect of wearing the cowl has already calmed down . . . I don't want anything worldly to disturb me, Lord, nor do I want to let anything to do with creatures rob me of the peace and calm of loving Your will alone.

And so, Lord, I see that all is vanity. You are not in a habit or a crown. Where, then? You, Lord, are in the heart that is detached from everything.

You, good Jesus, my divine Beloved, find joy in . . . Oh, Lord, what can I say! . . . in the human heart . . . I offer You mine.

Let me make my cell in Yours. Let me make my bed there, too. Let me live alongside Your Divine Heart, alone and stripped of everything. Then I'd have a laugh at all the habits and crowns and the beards of all the lay brothers in the whole world.[4] I'll always be the same to You, Jesus, won't I?

How foolish and childish the world is! A piece of cloth will cheer us up, while a cloud will get us down! One silly thing will easily make us think we are happy, and the next silly thing will make us downcast and discouraged!

How trifling we are . . . we live for exterior things, not realizing that it's all nothing . . . except loving and serving You, my Jesus!

Lord, I want to spend this Lent dying, little by little, to the many things I still have left, so that I might live for You alone, and so that one day, Lord, You will let me enter into the wound in Your side and make a little cell there next to Your Divine Heart . . . Won't You let me? I ask the Blessed Virgin Mary for this fervently. May it be so.

(You can't make a silk purse of a sow's ear.)

One day, when the *little* cross Jesus sent me was seeming very big . . . One day, when I was thinking of how much life I have left . . . to live as a Trappist, locked up in here forever . . . and it seemed as though it would be very long . . . One day, when I was suffering because I *thought* my path was very long and painful, I read these words . . .

NOTHING THAT COMES TO AN END IS OF GREAT VALUE

---

4. At the time, lay brothers wore beards (OC 911).

191. God and My Soul

Virgin Mary, I Offer You My Will

La Trapa, March 9, 1938

My most beloved Jesus,

I can see that humility and patience are the two things I need most right now.

After a little over an hour in Latin class with the oblates,[1] I left with an exhausted spirit and tense nerves. How often, Lord, I grasp the crucifix and make an act of submission to Your will . . . but Lord, I cannot get my nerves under control. If only I had true and perfect patience!

Most Holy Virgin Mary, I offer this little suffering to You in reparation for all the times I've offended You in my studies and in university classrooms.

Virgin Mary, I offer You the *difficulty of paying attention* in reparation for all the time I wasted as a student. Virgin Mary, I offer You my humble obedience in class in reparation for all the sins of pride that I committed in the world.

Finally, Virgin Mary, I offer You my entire will and my submission to the divine desires of Your Son, so that You might present them to Jesus.

Receive it all, my Mother, as I place it in Your hands, even though none of it is so pure as I'd like it to be. Virgin Mary, look not on the offering itself, which is worth nothing, but rather upon my intention, which I do hope is to Your liking. Amen.

---

1. Other than Rafael, the oblates who lived at the monastery during this period were children who were raised and educated by the monks. While those preparing for ordination would normally study Latin separately from the oblates, the monastery was short on teachers during this period, so Rafael attended the same class as the children (OC 912).

192. Dedication of a Holy Card to Br. Damián Yáñez[1]

La Trapa, March 9, 1938

✠ May the Most Holy Virgin Mary help you while you are away from the monastery. Such is the fervent prayer of this oblate who, even though he is not able to accompany you at the front, is nevertheless *fighting* in his own way for God and Spain.

Your most humble brother in Jesus and Mary,

Brother María Rafael

---

1. Rafael's former co-novice, Br. Damián Yáñez, visited the monastery for a few days while on leave from his military service (OC 913).

193. *God and My Soul*

Lord, How Hard It Is to Live!

La Trapa, March 13, 1938

In the name of the Father and of the Son and of the Holy Spirit.

Lord! How is it possible to keep on living, when you're waiting for what I'm waiting for? How could I possibly think about all the created things that surround me, when I have You? I'm amazed that Your grace hasn't killed me. There's so much of it, in such abundance!

I dream of Your glory. Sometimes, I'm just living in a daze, not knowing what I want . . . because I love You so much.

Creatures exhaust me so much, my Lord and my God! What great displeasure I feel whenever I have to deal with things of this world, talk about temporal concerns, hear news! . . . Oh, Lord! I don't want to know anything, or hear anything . . . Only You, Lord, only You.

Nothing satisfies me . . . My soul desires nothing . . . not even joy, nor suffering . . . It just wants to love madly. Only the thought of You satisfies it . . . Such great longing, Lord . . . how hard it is to live!

Before, *everything* pointed me toward You . . . Everything spoke to me of Your great goodness, of Your grandeur. I praise You in Your creatures now too, Lord, but . . . the sun seems small to me . . . the blue sky is beautiful, but it isn't You, the beauty of all the world . . . in comparison, it's such a small thing.

You are changing my soul so much! . . . What a wonderful miracle. Creatures say nothing to me now . . . it's all noise . . . Only in silence, apart from everything and everyone, can I find the peace that is Your love . . . It is only in the humble sacrifice of my loneliness that I find what I am searching for . . . Your cross . . . and You are on that cross, and You are alone, with no light, no flowers, no clouds, no sun . . . Creatures abandoned You; the sky darkened. All that remained was the silence of Golgotha, a God nailed to the cross.

Lord Jesus . . . look at me, at Your feet, adoring Your agony, kissing Your wounds, wiping away Your divine blood with my pain . . .

Lord, I so wish to die of love at Your feet . . . forgotten by all; not making any noise; in silence; not thinking about people, who are creatures; not dreaming about the world that abandoned You; not turning my gaze toward the sky, or the flowers, or the birds, or the sun.

Lord, I wish to die of love at the foot of Your cross. What divine miracle did you perform in my soul? Where have my sufferings gone? . . . What about my joys? And my hopes and expectations? . . . They've all flown away.

My sufferings were just selfishness . . . My joys, vanities . . . My hopes and expectations, swept away at the touch of Your love. You showed me human beings and said to me, "What can they give you that I cannot?" . . . And I saw miseries that made me cry . . . I looked for comfort and did not find it. I looked for love and . . . Lord, what can I say? I found it only in You.

Nothing matters to me anymore . . . The only thing that is making me suffer is the wait . . . the fear of losing You . . . having to keep living.

I no longer mind living all locked up within these walls, not being able to see sunsets or enjoy the sea breeze or fly around the world on the wings of freedom. Those are all small things, they're nothing. I would rather have Jesus in my solitude.

I no longer care about creatures, and human weaknesses no longer hurt me . . . They're human, that's all. I find my refuge in God alone; I must look for love in Him alone.

I no longer care about my life, or whether I'm healthy or sick . . . I find consolation only in doing His will . . . and that fills me with such joy. Sometimes my heart is so full that it's as if it were going to burst . . .

How good God is, how great is His mercy . . . how wonderful is Jesus' love for me . . . How far will it go?

I don't know, Lord . . . I am stunned and stupefied. I bury myself in my littleness and yearn to be able to offer You even a little bit of love. I am nothing, I am worth nothing, all I have is misery and sin . . . and despite it all . . . You, Lord, care for me and console me . . . You draw me apart from other creatures and fill me with Your love . . . What can I say?

I would rather fall silent . . . but even if perhaps no one will read it, writing about this great miracle that You are performing in my soul makes me feel as though I am giving You a little bit of glory, for my writing is often a prayer.

Lord Jesus, how good You are.

One of the great things You have done is a transformation in my soul with respect to love of neighbor. I will explain.

Before, when I looked for a *monk* and instead I found an *ordinary human being* . . . I suffered so much, my good Lord!

When a brother would unknowingly humiliate me (humiliate *me* . . . what a contradiction!), I would suffer then, too . . .

When my soul did not find what it was looking for . . . even if it was just education . . . I've spent so much time at the foot of the cross . . . as You know, Lord.

I lost hope . . . and during such times of distress, I would think . . . it's better this way . . . I must detach my heart from human beings, and give it over to God alone . . . There were days when I didn't even want to make signs[1] . . . And amidst all that (I have come to see this clearly now), there was a great deal of pride, a lot of vanity, and just massive self-love . . . Sweet and gentle Jesus . . . forgive me, I did not know what I was doing . . . I am alone, without a guide . . . if You do not help me, I will stray a thousand times over from the true path, which is the love of Christ.

Something strange happens to me now. Some days, when I leave prayer, even if I feel that I didn't do anything while I was praying, I have such a great desire to love all the members of the community with such great longing . . . as Jesus loves them.

Some days, after receiving the Lord in communion, and realizing that He loves me *despite what I am*, I feel like enthusiastically kissing the ground that the monks walk on. I have such a great desire to humiliate myself before those who I thought had humiliated me.

They are monks at God's service . . . Jesus loves them . . . I am the last, the most worldly, and the most burdened with sins . . . Oh, if only the world knew what I once was!

Oh, Lord! In such moments, I wish everyone would trample on me. I feel such great love and charity toward all that I wouldn't mind if the very least among them were to order me to do the most humiliating of

---

1. That is, communicate using Cistercian sign language.

things . . . I see no weakness or misery in anyone . . . *I see only my own wretchedness, loved by God* . . . and looking at that, what would I not do so that I might imitate Him? . . . And so I must love my neighbor dearly!

How great is Your mercy, Lord! What credit is it to us if we love those who are good and holy?[2] Was Jesus not nailed to the cross for sinners' sake?

Good Jesus, fill my soul with love . . . It is the only food that can truly nourish me in this life . . .

I don't know if I'm explaining this well . . . but *I understand very well* what is happening to me.

Oh, Lord! I feel great peace in such moments . . . While I used to get upset over a brother's fault or weakness before, and feel almost *repulsed* by him, now I feel great *tenderness* toward him . . . and I want to do whatever I can to make reparation for that fault . . . He is a soul loved by Jesus. He is a soul for whom Jesus is bleeding on the cross . . . Who am I to scorn him?! . . . God forbid . . . Rather, I feel great love for this soul. This isn't just hot air, it's actual fact, and I am positive that I am not the one who has done this, but rather Jesus has done this in my soul . . . And that is the tremendous miracle.

I can see clearly now. Love alone can make you happy . . . In love alone can meekness and peace be found . . . In love alone can true humility be found, and in love alone can we live peacefully and happily in community. There are so many things I'd say, if only I knew how to write!

But I don't know how to, and faced with my inability to express what my soul is feeling, I'd rather be silent.

The Most Holy Virgin, who understands me without any need for noise or words, is my great consolation.

I place my silence before Her. Amen.

2. Matt 5:46; Luke 6:32.

194. *God and My Soul*

To Die for Jesus and Mary

La Trapa, March 19, 1938
The Glorious Feast of Saint Joseph

Blessed Jesus, I don't even understand myself. I no longer know what I want, or what I desire, or if I desire or want at all . . . My soul is a whirlwind. Sometimes I think my heart has been emptied of everything, and at other times I realize that it hasn't been . . . Which one is it?! . . . I don't know.

Lord, I have an *intense* desire to do Your will and only Your will; to immerse myself in Your will; to love it even if it kills me; to drown myself in it, and live only to follow it . . . *This is true.*

At the same time, I have some desires *of my own* for mortification and penance. I have such a great longing to suffer something for You, my good Jesus.

I wish I could die of hunger, if they'd let me . . . I wish I could stop breathing and talking, and just keep staring at the ground . . . I wish I could stop sleeping, or even lying down . . .

I wish I could stay on my knees before Your tabernacle all day and night . . . Oh, Lord! It's so hard for me to leave the church sometimes . . . and have to go deal with people.

Lord, whether I live or die, I wish I could do *something* for Your love . . . it's terrible, this useless life of mine.

I'm very fearful of my current situation. I'm being shown far too much *consideration*. They're going to give me the cowl, and nobody will trample me as I deserve.

I wish I could live in some corner of the monastery, wearing a sack, eating only the rinds of cheese left behind by the community . . .

Lord, I wish I could do crazy things . . . Instead of living as I do, I wish I could be forgotten, despised, even repulsed.

All of this is true. Does it conform to Your will? I don't know,[1] at least
not right now. Sometimes I think it doesn't, and sometimes I think I just
don't have the courage and resolution to take the leap and jump over it all.
Sometimes I think God is calling me down a path of greater penance and
prayer. More mortification, and less attention to my illness, or none at all.

Since they wouldn't let me carry on such a life in community, I could
do it under bridges or in the porticos of churches . . . wearing wooden
clogs with a sack over my shoulder . . . and disappear from the lives of
everyone who knows me, whether parents, or friends, or monks . . . no
one but God and me. They say that Saint Benedict Labre starved to death
in a church.[2]

I have given this all serious thought.

All my confessors, superiors, and teachers have to offer is prudence . . .
prudence and more prudence. They order me to eat, sleep, and refrain
from work . . . I am a delicate flower, good for nothing, not even a scent.

Meanwhile . . . I'm waiting to know what I ought to do. Will I know
it for *certain* someday? In God and Mary, I do hope so.

Lord, this is such a comfortable life! I've got my room; my bed, which
is a little hard, sure, but I'm used to it by now . . . I've got books; I'm
a little bit hungry, sure, but it's not killing me. In fact, it's the other way
around, I think I'm better now than I was when I got here. They don't give
me hard work to do . . . I have silence whenever I want it, because all I
have to do is retire to my room . . . In short, other than a few little things,
what more could I ask for! . . . And I feel something inside of me saying:
mortification . . . penance . . . sacrifice . . . *I'm not doing any of that.*

I set two things against this calling: 1. *Myself.* 2. *Prudence.* Flesh and obedience. My nature finds obeying perfectly *reasonable.* It's so comfortable!

"Father, can I get up for Vigils?"

"No, my son, you need to rest."

"Father, can I eat less?"

"No, my son, you need nourishment."

---

1. I don't know: in the original, Rafael circled this phrase.
2. Saint Benedict Joseph Labre (1748–1783) was a Franciscan tertiary from France who
lived as a mendicant. He did die of starvation in Rome, though not in a church, but rather
in a residence near a church where he had collapsed.

"Father, can I go out to work in the fields?"

"No, my son, you'll get tired."

Fine, then, I'll obey . . . and sometimes I obey while desperately wanting to do the opposite . . . to jump past all that prudence and . . . die for Jesus and Mary.

195. God and My Soul
I Am So Tired, Lord!

La Trapa, March 20, 1938
Third Sunday of Lent

I am so tired, my Lord and my God! *How long, O Lord? Will You forget me forever?*[1] . . . My soul delights in those psalms of David in which he weeps, weary of still living on earth and sighing for You . . . *Incola ego sum in terra*,[2] I say to myself over and over again, yearning for heaven, feeling like a foreigner and pilgrim on this earth.

I am so tired, Lord! It's so hard for me sometimes to have to deal with creatures who will talk to me about everything but God . . . Sometimes I have to seriously force myself not to start shouting, calling on God for help in this exile where, as Saint Teresa says, everything is an obstacle to enjoying Him.[3]

How long, O Lord!

People exhaust me, even the good ones . . . they have nothing to say to me. I yearn for Christ all day long, and in the midst of my desire for heaven and my love for Jesus, I have to drag this life of mine around, still subject to the world. I have to force myself to pay attention to eating and sleeping . . . Ugh! Forgive me, Lord . . . You want it this way.

I don't know what I'm saying . . . I don't know what I'm feeling . . . Forgive me, Lord . . . I'm so tired! My soul is suffering as it finds itself deprived of Your affection, trapped within this miserable body . . . I am sick, Lord, have mercy on me . . . I have been a great sinner. I don't know what I want, I don't know what is happening to me . . . Forgive everything

---

1. Ps 13:1.

2. I live as an alien in the land (Ps 119:19).

3. "My God, how sad is / Life without You! / Longing to see You, / Death I desire. / This earth's journey / How long it is; / A painful dwelling, / An exile drear. / Oh, Master adored, / Take me away! / Longing to see You, / Death I desire" ("Sighs in Exile," STA 3:382).

I'm saying, Lord . . . You know the depths of my heart, You can understand . . . People can't, but that doesn't matter to me . . . Let them keep busy with their things, their world, their worries . . . their vanities . . . Lord, I want nothing, I care about nothing . . . only You . . . Don't pay attention to anything I'm saying, I go crazy sometimes.

Yesterday, I wanted to die by penance; today, I understand that I can do nothing that You do not want . . . I am bound to Your will . . . what a joy!

Don't pay me any mind, Lord . . . I'm a whimsical child . . . But it's Your fault, my God . . . if only You didn't love me so much!

You must understand, my Jesus, given how much You love me and how much I love You, it's so painful to live like this . . . and of course, You'll understand why sometimes I have those desires to be freed from this body that causes me so many difficulties and to leave behind all these creatures *who are not You* . . . and why I get tired of waiting . . . As You can see, Lord, I'm weak and miserable . . . I don't know <u>how</u> to suffer, I don't know <u>how</u> to do Your will . . .

I'm just a poor man who wants to do *only* what You want and desire, and at the same time longs to fly to You and yearns to see the Virgin and the saints . . .

What a joyful day that will be, when I can see Mary, and Saint John the Evangelist, and Saint John of the Cross, Saint Bernard, Saint Francis of Assisi, and Saint Joseph, who are my protectors . . . and those two saints who loved You so much, who have taught me so much: Gertrude and Teresa of Jesus, and Saint Thérèse too . . . and all the angels . . . and the glorious Saint Raphael . . . and my guardian angel . . . And . . . well, You, Lord, whom I desire so much, whom I adore, whom I love above all things, for whom I long and pine and weep, and for whom, as You well know, my good Jesus, I want to lose my mind.

Lord, as You can see, I have all this inside me, and it's not possible for me to keep on living like this. I'm serious, Lord . . . I'm hopeless.

But forgive my boldness . . . who am I to say such things? I don't know . . . ignorant people say all sorts of things, and I am often ignorant of what I am and what I have been . . . shed light upon my darkness, that I might know myself better, and, in Your light, see all my miseries and sins and wickedness for which I still need to weep on this earth for a long time.

Pay me no mind, Lord, until I am made clean . . . Give me Your light, to understand. Holy compunction, to weep. Faith, to trust in it alone. Hope, to sustain me in my weaknesses . . . And above all, reigning over it all, Lord, fill me with Your boundless charity, with Your love . . . May it fill me, flood me, overflow from me, the joy of Your limitless love . . . and make me go mad for real.

Forgive me, Lord . . . I don't know what I'm asking for.

Mary, my Mother, be my help and my guide. Amen.

196. God and My Soul

A Visit with His Brother Luis Fernando[1]

La Trapa, March 25, 1938

My Jesus, how good it is to suffer at Your side, here in the hidden life of a monastery! . . . I feel so sorry for those in the world!

My brother came to visit me . . . I love him so much. He is an angel from God. His Christian way of thinking edifies me, as does his conduct, so serious and formal. There is so much raw material in his soul to be built up, and a heart ready for God . . . That's my brother, the kindly lieutenant.[2]

He came here on leave from the front, and . . . we talked . . . we talked about the world, and we talked about God.

Having spent the day with him, now that I am in the quiet of my cell, I am thinking about how good God is to have brought *me* into religious life, far from the world, to the feet of Jesus.

How happy I am, amid all my sufferings and sacrifices . . . How happy I am to be able to be a soul that suffers for Christ . . . How happy I am to be able to place my longings, desires, and even my weaknesses at the feet of Jesus in the tabernacle.

My brother and I talked about the world . . . and I came to realize what I'd already thought on other occasions: the vanity of the things of the world.

He talked about my family . . . their worries and concerns . . . We talked about future projects . . . He told me the details of my family's

---

1. Luis Fernando later testified about this last visit: "I asked him how he could spend all his time surrounded by the same people who were so different from him in their ways, and why didn't he go become a Carthusian so he could live in solitude. He told me, 'Luis Fernando, I cannot bear loneliness. I have to see faces, even if they make me suffer. You will be able to bear the solitude. With your temperament, you could be a Carthusian.' At the time, I hadn't even thought about being a Carthusian, so as usual I just said, 'typical Rafael.' But with time, the most curious thing happened: I became a Carthusian" (OC 926).

2. Luis Fernando was promoted from sub-lieutenant to lieutenant in the artillery corps on February 3, 1938.

new life, changes around the house. He talked about dogs and horses and cars . . . God knows what else.

How good God is to have separated me from all that . . . There is no longer anything that interests me . . . How happy I am with just God and my cross.

In the world, people are suffering . . . all those ambitions, desires, hopes . . . so rarely realized. In the world, there is weeping over material interests, so evil and despicable . . . In the world, *there is little weeping for Christ.* In the world, *there is little suffering for God.*

I feel such pity for the world! . . . People waste time on trifles. They waste time weeping over this life, which is just a mere breath in the midst of a tempest, a mere grain of sand in the sea . . . an instant in eternity.

I envy no one . . . I don't want freedom if all it has to offer is to make me forget about the only thing that is necessary, which is loving Jesus on the cross.

I feel such pity for the world! Amid all its desires for pleasure and happiness, it doesn't know that the only true fortune is to die embracing the cross of Jesus, among tears of pain, yearning and longing for heaven and for love.

I suffer a great deal . . . it's true. Sometimes, the weight I have placed on my weak, sick shoulders feels very great indeed . . . I look behind me and . . . it's so hard to live in poverty when you had everything and wanted for nothing . . . I look ahead and . . . the hill that I must climb looks so steep. Sometimes Jesus hides Himself away so completely! My life has become a *continual renunciation in all things.* And that is not easy for a creature as fragile and frail as I am . . . That's why I suffer.

Nevertheless . . . Oh, wonders of divine grace! I understand why I suffer, and that what is happening to me is the work of grace. (I don't know if I'll manage to put this into words.)

It gives me great joy to be able to suffer for Jesus, greater than I could have ever imagined. I love my cross more and more every day . . . and I wouldn't lay it down for all the world.

I remember when I was happy in the world, very happy. I had Christian parents, well-being, health, freedom . . . everything was smiling upon me. Who could think about suffering?

Jesus calls me. Loneliness, poverty, illness, all locked up without sunlight . . . at times, something very dark takes over and makes me cry . . . I don't know what it is.

I don't see God . . . and in the midst of it all, I shout with all the strength in my heart . . . "How happy I am!! I am suffering so much for Jesus!!" I don't want the world's happiness, I'd be miserable if I had it . . . I want to suffer for Him, even without seeing Him . . . it's enough for me to know that I'm doing this for Him.

The world cannot understand this . . . it's very hard. I know this is a grace from God, but I don't know how to explain it.

Today, with my brother, we talked about the world. I was sad . . . I felt far away from everything my heart loved, and loves still. I don't think that's wrong. Can anyone with a heart not love their home?

Even so, God continues to work in my soul. Deep within me, I feel a certain distance from everything that I cannot explain.

I have a very sweet and tender affection for my family, but it's different than it was before.

I take more joy in not feeling the love of Jesus than anyone could take in feeling the love of creatures. My *loneliness* makes me sad, it makes me suffer, and I wouldn't *leave it behind* for all the world.

I don't know if anyone will understand this.

It's so hard to explain why suffering can be loved! But I think it can be explained, because it's not a question of loving suffering *itself*, but rather what suffering is in Christ. Those who love Christ love His cross. I don't know how to bring this to a conclusion, but I do understand it.

And I love Jesus so much that I don't want anything other than Him. And I know that Jesus loves me so much that He would die of sorrow if He learned that I loved someone more than Him.

I feel so united to His will that when I suffer, I cease to suffer when I come to understand that He wants it this way.

I find myself in such a state that when I think about this, I get confused . . . I hope in Jesus that I will soon have a guide to explain all this and put my soul in order, because if not, I'm going to go crazy.[3]

Oh, Lord Jesus, I love You so much! If I had a thousand lives, I'd give them all to You . . . With Your divine grace and Mary's help, I can do all things. May You be blessed.

---

3. Rafael was without a spiritual director at this time (OC 590).

197. God and My Soul
A Little Piece of His Cross

La Trapa, March 28, 1938

Today, at Holy Communion, I asked the Lord for a little piece of His cross . . . I asked Him to be able to help Him in His agony, to make me a participant in His suffering, to give me a little piece (and it does have to be little, because I'm weak) of His most holy cross.

Jesus heard me.

I felt the cross upon my shoulders . . . it weighed down on me, and I cried, feeling abandoned and lonely . . .

After breakfast, I paced the hall in the infirmary with my little burden. A very great sadness came over me. I felt far too sick, alone, and weak to suffer what Jesus was asking me to suffer. I sat down, exhausted by everything and everyone, and I cried, overwhelmed and in pain.

I felt intensely abandoned, both physically and spiritually.

There is no one who can offer me relief. Sometimes that is a very great consolation, and sometimes it is also a source of very deep pain. Especially when we are sick. In such moments, a single word spoken to the heart can relieve so much pain, and it can even provide strength to endure the scourges and miseries of illness . . . But I don't even have that. Blessed be God.

It is so painful to experience bodily need when you also have spiritual needs, and meanwhile God is hiding Himself and leaving you alone with the cross . . . Is it any wonder that the soul should suffer and weep?

This morning, at that moment, I didn't remember what I'd asked Jesus for in communion . . . a little piece of His cross.

If only the infirmarian[1] realized how much hunger I am enduring! He doesn't really know or understand my illness, and he makes me suffer

---

1. Brother Domingo García, the acting infirmarian in Brother Tescelino's absence during the war, was not medically trained.

so much. God ordains it thus, and so He has provided. I do not complain, and I kiss the infirmarian's hand, which to me is the hand of God.

Hunger in loneliness and silence. . . sometimes I think I won't be able to keep going, but God helps me, and I get the feeling that everything will come to an end soon. On the one hand, I desire it. On the other hand, it's all the same to me, and I desire only to do God's will.

The day has passed, and with it . . .

I am at peace now. I adore and bless God, who is storing up these little pieces of His cross for me in heaven, and sending them to me whenever He wants. How great is His mercy toward me! If I weren't suffering in La Trapa, what purpose would my life serve?!

If you have such a strong desire for penance, what are you crying about?

Lord, these are not tears of rebellion . . . Lord, I wouldn't trade my tears for anything . . . Receive them, for I have to repay You somehow. You too suffered hunger, thirst, and nakedness. You too wept when You were abandoned.

Lord . . . I am so happy to suffer. I wouldn't trade places with anyone . . . but . . . *how long, O Lord?*[2]

2. Ps 13:1.

198. God and My Soul

When Will You Begin?

La Trapa, April 1, 1938

Always good intentions . . . Always a desire to be better . . . Always a desire for mortification . . . but they never become more than just desires . . .

What a poor man you are, Brother Rafael!! When will you begin? When will the moment arrive when you really start to be what you promised Jesus you would be?

It's still good for you to humble yourself in your own weaknesses . . . You still need to experience being incapable of anything good . . . What can you do on your own? Fall, and never get back up . . . Retreat, rather than advance. With Jesus, consider what you are, and come to know yourself. That way, you will not be proud. In your own humiliation, you'll learn something of humility, which you do not yet understand, and it is necessary that you learn it.

199. God and My Soul

Relishing the Cross

La Trapa, April 3, 1938
Palm Sunday

Today the community was fortunate to hear from the Bishop of Tui,[1] who came here for a few days of retreat. He gave us a short talk in chapter and spoke about the cross of Christ.

How can I express what my soul felt upon hearing such a holy prelate touch upon my foolishness, my absolute happiness in my exile . . . that is, love for the cross!

Oh, if only I could express myself as the bishop does! Oh, if only I had David's tongue, that I might put into words the wonders of loving the cross! Oh, if only my pen were made of spirit rather than physical, hard steel, and if only it could write what my soul really feels rather than clumsy words.

Oh, the cross of Christ! What more can I say?

I don't know how to pray . . . I don't know how to be good . . . I don't have a religious spirit, because I'm full of worldliness . . . I know only one thing, and it fills my soul with joy despite being so poor in virtue and so rich in misery . . . I know only this: I have a treasure I wouldn't trade for anything or anyone . . . my cross . . . the cross of Jesus. That cross is my only rest . . . how can I explain it! If you haven't experienced this . . . you can't even begin to imagine it.

If only every human being loved the cross of Christ . . . Oh, if only the world knew what it was to embrace the cross of Christ *entirely*, for *real*,

---

1. Antonio García y García, the former bishop of Tui, was appointed the new bishop of Valladolid on February 3, 1938. The diocese of Tui (now Tui-Vigo) is located in Galicia in northwestern Spain, while the Diocese of Valladolid is located immediately to the south of La Trapa.

with *no reservations*, loving it *madly* . . . ! How many souls, even religious ones, do not understand this . . . What a shame!

How much time is wasted on talks, devotions, and exercises that are holy and good . . . but they are not the cross of Jesus, they are not *the best thing* . . .

Oh, if only I could speak or cry out to people, telling them how sublime it is to love the cross! . . . You poor man, worth nothing, good for nothing, what crazy ambitions you have.

You poor oblate, dragging your life around, following the austerities of the Rule as best you can, let it be enough for you to conceal your ardor in silence. Love madly what the world despises because it doesn't know any better. Adore in silence the cross that is your treasure, but let no one notice. Meditate before it in silence upon the greatness of God, the wonders of Mary, and the miseries of human beings, from whom you should expect nothing . . . Carry on with your life in silence, loving, adoring, and uniting yourself to the cross . . . What more could you want?

Relish the cross . . . as the Bishop of Tui said this morning.

Relishing the cross . . .

Oh, Lord Jesus! . . . How happy I am . . . I have found my soul's desire. It is not human beings, or creatures . . . it is not peace, or consolation . . . it is not what the world thinks it is . . . it is what no one could imagine it to be . . . it is the cross.

How good it is to suffer! . . . At Your side, on Your cross . . . seeing Mary weep. If only I had the strength of a giant, to be able to suffer more!

Relishing the cross . . . Living as a sick person, ignored and abandoned by everyone . . . Only You, and on the cross . . . How sweet is bitter sorrow, loneliness, pain, when devoured and consumed helplessly in silence. How sweet are the tears shed before Your cross.

Oh, if only I could tell the world where true happiness is to be found! But the world does not and cannot understand this, for in order to understand the cross, you must love it, and in order to love the cross, you must suffer, and you must not only suffer, but love suffering itself . . . and so few are willing to follow You to Calvary in this way, Lord!

My Jesus, I wish I could make up for what the world will not do . . . Lord, I want to love Your blessed cross with all the longing that the whole world does not have for it, but would, if only they knew what treasure You have hidden away in Your wounds, Your thorns, Your thirst, Your agony, Your death . . . Your cross.

If only I could suffer next to Your cross, to relieve Your pain.

Look at me, Lord, kneeling at Your feet. I'm crazy, I don't know what I'm asking for or what I'm saying. I'm afraid to attempt something that is too much for me . . . Is it unwise for me to even try?

Lord, guide me down the path of humility . . . and that is all . . .

I am afraid, even though . . . forgive me, my Jesus. With You at my side, letting You do as You please . . . what do I have to fear?

Kill me if You want . . . Take my life and use it as You will. Open it, cut and carve me up, tear me to pieces, take me apart and put me back together . . . rip me to shreds . . . do whatever You want. I want only to love You madly, with wild abandon . . . To adore Your will, which is my own, transfixed by Your great mercy toward me . . . I see how much You love me . . . and I see what I am . . . and not daring to even look at the ground, I don't know if I should laugh or cry . . . I just want to die of love.

Anyway, I'm saying such crazy things . . . but Jesus does so many things for me that it's impossible to remain passive.

Nothing I've said makes any sense at all . . . but this is how I feel, that's all.

If I said that sometimes I have a great desire to start shouting . . . "Jesus . . . Jesus . . . Jesus!" like a crazy person, nobody would believe me. And then other times I want to lie down on the floor with my face to the ground, beg aloud for God's mercy, and never get back up again.

Still other times, I want to disappear, leaving behind human beings and flying to God, who is waiting for me . . . I don't know, I don't want to talk nonsense here.

My Lord Jesus . . . it's so difficult to live, and yet there are still people who love this miserable life and call themselves religious. Lord, I'm not a religious, I'm nothing and no one . . . I am the least of all . . . but Lord, I want to love You as no one else does . . . I despised the whole world for You . . . let me also despise the only things I have left: my will and my life.

But Lord, there's nothing meritorious about that, because forsaking the only thing that separates me from You is no great feat, and eagerly awaiting for whatever will get me close to You is no virtue. What credit is it to us if we hate our lives and wait for death?

But Lord, I don't want to hate anything You have given me, or want anything that You do not. May Your will be done, my Jesus. Just let me stay by Your cross . . . Virgin Mary, do not abandon me when I fall . . .

I will not seek comfort or rest . . . I want only to love the cross . . . to feel the cross . . . to relish the cross.

My Plan to Live Holy Week:

I will not part from Jesus' cross for even a moment.

While I sleep, walk, study, pray, and eat, I will be ever mindful that Jesus is looking at me from the cross.

When I wake up, I will adore the cross. When I go to bed, I will place my bed on Calvary right next to it.

Communion, prayer, and Holy Mass will all be offered in reparation for the whole world, which is *not availing itself* of the merits of Christ's passion.

I will pray the Divine Office thinking of my beloved Jesus, nailed to the cross.

May the Most Holy Virgin help me and accompany me . . . Amen.

200. God and My Soul

How Good It Is to Live Close to the Cross of Christ!

La Trapa, April 7, 1938

My Jesus, kneeling humbly at the foot of Your most holy cross, I earnestly beg You to give me the virtue of patience, to make me humble, and to fill me with docility . . . My Jesus, I need these three things so much.

I was slighted by one of the brothers yesterday . . . he made me cry. If You hadn't taught me from the cross to forgive, I might have committed an offense. How difficult it was to overcome myself! . . . But I slept more peacefully.

Blessed Jesus, what could human beings teach me that You are not teaching me from the cross?

Yesterday I came to see clearly that one can only learn by turning to You. Only You can strengthen us in our trials and temptations, and it is only at the foot of Your cross, seeing You nailed to it, that we can learn forgiveness, humility, charity, and docility.

Forget me not, Lord . . . look at me, kneeling at Your feet, and grant my request.

Come what may, slights, humiliations, or scourges from creatures . . . what do I care! With You at my side, I can do anything . . . The magnificent, admirable, extraordinary lesson that You teach me from the cross gives me the strength for all of it.

They spat on You, insulted You, scourged You, and nailed You to a cross, and Your response, God, was to forgive, humbly remain silent, and even *offer Yourself up* . . . What can I say about Your passion?! . . . It's best that I say nothing, and instead meditate within my heart upon that which human beings can never fully comprehend.

Let me be satisfied with loving the mystery of Your passion deeply and passionately. May I learn to suffer the way You suffered. I know that's the most impossible of impossible requests, but consider my intention, Lord Jesus.

How sweet is the cross of Jesus! How sweet it is to forgive while suffering!

How sweet it is to suffer while abandoned by human beings, embracing the cross of Christ!

How sweet it is to cry a little bit over our sufferings, and unite them to Jesus' passion!

How good God is for testing me this way, and teaching me from His holy cross! He shows me His wounds, pouring innocent blood; He shows me a demeanor that does not complain in the midst of agony and pain, but instead offers words of love and forgiveness. How could I not go crazy?! . . . He shows me His heart, open to all human beings, and yet despised . . . Has anyone ever seen or even dreamed of suffering that compares?!

How good it is to live in the heart of Christ! Who could complain about their suffering?

Only fools who fail to adore Christ's passion, Christ's cross, Christ's heart, could let their own suffering drive them to despair . . .

But those who truly love, those who experience what it is to unite themselves to Jesus on the cross . . . they can truly say that their suffering is delightful, that their pain is as sweet as honey, that it is a great consolation to suffer loneliness, boredom, and sadness at the hands of human beings.

How good it is to live close to the cross of Christ!

Christ Jesus, teach me to suffer . . . Teach me the science of loving scorn, injury, abjection . . . Teach me to suffer with the humble joy of the saints, never crying out . . . Teach me to be docile with those who do not love me, or who despise me . . . Teach me the science that You proclaim to the whole world from atop Calvary.

But I already know it . . . a very gentle interior voice explains it all to me . . . something I feel inside me, something that comes from You and that I cannot explain, unravels such a great mystery that human beings cannot understand it . . . In my own way, Lord, I do understand it . . . it is love . . . it contains everything . . . I know now, Lord . . . I need nothing more, I need nothing else . . . it is love. Who can put the love of Christ into words? . . . May human beings fall silent, may creatures fall silent . . . May we all be silent, so that in that silence, we might hear those whispers of Love, of the humble, patient, infinite, boundless Love that Jesus is offering us with open arms from the cross.

This mad world doesn't listen . . . Crazy and foolish, it rushes about, drunk on its own noise . . . it doesn't hear Jesus, who is suffering and loving from the cross.

But Jesus needs souls who will listen to Him in silence.

Jesus needs hearts who, forgetting themselves and going far away from the world, will adore His heart, injured and ripped apart by so much neglect, and love it madly, with wild abandon. My Jesus, sweet master of my love, take mine.

I place my heart at the foot of Your cross . . . next to Mary's. Take it, my Jesus . . . Show me Your wounds . . . Show me Your sufferings and bitter sorrows. Show me Your treasures, that I might learn to despise the world and everything that is not You . . . Show me Love . . . Place my heart next to Yours, that it might be besotted with Your delights once and for all, and be soaked in Your most pure divinity.

Virgin Mary . . . I'm crazy, I don't know what I'm asking for . . . My soul is talking nonsense . . . I don't know what I'm feeling. My words are clumsy and poorly arranged, but You, Virgin Mary, my Mother, see the desires of all your children, and so You will be able to understand.

I know I'm asking for a lot, because I'm asking for everything.

For my part, Mary, I have given Him everything. If I have *anything* left, take that too, Mary, and give it to Jesus. I know that even if I had a thousand lives, and even if I gave them all to Him, I still would not be worthy to receive even one good thought from God, but that's just how I talk . . . I know I've given Him everything and it's all . . . nothing. And so I do not claim to have what the world considers to be merits, that I might ask Jesus for a little bit of love. He gives love when He pleases, to whom He pleases. And since the sacrifices and renunciations I have made for Jesus are not enough . . . I offer You, Mary, something that You cannot refuse, something that means You must hear me, something that will make the heavens open, upon which the Father Himself will look pleased . . . and that is, Mary, the passion of Christ Your Son . . . It is the blood of Christ; it is the cross upon which the Son of God died.

See, O Virgin Mary? . . . With the cross, I can do anything.

Forget me not, Mother . . . and forgive this poor Trappist oblate's madness. He wants to go truly mad for love of You, Virgin Mother, and for love of his obsession . . . which is the cross of Jesus, his divine model. Amen.

201. God and My Soul
Palm Sunday

La Trapa, April 10, 1938[1]

Today, I take up my pen to keep praising God as always. I'd like to not talk about myself . . . and talk only about Jesus, but my God is so deep within me!! The work He is doing in my soul is so wonderful that in talking about myself, a poor and miserable sinner, and sharing what is happening in my relationship with Him . . . I am giving Him glory!

I'd like to disappear, and I am, in a way, because He fills everything . . . How good God is! I did nothing for Jesus, and yet . . . how great is His mercy! I don't know what else to say, and I don't know how to move forward, either.

My soul loses itself in this great wonder, and goes mute. All I can see is a poor creature, removed from the world (and what a world!) by grace, and only by God's grace, and brought into solitude in order to cooperate with one of God's greatest, most wonderful glories . . . almost without even realizing it.

And what is this wonder? This wonder is a stupendous miracle: that a soul like mine, poor, naked, full of the world and its vices . . . that a soul like that should be *loved* by God and *led* by Him down the humble path of penance, *upheld* by Him in its many weaknesses, miseries, temptations, and sorrows . . .

God, doing His work in my soul . . . transforming my heart and lifting it up to Himself, prying it loose from creatures and filling it with His love . . . God, the Eternal One, leading and guiding *me* . . . Who could not wonder at this? Who could not be astonished?

Oh, if only the world knew me and saw me for what I am! . . . If only people could see my ineptitude and hardheartedness, they would be in awe of the greatness of Jesus, who does not refuse to care for this poor man,

1. Rafael turned 27 on April 9, 1938.

more worthy of pity than love . . . And God loves me . . . Oh, and how He loves me! . . . I know it, and no one else does. If only I could share it! . . . If only I had the right words to express this!

But I don't know . . . I'm so inarticulate, especially when it comes to talking about this . . . And if I'm being honest, I'd rather roar or bellow like a bull than talk . . . How great God is!

Indifference is one of the transformations that Jesus has brought about in my soul. I am amazed at this myself, because I'm realizing that I've come to understand something I didn't before.

I knew that desiring nothing is very pleasing to God, and that this is the way to follow His will . . . But I only *knew* that because of the light of intelligence . . . I understood this sublime doctrine with my reason. I *wanted* to obtain that virtue of holy indifference, and I asked Jesus for it.

There's nothing meritorious about desiring nothing if you love God. It's the most natural thing in the world. That's how I see it now.

How can one love vanity while loving God? And everything we desire that God does not desire is vanity. It's only logical for those who truly love God to want only what God wants . . . Our desires *do not exist* outside of His desires . . . if we do have any, they are conformed to His will; if not, then our will is not united to His . . .

If we are truly united in love to His will, we will desire nothing that He does not desire, we will love nothing that He does not love, and *abandoning* ourselves to His will, we will be indifferent toward everything He sends us, any place He might put us . . .

We will not merely be indifferent to everything He wants from us, but rather, we will be pleased by it. (I don't know if I'm wrong about any of this; in everything, I submit to those who understand. I'm just saying how I feel, which is that I truly don't want anything except to love Him, and I give Him back everything else. May His will be done.)

Every day I am happier to have completely abandoned myself in His hands. I see His will in even the smallest, most trivial things that happen to me.

From all of it, I take away a lesson that helps me to better understand His mercy toward me.

I love His designs dearly, and that is enough for me. I am a poor man who doesn't know what's best for him, and God takes care of me better than anyone could imagine.

What's so special about my not desiring anything, if placing my desire in God alone and forgetting everything else is so good for me?

Rather, it's not that I forget my desires, but that they have become so unimportant and irrelevant that they are not simply forgotten but in fact *disappear*. My spirit is left only with a great contentment, realizing that all it earnestly desires is to do what God wants from me, and a great joy, realizing I have been relieved of a very great burden and that I am free from my will, which I have laid down next to that of Jesus.

The only desire I have left is a very great longing to *obey*. I don't want to decide anything for myself, but rather to be ordered to do absolutely everything. I still have a lot of freedom, and since I don't have a spiritual director, sometimes I'm very afraid of being wrong and mistaking my mere whims for God's will.

My Jesus, help me.

Virgin Mary, don't leave me.

If someone were to tell me in detail what I must do in order to be holy and pleasing to God, I think that with the help of God and Mary, I would do it all.

With Jesus at my side, nothing seems difficult to me, and the path toward holiness looks simpler and simpler. I think it's a matter of subtracting things, rather than adding them. It's about cutting down toward simplicity, rather than cluttering with new things.

And I think the more we detach ourselves from disordered love for creatures and for ourselves, the closer and closer we get to the only love there is, the only wish, the only desire in this life . . . true sanctification, which is God.

How good God is, to go about teaching me all this! . . . How good God is to me! . . . Will I repay Him as I ought?

Lord, do not look upon my actions or my words, but rather my intentions, and when they are not directed toward You, right them. Do not permit me, my Lord, to be ungrateful or waste time.

How good it is to live far away from human beings and close to You . . . When I hear the noise that the world is making, when I see the sun flood the countryside, illuminating the birds flying free, when I remember the happy days I lived at home . . . I close my eyes and ears, quiet the voice of my memory, and say . . . "What happiness, to live with Christ

. . . I have nothing, and I have Christ . . . I possess and want nothing, and I possess and want Christ . . . I enjoy nothing, and Christ is my joy."

And deep within my heart, I am absolutely happy, although that's not really the word that best describes the state of my soul.

Creatures are of no importance to me, if they don't point me toward God. I don't want freedom, which doesn't lead me toward God. I don't want consolations, joys, or pleasures. All I want is solitude with Jesus, love for the cross, and tears of penance.

My Jesus, my sweet love, do not permit me to be parted from You.

Mary, my Mother, be my only consolation.

The other day I tried on the cowl that Reverend Father Abbot will let me wear beginning on Easter, as a special favor. It was always such a big dream of mine to be able to wear the Cistercian cowl someday. But . . . it's so new and so white that later I felt so embarrassed and ashamed to have had that childish desire. *For me*, this is nothing but a vanity with regard to human beings.

Now, when Christ, my Master, is being stripped in front of the crowd as they insulted him . . . this is how they dress me . . . Does this really give me something to brag about? . . . I'd be a fool if I were not to find it deeply humiliating for <u>me</u>, the last among Christ's disciples, to present myself to the community on Easter with a shiny new Cistercian cowl . . . It would've been better if they'd given me a sack to wear.

But that too would have been a childish vanity, and to be honest, today I came to the conclusion that it's all the same to me. At the end of the day, whether I'm wearing silk or wool or a sack doesn't change my heart, which is all that will matter in God's eyes someday. Everything else is external and might matter in the eyes of human beings, but they are not the ones who will be judging me.

Lord . . . Lord . . . what fools we human beings are!! A piece of cloth can please us, and a grain of sand can pain us.

Have mercy on us human beings, Lord!

202. God and My Soul
Holy Tuesday

La Trapa, April 12, 1938

I only find what I'm looking for in God, and I find it in such abundance that I no longer mind that I cannot find what I once dreamed of in human beings. That dream has come and gone . . .

I looked for truth and I didn't find it. I looked for love, and all I saw in human beings was a few drops that wouldn't satisfy my thirsty heart . . . I looked for peace, and I realized that there is no peace on earth.[1]

That dream came and went, but quietly, before I'd even realized . . . The Lord, who tricked me in order to draw me closer to Himself, is the one who made me realize it . . .

How happy I am now! "What are you looking for among human beings?" He says to me . . . "What are you looking for on this earth, where you are a pilgrim? What kind of peace do you want?" . . . How good is the Lord, who separates me from creatures and vanity!

I can see clearly now that true peace is to be found in God . . . that true love is to be found in Jesus . . . that the only Truth is Christ.

Today, at Holy Communion, while I had Jesus in my heart, my soul swam in the boundless, immense joy of having the Truth . . . I felt as if I possessed God, and God possessed me . . . I desired only to profoundly love the Lord who, in His great goodness, was consoling my heart, which was thirsty for something *I couldn't name* and searched for among creatures in vain. Without the noise of words, the Lord helped me to understand that He is what my soul desires . . . That He is Truth, Life, and Love . . . And that so long as I have Him . . . What am I looking for? What am I asking for? . . . What do I want?

1. Jer 6:14; 8:11.

Nothing, Lord . . . this world is too small to contain everything You give me. Who could explain what it's like to possess the ultimate Truth? Who could find the words to express what this means: "I desire nothing, for I have God"?

My soul almost weeps for joy . . . Who am I, Lord? Where can I put my treasure so it doesn't get tarnished? How could I possibly live in peace, without fear of getting robbed? What can my soul do to thank You?

Poor Brother Rafael, you'll have to answer to God for the great many blessings He has given you here! You must have a heart of stone not to weep for your great ingratitude and scorn for divine grace.

My Lord, I spend my life wallowing in my own misery, and at the same time I don't dream of anything but You, I don't live for anything but You. How does that make sense?

I am thirsty for You . . . I weep for my exile, I dream of heaven; my soul longs for Jesus, in whom it finds its Treasure, its Life, its only Love; I expect nothing from human beings . . . My Jesus, I love You like crazy, and even so, I eat, laugh, sleep, talk, study, and live among human beings without doing anything crazy. I'm ashamed to say I even . . . look for comfort. What explanation is there for this, Lord?

How is it possible that You have placed Your grace within me? If I made a return to You somehow . . . then maybe that would explain it.

Forgive me, my Jesus . . . I should be holy, and I'm not. And I'm the one who used to be scandalized by some of the miseries of human beings? Me? . . . Ridiculous.

You've already given me *light* so that I might see and understand, Lord; now give me a very, very big heart so that I can *love* human beings, who are Your children, and my brothers and sisters. My great pride saw flaws in them, while I was blind to my own.

And if You were to give the least of them what You have given me? But You do all things well . . . My soul weeps over its bad habits in the past, its old ways . . . It no longer looks for perfection in human beings . . . it no longer cries about not finding *a place to rest* . . . it has all of that now.

You, my God, are the one who fills my soul; You are my joy, my peace, and my calm. You, Lord, are my refuge, my strength, my life, my light, my consolation, my only Truth and my only Love.

I'm so happy. I have it all!

I am filled with such tenderness when I think about these fathomless favors that Jesus grants me. My soul is filled with true love for human beings, for my weak, sick brothers and sisters . . . It is understanding now, and sweetly forgives the weaknesses that used to make it suffer when it would see them in its neighbor . . . Oh, if only the world loved God a little, they would love their neighbor too.

When you love Jesus, when you love Christ, you also *necessarily* love what He loves. Did Jesus not die of love for human beings? As our hearts are transformed into the heart of Christ, then we too feel this and note its effects . . . and the greatest of them all is *love . . . love for the Father's will . . . love for everyone* who suffers and struggles, whether they're a father or a far-off brother, whether they're English, Japanese, or Trappist . . . *love for Mary . . .* In short, who can comprehend the heart of Christ? No one. But there are those who have tiny pieces of it . . . very hidden away . . . very much in silence, without letting the world notice.

My Jesus, how good You are. You do everything so wonderfully well. You show me the way; You show me the end.

The way is the sweet cross . . . it is sacrifice, renunciation, and sometimes the bloody battle that ends in tears on Calvary or in the Garden of Gethsemane; the way, Lord, is to be the last, to be the poor, sick, Trappist oblate who suffers by Your cross sometimes.

But it doesn't matter. To the contrary . . . one can only enjoy the gentleness of pain through humbly suffering for You. Tears shed at Your cross's side are a balm in this life of continual renunciation and sacrifice, and those sacrifices and renunciations are made pleasant and easy when the soul is alive with love, faith, and hope.

This is how You turn thorns into roses. So then, what is the end? . . . You are the end, and only You. The end is eternal possession of You in heaven with Jesus and Mary and all the angels and saints. But that will happen in heaven. And to encourage those of us who are weak, feeble, and fainthearted like me, sometimes You reveal Yourself to our hearts and say . . . "What are you looking for? What do you want? Who are you calling out for? . . . Take Me, consider who I am . . . I am the Truth and the Life."[2]

2. See John 14:6.

And then You flood the soul with delights that the world doesn't know about or understand. Then, Lord, You fill the souls of Your servants with ineffable sweetness, which they ponder in silence. Human beings hardly dare to begin to explain this . . .

My Jesus, I love You so much, in spite of what I am . . . and the worse and more miserable I am, the more I love You . . . and I will always love You, and I will cling to You and never let You go,[3] and . . . I don't know what else I was going to say.

Help me, Virgin Mary!

3. See Song 3:4.

203. God and My Soul
Holy Wednesday

La Trapa, April 13, 1938

My dearest Jesus, my God. I can see, Lord, that I am not doing anything in Your service. I fear that I am wasting time . . . The hours, days, and months are passing me by, and it's all just good words and good desires. The actual works never appear.

Today, Lord, during Holy Mass, I saw my great uselessness, and as always, I meditated upon Your great blessings . . . In your boundless mercy toward me, You watch over me, allowing me to approach the holy sacrifice *day after day*. And in contrast, I am a mere simpleton. My Jesus, when will I begin to serve You for real?

I'm always beginning, and never actually doing anything. I live a comfortable, pleasant, unmortified life . . . In part (and only in part) because my superiors won't let me do otherwise, and in part (the greater part) because I haven't made an effort, and austerity scares me. As a result, I'm not a layman because I live among religious, but I'm not a religious either, because I live like a layman . . . What am I then, my God? . . . I don't know, and sometimes when I think about this, I figure I don't care about being anything in particular . . . but what I do care about, and what I do worry about, is that either way I'm not doing as much as I should when it comes to mortifying myself, renouncing myself, and living more for You than for others or for myself.

I seek out so many comforts . . . I'm still very attached to my preferences and opinions . . . I often see that I am still that worldly Rafael, puffed-up, vain, and critical, whose whole life was about meals and fashion and vice . . . Oh, Lord! When I remember . . . let's leave it at that for today.

My Lord, I can see that while I might not be doing anything bad now, I'm certainly not doing anything good, either . . . I'm living the life of a

simpleton, in a monastery. I don't serve God physically or spiritually. All I do is say: how good God is, I love Him so much, He loves me so much . . . and just drooling over Him.

When I think about my uselessness, I truly start to worry. I owe God so much!

I don't do prayer, meditation, or reading right. As for work . . . I hardly work. When I eat and sleep, that's all I do . . . eat and sleep as an animal does. And I can't go on like this . . . I shouldn't go on like this. But I'm useless and sick . . . what can I do? Poor Brother Rafael! Let it be enough for you to purify your intentions *at all times*, and love God *at all times*, and do everything for love and with love . . . The act itself is nothing, and is worth nothing. What is worth something is the way you do it . . . When will you understand this? You're so hopeless.

When will you understand that virtue is not about eating onions, but eating onions for love of God? When will you understand that holiness is not about doing external acts, but rather the internal intentions behind any given act? . . . If you know this, why don't you put it into practice?

I do, Lord, but badly. I lack humility, and I want to follow my own whims . . . and do my own will, even when it comes to penance . . .

My God, my God, help me to humbly do Your will. Help me to serve You, loving my own weakness and uselessness . . . Lord, Lord, look at my intentions, and *purify them*.

What can I do without You? Even if I were to cut my own throat in the name of penance, what would be the point, if You didn't want me to and if I found vanity and self-interest in it?

Do with me as You will, Lord, but listen, my Jesus: do not permit the devil to deceive me. Show me what You want so that I can do it, and give me a humble spirit so that I can see it and do it. My Jesus, do not permit me to refuse Your divine intimations.

I understand that I can do more than I am now, and that You will accept it.

Give me strength, Virgin Mary!

204. God and My Soul
Holy Thursday

La Trapa, April 14, 1938

Today was a happy day for me. At Holy Communion, I promised not to abandon the Lord during the coming days of His holy passion. Forever at my side, very deep within my heart, very united to the suffering of Your cross. My Jesus, do not permit me to be parted from You. I love You so much, my sweet Jesus!

When I approached for communion, I remembered Saint John the Apostle, whom You allowed to lean against Your breast at dinner. Ought I to envy him? His virtues, yes, but not Your love . . .

My Jesus, I am not worthy, as You well know, and even so, You let me rest next to Your divine heart just like the beloved disciple. I promise to love You very much, like nobody else in the community, like all of them put together, and never to abandon You in Your sufferings or Your most sacred passion.

Virgin Mary, help me to be faithful to my good Jesus.

The day has passed . . . One more day toward the final count, one fewer day in exile in this life . . . Holy Thursday has passed, and with it, the consolation of having lived for God and with God. What will tomorrow be like? . . . I am afraid. I don't trust myself. I'm very afraid to be this happy with Jesus, and only with Jesus.

I've suffered so much over the past four years! My soul has been torn apart for so long! . . . And now that I can see <u>how necessary that was for this to happen</u> . . . I'm afraid, and I don't know what I'm afraid of.

Not suffering, it's not that. I'm not afraid of anything that comes from human beings. But now that I've had God . . . I'm afraid of losing Him. How good it is to live like this!

Today, Holy Thursday, when the Lord gathered His disciples and promised to remain with them forever, I too approached Jesus in my littleness, asking Him to remain with me, and welcome me at His table, and allow me to live with Him, and to follow Him everywhere like a shadow . . .

I asked Jesus to let me lean my head against His breast like Saint John . . . I asked Him not to push me away, even though I looked so weak and miserable . . . I asked Him to hear my petitions . . . I traversed the whole world showing Jesus everything that I wanted Him to take care of: Spain . . . the war . . . my brothers, my sister, so many people I love . . . my parents . . . Oh, what do I know?

I showed Jesus all this and told Him: Lord, *take me and give Yourself to the world.* Take what You have given me and give it to them . . . Let me distribute the treasure I have to the needy of the world . . . there are so many! Let me be poor at Your side . . . I want nothing more than Your love, Your friendship . . . Your companionship . . . Take me, Lord, as I am: sick, useless, lax, and negligent.

And the Lord heard me . . . I felt His love deep within me, so deep . . . I saw my boundless treasure, and I fear losing Him.

What am I to do? . . . I don't know . . . I hear people talking, arguing . . . I see them and their ambitions, bound to the earth . . . nobody is talking about God . . . It's all noise, even in La Trapa.

Lord, I wish I weren't living, so that the longing for love in my soul would remain undisturbed . . . for I am the one making the most noise . . . Clutching my crucifix, I want to die.

Everything upsets me . . . Only You, Lord! . . . Only You!

I am so afraid of losing You, my good Lord! I can see that You love me, but I can also see what I am, and what I have been.

How good it is to live with You! If only the world knew!

Tomorrow, Good Friday . . . I will be at Your cross's side. I don't mind that I won't receive You tomorrow in communion, because today we agreed that I wouldn't separate myself from You, and You seemed pleased with that. Today's communion will be good for today and tomorrow.

Oh, I don't know how to write! If I did keep writing, I would just say crazy things . . . It's best that I be silent.

205. *To Toribio Luis (Tescelino) Arribas*

La Trapa, April 15, 1938
Good Friday

Ave Maria
My dear brother Luis Gonzaga,[1]

Complying with obedience once again, I am replying to the last two letters you sent Reverend Father. Thanks be to God, he is better from his previous illness, although he is still on a very strict diet.

On his behalf, I thank you for your great efforts in response to all the requests that were made of you . . . The Lord will repay you for all of it. We will try to make the ointment you described using the gram and a half of chloramine you sent.

Indeed, it's very difficult to find medicine these days, but everyone's goodwill makes up for it.

That is all Reverend Father asked me to tell you . . . I am not authorized to send you his blessing, but I am sure you have it. All this poor oblate can send you are his many prayers to our Mother Mary.

Since I have quite a lot of paper left, and poverty commands us not to waste anything, I'll make use of holy obedience to write you a note of my own creation.

First of all, my dearest brother, *tú* and *usted* are of little importance among those who possess Christ's love, which Cistercian brothers like us ought to have.[2] Love in God knows nothing of formalities. One form of address or another is all the same to those who love one another in the heart of Jesus.

---

1. Luis is the Spanish spelling of Saint Aloysius Gonzaga's first name. The former Br. Tescelino reverted to his baptismal name Luis while away from the monastery on military duty (see #166, n. 1).

2. While Rafael and Luis were both outside of the monastery, they addressed each other using the informal *you* (*tú*) in their letters. Now that Rafael had returned to La Trapa, where the custom was exclusively to use the formal *you* (*usted*), he addressed Luis using *usted* in this letter.

As for your letter, all I can say is that the confidence you have in my prayers embarrasses me a great deal, as does Reverend Father's order to pray for my brother while he is away . . . God alone knows I do, but I dare not imagine the results of my poor prayers.

Take heart, my brother . . . don't give up. I know from experience what it's like to suffer while fighting against the world, and I also know that only a very deep trust in Jesus and Mary leads to triumph.

Meanwhile, how sweet is the peace in the house of the Lord afterwards.

Everything will come to pass, even the end of this exile that the Lord wants us to dwell in for just a little while . . . Take heart and don't give up, brother.

I wish my clumsy words would reach your heart, leaving a tiny little glimmer of peace in Jesus and trust in Mary there . . .

I wish to give my brother in the world a gentle reminder of the peace of the Trappist cloister. Surely that will help you fight and triumph over the world (I have no doubt about that), but . . . why explain what you already understand perfectly well?

All I can say for now is that it is very hard to leave freedom behind in order to embrace the cross, but once we do so generously, not even the whole world, or a thousand worlds, could possibly separate us from it.

How sweet it is to live close to the cross of Christ! God asks so *little* of us, considering how much He gives us!

Anyway, I don't want to go on too long; I don't think it's necessary. May Brother Luis be satisfied with Brother Rafael's humble intention, which is just to send you at Easter what I already said: a reminder of our dear, sweet Virgin of La Trapa . . . A smile from our blessed Mother, who is *waiting here for you*, not so that you can rest, but so that you can keep fighting under Christ's standard, embracing the cross and awaiting . . . whatever He wants.

Take heart, brother. You will always have my poor prayers, since you want them so much; their good faith will do more for you than my words. Don't you forget about this poor sick man either. He is at the foot of the tabernacle, hoping to see you back here again in your brown habit, praising God with a syringe in your hand.[3]

3. Luis Arribas did not return to the monastery after the war, instead continuing his medical practice as a layman. He moved to the United States, where he married, had two daughters, and had a long professional career in psychiatry. After being diagnosed with

I read your mother's article . . . She must be very good, and her way of thinking reminds me of my own mother. Don't worry about upsetting her again[4] . . . The last time I left my mother, the Virgin Mary put everything right.

Fr. Francisco asked me to give you his regards.[5]

Until obedience commands me to write again, a big hug and goodbye from your brother in Jesus and Mary,[6]

Brother María Rafael
☩

---

colon cancer, he experienced a profound conversion through the intercession of his old friend Rafael. Writing to his sister, Luis reflected, "It's not all suffering; on the other side of the coin, there is the joy of having renewed my friendship with Brother Rafael, who has taken me by the hand and helped me to rediscover the Master" (OC 292). Luis died on February 28, 1992.

4. That is, by returning to the monastery after the war.

5. Fr. Francisco Díez, sub-master of novices.

6. In this last line, Rafael forgot about the customary formality and addressed Luis as *tú*.

206. *God and My Soul*

Easter Sunday

La Trapa, April 17, 1938

Today, Reverend Father Abbot gave me the cowl and the black scapular. I'd be lying if I said I didn't let myself get carried away with vanity today. What a poor man I am!

Lord, Lord, have mercy on me. I am no greater or lesser in Your presence for being here or there, wearing this or that . . . We human beings are very childish, and so we play like children . . . We put our hopes in things that make the angels laugh. Lord, give me Your holy fear, fill my heart with Your love, and as for the rest . . . *Vanitas vanitatem.*[1]

I expect less and less from human beings . . . God's mercy is so great! He more than makes up for what they cannot give me.

I am coming to see, with complete clarity, that those who focus on earth and its creatures are wasting their time . . . Only Jesus can fill the heart and soul.[2]

1. *Vanity of vanities* (Eccl 1:2). Rafael makes a slight Latin error; this should read *vanitatum*.

2. These last two paragraphs were written in pencil, while the rest was written in ink. Mercedes Barón and Fr. Teófilo Sandoval agreed that it was probably added at a later date, making these two paragraphs the last things Rafael ever wrote (OC 964).

207. To Leopoldo Arnaiz Barón

La Trapa, April 17, 1938
Easter Sunday

Ave Maria
My dearest brother Leopoldo,

I'm addressing my Easter letter to you because I figure by now you're "in charge" enough to receive the paschal greetings this monk sends to his dearest family.

First of all, I should say that I received both packages of insulin that my father sent me . . . May God repay him. I hope to see him here soon, since Fernando told me he would be going to Oviedo shortly.[1]

Fernando, in all his brevity, hardly told me anything about what you were up to in Villasandino . . . Besides, he didn't learn much while he was there with you. He told me you were going to sell the horse, that you were building a water tank, that Francisca's[2] pig had fattened up, and that you were otherwise very happy.

I praise God for all of it, and all I ask Him is that you have more peace than abundance . . . I think He'll hear this poor Cistercian oblate's prayers.

Today, on Easter, Father Abbot gave me the black scapular and cowl, so other than the crown, I look just like a real monk now.

I'm so happy with my long sleeves that I don't know what to do with them. Oh, my dear brother, if only I had as much love for God as I have excessive fabric! . . . I have almost nothing to tell you, because as you can imagine, monastic life doesn't have much to offer in the way of news.

My life carries on amid studying Latin, holy reading, and singing in choir, praising Jesus and Mary.

---

1. Rafael's father visited him at the monastery on April 22, 1938 (OC 965).

2. Francisca was married to Eutiquio, the gardener at the Arnaiz-Barón residence in Villasandino (OC 966).

Some days, my work involves a pencil and paintbrush, when Reverend Father Abbot asks me to use them for an assignment. Other days, a broom, to help the infirmarian[3] . . . I assure you that I live a happy life, and I don't even notice the days flying by.

I hope the war ends soon and everything goes back to normal so you all can come visit me in the new car[4] you'll get. Make sure it's very small and slow . . . speed is very dangerous.

I imagine the work in the fields is almost back to normal by now . . . Anyway, when you write, give me all the details. I may be a Trappist, but I'm still interested in everything back home . . . because, as you well know, I just want good things for all of you . . .

Of course, God above all. Everything else is secondary. But often, those *secondary* things are needed in order to be at peace and love God . . . Look, brother, we are human beings! . . .

There are so many things I'd tell you, if only I had enough time and paper, but I don't think it's necessary. Right? When you come here next, then we can talk about harvests and tractors and . . . God.

Look, I'm sending you some holy cards I painted periodically on Sundays.[5] I don't know if you'll like them, but I think you will, even if it's just because your brother was the one who painted them. I'm sure you'll understand the meaning of all three . . . it's pretty simple.

Since monks are nourished by the Psalms, it won't surprise you that I have taken them up as subjects . . . Oh, if only I knew how to paint! But look, there are some things in the interior life that cannot be expressed. Only sacred Scripture can say in just a few words what a human being would need many speeches to fail to get across.

Listen, dear brother, if you managed to truly *live* what these three images represent, you'd be a sage and a saint. But how quickly we forget!

The first, you'll see, shows a humble lay brother who has chosen the way of truth, *viam veritatis elegi.*[6] In the world's dark night, only the cross of Christ sheds light upon the path of life . . . This is the only truth, which

---

3. The infirmarian: Br. Domingo García.
4. The family car was requisitioned by the military during the war (OC 967).
5. For images of the three holy cards Rafael describes in this letter, see the color insert.
6. I have chosen the way of truth (Ps 119:30).

gives the peace we need to hope, the strength to keep going, and the trust to keep from going astray.

Christ and His cross are the Truth, the Way, and the Life.[7] He said so Himself, and His words are fulfilled in the serene peace of the little monk who walks in the way of Truth in search of Christ.

The second shows a soul adoring God in the greatness of His creation. Looking out at the world, contemplating the beauty of creation, he asks all creatures to adore Him: *omnis terra adoret te.*[8] The shadow of this soul who loves God in beauty is a cross.

The third shows a monk who, high up on a cliff, is contemplating the world. Thirsting for divine love and longing for heaven, he cannot help but exclaim: *incola ego sum in terra . . .* I am a stranger and a pilgrim on earth.[9]

My dearest Leopoldo, whether we like it or not, we are indeed pilgrims. Why seek our permanent place here? Like the little monk in the drawing, let us look at the world in which foolish people place their hopes, where they wage their wars and greedily hide their miserable, perishable treasures . . .

How fortunate, brother, are those who truly consider themselves foreigners in this world and dream only of God and their true homeland . . . Their lives will consist of serene peace, for peace is only to be found in detached hearts . . . They will work with their eyes fixed on God, and their work will be blessed. They will deal with human beings, and their dealings will be grounded in charity . . .

Anyway, I don't want to be tiresome. I figure I have sufficiently explained the holy cards this poor monk is sending you, along with so much affection . . . "Typical monk," you'll say, and that's true, but listen. My life is spent thinking, meditating, and ruminating on these things, and . . . I give from what I have.

My next letter will be for Mercedes.[10] I'll say nothing more, for I don't think I have to tell you to give my parents a big hug for me. As for everyone

7. See John 14:6.
8. *All the earth worships you* (Ps 66:4).
9. Ps 110:19.
10. Mercedes: Rafael's sister.

else, whatever you want. As for you, receive what your brother cannot send by letter; you can imagine what it is.

Bye, Leopoldillo. Be good, your brother asks that of the Most Holy Virgin often. And don't you forget about your poor brother who loves you so much,

Brother María Rafael

Greetings from Father Abbot and Father Master. And Father Armando[11] too, he's been sick, and when he saw that I was writing, he told me to give my parents his regards . . . so please do.[12]

---

11. Dom Félix Alonso García, abbot; Fr. José Olmedo Arrieta, master of novices; and Fr. Armando Regolf Santcher.

12. On Easter Friday, April 22, 1938, Rafael fell into a diabetic coma characterized by intense thirst, periods of delirium, and an extremely high fever. He received Anointing of the Sick on Monday, April 25, but was unable to receive Viaticum. He died on April 26, 1938 (OC 971–72).

208. Chapter of Faults[1]

Making noise bounding up the stairs.
Not bowing in chapter.[2]
Turning my head during Mass.
Making signs during the Great Silence.
Running, failing to show respect in the church.
Speaking while making signs to a professed monk.
Not immediately obeying the bell.
Mistake in choir, didn't prostrate myself.[3]
Showing external signs of impatience.
Wasting time at work.
Wasting time looking out the window.
Wasting time during intervals.
Making exaggerated gestures like a layman.
Being careless with my room in the infirmary.
Unnecessary talking.
Being careless by making noise when using stairs and closing doors.
Getting distracted in choir and not bowing on time.

1. Chapter of faults: A gathering of the community in chapter to acknowledge failings and ask forgiveness. This piece of paper was found in one of Rafael's pockets when he died, with all but the last four items crossed out.

2. "In entering and leaving [the chapter room], a moderate inclination is always made to the crucifix" (*Regulations of the Lay Brothers of the Order of Cistercians of the Strict Observance, Approved by the General Chapter of 1927* [Dublin: M. H. Gill & Sons, 1934], 122).

3. "Should anyone make a mistake in a psalm, responsory, refrain, or reading, he must make satisfaction there before all" (RB 45.1).

IX. Never Stop Looking to the Heights

Prayers and Other Undated Passages

209. Passages from Notes I[1]

God has not made anything useless. The king's secret is sullied the very moment it is made known.[2]

How difficult it is to walk among thorns without letting your clothes get caught in them . . . but knowing that it is the hand of God that is helping and upholding you, how pleasant it becomes to avoid danger.

Prayer is pride's grave.

Let's not await justice in this world; human beings don't know how to administer it . . . Trust Him, trusting that all the tribulation you endure down here with a happy heart will be repaid with Love once you're up there . . . Never stop looking to the heights.

God willed that every life should have its trials, that all should have their thorns, and each soul should have its own hidden grief . . .[3]

Silence is more pleasing to God than speech, even in regard to spiritual things (see Saint Benedict's Rule).[4] No one is more worthy of being judged kindly than someone who is suffering.

Unless you fight, you cannot win.

---

1. Rafael created three notebooks of spiritual advice from his favorite saints and writers by copying their texts, illustrating them with pasted-in holy cards, and adding occasional notes of his own (Juan Antonio Martínez Camino, *Mi Rafael: el Beato Rafael Arnáiz, según el Padre Teófilo Sandoval, su confesor, intérprete y editor* [Bilbao: Desclée de Brouwer, 2003], 156–57). His editors later designated these notebooks Notes (Anotaciones) I, II, and III. In addition to the undated original passages translated here, Notes I included many copied texts from other authors, a full list of which can be found at OC 1067. The only dated original composition in Notes I is #7, Impressions of La Trapa.

2. See Tob 12:7, which Rafael also paraphrases in #140, n. 1.

3. Rafael wrote this sentence in French. Translation assisted by Tim Markatos.

4. See RB 6.1-6. The parenthetical note is in Rafael's original.

210. *Passages from* Notes II[1]

Jesus, I see suffering and I suffer, I see weeping and I weep . . . Make me bleed, and in me, relieve all the sorrows of those around me.[2]

Lord, if I need a cross in order to love You, send me one; for I can clearly see that the greater a cross I have, the more I love You. You know that loving You is my only concern on this earth, and the more I love You, the more joy I give You. O Most Holy Virgin, who brought me to La Trapa that I might learn to love Your Son, help me in my aim to love Him more and more every day. What little humility I have . . . ! I dare such things!

Lord, look at Your servant Rafael . . . You know his life and his entire soul belong to You. He gave them to You one day, and You, as Master and Lord, accepted them. You saw that they were unclean, and You wanted to purify them. I gave You all I had, but *all I had* were sins, miseries, and imperfections, and that was not worthy of You.

Do You want to purify me through sacrifice? . . . Sacrifice me, Lord! Do You want my suffering? Take it, Lord! I don't want to obstruct Your divine work. But Lord, don't forget about me. Look at me. I am very miserable, and I won't be able to resist. Well . . . Lord, pay me no mind, and do with me as You will. All I can do is not get in Your way, and *in all humility*, let myself be molded . . . and besides, how simple and pleasant that is!

Lord, with each passing day, I am coming to see more clearly what I must do in order to become holy. Wretch that I am, I used to think that I was the one who brought about virtue, and that if I did something good, I was the

---

1. For the Notes series, see #209, n. 1.

2. Unlike the rest of the passages here, Rafael added a date and location to this paragraph: Torrelodones, August 27, 1935. At the time, he and his mother were accompanying his sister Merceditas as she pursued medical treatment for a life-threatening case of peritonitis (see #62, n. 3).

one doing that too. . . But no. . . O Lord! No, it's not like that. You bring about all that is good. . . *in my whole life, I have brought about nothing but sins*. . . As such, *Lord*, it's best to let You work in my life. . . I surrender myself entirely to You. I don't want to have even desires to be good, if that is not Your desire. I don't want anything. I want to be nothing to the world. I want to be entirely Yours. I give You even my sins, for they are all I have left that is entirely my own. Are you pleased, Lord?. . . I know I am.

The greatest consolation is to have none at all.[3]
Suffer and rest in Me. . .
It's not yet time. . . keep trusting.
I enjoy your company. Be with Me.
What more do you want?. . . What are you asking for? Why are you yearning and weeping? Don't I love you?. . .
Who am I, Lord, that You should regard me so?

A Prayer for Spain, inspired by the sacred Scriptures
Hear a just cause, O Lord; attend to my cry, give ear to my prayer from lips free of deceit.[4] O Lord, who wept for Lazarus, whom You loved, be stirred to compassion by the pain of Your children in Spain, who are weeping and suffering amid the turmoil of war. O Lord, do not reject the people as we cry out to You in their affliction.
O God, do not keep silence; do not hold your peace or be still, O God.[5] *Even now your enemies are in tumult; those who hate you have raised their heads.*[6] *O my God, make them like whirling dust, like chaff before the wind.*[7]
Fill their faces with shame, so that they may seek Your name, O Lord. Let them be put to shame and dismayed forever; let them perish in disgrace. Let them know that You alone, whose name is the Lord, are the Most High over all the earth.[8] *Blessed be the Lord, who has not given us as prey to their teeth.*[9]

3. See #63, n. 2, and #181, n. 1.
4. Ps 17:1.
5. Ps 83:1.
6. Ps 83:2.
7. Ps 83:13.
8. Ps 83:16-18.
9. Ps 124:6.

We, the Spanish people, are crying out to You, O my God, with David's words: *Rise up, O Lord! Deliver me, O my God! For you strike all my enemies on the cheek; you break the teeth of the wicked. Deliverance belongs to the Lord; may your blessing be on your people!*[10]

Regina pacis . . . Ora pro nobis . . .[11]

The logic of great souls is the foolishness of the cross. Maybe we are meant for more than happiness.

10. Ps 3:7-8.
11. "Queen of peace, pray for us" (Latin).

211. Passages from **Notes III**[1]

I invoke God and the Most Holy Virgin, that the words of this note-book might inspire my soul during the difficult moments of my life, and lift it up to the Lord. May they lead me toward consolation on some occasions and meditation upon others, and may I always find in them a *way* to be better, to be more detached from the world and closer to God.

Before the Tabernacle
Lord, I don't know what I'm doing here . . . Nothing, because I don't know how to do anything . . . I wish I could pray . . . I don't know, but it doesn't matter . . . I don't pray because I don't know how. Lord, I don't know what I'm doing here, but I am with You . . . that is enough for me, and I know that You are here in front of me . . . Lord, I wish I could see You . . . but *how long, O Lord?*[2] . . . And in the meantime? . . . How will I endure? . . . I am weak, I am feeble, I am sin, I am nothing . . . But Lord, I want to see You, even though I know I don't deserve to.

How often I come before You, O Lord, and my immediate feelings are those of shame! Lord, You know why. But then—O God, how good You are!—after looking at myself, I look at You. Then, as I contemplate Your mercy, which does not turn me away, my soul is consoled and happy.

To think that I offended You, and in spite of that, You love me and allow me to be in Your presence, rather than annihilating me with Your just wrath . . . Lord, give me David's tears, that I might weep for my faults; and at the same time, give me a very, very big heart . . . that I might be able to return the great love You have for me, even if it's just a little . . . a very little bit.

1. For the Notes series, see #209, n. 1.
2. Ps 13:1.

IX. Never Stop Looking to the Heights

Lord, what do You want from me? There are so many things I'd like to tell You, but so few words are coming to my lips . . . So listen to my heart instead. Without words or noise, it will find a way to tell You how much I love You and everything You are to me . . . My light, my guide, my only love, my hope, and my only reason for living, for if I lost You, Lord, my life would be extinguished like a flame without oxygen. You are my nourishment, the air I breathe and the bread I eat . . . What do You want from me, Lord? Do You want me to love You more? . . . And how can I, Lord . . . if I have such a wicked, miserable little heart? Make it big and generous for me. Make me all heart, so that I may be all Yours, and that I may love You, love You so much, as nobody has ever loved You before.

My Lord and my God, You can do this if You want to, and I can't do anything if You don't help me. Quench this thirst I am feeling, because I can't live like this. My soul is full and running over. You've put so much love into such a miserable little soul, Lord! If You, Lord, are causing the injury, please kindly cauterize it too. But don't leave me in this state, because I won't be able to go on . . . Jesus, Joseph, and Mary! . . .

212. A Prayer in Time of War[1]

Hear a just cause, O Lord; attend to my cry, give ear to my prayer from lips free of deceit.[2]

O good Jesus, who wept when they told you *he whom you love is ill,*[3] I confide this in You: Lord, Spain is at war.

O all-powerful God, do not reject us, the people that cries out to You in our affliction. Our enemies are Your enemies.

O God, do not keep silence; do not hold your peace or be still, O God.[4]

Even now your enemies are in tumult; those who hate you have raised their heads.[5]

O my God, make them like whirling dust, like chaff before the wind. Fill their faces with shame, so that they may seek Your name, O Lord. Let them be put to shame and dismayed forever; let them perish in disgrace. Let them know that You alone, whose name is the Lord, are the Most High over all the earth.[6]

May peace reign, and may Your name be praised.

Why do the nations conspire, and the peoples plot in vain? Why do the kings of the earth set themselves and the rulers take counsel together against the Lord and His anointed?[7]

They say, *Let us burst their bonds asunder, and cast their cords from us.*[8]

---

1. This loose, undated sheet of paper was found separate from Notes II, the notebook that contains a similar prayer for Spain at war (see #210).

2. Ps 17:1.

3. John 11:3.

4. Ps 83:1.

5. Ps 83:2.

6. Ps 83:13, 16-18.

7. Ps 2:1-2.

8. Ps 2:3.

He who sits in the heavens laughs; the Lord has them in derision. Then he will speak to them in his wrath, and terrify them in his fury.[9]

Lord, Your enemies are our enemies.

Stay your hand,[10] and do not unleash Your fury. *Peace be within your walls*, O Jerusalem.[11] Bring forth songs from our lips: *If it had not been the Lord who was on our side, then they would have swallowed us up alive. The flood would have swept us away, then over us would have gone the raging waters.*[12]

Blessed be the Lord, who has not given us as prey to their teeth.[13]

But, Lord, free our captive brothers and sisters from slavery. Grant us peace, Lord.

9. Ps 2:4-5.
10. 1 Chr 21:15.
11. Ps 122:7.
12. Ps 124:1a, 3, 4a, 5.
13. Ps 124:6.

213. Dedication of a Holy Card to María Osorio

When you look at this holy card, Aunt María, don't think of me, because I don't deserve it and it's not necessary. Instead, look to the Most Holy Virgin, and She will tell you better than I can what is best for you.

We creatures can console one another . . . but since we are creatures, we always do so in a weak, human way. Conversely, Aunt María, I know that if we turn to Her in our pain, our tears will become laughter and our bitter sorrow will become holy joy . . . That is what I wish for you, always. Pray to the Virgin, asking for that for me too. Your nephew and brother,

Rafael

214. Dedication of a Holy Card to Rosa Calvo[1]

On this holy card, a young man offers the Virgin a lily. My dear Rosa, what will we offer Her? It doesn't matter what it is, so long as we do it cheerfully, for then, as Saint Paul says, God will love us.[2]

The Virgin accepts it all, and the more humble our offering, the better. She doesn't need great things or huge sacrifices . . . as you can see, a simple lily is enough for Her to look on us with love, and make us pleasing in Her eyes.

All for God, and all through Mary,

Rafael

1. Rafael's friend from Toro (see #8, n. 1).
2. *God loves a cheerful giver* (2 Cor 9:7).

215. Loose Paper Written in Pencil

Lord . . . Lord!!! Your servant's prayer is a short one . . . I wish I had the heart of the holy king David, that I might implore Your aid with beautiful words, and sing hymns in Your honor to the tune of stringed instruments . . . but I am not like David. My heart has so many things to tell You, but it doesn't know how to say them . . . Only one word comes to my lips: Lord, look at me. I ask You for nothing else, and I know not what else to ask of You . . . You delight in the saints of heaven as well as those on earth. In them you see Your glory reflected, and You take pleasure in them . . . and I, Lord, am a poor sinner who neither praises nor glorifies You. Rather, what I do is offend You . . . My heart is not yet completely detached from creatures, that I might offer it to You free of earthly affections . . .

In the meantime, Lord, do not turn Your gaze from Your servant. Though he is a sinner, he hopes in Your mercy, that he might one day be able to contemplate You for all eternity . . . Meanwhile, Lord, look at Your servant.

216. Note in Rafael's Bible[1]

It's not the solitude of the body that is pleasing to God . . . That is pleasing to our bodies . . . What draws us closer to Jesus is the solitude of the heart that is detached from the world and from its creatures and from its own will . . . That is what it means to deny yourself . . . that is death, that is the cross. But blessed be the cross whose suffering is the source of eternal life.

Loving God in silence and solitude, with a heart detached from the world and only one will: that of Christ. With these three things . . . one can become perfect, so long as one doesn't forget about Mary.

Salus infirmorum . . . Ora pro nobis[2]

1. This note was found on a loose sheet of paper tucked into Rafael's copy of the Bible. He used the following edition: *La Sagrada Biblia,* trans. Félix Torres Amat (Barcelona: Imprenta y Librería de Subirana Hermanos, 1894).
2. "Health of the sick, pray for us" (Latin).

217. Gloss on Psalm 6[1]

The first penitential psalm.[2] A psalm that's worth memorizing, in order to whisper it and meditate upon it at any moment during the day . . . If we kept this beautiful psalm's words in our hearts, what consolation would we lack, as we find ourselves flooded with weakness, misery, and infidelity toward God and say to Him, *Domine, ne in furore tuo arguas me.*[3] We ought to exclaim these words as we realize our sins. *Exaudivit Dominus deprecationem meam,*[4] we will cry out when we see that God, even in the midst of our misery, hears us.

1. In addition to his Bible, Rafael had a separate book of the Psalms (*Libros Sapienciales,* vol. I: *El libro de los Salmos,* trans. P. Ruperto María Manresa, OMC [Barcelona: Librería Bastinos de José Bosch, 1935]).

2. The seven penitential psalms (Pss 6, 32, 38, 51, 102, 130, 143) are often prayed together as an expression of repentance. Rafael recommended this spiritual practice in #50, n. 1.

3. *O Lord, do not rebuke me in your anger* (Ps 6:1).

4. *The Lord has heard my supplication* (Ps 6:9).

218. Dedication of a Holy Card
to Fernando Barón Osorio[1]

JHS. Fernandito, on this holy card, I wish you great tenderness for the Child Jesus, who, as you know, loves you very much. You'll see, as I'm going to pray to the Most Blessed Virgin for you so much, I am sure you'll always be very good.

Brother María Rafael

---

1. Rafael's cousin, the son of Leopoldo Barón and María Osorio.

219. Dedication of a Holy Card

Pray for this poor Cistercian novice sometime, that this Christmas, he might offer the divine Child the only thing he has, which is a poor heart with a little bit of love for God.

Rafael

Addressees

Family

Rafael Arnaiz Sánchez de la Campa	Rafael's father
Mercedes Barón Torres	Rafael's mother
Luis Fernando Arnaiz Barón	Rafael's brother, addressed as Fernando
Leopoldo Arnaiz Barón	Rafael's brother
Mercedes Arnaiz Barón	Rafael's sister, addressed as Merceditas
Leopoldo Barón	Rafael's maternal uncle, who lived in Ávila, addressed as Uncle Polín; Duke of Maqueda by marriage
María Osorio	Rafael's aunt, married to Leopoldo Barón; sometimes addressed by Rafael as Sister; Duchess of Maqueda
Dolores Barón Osorio	Rafael's cousin, Leopoldo and María's daughter
Fernando Barón Osorio	Rafael's cousin, Leopoldo and María's son
Fernanda Torres	Rafael's maternal grandmother, who lived in Toro
Leopoldo Torres	Rafael's maternal great-uncle, Fernanda's brother; known by his title, Marquess of San Miguel de Grox

Friends

Toribio Luis (Br. Tescelino)
      Arribas
As Br. Tescelino, second infirmarian at San Isidro; left the monastery in 1937 for military service, reverting to his baptismal name of Luis

Rosa Calvo
Rafael's friend, who worked at the lottery in Toro; addressed as Aunt Ropi

W. Marino del Hierro
Rafael's pen pal, an acquaintance of Luis Arribas

Monks of San Isidro de Dueñas

Dom Félix Alonso
      García
Abbot, sometimes addressed as Reverend Father or Father Abbot

Fr. Marcelo León
Master of novices when Rafael was first accepted to the monastery; addressed as Father Master

Fr. José Olmedo
Master of novices as of July 1935; also addressed as Father Master

Fr. Francisco Díez
Sub-master of novices; addressed as Father Sub-Master

Fr. Buenaventura Ramos — Porter

Fr. Vicente Pardo — Infirmarian

Br. Damián Yáñez — Rafael's co-novice

Br. Ramón Vallaure — the brother of Rafael's closest friend, Juan Vallaure

Br. Jesús Sandoval — An oblate

Time Line

1911 April 9   Rafael is born in Burgos.

April 21   Rafael is baptized at the Church of Saint Agatha (*Santa Águeda*), Burgos.

1913 December 1   Rafael receives the Sacrament of Confirmation at the School of the Child Jesus (*Colegio del Niño Jesús*), Burgos.

1919 October 25   Rafael receives First Communion at the Monastery of the Visitation (*Monasterio de la Visitación*), Burgos.

1920 October   Rafael begins his schooling with the Jesuits in Burgos.

1922 Rafael's family moves from Burgos to Oviedo for his father's work.

1923 Rafael continues his schooling with the Jesuits in Oviedo.

1926 Rafael begins painting lessons with his tutor, Eugenio Tamayo.

1930 September 30   Rafael makes his first visit to the Cistercian Monastery of San Isidro de Dueñas (La Trapa).

1930 September 17   Rafael moves from Oviedo to Madrid to begin studies at the Higher Technical School of Architecture of Madrid (*Escuela Técnica Superior de Arquitectura de Madrid*).

1932 July 17–26   Rafael makes a retreat at La Trapa.

1933 January 25–July 26 Rafael completes his obligatory military service in the Corps of Engineers.

1934 January 16   Rafael is received into the novitiate at La Trapa.

> May 26   Because of grave illness from diabetes, Rafael is forced to leave the monastery and moves back in with his parents in Oviedo to recuperate.

1936   January 11   Rafael re-enters La Trapa as an oblate.

> September 29   Along with other monks of military age, Rafael is forced to leave the monastery to report for military service during the Spanish Civil War.

> December 6   Having been found medically unfit to serve, Rafael returns to La Trapa.

1937   February 7   Rafael is once more sent away from the monastery to treat a relapse in his diabetes. He moves in with his family once more, now living in more remote quarters in Villasandino, in the province of Burgos.

> December 15   Rafael returns to La Trapa for the last time.

1938   April 26   Rafael dies from diabetes.

1960   The Monastery of San Isidro de Dueñas begins the process for Rafael's beatification.

1983   January 15   After a thorough examination of his life and writings, Rafael is declared a Servant of God.

1989   September 7   Rafael is declared Venerable by Pope John Paul II.

1992   September 27   Rafael is beatified by Pope John Paul II in St. Peter's Square. His feast day is set for the day of his death, April 26, though it is observed on April 27 on the Trappist calendar and in certain dioceses in Spain.

2009   October 11   Rafael is canonized by Pope Benedict XVI in St. Peter's Square.

Photographs

Page ii: Rafael, smiling, in his novice's habit. Source: LPM 5.

Photo of Rafael as a child with his father. Source: OC 160.

Photo of Rafael with the stained-glass windows he painted at his aunt and uncle's estate, Pedrosillo. Source: LPM 47.

Photo of Rafael as a student in Madrid. Source: OC 160.

Photo of Rafael with his aunt, María Osorio. Source: *Espiritualidad del Hermano Rafael: Conferencias* (Valladolid: Abadía Cisterciense de San Isidro de Dueñas and Gráficas Andrés Martín, 1984), 137.

Photo of Rafael as a novice at La Trapa with his brother Leopoldo (left), mother Mercedes, and father Rafael. Source: *Espiritualidad del Hermano Rafael: Conferencias* (Valladolid: Abadía Cisterciense de San Isidro de Dueñas and Gráficas Andrés Martín, 1984), 137.

A sample of Rafael's handwriting (text of #179). Source: Rafael Arnáiz Barón, *Dios y mi alma: Notas de conciencia*. Edición facsimilar (Burgos: Editorial Monte Carmelo, 1997), 59.

Rafael as a child with his father (OC 160)

Rafael with the stained-glass windows he painted
at his aunt and uncle's estate, Pedrosillo (LPM 47)

Rafael as a student in Madrid (OC 160)

Above: Rafael with his aunt María Osorio

Below: Rafael as a novice at La Trapa
with his brother Leopoldo (left), mother Mercedes, and father Rafael

Image source: *Espiritualidad del Hermano Rafael: Conferencias*
(Valladolid: Abadía Cisterciense de San Isidro de Dueñas
and Gráficas Andrés Martín, 1984), 137.

Una de mis mayores penas, es el ver que estoy abrazado a la Cruz de Jesús, y que no la amo como quisiera.

Dios mío.... Dios mío; enséñame a amar tu Cruz, enséñame a amar la absoluta soledad de todo y de todos..

Comprendo Señor, que es _así_ como me quieres, que es así; de la única manera que puedes doblegar a ti ✕ este corazón tan lleno de mundo y tan ocupado en vanidades. _Así_ en la soledad en que me pones, me enseñarás la vanidad de todo, me hablarás tú solo al corazón y mi alma se regocijará en ti.

Pero sufro mucho Señor.... cuando la tentación aprieta, y tú te escondes.... ¡como pesan mis angustias!

¡Silencio pides!.... Señor, silencio te ofrezco.

¡Vida oculta!...... Señor, sea la Trapa mi escondrijo

¡Sacrificio!....... Señor, ¿que te diré? todo por ti lo te dí

¡Renuncia!.... Mi voluntad es tuya Señor

¡Que queréis Señor de mí!

¡¡Amor!!— Ah! Señor, eso quisiera poseer a raudales. quisiera Señor amarte como nadie... quisiera Jesús mío morir abrasado en amor y en ansias de ti.

¿Que importa mi soledad entre los hombres?

Bendito Jesús, cuanto mas sufra..... mas te amaré.

Mas feliz seré, cuanto mayor sea mi dolor.

Mayor será mi consuelo, tanto mas carezca de él.

Cuanto mas solo esté, mayor será tu ayuda.

Todo lo que tú quieras seré.

Mi vida quisiera, que fuera un solo acto de amor.... un suspiro prolongado de ansias de ti. Quisiera que mi pobre y enferma vida fuera una llama en la que se fueran consumiendo por amor... todos los sacrificios, todos los dolores, todas las renuncias, todas las soledades.

Quisiera de tu vida fuera mi única Regla.

Que tu "amor eucarístico" mi único alimento.

Tu evangelio mi único estudio.

Tu amor mi única razón de vivir.

Quisiera dejar de vivir, si vivir pudiera sin amarte.

Quisiera morir de amor, ya que solo de amor vivir no puedo.

A sample of Rafael's handwriting (text of #179).

Image source: Rafael Arnáiz Barón, *Dios y mi alma: Notas de conciencia,* edición facsimilar (Burgos: Editorial Monte Carmelo, 1997), 59.

Bibliography

Alcalá-Zamora y Torres, Niceto, and Álvaro Albornoz y Liminiana. "Ministerio de Justicia: Decreto." *Gaceta de Madrid* 24 (Jan. 1932): 610–11.

A. M. D. G. [Jean-Nicolas Loriquet, S.J.]. *Él*. Trans. el Duque de Maqueda [Leopoldo Barón y Torres]. Madrid: Editorial Voluntad, 1930.

Arnáiz Barón, Rafael. *Dios y mi alma: Notas de conciencia*. Edición facsimilar. Burgos: Editorial Monte Carmelo, 1997.

Arnáiz Barón, Rafael. *Escritos y datos biográficos de Fray María Rafael Arnáiz Barón, monje trapense*. Ed. Mercedes Barón y Torres. Oviedo: [s.n.], 1947.

Arnáiz Barón, Rafael. *Hermano San Rafael: Obras completas*. Ed. Fr. Alberico Feliz Carbajal. 6th ed. Burgos: Edición Monte Carmelo, 2011.

Arnáiz Barón, Rafael. *Vida y escritos de Fray María Rafael Arnáiz Barón: monje trapense*. Ed. Mercedes Barón y Torres. Madrid: P. S. Editorial, 1974.

Augustine of Hippo. *Expositions on the Psalms*. Trans. J. E. Tweed. Nicene and Post-Nicene Fathers. Ed. Philip Schaff. Buffalo, NY: Christian Literature Publishing Co., 1888. New Advent Church Fathers Database, ed. Kevin Knight, https://www.newadvent.org/fathers/1801.htm.

Beltrame Cuattrocchi, Paoline. *Fascinado por el absoluto*. Trans. Tomás Gallego Fernández. Madrid: Paulinas, 1991.

Benedict. *RB 1980: The Rule of Saint Benedict in English*. Ed. Timothy Fry. Collegeville, MN: Liturgical Press, 2019.

Bernard of Clairvaux. "Sermon for the Nativity of the Blessed Virgin Mary." In *Sermons for the Autumn Season*, translated by Irene Edmonds. Cistercian Fathers Series 54. Collegeville, MN: Cistercian Publications, 2016.

Bernard of Clairvaux. *The Steps of Humility and Pride*. Trans. M. Ambrose Conway. Cistercian Fathers Series 13. Kalamazoo, MI: Cistercian Publications, 1989.

Bourg, Dom Antoine de. *Del campo de batalla a la trapa: El hermano Gabriel (1835–1897)*. Trans. the Duke of Maqueda. Madrid: Librería Religiosa Hernández, 1931.

Brenan, Gerald. *St. John of the Cross: His Life and Poetry*. Poetry trans. Lynda
Nicholson. Cambridge, UK: Cambridge University Press, 1973.

Calderón de la Barca, Pedro. "The Great Theater of the World." Trans. Rick Davis.
Theater (New Haven, CN) 34, no. 1 (Jan. 2004): 129–54.

Carmelitas Descalzos, PP., ed. "Poesías de nuestro Padre San Juan de la Cruz que
no están en sus obras." *S. Juan de La Cruz: Revista Carmelitano-Teresiana*
1, no. 1 (Nov. 1890): 311–12.

Catechism of the Catholic Church. Vatican City: Libreria Editrice Vaticana, 2003.
https://www.vatican.va/archive/ccc_css/archive/catechism/ccc_toc.htm.

Chrysologus, Peter. *Selected Sermons*. Vol. 2. Trans. William B. Palardy. Washington, DC: Catholic University of America Press, 2004.

Cobos Soto, Antonio. *La pintura mensaje del Hermano Rafael: Estudio crítico de
la obra pictórica del venerable Rafael Arnáiz Barón, monje trapense*. Burgos:
Monte Carmelo, 1989.

Conrad of Eberbach. *The Great Beginning of Cîteaux: A Narrative of the Beginning
of the Cistercian Order: The* Exordium Magnum *of Conrad of Eberbach*.
Trans. Benedicta Ward and Paul Savage. Ed. E. Rozanne Elder. Cistercian
Fathers Series 72. Collegeville, MN: Cistercian Publications, 2012.

Constitutiones Ordinis Cisterciensium Strictioris Observantiae a Sancta Sede Approbatae et Confirmatae. Westmalle, Belgium: Ex Typographia Ordinis, 1925.

Constitutions of the Order of Cistercians of the Strict Observance. Dublin: M. H.
Gill & Sons, 1925.

*Constitutions and Statutes of the Monks and Nuns of the Cistercian Order of the
Strict Observance and Other Legislative Documents*. Rome: Cistercian Order
of the Strict Observance, 1990.

Dante, Giulio. *Summarium*. In *Palentina Canonizationis servi Dei Raphaélis Arnáiz
Barón, Ordinis Cisterciensium Reformatorum Oblati, Positio super virtutibus*
by Congregatio pro Causis Sanctorum. Rome: Tip. Guerra, 1987. 1–265.

Espiritualidad del Hermano Rafael: Conferencias. Valladolid: Abadía Cisterciense
de San Isidro de Dueñas and Gráficas Andrés Martín, 1984.

Faber, Frederick William. *The Creator and the Creature; Or the Wonders of Divine
Love*. London: T. Richardson and Son, 1857.

Fernández, Carlos. "El derribo del Atlántico." *La Voz de Galicia*, June 3, 2006. https://
www.lavozdegalicia.es/noticia/coruna/2006/06/03/derribo-atlantico
/0003_4830956.htm.

Fernández, María Gonzalo. *God Alone, A Spiritual Biography of Blessed Rafael
Arnáiz Barón*. Trans. Hugh McCaffery. Monastic Wisdom Series 14. Kalamazoo, MI: Cistercian Publications, 2008.

Fleming, David L. *The Spiritual Exercises of Saint Ignatius: A Literal Translation & A Contemporary Reading*. St. Louis, MO: The Institute of Jesuit
Sources, 1978.

Foto Delespro. *Barrio de las Adoratrices destruido (Oviedo, Asturias)*. Dele-
gación del Estado para Prensa y Propaganda, 1937. Biblioteca Nacional Española, GC-CAJA/68/5. http://bdh-rd.bne.es/viewer.vm?id
=0000137935&page=1.

Francis de Sales. *Introduction to a Devout Life*. Trans. John K. Ryan. New York:
Harper & Row, 1966.

Gertrud the Great of Helfta. *The Herald of God's Loving-Kindness*. Trans. Alexandra Barratt. 5 vols. CS 35, 63, 85, 86. Kalamazoo, MI, and Collegeville,
MN: Cistercian Publications, 1991, 1999, 2018, 2020.

Graham, Helen. *The Spanish Civil War: A Very Short Introduction*. New York:
Oxford University Press, 2005.

Ignatius of Loyola. *The Spiritual Exercises*. Trans. Elder Mullan. Santa Cruz, CA:
Internet Sacred Text Archive/Evinity Publishing, 2009.

Jerome. *Dogmatic and Polemical Works*. Trans. John N. Hritzu. Washington, DC:
Catholic University of America Press, 1965.

John of the Cross. *The Collected Works of Saint John of the Cross*. Trans. Kieran Kavanaugh and Otilio Rodriguez. Washington, DC: ICS Publications, 1991.

Kempis, Thomas à. *The Imitation of Christ*. Trans. Ronald Knox and Michael
Oakley. New York: Sheed and Ward, 1960.

La vida cisterciense en el monasterio de San Isidro de Dueñas. Burgos: Tipografía
de «El Monte Carmelo», 1923.

Ledohey, Vital. *A Spiritual Directory for Religious*. Trappist, KY: Abbey of Our
Lady of Gethsemani, 1946.

The Life of Father Maria Ephraim. Philadelphia: H. & C. McGrath, 1856.

Manresa, P. Ruperto María, trans. *El libro de los Salmos: versión según el texto
hebreo, vol. I*. Barcelona: Librería Bastinos de José Bosch, 1935.

Maqueda, Duque de [Leopoldo Barón y Torres]. *Un secreto de la Trapa: El hermano Rafael*. Madrid: Librería Religiosa, 1944.

Marcos del Olmo, María Concepción. "La movilización eclesiástica en defensa
de sus haberes: una reacción ante la política religiosa republicana (1931–
1934)." *Diacronie: Studi di Storia Contemporanea* 41 (January 2020): 1–21.

Martín Fernández-Gallardo, Antonio María. *San Rafael Arnáiz Barón: Vida y
mensaje del Hermano Rafael*. 2d ed. Madrid: Edibesa, 2009.

Martínez Camino, Juan Antonio. *Mi Rafael*. Bilbao: Desclée De Brouwer, 2003.

Meléndez Valdés, José. "Romance XV: Los segadores." *Poesías*, vol. 2. Madrid:
Imprenta Real, 1820. 70–71.

Menéndez, Carolina. "Sabores monacales." *La Nueva España*, 26 Aug. 2012. https://www.lne.es/oviedo/2012/08/26/sabores-monacales-20823612.html.

Merton, Thomas. *Charter, Customs, and Constitutions of the Cistercians: Initiation into the Monastic Tradition 7*. Ed. Patrick O'Connell. Monastic Wisdom Series 41. Collegeville, MN: Cistercian Publications, 2015.

Merton, Thomas. *Monastic Observances: Initiation into the Monastic Tradition 5*. Ed. Patrick F. O'Connell. Monastic Wisdom Series 25. Collegeville, MN: Cistercian Publications, 2010.

Montfort, Louis-Marie Grignion de. *True Devotion to Mary*. Charlotte, NC: Saint Benedict Press, 2010.

Officium Parvum Beatae Virginis Officiumque Defunctorum auctoritate RR. Domini Sebastiani Abbatis Generalis Ordinis Cisterc. Reformatorum B. M. V. de Trappa editum. Westmalle, Belgium: ex typographia Ordinis Cist. Reform. B. M. V. de Trappa, 1897.

O'Rahilly, Alfred. *Father William Doyle, S.J.* London: Longmans, Green & Co., 1922.

O'Rahilly, Alfred. *Vida del P. Guillermo Doyle, S.J.* Trans. Aurelio Ubierna. Ávila: Imp. Casa Social Católica, 1929.

Pemán, José María. "Balada de las dudas del lego." *Poesía: nueva antología, 1917–1959*. Madrid: Escelicer, 1959. 67.

Pemán, José María. *A Saint in a Hurry: El Divino Impaciente: The Story of Saint Francis Xavier*. Trans. Aodh De Blácam. London: Sands and Co, 1935.

Preston, Paul. *The Spanish Civil War: Reaction, Revolution, and Revenge*. Rev. and exp. ed. New York: W. W. Norton, 2007.

Prieto, Indalecio. "Sección de Personal." *Diario Oficial del Ministerio de Defensa Nacional*. Número 203, de agosto de 1937.

Regulations of the Lay Brothers of the Order of Cistercians of the Strict Observance, approved by the General Chapter of 1927. Dublin: M. H. Gill & Sons, 1934.

Regulations of the Order of Cistercians of the Strict Observance Published by the General Chapter of 1926. Dublin: M. H. Gill & Sons, [1927].

Roelandts, Rik. "The History of Phototherapy: Something New under the Sun?" *Journal of the American Academy of Dermatology* 46, no. 6 (June 2002): 926–30. *ScienceDirect*, doi:10.1067/mjd.2002.121354.

Ruano, Lucinio, and Crisógono de Jesús Sacramentado. *Vida y obras de San Juan de la Cruz*. Madrid: Editorial Católica, 1974.

La Sagrada Biblia. Trans. Félix Torres Amat. Barcelona: Imprenta y Librería de Subirana Hermanos, 1894.

Santa Teresa, Silverio de, ed. *Procesos de Beatificatión y Canonización de Sta. Teresa de Jesús*. In Biblioteca mística carmelitana, vol. 18. Burgos: Tipografía de «El Monte Carmelo», 1934.

Tattersall, Robert B. "The History of Diabetes Mellitus." *Textbook of Diabetes*. Hoboken, NJ: John Wiley & Sons, Ltd, 2010. 1–23. Wiley Online Library, doi:10.1002/9781444324808.ch1.

Teresa of Ávila. *The Collected Works of St. Teresa of Ávila*. Trans. Kieran Kavanaugh and Otilio Rodriguez. Vols. 1–3. Washington, DC: ICS Publications, 1976.

Teresa of Ávila. *The Way of Perfection*. Study Edition. Ed. and trans. Kieran Kavanaugh. Washington, DC: ICS Publications, 2013.

Thérèse of Lisieux Martin, Saint. *The Story of a Soul*. Trans. John Clarke. Washington, DC: ICS Publications, 1996.

Thérèse of Lisieux Martin, Saint. "The Story of a Soul." In *Soeur Thérèse of Lisieux: The Little Flower of Jesus*, translated by Thomas Taylor. London: Burns, Oates, & Washbourne, 1922.

Townson, Nigel. *Is Spain Different? A Comparative Look at the 19th and 20th Centuries*. Eastbourne, UK: Sussex Academic Press, 2015.

Usos de la Orden de los Cistercienses de la Estrecha Observancia precedidos de la Regla de San Benito de la Carta de la Caridad y de las Constituciones. Westmalle, Belgium: [General Chapter of 1926], 1928.

Valenciano Gayá, Luis. *La asistencia al enfermo mental*. Madrid: Publ. de Archivos de Neurobiología, 1933.

William of Saint-Thierry, Arnold of Bonneval, and Geoffrey of Auxerre. *The First Life of Bernard of Clairvaux*. Trans. Hilary Costello. Cistercian Fathers Series 76. Collegeville, MN: Cistercian Publications, 2015.

Zorrilla, José. *Don Juan Tenorio*. Translated by N. K. Mayberry and A. S. Kline. Project Gutenberg, 2001.